Spanish identity in the age of nations

Manchester University Press

Spanish identity in the age of nations

José Álvarez-Junco

Manchester University Press

Manchester and New York

distributed in the United States exclusively by Palgrave Macmillan

Published by Manchester University Press
Oxford Road, Manchester M13 9NR, UK
and Room 400, 175 Fifth Avenue, New York, NY 10010, USA
www.manchesteruniversitypress.co.uk

Distributed in the United States exclusively by
Palgrave Macmillan, 175 Fifth Avenue, New York,
NY 10010, USA

Distributed in Canada exclusively by
UBC Press, University of British Columbia, 2029 West Mall,
Vancouver, BC, Canada V6T 1Z2

British Library Cataloguing-in-Publication Data
A catalogue record for this book is available from the British Library

Library of Congress Cataloging-in-Publication Data applied for

ISBN 978 0 7190 7579 7 hardback

First published 2011

Typeset in 10.5/12.5 Plantin
by Servis Filmsetting Ltd, Stockport, Cheshire
Printed in Great Britain
by the MPG Books Group, Bodmin

Contents

Introduction

Few historical questions have provoked such passionate debate over the last three or four decades as nationalism. The many dimensions of the national phenomenon, from the forging of identities and the invention of traditions to the nature of the relationship between state and nation, the legitimacy of large nation-states and the viability of the small, have been subjected to extensive research and analysis. The recent bibliography alone is overwhelming. This outpouring of scholarly studies notwithstanding, Spanish identity has, until not long ago, elicited little interest. In 1985, the sociologist Juan Linz criticised the widespread conviction that 'specifically Spanish nationalism is not worthy of study and analysis'. 'The fact that', he underlined, 'there is no book, let alone a handful of articles, on Spanish nationalism in its diverse dimensions, on its triumphs and disasters over the course of the [nineteenth] century and on its intellectual articulation', makes it impossible to understand 'the difficulties experienced by the Spanish State and ruling classes . . . in the [twentieth] century'. Despite the important contributions of Andrés de Blas, Juan Pablo Fusi, Borja de Riquer, Xosé M. Núñez Seixas and Juan Linz himself, there is no book on Spanish nationalism comparable to those of Eugen Weber on France, George Mosse on Germany or Linda Colley on Britain. Furthermore, comparative studies, such as Liah Greenfeld's wide-ranging examination of nationalism in the early modern era, tend to eschew the Spanish case. Indeed, Greenfeld's book, which addresses the three countries cited above in addition to Russia and the United States, not only excludes 'Spain' as the topic of a chapter but even as a reference in the index. Still, the fault does not lie with the author, but with the historians of Spain, who have been unable to furnish the appropriate material. The research on Spanish nationalism even suffers in comparison with that on the regional variants within Spain, which have received an extraordinary amount of attention. Thousands of articles and books have been dedicated to the Basque, Catalan and Galician identities, while the Spanish one has been largely ignored. In short, the paucity of work on Spanish nationalism contrasts starkly not only with the mass of publications on the peripheral nationalisms of Spain, but also, and more broadly, with that on other nation-states.

The principal reason for the patent neglect of Spanish nationalism is political. Under the Franco dictatorship of 1939–1975 all regional identities, especially the Basque and Catalan ones, were repressed in favour of the regime's centralised, Catholic-conservative version of Spanish identity. The protest of the Basque and Catalan nationalists at the centralising prerogatives of the dictatorship merged into the wider anti-Francoist opposition to the extent that ETA, the Basque terrorist group, was applauded as an anti-fascist hero, as shown by the widespread support for it during the Burgos trial of 1970 and for its audacious assassination of Franco's right-hand man, Admiral Carrero Blanco, in 1973. During the transition to democracy of 1975–1978, there was a redoubtable backlash not only against the centralised political and administrative structure of the dictatorship, but also against any form of Spanish nationalism, whether or not it coincided with the particular Francoist vision. Accordingly, Spanish identity rapidly became synonymous with Francoism, especially in its militaristic and fascistic dimensions. Even today, any manifestation of Spanish nationalism is regarded in many regionalist and certain progressive circles as inherently reactionary and untrustworthy.

As a result, the proliferation of studies on the regional nationalisms of Spain is motivated in large measure by an implicit or explicit hostility to Spanish identity. Not to speak of 'Spain' is itself a way of denying the existence of the nation that goes by that name. Recognition of the 'Spanish state' alone implies that this is an artificial and even innately oppressive construct. This approach has its rationale insofar as it seeks to delegitimise the central authority and to offend Spaniards, but it can also be regarded as counterproductive as it suggests that the disproportionate effort devoted to the study of the peripheral nationalisms is due to their very exceptionality. The overriding focus on the Basque country, Catalonia and Galicia might indicate that these cases merit research precisely because they are 'oddities', while the Spanish one does not require the same scholarly dedication as it is a 'natural' phenomenon.

The guiding principle behind this book, however, is quite the opposite: Spain has not been an eternal or timeless entity. Still, the thesis defended here is that for five centuries there has existed in Europe a political structure that has responded, with slight variations, to the name of 'Spain', that the frontiers of this structure have been generally stable throughout this time and that 'Spain' is not merely worthy of study but can even be regarded as an exceptional case when set against the constant changes to the boundaries of many other European nation-states during this period. Whatever the vicissitudes of Spain in the twentieth century, the Spanish political identity has enjoyed the greatest success of all those that have emerged in the Iberian Peninsula over the last millennium or so, and for this reason alone it merits careful scholarly study.

It should go without saying that this book does not aspire to fill the huge gap that exists in relation to the study of Spanish nationalism. My focus is largely on the nineteenth century, although I do trace the development of the idea of Spain from its very earliest origins. Neither does this work aspire to the heights of what was once pretentiously dubbed 'total history'. References to economic or socio-economic history, to legal and institutional history, do not abound. These are not my areas of expertise, but neither do I consider them essential tools of analysis for this topic. In reality, this study is a product of cultural history, or, if you like, politico-cultural history. The human being, as Ernst Cassirer observed, 'does not only live a physical world but in a symbolic world. Language, myths, art and religion are constituent elements of this world. These are the different threads that make up the symbolic fabric, the complex web of human existence . . . Man does not accede to reality in a direct fashion: he cannot see it, shall we say, face to face . . . He has surrounded himself with linguistic forms, artistic images, mythical symbols and religious rites, and cannot see or know anything without first passing through this artificial medium'. Consequently this book is about the world of symbols; that is to say, the one in which the nationalist phenomena of the modern era have unfolded.

The aim of this book is *not* to provide an encyclopaedic account of Spanish nationalist culture but to present an interpretation of the emergence and evolution of Spanish national identity. The first part of the book covers, albeit relatively briefly, the ancient, mediaeval and early modern periods. The entire second part is dedicated to the culture of nineteenth-century Spain: its history, literature, painting, music, archaeology, anthropology and so on. In the third part, I tackle the immense issue of the relationship between Spanish nationalism and Catholic culture and belief. In the final part, I offer an overall analysis of the political role of Spanish nationalism in the nineteenth century and even make a few suggestions in relation to its consequences for the twentieth century.

Many other disclaimers could be made for this book. It should at least be pointed out that it is written to a great extent from the perspective of Madrid; this is not to say that this is a book about the political culture of Madrid – and thereby written in isolation from the rest of the country – but one about a culture that was principally elaborated in Madrid, whether by Galicians, Valencians, Basques, Catalans or *madrileños* (people from Madrid), and then absorbed and felt as their own by extensive parts of the territory subject to the influence of the capital. Despite this, I am convinced that the process adopted different forms in Bilbao, Valencia, La Coruña, Seville and above all Barcelona, not to mention the rural domain. Everything that I affirm would probably require serious qualification in order to explain how the process developed in the distinct Iberian cultural worlds. But I am concerned with the evolution of Spanish nationalism in its totality, as it emanated from its central nucleus, and to have included distinct, regionally located visions would have made the study unmanageable. In other words, this is a synthetic interpretation of a very broad subject and not an exhaustive examination of every aspect of the question. Primary research has been limited to a number of crucial issues which lack previous studies, but for the rest of the book I have drawn on the existing secondary literature.

It may be something of a cliché, but no one is the sole author of his or her work. This could not be truer in the case of *Spanish identity in the age of nations*, as not only have I drawn heavily on the secondary literature but I have also benefited enormously from the constructive criticism of a great many colleagues. I am extremely grateful to the members of the history seminar at the Ortega y Gasset Institute, above all Mercedes Cabrera, Luis Arranz, Demetrio Castro, Miguel Martorell, Juan Pan-Montojo and Paloma Aguilar, for allowing me to discuss the book-in-the-making with them on a number of occasions. Various parts of the manuscript were also commented upon by Edward Baker, Antonio Cazorla, Julián Casanova, Rafael Cruz, Josep María Fradera, Santos Juliá, Carmen López Alonso, Manuel Pérez Ledesma, Fernando del Rey, Javier Ruiz Castillo and Eva Velasco. I owe all of them a heartfelt *gracias* for greatly improving the original draft. None, of course, is responsible for the remaining errors and omissions.

The book was mostly written in Boston, where I not only enjoyed the support of the History Department at the University of Tufts but was also privileged to have access to its exceptional bibliographical resources, particularly the Widener Library at Harvard. I also owe an immense debt to Plácido Arango, patron of the Prince of Asturias Chair in Spanish History which I occupied at Tufts, for his generosity and his unflagging interest in Spanish culture and Spanish history. Thanks to him, I was able to organise seminars with some of the leading historians of Spain, such as Carolyn Boyd, Juan Linz, Edward Malefakis, Stanley Payne and Adrian Shubert, and discuss my ideas with them. I am indebted to them all.

I should also like to thank the anonymous reader at Manchester University Press and my editors at the press for their guidance in ensuring the publication of *Spanish identity in the age of nations*. Lastly, the translation of the Spanish original text has been a drawn-out process. Patricia Newey produced a first draft, but this was then revised and adapted by fellow historian Nigel Townson, who also encouraged me to present the Spanish version of this book to Manchester University Press. Indeed, my greatest debt is to Nigel for his constant support and in particular for the many hours which he devoted to this book.

Part I

The origins of the nation

1

Ethnic patriotism

The birth of the nation

Citizens of Madrid: With the imminent approach of the anniversary of the day that is the most glorious for our people and the most memorable in the annals of the Spanish nation, your constitutional town hall addresses you to announce that the day of the most noble and heroic remembrances, THE SECOND OF MAY, has arrived. On that day, in the name of independence, you made the throne of the most successful soldier of the century tremble beneath him, and, by offering your lives for the sake of your *patria*, you declared to the universe that a people determined to be free disdains all tyrants.[1]

The town council of Madrid in 1837 had no need to specify the year of the day to which it referred in its proclamation. Every last one of its citisens knew that the Second of May was the 'glorious' day (as it was ritually described) of 1808 on which the people of Madrid had risen up against the French army which had occupied the country as a result of the shameful agreement reached in Bayonne in late 1807 between Napoleon and the Spanish prime minister, the infamous knave Manuel Godoy. Throughout the long afternoon and night of that day, the French troops overran the city, crushing the uprising and executing not only the insurgents but innocent bystanders too. The capital was put to the sword, but its rebellion was to be the catalyst for the visceral resistance that, in a matter of weeks, was to overwhelm the entire country and which would eventually result, six years later, in the defeat of the hitherto invincible Emperor of the French and, as a result, in the 'independence of Spain'.

A quarter of a century after these events, the conflict was to become known in the history books as the 'War of Independence'. Upon this foundation the dominant nationalist mythology of the nineteenth and much of the twentieth century would be built. Thus the Spanish Second of May is the equivalent of the American Fourth of July, the Argentinian Twenty-Fifth of May or the French Fourteenth of July. It was the dawn of the Spanish nation, the great initial affirmation of its existence.

The war fought in the Iberian Peninsula between 1808 and 1814 was of huge complexity, but there is no doubt that those leading the struggle against the new king of Spain, Joseph Bonaparte (brother to the Emperor), deployed a rhetoric that verged on the national. From the outset it was claimed that the rebellion was in defence of 'what is ours', 'what is Spanish', as well as the dignity and freedom of the '*patria*', while those who opposed Napoleon were called 'patriots'. Although it took some time to invent a name as resonant as the 'War of Independence', there was talk at the time of a 'rising' or an 'uprising' (sometimes described as 'national'), a 'war with France' or 'against the French', a 'holy Spanish insurrection', 'our sacred struggle', and a number of other expressions that contained references to a sacralised collective identity.

Of those motives deemed to have inspired the struggle, the term 'independence' found a place alongside those of 'freedom' and 'the dignity of the *patria*'. It may well be that, at the time, the word meant little more than 'insubordination', 'integrity' or 'strength of character'; it was certainly a long way from referring to the political self-determination of an ethnocultural group, as it subsequently came to mean in the era of nationalism.[2] But nobody can deny that it constituted, at the very least, language bordering on what can be identified as 'national'. To explain the resistance of Zaragoza and Gerona to the French army, the legendary resistance to the Carthaginians at Saguntium or to the Romans at Numantia were invoked. This permitted a connection to be made between the conflict of 1808–1814 and the remote past, which was supposedly characterised by the Spaniards' unyielding resistance to all attempts at foreign domination and which thereby produced the 'Spanish character', one that was distinguished by an obstinate affirmation of its own identity in the face of the invader. It should also be underlined that in response to the questions 'what are you?' and 'what do you call yourself?', as revealed in the *Catecismos Políticos* published during the war, there was a surprising unanimity: 'Spanish'. By contrast, some years earlier the answer would have probably been 'loyal vassal of the King of Spain'. All discourse now revolved around the national entity, and as a result the anti-Bonapartist leaders won the propaganda battle by a wide margin, defeating those who chose to serve the new, French dynasty.[3]

As has often been observed, it was when *las Cortes* (the Spanish parliament), retreated to the south-westerly port of Cádiz in 1810 that the inherited terms of *kingdom* and *monarchy* were replaced by *nation*, *patria* and *pueblo*.[4] '*Patria*' and 'love of one's *patria*' were words originating in classical antiquity, but 'patriotism', an eighteenth-century innovation that referred to the predisposition to sacrifice oneself for the community, received a decisive impetus from the constitutionalists in Cádiz. The *Catecismos Políticos* mentioned above included emotional references, such as '*our* patria' (not *the* patria), 'the nation in which *we* have come into the world', or as '*our common mother* who took us to her breast at birth and since our infancy has secured our well-being'.[5] The *patria*, presented as a loving mother who welcomes and protects us and, in the process, transcends our lives while giving meaning to our miserable finite condition, resulted in the demand for 'us' to be willing to shed our last drop of blood on her behalf. And that was just the kind of emotion required to motivate the Spanish people in their struggle against the French invader. With an unconventional war under way – one that was neither organised nor sustained by the powers of the State but depended on the spontaneous response of the people – it was essential to convince individuals to risk both their lives and their possessions in favour of collective independence and freedom. This sacrifice could only be demanded in the name of patriotism, the new virtue that, in the words of the contemporary poet José Quintana, was 'an eternal source of political heroism and prodigies'.

In the besieged city of Cádiz, the *Café of the Patriots* was opened and immediately became popular for staging plays with a patriotic content. Literary critics recommended that the plays should aim to teach the history of Spain; the press suggested that they should end with the singing of patriotic songs; and the first flight of Joseph Bonaparte from Madrid in August 1808 was celebrated by dressing up the city's councillors 'in the ancient and majestic dress that recalls the glory, perseverance, and courage of our magnanimous forebears.'[6] It was a complete change of emphasis, perhaps best expressed by the chants and catchwords most frequently heard: in contrast to 'Long live Fernando VII' or 'Death to the French', which had resounded in the insurgent Madrid of May 1808, 'Long live Spain' soon prevailed in Cádiz some months later. Still, for the eminent patriotic publication *El Revisor Político* nothing was sufficient, and it continued to complain that 'in Spain, love of the *Patria* has still not achieved the necessary level and substance', while recognising that 'national hatred and many other things have already become part of our revolution.'[7] This reflected the first stirrings of Romanticism, and it would soon be claimed that any human being of an elevated nature should feel an emotionally, even morally, charged 'passion' – transcending any other experience – for the place or country they called the '*patria*'.

Historians have long argued over the motives for, and ultimate significance of, the war of 1808–1814, and probably will long continue to
do so. What is in no doubt, however, is the violent chain reaction triggered by the actions of the French troops in Madrid, which spread like
wildfire throughout the kingdom from late May 1808, generally flaring
up as soon as news came through of the massacre in the capital. Neither
is there any doubt that, parallel to the conventional war, there was a
military mobilisation of a barely planned nature that remained constant
throughout the six years of the war and whose impact on contemporary
observers was such that it led to the incorporation of the term 'guerrilla'
into everyday language. Moreover, the guerrillas would not have survived without widespread popular support, people thereby risking their
lives in order to provide the insurgent groups with shelter, food, money
and intelligence.[8]

The hundreds of thousands who rose up against the invading army,
and the millions who supported their actions, shared a deep-seated
hatred of the 'French', while appearing to accept a definition of themselves as 'Spanish'. Further, the call to rebellion sounded by those
groups most capable of articulating their convictions were made in the
name of 'Spain'. One can therefore start out with the hypothesis that,
in 1808, there existed a collective identity that was characterised as
Spanish and that this originated in the early modern period, prior to the
era of nations.

The fundamental question addressed in this first part of the book
derives from that hypothesis. What did it mean to be 'Spanish' to
those people who fought, killed, and died while invoking that name?
In other words, what did it mean to those people who believed in
an identity that, to judge by their behaviour, they considered superior to their individual lives and interests? In Chapter 1, this issue is
addressed by examining the political and cultural factors that contributed to the creation of this identity in earlier centuries. In Chapter
2, the most important obstacles from the early modern age to the
formation of a national identity in the nineenth century will be examined. Chapter 3 centres on the war of 1808–1814 and analyses its
subsequent mythification as the 'War of Independence': that is to say,
as a struggle governed by a spirit of national emancipation in the face
of an attempt at foreign domination. Chapter 3 also scrutinises the
difficulties that lay ahead for the liberal élites which sought to deploy
the Spanish identity which had been inherited, reinforced and reformulated during the Napoleonic Wars in the service of their mission
to modernise 'Spain'.

The distant past: from 'Hispania' to 'Spain'

Only an ardent nationalist would claim today that national identities are eternal creations preordained by divine intervention since the beginning of time. However, in the nineteenth century, and even the first half of the twentieth, when nationalism in Europe was at its peak, many people did indeed believe that claim. The histories written during this period accepted that there had been 'Spaniards' in 'Spain' since virtually the Creation. That was how the primitive inhabitants of the Peninsula were referred to by the great majority of authors, from Tomás de Iriarte at the end of the eighteenth century ('the Spanish offered resistance' to the Carthaginians) to Dalmau Carles in the mid-twentieth ('the Spanish defended their independence' against the Romans). Between these dates, it was a truism uttered by everyone. For the influential and erudite mid-nineteenth-century historian Modesto Lafuente, 'the Spanish attack on the Phoenicians [was] the first protest in defence of their independence'. More subtly, Miguel Cervilla distinguished between the 'original' inhabitants of Spain (who had arrived from elsewhere – the Iberians, according to him, were from India) and the 'foreign peoples' who invaded afterwards, such as the Phoenicians, Greeks and Carthaginians.[9]

This book is based on the opposite assumption: that the Spanish identity has not existed since time immemorial. Neither, it should be added, was it an invention of the nineteenth century, as has recently been claimed. To start with, the name 'Iberia' in Greek, or 'Hispania' in Latin, dates from classical antiquity, although its significance has of course varied with the passage of time. Both words had an exclusively geographical content and referred to the Iberian Peninsula as a whole – i.e., they always included what is today Portugal. It was a Peninsula that, for a very long time and due to its remoteness from the first European civilisations, was seen from afar as a distant territory where the *Finis Terrae*, or limits of the known world, were to be found. As the ultimate frontier it was a land of danger and adventure in which legend locates several of the twelve Labours of Hercules.

'Hispania' only appeared on the principal stage of history at the beginning of the Second Punic War (214 BC), when Roman legions reached the Peninsula. From then on, and during the last two centuries before the Christian Era, the first reliable reports and descriptions from travellers and visitors began to trickle out. Following the Peninsula's complete conquest by Caesar and Octavian at the end of this period, the Peninsula was fully incorporated into the Roman world over the course of the next five centuries, to which the cities, roads, bridges, aqueducts

and even the majority of languages still spoken today in the Peninsula
bear witness. Those 500 years went by without any significant manifestations of a specifically 'Hispanic' personality emerging in contrast
to that of the other Roman territories. Not only did there not exist a
political unit that encompassed the whole of the Iberian Peninsula, but
in addition there never existed an administrative unit or a province of
the empire that corresponded to the name 'Hispania'. References to
'ancient Spain' or 'Roman Spain' are therefore unwarranted distortions of the remote past, governed by an interest in uncovering early
examples of a modern national identity and which lack any historical
meaning in the same way as references to a 'Roman Portugal' or a
'Roman Catalonia' do.[10]

It was only with the arrival of the Visigoths in the fifth century AD
that 'Hispania' began to acquire an ethnic meaning in addition to its
geographical one, as can be seen in the expressions of pride in the land
and its peoples exemplified in the '*Laus Hispaniae*' by Bishop Isidoro of
Seville. He was so passionate in his praise of a land of such incompa-
rable beauty and fertility that, he claimed, it was worthy of the violent,
amorous rapture of the invincible Goths, successors to glorious Rome
in their domination of the Peninsula:

> You are the pride and ornament of the world, and the most illustrious
> part of the earth, in which the glorious fecundity of the Gothic people
> rejoices and flourishes most splendidly. In all justice, indulgent nature
> blessed you in great abundance with all things created. You are rich in
> fruits, plentiful in grapes, joyful in harvests; you clothe yourself in corn,
> shade yourself in olive trees, crown yourself with vines. You are fragrant
> in your fields, leafy in your hills, plentiful in fish along your coasts. With
> good reason were you coveted by golden Rome, leader of peoples. But
> although the victorious heirs of Romulus were the first to espouse you, at
> last came the flourishing nation of the Goths, after innumerable victories
> throughout the world, and it conquered you in order to love you; and
> since then, among regal emblems and abundant treasure, it has enjoyed
> you in the joyous safety of the empire.[11]

The nationalist ideologues of the nineteenth and twentieth centuries
were to magnify this change to the point of transforming the Visigoths
into the creators of a political entity that was defined as 'Spanish', partly
because it coincided with the peninsular territory, partly because it
was independent of 'foreign' powers and partly because, following the
conversion of king Reccared in 589, its inhabitants could collectively be
identified with the Catholic religion. The conservative thinker Ramiro
de Maeztu even stated that 'Spain came into being on the conversion of

Reccared to the Catholic religion', while García Morente wrote that the Councils of Toledo, the ecclesiastical council-cum-parliament of the sixth and seventh centuries, had been the first expression of 'national awareness'.[12] Neither Maeztu nor Morente was a historian, but many historians of the period allowed themselves to be seduced, though in a more sophisticated way, by this 'Spanish' vision of the Visigothic world. Even today, in the central *Plaza de Oriente* in Madrid, there is a series of statues dedicated to the kings of Spain, of which the first is Ataúlfo, a nomadic Visigoth leader who did no more than set foot in the north-eastern corner of the Iberian Peninsula during the last months of his life. There are no monuments, however, to the Cordoban Omeyyads who dominated the greater part of the Peninsula for more than three centuries, but who were alien to a Christian faith that was considered to be consubstantial with Spanish nationhood.

This vision of the Visigothic world as a period of political, religious and even legal unification, in which the 'Spanish nation' came to life, is nothing but an idealisation. First, because the territorial limits of the Visigothic kingdom were different not merely from those of contemporary Spain but even from those of 'Hispania' or the Iberian Peninsula. For almost two of the three centuries of Gothic domination, the Suevi occupied Galicia in the north-west, while the Byzantines controlled the southern and south-eastern parts of the Peninsula from Seville to Cartagena. And for a long time, the Visigoths chose to establish their capital in the south of France while calling their monarchy *regnum Tolosanum*. As regards religion, the adoption of Catholicism as the official religion took place in AD 589, when almost two-thirds of the Gothic era had already run its course. To this must be added the instability, civil wars, palace plots and other political crises that distinguished the period. However, even in the seventh century, and more so in the following ones, the process of its idealisation had already begun, despite the disappearance of the monarchy set up by Ataúlfo. We should not forget that nobody benefited more from the system of power established in the last century of Visigothic rule than the Catholic Church, whose Councils of Toledo not only passed legislation but even selected the successor to the throne. It is understandable that the bishops and monks who chronicled these events made an effort to create an awareness of an identity based on that particular monarchy and its faith, presenting the Catholic kingdom as united, flourishing and master of the entire Peninsula. But any present-day mediaevalist with a sense of history would take issue with this interpretation of the Visigothic world as the initial, idyllic manifestation of Spanish identity.

The catastrophic battle of Guadalete in 711, when the Visigoths were defeated by an invading Muslim army, not only put an end to the Visigothic monarchy but also shed much light on its political system. One aspect was the disloyalty of the élites towards their own community, as they had no qualms about calling in their Muslim neighbours to resolve an internal dispute. Another was the astonishing ease with which a people with a excellent fighting reputation was crushed in a single battle by a relatively modest Muslim army. Yet a third was the passivity that characterised the rest of the country, whereby all the cities opened their gates to the Muslim invader with no hint of mass resistance. This is in stark contrast to the supposition of an enduring 'national character' marked by fierce opposition to foreign domination. Lastly, the relative scarcity of buildings, *objets d'art* or even linguistic survivals from the Visigothic era indicates how weakly rooted the culture was within the Peninsula.

In spite of all this, what certainly was kept alive in the monasteries and bishoprics was an idealised memory of a Visigothic Hispania unified under a single king and assimilated into a single faith. When those centres of resistance still holding out against the Muslims achieved sufficient strength and stability to proclaim themselves Christian kingdoms and to prepare for their expansion, clerics and jurists hastened to provide them with a past to consolidate their legitimacy. First the leaders of the Asturs, and later those of the Navarrans, Aragonese, Catalans and Portuguese, declared themselves to be successors to the Gothic kings because they understood that it made them heirs to a power base illegitimately wiped out by a foreign invader. Insofar as they were able to express their pretension, it was that Christian dominion over the whole Peninsula should be consistent with the historic rights of the Visigoths. This pretension was first presented in the chronicles of the time of Alfonso III, which were written during the last third of the ninth century, some 200 years after the landing of the Muslim leaders Tarik and Muza. Later still, the poets were to add feelings of nostalgia, based on the idea of the 'loss of Spain' at Guadalete, that served to reinforce this construction from a sentimental point of view.

The arrival of the Muslims was decisive for the construction of a 'Spanish' image from other perspectives. Because their defeat at the hands of Charles Martel at Poitiers in 721 forced the Muslims to retreat south of the Pyrenees, the Iberian Peninsula became a frontier once more and, as a result, an exotic and fantastic place, just as in pre-Roman times. It is no coincidence that the great French epic poem of the late Middle Ages, the *Chanson de Roland*, was situated in *Espagne* (and in which, incidentally, Zaragoza is confused with Syracuse in

Sicily – both distant lands ruled by Muslims). Many of the German epic poems were the result of pilgrimages to Santiago de Compostela, and the name Santiago – Saint James – likewise appears in Nordic sagas. The mediaeval Hispania once again became a remote place of danger and adventure in European imagery. One travelled there to fight, to earn special indulgences, to study the art of necromancy. It was a land almost permanently at war and, accordingly, with possibilities for advancement, but it was also a land of confusion caused by the typical mix of races and religions of a frontier milieu. Consequently it was a perilous place, but also one that had the attraction of being the conduit for jewels and fabrics from the East, along with illuminated classical Greek texts, translated into Latin from Arabic.

A fundamental element of Hispanic identity, and a magnet for Europeans, was the tomb of Santiago. The legend that this apostle was the first to preach the Gospel in Roman Hispania, supported in a moment of weakness by none other than the Virgin Mary herself (who appeared to him on a column in Zaragoza), was firmly established by around the twelfth century. He was then supposed to have returned to Jerusalem where, we are told in the *Acts of the Apostles*, he was the first of the direct disciples of Christ to die, executed as early as AD 44. Apart from this last fact, the legend passed down about Santiago is totally lacking in historical truth, and any connection with the Iberian Peninsula in particular has no bearing on reality. It was simply not possible to travel to the other end of the Mediterranean and carry out an effective evangelising mission there in such a short period. Neither is it comprehensible that, having died in Jerusalem, the apostle's body should have been buried in Galicia. Moreover, prior to the ninth century, ecclesiastical histories did not link Santiago to Hispania, a land whose early evangelisation was attributed to seven bishops or preachers sent by Jesus' disciples from Rome.

The legend actually took shape in the ninth century, during the reign of Alfonso II, at a time when the Astur kings were desperately in need of miraculous elements to support their political and military enterprise against the Muslims. It was a very long time, however, before it was accepted by the rest of Christendom, including Hispanic political and ecclesiastical circles. The main impetus for the cult of Santiago only came at the end of the eleventh century, under Alfonso VI, at a crucial moment when the spirit of crusade had penetrated Hispania at the same time as the balance of military power finally tipped in favour of the Christians. From the year 1000 onwards, after the death of Almanzor and the break-up of the Caliphate of Córdoba, three powerful kings in succession were able to expand their territories and unify the Christian north of the Peninsula in a manner that not one of their predecessors had been able to do: they were Sancho the Elder of Navarre, his son Fernando I of Castile and León, and the latter's son Alfonso VI of Castile. These kings also established links with Christendom on the other side of the Pyrenees and, in particular, with the ducal house of Burgundy and its protégés, the Cluniac monks. This order was embroiled in a struggle with Rome for the reform of Christendom. The reformers understood the importance of the holy relic that was venerated in Galicia: it was an excellent instrument for launching the idea of a crusade in the Iberian Peninsula while undermining papal pretensions by becoming guardians of the only tomb with the complete body of a direct disciple of Christ. The Church of *Saint Jacques* was built in Paris as the point from which the majority of pilgrims set out. They followed the street known as the *rue Saint Jacques*, which led away from the church and through the city in a south-westerly direction, finding shelter at the Cluniac monasteries along the way. It was a French Pope, Calixtus II, who sanctioned the *Liber Sancti Jacobi* or *Codex Calixtimus*, a résumé of the life and miracles of the Saint that included a sort of itinerary or guide for pilgrims, including practical advice and explaining spiritual rewards. This is why the route became known as *the French road*; why the towns along the way were filled with exquisite Romanic churches (built by the master-builders brought by Cluny), and why there were streets and neighbourhoods in these towns known as *of the Franks*. The pilgrims' songs that have come down to us, when not written in Latin, are in Parisian French or Occitan.

Under the Burgundian and Cluniac influence, both the significance of the saint as well as the struggle against the Muslim underwent a sea change. From being an enterprise for the recovery of territory that had been wrenched from the Visigoths by the Muslim invader, it became a religious struggle or *crusade* – a term recently invented by the Papacy – which was the Christian equivalent of the Islamic *jihad*. Alfonso VI himself asked for, and obtained, international assistance against the second wave of Muslim invaders, the Almoravides. And the Santiago who reappeared after so many centuries of obscurity was no longer the peaceful Galilean fisherman whom no one ever saw on horseback or wielding a sword, but a warlike horseman, the hammer of the Saracens. The new phase of the fight against Islam required supernatural support and, from his place in heaven, Santiago was willing to come to the aid of the land he himself had evangelised and was now seeing suffer under the yoke of the infidel. Against a backdrop of clouds and mounted on a white horse, in the same way as the Book of the Apocalypse described Christ's descent from the heavens for the last battle, Santiago appeared in the heat of the battle against the Muslims and decided its course.

Just as the idea of the crusade was the Christian adaptation of the Muslim 'holy war', the mediaeval Santiago was its answer to Mohammed. But his transformation was to continue until he became the incarnation of a patriotic, later *national*, identity and, more particularly, of the *martial* aspect of that identity. Santiago was not only *'matamoros'* (the Killer of Moors), he was the saviour of Spain (or Hispania, we should say, for the latter continued to include Portugal),[13] the patron saint or heavenly intercessor of Spain. The kings of Castile and León, early aspirants to pre-eminence in the Peninsula, proclaimed themselves to be 'the standard-bearers of Santiago'. At the end of the twelfth century, the Order of Santiago was created. It was a Hispanic version of the Order of the Temple, both of which were dedicated to administering the vast resources that kings and the faithful assigned to the Crusade. His name was taken up as a battle cry by the Spanish not only in the Middle Ages but in the conquest of America, as demonstrated by Pizarro, the conqueror of the Incas, whose words at the decisive moment when facing the Inca emperor Atahualpa were *'¡Santiago y a ellos!'* ('For St. James, up and at them!'). It was actually in America where the apostle lived on in the many important cities founded in his name. Centuries later, during the conflict of 1808–1814 when modern national Spanish sentiment was born, Santiago was to reappear yet again, invoked by the clergy as a guarantee of victory over the French who, curiously enough, were descended from those who had endorsed the tomb of the Apostle and launched the Jacobean road on its way centuries earlier.[14]

The ironies of history do not cease here. Philologists have maintained that it was north of the Pyrenees, in the period of the initial success of the cult of Santiago, that the adjective *'español'* was invented and that it was used to refer to those belonging to the national entity whose remote origins are the subject of these pages. The logical evolution of the word *hispani*, the Latin name for the inhabitants of Hispania, in passing into the romance language most widely spoken in the Iberian Peninsula, should have given rise to *'hispanos'*, *'espanos'*, *'espanienses'*, *'espanidos'*, *'españeses'*, or *'españones'*. Yet the termination that triumphed was *'ol'*, typical of the Provençal family of languages and very rare in Castilian. Although the controversy between specialists has been intense, and still cannot be considered conclusive, it seems logical to assume that it would not have been easy for the generic name referring to such a large and diverse human group, comprising the inhabitants of all the kingdoms of Hispania, to have been derived from those living there: they had neither the perspective nor the necessary maps. It seems far more likely that outsiders, particularly from what is today France, which was so deeply involved in the creation of the *Camino de Santiago*, would feel the need to name those Christians living south of the Pyrenees. This they duly did by referring to '*espagnols*' or '*espanyols*'. Within the Peninsula, when a king as European in outlook as Alfonso X *el Sabio* (the Wise) ordered the *Crónica General*, which was nothing less than the first *Estoria de Espanna* (History of Spain), to be written in the future national language, he decided to have all the passages in which his sources had written '*hispani*' translated as '*espannoles*'. The term, there-fore, did not emerge as a result of the development of everyday language – the usual path – but took a radically different route in that it originated from an outside source and was turned into common currency by the educated classes within.[15]

If nationalists read something other than their own literature, they would probably relativise the sacrosanct nature of their idols and legends to a far greater degree. It is a huge irony that the myth of Santiago, the personification of Spain and an instrument of anti-Napoleonic mobilisation, should owe its initial success to a court and monks whom we would now, with our vision of a world divided up into national entities, be obliged to call 'French'. It is no less ironic that the community to which Europeans would later attribute an innate 'crusad-ing spirit' was, in the Middle Ages, a world of coexisting cultures, and that the idea of 'holy war' should be imported from central Europe. Lastly, it is verging on the satirical that the very term designating the members of a nation has, in its origins, all the appearance of being what a purist would have to admit is an *extranjerismo* or foreign expression.

The more recent past: the empire of the *Spanish* Hapsburgs

It seems undeniable that, throughout Antiquity and the Middle Ages, an identity was gradually forged for the Iberian Peninsula and its inhab-itants that differentiated it from its neighbours and as a result of which the place became known as '*España*' and its people as '*español*'. Until the reign of the Catholic Kings in the late fifteenth century, however, the division of the Peninsula into several independent kingdoms of similar power and unstable borders prevented these terms from acquir-ing any political significance. Still, at the beginning of the early modern age, the Catholic Kings held the crowns of most of these kingdoms, thus forming a monarchy whose borders coincided almost exactly with those of present-day Spain, thereby providing an example of extraor-dinary territorial stability in view of the constant changes to European frontiers over the last five hundred years. This is sufficient for us to consider that, in principle, Spanish identity – and I stress, not Spanish *national* identity – has endured in a manner comparable to the identities of the French and the English, which were the earliest in Europe (and, at the time, not national either).[16] Moreover, during the early stages of this process the monarchy, in all of these cases, was the backbone of the future nation.

Fernando and Isabel not only united their kingdoms but, almost simultaneously, established the new monarchy as a great Christian power. This 'Spanish' hegemony in Europe was a strange phenomenon, since the lands of the Iberian kingdoms were neither especially fertile nor well-populated and, with the exception of Aragón, they had played only a marginal role on the European stage during the mediaeval period. Their sudden promotion to the leading ranks of continental politics towards the year 1500 can be partly explained by what their contemporary Machiavelli called the *virtù* of the King and Queen – their ability and determination to extend their power – and partly as a result of what the astute Florentine called *fortuna*, or the combination of unplanned, fortuitous events.

One of the earliest events that no one attributes to chance but to the ambition, audacity and farsightedness of the two future monarchs of Castile and Aragón, was their marriage itself, which created the initial foundation for the power of the new monarchy. After the death of Enrique IV of Castile, who was revealingly dubbed *The Impotent*, the succession to the throne was disputed by two women. One was his sister, Isabel, with the support of her cousin, Don Fernando of Trastamara, prince and heir to the throne of Aragón; the other was Juana, recognised by law as the legitimate daughter of Enrique and his wife but whose true paternity was attributed to the Queen's lover, a courtier by the name of Don Beltrán de la Cueva – which is why Isabel's supporters nicknamed her *la Beltraneja* – and whose claim had the support of the King of Portugal. Of these two couples, it was Isabel, the sister of the dead king of Castile, and her suitor, Fernando of Aragón, who displayed the necessary determination and political and military abilities. Not only did they marry in haste, falsifying a papal dispensation because they were cousins, but they triumphed over the armies of the Portuguese, or pro-*Beltraneja*, party in the war that inevitably followed.

The aggregation of territories was to continue with the war against Granada, which brought about the downfall of the last Moorish kingdom in the Peninsula in 1492, and the consolidation of Aragonese power in Sicily along with its expansion into Naples, thanks to a combination of the diplomatic cunning of Fernando and the military innovations of his generals. The Castilian infantry, which until the 1490s had never fought outside the Peninsula, was first taken to Naples under the leadership of the *Gran Capitán* Gonzalo de Córdoba and was thereafter to become the most fearsome fighting force in Europe for the next century and a half. After Isabel's death in 1509, Fernando continued to increase his kingdoms with the annexation of Navarre, which was justified by his second marriage to Germaine de Foix and accompanied by the usual armed intervention. Those commentators who have presented the matrimonial policy of the Catholic Kings as an operation designed to achieve 'Spanish national unity' overlook the fact that one of the clauses in the matrimonial agreement between Fernando and the Princess of Navarre obliged him to bequeath his Aragonese kingdoms to the potential offspring from the marriage, separating anew what had cost so much to unite. In fact, this segregation almost came about when Germaine gave birth to a male heir, but the opportune intervention of *fortuna* led the baby to die within a few hours of birth.

The most momentous territorial expansion of the newly unified monarchy was, to some extent, also due to *fortuna*. Christopher Columbus, the Genoese navigator who hawked his services around the courts of Europe with a view to exploring the western route to India, discovered vast lands unknown to Europeans because of his mistaken calculations as to the size of the planet. The Portuguese, experts in geography, had already rejected his plan: they accepted that the Earth could be circumnavigated but rightly maintained that the shortest route to India was still that which skirted the African coast in a southerly direction. In spite of the fact that the University of Salamanca expressed an opinion as unfavourable as that of the Portuguese geographers,[17] Queen Isabel in Castile decided to finance Columbus's expedition. He went on to discover land, more or less where he had expected to do so, and died in the conviction that events had proved him right and that he had sailed westwards to 'the Indies'. Shortly afterwards, a shrewd Florentine by the name of Amerigo Vespucci interpreted correctly what had happened: the Castilian caravels had stumbled upon a continent hitherto unknown to Europeans. As they had returned without naming it, he gave it his own name, in its Castilian version, and in the feminine, as befitted a continent: America. If the renowned Genoese adventurer had not been so obstinate, the continent would no doubt be known as Columbia. As to how it affected the meteoric rise of the Hispanic monarchy, the unexpected discovery of these boundless lands was to provide the Castilian crown with a huge income, mainly in the form of silver ingots, for several centuries, and this played no small part in maintaining its European hegemony.

Fate, or fortune, also played a part in shaping the results of the matrimonial policy of the Catholic Kings. Many felt that the alterations to their plans led to the imperial splendour which distinguished the royal house under subsequent kings, while for others they were the cause of the many collective misfortunes that were to befall it. As already mentioned, the untimely death of the son of the Aragonese King Fernando and Germaine de Foix meant that the territories brought together by his marriage to Isabel remained united. However, the only son born of that earlier Castilian-Aragonese union, the prince Don Juan, who was the heir to the whole legacy, also died in the fullness of youth. To quote Roger Merriman, it was a 'terrible catastrophe' for the Catholic Kings, who 'must have felt inexpressible things'.[18] He was survived by his four sisters, whose marriages had been carefully arranged by a King and Queen who were fully aware of the benefits of an advantageous union. With the aim of uniting the peninsular kingdoms under a single crown, two of them were married off to the scions of João of Portugal; and with the aim of isolating France, one of the other two was wedded to the son of the Tudor King Henry VII of England and the other to the son of the Hapsburg Holy Roman Emperor Maximilian, both of which powers were traditional enemies of France. These aims were achieved: never before had France been surrounded by so many enemies nor defeated as it was in the succession of wars that took place during the sixteenth century, while the Portuguese crown adorned the brow of Felipe II, the great-grandson of Fernando and Isabel. Nevertheless, a succession of deaths, particularly that of the heir to the throne, led to an unexpected change in the dynasty: the Castilian and Aragonese Trastamaras were to see their heritage pass to the Hapsburgs, successors to the Holy Roman-Germanic Empire, who vied with France for the lands of Burgundy.

Consequently, the vast dominions acquired by Carlos V in 1516 derived from four inheritances: the Imperial one, the Burgundian one, the Aragonese one – including Sicily and Naples – and the Castilian one, with its recently discovered American territories. The defence alone of this fabulous ensemble of territories forced him to embark upon an interminable series of military campaigns, which were neither limited to the Emperor's reign nor to the period of hegemony experienced by his immediate successors. From the time of the *Gran Capitán* to the Napoleonic invasion or, in other words, during the reigns of all the Hapsburgs and the first four Bourbon kings, the Catholic Monarchy – the title that had corresponded to the new collection of kingdoms since the conquest of Granada in 1492 – participated in *all* the European military conflicts of importance. While any king of that era expected to wage war indefatigably against other rulers in order to survive, or to enlarge his dominions, it was a more acute and perpetual problem for those who believed it their destiny to occupy the principle seats of power in Europe.

This aspect is of direct relevance to our subject because the 'nationalising' function of the monarchy was exercised primarily through the wars in which it was constantly engaged. Not that the wars were waged in the cause of national interests, because it was the king who won or lost territory; there was still no 'national essence' staking its prestige on every new conflict, as occurred with the colonial wars of the nineteenth century. The troops were fighting *in the service of the king*, and although, for a very long time, the crack troops of His Catholic Majesty's army were the Castilian *tercios*, these were a minority, swamped by the multitudes of Italian, Swiss and Walloon soldiers. It was not a national army, nor did it exhibit national or even pre-national sentiments: its 'soldiers' were, above all, professionals – mercenaries – who could pass from the service of one master to another overnight on receipt of their wage. This situation, however, was beginning to change, as it was principally the effect of war on the population that had a necessarily nationalising impact. Wars led to the existence of common enemies and the emergence of a collective image of both oneself – imposed by the enemy – and the 'other', creating bonds of unity and contributing to the rise of a collective identity that would soon come to be called national, as early modern specialists have demonstrated in the case of other European States.[19] Moreover, as any researcher into national phenomena is all too aware, nothing unites a people like a common enemy. It is therefore reasonable to suppose that the fact of having not just one but numerous external enemies for a very long period – the greater part of three hundred years – and living in permanent tension with neighbouring kingdoms made a profound impression on the subjects of that monarchy. This is in contrast to the very few wars waged between the peninsular kingdoms (only two, in 1640 and 1700, though each one lasted some twelve years).

This unifying, warring monarchy required a level of resources that inevitably affected all its kingdoms, but without question Castile more than any other. This territory became the central nucleus of the monarchy and its principal source of men and money, especially from the moment that the defeat of the 1521 uprising of the towns of Castile, known as the revolt of the *Comuneros*, left its representative institutions defenceless before the exigencies of the crown. The monarchy's demands on the peripheral kingdoms, which were less tightly controlled politically, led to mounting tensions that erupted into attempts at secession, such as the crisis of 1640, the year of the Catalan and Portuguese uprisings. The former failed, while the latter succeeded. But not all was dissension. The Catholic Kings and the early Hapsburgs could also boast of an apparently interminable series of diplomatic and military successes to their subjects. Under the Catholic Kings, there were already messianic songs and millenarian prophecies expressing pride in the amazing events that the people had lived through, with a tendency to attribute them to divine favour in accordance with the providential vision of history prevailing at the time. There was a feeling that the history of the world had taken a new turn, that a new empire had arisen which was comparable with that of the Persians or the Romans, and even that the universal monarchy, the culmination of all history, had arrived. The apologists of Fernando and Isabel prophesied that the crowning achievement of their reign would be the conquest of Jerusalem, as the prelude to the second Coming of Christ. Empires, they observed, were moving from East to West, following the course of the sun: originating in Assyria and Persia, embodied successively in Greece and Rome, they now culminated in Spain, a *Finis Terrae* that would also be the *Finis Historiae*.[20] Pedro de Cartagena, in his zeal to praise Queen Isabel, explained this, on the basis of the letters of her name: '*la I denota Imperio / la S señorear / toda la tierra y la mar . . .*' [the I denotes Empire / the S Seigniory / over all the land and sea . . .]. When he reached *Regina*, anticipation soared:

> Dios querrá, sin que se yerre, / que rematéis vos la R
> en el nombre de Granada . . . / No estaréis contenta bien
> hasta que en Jerusalén / pinten las armas reales.[21]

Although the protagonist of this millenarian promise was the monarchy, and not 'the Spanish people', early hymns to the greatness of the people or *nation* can also be found. It must be remembered that the first foreign military expedition of the Catholic Kings marched on Renaissance Italy, where it was received as a barbarous invader. Thus, both the monarchs and their supporters had a vested interest in demonstrating not only that they were militarily superior, but also that they were the rulers of a highly cultured country. The Gothic myth – that of being successors to the Visigoths – had come to the end of its useful life after the disappearance of the Kingdom of Granada and was hardly likely to impress the descendants of the Roman Empire. Neither could the Castilian language, which was widely spoken within the Peninsula but not outside it, be of service in changing the image of the country in the eyes of the rest of Europe. The upshot was that the Catholic Kings, in contrast to

Alfonso *el Sabio* (the Wise), ordered their chroniclers to write in Latin, even having the histories written hitherto in Castilian to be translated into Latin. What characterised these histories was the obsessive stress on the millennial antiquity of the Spanish monarchy, dating back – they insisted – beyond that of the Romans. The *Comentarios*, published in 1498 by the humanist Annio de Viterbo, were most timely, as they claimed that the Spanish monarchy originated six hundred years before the founding of Troy, no doubt in order to flatter the new rulers. This was also the line taken by Lucio Marineo Sículo, another Italian humanist imported by the King and Queen for this purpose, along with the Catalan Joan Margarit and the Castilians Rodrigo Sánchez de Arévalo and Antonio de Nebrija. All of them praised the exploits of the soldiers who had conquered Granada and were then securing victories in Italy, portraying them as the continuation of the race of heroes which began with Hercules and Tubal, later resisted Rome, and which, finally, rebelled against the Muslims. However, it was Nebrija, 'extraordinarily sensitive to the disdain shown by Italian scholars towards the cultural traditions of Spain', who published the first book of Castilian grammar and who established in his prologue the famous parallel between the expansion of political domination and its linguistic counterpart ('language was always a companion of empire'), a language whose perfection and sonority he considered a source of pride for its speakers. This puts him several centuries ahead of his time in making the connection between State power and official culture which is typical of all nationalisms.[22]

Under Carlos V, identification of the successes of the monarchy with 'Spain' became more difficult. Not only was the King unmistakably Flemish but he held the imperial crown in far higher esteem than those of Castile, Aragón, Navarre or Granada. His Chancellor, the Italian Mercurino de Gattinara, was driven by the Dantean ideal of universal monarchy, which was shared by even the Hispanic counsellors and thinkers surrounding the Emperor, such as Alfonso de Valdés and Bishop Guevara. Valdés himself explained the imperial mission the day after the battle of Pavia (1525) in these terms: 'God has miraculously given this victory to the Emperor . . . so that, as is prophesied by many, under this Most Excellent Christian Prince all the world will be received into our Holy Catholic Faith and the words of our Redeemer will be fulfilled: *Fiet unum ovile et unus pastor.*'[23] This image of the shepherd and his flock would be repeated by Hernando de Acuña, a soldier and poet in the style of Garcilaso de la Vega, in a vibrant sonnet dedicated to Carlos V, which expresses like none other the universalist, messianic imperial optimism of his court, and whose two quartets proclaim:

Ya se acerca, señor, o ya es llegada
la edad gloriosa en que promete el cielo
una grey y un pastor sólo en el suelo
por suerte a vuestros tiempos reservada.

Ya tan alto principio en tal jornada
os muestra el fin de vuestro santo celo,
y anuncia al mundo para más consuelo
un monarca, un imperio y una espada [24]

It was a poem much to the liking of twentieth-century Falangist or fascist poets, who interpreted it as an expression of the *españolismo* or Spanishness of the imperial era. Note, however, that there is no mention of Spain, only of an Emperor who rules the globe in the name of Christ. This is not only a mediaeval idea, but also one which is entirely alien to the Hispanic tradition, since lawyers at the Peninsular courts had been insisting for centuries that each king was an emperor in his own kingdom, in defiance of imperial pretensions of supremacy. This was ratified by the scholars of the sixteenth century, such as Francisco de Vitoria, Francisco Suárez and, more than any other, Domingo de Soto.[25] Driven by his ecumenical ambition, Carlos V actually turned his back on Peninsular tradition, even that which prevailed in his own time. Consistent with the idea of his mission, he spent his time travelling constantly around his European territories and lived less than one-third of his life in the Peninsula. His ministers and advisers, apart from Gattinara, were Granvelle, Adrian of Utrecht, Charles de Lannoy, Guillaume de Croy and the Count of Nassau. Although he had generals called Alba and Leyva, others were called Savoy, Pescara, Farnese, Bourbon and Orange. His bankers, once the Jews had been expelled from Spain, rejoiced in only German or Italian names: Fugger, Welser, Schetz, Grimaldi, Marini, Centurione. And although there were Castilian *tercios* in his armies, there were also German lansquenets and Swiss mercenaries. In no way could this Empire be called a Spanish, or even a Hispanic, monarchy: during the reign of Carlos V, the most appropriate title was the Empire *of the Hapsburgs*, and, from the next generation onwards, in order to distinguish it from its imperial Austrian cousins, the monarchy of the Spanish Hapsburgs (as long as it remains clear that this referred to Hispania or Iberia).[26]

The progressive identification of the monarchy with Spain gathered pace in the harsh political climate of the Counter-Reformation. It forced the Emperor himself to take refuge in his Peninsular territories in 1555, where he had not set foot in the previous thirteen years, but which had, by then, become the safest of his broad dominions in which to end his days. The tendency was accentuated by his son who, after travelling in his youth, spent the last forty years of his life without leaving the Peninsula, which was completely under his dominion from 1580 onwards with the incorporation of Portugal, from which point on the Catholic Monarchy became increasingly defined as Hispanic or Iberian. Thus, the universalist imperial messianism became progressively replaced by an identification with 'Spain' as the chosen nation.[27]

The intellectuals of the time tended, in effect, to liken the glories of the Hapsburg monarchy to the legendary episodes attributed since time immemorial to *Hispania*. Between the mid-sixteenth and mid-seventeenth centuries, there was a period of huge cultural creativity, particularly in the spheres of literature and painting, known as the *Siglo de Oro* (literally, the Century of Gold) of Spanish culture, which continues to be analysed by literary and art historians in innumerable publications. In the field of painting, Diego de Velázquez and Bartolomé de Murillo are only two of the great names of that era and their canvases reflect the splendour of the royal house and the martial glories of 'Spain', among other subjects. But it was, above all, a glorious moment for literature, with Pedro Calderón de la Barca and Lope de Vega writing plays that made an illiterate public feel proud of what it was to be 'Spanish'. Such literature identified Spain with a hierarchical social order under the protection of the king and defended this as the natural order consecrated by God. A renowned early modern specialist, Ricardo García Cárcel, concludes that, during the sixteenth century, the word 'Spain', 'used until then in an almost exclusively geographical sense, began to take on political connotations', and the term, particularly in the historical sense, was 'used preferentially by poets . . .; epic poetry was passionate in its exaltation of the imperial deeds of the Spanish and invented a singularly exaggerated Spanish narcissism'.[28]

All the plays and poetry of the *Siglo de Oro* are sprinkled with references to the glories of the monarchy, which are simultaneously presented as 'Spanish', in which battles from the early modern era are mixed up with legendary acts or actors from the Middle Ages, or even Antiquity, such as Viriathus, Numantia and El Cid. Outstanding in this endeavour was Lope de Vega, due to the directness of his style and his indisputable popular appeal. Lope repeatedly invoked Spain in his poetry, and in his plays he often located the action in Flanders, and either had Don Juan de Austria put in an appearance or even Felipe II himself (with the world at his feet), or else simply included a character called 'Spain'. In *Jerusalén conquistada*, he attempted to write the great epic poem of the nation, which was in turn that of the monarchy:

> también donde el Jordán los campos baña
> pasó el castillo y el león de España.

There are no lack of references in the poem to the 'loss of Spain' at Guadalete (a theme to which Fray Luis de León had also dedicated his 'Profecía del Tajo') nor is any opportunity missed to express a very 'Spanish' pride bordering on intolerable boastfulness:

> Teme a español, que todas las naciones
> hablan de sí, y al español prefieren . . .
> Todas grandezas del español refieren;
> español vence en todas ocasiones . . .
> El español no envidia, y de mil modos
> es envidiado el español por todos.[29]

With less of a swagger, Miguel de Cervantes also sketches a collective 'Spanish' stereotype based on the Numantians in his *El cerco de Numancia*. One of their traits is religiosity, which dates back to the Goths *('católicos serán llamados todos / sucesión digna de los fuertes godos')*, but the most outstanding one is courage:

> indicio ha dado esta no vista hazaña
> del valor que en los siglos venideros
> tendrán los hijos de la fuerte España,
> hijos de tales padres herederos . . .
> ¡Qué envidia, qué temor, España armada,
> te tendrán mil naciones extranjeras . . .!'[30]

This was no longer the ecumenical climate of Carlos V. Cervantes was certainly talking about a powerful empire whose existence was devoted to the 'universal good' – who could doubt it? – but it existed in competition with the other 'thousand foreign nations'. The monarchy of the Hapsburgs was coming to be defined as a limited one and the adjective that characterised it was *Spanish* or *Hispanic*.

Although ecumenism was on the wane, this did not affect either the élites' sense of providentialism or their awareness of being the chosen people. The political works of Ginés de Sepúlveda and Francisco de Vitoria, who rationalised imperial expansion in America, dated from the high point of imperial power; as did those of Alfonso de Valdés and Guevara, who elaborated upon the ideals of imperialism and justified the Sack of Rome as divine punishment. Later on, when the differences faced by the empire began to mount, the works of Gracián, Saavedra

Fajardo and Quevedo defended the kings against their European rivals. In the first half of the seventeenth century, when the imperial edifice was beginning to show signs of collapse, the ideologues of the minor Hapsburgs – made up almost exclusively of the Catholic clergy – still continued to express their faith in the messianic nature of the *Spanish* people, which was identified with the Catholic Monarchy. In 1612, the Dominican Juan de la Puente interpreted the prophecies of Isaiah on Mount Zion as referring to Toledo; seven years later, Juan de Salazar, a Benedictine, insisted on identifying the Spanish people as the Chosen People of the Lord; in 1629, yet another Benedictine, Benito de Peñalosa, published his *Libro de las cinco excelencias del español*, in which there is a whole chapter entitled 'How the Spanish spread the Catholic Faith, Office and Prerogative of God's Chosen People'. And in 1636, another priest, Juan Caramuel, wrote a *Declaración mística de las armas de España* in a similar spirit.[31]

Together with the polemical and apologetic works, a whole new literary genre began to grow up under the heading of 'The History of Spain'. Already, in the time of Carlos V, alongside the traditional chroniclers dedicated to praising the memorable deeds of the monarch,[32] historians began to eulogise not so much the king as the kingdom of Castile, which was frequently identified with 'Spain'. The earliest of these, Florián de Ocampo, wrote a *Crónica General de España* that only covered the period up to the Romans and merely reproduced the fables invented by Annio de Viterbo. At the same time as Ocampo, Pedro de Medina, Lorenzo Padilla and Pedro de Alcocer were also writing 'general histories' or 'chronicles' of 'Spain', and those written by Esteban de Garibay and Ambrosio de Morales, who succeeded Ocampo as official chroniclers in the time of Felipe II, bore similar titles.[33] Not only did these histories have a wider readership than the mediaeval accounts because they were printed, but also their contents were substantially different to those of the purely royal chronicles because they began with the exploits of the *nation* in antiquity.

Not one of these authors could rival in importance the Jesuit Juan de Mariana, who in 1592 began publication of his *Historia de Rebus Hispaniae*, translated into Castilian from 1601 onwards as a *Historia general de España*. Mariana was a true intellectual and he set out to produce a more rigorously accurate work than that of his predecessors, leaving out the kind of inventions to be found in Annio de Viterbo.[34] This, however, did not mean that his work was in any way impartial. The inscription itself signalled a personal identification with the glories of the *patria*, which was not exempt from a certain tone of vindication: 'I was encouraged to take up the pen by the urge I held within me during those years when I journeyed beyond Spain, through foreign lands, to understand our own affairs and the origins and the means which placed it on the road to the greatness it enjoys today'. History, for him, is a source of collective pride: the pride of 'lineage', a term which he employs in preference to race, people or nation. And the history of a lineage is, in effect, what he provides: a genealogy of illustrious men and a chronicle of the glorious feats of arms of forebears, both of which illustrate the superior quality of their blood. As a result, although he refuses to give credence to some of the mythological fables of ancient Iberia, he begs indulgence for including many others because 'to all and by all is granted the establishment of the origins and beginnings of their people and to make them much more illustrious than they are by mixing falsehoods with truth'. And 'if some people can be granted this liberty, the Spanish, for their nobility, should be more than others because of the greatness and antiquity of their doings'. Consequently, repeating the words of San Isidoro, Mariana claimed that Tubal, son of Japheth, had been the 'first man to reach Spain' and was the founder of 'the Spanish people and their valiant empire'; and that no less than a procession of gods and heroes – Osiris, Jason, Hercules and Ulysses – followed him to the Peninsula.[35] This was a means of tracing the Spanish people back to one of the original 'lines' or 'peoples' of the world, so that there was no possibility of a greater antiquity. Indeed, they were even earlier than the Romans. Mariana and all the intellectuals educated in Italy may have felt a great reverence for the Romans, but they were equally committed to the task of creating a patriotic identity.

It is clear that Mariana's work represents a huge step forward in the creation of the identity of what he himself calls the 'nation'. Still, the leading figures continued to be the monarchs. It is true that the bedrock underlying royal succession is 'Spain', but this is an ambiguous term which, at times, possesses little more than a geographical significance, while at others it clearly has a racial or group connotation in which Mariana demonstrates an undeniable pride. In addition, the rationale behind his pride is complicated: in his description of the collective nature of the Spanish he is unable to avoid emphasising their martial prowess yet, even as he does so, one can detect a faint note of disgust. Although he considers Numantia to represent the 'glory and honour of Spain' (because it struck 'fear and terror in the hearts of the people of Rome'), he describes the primitive inhabitants of the country as 'more like wild beasts than men', and though no doubt loyal and excellent warriors, they were 'contemptuous of the study of the sciences'. There is little sense of pride in these lines. It should not be forgotten that Mariana wrote this work in Latin and that, only against his better

judgement ('far removed from what I anticipated at the beginning'), did
he translate it into Castilian ('corrupt Latin'), all of which distances him
from the pride in Castilian of, for example, Nebrija.[36]

Juan de Mariana's *Historia general de España* proved to be a watershed. The work was republished many times over the centuries, with
additional appendices. It became the fundamental point of reference for
studying the history of the *patria* for two hundred and fifty years. Not
many books can lay claim to such a legacy.

A question of terminology

This chapter has examined the main features of the formative process
of a collective identity prior to the modern era, the existence of which
– at least among the educated élites – is unquestionable, to judge by
the amount of surviving evidence. What is the most appropriate term
to describe this identity and the expressions and feelings of pride which
it generated? When Cervantes speaks of the envy that a 'thousand
foreign nations' feels towards Spain, or when Father Mariana says that
in his wanderings through 'foreign nations' he was moved by the desire
to know 'of our own affairs', in what sense are they using the word
'nation'? Are we perhaps talking about *nationalism*?

The answer, in essence, is that we are not. *Natio* was a term used in
classical Latin to designate the foreign communities, usually composed
of merchants, which were established in the outlying suburbs of imperial Rome. The same word was applied to the various linguistic group-
ings in the few mediaeval centres or meeting places of European scope,
such as the great universities and the ecclesiastical councils. *'Nation'*
must therefore be interpreted as a human group that is characterised
by having been *born* in the same territory, with the result that all its
members speak the same language. Many stages are required in order
to make the transition from nation, in this sense, to nationalism. First,
there is the necessary attribution of common psychological features to
such peoples, which generally occurred during the sixteenth century.
Many of these alleged psychological traits already contained ethical
judgements, so that nations went on to become ideal moral collectives.
A people then had to be transformed into the 'voice of God' – as in
the case of Protestantism – and presented as being in opposition to the
monarch who had, until then, been the earthly incarnation of divine
authority in competition with none other than the Papacy. One such
event took place with the Cromwellian Revolution in the England of the
mid-seventeenth century.[37] Next, the process had to attain intellectual
acknowledgement from men such as Hobbes or Locke, the thinkers

behind the theory of the 'social contract', culminating in Jean-Jacques Rousseau, who defended the existence of a 'common "I"' endowed with a 'general will' different to the sum of the individual wills that comprise society. The conviction that this collective being was the only legitimate subject of sovereignty, rather than the monarch, was the result of the enlightened intellectual environment that led up to the rebellion of the British colonies in North America in 1776 and France in 1789. Only when the collective being becomes the subject of political rights does one come to the onset of nationalities, or the demand for the alignment of a State with a previously defined ethnic entity. This necessity was not felt until the nineteenth century and there was no attempt to apply it in any systematic way until after the First World War. Strictly speaking, it was only in these latter stages, when a logical or necessary link was established between a people or *ethnos* and its dominion over a territory, that one can talk about *nationalism*, a doctrine whose fundamental core consists of making the nation the depository of supreme political power. It was also at this point that States *officially* adopted and promoted a culture that they considered identifiable with whichever people or *ethnos* they believed themselves to be representative of in order to ensure their legitimacy.

Although the development of nationalism is subsequent to the era discussed, it must be understood that a nation, like any other viable mobilising identity, cannot be invented or constructed *ex nihilo*. There is no doubt that the term *Hispania* is the origin of 'Spain', a word that identifies the cultural and political entity whose evolution in the nineteenth century is the main theme of this book. Neither that over the centuries Latin, the language of Roman origin that came to dominate the Peninsula, would become Castilian or 'Spanish', one of the cultural foundations of this national identity. In other words, in the pre-modern world there was no nationalism but there were collective identities whose cultural components – whether geographical, religious, linguistic, of estate, lineage or 'historical memory' – were subsequently introduced by nationalists as elements of their political agenda. Accordingly, the purpose of this chapter has not been to tackle Spanish nationalism as such but to explain the admixture of collective identities prior to the emergence of a truly national identity, a condition *sine qua non* for the development of Spanish political nationalism.

The fact that these identities preceded nationalism does not necessarily mean *pre-* or *proto-nationalism*, as many historians and political scientists have done. It is true that these phenomena culminated in the nationalism of the nineteenth and twentieth centuries, but they might not have done. A seed does not necessarily grow into a tree; a child does not always reach adulthood. To define them as *pre-tree* or *pre-adult* is not only inadequate (as it is deterministic), it also implies a lack: to talk about 'pre-' or 'proto-' is to refer to an absence, to define something by what it has not yet become or by what it has already ceased to be. The usage of this kind of prefix reflects an Aristotelian vision of reality, a definition of entities in accordance with their assumed purpose. An exact language should aspire to name each phenomenon at each stage without reference to its assumed evolution.

In a bygone age, one talked of 'love of one's *patria*', an expression originating from Latin. During the early modern period, the idea of the '*patria*' was used less and less to refer to the *patria chica* (one's home town or local area) and increasingly to the global political unity of which it formed a part. In the eighteenth century, the word 'patriotism' first appears, a term which can be applied to this kind of sentiment. Moreover, expressions of dynastic loyalty to the monarch or the royal house gradually became indistinguishable from loyalty to the group, which was defined in cultural or ethnic terms. Still, such terms were closer to those of the clan, *genus* or lineage because collective identities adopted the forms and sentiments previously reserved for aristocratic lineages and families. It is therefore not incorrect to talk of a growing 'ethnic patriotism', a pride in one's *ethnos* or cultural group. It is a *patriotic* and also an *ethnic* feeling because it is related to the genus, lineage or 'nation', but it is not *nationalist* because two crucial links are absent: the first is that between an official culture and State power and the second is between the legitimacy of the State and its sanction by the collective or popular personality.[38]

This adhesion to a human group which believes itself to be imbued with its own cultural identity and which merges with the political structure of the monarchy is what can be termed more accurately as *ethnic patriotism* rather than *nationalism* or *pre-nationalism*. It is the development of this phenomenon that has been traced here, from the *Laus Hispaniae* of Isidoro to the history of the 'nation' by Juan de Mariana. The feature common to all these outpourings was an exaltation of the deeds of 'the Spanish' in terms similar to those praising the great noble houses: for their antiquity, for the martial exploits of their ancestors, for the fertility and abundance of their lands and for the religious devotion of their inhabitants, all of which was made manifest by the riches that they bestowed upon the Church or by the miraculous relics – sure signs of divine grace – that they treasured. In short, the paradigm had been established by Isidoro, Bishop of Seville, in his eulogy to the Visigoths who, after a long, arduous courtship had conquered the favours of radiant *Hispania*.

Notes

1 Manifest of the constitutional Madrid City Council, 1–V–1837. The Spanish word *Patria* combines a masculine meaning from the Latin, *pater* – father – with a feminine 'a' ending. Its significance is a combination of fatherland, motherland and even homeland. As no single one of these words captures its essence, it has been left untranslated.

2 See for instance A. Flórez Estrada, *Introducción para la historia de la revolución de España*, London, 1810 (Biblioteca de Autores Españoles [B.A.E.], Madrid, 1958, p. 260), or *El Procurador General de la Nación y del Rey*, 108, 1814, p. 997.

3 V. Gebhardt, *Historia general de España y de sus Indias*, Barcelona, 1860–1873, Vol. 6, p. 468; or B. J. Gallardo, *Alocución patriótica en la solemne función con que los ciudadanos del comercio de Londres celebraron el restablecimiento de la Constitución y la libertad de la patria*, London: A. Taylor, 1820, p. 22. On the persistence of the essential traits of character, see Pardo de Andrade's manifesto in December 1811: 'Numantia and Saguntum are reborn in the ruins of Zaragoza, Gerona . . .' (G. Lovett, *Napoleon and the Birth of Modern Spain*, New York: New York University Press, 1965, Vol. I, p. 402).

4 Words with very different meaning, certainly, since *nación* is used in official documents with a juridical content, while *patria* is more emotional and therefore used in military or political speeches with mobilising aims, while *pueblo* is preferred by Liberal radicals (according to F.-X. Guerra, *Modernidad e Independencias*, Madrid, 1992, p. 335, in Jacobin pamphlets it almost replaced 'the word nation and its ambiguities').

5 *Catecismo católico-político*, 1808 (*Catecismos políticos españoles*, p. 38). On 'patria' and 'patriotismo', see M. C. Seoane, *El primer lenguaje constitucional español*, Madrid, 1968, pp. 78–80; or M. P. Battaner, *Vocabulario Político-Social en España (1868–1873)*, Madrid, 1977.

6 Quintana, in 'Reflexiones sobre el patriotismo', *Semanario Patriótico*, 3, 15–IX–1808 (cf. F.-X. Guerra, *Modernidad e Independencias*, Madrid, 1992, p. 242). R. Solís, *El Cádiz de las Cortes*, Madrid, 1969, pp. 345–346 and 349–350 (Café de los Patriotas, p. 136); and *Semanario Patriótico*, 5, 29–IX–1808 (quoted by Guerra, *Modernidad*, p. 328).

7 Solís, *El Cádiz de las Cortes*, p. 80.

8 Guerrillas as a revolutionary war, in M. Artola, *La España de Fernando VII*, Vol. XXXII de la *Historia de España Menéndez Pidal*, Madrid, 1992. Cf. A. Moliner Prada, *La Guerra de la Independencia en España*. Barcelona, 2007.

9 J. Dalmau Carles, *Enciclopedia de grado medio*, Gerona and Madrid, 1954, p. 325. On historians, see below, Chapter 4.

10 Roman provinces – Lusitania, Tarraconense, Gallaecia, Cartaginense, Baetica – did not coincide with future political or administrative units, such as Portugal, Catalonia, Galice, Castile or Andalucía.

11 See Isidoro of Seville's *Las Historias de los Godos, Vándalos y Suevos*, ed. C. Rodríguez Alonso, León, 1975; A. Castro, *La realidad histórica*

de España, Mexico, 1966, p. 82; R. Menéndez Pidal, preface to *España Visigoda*, Vol. III, *Historia de España Menéndez Pidal*, pp. XXXIV–XXXV; or J. L. Romero, 'San Isidoro de Sevilla: Su pensamiento histórico-político y sus relaciones con la España visigoda', *Cuadernos de Historia de España*, 8 (1947): 5–71.

12 See R. Valls Montes, *La interpretación de la historia de España y sus orígenes ideológicos en el bachillerato franquista (1938–1953)*, Valencia, 1984.

13 Saint James fights for 'Spain', for instance, in Coimbra. Petrus Hispanus, the only mediaeval pope who bore that patronymic, was born in Lisbon.

14 B. Bennassar, *Saint-Jacques de Compostelle*, París, 1970; J. Herrero, *Los orígenes del pensamiento reaccionario español*, Madrid, 1971, pp. 227–228.

15 See P. Aebischer, *Estudios de toponimia y lexicografía románicas*, Barcelona, 1948; A. Castro, *Sobre el nombre y el quién de los españoles*, Madrid, 1973.

16 See J. J. Linz, 'Early State-building and Late Peripheral Nationalism against the State: the Case of Spain', in S. N. Eisenstadt and S. Rokkan (eds), *Building States and Nations*, London, 1973, Vol. 2, pp. 32–109.

17 The Salamanca geographers agreed with Columbus on the round shape of the Earth, but they disagreed on its size. See F. Fernández Armesto, *Columbus*, Oxford: Oxford University Press, 1992, pp. 53–54; or W. and C. Phillips, *The Worlds of Christopher Columbus*, Cambridge: Cambridge University Press, 1992, pp. 110, 121–122. On Vespucci, L. de Matos, *L'Expansion portugaise dans la littérature latine de la Renaissance*, Lisbon, 1991, pp. 277–318.

18 R. B. Merriman, *The Rise of the Spanish Empire, in the Old World and the New*, New York, 1962, Vol. II, pp. 320–21. On the matrimonial policies of the Catholic Kings, a good synthesis in J. H. Elliott, *Imperial Spain, 1469–1716*, London, 1970, Chaps 1–3; marriage to G. de Foix, p. 138.

19 For the British case, L. Colley, *Britons. Forging the Nation 1707–1837*, New Haven, CT: Yale University Press, 1992. Western Europe in general, in Ch. Tilly (ed.), *The Formation of National States in Western Europe*, Princeton, NJ: Princeton University Press, 1975, especially introduction and chapter 9 (by Tilly), S. Finer, 'State and Nation-Building in Europe: The Role of the Military', pp. 84–163, and S. Rokkan, 'Dimensions of State Formation and Nation-Building: A Possible Paradigm for Research on Variations within Europe', pp. 562–600.

20 See J. Cepeda Adán, 'El providencialismo en los cronistas de los RR CC', *Arbor*, 59 (1950). On Nebrija, E. Asensio, 'La lengua compañera del imperio', *Revista de Filología Española*, 43(3–4), 1960: 398–413. D. Catalán, in his preface to Menéndez Pidal's *Los españoles en la historia*, Madrid, 1991, p. 52, observes that most of these writers belonged to a first generation of *conversos*, prone to assign some providential mission of the Iberians rather than accepting the antiquity and superiority of the Romans.

21 Quoted by O. H. Green, *Spain and the Western Tradition: The Castillian Mind in Literature, from El Cid to Calderón*, Madison, WI: University of Wisconsin Press, 1963–1966, Vol. I, p. 97. Cf. P. Marcuello (on the

conquest of Granade *and Jerusalem* by Ferdinand), or A. Hernández, both quoted by R. del Arco y Garay, *La idea de imperio en la política y la literatura españolas*, Madrid, 1944, pp. 111–112. Nebrija also calls Fernando and Isabel 'orbis moderatores': see R. B. Tate, *Ensayos sobre la historiografía peninsular del siglo xv*, Madrid, 1970, p. 210.

22 Tate, *Ensayos*, pp. 27, 185, 194, 209 (on Annio de Viterbo, pp. 25–27; on Sánchez de Arévalo and Nebrija, pp. 22 and 191). On Annio de Viterbo, see also J. Caro Baroja, *Las falsificaciones de la historia (en relación con la de España)*, Barcelona, 1992, pp. 114–120. More on Nebrija, E. Asensio, 'Lengua compañera'. Quotes of J. del Encina, C. de Castillejo, V. Espinel, J. de Valdés or A. Laguna in Green, *Spain and the Western Tradition*, I, pp. 250, 257, 264.

23 Valdés, *Diálogo de Mercurio y Carón*. See also J. A. Maravall, *Carlos V y el pensamiento político del Renacimiento*, Madrid, 1960, especially pp. 183–226, and *Utopía y reformismo en la España de los Austrias*, Madrid, *Siglo XXI*, 1982: 346–354; or R. Menéndez Pidal, *Idea imperial de Carlos V*, Madrid, 1963. The idea was kept throughout the sixteenth and early seventeenth centuries; in 1621, the count of Villamediana addressed a famous sonnet to Felipe IV's coronation, with the prophecy: '. . . *uno el redil, una la ley perfecta, / habrá un solo Pastor y un solo Imperio*' ('there will be one sheepfold, one perfect law, one Shepherd, one Empire') quoted by Green, *Spain and the Western Tradition*, IV, p. 5.

24 'The time has come when Heavens have promised one single herd and one shepherd . . . one king, one Empire, one sword'. Hernando de Acuña (c.1519–1580), poet and soldier, fought at San Quintín, 1557. The most perfect expression of the so-called 'imperial poetry' was Fernando de Herrera (1534–1597); in his ode to the Lepanto victory, he refers to the 'claro Español, y belicoso' and compares the Spanish lion to Babylon, Egypt or Greece.

25 See J. A. Maravall, *El concepto de España en la Edad Media*, Madrid, 1954; or Arco y Garay, *La idea de imperio*, pp. 133–144.

26 Although future nationalist historiography presented as 'Spanish victories' battles such as Pavía's (1525), where most of Carlos V's troops were German *landsknecht*, writers of the time, such as Gutierre de Cetina, spoke of the honour that these victories would report to 'Spain' because they were commanded by 'gentlemen from Spain' (Arco y Garay, *La idea de imperio*, p. 175). On bankers, see R. Carande's *Carlos V y sus banqueros*, Madrid, 1965. See also K. Brandi, *The Emperor Charles V*, London, 1965; P. Chaunu, *La España de Carlos V*, Barcelona, 1976; and, above all, H. Kamen, *Imperio: La forja de España como potencia mundial*, Madrid, 2003. B. Bennassar, *Historia de los españoles*, Barcelona, 1989, Vol. I, pp. 372–379 concludes: 'the Spanish monarchy at its peak was led by a real *International*, both in its monarchs, their counsellors and its military or financial chiefs'.

27 The young Carlos V, asked by the Castilian Cortes not to appoint as his aids anyone but 'people born in these Kingdoms', coldly replied that his

intention was to take advantage of 'all nations from his Kingdoms'. Forty years later, the situation had changed and his son Felipe II declared before the Cortes, in Toledo, his open preference for Castile (see Arco y Garay, *La idea de imperio*, pp. 145, 231 and 178). When Carlos V dictated a kind of memoirs, or rather a list of his travel and battles, he seems to have done it in French (see *Carlos V: Memorias*, ed. M. Fernández Álvarez, Madrid, 1960).

28 R. García Cárcel, 'El concepte d'Espanya als segles XVI i XVII', *L'Avenç*, 100 (1987): pp. 38–40. On this, J. A. Maravall, *Teatro y literatura en la sociedad barroca*, Madrid, 1972, and *La cultura del Barroco*, Barcelona, 1975.

29 'The river Jordan also saw the lion and castle of Spain'; 'Fear the Spaniard, for all nations refer great feats accomplished by him; the Spaniard does not envy anyone, but all envy the Spaniard' (Arco y Garay, *La idea de imperio*, pp. 300 and 310).

30 'This unseen feat has indicated the sons of Spain's valour in future centuries; one thousand foreign nations will fear and envy you, armed Spain', *El cerco de Numancia*, 1584. Other patriotic references in Cervantes' poems in Arco y Garay, *La idea de imperio*, pp. 286–299: in some, Spain is referred as a 'mother' (sorrowful mother, at times), although in general is a glorious, famous warrior.

31 De la Puente, in A. Milhou, 'La cultura cristiana frente al judaísmo y al islam: identidad hispánica y rechazo del otro (1449–1727)', *Monarquía católica y sociedad hispánica*, Fundación Duques de Soria, 1994, pp. 33–34; Salazar, in F. Castillo Cáceres, 'El providencialismo y el arte de la guerra en el Siglo de Oro: la 'Política Española' de fray Juan de Salazar', *Revista de Historia Militar*, XXXVII(75) (1993): pp. 135–156; Peñalosa, in M. Herrero-García, *Ideas de los españoles del siglo XVII*, Madrid, 1928, pp. 16–17; Caramuel, in R. García Cárcel, 'El concepte d'Espanya', p. 46.

32 For instance, Alonso de Guevara, Ginés de Sepúlveda, Pedro de Mexia, Luis Ávila Zúñiga, Alonso de la Cruz, and among the Aragonese historians, Jerónimo de Zurita.

33 L. Padilla, *De las Antigüedades de España*, 1538; P. A. Beuter, *Crónica general de toda España y especialmente del reino de Valencia*, 1546; P. M. Carbonell, *Chroniques d'Espanya fins ací no divulgadas* . . ., 1547; P. de Medina, *Libro de grandezas y cosas memorables de España*, 1548; F. Tarafa, *De origine ac rebus sestis regum Hispaniae*, 1553; P. de Alcocer, *Historia, o descripción de la Imperial ciudad de Toledo* . . . *Adonde se tocan* . . . *cosas notables de la Historia general de España*, 1554; E. de Garibay, *Compendio historial de las crónicas y universal historia de todos los reynos de España*, 1571; A. de Morales, *Crónica General de España*, 1586; etc. See Tate, *Ensayos*, pp. 29–30; or G. Cirot, *Études sur l'historiographie espagnole: Les histoires générales d'Espagne entre Alphonse X et Philippe II*, Bordeaux, 1904.

34 Truth is 'the first law for a historian'; 'I am determined to write what is correct according to the laws of history, rather than what will please our people' (Mariana, *Historia general de España*, Preface and Chapter X). On

Mariana, see G. Cirot, *Études sur l'historiographie espagnole: Mariana, histor-ien*, Bordeaux, 1905.

35 Preface and chapter I; 'I will not dare to deny what other serious authors said and testified' (Book I, Chapter 7).

36 *Ancient Spaniards*, Book I, Chapter 6. *Numantia*, III, 1, 6 and 10; *Saguntum*, II, 9; Viriathus, 'de nación lusitano', 'was almost the liberator, one could say, of Spain' (III, 3–5). Geographical meaning of the word 'Spain' in the preface, but there are references to 'the greatness of Spain'. 'Corrupt Latin', Book I, Chapter 5.

37 See G. Zernatto, 'Nation: The history of a Word'. *Review of Politics*, 6(3) (1944): pp. 351–366. In Castilian Spanish, the word was used in the first half of the sixteenth century. The *Diccionario de autoridades*, by the Spanish Royal Academy, in the eighteenth century, keeps the meaning of 'nación' as 'foreigner' ('he is fair haired; he must be a nation'). *Fernán Caballero*, in her novel *Clemencia*, still uses it in this sense (Madrid, 1852, Vol. I, p. 165).

38 It could be defended, though, that the connection between nation and sov-ereignty is sketched by Mariana in his *De Rege et Regis Institutionis*, as well as in other works by Spanish scholastic political philosophers, if we interpret 'pueblo' or 'regnum' as 'nation'.

2

Factors conditioning inherited identity

The formation of the 'Spanish' identity was centred upon the monarchy in a fashion similar to practice in France or England, the two classical examples of State nationalism in Europe. From the end of the fifteenth century, feudal divisions in Spain were overcome by the monarchy through the creation of a broader political community, thereby giving the initial geographical and cultural significance of the word 'Spain' a political dimension. Thereafter, millions of subjects who obeyed different laws and spoke different languages – meaning that they belonged to different kingdoms *and* to different *nations* – had a common point of reference: their submission to the same political master, the King of Spain. In addition, this new political structure was to become hegemonic: Spain was to be the leading figure on the European stage from the early sixteenth century until the mid-seventeenth century, while playing a central role in America for yet another 150 years, until the Napoleonic wars. This military hegemony led to expressions of loyalty towards, and pride in, what was 'Spanish', something which was always based on a self-justificatory account of the past and which gave rise to a manifest consciousness of superiority in relation to others, and even to a belief in being God's 'chosen people'.

Thus *Spain* became one of the earliest identities in Europe, emerging at roughly the same time as those in France and England. Assertions of Spanish ethnic patriotism also correspond to those made in relation to the other two countries. Initially, therefore, Spain was as capable as France and England of becoming a modern nation; and yet, even in that embryonic phase, a number of factors can be detected in the Spanish case that at once conditioned and complicated the process of constructing a national identity. Still, it should be stressed that these problems or conflictive issues were not substantially different from those affecting the formation of other identities – which later became national – in the early modern age, including the most successful ones.

A Nation or just a Monarchy?

The first thing one notices in the early expressions of identification and pride in relation to *Spain* is the alternation between glorification of the *monarch* or *dynasty* and what I have termed *ethnic patriotism*, or praise of the *collective* identity, upon which the future national identity would be based. It is extremely difficult to establish with any accuracy the role played by the throne in creating Spanish national identity, or, to put it another way, the relationship between a monarchy that increasingly came to be defined as 'Spanish' and the collective subject that responded to the same name. In general terms, the process evolved from the dynastic, which predominated in the early stages, to the ethnic, which prevailed in the final phase.

The monarchy/nation dichotomy does not initially appear to have concerned the writers of the Golden Age, who facilely identified their King with Spain. In his *El Cerco de Santa Fe*, Lope de Vega has 'Fame' declaim:

¡Oh, España amiga! ¡Oh, España belicosa!
¿Quieres de mi pendón alguna cosa?
Que tengo aquí tres raros españoles:
a Bernardo el Carpio, al Cid famoso
. . . y al gran Pelayo, norte luminoso;

who are soon followed by 'Isabel and Fernando, light of the world' and by 'a Carlos V, a great Felipe.'[1] The modern kings of the royal houses of Trastamara and Hapsburg are added seamlessly to this list of legendary 'Spanish' heroes.

In a similar way, Cervantes, at the end of his *Cerco de Numancia*, makes the River Duero itself rise up alongside the ruins of the devastated city to console the 'lonely and unhappy Spain' and prophesies future greatness under a king, the 'second Felipe, second to none', who would bring even Portugal under his sceptre:

Debajo de este imperio tan dichoso
serán a una corona reducidos,
por bien universal y a tu reposo,
tus reinos, hasta entonces divididos.
El girón lusitano, tan famoso,
que un tiempo se cortó de los vestidos
de la ilustre Castilla, ha de asirse
de nuevo, y a su antiguo ser venirse.[2]

Thus the splendour of Felipe II made up for the humiliation suffered by 'Spain' at the hands of Rome seventeen centuries earlier.

Unfortunately, it is not known whether these monarchs, their ministers and their advisers thought the same. Were they just as eager to
embrace these peons to the legendary exploits of 'Spain' as a nation
or as a people whose history preceded, and was different to, that of
the royal house? The monarchs seem to have been not merely concerned, but obsessed, with the defence of their dynastic rights. The
main enemies of such rights were, of course, neighbouring kings, but
ancient disputes also smouldered with aristocratic families or privileged corporations from within the territory. If historians extolled the
personality of the kingdoms over which the monarch exercised power,
it might seem to the latter like an assertion of prerogatives or interests
that did not necessarily coincide with his or her own. The *comuneros*
rebelled against Carlos V in the 1520s in defence of local rights, while
a century later English Parliamentarians dethroned and beheaded a
Stuart king in defence of parliament. This explains the ambiguity of
the court's attitude towards the process of ethno-patriotic construction,
which was certainly neither planned nor controlled by it – nor anyone
else – although it did serve the monarchy's objectives of expansion and
the domination of neighbouring monarchies admirably. Incidentally,
Hapsburg foreign policy is a prime example of how the preservation of
the family inheritance came before the interests of the territories ruled
over: the uncompromising defence of the Flemish territories was undertaken in spite of its devastating cost to Castile. The Hapsburgs had no
reservations about squandering one part of their 'patrimony' in defence
of another that they refused to give up.

It was during the early modern period, however, when this narrow
vision of dynastic interests began to change. What was beneficial for the
Crown began to coincide with what was desirable for the State, primarily because the wars of the early modern era were far more frequent,
lengthy and costly than those of the Middle Ages. The last Hapsburgs,
and particularly the first Bourbons, mobilised ten times the number of
troops under the command of the Catholic Kings or even Carlos V.
Without a strong economy filling the State coffers, and without the subjects willing to serve at the king's command – or at least not to oppose
it – there was not a single throne that was able to survive, much less
subdue, its enemies. From this point of view, the emergence of ethnic
patriotism must have been welcomed at court because it coincided with
the latter's pro-statist stance. Moreover, the monarchy had no reason to
feel threatened by the exaltation of a collective pride which so insistently
identified itself both with the institution of royalty and with the Catholic
Church. In exchange for society's support for his enterprises, the king
could therefore approve of this kind of collective exaltation. He would

not, of course, consent to any diminution of the glory owed to him and his family, but he could accept that the Spanish *ethnos* was superior to that of the rest of the human race. This was especially true if it is borne in mind that from the sixteenth to the eighteenth centuries *ethnos* was understood in very similar terms to those of 'ancestry' or 'lineage', concepts which were so beloved of aristocratic society, of which the royal family was both the leader and supreme expression.

Some light can be shed on this issue by scrutinising the regal titles and symbols with which the Hapsburgs adorned their persons and their residences. Carlos V called himself *Augustus Imperator Caesar* far more often than *Hispaniarum Rex,* and around his person he displayed the two-headed eagle, the laurel crown and golden fleece in preference to the coats of arms of the peninsular kingdoms. It is not so easy to analyse the symbols of the Emperor's principal residence as he never had a permanent one. He solved the problem of his self-glorification by carrying around two vast series of Flemish tapestries depicting his triumphs at Pavia and Tunis, which were hung in a succession of temporary residences. Felipe II, though less of a wanderer than his father and more clearly identified with the *Spanish* throne, showed a similar taste in decoration in his palaces – namely, representations of the battles in which either the Emperor or he himself emerged victorious, among which were two magnificent paintings by Titian: *Charles V at Mühlberg* and *Allegory of the Victory at Lepanto.* As well as these battle scenes, classical mythological references, portraits of the royal family and a series of works eulogising the virtues of the prince in an allegorical manner – including the traditional virtues of Fortitude and Temperance together with the Catholic ones of Faith, Hope and Charity[3] – could be seen at the palaces of El Pardo and Aranjuez, and at the Alcázar in Madrid. The great architectural achievement of Felipe II was San Lorenzo de El Escorial: not only was it a monastery and pantheon but also the court and the supreme symbol of the monarchy. He ordered statues of biblical kings, with Solomon and David at the centre, to be placed in the main inner square, thereby projecting the belief which the Hapsburgs held of themselves as continuing the work of the builders and protectors of the divine temple par excellence. However much he might consider himself King of Spain – a title not used formally by any monarch until much later – Felipe II regarded himself in biblical and universal terms while eschewing any reference to Spain, to its mythical heroes, to those who resisted Rome, or even to those Visigoths whose idealisation had legitimised the anti-Moorish struggle.

Fifty years later, the grandson of the Prudent King, who was the fourth Felipe in the Hapsburg line, ordered the building of the Palace of the Buen Retiro, in the eastern part of Madrid. Its decoration was carefully planned by the Count-Duke of Olivares and has been no less carefully studied by Jonathan Brown and John Elliott. It is clear that the 'Histories of Spain' compiled in the previous century, and particularly the work of Mariana, had left their mark. Exaltation of the glories of the dynasty, its victories in war and the virtues of its princes did, of course, continue to be the central themes on display. This is evident from the prominent position assigned to the statues of Carlos V and Felipe II, cast in bronze by the Leoni brothers and currently on display in the Prado Museum, and the equestrian statue of the reigning monarch, to be seen today in the Plaza de Oriente in Madrid, which was added to that of Felipe III, now installed in the capital's Plaza Mayor. In what is known as the 'Hall of Kingdoms', a room of major symbolic significance where ambassadors were received and the most formal ceremonies held, it was decided yet again to install huge commemorative paintings of recent military actions, all of them victories over heretics – including the wonderful *Surrender at Breda* by Velázquez – together with portraits of the royal family. A smaller series of works portraying the Labours of Hercules was also commissioned from Zurbarán to be hung above the doors. Of all the figures from classical mythology, why was Hercules chosen? Because Mariana and others had included him among the kings 'of Spain' and even considered him to be the founder of the 'Spanish' monarchy. Hercules, moreover, complemented the statues of the Roman emperors who were called 'Spanish' (because they were born in the Roman province of Baetica) that stood in the 'Garden of the Emperors' of the Alcázar or fortress on the banks of the River Manzanares. Rodrigo Caro, in his 'Song to the ruins of Italica', dedicated a number of verses to the statue of Trajan that were unequivocal in their meaning:

> Aquí nació aquel rayo de la guerra,
> gran padre de la patria, honor de España,
> pío, felice, triunfador Trajano,
> ante quien muda se postró la tierra . . .[4]

Although the cult of the dynasty continued to take priority, it is possible to distinguish the first signs of another type of cult, which referred to royalty in a different sense: as the expression of a people. To praise Hercules or Trajan was to praise the deeds of hero-kings with no link to the reigning monarchy other than their qualities as leaders and as representatives of a lineage or race distinguished by martial glory. This, at least, was the interpretation of contemporaries. The Ambassador of the Grand Duke of Tuscany explained that the Battle of Nordlingen was absent from among those represented in the 'Hall of Kingdoms' because, in spite of being more important than some of those included, 'it had not been won with arms from there alone, but also with those of the Emperor.'[5] The idea, therefore, was to extol the glories of 'the Spanish'. It was in fact the Medici, the Grand Dukes of Tuscany, who bestowed upon Felipe III and Felipe IV the two magnificent equestrian statues mentioned above, which, on the demise of the Austrian dynasty, became the only political monuments to remain in the capital of the kingdom – an indication that exaltation of the monarchs continued to take pride of place.

In their eagerness to reinforce monarchical power, the Bourbons of the seventeenth century undertook a renewal of the symbols designed to represent the State, a body that had to manifest itself visibly in order to facilitate its identification and popular support among its subjects. This was most apparent in the reign of Carlos III, when a new flag was designed for the navy which would henceforth consist of three horizontal bands: the upper and lower ones were red while the central one was a double width of yellow. It was to become the future 'national flag', the literal phrase used in the Caroline decree of 1785 and which, by the express wish of the king, did not include a trace of the colour of the royal house, Bourbon white, or the fleur-de-lis. It was also during Carlos's reign that the 'Grenadiers' March' was adopted for royal occasions, although this only became the national anthem much later, after a long and complicated history. Nonetheless, in the symbolic representations of the eighteenth century, the nation appeared to be gaining ground and, in its attempts to legitimise and glorify the monarchy, the nation was also developing, although there were manifold ambiguities and regressions. Hymns to the collective identity could be equated with those in praise of dynastic glories. And although the first two Bourbons created academies in order to foster a culture that would become the 'national' or official State culture, these institutions were not called 'national' but 'royal', signifying that such a culture should not be considered as being linked to the State – even less so to the nation – but rather as being directly related to the patronage of the king.[6]

As for the development and embellishment of Madrid, which is associated above all with Carlos III, was this because the city was the *capital* of the nation-State or rather because it was the location of the *court*, the king's residence? What 'the best Mayor of Madrid' erected in the new Paseo del Prado (Prado Avenue) were statues of Neptune and Cybele, mythological gods similar to the ones that his great-grandfather, Louis XIV, had had installed at Versailles, and therefore devoid of any reference whatsoever to national glories. Neither was there any allusion to

them in the groups of sculptures with mythological or allegorical themes
that were placed in the gardens and fountains of the Palaces in Aranjuez
and La Granja, built or enlarged by the Bourbons along lines that
showed no substantial alteration from the decorative style chosen by
Felipe II for the gardens of his Palaces of El Pardo and El Bosque.[7] The
same doubts characterise all the symbology of the *ancien régime*, including that which signalled the most evident progress in the affirmation of
a pre-national identity. Can the strengthening of the State, and of the
symbols and culture associated with it, be interpreted as representations
of the *nation?* Or was it an attempt to exalt the power and glory of the
crown? All the activities undertaken by the State to further the modernisation of society and the economy can be regarded as an attempt
to increase the resources of the monarch in his dynastic conflicts. Even
the promotion of Castilian as the *lingua franca* of the monarchy could
be considered merely as a pragmatic measure, inspired by the desire to
increase the efficiency of the administration and the control of the king
over his subjects. Greater control was certainly what Olivares wanted,
but this was a long way from identifying the State with an *ethnos* or a
culture. As for the symbols, it must be remembered that, for a long
time, the future national anthem was simply the 'Grenadiers' March'
or the 'Royal March'; and that the same Carlos III who had signed the
decree creating the 'national' flag declared in 1760 that the patron saint
of Spain was to be the Immaculate Conception, a deity or mystery that
is difficult to nationalise.[8]

   Other indications can be surmised from the royal palace that the
new Bourbon dynasty had built in the Plaza de Oriente, which replaced
the old Alcázar of Madrid, intimately linked to the memory of the
Hapsburgs but irreparably damaged by fire. Initially, in the 1740s,
Felipe V had thought of adopting the decorative plans of the sculptor
Oliveri, by virtue of which the royal family was eulogised alongside
characters from the Holy Scriptures (the strong women of the Bible)
and from classical Antiquity (mythological heroes and Roman generals), together with allegories of the four parts of the world. If this plan
had been executed, it would have been sadly lacking in innovation in
terms of ethno-patriotic identity. Later, however, the royal confessor
Father Fèvre and the Benedictine Father Sarmiento were asked to
review these plans. Father Fèvre proposed a series of allegorical scenes
portraying the major events of the kingdom together with a representation of the kingdoms of the crown; thus far there were no elements
indicative of a national sensibility, except that the only kingdoms to be
included were the peninsular ones. But he went on to propose a collection of statues of the great figures in the history of Spain that included

Scipio, Hannibal, Pompey, Trajan, Theodosius, El Cid, Gonzalo de Córdoba (The 'Gran Capitán' or Great Captain who defeated the French in Italy), Cisneros, Columbus and Hernán Cortés; a curious list of 'Spanish' heroes, the majority of whom (six out of eleven) an Italian nationalist would have had no hesitation in claiming for his own. In his proposal, Father Sarmiento suggested some fifty tapestries of the battles of Felipe V himself, together with others depicting his birth and that of his two sons (who would also become kings). To all this, he added classical 'Spanish' themes such as the heroic resistance to the sieges of the Carthaginians and Romans at Saguntum and Numantia respectively, as well as the battles of Covadonga and Clavijo. It is true that a large number of these themes dated back to the old chroniclers, and it could be said that they were of as much interest to the legitimacy of the crown as to the construction of the nation. Nevertheless, it is also worth observing how the traits of collective characterisation already outlined in the previous stage continued to be emphasised, including love of independence (Saguntum, Numantia), the innate Christianity of the Spanish nation (the Councils of Toledo, Spanish saints), the pre-dominance of Castile over all the other peninsular kingdoms, and the protracted struggle against the Muslims during the Middle Ages.

In short, although Christianity and the monarchy continued to be the principal foci for a definition of collective identity in these projects, there can be no doubt that national history was gaining in strength with each new project to the detriment of Graeco-Roman mythology and the traditional allegories of generic virtues that were ritually attributed to each ruler or ruling family. Father Sarmiento, confessor to the new King Fernando VI and a man with a good understanding of the pedagogical functions of paintings, which he described as 'books clear to everyone', seems to have played a special part in this evolution. Of undeniable significance, for example, were the decisions to bury books and objects referring to the history of Spain (not to the dynasty) in the walls of the royal chapel, and to have palace inscriptions written in 'ordinary Castilian' instead of Latin. The general guidelines were also explicit: 'insofar as possible' the adornments had to be chosen to 'represent persons, things and actions of the Spanish nation'; and, as regards images, only those which were 'suitable to the palace of a Spanish monarch, and not to any other palace' could be displayed.[9]

Under the first Bourbons, one can detect a growing tendency to present power in terms of lineage or collective culture, which furthered the development of the ethnic patriotism initiated under the Hapsburgs. Nevertheless, oscillation between the two loyalties, the *patria* and the king, continued. A step forward in terms of the construction of the

ethnos or nation, in the modern sense of the term, required the glorification of the Spanish *people*, represented by Viriathus, El Cid and
other figures, whether warriors or men of peace. Of course, this aspect
becomes increasingly difficult to distinguish from mere dynastic self-
glorification because the king and the royal family figured more and
more often as the leading and most distinguished members of the
people. No doubt this was the aim of many of the intellectuals who
were collaborating with enlightened governments in the development
of a pre-national consciousness. It is more doubtful, however, that this
representation of the Spanish nation was understood by either the royal
family and its entourage or, above all, by the common people, still overwhelmingly characterised by reverence and submission to the monarch
as the supreme incarnation of public authority.

The conclusion of this brief overview is that, long before 1808, a
Spanish identity was being formed, an embryo of the nation that was
about to spread its wings. For the educated élites, this identity was
linked to the exploits, somewhat embellished by historians, of the
collective entity known as 'Spain'. Outstanding among these were
the achievements, both political and cultural, of the *Siglo de Oro*, the
Golden Age. Among the populace, however, it is probable that their
loyalty was first and foremost to the local community and, in global
political terms, was related almost exclusively to the monarchy, and
in particular to the successes and failures of the royal armies. Religion
aside, the monarchy seems to have been the focal point of the anti-
French mobilisations of 1808. Documents indicative of the sentiments
prevailing during the uprising certainly maintained the king-nation
duality, but invocations of the former are far more frequent than
those of the latter. If we are to believe these texts, those involved in
the uprising undoubtedly felt themselves to be Spanish, but what they
worshipped was not an abstract idea but an actual person, Fernando, a
sacrosanct figure immune to all criticism. Thus they followed the time-
honoured secular tradition of invoking the king as the personification
of the collectivity, particularly in time of war. As Gabriel Lovett has
observed, not even the king's absence during the war diminished his
prestige because 'the government of national resistance always referred
to the king with the greatest devotion, and since all decrees were rendered in his name, the people had no reason to lose their extraordinary
faith in what they felt to be the symbol of their salvation.'[10]

Of interest, though of no special significance, is the oft-repeated
anecdote that the Constitution of Cádiz was affectionately nicknamed
la Pepa because it was promulgated on 19 March 1812. The novelist,
Benito Pérez Galdós, appositely titled the *Episodio Nacional* with which

he began his tale of the War of Independence, 'From the Nineteenth of March to the Second of May'. These two dates were the object of a proposal presented to the *Cortes* in the spring of 1814, after Napoleon's defeat, for a monument. The President of the Cortes emphasised that 'among the most glorious days that a Nation must acknowledge is the one on which it takes its first step towards liberty and independence. For us, that day is 19 March 1808, a great, memorable and glorious day on which the lion of Spain awoke and broke his shackles.'[11] It is merely coincidental that 19 March happens to be St Joseph's Day, not because Spanish society and the institutions of the day felt a special devotion towards the good carpenter who passed into history as the nominal father of Christ. In fact, 19 March was the date of the insurrection of Aranjuez, which led to the fall of Godoy and forced Carlos IV to abdicate in favour of his son, Prince Fernando. In other words, for some time, the latter's accession to the throne was a cause for celebration of similar importance to that for the uprising against the French in Madrid, which was to become a national holiday.[12]

It would appear that the liberal *diputados*, or members of the *Cortes*, were unable to comprehend sufficiently either the enormous magnetism of Fernando *the Desired One* (as he was popularly known) or the fact that those who took up arms against the French had done so for the monarchy rather than for the nation. It was a mistake for which they were to pay dearly. A similar state of affairs confounded their successors, the liberals of the 1830s, whose struggle to overcome the followers of Don Carlos was so difficult partly because they were unable to oppose him with a figurehead of comparable strength. This personalisation of politics around a warlike leader, obviously male and of royal blood, was to shape all the major political conflicts during the greater part of the nineteenth century.

United kingdom or spineless confederation?

A second problem relating to the construction of a pre-national identity in Spain during the early modern period has recently been subjected to scrutiny. It is the fact that the Hispanic monarchy was not a united State but a disparate collection of kingdoms and feudal domains, with subjects who spoke a variety of languages, who were characterised by substantial differences as regards laws and taxes, and who even had to pay tolls when they journeyed between the different territories. The growth of any sense of cohesion between the individuals who coexisted beneath the supreme monarchical authority was therefore made difficult – if not impossible – by the persistence of identities relating to the old mediaeval kingdoms and to even smaller entities such as regions, valleys or municipalities, and rooted in loyalty to their institutions and local customs. People would have undoubtedly regarded these entities as 'their own' and as being more authentic than any larger territorial framework.

It is indisputable that the monarchy to which the cultural creation of Spain was so closely linked was highly decentralised. In effect, the Hapsburgs were never the rulers of a 'kingdom' in Spain but only of a monarchy, which is a dynastic union or a mere aggregation of crowns. The process of aggregation had been long and complicated and was usually based on matrimonial unions or inheritances, frequently combined with some kind of military intervention. Nevertheless, it was always agreed to respect, if only partially, the traditional laws and taxes of the territory that was incorporated into the whole, as well as to maintain the internal representative institutions. These were usually *Cortes* or chambers made up of the members of the great families and some prelates and representatives of privileged corporations. In this respect, the Hispanic Monarchy was no exception within Europe. Other *ancien régime* political entities exhibited few differences in comparison with those of Hapsburg Spain: all were governed by some form of decentralised organisation and all were characterised by exceptions and privileges because all had acquired territory in a similar fashion. The highly complex system of the Spanish Hapsburgs displayed the closest similarities to that of the Holy Roman Empire, which was ruled by their Austrian cousins and which later became the Austro-Hungarian Empire. This was one of the great political constructions of the *ancien régime* which, unable to transform itself into a nation-State, finally imploded in the modern era.[13]

However, the Hispanic Monarchy did possess some features that gave it a certain homogeneity. To begin with, it had one institution common to all the kingdoms, namely the Inquisition, which had a proven capacity to shape habits and collective beliefs and was without parallel in any other monarchy, including the Holy Roman Empire. Second, it had a central power base, the Kingdom of Castile, the richest, most highly populated and belligerent of all the kingdoms at beginning of the process, even though it was to be left in ruins by the end. Castilian contributions to the Hispanic monarchy were soon augmented by the wealth from mining and trade with the Americas, which furnished the central government with greater resources – and greater independence from the representative institutions of the kingdom – than those possessed by any rival monarchies. Even then, the highest authorities of the Hapsburg monarchy could not, or would not, legislate for, or impose homogeneous institutions on, their collection of kingdoms.

The Count-Duke of Olivares, obsessed by the struggle between the Monarchy and its rivals for European power, believed that this was one of the weaknesses of the empire. In his famous 'Instruction' sent to the young Felipe IV, he argued with enviable clarity in favour of the centralisation and standardisation of the system: 'Let Your Majesty make it the most important business of your Monarchy to become King of Spain; I mean to say, Sire, that Your Majesty should not be content to be King of Portugal, of Aragón, of Valencia, Count of Barcelona, but that you should work in secret and silent counsel, to reduce those kingdoms which make up Spain to the style and laws of Castile, with no difference, and that if Your Majesty achieves this, you will be the most powerful Prince on earth'. Some years later, this idea of Olivares would materialise in the 'Union of Arms', a plan which was designed to extract a greater supply of men and resources from the non-Castilian kingdoms for the accursed 'Thirty Years War'. Such a plan was doomed to failure: Portuguese and Catalan resistance led to war in 1640, and not only were the plans of the Count-Duke put aside, along with Olivares himself, but Portugal achieved its independence as a result. Olivares's rival, Cardinal Richelieu, faced similar revolts – and outright civil war – when he demanded greater resources from the more wealthy areas or families for the same war, but he proved capable of controlling the situation with greater success than Felipe IV's minister. And France, in the words of Domínguez Ortiz, 'made faster progress towards the modern structure of the State than Spain'. If 'modern' is understood as a more centralised and homogeneous structure, this was undoubtedly true.[14]

Olivares's successors did not adopt his centralising strategy, and when Barcelona fell to the royal troops in 1653, they did not substantially modify the Catalan *fueros* or laws, and no one thought of limiting the use of the Catalan language. In fact, as regards cultural standardisation, official attempts to impose the language of the court in non-Castilian-speaking territories before 1700 were practically non-existent. The only cultural area which really concerned the rulers of the sixteenth and seventeenth centuries was religion, not language.

If neither monarchs nor their ministers were aware of the political importance of language in the first centuries of the early modern age, there are signs that intellectuals had a clearer understanding of its importance for the political legitimacy of the future nation. Before the end of the fifteenth century, Antonio de Nebrija had penned his famous phrase, 'language always accompanies empire', in the prologue to his Castilian grammar book, in order to convince Queen Isabel of its usefulness. A similar attitude led to a 'defence' of the Castilian language by Aldrete and Covarrubias in the seventeenth century and to the pride expressed in it in the eighteenth century by the Valencian Mayans and the Catalan Capmany, both of whom described it as a sonorous language with a rich 'literature' (referring to written culture in general). The Castilian language began to take precedence over Latin and the other languages spoken in the Peninsula between 1500 and 1700 (one of which, the Aragonese variant of Occitan, practically disappeared during the early modern age), especially from the moment the court decided to settle permanently in Castile and to employ Castilian as the language of the upper ranks of the bureaucracy. Although there are no reliable figures, it is likely that at the time when Felipe V proposed the linguistic standardisation of his kingdoms (that is, after Portugal and the Italian and Flemish territories had broken away from the Crown of Spain), some two thirds of the monarchy's inhabitants spoke Castilian. In addition, after the great literary creations of the *Siglo de Oro*, the language was accepted by the political and cultural élites of the other kingdoms as a form of educated expression common to all and, last but not least, it was the only language spoken by the colonisers of the Americas. As a result, a single language came to dominate within the Spanish monarchy to at least the same extent, and probably with a greater degree of standardisation, than in either the English or French cases. Regional and social differences resulted in far greater levels of incomprehension between the politico-social élites and the peasantry in France and England than in Spain.[15]

While the cultural fragmentation of the Spanish Monarchy should not be exaggerated, it none the less began to be seen as a political problem on the accession of the new Bourbon dynasty in 1700, and rulers began to introduce measures to combat it. The monarchy's title of *Spanish* took over from *Hispanic*, and there was even talk of the *kingdom* of Spain (although it is both curious and significant that the title was not officially adopted until the time of Joseph Bonaparte). The new centralising mentality led to the elimination of the *fueros* of the kingdom of Aragón, with reforms introduced in the so-called *Nueva Planta* of the early eighteenth century. This did not merely represent a new means of organising the administrative apparatus but also a new conception of culture based on standardisation. The decrees of Felipe V included measures designed to impose Castilian as the exclusive language of officialdom. Similarly, the University of Barcelona was transferred to the small town of Cervera, near the Aragonese border, where classes were taught only in Castilian.

In addition to prohibitions and sanctions against the use of regional languages, incentives were introduced in order to encourage the use of Castilian and to promote what was beginning to be considered as the *official* State culture, though without being called as such. A major stimulus was the foundation of the Royal Academies, which were *royal* institutions not because they were founded directly by the monarch (originally they were private institutions), but because the Crown agreed to be their patron. Their aims went far beyond dynastic glorification. The first to be founded, in 1713, bore the grand title of the Royal Spanish Academy, combining in those two adjectives, the two pillars – dynastic and ethnic – on which legitimacy was now based. Its motto '*limpia, fija y da esplendor* (it cleanses, establishes and enhances)' expressed its aim of purifying and preserving the official forms of expression of the monarchy, a crucial part of the cultural canon that had to be assimilated by all the subjects of the nation-State that it defined. It was time for the national language to affirm its autonomy and become definitively divorced from Latin in the same way that national Law had to become independent of Roman Law. To accomplish the latter, Felipe V set up Chairs of Spanish Law, announcing that 'it is by this, and not by Roman Law, that future judges must decide and substantiate legal cases'.[16]

Another affirmation of independence was forthcoming in the field of history, a cultural dimension that has always been crucial to nationalism. It was felt necessary to define what was 'Spanish' from among the myriad events transmitted by the chronicles and to transform the 'nation' into the main protagonist of the past. This was the task allotted to the Royal Academy of History, also founded under the first Bourbon monarch, in 1738. It was an undeniably modern institution inspired by the new historiographical perspectives that had emerged from the intellectual revolution of the previous century, and it performed a most praiseworthy job in eliminating the mythological elements that still persisted in the works of Mariana and other historians of the sixteenth and seventeenth centuries. However, not all its concerns were scientific. It was not called a National or Spanish Academy, nor did it produce any documents referring to a collective, permanent entity, and yet all its activities were based on the assumption that the nation was the essential subject of history. Its founding statutes declared that the aim of the institution was to write a 'universal critical-historical dictionary of Spain', cleansing the history 'of *our* Spain from the fables that discredit it'. Its members, who were certainly the best historians of the 1700s, even ventured to organise historical time in a new way, setting up nothing less than their own chronology or 'Hispanic era', commencing with the pacification of the Peninsula by Augustus some forty years before Christ. In this way, 'Spain' was located within a specific, secular time-frame of its own. It replaced the universal, sacred framework prevailing until then, which had established on the basis of the Biblical texts that the world was 6,000 years old.[17]

In order to establish a national historical canon, the Royal Academy of History sponsored works on the Gothic period and the origins of the Castilian language. This reinforced Castilian superiority and Gothic mythology as the foundation of the Spanish identity invented in mediaeval times. It also drew up reports of symbolic importance, such as establishing 'which of the Gothic kings was and should be considered first of their nation in Spain', which was used for deciding which statues should be placed on the cornices of the new royal palace. It might be assumed that crowning an edifice with statues of 'all the Spanish kings', as was initially planned, was merely a technical or economic problem. In fact, it involved conceptual decisions: it was necessary to define what a *Spanish king* was – in other words, to interpret 'Spanish' in time and space – and this was exactly what the Royal Academy set out to do. As proof of the new critical spirit of historical enquiry, Tubal, Hercules and Argantonio were eliminated, as were the Roman emperors born in Hispania (so that the umbilical cord to Italy could be severed). Don Pelayo was included, but not as the first king. By decision of the august Academy, pride of place as the first 'Spanish' monarch fell to Ataúlfo, with Pelayo as a successor. The first 'Spanish' kings were therefore the Visigoths, followed by the Asturians. There was no discussion of the equal claims to legitimacy of the Navarrans or the Aragonese, whose lineage also passed down through the Visigoths, while the Muslims, as 'foreign invaders', did not even merit a mention. So it came about that a highly imaginative statue of Ataúlfo is the first in the set of 'Spanish' monarchs celebrated in the Plaza de Oriente of Madrid.

In the field of art, the Royal Academy of San Fernando was established in 1752 with the explicit purpose of promoting patriotic art. This was accomplished by holding competitions in painting and sculpture in which historical 'Spanish' themes now ousted the traditional allegorical and mythological ones and even, to a degree, religious ones. It was not an attempt to promote the arts in general but to consecrate a national iconography, to entrust to artists 'the uplifting mission of reproducing the glories of the *patria*, representing them faithfully in marble and on canvas', as one chronicler of the time described it. The latter went on to say that the compositions reconciled 'the inspirations of patriotism with the circumstances demanded by Art', uniting 'the education of the citizen with that of the artist' and keeping alive 'the love of painting and sculpture as well as the memory of the most heroic actions of our forefathers'. The historical themes were generally taken from Mariana's *History*, and among these, the Visigoths, the Middle Ages and the Catholic Kings tended, once again, to predominate. Legitimisation of political unity and collective identity continued to be based on the anti-Muslim struggle, interpreted as a recuperation of the Gothic monarchy, while the confusion between political and religious identity continued to reign, as demonstrated by the prevalence of themes such as the 'Spanish' Christian martyrs, the Councils of Toledo, and figures such as Recaredo and Fernando III, the first a great benefactor of the Church, and the second a saint as well as king.[18]

In short, the eighteenth century was an era in which important steps were undertaken not only in terms of cultural homogenisation, but in relation to administrative standardisation and centralisation, these being aspects of the period on which historians tend to concentrate. Overall, the change in respect of earlier periods could not have been more marked. Hitherto, the Church, the nobility and the monarchs themselves – as powerful lords rather than as Heads of State – had patronised cultural creations designed to glorify them and uphold their rights. The official, standardised culture now fostered by the royal academies and other enlightenment institutions was designed as the representation of a collective entity, 'Spain', the nation whose reality justified the existence of the State. It was an unmistakable symptom of the new era that was dawning.

The enlightened élites were generally enthusiastic participants in this cultural process. When the Napoleonic invasion of 1808 unexpectedly placed the fate of the country in the hands of the *Cortes* gathered in Cádiz, it was not considered necessary to alter direction but simply to accelerate the process by extending official culture across a broader social spectrum. This was not very different to the ongoing standardisation taking place in the juridical and territorial spheres, although in relation to the latter the efforts of the enlightened monarchy appeared frankly insufficient to the *diputados* of Cádiz, who debated the reform of the political and social structures of the country. The majority of the constitutionalists considered the fragmentation of the kingdom to be one of the most scandalous malformations inherited from the *ancien régime* and in need of urgent reform. Consequently they pressed on with the work that Felipe V had embarked upon with, in their opinion, excessive caution. In other words, there was continuity in the Spanish case between Enlightenment and revolution, much as de Tocqueville found in France.

Even before the *Cortes* assembled in 1810, one of the instructions from the *Junta Central* or Central Junta, written by Gaspar de

Jovellanos, the prominent politician and polymath, stated that 'as no political constitution can be good if it lacks unity, and there is nothing more contrary to this unity than the diverse privileged and municipal constitutions of some peoples and provinces . . . the Legislative *Junta* will investigate and propose the means of improving this part of our legislation, seeking the most perfect uniformity'. Let there be no mistake: not just *unity*, but *the most perfect uniformity*. Manuel José Quintana, the poet and political thinker, was of the same opinion. He maintained that the *Cortes* should draw up a constitution that made 'of all the provinces that comprise this vast Monarchy truly a single Nation . . . In it there should cease to be differences between Valencians, Aragonese, Castilians, Biscayans in the eyes of the law: all should be Spaniards'. The Alavese lawyer Pedro Egaña had no argument with this. Before the drafting of the Constitution, he had underlined that 'there was not a true political association between us' since 'the Nation was completely separated, disunited and divided. Each Province had its own particular laws and *fueros*, its own government and administration'. With the constitutional charter, on the other hand, 'everything has changed. The laws and *fueros* peculiar to each province no longer exist: for each one, the government is the same and the administration is uniform . . . Everyone is subject to the same law and everyone bears the same burden of the State. We all belong to a family and we make up a single society. The Spanish, imperfectly constituted under the *ancien régime* . . . now form a true body politic and we are indeed an independent, free and sovereign Nation.'[19]

The necessity of moulding the nation into a unified, homogeneous model seemed like a truism to many of the liberal *diputados*, since the essential attribute of *unity* was implicit in the very concept of *national will*. The solidity and exclusivity of the subject required, above all, the dissolution of divisory historical inheritances such as kingdoms and privileged corporations with their own institutions and laws and, though unconnected, their languages and cultures. However much the constitutionalists in Cádiz tried to dress up their projects as a return to mediaeval laws and freedoms, they did not disguise their intention to sweep away the old legislation specific to the kingdoms and divide up the territory in a new, uniform way.[20] The nation was called a 'moral body' by the deputy and poet Juan Nicasio Gallego, by which he meant a single, compact block, proof against internal divisions. That 'the kingdom should be one and indissoluble' was, according to the historian and deputy Martínez Marina, the 'fundamental law of the Spanish Monarchy'. The deputy Agustín de Foronda requested that the Constitution expressly declare the abolition of 'all the privileges of provinces, cities, for they are all Spanish and thus none should have advantages not enjoyed by others'. More radical than anyone else, Foronda confessed that, if he could, he 'would divide Spain up into eighteen square sections numbered *number one, number two,* etc.' and he 'would remove the names of Vizcaya, Andalucía, etc. as the origin of cruel, puerile and ill-fated disputes, since the Spanish should all be as one'.[21]

The alternative possibility would have been to go down the same road as Switzerland or the United States, namely, to move towards the construction of a new political framework by means of a federalising process that would start out by recognising the legitimacy and diversity of the pre-existing kingdoms or fiefdoms. The Count of Toreno summed it up well: 'The broad expanse of the nation impels it towards federalism under a liberal system; and if we do not prevent this it will come to form, especially with the overseas provinces, a federation like that of the United States, that will imperceptibly come to imitate the most independent of the old Swiss cantons, and end up by constituting separate states'. However, a number of *diputados* in favour of the federal solution, especially those from the kingdom of Aragón, played on fears of a centralised despotism such as France had experienced under the Jacobins. But the majority of reformers were more attracted by Napoleonic Cartesianism than Anglo-Saxon organicism: according to them, the elimination of inequalities required administrative standardisation; or, to put it another way, the establishment of legal equality demanded the elimination of *diversity*. On this point, the legislators of Cádiz displayed general agreement, against which there were only rather timid objections raised by some of the representatives of the traditional *foral* territories.[22]

Those who opposed the reform of territorial limits were put firmly in their place by the liberal deputy and priest Diego Muñoz Torrero, who maintained that they were talking 'as though the Spanish nation were not one, as if it had different kingdoms and states. It is necessary that we recognise that all these divisions of provinces must disappear, and that in the present constitution all the fundamental laws of the other provinces of the monarchy must be rewritten . . . The Commission has proposed to equate them all . . . so that together they make up a single family with the same laws and government . . . I want us to agree that we form a single nation and not an aggregate of nations.'[23] It would be difficult to imagine a clearer statement of intent by the liberals in Cádiz in relation to their project for the reorganisation of the State. They wanted to build a united State that was legitimised by the existence of a single nation.

In spite of the occasional objections to this unifying project, the underlying support for it by the Catalans, Aragonese and Navarrans, and the creation of the mythology that underpinned the so-called 'War of Independence', should not be forgotten. Napoleon's attempts to foment Catalan and Basque 'identities' as a means of undermining the unity of those opposing his dominion were a failure, in contrast to the success of similar stratagems which had led to confrontations between the inhabitants of Württemberg and Swabia, on the one hand, and Bolognans and Romans, on the other. In the Spanish case, however, many Aragonese and Catalan names were linked to the 'epic' struggle against the French; and a Catalan as renowned as Antonio de Capmany was to write some of the most sensational anti-French speeches. Moreover, 'Juan Español' – the Spanish equivalent of John Bull – was usually dressed in traditional Aragonese style. During the war, the *jota*, a traditional Aragonese dance, came to represent national folklore, and the lyrics of one of them are very famous:

> La Virgen del Pilar dice / que no quiere ser francesa;
> que quiere ser capitana / de la tropa aragonesa.

The *jota* was a symbol of Aragonese, not Spanish, opposition to the French, and the great heroine of the war was called Agustina *Zaragoza*, or Agustina *de Aragón*, but not Agustina *de España*. However, Aragón and Spain were definitely not mutually exclusive terms. Indeed, asserting one's Aragonese identity between 1808 and 1814 was a way of proclaiming oneself to be Spanish.[24] To judge from the behaviour of the kingdoms of Aragón during the Napoleonic war, their confrontation with Felipe V a century earlier did not appear to have left many scars.

The national sentiment created during, and by, the war of 1808–1814 was to last for the greater part of the nineteenth century. It was a case of collective self-suggestion, which is what national identities actually are. It was generally accepted that the massive uprising against the French demonstrated the existence of a solid and united Spanish nation, while the projects for reorganising cultural life and the political system on a nationwide basis were rooted in this belief. It meant giving a 'national' culture precedence over 'dialects' and 'regional variations'. It also meant putting an end to the legal inequalities that existed between citizens because, in short, 'we are all Spanish'. Lastly, it meant dividing up the territory in the most uniform way possible in order to eliminate the differences – the 'privileges' or *privatae leges*, which were the special laws – between the old kingdoms and feudal entities. Throughout the nineteenth century, an effort was made to accomplish all of this. That this unifying endeavour was not wholly successful was due more to the weakness of the State itself than to the existence of forces that questioned the unity of the nation.

The possible alternatives: a digression on the (turbulent) nobility

Let us return briefly to the *ancien régime*. It is clear that, during the two hundred years of Hapsburg rule, the kings, their ministers and their central bureaucracy had barely attempted to impose a uniform administration or culture that would facilitate the formation of a collective identity. Moreover, the attempts of the Bourbons in this respect seemed manifestly insufficient to the liberals in Cádiz. Would it have been possible for some other sector of society to have created this identity under the *ancien régime*? Could some other sector have represented 'the kingdom' or 'kingdoms', or the estates? In other words, did the élites who opposed Carlos V in the war of the *Comuneros* of Castile or who defended Aragonese privileges against Felipe II, or the Catalans who fought Olivares, or the nobles opposed to Bourbon centralisation, perhaps consider themselves to be speaking on behalf of the 'kingdom'? Did they look upon their role as similar to that of England's Members of Parliament, for example?

The answer has to be a resounding 'no' and, as a result, this brings us to yet another problem with the origins of Spanish nationalism. To quote De Blas and Laborda, 'in Castile in the early modern age, the dual constitution defined by Otto Hintze of the *Rex* and the *Regnum* did not exist. Royal supremacy was not counterbalanced by a representative organ of the estates as in other countries.'[25] There were parliamentary traditions in the various peninsular monarchies which, although not enjoying the strength of the English one, were not to be dismissed lightly. An indication of the ability of a parliament to stand up to royal power is to be found in the harsh war between the Castilian *Cortes* and Charles of Ghent in 1520–1521. It could be argued that the adverse outcome of that conflict was proof that parliament's strength was less than it thought, or, conversely, that its attempt to take power was premature precisely because of its exceptional self-confidence. Whatever one's interpretation, it cannot be denied that from then on, the situation that developed was exactly the opposite of that in England during the following century: instead of parliamentarianism being reinforced thanks to successive victories over the monarch, the defeat of the *Comunero* rebellion increased royal absolutism. In just a few years, the representative institutions of society in Castile, of the *kingdom* as opposed to the *king*, collapsed. The Castilian *Cortes* not only saw their

powers drastically reduced under Carlos V but, after 1538, representatives of the nobility and the clergy were not summoned.[26]

The representative institutions of the kingdoms of Aragon, Catalonia
and Valencia maintained their prerogatives for longer, although the
first two had them cut back after the affair of Antonio Pérez and Juan
de Lanuza in 1590 and the *dels Segadors* insurrection in 1640 – two
major uprisings against the centralised monarchy – while Valencia
was subdued after the *Germanías* revolt in the 1520 and the expulsion
of the *Moriscos* in 1610. Moreover, the Aragonese kingdoms neither
considered themselves the centre of the monarchy nor assumed a
guiding role in relation to the development of Spanish identity – which,
without occupying the geographical centre, Prussia did in Germany,
and Piedmont did in Italy. On the contrary, they confined themselves
to rising up in defence of their privileges in the face of enforced integration and centralisation, but only managed to delay their subjection to
monarchical absolutism, which finally enveloped them during the War
of Succession (1700–1713). Thus, the life of these institutions finally
came to an end in the early 1700s. It should not be thought, however,
that this signalled the defeat of the universal right to representation, for
the simple reason that this was not what the parliaments had defended.
They had only defended the liberties and privileges of certain territories within the State. The Bourbons made it impossible to defend such
fragmentation except in the Basque provinces and Navarre, where privileges were respected and whose people were, for the time being, content
to survive on the periphery of the system.

A prominent sector of society absent from the 'Spanish' process
of politico-cultural construction was the nobility. In one of his most
famous works, José Ortega y Gasset maintained that the principal
'abnormality' of Spanish history had been the 'absence of the best'.
According to him, the lack of 'eminent minorities' was the 'secret of
the evils' of Spain, the obstacle that had prevented it from being 'a sufficiently normal nation.'[27] Such an ambitious interpretation of Spanish
history is hardly justified on the basis of the scanty information put
forward by the illustrious essayist. Nevertheless, within the European
context, it is anomalous that the Spanish nobility not only played no
part in the creation of a national identity but that, amazingly, it played
an equally irrelevant role in the construction of the State. This is in
stark contrast to the other major powers: in England, for example, the
aristocracy assumed a corporate role in the name of the nation in both
parliamentary houses. In France, it was involved in an ongoing though
isolated and sporadic struggle with the monarchy throughout the early
modern age, and some of its members even espoused revolutionary

ideals at the end of the process. In Russia and Prussia, nobles held the highest positions of command in the army and were charged with imposing royal authority in their territories. Even in Portugal and Hungary, the nobility upheld their 'own' identity, in opposition to domination by an imperial power which they were astute enough to represent as 'foreign.'[28] In some cases, the nobility acted in the name of the *kingdom* against the absolutist pretensions of the *king*; in others, it collaborated with the State, sending its scions to serve in the army or the navy and representing State authority in the latter's dominions; in some cases, it did both. In my opinion, the Spanish nobility failed to do either.

In comparison with other aristocracies, the Spanish one was far more 'domesticated'. Lacking their own corporate institutions similar to the English ones, the estates were deprived of their mediaeval function, and their political powers were steadily trimmed back as those of the monarchy increased. When the aristocracy did achieve a certain degree of influence, such as in the second half of the seventeenth century, all it did was to 'refeudalise' power, to quote José Antonio Maravall, or to aspire directly to the fragmentation of the State, as occurred with the conspiracies of Híjar and Medinasidonia in the time of Felipe IV.[29] Entrenched within their local power bases, nobles only fought to uphold or extend their private jurisdictions. Faced with the Bourbon reforms of the eighteenth century, the aristocracy put up a tenacious resistance to the 'recovery' of royal prerogatives embarked upon by the monarchy. Only towards the end of the century, when the first signs of the liberal revolution were glimmering on the horizon, did some nobles, notably the Count of Teba in his manifesto of 1794, try to present their estate as the upholder of liberty in opposition to absolutism. Nonetheless, when the opportunity arrived to transform the system into a constitutional one some fifteen years later, it was not the nobility, as a group, who led the way.[30]

Attempts to turn the sons of the most illustrious families into high-ranking administrators or military commanders, like the Russians and the Prussians, were also a failure, even when promoted by the monarchy. Olivares was also relatively unsuccessful in his patronage of academies for training the sons of noble houses. Even the military functions that were still performed by the aristocracy in the sixteenth and seventeenth centuries gradually lost any significance, and virtually disappeared in the eighteenth century as a result of the professionalisation of first the navy and then the army. As the Venetian ambassador Cornaro observed in surprise in 1683, 'all power resides in the grandees' – referring to political as well as social power – but they 'have no care for the public cause nor for the interests of the crown'. A century later, a perspicacious British traveller, Joseph Townsend, also expressed his astonishment at the fact that, in Spain, among 'the most important appointments' there was not 'a single man of elevated birth' to be found, whereas in England 'the most able ministers are individuals who belong to the leading nobility.'[31] He thus confirmed the continuing lack of interest in State matters which Ambassador Cornaro had observed before. Fernández de Bethencourt, a genealogist prone to applauding the nobility, admitted in the early twentieth century that 'the leading Spanish nobility, like none other in Europe . . . has turned its back on the army . . . turned its back on politics . . . has turned its back on the toga . . . turned its back on the great commercial enterprises.'[32]

Whatever the facts, it is undeniable that the nobility had an abominable political reputation. In the chronicles of the kingdoms as well as the general histories of Spain, their role in building a collective identity is systematically discredited, being described in terms of stereotypes such as the '*turbulent* aristocracy', 'noble *anarchy*', 'seigniorial *factions*', and the '*weakness*' of the monarchy in the face of the '*arrogance*' of the grandees. The figure of the 'nobility' is almost inextricably linked to 'disturbances', 'troubles', 'civil war', and to the mean and selfish impulses that led to such *fratricidal* struggles. This is in direct contrast to the monarchy, the representative of authority, justice, order and internal peace. The only cause for reproach was the kings' repeated, though not ill-intentioned, mistake of apportioning their kingdoms among their heirs, the inevitable cause of new quarrels. The mid-nineteenth century historian Antonio Cavanilles, for example, in his chapter on the Catholic Kings, reels off the usual eulogies of their many ventures and concludes, in lapidary style: 'feudalism came to an end; the magnates bowed their heads; the law prevailed'. The law, a fundamental feature of the modern State, came to be associated with monarchical unity whereas 'feudality' meant disorder. Mariana had recognised this paradigm long before, and it is symptomatic of the nobility's attitude to the project of national construction that his history should have provoked such a furious reaction from the Dukes of Frías, Constables of Castile and León, that they ordered a rejoinder from their secretary, Father Mantuano. He obliged by scrutinising the tomes written by the Jesuit with a critical eye, guided by a single premise: that the glory of the noble houses, and especially that of his patrons, was inadequately described. Thus the Castilian nobility cast doubts on the first great *Historia General de España*, the maximum expression of ethno-patriotic or *pre-national* historiography. This had no effect on its immense success and its endurance as *the* work of reference for two and a half centuries.[33]

The Spanish nobility entered the nineteenth century burdened with a negative image that not even the Napoleonic wars nor the subsequent political disturbances did much to improve. Hardly any aristocrats led military actions between 1808 and 1814, and their contribution to the legislative discussions held in Cádiz was equally unimpressive. For the remainder of the nineteenth century, all that can be said about the nobility generally is that, once their legal privileges were removed, the untitled faded into obscurity and, of those with titles, the most important tended to give up their old lifestyles and become integrated into urban centres as the upper class. The minor local nobility, to the extent that it survived, resisted the modernisation of the State and the nationalisation of politics from its local strongholds, either by supporting the Carlist cause or by turning to *caciquismo*.[34]

One last fact of interest is the curious contradiction between the poor image of the aristocracy as a social group and historical agent, and the overabundance of noble rhetoric in political discourse. The negative role assigned to nobles in collective life was no obstacle to a deep interiorisation of aristocratic attitudes. During the conflict with Napoleon, the most commonly repeated expressions of repugnance at French aggression concerned the invaders' lack of integrity and honour, accusations which are among the most traditional social values of the aristocracy. Faced with French *villainy*, with their *treacherous* attack, the Spanish reaction was conspicuous for its *nobility* and *chivalry*, and for its *heroism* and *bravery* in comparison with the *cowardice*, the *deceitfulness* and the *perfidy* of the enemy.[35] Fray Simón López, in his *Despertador cristiano-político*, declared that the 'weapons of Napoleon and the French empire' are not 'valour and strength but deceit, cunning and scheming, intrigue and perfidy'. Antonio de Capmany, in referring to the French, reviles them for 'perversion' and 'monstrosity'. The history compiled by Francisco X. Cabanes also refers to 'the most horrible perfidy' and the 'horrendous attack' by the French. On the other hand, 'all the nation did', affirmed the Marquis de las Amarillas, 'was nobly done'. For Díaz de Baeza, the rebellion was 'prompted by honour and fidelity' and was a 'glorious war, that made the name of Spain immortal'. The Count of Toreno described the Asturian decision to join the rebellion as a 'noble' resolution 'founded on the desire to preserve their honour'. In 1812, Fray Manuel Martínez, a preacher from Valladolid, referred to the 'great Nation . . . carried away by that noble impulse of honour, virtue and patriotism'. Another historian-friar, Father Salmón, who published an account of the conflict while the cannons were still roaring, explained that in the artillery park at Monteleón, the French had behaved with 'unprecedented cruelty' because 'under cover of words as sweet and gratifying as *peace*' they had entered 'without opposition from the aforementioned officials of this arm, Velarde and Daoiz, and approaching them as if to embrace them, they inhumanly murder[ed] them with their sabres . . .'. Significantly, the place where a monument was erected to those who died on the Second of May, on one side of the Paseo del Prado in Madrid, is called the '*Campo de la Lealtad*' (the Field of Loyalty). It would later be said that Daoiz and Velarde had sacrificed their lives for the *patria* and that they were heroes of 'national independence', but at the time they were praised for their 'loyalty', the supreme virtue of a knight.[36]

Much could be said about the knightly traits of the Spaniards in the Napoleonic war, from the surprise attacks to the slaughter of defenceless prisoners, all so typical of guerrilla warfare. The fact is that Napoleon's troops had advanced into Spain under false pretences, but *in connivance with the Spanish government*, which had consented to, and cooperated fully with, the strategy: conquer Portugal and deliver a blow to the common English enemy. The nationalist version, however, could not tolerate a stain on the country's good name, and reinterpreted the conflict in a way that would have done Quevedo proud back in the early seventeenth century: 'Spain' had acted in a noble, courageous and ingenuous manner, involving not the slightest selfishness, while it had been attacked in a manner 'lacking in nobility'.

It is evident that the chivalrous rhetoric, accepted and interiorised by all, was one thing, and the generally negative opinion of the nobility as a social group was another. So much so that the *Cortes* of Cádiz simply decided to eliminate it as a political actor. Aristocratic privilege, associated with inequality and internal quarrels, had to be suppressed *in order to build the nation*. At the start of the discussion on aristocratic jurisdictional and seigneurial rights, the *diputado* from Soria, García Herreros, asked that a law be passed 'which restores *to the nation* the enjoyment of its natural, inherent and imprescriptible rights'. The majority of the members supported the motion, explains Pérez Ledesma, moved by 'the desire to constitute a new body politic of citizens equal in their rights'. And the order for the elimination of all public symbols of serfdom was based upon the argument that 'the peoples of the Spanish nation do not recognise nor will ever recognise any jurisdictional rights other than *that of the nation itself.*'[37] Not only are the aristocracy described in the national histories as an obstacle on the difficult road to unity, but also, at the glorious moment of the birth of the nation, its midwives, the members of the *Cortes*, considered the symbols and powers of the aristocracy to be contrary to the new collective identity.

Those obsessed with the *unity* of the nation not only made an issue of the nobility and of *divisive* regional and local identities, but were also opposed to political divisions *in general*. An observation published in *El Redactor General* as early as the summer of 1812 drew attention to this concern: 'In the midst of our rejoicing, let us not lose sight of an object which we judge of the greatest interest . . . the union, the indissoluble union that we must possess in order to harvest the fruits of our sacrifices . . . Let the quarrels, the partisan pretensions disappear from among us, and let us move towards the great purpose of saving the *Patria* and of establishing in all parts the judicious Constitution'. Shortly afterwards, when liberal parliamentarianism was put into practice, the political leaders, their parties, and the parliamentary system itself were constantly discredited because public opinion perceived that, contrary to what had been promised, they indulged in dissension and the confrontation of private interests rather than working for the common good. The *Diccionario de los Políticos* by Juan Rico y Amat was to reflect the general feeling at mid-century when it stated that 'in politics' patriotism is 'what is most talked about and least felt.'[38] The parties, the politicians, democracy, lacked 'patriotism' precisely because they fought among themselves. To some extent, the distrust heaped upon the *turbulent* nobility of earlier times was projected upon 'the politicians' of the nineteenth century.

With no tradition of representative institutions, given that these had been lost long ago, true parliamentary politics did not come naturally and very soon suffered from a loss of prestige. Instead of being viewed as a forum where the diverse interests and points of view existing within society could be aired in a relatively innocuous manner, it was considered a battlefield that encouraged struggles, motivated by self-interest, between immoral party ambitions. The existence of debate, of conflicting opinions, was seen in negative terms, while *efficient* management, which *united* the country, continued to be associated with the monarchy, and particularly that of the Catholic Kings. It could be claimed that this came to be one of the problems of contemporary Spanish political culture, based on myths of unity, harmony and collective redemption rather than on respect for individual rights and liberties and the development of institutions where conflicts of interest could be debated and resolved.

Further shortcomings of the inherited culture

There were other factors that conditioned and limited the development of a 'Spanish' identity under the *ancien régime*. One of these was élitism, or the very restricted access of the populace to the images that were

transforming the representation of the collective body. If we consider
the small minority of the subjects of Felipe III or Felipe IV who could
visit Madrid and enter the gardens of the royal palaces to see the equestrian statues of the monarchs, and the even smaller number who would
be granted access to the Hall of Kingdoms to contemplate the *Surrender
of Breda*, then we can form an idea of the limited diffusion of the works
which, in the previous chapter, were considered as representative of the
emerging political identity under the Hapsburgs. For this reason alone,
early expressions of ethnic patriotism were substantially different to
the multitudinous national phenomena of the nineteenth century that
could be transmitted through daily editions of the press, not to mention
the fascist fervour of the twentieth century that was transmitted over
the radio. The diffusion of this nationalistic identity or 'imaginary community' was actually so limited as to bring into question whether the
term 'collective' or 'popular' can be applied at all prior to 1800. But of
course it was a feature that applied equally to all the European societies
of the period.

It is clear that the first steps towards a collective 'Spanish' image,
and that of other mediaeval *nations*, were taken from within very small
circles: royal chancelleries, bishoprics or monasteries where manu-
scripts were produced, copied and interpolated, or courts where reports
would come in from some person of high standing, who had perhaps
been an ambassador to the peninsular kings or left a memoir of his or
her pilgrimage to Santiago. The information that we possess about
forms of self-identification among the lower classes indicates that they
did not subscribe to political identities. Apart from family names or
nicknames and those referring to a trade (smith, potter, tailor) or an
estate (knight, gentleman), names sometimes included reference to a
location but, given the difficulty of communications and the fragmentation of cultural spaces, these rarely mentioned more than a hamlet,
a village, a region or a valley (*alcarreño, pasiego*). Only the widely travelled, and particularly those who lived far from the land of their birth,
would include an indication that they belonged to one of the kingdoms
(*aragonés, navarro*) in their name. Something similar occurred with
the pre-national terms of most interest to us, '*español*' and '*hispano*'.
Not many used them during the Middle Ages but the most important
person of all those who did, namely the priest who prior to being raised
to the papal throne was known as Pedro *Hispano*, was not 'Spanish' as
we understand it today but Portuguese, because he was born in Lisbon.
This appears to demonstrate the name's geographical, rather than
political, significance.

With the introduction of the printing press, cultural identities began to extend across a broader spectrum of society, as Benedict Anderson has observed. It is an issue that will be dealt with in Part III, on religion, because political debates in the early Modern Age were inevitably expressed in theological terms. In Spain, as we shall see, in spite of the ecclesiastical distrust of popular opinion in relation to questions of dogma, a political identity was transmitted largely by means of religious ceremonies and symbols: masses, processions and inquisitorial autos-da-fé. Another, very different, type of political influence in people's lives was that of war, the great creator of identity in the face of a common enemy, though it should not be forgotten that, until the second half of the seventeenth century, the conflicts were unleashed on battlefields far from the Peninsula. A further means of spreading the identities emanating from intellectual circles to the populace at large was undoubtedly theatrical performances, many of which, such as the mystery plays, were charged with ideological content. Lastly, it should be remembered that, according to studies by Richard Kagan, Spanish society had a very large university population in comparison with the European average in the sixteenth and early seventeenth centuries. Kagan states that, towards the end of the sixteenth century, some 20,000 students attended peninsular universities, and they would undoubtedly have studied the *Historia General de España* by Mariana, as well as the literary works of the *Siglo de Oro*. From this fertile breeding ground came the public officials who filled the councils, offices and tribunals of the kingdom, the clergy, the tutors to the sons of the aristocracy, and the lawyers and doctors whose ideas and behaviour must have influenced the rest of the population.[39]

This situation was to change over the last two-thirds of the seventeenth century and throughout the eighteenth. Of the nationalising factors already mentioned, the only one that remained constant was war. Theatrical production was slashed, as was artistic production in general. As for the universities, Kagan has shown how they went into decline from 1630 onwards, with many of them being closed down. From the scientific point of view, Spain's backwardness in relation to a Europe revolutionised by Cartesian rationalism and Newton's physics was nothing less than abysmal. As for historiography, the pioneering work of Juan de Mariana found no adequate replacement until that of Modesto Lafuente in the mid-nineteenth century. Between 1600 and 1850, anyone who took an interest in the field that the Jesuit had defined as the 'history of Spain' had to make do with the tomes written by him in the times of Felipe II, to which appendix after appendix was added as one reign succeeded another.

Alongside this intellectual decadence, there was marginalisation and a loss of political power in relation to that of the triumphant Europe of the modern period. Why did this happen to the Spanish monarchy but not to the other European monarchies that evolved into nation-States? Clearly, the most traumatic and intense period in the formation of the ethno-patriotic Spanish identity, and which was to have the greatest effect of all on the creation of that identity, coincided with the rule of the *Spanish* Hapsburgs at the height of their struggle against Protestant, Anglo-Saxon, northern Europe; and it was there that capitalism, parliamentarianism, tolerance of dissidents and the scientific revolution of the seventeenth century were to take place, providing the impetus for the technological discoveries and industrial revolution in the eighteenth. Within these societies, the 'Spanish' Monarchy was held in abhorrence, associated with monarchical absolutism, the intolerant Catholicism of Trent, and the Inquisition. Without entering into the rights and wrongs of this debate, it is enough to say that the aversion was mutual and that from the viewpoint of reinforcing national identities, this kind of antagonism is far from counter-productive. The difficulty was that, from the seventeenth century onwards, the form of political and social organisation, as well as the mental world represented by the Catholic Monarchy, suffered one defeat after another, adding to the old xenophobia and, in particular, to the hatred felt towards the buoyant northern European world. They brought feelings of incomprehension, failure, isolation and *resentment*;[40] in other words, feelings of being unjustly scorned and attacked by everyone else, and particularly by the more successful powers. Once the relatively brief phase of the Catholic Kings and the two 'elder' Hapsburgs had passed, collective self-perception of 'Spaniards' was dominated by a sense of inferiority and self-commiseration based not only on their awareness of *decline* but on the perplexity that this decline produced in them, and for which they could find no better cause than the malevolence of diabolic powers.

All political commentators had perceived the Catholic Monarchy's loss of power by 1630, at the very latest. There had been talk of decline, the depletion of resources, and the impossibility of maintaining hegemony since the 1580s, but no one could explain such an astonishing turn of events. How could the Spanish Monarchy, as the faithful agent of the will of Almighty God, be so unlucky in war? It could be due simply to the inevitable corruption of all things human, something which one had to accept with fatalistic resignation in the typically stoical vein of Quevedo. Or perhaps it was due to the growing 'fondness for luxury' (a term that classical historians attributed to the decadent Roman empire and had applied, in the history of Spain, to the reign of the last Goths) which was now linked to empire and the wealth of the Americas. Such wealth had undermined morality and corrupted the virtue of the

Spanish people. As Quevedo wrote, in his unsurpassable prose: 'poor, we conquered the riches of others; rich, those riches conquered us. To what vices does avarice not open the door with a key of gold?' The final explanation was that Spanish hegemony had been undermined by diabolical powers. Lucifer had been at work, perhaps through foreign influences, by teaching the Spanish vices which were unnatural to them or by adopting the oldest of his incarnations, the female form: women were at fault for demanding finery and jewels, leading to the importation of luxury articles on which – Quevedo speculates again – money, 'that is the sinew and substance of the kingdom', was ill-spent.

It is no coincidence that there are so many quotations from Quevedo, because his early work, *España defendida, y los tiempos de ahora: De las calumnias de los noveleros y sediciosos*, is the paradigm of this attitude, bordering on paranoia, to the problems facing the Spanish Monarchy and the incomprehension it encountered beyond its frontiers. The epigraph to this work, taken from 'The Lamentations of Jeremiah' in the Bible, was eloquent: 'All thine enemies have opened their mouth against thee'. So too was the dedication to King Felipe III, where the poet declared himself 'tired of witnessing the suffering of Spain for she has let so many foreign calumnies pass unpunished'. He recognised that the Spanish were detested everywhere, but this ill will was, according to him, totally unjustified: 'Oh unhappy Spain! A thousand times have I turned over your antiquities and annals in my memory, and yet I have found no cause that you should be the object of such bitter persecution'. Certainly it was difficult for him to identity a reason because he simply believed that Spain had no defects. Taking to extremes the *Laus Hispaniae* of Isidoro, he was convinced that it was a land of natural abundance and inhabited by an exceptionally religious people of martial courage and loyalty towards their rulers; its antiquity was unsurpassable; its language, only accidentally related to Latin, was linked to biblical Hebrew; and in warfare, the Spanish had emulated Alexander the Great. They were, in short, God's chosen people. Instead of recognising this superiority, her rivals, spurred on by envy, hated Spain with a fury that had recently turned into universal aggression. I say 'universal' because, to Quevedo, everyone was its enemy: France, Italy, Holland, Denmark, Flanders, Norway, Germany, Greece, the Turk . . .: 'Who does not call us barbarians? Who does not say that we are crazy, ignorant and arrogant?' Spain, on the other hand, was the messianic martyr as well as the chivalrous nation that suffered insults with patience and even forgave their perpetrators. Thus spoke Quevedo, although he gave free rein to his own language, calling the enemies of his *patria* 'insolent, slanderous and shameless.'[41]

This perplexity in the face of international hostility was related to an inability to analyse the causes of Spain's decadence. In the same way that 'Spain' was unable to recognise mistakes or internal problems, believing itself to be the champion of the divine cause, neither could it find an explanation for its bad reputation abroad except for envy – an abidingly ungenerous sentiment – or direct diabolic intervention. All this led the Hapsburg ideologues to reaffirm the dogmatism of the Counter-Reformation. Save for personal attacks on the Count-Duke of Olivares and some of his successors, intellectuals did not question the main structure of the political edifice or the fundamental strategy of the monarchy, even when decadence was upon them. The times when Bartolomé de las Casas had dared to criticise the American conquests were long past and there was no longer a place for questions, such as those posed by the scholastic thinker Francisco de Vitoria, about the legitimacy of imperial expansion. Even proposals for constitutional limits on royal power, in the style of Mariana, were silenced. At the moment of truth for the monarchy, the slightest criticism was treason.

It is worthwhile comparing the poverty of the arguments of apologists and publicists of the Hispanic Monarchy with those of their antagonists, who were fast learning the use of political propaganda. They denounced the cruelty of the Spanish *tercios* and the threat that the arrival of the latter posed to the lives of their enemies, to freedom of conscience, to traditional liberties and institutions, to possessions and wealth (exaggerating when convenient in order to maximise the impact). The critics were appealing to a sense of order, of property and of liberty: to modern values which were both comprehensible and shared by their public, the gentry and middle classes of Flemish, English and Italian towns. In contrast, the Hapsburg ideologues continued to base the glory of their monarchs and the legitimacy of their rule on martial and religious values. At a time when the armies of the Catholic Monarchy were active on many fronts in Europe, not only did they not consider themselves to be the aggressors but they boasted of their deeds: they were invincible warriors and they would be remembered forever. So drunk were they on their own warlike logic that they did not even strongly criticise the English, for example, for their sackings of La Coruña and Cádiz, attacks which were considered just, legitimate and even the acts of gentlemen. Conversely, they thought that the intellectual aggression, the propaganda, the 'slanders' against Spain, were intolerable; such tactics were 'ignoble', 'Machiavellian' and 'insulting' to the principles and good name of their adversaries. Quevedo himself, a writer of such immense ingenuity and dialectical passion that he would have made a great modern polemicist, gave it all up because he mistrusted intellectual sparring as much as he trusted the martial variation: empires were built up by soldiers and torn down by scholars, he said. 'While Rome had someone to fear and enemies', he continued, what different customs it had! ... What courageous chests it exposed to the world! But when they honoured its indolent desires for bestial leisure with the name of Holy Peace, what vices did not overcome it!' Despising the new weapons of politics, his writings became mere outlets for his personal distress.[42]

As the writer Francisco Ayala once observed with some delicacy, what this attitude revealed was the inferiority of the Spanish dialectic in this debate. Although the Spanish Monarchy was acting in accordance with reasons of State, just like all the other powers of the time, its apologists obstinately insisted on defending an 'anti-Machiavellianism' that openly contradicted the needs and customs of the age. Ultimately, one has to recognise a certain amount of truth in the '*Leyenda Negra*', or Black Legend, of Spain: by clinging to an earlier cultural tradition, in which martial values and the defence of religion continued to be the only measures of political legitimacy, the Spanish were incapable of understanding either their own failures or their bad international image. All of this led to the perplexity, the anger, the lamentation and the despondency typical of the ideologues of the Hispanic Monarchy at a time of confrontation and decline.[43]

The problems underlying this formation of a 'Spanish' identity were fully exposed when the new Bourbon dynasty arrived in the eighteenth century and embarked upon a series of reformist projects that were essential to reverse the decline of the monarchy. The programme that was adopted did not initially seem problematical: it was an attempt to imitate the French model which had proved such a dazzling success under Louis XIV. It required rebuilding the navy, centralising the administration, improving roads, building canals, setting up royal manufactories to prevent the kingdom from being emptied of precious metals, and fomenting the spread of the new scientific ideas in the works of, for example, Feijóo. As these changes represented the will of the King and he was not only absolute master but had just won the War of Succession in order to accede to the throne, it was not easy to question his legitimacy nor to insinuate that he might be going against the grain of a 'Spanish' identity that had been forged over the course of centuries. What was good for the monarchy was good for Spain – and what had revitalised the French monarchy was bound to be equally beneficial to the Spanish one. As the government's new plans also enjoyed the support of the modernising élites, hardly any voices were raised in protest.

However, as the rulers embarked on these reforms, they began to introduce changes into the legitimising discourse. Until then, power had been based on what could be called a mixture of the 'traditional' and 'charismatic' types established by Max Weber, which Justo Beramendi has ventured to refine by distinguishing between *traditional* legitimacy (the king inherited the power passed down from father to son for centuries), *volitive-transcendent* or *charismatic* legitimacy (based on a factor which was external and superior to society itself, such as divine will) and legitimacy based on *right of conquest* (related to the military successes of the monarchy). Without relinquishing these classic justifications, the Bourbons sought to add yet another type, which falls within the orbit of what Weber calls 'legal-rational': the king, a great warrior who had inherited his throne and defended the true faith, now proposed to be *useful* to society, to be the driving force behind measures to improve the welfare and safety of his subjects, or, in the terminology of the period, to act in the cause of *public happiness*.[44]

The ideologues of the new dynasty believed that their new formulations were compatible with maintaining inherited traditions. It was well and good that the king should be an instrument of progress for society and the happiness of its subjects; but he was not going to abandon either his rights based on the legitimacy of the hereditary line or the support received by the representatives of the true faith. Nobody appeared to notice that the new justification of power in the name of progress and modernity might come into conflict with the old ideas, far less that this might affect the process of building an identity begun in an earlier period. Nevertheless, this is exactly what happened.

The eighteenth-century reforms were inspired by motives that can be described as *patriotic*, as well as by a desire to reinforce royal power. Strengthening the monarchy was essential to recovering the prestige of the collectivity, to demonstrating to the world the injustice of its contempt for the *nation*. Not for nothing were enlightened thinkers known as 'Friends of the *Country*'. As José Antonio Maravall and François Lopez have observed, however much conservative historians persist in defining the eighteenth century as 'anti-national', it was a patriotic century when the old *amor a la patria* became the impulse for individuals to sacrifice their private interests for the public good.[45] The 'patriot' was more than just someone who felt himself to be part of a 'nation' or linguistic group, just as he was more than the vassal of the prince: the patriot was not only loyal to the king, nor confined his pride to belonging to an *imaginary community*, but considered that it was his duty to be useful, or *beneficial*, to the human group that he accepted as his own. The greatest men of this enlightened élite – even though some of them became *afrancesados* – insisted on their link with 'the holy name of patriotism'. Pedro Rodríguez de Campomanes claimed that he wrote to fulfil his obligations as magistrate and patriot, while Cadalso defined patriotism as 'the noble enthusiasm . . . that has guarded States, halted invasions, safeguarded lives and produced the men who are the true honour of the human race'. It is difficult to think of another period in which the literary élites, and intellectuals in general, have devoted so much attention to the solution of the problems of their *patria*, and collaborated so closely with the State. It is true that these intellectuals looked to Europe, and to France in particular, but they did so in search of standards and solutions for the evils of *their* country.[46]

Rulers and intellectuals of the Enlightenment also strove to build a *national* culture, something which had never existed under the previous dynasty. They founded royal academies, re-launched the history of Spain, wrote plays about Viriato, Pelayo, El Cid and Guzmán el Bueno and created the flag and the anthem that would become national. The enlightened élites were motivated not just by their dynastic loyalty but also by the creation of a national culture. Nobody refused to join the Royal Academies or support the *Sociedades de Amigos del País* (Societies of Friends of the Country). Even a significant number of the higher clergy and the aristocracy were persuaded to become involved in these institutions and to patronise salons and scientific meetings, although to a lesser extent than in the case of the English and the French. At first sight, the reformers appeared to form a solid block, without fissures or 'contradictions'. Everyone was concerned about the ignorance that characterised the lower orders of the clergy and the prejudice against doing useful work, which was believed to be the source of the country's stagnation. This meant that the circumstances that prevailed in enlightened Spain, particularly towards the end of the reign of Carlos III (1759–1788), were far more propitious regarding a peaceful and harmonious evolution towards modernisation than, for example, in France. There had been none of the alienation between government and cultural élites which Crane Brinton called 'the loss of intellectuals' loyalty' and which he established as one of the prerequisites for revolution.[47] In 1788, the year that Carlos III died, there were no signs in Spain of the revolutionary upheavals that were about to erupt in France. The process of creating a pre-national identity followed its course with no apparent incompatibility between it and the modernisation of State and society undertaken by the Bourbon rulers and supported by enlightened intellectuals.

Such tranquility, however, came under threat in two ways. First, reformist aims encroached upon the privileges and interests of traditionally powerful groups. Manuel de Godoy, for example, pushed through an early disentailment of considerable scope, while the rights of the Mesta and the legal privileges of the aristocracy, among other issues, were constantly targeted by enlightenment critics. It is hardly surprising that resistance grew, apparently led by the lower clergy and sections of the nobility. Still unaccustomed to thinking in national terms, the conservatives initially confined themselves to dusting off the weapons of the Counter-Reformation and accused their enemies of heresy – *regalism*, or rather *Jansenism*, which was the doctrinal deviation in fashion at the time –, notching up some successes, such as the removal of certain enlightened ministers. As for Godoy, they accused him of being an *arriviste* and of immorality, referring to his lack of noble pedigree and his intimate relationship with the royal couple: the puritanical Carlos III and his respectable ministers had at least been able to protect themselves from such accusations.[48]

The enemies of reform came to realise that it was not enough to cast suspicion on the religious orthodoxy or private morals of the reformists in times of unbelief. They began to comprehend the conflict between modernisation and national tradition, which leads us to the second threat; namely, that the reforms appeared to give credence to the '*Leyenda Negra*'. This damning image of the country, far from dying away, had persisted into the eighteenth century and acquired further nuances along the way. As the political battle against absolutism and intolerance swept across Europe, national stereotypes were used more and more frequently. On the one hand, they required little mental effort: 'the Spanish are fanatics' is not a complex idea. On the other hand, they were readily accepted, given the ignorance and prejudice against all things foreign. Moreover, by apparently directing criticism at foreign countries, stereotypes were able to avoid censorship with ease. Last, but not least, following the loss of power experienced by the Catholic Monarchy, the heaping of all religious intransigence and absolutism on 'Spain' had an added advantage: it demonstrated beyond question that intolerance, cruelty and a disdain for productive work resulted in decadence. The policies of the Spanish Hapsburgs proved the causal relationship between intransigent religiosity, monarchical absolutism, and aristocratic values, on the one hand, and backwardness, impoverishment, loss of hegemony, and the inability to join the train of *progress*, on the other. As François Lopez observed, for the first time, authors writing in the eighteenth century 'established a systematic relation between misery, laziness, ignorance, pride . . . with a particular way of conceiving and defending Catholicism'. It was enough for the *philosophes* to write the word 'Spain' to evoke, without further explanation, the errors and self-destructiveness of clerico-monarchical obscurantism, a lack of liberty, and the rejection of modern science and free thinking. There was not a country in which the enlightened minority did not use the example of Spain for internal debate, indirectly warning their kings that, if they did not wish to sink into decline in a similar way to the Spanish Monarchy, they should avoid its mistakes.

The eighteenth century was also the time of travel guides, which had become fashionable in Europe due to the growth in popularity of the Grand Tour, upon which families of high standing would send their sons in order to complete their worldly education before getting married. Although Italy was the preferred destination, some English and French travellers also visited Spain and more than one left a record of their impressions that only confirmed the prejudices and stereotypes with which they had set out. All of them were horrified by the bad roads, the unhealthy inns, the beggars in the streets, the superstition and fanaticism of the religious festivals, the savagery of bullfights, the low cultural level of social gatherings (where the only activity was gambling), and the particular ignorance of women, including ladies of the highest society, who were incapable of holding an educated conversation. It was, in short, a country of indolence, a product of the hot climate, no doubt, but also of its aristocratic values and its disdain for meaningful work; a country full of Catholic superstition, intolerance and ignorance, which was a sufficient cause for all the rest; and a country of cruelty, so evident in the spectacle of bullfighting, so similar to the Roman circuses described in so many Christian accounts and in consonance with the infamous *behaviour* of the merciless conquerors of the Americas.[49]

As Spain no longer inspired terror, it was easy to add ridiculous traits to its negative image. The Spanish ambience had already been used as a literary ingredient of the gothic novel in northern Europe, which, in order to cause maximum effect, only had to invoke the dungeons of the Inquisition. Shakespeare himself had already sketched an outlandish Spaniard in the character of Don Adriano de Armado in *Love's Labours Lost*. He was to become the prototype that would be all the rage in eighteenth-century Europe: the Spanish, authors of their own disgrace and, moreover, presumptuous and obsessed with their noble ancestry, were, by definition, absurd and laughable. Beaumarchais created the cuckolded marquis in his play, *The Barber of Seville*, transposed into an opera by Mozart, both of which received huge critical and popular acclaim. The Italians, especially, took the opportunity to take revenge on two centuries of Spanish military presence and political domination by creating the *bragadoccio*, Captain Spavento. 'It was also the time when the affairs of Spain assumed an antiquated, conceited, affected, almost ridiculous air', affirmed the Italian historian and philosopher Benedetto Croce, and it was around then that the word *spagnolata* entered the vocabulary to mean bad taste, boastfulness, or ceremonial absurdity.[50] Not even Casanova, who could find amorous adventure and pleasure in every corner of the world, could discover anything more than inquisitorial prisons and repressed and affected manners in Spain.

Nobody presented the Spanish stereotype in more ridiculous terms, nor put it to such efficient use, as Montesquieu, the most widely read political author of his time. He firmly believed in a 'national character', and found none so negative as the Spanish one, based on *pride*. Even honour and fidelity, for which he gave it credit, when mixed with pride – the source of indolence and solemnity – resulted in neglect and destruction.[51] The predominant features in his description of an imaginary journey through Spain and Portugal were laughable: the Iberian peoples were 'phlegmatic and serious', full of haughtiness as a result of such banal things as owning 'a big sword', or of being 'old Christians': that is to say, not being descended from 'those who had been *persuaded* by the Inquisition to embrace the Christian religion in recent centuries'. The possessors of these qualities or instruments did no work, 'concerning their dignity with the repose of their limbs' and demonstrating their nobility by 'sprawling in a chair': it was a country where 'he who sits for ten hours of the day is held in double the esteem to him who sits for only five'. This had led to the conspicuous consumption that had brought ruin on imperial Spain, where fictitious wealth such as gold and silver had been more highly valued that true riches like corn, wine and cloth. Thus the 'internal vices of the system' had made it impossible for Spain to take advantage of the resources imported from the Indies. 'They say the sun rises and sets on their dominions', he concluded, 'but it must also be said that, as it crosses the sky, it only shines on ravaged fields and barren lands.'[52]

What is most reprehensible about Montesquieu's account is that, when criticising specific policies, he does not blame the monarchy or other Spanish institutions but the *character* of the whole nation. For example, his criticism of the atrocities committed during the conquest of America were based on old reports drawn up by Las Casas and passed on down by Protestant propaganda. The French writer was actually less interested in the fate of indigenous Americans than in the political role of religion in Europe. He believed that religion was useful to social life, especially as a moderator of absolute power; but that, in the Spanish case, where Catholicism bordered on the fanatical and had spawned the Inquisition, it had led to the cruelty of the 'destroyers of America', 'very devote . . . bandits' who took advantage of their religion to 'reduce to slavery those who do not profess it'. The 'Spanish', explained Montesquieu, had 'decided' to exterminate the indigenous population of America due to the impossibility of overcoming it by force, 'and never has such a hideous project been put into effect with such precision; a people as numerous as all those of Europe together disappeared from the face of the earth with the arrival of these barbarians', who appeared to want to show the world 'how far human cruelty could go'. Another consequence of inquisitorial fanaticism was a contempt for culture that had created a genuine intellectual vacuum among the Spanish, which they filled with magical fears: 'look at one of their libraries: novels on one side, school books on the other', a collection that seemed to be put together by 'a secret enemy of human reason'. 'The only good book they have is the one that makes you see how ridiculous all the rest are', Montesquieu claimed, referring to *Don Quijote*. In short, the Spanish, who had made such immense discoveries in the New World, did not even have a map of their own country: 'on its rivers, there are ports that have not yet been discovered, and unknown peoples in its mountains.'[53]

Montesquieu's sole purpose in holding 'Spain' up as an example of the crassest contempt for modern knowledge was to explain to European rulers that a society dominated by aristocratic prejudice, clerical intolerance and unlimited monarchical power would necessarily lead to decadence and, ultimately, paralysis. In the course of this lesson, however, he portrayed the 'Spanish' identity in almost indelibly negative terms. He confirmed the *Leyenda Negra*, and the features he attributed to the 'Spanish' as a human group rather than to their political system went on to become an article of faith for most authors of his century.

However much enlightened Spaniards may have agreed with this analysis of the decadence of nations by the best thinkers of their age, they could not allow such sweeping criticisms to go unchallenged. García Cárcel writes that, in the eighteenth century, 'there loomed a permanent need to write a history of Spain that refuted the negative opinions of foreigners'. And it was not only history. All the political literature is dominated by a clear awareness that a huge effort was needed in order to overcome the ignorance and prejudices held by foreigners about Spain. As early as 1714, an anonymous work complained about the 'innate aversion, inherited antipathy, and deadly spite with which all foreigners had always viewed Spain', and begged for someone to write 'our history' with a renewed sense of national fervour.[54] Feijóo, an intellectual with few complexes, felt he had to devote part of his work to defending Spanish culture from the disdain of foreigners, exerting himself to reveal a country whose glories were not only military but cultural. But not all eminent men found it such an easy problem to solve: among many of them, one can detect an internal struggle, an ambivalence towards inherited tradition, doubts about their own identity, and an ambiguity that, much later, would be typical of the political reformers of the nineteenth and twentieth centuries. In the reign of Felipe V, his minister, José del Campillo, wrote *Lo que hay de más y lo que hay de menos en España para que sea lo que debe ser y no lo que es* (What there is too much and too little of in Spain so that it becomes what it should be and not what it is), a work full of anxieties and paradoxes in the style of Unamuno. 'I am going to write about Spain, against Spain and for Spain' declared Campillo; 'for Spain', because he wanted to put the decadent ship of state back on course and 'against Spain' because he identified the nation with certain aspects of a traditional way of life that would have to undergo reform. Modernising or progressive ideology, even placed at the service of the 'Spanish' monarchy, came into direct conflict with the national mythology as it had been created under the Hapsburgs in the same name of 'Spain.'[55]

It is ironic that voices should have been raised in criticism just at the time when Spanish rulers were making a serious effort to introduce enlightened reforms. The ministers of Fernando VI and Carlos III, just like the modernising élites who supported them, were perfectly in tune with their European counterparts, the ministers of Joseph II of Austria or Catherine the Great of Russia. However, enlightened opinion generally refused to recognise this fact, except for a few lone Frenchmen who, in a paternalistic way, registered the recent successes of Spanish politics as a credit to their own culture. The rigidity of national stereotypes, which made it impossible to believe in radical changes of direction within a country, even damaged those who most agreed with their critics.

An excellent example of the strength of nationalist sensibilities in this era was the reaction of the Jesuits who were expelled from Spain by Carlos III. On reaching Italy, they were overwhelmed by the contempt in which Spain was held. When they read the recently published histories of Italian literature written by Bertinelli and Tiraboschi, who blamed Spain for the cultural decadence following the Renaissance, both Juan Andrés and Javier Lampillas wrote several works in refutation. Juan Francisco Masdeu declared in the Introduction of his *Historia Crítica* that he wanted to examine 'the defects usually attributed to Spanish naivety' and was very indignant that 'in their writings, the Dutch, the English, the French, the Italians and the Germans believe

that they have the right to call Spain a nation that is idle, lazy and neg-
ligent in character; a nation of men careless in their cultivation of the
land, without diligence in the Arts and with no head for business. This
has been read since those times in books, this is copied in all the daily
papers, this is heard even in the mouths of common people'. These
three authors were all Catalan Jesuits, and all three had been expelled
from the country by the Spanish government, yet their wounded patriotic sensibilities – which recall those of Mariana, another Jesuit who
lived and wrote in Italy in defence of Spain – prevailed over other cultural and institutional bonds, and even over their natural resentment
at their expulsion. Among the many other rejoinders in the same style
which were forthcoming during the eighteenth century, it is also worth
mentioning the *Viaje Literario* by Antonio Ponz, written to vindicate
Spain against the *Lettere d'un vago italiano*, by Norberto Caimo. Even
the Count of Aranda, who was so closely connected to enlightenment
circles, felt obliged to respond and – as he was the Spanish ambassador
in Paris – to take legal action against the Marquis de Langle, or false
'Figaro', who had published a story of travels through Spain loaded
with negative stereotypes.[56]

However, none of this criticism wounded enlightened Spaniards
as deeply as those that were made by their beloved Montesquieu.
Outstanding among the many who came forward to refute him was
José de Cadalso, a great admirer of the author of the Persian Letters,
from whom he took many ideas and whose literary style he imitated in
his own *Marruecas*. This did not prevent him from writing a juvenile
Defensa de la nación española, in which he set out to refute, paragraph
by paragraph, the content of one of the *letters* by the master, in which
'the religion, valour, science and nobility of Spaniards' were impugned.
Cadalso did not accuse the great French thinker of ill will or envy –
'quite unlike the quarrels in Quevedo's time', as Maravall points out
– but of ignorance of his subject and superficiality. He claimed that
Montesquieu's mistakes were not 'born of intention, but of the false
reports offered him by certain individuals, not worthy of dealing with
such a distinguished gentleman on such a serious subject as the criticism
of a nation'. Despite sparing Montesquieu, he is no less determined to
defend Spain, contrasting the stereotype put forward by the Frenchman
with one of a national character based on fidelity, religiosity and valour.
He agrees with the political criticism, but is offended by the humiliation of his nation. And as he also feels himself to be misunderstood
within his own country, he concludes that he has gained no benefit
'by thinking with a patriotic fervour unusual in our Spain ... I have
already seen how useless it is to live with the love of one's *patria*, or to

set out to die for it.'[57] Cadalso is the perfect embodiment of the internal struggle going on in the minds of enlightened Spanish thinkers: believers in progress and reform, but not at all inclined to renounce a feeling of belonging and pride in a national entity of which they are unable to conceive except in the terms established in the previous century. As the writer *Azorín* pointed out, it set a precedent for the Generation of '98. Bernhardt Schmidt has defined Cadalso's work along the lines of 'Spain grieves me', which runs from Quevedo to Larra, while Maravall believed it to be an example of the anguished personal relationship with national problems typical of the era.

One story that illustrates the situation like no other is the reaction to the famous article on Spain by Masson de Morvilliers in the *Enciclopédie Méthodique,* edited by Joseph Panckoucke in 1782. The content of this encyclopaedia was similar to the more famous one by Diderot and D'Alembert but less ideological and polemical. This made it highly suitable for the needs of the enlightened government of Spain in the time of Carlos III, desirous of broadening horizons without questioning the paternal absolutism of the monarchy. Consequently, all obstacles for its importation were removed, and once several hundred people had taken out a subscription, the volumes began to arrive. However, a scandal erupted in the summer of 1783, when they received the volume on *Géographie Moderne,* which included an article on *'Espagne',* signed by one Nicholas Masson de Morvilliers. The article began with boundless praise of Spain, soon revealing the author's banality: 'What people inhabit such a beautiful country, have such a rich language, have such fabulous mines, such vast possessions? What nation was endowed with so many moral and physical qualities?' So much adulation merely served as rhetoric in order to contrast the country's favourable natural conditions with its current lamentable state. This 'colossal nation' had become a 'country of pygmies . . . The proud and noble Spaniard is ashamed to be taught, to travel, to deal with other peoples'. Initially, it might be thought that such a transformation was due to political causes ('a bland, lethargic administration', 'its priests, its friars . . .'), but the ultimate explanation was due to the collective character, described along the same lines as those of Montesquieu: the Spanish, 'sober, serious . . ., loyal, good soldiers' were also 'indolent', and dominated by a 'shameful apathy' that Masson, in completing his long list of stereotypes, attributed to the 'hot climate'. The core of the article was its damning evaluation of the contribution of Spanish culture to the progress of humanity: namely, that, in recent centuries, all peoples, even those of Russia and Poland, had contributed to 'the sciences and the arts' – except for Spain. 'What do we owe to Spain? For two centuries, for four, for ten, what has she done for Europe? Spain today is like those weak, unfortunate colonies that have a permanent need of the protective arm of the metropolis . . . In Spain, there are no mathematicians, no physicists, no astronomers, no naturalists. Without the assistance of other nations they do not even have what they need to make a chair.'[58]

'*Depuis deux siècles, depuis quatre, depuis dix, que doît-on à l'Espagne?*'. This line caused uproar at the time and has continued to resonate in the ears of Spanish intellectuals ever since. Menéndez Pelayo unearthed it a century later and it has been invoked every time Spain has had reason to contemplate the long list of insults drawn up by France and the rest of the world. At the time, in 1783, it launched modern Spanish national sentiment. Vindications of the Spanish contribution to European culture soon appeared, one of which was signed by Antonio Cavanilles, a Valencian botanist working in Paris, and another by Carlo Denina, an Italian priest resident at the court of Frederick II of Prussia.[59] The government of Carlos III made an official protest to the French government as a result of the Masson de Morvilliers article and demanded that measures be taken against those responsible for the offence. The Royal Spanish Academy announced a competition in response, with a prize for the 'best apology or defence of the nation, referring only to its advances in the arts and sciences', which would be duly published by the royal printing press and added to the next volume of the *Encyclopédie* as an appendix. The winner was Juan Pablo Forner, whose work was entitled *Oración Apologética por la España y su mérito literario.*[60]

Forner was a lawyer and man of letters of about thirty years of age from Extremadura, who believed that nations were the subjects of history. Maravall explains that, for him, 'love of the *patria* was the fundamental trait of a civil man' on which all his moral impulses and civic values, such as the duty to work or to 'promote public happiness', were based. All of which is highly typical of the enlightenment era. Maravall insists that Forner, in contrast to Quevedo or Mariana, conceived of Spain as a *nation* in the fully modern sense of the word; that is to say, as a territory and as a people characterised by a set of collective values and a political will. However, in his obsession to defend Spain, he presents her identity in very traditional terms, contradicting the attitudes prevailing in the enlightened eighteenth century. He denied that the 'scientific prestige of a nation' should be measured by 'its advances in superfluous or prejudicial things' which, according to him, is what characterised the period. It was a 'century of the oracle', of impertinent small-time writers, an era that, 'giving itself the magnificent title of philosophical, scarcely appreciates the proper modes of thought and judgement'.

Against this culture 'of vacuous thought systems', of 'sophisms and unverifiable opinions', he declared himself in favour of a true philosophy that, as well as being enlightened, would serve as the basis for a public morality. On this he based his enumeration of the 'glories' of Spain, which 'has not had Cartesians or Newtons' but has had 'very just legislators and excellent practical philosophers' who, while not creating 'imaginary worlds', have created 'real and effective worlds'.[61]

This kind of defence only aggravated the problem. It brought an angry reply from Luis Cañuelo, editor of the newspaper *El Censor*, who decided to intervene in order to clarify that patriotism was one thing but an attack on modern culture was quite another. Patriotism was all well and good, he declared, as long as it did not waste its time bragging about qualities that the country did not possess, as Forner had done. In that case, he went on, it could become a petty and misunderstood sentiment. It had to be recognised that Spain's contributions to the sciences and the arts did not merit a very 'positive' verdict and that true patriotism should concern itself with denunciation of the privations and defects of the nation as the only means of setting them right. Forner, on the other hand, having given such a passionate defence of Spanish culture, was aligning himself with the interests of the individuals and corporations who were obstructing the advance of the sciences in Spain. Cañuelo had thereby managed to raise the level of the debate. Although he continued to defend 'Spain', it seemed more important to him to highlight the prejudices that were hindering the country's progress. Principal to this were religious preoccupations that deflected attention from an improvement in living conditions. He showed how such prejudices, together with private interests, manipulated offended national sensibilities in order to reject all reform on specious grounds. Faced with Forner's reply, which exonerated religion from any responsibility for Spanish decadence, Cañuelo nonetheless admitted defeat and ended the controversy by expressing his 'sorrow' at not having made himself understood by 'those barbarians'.[62]

The importance of the *affaire Masson* has little to do with the content of the article in the *Encyclopédie*. Its author was an intellectual of no account, and it would have been of small advantage to the Spanish government to have had him sent to prison or fined him for his insolence. What was so serious and truly offensive was that, apart from the vain, bombastic style, there was nothing personal in what he wrote; he had merely recited the litany that any enlightened European thinker would have said of 'Spain', the paradigm of a cultural and political identity incompatible with progress. This was the gulf that reformist Bourbon governments were attempting to bridge, and what intellectuals favourable to them were trying to conceal. They venerated Locke, Montesquieu and Voltaire, from whom they had learned that reason was the driving force behind human progress, but they found it intolerable that these idols should belittle Spain's – that is to say, *their* – politico-cultural identity.

Conservative circles soon grasped that the Bourbon reform programme was incompatible with Spain's inherited identity. Changing their tactics, they decided that, instead of denouncing heretical beliefs, they would attack the '*afrancesamiento*', or 'Frenchification', of ministers and reformers, and their dependence on foreign models. The xenophobia stirred up in the earlier period was fertile soil in which to plant the idea that a group of idle young men, out of no more than a pedantic desire to be *à la mode*, were attacking the institutions and attitudes consubstantial with the national *way of life*. The modernisers were *introducing foreign customs*, which were *anti-Spanish* and *afrancesados*. Francophobia was to be expressed in many ways throughout the century: from the introduction of contemptuous words such as *petimetre* (a dandy) to more elaborate intellectual arguments as well as popular movements in which xenophobic feelings were harnessed in order to oppose enlightened reforms. These included the revolt against Squilace of 1766 and the mobilisation against Godoy, the latter scarcely two months before the anti-Napoleonic uprising.

When war broke out in 1808, the epithet *afrancesados* proved a powerful weapon with which to destroy the reputations of those who collaborated with Joseph Bonaparte. Meanwhile, the 'patriotic' liberals, in the mistaken belief that the insurgents sympathised with their reformist intentions, drew up a Constitution that established a rigid division of powers, with severe limitations on the royal will and strict guarantees of individual rights. It was an enormous contradiction that, in the very country which Montesquieu had presented as the most harrowing example of the effects of absolutism and intolerance not long before, there should now be an attempt to introduce the most advanced Constitution in Europe. Reality soon brought home to these liberals how right the Frenchman had been: the text would not easily be put into effect in Spain.

Just as Napoleon's generals discovered in desperation how effectively the cultural identities and traditions carried over from the *ancien régime* could be mobilised, the liberal élites, who shared so much of their rationalist vision of the world with the *afrancesados* and those very same generals, were to come up against the same mentality over the next few decades. However much they invoked the name of 'Spain' in their proclamations, and however much warmth and sincerity they displayed, the ability to juggle in a progressive way with the mythical identity born of the Counter-Reformation was beyond them. Even if they had been capable of doing so, the constitutionalists of Cádiz did not actually believe that it was necessary to win popular support for their political and cultural project. So their patriotism was of no use whatsoever. Conservative sectors found it easy to slander them for being 'anti-patriotic' and 'foreign sympathisers' in the same way that they had accused enlightened reformers and Bonaparte's collaborators. Labelling them as such, or as the enemies of national traditions, as well as being heretics or atheists, proved highly effective. On his return, Fernando VII annulled all the laws passed by the *Cortes* of Cádiz and had their authors imprisoned or sent into exile, while crowds sacked their houses, dragging the bodies of those they encountered through the streets and cheering the returning monarch with enthusiasm.

The modernising élites lived under the shadow of their doubtful *Spanish* affinity until well into the twentieth century. This was one of the problems of a nationalising process that did not coincide with the principal European models. Spain's trajectory was characteristic of peripheral countries, in which the modernising project was based on exogenous models, and it could therefore be presented by conservatives as a *betrayal of the inherited identity*. Russia was the most typical case, where debates on modernisation were disguised as debates over national identity and gave rise to interminable arguments between *Occidentalists* and *Slavophiles*. In Spain, in a similar vein, *Europeanists* were to be opposed by *Casticistas*.

Notes

1 R. del Arco y Garay, *La idea de imperio en la política y la literatura españolas*, Madrid, 1944, pp. 299–300 (*Bellicose, friendly Spain, do you need any glory from my flag? I have three rare Spaniards: Bernardo el Carpio, the Cid, the great Pelayo*).

2 *El cerco de Numancia*, ed. R. Marrast, pp. 47–49, 109 (*Under this glorious and happy empire, your kingdoms will be united in one crown. The famous Portuguese segment will come back to its ancient being, the illustrious Castillian dress*).

3 J. Brown and J. Elliott, *A Palace for a King*, Yale University Press, 1980, pp. 147–152. The monarch's virtues were the central topic in a king's funeral: see J. Varela, *La muerte del rey: El ceremonial funerario de la monarquía española, 1500–1885*, Madrid: Turner, 1990.

4 Brown and Elliott, *Palace*, pp. 109ff. (statues) and 123ff. (paintings). To these authors, nevertheless, Hercules was a symbol of Virtue and Force (pp. 157–158). But they point out that this hero was also the forerunner of the

Spanish dynasty. Among the Roman emperors, only the so-called *Spanish* ones were included (because they had been born in the Baetica region), as T. Pérez Vejo observes in his *Pintura de historia e identidad nacional en España*, Madrid: Universidad Complutense, 1996; the Spanish kings were also considered heirs to the Roman empire.

5 E. Tormo, 'Velázquez, el Salón de Reinos del Buen Retiro', *Boletín de la Sociedad Española de Excursiones . . .*, 1911–12, quoted by T. Pérez Vejo, *Pintura de historia e identidad nacional en España*, Madrid: Universidad Complutense, 2001, p. 259.

6 The Biblioteca *Nacional*, already in the late nineteenth century, would be the opposite example. Its predecessors had been called the Real Librería or Biblioteca Real: see J. Fernández Sánchez, *Historia de la Bibliografía en España*, Madrid, Compañía Literaria, 1994, pp. 96–108.

7 Brown and Elliott, *Palace*, pp. 31, 38–41 and 48.

8 What diminishes the importance of the bellicose Saint James, partially replaced by Santa Teresa in the seventeenth century and the Immaculate Conception in the eighteenth: see T. D. Kendrick, *Saint James in Spain*, London: Methuen, 1960.

9 Pérez Vejo, *Pintura de historia*, p. 296.

10 G. Lovett, *Napoleon and the Birth of Modern Spain*, New York: New York University Press, 1965, Vol. 2, p. 834.

11 *Diario Sesiones Cortes*, 19–III-1814, pp. 146–147. As to the *Pepa*, it is the feminine form (the word 'constitution' in Spanish is feminine) of *Pepe*, the nickname of *José* or Joseph, and 19 March is St Joseph's day.

12 On the different uses and meanings of the terms '*nacional*' and '*real*' see M. C. Seoane, *El primer lenguaje constitucional español (las Cortes de Cádiz)*, Madrid, 1968, pp. 64–67, and M. P. Battaner Arias, *Vocabulario político-social en España (1868–1873)*, Madrid, 1977, pp. 63–64 and 214–215.

13 See J. M. Jover Zamora, 'Sobre los conceptos de monarquía y nación en el pensamiento político español del siglo XVII', *Cuadernos de Historia de España*, XIII, 1950: 101–150; cf. Brown and Elliott, *Palace*, p. 9: 'known to later generations as the Spanish Empire, but to contemporaries as the *monarquía*, the Spanish Monarchy'. The Spanish case was not exceptional at all at the time, according to J. J. Linz, 'Early State-building and Late Peripheral Nationalism against the State: the Case of Spain', in S. N. Eisenstadt and S. Rokkan (eds), *Building States and Nations*, London, 1973; M. Artola, *La Monarquía de España*, Madrid, 1999; or A. de Blas and J. J. Laborda, 'La construcción del Estado en España', in F. Hernández y F. Mercadé (eds), *Estructuras sociales y cuestión nacional en España*, Barcelona: Ariel, 1986, p. 467.

14 A. Domínguez Ortiz, *La sociedad española en el siglo XVII*, 2 vols. Madrid, 1963, Vol. I, p. 217.

15 See D. Laitin, C. Solé and S. Kalyvas, 'Language and the Construction of States: The Case of Catalonia in Spain', *Politics and Society*, 22(1), 1994, pp. 5–29. For mistrust in the Aragonese kingdoms about the growing

Castilian monopoly of the monarchy, see R. García Cárcel, 'El concepte d'Espanya als segles XVI i XVII', *L'Avenç*, 100 (1987): 49.

16 R. Kagan, *Students and Society in Early Modern Spain*, Baltimore, 1974, p. 226.

17 See *Catálogo de las obras publicadas por la Real Academia de la Historia*, Madrid: Tipografía Fortanet, 1901, pp. 3–4. On the Royal Academy of History, see E. Velasco Moreno, *La Real Academia de la Historia en el siglo XVIII: Una Institución de sociabilidad*, Madrid, 2000.

18 Nevertheless, the growing importance of the Cid must be underlined. He was a kind of *populista heroe*, confronted with the Kings and the apostle St James. (The quote of the chronicler Caveda, reproduced by Pérez Vejo and repeated by me, appeared in the *Memorias para la Historia de la Real Academia de San Fernando.*)

19 Jovellanos, quoted by M. Artola, *Los origenes de la España contemporánea*, 2 vols. Madrid, 1959, Vol. I, pp. 267–268. Quintana, in *Semanario Patriótico*, Madrid, IV, 22–IX–1808, quoted by F.-X. Guerra, *Modernidad e Independencias*, Madrid, 1992, p. 233. Egaña, quoted by J. Fernández Sebastián, 'España, monarquía y nación: Cuatro concepciones de la comunidad política española entre el Antiguo Régimen y la Revolución liberal', *Studia Histórica. Historia Contemporánea*, 12 (1994): 59–60.

20 Guerra, *Modernidad*, p. 344. Cf. the 1793–1795 war, where there were calls for the unity of all Spanish kingdoms against the French, but on behalf of the *monarchy*, not the *nation* (see J.-R. Aymes, *La Guerra de España contra la Revolución Francesa, 1793–1795*, Alicante, 1991, p. 421).

21 Quoted by J. A. Maravall, 'El mito de la "tradición" en el constitucion-alismo español', *Cuadernos Hispanoamericanos*, 329–330 (1977): 556. Previous quote from Gallego, in A. Morales Moya, 'El Estado de la Ilustración', in *Las bases políticas, económicas y sociales de un régimen en transformación (1759–1834)*, Vol. XXX of *Historia de España Menéndez Pidal*, Madrid, 1998, p. 192. Martínez Marina, in J. I. Lacasta, *Hegel en España*, Madrid, C.E.C., 1984, p. 281. Joseph Bonaparte's followers were using the same language, according to Gérard Dufour, 'Le centralisme des *Afrancesados*', in *Nationalisme et littérature en Espagne et Amérique Latine au XIXe siècle*, Presses Universitaires de Lille, 1982, pp. 11–23.

22 See J. M. Portillo Valdés, 'Nación política y territorio económico: El primer modelo provincial español (1812)', *Historia Contemporánea*, 12 (1995): 247–277; Toreno, quoted on p. 271; fears of Jacobin centralism, pp. 264–66. See also A. Gallego Anabitarte, 'España, 1812: Cádiz, Estado unitario, en perspectiva histórica', *Ayer*, 1 (1991): 140–143.

23 Quoted by Gallego Anabitarte, 'España, 1812', pp. 141–142; and Portillo, 'Nación política y territorio', pp. 266–267.

24 J. Tone, *The Fatal Knot: The Guerrilla War in Navarre and the Defeat of Napoleon in Spain*, Chapel Hill, NC: University of North Carolina Press, 1994, p. 153. A. Capmany, *Centinela contra Franceses* (London, 1988), also explains Spanish resistance against Napoleon because Spaniards are

a nation, unlike the Germans or Italians. The *jota* words: *The Pilar Virgin does not want to be French; on the contrary, she wants to be the captain of the Aragonese troops.*

25 Blas and Laborda, 'Construcción del Estado', p. 483.

26 J. A. Maravall, *Las Comunidades de Castilla: Una primera revolución moderna*, Madrid, 1963; J. Perez, *La Révolution des 'Comunidades' de Castille (1520–1521)*, Bordeaux, 1970; J. I. Gutiérrez Nieto, *Las Comunidades como movimiento antiseñorial*, Barcelona: Ariel, 1973.

27 J. Ortega y Gasset, *España invertebrada*, Madrid, 1921, Chapter 6.

28 See L. Greenfeld, *Nationalism: Five Roads to Modernity*, Cambridge, MA: Harvard University Press, 1992, *passim.*

29 Nobility 'domesticated', in Domínguez Ortiz, *Sociedad española*, Vol. I, p. 217; 'refeudalisation' in J. A. Maravall, *Estado moderno y mentalidad social (siglos XV a XVII)*, 2 vols. Madrid, 1972, Vol. II, pp. 450–451.

30 See the duke of Medinaceli's manifesto, in 1707, in Morales Moya, 'Estado de la Ilustración', p. 85. The count of Teba's *Discurso sobre la autoridad de los ricos hombres sobre el rey*, quoted also by Morales Moya (ibid., pp. 120 and 397) maintains that the Spanish monarchy had become absolute with the Catholic Kings, who took all political power away from the aristocracy.

31 Townsend, 'Viaje a España hecho en los años 1786 y 1787', in J. García Mercadal, *Viajes de extranjeros por España y Portugal*, Madrid, 1962, Vol. III, p. 1519. On the possible conversion of nobles in high public servants, see Morales Moya, 'Estado de la Ilustración', p. 107. Their diminishing military role in J. A. Maravall, 'Élite y poder político en el siglo XVII', *Annuario dell'Istituto Storico Italiano per l'età moderna e contemporanea*, Vols XXIX–XXX, 1979, p. 41.

32 Quoted by A. Morales Moya, 'Nobleza y sociedad liberal', in C. Iglesias, *Nobleza y sociedad en la España moderna*, Oviedo, 1996, Vol. I, p. 331. See additional bibliography on this topic in that article.

33 A. Cavanilles, *Compendio de Historia de España*, 5 vols. Madrid, 1860, Vol. IV, p. 273. P. Mantuano, *Advertencias a la Historia de Juan de Mariana*, Milan, 1611.

34 See J. Pro Ruiz, 'Las élites de la España liberal: clases y redes en la definición del espacio social (1808–1931)', *Historia Social*, 21 (1995): 47–69.

35 See the *Colección de bandos, proclamas y decretos de la Junta Suprema de Sevilla y otros papeles curiosos*, Cádiz, 1808, pp. 17, 22; *Catecismos políticos españoles*, pp. 17–19; *La música y la Guerra de la Independencia*, Madrid, 1995, pp. 45–59. Cf. the excellent study by J.-F. Botrel, 'Nationalisme et consolation dans la littérature populaire espagnole des années 1898', in, *Nationalisme et littérature en Espagne et Amérique Latine au XIXe siècle*, Presses Universitaires de Lille, 1982, p. 69.

36 Fr. S. López, *Despertador Cristiano-Político*, Mexico, 1809, p. 15; Capmany, quoted by J. Herrero, *Los orígenes del pensamiento reaccionario español*, Madrid, 1971, pp. 239–240; F. X. Cabanes, *Historia de la Guerra de España contra Napoleón Bonaparte*, Madrid, 1818, p. X; Marquis de las Amarillas,

Recuerdos (1778–1837), Pamplona, 1978, p. 284; J. Díaz de Baeza, *Historia de la Guerra de España contra el Emperador Napoleón*, Madrid, 1843, pp. 38 and 395; Conde de Toreno, *Historia del levantamiento, guerra y revolución de España*, ed. B.A.E., 1953, p. 43; Fr. M. Martínez, in R. Serrano García, *La revolución liberal en Valladolid (1808–1874)*, Valladolid, 1993, p. 45; P. Salmón, *Resumen histórico de la Revolución de España*, Cádiz, 1812, p. 73.

37 M. Pérez Ledesma, 'Las Cortes de Cádiz y la sociedad española', *Ayer*, 1 (1991): 195, citing García Herreros p. 192.
38 Quoted in Battaner, *Vocabulario político-social*, p. 546. *El Redactor General*, 26-VIII-1812.
39 According to Kagan, *Students and Society*, about 3.7% of Spaniards between 15 and 24 years of age attended a university around 1580, the peak of the period. J. J. Linz, 'Intellectual Roles in Sixteenth and Seventeenth-Century Spain', *Daedalus*, 101(3), 1972: 59–108, around 60% of the 321 authors included in Nicolás Antonio's *Bibliotheca Hispana Nova* had gone to college.
40 Greenfeld, *Nationalism*, pp. 15–17.
41 F. Quevedo, *España defendida, y los tiempos de ahora: De las calumnias de los noveleros y sediciosos*, 1609, in *Obras Completas*, Madrid: Aguilar, 1941, pp. 325–328 and 355–358. Spanish valour also exalted by Mártir Rizo and others (see R. García Cárcel, *La Leyenda Negra: Historia y opinión*, Madrid, 1992, pp. 106–110). On Spaniards as the Chosen People, see R. Lida, 'La "España Defendida" y la síntesis pagano-cristiana', *Letras Hispánicas. Estudios. Esquemas*, México: FCE, 1958, pp 142–156; and 'Quevedo y su España antigua', *Romance Philology*, XVII(2), 1963: 253–271. B. Schmidt, *El problema español, de Quevedo a Manuel Azaña*, Madrid: Edicusa, 1976, pp. 29–70, considers this work a forerunner of 1898 literature on the 'Spanish problem'.
42 R. Lida, 'La "España Defendida"', p. 148, and 'Quevedo y su España', p. 271.
43 F. Ayala, *La Imagen de España*, Madrid, 1986, pp. 79–84, and *Razón del mundo*, Xalapa, Mexico, 1962, pp. 98–101. On Machiavelli's influence in Spanish political thought, see J. A. Maravall, *Estudios de historia del pensamiento español. Siglo XVII*, Madrid, 1975, pp. 39–76 and 107–124.
44 J. Beramendi, 'Historia y conciencia nacional', *Ayer*, 30 (1998): 128–129; and J. A. Maravall, 'La idea de felicidad en el programa de la Ilustración', in *Estudios de Historia del pensamiento español (siglo XVIII)*, Madrid, 1991, pp. 162–189.
45 *Patria, patriota* or *patriotismo* are widely used in the second half of the eighteenth century, according to F. Lopez, *Juan Pablo Forner et la crise de la conscience espagnole au XVIIIe siècle*, Paris, 1976, or Maravall, *Estudios (siglo XVIII)*, pp. 32–33, 36–37, 49.
46 See J. A. Maravall, 'Sobre el sentimiento de nación en el siglo XVIII: la obra de Forner', *La Torre*, XV(57) (1967), pp. 36–37, and 'De la Ilustración al Romanticismo: el pensamiento político de Cadalso', in

Mélanges à la mémoire de Jean Sarrailh, Paris, 1966, pp. 81–96; J. de Cadalso, *Cartas Marruecas*, Madrid, 1984, p. 256; and Fernández Sebastián, 'España, monarquía y nación'; according to the latter, p. 50, taking part in this nation-building process were Andalusians (Cadalso), Basques (Zamácola), Catalans (Masdeu, Lampillas, Capmany), Madrilenians (Quintana), et al.

47 C. Brinton, *The Anatomy of Revolutions*, New York, 1938, Chapter 2. On Spain, see J. Marías, *La España posible en tiempos de Carlos III*, Madrid, 1963.

48 A. Mestre, *Despotismo e Ilustración en España*, Barcelona, 1976. R. Herr, *The Eighteenth-Century Revolution in Spain*, Princeton, NJ, 1969.

49 See M. F. Bacigalupo, 'English Travel Accounts of Spain, 1750–1787', *Dieciocho*, I(2) (1978): 116–126; on French travellers, F. Lopez, 'La Leyenda Negra en el siglo XVIII', both in special issue 'La Leyenda Negra', *Historia 16*, 193 (1992): 103–112.

50 B. Croce, *La Spagna nella vita italiana durante la Rinascenza*, Bari, 1949, p. 269. On Gothic novel, see P. Powell, *Tree of Hate: Propaganda and Prejudices Affecting U.S. Relations with the Hispanic World*, New York, 1971, pp. 109–110.

51 The opposite to pride was *vanity*, typical of the French, according to Montesquieu, source of consumption and incentive for work and progress; see *L'esprit des lois*, XIX, X; and *Lettres persanes*, XXIV.

52 *Réflections sur la monarchie universelle*, chap. XVI, and *Lettres persanes*, LXXVIII (see also *Lettre* CXVII).

53 *Lettres persanes*, XXIX, CXXI and LXXVIII; *L'Esprit des lois*, XV, III.

54 R. García Cárcel, 'La manipulación de la memoria histórica en el nacionalismo español', *Manuscrits*, 12 (1994): 180.

55 See B. J. Feijóo, 'Glorias de España', in *Teatro Crítico Universal*, Biblioteca de Autores Españoles, LVI, pp. 194–230. J. del Campillo, *Lo que hay de más y lo que hay de menos . . . en España para que sea lo que debe ser y no lo que es*, 1742; cf. G. Anes, 'España como nación en el Siglo de las Luces', in Real Academia de la Historia, *España como nación*, Madrid, 2000, pp. 193–194.

56 See M. Batllori, *La cultura hispano-italiana de los jesuitas expulsos*, Madrid, Gredos, 1966. Lampillas, *Saggio Storico-Apologetico della Letteratura Spagnola*, was published in 1778–1781. Juan Andrés, *Origine, progresso e stato attuale d'ogni letteratura*, in 1782–1799. Masdeu's *Discorso storico filosofico sul clima di Spagna, sul genio ed ingegno degli Spagnuoli per l'industria e per la letteratura, e sul loro carattere politico e morale*, in 1781–1787. See also J. Sempere y Guarinos, *Ensayo de una Biblioteca española de los mejores escritores del reinado de Carlos III*, 6 vols. Madrid: Impr. Real, 1785–1789; and J. A. Ferrer Benimeli, *El conde de Aranda y su defensa de España: Refutación del 'Viaje de Fígaro a España'*, London, 1785.

57 Schmidt, *El problema español*, pp. 71–96. Maravall, *Estudios (siglo XVIII)*, p. 29.

58 'Espagne', in *Encyclopédie Méthodique*, Paris, 1782, Vol. I, pp. 554–568.

Included in García Camarero, *La polémica de la ciencia española*, Madrid: Alianza, 1970, pp. 47–53.

59 Cavanilles (1745–1804), author of *Observaciones sobre la historia natural, geografía, agricultura, población y frutos del reino de Valencia*, would become the director of the Royal Botanical Garden in Madrid. Masson's article was, according to him, 'a model of guilty ignorance and presumptuousness' (*Observations de M. l'Abbé Cavanilles sur l'article 'Espagne' de la Nouvèlle Éncyclopédie*, Paris, 1784; quoted by García Camarero, *Polémica*, pp. 54–57). Denina, *Discurso leído en la Academia de Berlín, el 26 de enero de 1786 . . ., por el señor abate Denina*, Madrid: Impr. Real, 1786, partially reproduced by García Camarero in *Polémica*, pp. 58–71.

60 Sempere y Guarinos, *Ensayo de una Biblioteca*. Forner's *Oración apologética por la España y su mérito literario* was published in Madrid, 1786. Cf. Herr, *Eighteenth-Century Revolution*, pp. 220–230. The Royal Academy's announcement, dated 30–XI–1784, in V. García de la Concha, *Historia de la literatura española: Siglo XVIII*, Madrid, 1995, Vol. II, p. 604–605.

61 Quoted by Maravall, 'Sobre el sentimiento de nación', pp. 42 and 50–53.

62 Mestre, *Despotismo e Ilustración*, p. 134. *El Censor*, 1786, CXIII ('Contra nuestros apologistas') and CLXV. In the end, Cañuelo would be tried by the Inquisition and banned from writing on any religious topic. See also L. de Arroyal's answer to Forner in F. Lopez, 'Leon de Arroyal, auteur des *Cartas político-económicas al conde de Lerena*', *Bulletin Hispanique*, 69 (1969): 26–55.

3

The 'war of independence': a promising beginning

The invention of the 'War of Independence'

The classification of the conflict unleashed in the Iberian peninsula between 1808 and 1814 as a 'war of independence', the term eventually bestowed upon it as a result of the nationalist narrative of these events, is highly questionable. If 'war of independence' is understood to mean an attempt at secession by the inhabitants of a territory integrated against their will into an empire, it should be borne in mind that Napoleon had no intention of turning the Spanish monarchy into the province of an empire ruled from Paris: he merely wished to replace the reigning dynasty. This was neither unusual nor unacceptable as regards Peninsular tradition: a hundred years earlier the Bourbons replaced the Hapsburgs without mishap and without the formal subordination of Spain to France. It is true that, in the course of the 1808–1814 war, Napoleon planned to annexe the provinces to the north of the river Ebro and then to compensate the Spanish monarchy with Portugal, but this was a short-lived project that was opposed by none other than the government of his brother, Joseph, as well as being put forward at too late a date to have been a cause for the uprising of 1808. At the insistence of the Spanish envoys, who considered the issue to be non-negotiable, the Treaty of Fontainebleau of 1807 explicitly stated that the territorial integrity of Spain – including the American colonies – would be respected, with both the existing borders and the independence of Spain guaranteed. Moreover, the first clause of the decree whereby the Emperor granted the Spanish throne to Joseph Bonaparte upheld the independence and integrity of Spain's states, this being ratified by the Statute of Bayonne in the summer of 1808.[1]

Hence the representation of the long and bloody conflict of 1808–1814 as a 'war of independence', or as a confrontation between 'the French' and a Spanish army of 'liberation', is a simplification characteristic of a nationalist (or any other doctrinaire) vision of the world, one which is always prone to explaining complex processes in Manichaean terms with a view to attracting and mobilising political support. In fact, the most recent and reliable historical interpretations tend to attribute these events to a highly complicated set of causes, and, in the last instance, to the convergence of a series of lesser conflicts which not only coincided in time but also fed off one another.

It is undeniable that this was an *international* war waged between France and Britain, the two great European and world powers of the time. With the exception of the Battle of Bailén (1808), all the major battles between 1808 and 1814 were fought between an Imperial army which, though incorporating Polish cavalry and Egyptian mamelukes, was essentially French and always under the command of French officers, and an Anglo-Hispano-Portuguese army whose Commander-in-Chief was the Duke of Wellington. This international dimension had in fact formed part of Godoy's plans, although the alliances anticipated by him, typical of the previous century (Spain and France against England and Portugal), were overturned unexpectedly by the popular revolt of 1808, after which the majority of Spaniards went over to the Anglo-Portuguese side. From this perspective, the struggle had nothing to do with an attempt at liberation or national independence.

Many aspects of the conflict also permit it to be classified as a *civil* war, a term used to describe it by, among others, Jovellanos. Although the nationalists would roundly deny any internal dissension within Spanish society in 1808, the élites were in fact profoundly divided. Whether or not the cause of the divisions was solely a disagreement over the dynasty or whether there were two opposing political projects[2] is open to argument. The latter interpretation is undermined by the fact that kindred spirits such as Meléndez Valdés and Jovellanos or Cabarrús and Floridablanca were to be found on opposing sides. Even anecdotal evidence, such as the French origins of the two dynastic claimants or the internal feuding within the Bourbon royal family, merely underlined the fratricidal aspects of the war.[3] Nevertheless, it is equally true that such differences only affected the ruling classes, as the masses overwhelmingly took sides against the French from the very beginning, while those of the élite faded away as the war's end approached. Barely had Joseph Bonaparte and his cohorts been expelled from Spain than identification with what was eventually to be called the 'War of Independence' became a positive move for any who considered themselves to be '*Spanish*'. The families of the *afrancesados* tried to forget the activities of their forebears as soon as possible.

One aspect of the conflict that might indicate a form of national affirmation was the degree of xenophobia – especially directed at the French

– evident in the popular reaction. According to the deputy José Canga Argüelles, during the course of the war the Spanish exhibited 'greater personal hatred of the French than enthusiasm for the cause'.[4] Existing evidence, for example, suggests that during the crucial Madrid uprising against the French of 2 May 1808 the common battle cry was 'Death to the French!', not 'Viva España!'. This hostility towards the French was reflected by the intellectuals: Antonio de Capmany, a relatively refined writer for his time, wrote that 'the Frenchman is an indefinable animal. He preaches virtue and has none; humanity and knows it not; desires peace and seeks war'.[5] Nonetheless, the negative significance of this factor should not be unduly exaggerated, as constructing a collective identity does entail the marking out of borders and the establishment of exclusions. At this stage, collective identity still amounted to a loathing of things foreign, particularly French things, rather than an as yet ill-defined sense of self-affirmation.

Though the origins of this Francophobia date back to the interminable wars of the sixteenth and seventeenth centuries between the two great monarchies of the Roman Catholic world, the Hapsburgs and the Valois/Bourbons, it was further accentuated in the eighteenth century despite the fact that a branch of the Bourbons occupied the Spanish throne and that, in consequence, the two monarchies were natural allies. The cause of the renewed animosity was French influence upon the Spanish political and cultural scene, especially upon the more traditional social sectors, which were deeply antagonistic to the reforms undertaken by the ministers of the new dynasty.[6] As we have seen, enlightenment reformers could very well be described as *patriotic*, not only for their efforts to promote an official culture that could be called *pre-national*, but also because, by introducing the French cultural and administrative model, they were trying to strengthen the political organisation of the Hispanic Monarchy and reverse the declining prestige of the country. Unfortunately, their political programme attacked many traditional institutions, including the ancient kingdoms' variegated legal systems, and required the eradication of many inherited cultural features and values such as the influence of the clergy or the dishonour associated with manual labour. Conservative circles attributed these reforms to the 'Frenchifying' of the court and its rulers and led them to rise in defence of what they considered to be their 'own' traditions. This is reflected in the fashion for *majismo* (originally the reaction of the common people to the perceived effeminacy of the nobility) which prevailed in some aristocratic circles at the end of the eighteenth century, as depicted by Goya, for example, in his 'cartoons for tapestries'. Thus, while political logic dictated that subjects of the Hispanic Monarchy

should direct their hatred towards the English – who were anti-Catholic
and secular historical enemies as well as competitors for the American
markets – the aversion to all things French was so deeply implanted in
the popular imagination that they began to detest their Catholic neighbour and ally almost as much as the 'perfidious Albion' and their eternal
enemy, 'the Moor'. Throughout the nineteenth century, the anniversary of the Second of May became, among other things, the occasion
for the Francophobia that led, year after year, to attacks on the '*gaba-
chos*' or 'frogs' who dared showed their faces in public on the day of the
celebration.

Another sentiment that proved decisive in mobilising many of the
combatants of 1808 was the Manichaean and personalist attitude they
held towards the political problems of the time. The struggle for power
between prime minister Godoy, favourite of king Carlos IV and his wife
María Luisa, and Godoy's opponents, supported by prince Fernando,
led to Godoy, a man styled the Prince of the Peace and who had controlled the destiny of the country from a position of absolute power
for the previous fifteen years, being popularly judged as the Wicked
Retainer, a figure who has gone down in history as the ambitious
courtier who duped the king and brought untold calamities upon the
kingdom. Regardless of Godoy's political performance, and it is true
that the final years of his mandate were beset by epidemics, famine and
defeat, culminating in the disaster at Trafalgar, his unpopularity owed
more to moral than to political censure as a result of the belief that, as
the queen's lover, he was cuckolding the king. And the appeal of the
future Fernando VII owed far more to the idea of an innocent prince
who was the unhappy victim of a weak father and a heartless mother
than to any ability he might have had to govern.[7]

This traditional moral attitude is linked to another of the causes
of the uprising: the crusade against modern Enlightenment-Jacobin
atheism; in other words, the counter-revolutionary motive. Restating
arguments employed in the war of 1793–1795, the popular *Despertador
cristiano-político* written by a priest named Simón López, claimed that
the Napoleonic troops were merely instruments of the revolution,
product of the 'coalition of the impious, the unbelievers, deists, atheists, heretics and apostates of France and of the whole of Europe' who
sought to carry out 'their long-standing grand plan to ruin the Throne
and the Altar'. Whether such thoughts were prevalent in the minds of
the rebels has been a source of argument ever since. It is one that has
generally been rejected by liberal historians who have always associated the patriotic uprising against the French with the desire for reform
of the country's institutions and, therefore, with an implicit protest

against absolutism. However, it is difficult to deny the extent of calls to defend the faith against the atheist revolutionaries, especially from the lower orders of the clergy, whom the French and their collaborators denounced as the principal agents of the insurrection right from the beginning. There was also a personalistic element insofar as the propaganda showed Napoleon as a modern Anti-Christ and the embodiment of the evils of modernity, especially those of the Revolution (with additional features that had been used for centuries to describe Luther). Though the issue is complex, it should be recognised that subsequent attitudes such as the popular enthusiasm for the return of Fernando VII after the latter's annulment of the work of the *Cortes* de Cádiz (1810–1812) indicate that many of those who took up arms against Joseph Bonaparte were anything but in favour of enlightened or liberal reforms.[8]

One apparently contradictory aspect to this was the element of *social protest*, expressed in a manner typical of the *ancien régime*. As a Catalonian historian has recently commented: 'politically, the fight against the French channelled a whole variety of energies generated by the sensation of general crisis . . .; existing social discontent turned into political complaint and action against the absolutist authorities – who had allowed the situation to happen – from the moment in which the presence of the invader made such behaviour possible'. This attitude of protest, which emerged as the traditional mechanisms of power collapsed, is revealed by resistance to the payment of seigneurial dues, by demands that 'the rich' should finance the war and by proposals even to 'put an end to rule by the rich'. Also worthy of mention are the anti-tax protests, riots against the cost of living, which led to an uprising against those authorities that supported the 'usurper king', as well as attacks on the belongings and mansions of aristocrats and wealthy families who were considered to be *afrancesados* or supporters of Godoy.[9]

One last aspect that challenges the *national* nature of the uprising is, to quote John Tone, 'the predominance of local patriotism over national unity', a particularism that in fact strengthened resistance to the French. Local loyalties were roused by the excesses of the occupying army and, together with the traditional obstacles to centralised control of provincial and regional institutions, proved to be a formidable source of opposition once the government had passed into the hands of Napoleon's Marshals. Tone's thesis seems reasonable: given what is known or intuited about the society of the *ancien régime*, it makes sense that individuals integrated into networks of patronage and community power could be mobilised by notables who appealed to highly localised identities. The juntas that emerged in the second half of 1808 were merely harbingers of later rebellious movements recurring throughout the century. It is true that the juntas merged into a 'Junta Central', and then into a *Cortes* that emphatically affirmed the essential unity of the 'Spanish nation', but the huge dispersion of the centres of power in the initial moments of the conflict must be acknowledged.[10] Rather than 'nationalism', or any sense of a Spanish identity, we are talking about community ties and local patriotism.

Naturally, a conflict of this complexity was not easy to give a name to. Every name had a political interpretation, and agreement was only reached after a long, conflictive process of invention. Initially, of course, people merely referred to the war in chronological or geographical terms ('the current war', 'the events of the last few months', 'the war in Spain'). The more traditional and less imaginative minds quickly took refuge in religious or noble references ('the holy Spanish insurrection', 'our sacred struggle', 'our glorious uprising', 'the heroic war against Napoleon'). The earliest openly ideological interpretations of the events resorted to apocalyptic images dating back to mediaeval millenarianism, representing Spain as 'the people of God' and Napoleon as the Beast announced by St John at the end of time.[11] Another equally traditional option was to call the conflict the 'War of Usurpation', emphasising the illegitimacy of Joseph I's claim to the throne. If these events had taken place a hundred or even fifty years earlier, it is conceivable that this name would have won the day, but more forward-thinking minds applied the recently invented term 'revolution' with greater, though short-lived, success: a *Colección de documentos para la historia de la revolución en España* appeared in 1809; in 1810, Álvaro Flórez Estrada published *Introducción para la historia de la revolución de España* and Eugenio de Tapia *Apuntes sobre los hechos principales de la Revolución de Sevilla en 1808*; the following year came a new *Colección de documentos para la historia política de nuestra revolución* as well as a *Memoria histórica sobre la revolución de Valencia* by Friar Juan Rico; and in 1812, Father Maestro Salmón began his *Resumen histórico de la revolución en España*, which eventually stretched to six volumes. After the end of the war, works of greater importance appeared, such as that of José Clemente Carnicero, *Historia razonada de los principales sucesos de la gloriosa revolución de España* (in four volumes), and *La revolución actual de España* by Martínez de la Rosa.[12]

The word 'revolution' continued in vogue even after the return of Fernando VII in 1814, although, given the dislike of the revolutionary metaphor in the renewed absolutist climate, the terminology became increasingly varied. The 'War of Spain against Napoleon', the

'Domination of the usurper government', the 'Defensive war against the invasion of the tyrant', the 'Last war between Spain and France', the 'Struggle against French domination' were all mixed in with 'Revolution', which remained predominant. It is significant that the first official history of the war, edited by Colonel Cabanes in 1818, was entitled *Historia de la Guerra de España contra Napoleón Bonaparte*.

Two phenomena were to modify the situation in the early 1820s. The first was the genuine revolution that shook Spain between 1820 and 1823 and introduced an almost unremitting period of instability over the next fifty years. The term 'revolution' then became inappropriate in reference to the conflict of 1808–1814. It continued to be used either to describe the whole process (1808–1823) or was used in the plural, as in 'the revolutions' in Spain (1808–1814 and 1820–1823). The second phenomenon was the rebellion of the American colonies, which began in 1810 and quickly intensified, becoming irreversible within ten years. The newly independent countries did not generally refer to these events as 'wars of independence' until much later: just like the Spanish, they spoke of 'revolution', although combined with more creative language such as 'emancipation' and 'liberators'. Seen from Europe, however, there could be little doubt that it was a question of American 'independence'.[13]

It was in the final phase of American independence that the Spanish began to apply the same term to the events of 1808–1814. The expression 'War of Independence' was first heard in the political debates of 1821–1822; in 1824–1825 it was used by Quintana in a letter to Lord Holland and by the ex-guerrilla fighter, Mina, in the first draft of his future memoirs, which were published in London. Nevertheless, five years later, in Canga Argüelles' review of Napier's *History of the War in the Peninsula*, the term 'War of Independence' is not once to be found.[14] However, in 1833 two books appeared with the expression in their titles, namely: *La Guerra de la Independencia, o sea, triunfos de la heroica España contra Francia en Cataluña* by Cecilio López; and the *Historia política y militar de la Guerra de la Independencia de España contra Napoleón Bonaparte, de 1808 a 1814* by José Muñoz Maldonado. An indication that the term was still not in common usage even then, apart from the length of the titles (necessary in order to explain their meaning), is the first sentence of Muñoz Maldonado's book, in which he states that the author's aim is to discuss 'the glorious revolution of Spain from 1808 to 1814'.

Leading figures from the conflict who were in the process of writing memoirs or strongly autobiographical historical accounts at the time were themselves resistant to using the new terminology. Most

important of these works was the justly famous account by the Conde
de Toreno, published in 1835, which immediately became the official history of the conflict, entitled *Historia del levantamiento, guerra
y revolución de España*. The review of this book published by Alcalá
Galiano, also a politician and historian of the period, displays a continuing imprecision in reference to the war: the review opens with 'at last
we have a Spanish historian who will remind posterity of the glorious
deeds of his *patria* during the war of Independence', but fails to use the
expression again, referring instead to the 'Spanish revolution of 1808',
'the Peninsular war', 'the war and revolution in Spain', the 'uprising
and defence (of Spain)', or the three nouns in Toreno's title. In his own
writings, Alcalá Galiano tended to keep to the traditional name, such as
in his *Índole de la revolución de España en 1808*, published in the *Revista
de Madrid* in 1839, where he explicitly rejected the idea that, 'comparing events in France . . . with those of Spain during the period called
the war of Independence . . . the latter [are] lesser and unworthy of the
title of revolution'.[15]

The imprecision continued until about the mid-1840s. E. de Tapia
in 1840, E. de Kosca Vayo in 1842, J. Díaz de Baeza a year later, and A.
Ramírez Arcas three years later, were all still unwilling to accept the new
name.[16] By the late 1840s, however, it is clear that the term had taken
hold. In 1844, the long-awaited history by Miguel Agustín Príncipe,
La Guerra de la Independencia, was finally published and became the
standard version until Gómez Arteche began publication of his *Historia
de la Guerra de la Independencia* in 1868. In 1860, Modesto Lafuente
brought out Volume XXIII of his *Historia General de España*, of which
Part III, Book X is entitled 'The War of Independence of Spain', indi-
cating its definitive adoption. It is interesting to note the evolution of
Alcalá Galiano, in whose late *Memorias* there are numerous undisputed
references to the 'War of Independence', a significant departure from
his earlier writing and, in particular, that of 1839.[17]

In short, by 1850, the war of 1808–1814 had acquired a durable
name.[18] An expression coined in the 1830s and 1830s (some twenty
years after the event) had achieved undisputed success in the 1840s
and 1850s. 'Spain', the Spanish people, had stood up as one against
'the French', or against Napoleon, in a 'War of Independence' and
emerged triumphant, revealing once again how strong Spanish identity
was, something which they had demonstrated many a time throughout
their history as successive waves of invaders swept across the Peninsula.
That sense of Spanishness, undeniable in the past, had been confirmed
in the present. It would have been difficult to find a more auspicious
beginning to the process of contemporary nationalisation.

'Spaniards, you now have a patria'

The first conclusion to be drawn from this analysis is hardly original: 1808 marked the turning point at which the *ancien régime* drew to its close and the 'modern' era dawned. 'Modern' is a word used in many senses, but one which is undoubtedly valid as regards the construction of national identity because, from that time on, one can begin to talk of nationalism in the modern sense of the term.

The second conclusion is that ethnic patriotism had moved on to become fully *national*, at least among the élites, during the Napoleonic War, and that this was unquestionably due to the work of the liberals. The disturbances that broke out against the French troops were initially scattered and disorganised. When the State collapsed, it became essential to improvise its reorganisation around a series of local juntas which would later be coordinated around a central body which, in turn, convoked the *Cortes*, an institution which had not assembled – except for formal ceremonies – for many centuries. The modernising élites took advantage of the occasion and tried to institute a programme of social and political changes, and the means they chose to defend the right of the *Cortes* to undertake such reform was to champion the revolutionary idea of the *nation* as the upholder of *sovereignty* in the absence of the monarch.

The national myth, put about by those abreast of the innovations in political language, was seized upon by everyone else as their best hope for salvation under such difficult circumstances. It was the most powerful magnet for attracting support, the most effective argument for persuading individuals to overcome their egoism and to sacrifice their belongings and even their lives in defence of the collective interest. At a stroke, a sense of national purpose succeeded in delegitimising both the Napoleonic army as *foreign* and *tyrannical* and the collaborators of Joseph Bonaparte as *afrancesados* or, in other words, *not Spanish*. Could anything worse be said of them? Could anyone trust such unnatural beings? This was quite enough for those who wanted to win the war without political reform and who wished to hear no further talk of the nation – which was, in short, a revolutionary idea, and French to boot – but harked back to tradition, faith and loyalty to the monarch. However, the followers of Enlightenment thinking, though far more radicalised by the impact of the French Revolution, wanted to grasp the opportunity offered by that myth to build a totally new political edifice. It is not by chance that *national sovereignty* became the *idée fixe* of the early – and decisive – sessions of constitutional debate. It was necessary to invent a credible political myth of sufficient power to rival the consecrated monarch. Just as seventeenth-century England and eighteenth-century America had invented 'the People', the voice of God and an invincible social force,[19] Spain, taking its lead from France, invented the 'Nation'. It was a device that nullified royal legitimacy and, consequently, all inherited privilege.

The rapidity and ability with which the constitutionalists of Cádiz overcame the obstacles that separated justification of the war against Napoleon from an affirmation of national sovereignty can only be cause for admiration. The first step in their argument was purely defensive and obvious to anyone: the abdication of the Bourbons, and in particular of Fernando *el deseado*, in favour of Napoleon. Though the abdication was endorsed by officially impeccable documents, this was considered inadmissible, having taken place under duress because the 'sovereigns' were being held prisoner in France by the Emperor, who had secured their signatures by force. The next step in the dialectic required a little more imagination: even if it could be demonstrated that the throne had been freely and willingly relinquished in Bayonne, rule by the Bonapartes continued to be usurpation *because it would have required the consent of the nation*. In accordance with the highly opportune unearthing of the mediaeval theory of the pact, the abdications and cessions of Bayonne were null and void because they had not been ratified by the *Cortes*. The deputies in Cádiz thereby began by making 'a solemn protest against the usurpations of Napoleon, declaring . . . that . . . the renunciation made in Bayonne was null, not only owing to the violence involved in that act, but *principally* because of the lack of consent of the nation'. The town hall of Mexico City, on refusing to recognise Joseph Bonaparte, argued that the 'ill-fated abdication' of Fernando had not only been 'involuntary, under duress' but that it was 'of no effect against the highly respectable rights of the Nation', which it 'deprives of the most precious prerogative that it possesses'; '*none can name him Sovereign* – it concluded – *without its consent and the universal [consent] of all its peoples*'[20] From that moment, the argument advanced inexorably towards a revolutionary conclusion. A phrase from the historian Francisco Martínez Marina sums up the third step: [though] the monarch is absent, the nation is not and neither does it cease to exist [and] within it, sovereign authority remains at its centre'. In other words, the nation has the right to defend and govern itself even without its monarch because sovereignty resides within it. A fourth step, formulated by the poet and politician Manuel José Quintana, completes the sequence: 'Kings are for the people, and not the people for the kings. The Spanish people achieved their freedom with their blood, they gave themselves kings in order to be governed in peace and justice'. In other words, the king was at the service of the nation and not the other way round: the nation had become *superior* to the king.[21]

Such was the thought process behind the passing of the celebrated Articles 2 and 3 of the Constitution: 'the Spanish Nation is free and independent and it is not nor cannot be the patrimony of any family or person'; and 'sovereignty resides essentially in the Nation and therefore it is [the nation's] exclusive right to establish its fundamental laws'. The formula did not break with tradition in a radical manner since a principle established by mediaeval scholastic doctrine and developed by Spanish doctrine in the sixteenth century had made the people the original depository of sovereignty, although this had been delegated irrevocably in the person of the monarch. This is why the absolutist deputies were prepared to accept Article 3 as long as the adverb 'essentially' was replaced by that of 'originally' or 'radically'. However, the liberals, determined to take advantage of the situation in order to enshrine the right of social forces to share power, insisted that sovereignty resided in the people in an 'essential' or irrevocable, and not merely 'original', way.[22]

In short, the liberal approach to the war consisted of transforming what was initially a repudiation of the tyrant Bonaparte into a stand against tyranny itself on principle and, consequently, against any person – foreign or Spanish – who attempted to take political decisions without acknowledging the will of 'the nation'. The phrase 'the end of despotism', which had been used somewhat lightly in the weeks after the fall of Godoy and before the Second of May, began to take on a more radical significance. For those who believed in the historic myth of the mediaeval freedoms crushed by Hapsburg absolutism centuries before, the time had come to rectify the course of history and recover them. Quintana declared that the moment for the 'restoration of collective virtues' had arrived, while Argüelles was even more graphic: 'the battle of Bailén redeemed the Spaniards from that of Villalar'. References to 1808 as the year of the 'regeneration of Spain' can be interpreted in a similar light. The rebellion against the French was a struggle for *freedom*. Quintana, once again, criticised those who, overcome by 'political egoism', 'shudder at the mere idea of reforming the kingdom' and want to restrict us to 'throwing out the French, as if it were only the French who oppress us'; the reforms were necessary specifically to ensure that 'after throwing them out', we shall see 'our rights established'.[23]

Writing in verse, Martínez de la Rosa declared that the people had not risen against Napoleon to defend 'the unjust laws / of a miserly master, nor the palaces / of a proud despot' but to honour the 'terrible holy vow / to rise up free or die with glory'. In the '*Sitio de Zaragoza*', he marries the defence of freedom to national identity:

> ¿Paz, paz con los tiranos? Guerra eterna,
> guerra a la usurpación; muramos todos
> sin libertad, sin patria arrodillados.
> Así gritó la muchedumbre: ¡guerra, guerra!

The young Duque de Rivas also took up this theme in '*El sueño de un proscrito*', a poem in which nostalgia combines with anger at seeing the *patria* ruled by a tyrant: '¡Patria! No existe / donde sólo hay opresos y opresores'. An idea he repeats in his 'Ode': 'Y cuando no tenemos patria, / ¿sus himnos entonar podremos?'[24]

The impossibility of feeling oneself to be a citizen in a republic with no free institutions was an ancient philosophical subject debated by Cicero in Rome.[25] The Spanish liberals, well-versed in the Graeco-Latin tradition, resorted to this classical identification between patriotism and the defence of freedom, turning it into a far more powerful rhetorical weapon than enlightened exhortations to a love of progress or philanthropy would ever be. Quintana explained that the ancients 'called *Patria* the state or society to which they belonged, and whose laws ensured their freedom and well being', whereas where 'the general will was enslaved to the will of only one' and 'there were no laws addressed to the interests of everyone', there might be 'a country, a people, a council of men; but there was no *Patria*'.[26] The connection between a sense of identification with the collectivity and political freedom was also established by Flórez Estrada when, on convoking the *Cortes*, he said that 'Spaniards find themselves without a constitution and therefore without freedom and without a *patria*'. The weekly journal *La Abeja Española* observed in 1813 that the war was inspired by 'patriotism', by 'the huge influx of love of the *patria*', but that that same patriotism required 'in terms of our independence to ensure our freedom forever', since Spain was facing 'the happy prospect of demolishing the monuments of execration and opprobrium, that . . . make empires wretched'. However, this did not only derive from Cicero and classical Rome but also from Robespierre and Jacobin France: while 'patriotism' and 'patriot' had enabled Enlightenment scholars to refer to a favourable predisposition towards sacrifice for the community, in the France of 1792–1793 the defenders of the revolutionary camp had been called 'patriots' in contrast to *les aristocrates* or *les légitimistes*. In Spain, fifteen years later, those who fought the French were the 'patriots'; which also meant that they were sacrificing themselves for the collectivity and in the fight for freedom. Argüelles used it in this sense when, on announcing the Constitution of Cádiz, he declared '*Españoles, ya tenéis patria*'.[27]

Élites and the common people

One of the main problems posed by the war of 1808–1814 to a historian of today is to distinguish between the thoughts of the Constitutionalists of Cádiz and those of the people at large. The nationalism of the former is clear, having its roots in the patriotic identity and sentiments created in the early modern age, but it is also evident that the entire cultural process had been a matter for the political and intellectual élites with limited popular involvement.

There is no reason to believe that, prior to the 1808 uprising, feelings of ethnic patriotism – let alone new nationalist ideas – had spread beyond the select political and literary circles close to the court. This was due not only to rural isolation and illiteracy but also to the fact that the educated classes exhibited little interest in promoting such ideas or sentiments among the masses. In none of the political debates or conflicts prior to the mid-eighteenth century, such as the *Comunidades*, the War of the Catalans or the War of Succession, was any attempt made by either side to involve the *people*, let alone appeal to them in the name of ethnic patriotism or turn them into a collective national subject.[28] As Max Weber observed in *Economy and Society*, the humanists of the Renaissance were very uncomfortable with the popular language employed by Lutheran preachers, and this appears to have been one of the factors that explains their lukewarm attitude towards them, even though they may have agreed with many of their theological positions and their critique of the Roman Catholic clergy.[29] The same could be said of the intellectual élites of the early modern age. They despised the masses and considered them ignorant and worthy only of taking orders. To attempt to mobilise public opinion to decide an issue one way or another would have been the last and worst possible resort. Common people, by definition, did not understand such things, and it was best if they did not try to do so. In Spain, the closest that political debate had come to the kind generated by the wars of religion in France or the Revolution in England had been the discussions of the critics (*arbitristas*) in relation to the causes of monarchic decline, while the greater part of their writings were merely 'memoranda' addressed in private to the king or his ministers and never intended for publication. Until the War of the Convention (1794) – or, if one prefers, the *Motín de Esquilache* – there were no proclamations and no papers or pamphlets directed at a public that, either implicitly or explicitly, went by the name of 'Spaniards!'. Judging from the records, chroniclers, while wary of the selfishness and factionalism of the nobility, expected no more than irrational, passionate, almost bestial reactions from the populace. It was one more reason to look to the monarchy as the only agent that represented order, equilibrium and the search for the common good.

It is true that the *ilustrados* brought a certain change in attitude insofar as they regarded the people as the ultimate beneficiaries of their political projects. However, they never believed that the people could ever contribute to social prosperity or uphold the monarchy without previously undergoing a long, intensive education. For enlightened reformers, ignorance amounted to an inability to perceive one's own interests, the result of which was as many vices as crimes, both of which were typical of the masses. 'Crimes are born of mistakes', wrote Cabarrús; and Jovellanos, the reformer most concerned about this issue, made it clear that 'where there is no education, there is nothing; where there is, there is everything'. Indeed, it was Jovellanos who drew up the very first national plan of education in the country in his *Memoria sobre la Instrucción Pública*, while it was his friend Meléndez Valdés who considered the possible creation of a Ministry of Education. However, this was still a far remove from allowing the people to have a voice in public affairs. When the ministers of Carlos III took higher education out of the hands of the Jesuits, they continued to hold the belief that the latter should be reserved for the nobility and the wealthy classes. For the working classes, schools or centres were set up in which they could be educated in a 'useful' manner, in other words, where they would receive technical training in order to improve their labouring skills. It was an idea thought up by Macanaz under Felipe V and put into practice by the *Sociedades de Amigos del País* (Societies of the Friends of the Nation) in the time of Carlos III. A political and moral education that centred on the new social values of tolerance, civic virtue and knowledge of one's own interests was reserved for the wealthy classes. Included in these values was national pride, based on a knowledge of national history.

The attitude of the élite towards the people underwent a sea change after 1808. It is perhaps best expressed by Antonio de Capmany who, in his *Centinela contra franceses*, warned of the corruption of Spanish moral life as a result of the Frenchifying of customs. He begged for traditional popular values to be protected, together with *fiestas* (including bullfights, which imbued one with particular 'ferocity'), the style of dress and, above all, language, because only thus would the country be preserved from the impiety and 'feminisation' typical of enlightened or revolutionary modernity. Capmany, in true pre-Romantic style, located the national essence in the popular instinct, in contrast to the élites who were corrupted by civilisation and cosmopolitanism. In an earlier work, the *Teatro histórico-crítico de la elocuencia española*, he had already expressed his conviction that the 'people' were not the dregs of the nation, but its true strength, both physical and moral: 'the science of a nation may be found in writers, in teachers, in those who govern and rule; but the origin of their talent has to be sought among the people, because only in them are reason and customs constant, uniform and common to all'. The people were the creators of the language, but they had something else: they had *numen*, the divine spark which determines national character and customs. In 1808, in his *Centinela*, he repeated that 'the people are the nation, for everything comes from their mass' and that they expressed the 'national spirit' in a spontaneous and instinctive way far better than the élites corrupted by culture. This was the crucial fact in the ongoing war: that the people, preserved from cosmopolitan 'contagion' by their 'lack of culture', had 'saved' the country; and by putting up such fierce resistance to Napoleon, Spain demonstrated that it was a 'nation', unlike Austria or Germany where 'there was an army but no nation', this being the reason why they had been so easily defeated. With great shrewdness, Capmany concluded that a new kind of war had been waged in Spain: 'it is a home-grown war, it is the war of a nation . . . rather than one of soldiers'.[30]

Miguel Artola has observed that there was a basic 'doctrinal antagonism' between Jovellanos and Capmany. The former reflected the spirit of the Enlightenment when writing to Lord Holland in 1810 that the 'wretched' people, who were 'day labourers', felt 'indifferent' towards the war 'with no sense of *patria*'. To this illustrious Asturian, human beings could only have patriotic feelings and become part of the citizenry through ownership and culture. In contrast, Antonio de Capmany, who represented the new romantic vision, revered the people precisely for their lack of culture, which led them to be ruled by their *heart*: 'neither books nor politicians nor philosophers will show you the path to glory. Your hearts spoke to you and led you from the plough and the workshop to the field of Mars'. In contrast to the philosophers, who 'have no *patria*', the nation was defended by 'the labourer, the farmer, the shepherd, the peasant', who were attached to their plot of land; 'it could well be said from experience that men feel greater love for their land the more uneducated and ignorant they are'. Ignorance, the source of vice for an *ilustrado*, had suddenly become a political virtue.[31]

At the time of the uprising, Capmany was the exception among the educated classes. Most *ilustrados*, such as Llorente, Moratín, Meléndez Valdés and Cabarrús, who had learnt not to expect anything of the people, went over to Joseph I, continuing the élitist, pedagogical tradition of the eighteenth century. Even the eminent figures who initially opposed the French felt a certain repugnance at the popular revolt. Toreno and other 'patriots' tried to placate the rebels on the Second of May, 'a day of bitter memory, of mourning and grief', and Goya, in his *Dos de Mayo*, reflects the barbarity and madness among the Spaniards as they set upon the Imperial lancers. The Inquisition itself – which, let us not forget, was a state institution whose most eminent members were appointed by the government – initially condemned the uprising. All this was to change very quickly. A few months after the outbreak of war, the idea that the people had saved the country at precisely the moment in which the *corrupt, anti-patriotic* élites had abandoned it had taken a firm hold. Everyone began to think that Capmany was right: that the true moral strength of the nation resided in the people and that only they were eternal. Endowed with a political instinct that was sometimes extreme but always accurate, it was the people – not the institutions – who had saved the *patria*, and that was because feeling ruled over reason or culture. The *afrancesado* Reinoso observed that the main actors of the war had been 'the least educated people', whose actions had been born 'of sentiment rather than calculation'. The future exile Blanco White stated that the people, if not 'thinking with clarity, do at least feel, and deeply'. When they 'spontaneously' made war, all went well and 'the French suffered severe setbacks', the guerrillas being successful 'because they did not have an army of pen-pushers ordering them around'. Elsewhere, he concludes that 'the poor part of the Spanish nation is the healthy part' and 'the filth is among the military commanders'. This at once fitted in perfectly with a growing romanticism and with the idea of *Volksgeist* while breaking with the élitist, pedagogical tradition of the Spanish reformism of the *ancien régime*.[32]

The inversion of the traditional image of the people is obvious in many of the statements emanating from beseiged Cádiz. 'Great and generous people!' exclaimed Quintana in his *Semanario Patriótico*. Fernández Sardino, in *El Robespierre Español*, emphasised the *exclusive* protagonism of the *common people* in the uprising: 'Only the common people raised the furious cry of *freedom* . . . Only the common people, whom the great in their fanatical pride call *base* . . . frightened the tyrant . . .Only the common people fearlessly destroyed the chains on the second of May; the nobility, terrified, deemed it too reckless an enterprise to resist the barbarous oppressor . . . Only the common people, overcome by holy fury, wrested victories from the enemy in the first campaign; astonished, the nobility could hardly believe its eyes'. In another edition of the paper, the same author published a 'Eulogy to the common people of Spain' in which he called them magnanimous, sublime, benign, honourable, incorruptible, generous, simple and courageous. They were 'like an immense torrent' when they ran amok, but they had now 'recovered their natural mildness'. Bartolomé J. Gallardo, in his *Diccionario crítico-burlesco*, distinguished two meanings of the word *pueblo*: in the 'highest and most sublime' sense it was 'synonymous with nation'; in the 'more humble' sense ('though never base', he hastens to add, 'for in Spain there are no lowly people'), it 'is understood as the majority of citizens who, without enjoying any particular distinction, income or job, live by their trade'; and it was these people who, on the Second of May, unarmed and abandoned by the government, raised the cry for Spanish independence: 'Eternal glory to the people of Madrid and all the peoples of Spain!'[33]

The populist volte-face performed by the liberals during the War of Independence was such a radical departure from their previous outlook that people accustomed to the latter could only think that the new discourse was a nonsense. How could ignorant people become the source of political and cultural inspiration? What could possibly be *learnt* from a people lacking in any sort of formative education? More than one declared that it was *Rousseauan* madness and, a little later, it was to be called *Romantic* madness. It *was* a madness, an undemonstrable truth that any *ilustrado* would have had difficulty in taking seriously, yet everyone now began to believe that the 'nation' was invincible. As the historian Padre Salmón explained, the popular uprising had demonstrated that 'Spain is unconquerable: without power, without armies, weapons or money, it is superior to the greatest forces of Napoleon . . . If, in such a state, and with only the weapons of their courage, constancy and patriotism, these men have been able to humiliate the enemy . . . [w]hat can we not expect of them when they become familiar with the roar of the cannon? They will bring the total destruction and downfall of despotism and tyranny to all the peoples of the world in a triumph such as has never been seen down the centuries. This is the inescapable result of a courageous and resourceful Nation that detests villainy and slavery. Spaniards, do not doubt that this is to be your ultimate destiny. You will suffer, you will endure, but you will conquer'.[34]

The way the élites viewed the masses, however, was not about to change overnight. Juan Francisco Fuentes has detected a 'dual language of liberalism' on this issue, whereby the élites veered between 'exaltation and execration' of the people, between 'populism' and 'egoism'. He reminds us how even such a radical thinker as León de Arroyal showed his contempt of the 'brutish masses', asserting their love of bullfights as evidence; and how even José de Marchena, an enthusiastic propagator of revolutionary ideals, was cautious in his references to Spain because he did not believe that the people were ready for progress. Once the war had begun, Flórez Estrada continued to show his lack of confidence in the people who, he admitted, had brought about the fall of Godoy, but who had not thought to demand measures to prevent the situation occurring again. He concluded that the common people 'have always been, and will be, victims of their ignorance, the only cause of all their misfortunes'.[35]

Still, the liberals had no choice but to accept and promote the myth of the people as heroic fighters in defence of the nation's liberty because the political results desired by the former derived from latter: namely, their right to participate in the decision-making that affected the collectivity. 'The decisive participation of the people in the insurrection against the French in 1808 conferred upon them a degree of prestige and power unimaginable before that date', writes Juan Francisco Fuentes. 'A people so magnanimous and generous can now only be governed by true laws', stated the *Junta Central* in justification of the convocation of the *Cortes*; and, as Fuentes has pointed out, the adverb *now* was expressive of the change of opinion among the enlightened minority regarding the political capacity of the people. It appears that the *Catecismos políticos* addressed to children and the inhabitants of rural areas, which proliferated during the war, were taking a similar line. Some radicals like Fernández Sardino tried to carry this conclusion to extremes by contrasting the 'magnanimous people' with the aristocratic 'traitors to the *patria*', against whom punitive measures should have been taken.[36]

Undoubtedly for the same reasons, the absolutists showed a distinct lack of enthusiasm over the people's participation. This demonstrated a certain lack of political vision because the idea of the 'people' could have been linked to the values of the *ancien régime*, as they were by Capmany and, later, by the writer Cecilia Böhl de Faber (known as 'Fernán Caballero'), who, in praising what was 'popular', interpreted it to mean traditional religiosity, respect for the established hierarchy, and anti-French, anti-revolutionary and, in sum, anti-modern xenophobia. During the war years, however, the conservatives tended to maintain their long-standing fear of the people. Fray Simón López, in his *Despertador cristiano-político*, said that the philosophers who tried to introduce the ideas that triumphed in France discovered 'insuperable obstacles in the Clergy, Monarchs and Nobility'; Spain was saved 'thanks to the loving providence of our God, thanks to the unity of the holy Catholic Religion ... thanks to the holy Inquisition'.[37] In neither statement does he mention the people. And when Fernando

VII returned and the absolutists could once again express their political beliefs openly, they made very clear the role reserved for the people in the *Manifiesto de los Persas*: they were to be kept in 'darkness' in order to avoid 'anarchy'.

The historians of today are not as convinced as those of the nineteenth century that the 1808–1814 war was quite so popular, so spontaneous or, above all, so inspired by patriotic feeling. John Tone has serious doubts about the traditional version. García de Cortázar and González Vesga claim that this 'popular' insurrection was actually encouraged by the Church and the nobility and that the activities of the deputies in the *Cortes* recall the measures taken by Enlightenment governments: 'as in the eighteenth century, they attempted to impose reform from above, without expecting assistance from the ignorant mass of the population'. For Pérez Ledesma, 'it was not the common people who headed the revolutionary movement after the first few months', and he goes on to observe that all the cities elected local notables to the Juntas, just as they sent public officials, intellectuals, the clergy and even members of the nobility to the *Cortes*, not artisans or the early rebels. We should also remember that in 1823, only fifteen years after the great uprising against Napoleon and only nine since victory had been declared, there was a new French invasion which did not cause any significant popular reaction. The reason is obvious: the networks that had mobilised the people in 1808 did not want to do so again in 1823. This raises as many doubts about the spontaneity of the uprising as about its strictly patriotic motivation.[38]

Nevertheless, what *actually* happened is less important than what people *believed* had happened. And the 'War of Independence' went down in history as a populist undertaking. Some decades later, Espronceda was overcome with emotion at the thought of it:

¡Oh! ¡Es el pueblo! ¡Es el pueblo! Cual las olas
Del hondo mar alborotado brama.
Las esplendentes glorias españolas,
Su antigua prez, su independencia aclama.[39]

And the novelist Pérez Galdós was to begin his great national saga with this war, protagonised by the people, in a very similar way to that of Tolstoy in Russia.

Throughout the nineteenth century, the populist myth was to reemerge at every key moment. On the eve of the revolution of 1868, Fernando Garrido, doubtless trying to stir up popular reaction to the forthcoming political changes, compared the 'grandeur and heroism' of the people in 1808 with the 'cowardice of their mandarins', who 'had at their command armies, squadrons and treasures' but left the defence of the *patria* to the 'unarmed, ignorant populace, accustomed for centuries to blind obedience'. For a whole century, the liberals, having written so much about this heroic 'defence of Spanish freedom' by the masses, continued to hope that the people would undertake a decisive act of political redemption or regeneration of the country. However many times they became disillusioned and frustrated, however much the crowds acclaimed Fernando VII and then supported Don Carlos, the myth lived on, at least in rhetorical terms: the people are liberal and, above all, patriotic; the true moral force of the nation lies within them; in desperate times, it is they, not the institutions, who salvage the *patria*; it was demonstrated in 1808 and will be demonstrated again when the time comes.

This confidence in the people on the part of the liberal élites was to prove misplaced and to be the cause of many future disappointments. In the end, the identity-building of the nineteenth century was to prove not to be radically different from that of the *ancien régime*. National loyalty was based on cultural constructs created and internalised by the elites, with little or no impact on the lower classes. The chasm between them persisted throughout the nineteenth century. After the Napoleonic wars, the change was little more than rhetorical: a nominal veneration of the people as the last bastion of patriotic sentiment and freedom. In the summer of 1898, this illusion led to generalised despair among the educated middle classes. As news came in of the sinking of the two Spanish fleets, they realised that the populace continued to attend bullfights as if nothing had happened. Even then, when everything seemed lost, Azorín, Baroja, Marquina and other intellectuals joined in a homage 'To the People' for their sacrifices during the Cuban War.[40]

The nation on its way

To conclude, the revolt of 1808 saw the launch of contemporary Spanish nationalism and, to all appearances, it was an auspicious beginning. The Spanish people had successfully rebelled against the most powerful foreign army ever to attempt to subdue it and had thereby demonstrated their fierce independence and their deep-rooted national identity, just as they had in earlier centuries against the Romans and the Moors. The consecration of the 1808–1814 conflict as a *War of Independence* by the liberals gave rise to an almost perfect national myth which transcended all party political interests. The liberals continued to base their attempts at building a political edifice on the idea that the people had been fighting for their sovereignty, but the conservatives had no compunction in claiming that these anti-Napoleonic heroes were in fact fighting in defence of age-old traditions.[41] In addition, the Catalans and Aragonese had distinguished themselves in the fighting. Zaragoza, Gerona and the Bruchs entered legend as crucial factors demonstrating the 'Spanishness' of all the 'regions'.

The victory over Napoleon was to become the foundation of national pride and the cornerstone of the mythology that haloed the newborn national State. In spite of all the blows to Spaniards' self-esteem in the nineteenth century, memories of the War of Independence allowed them to maintain a minimum degree of collective dignity. It is no coincidence that the Second of May was declared a *national* holiday or that monuments were set up in honour of the *martyrs* of the revolt, the first and most important public symbol of political significance of the century, whereas the statues of kings were the only legacy from the previous era.[42] When Benito Pérez Galdós began publishing his great historical saga *Episodios nacionales* in 1873, he did not start with the Reconquest of Granada, the sailing of Columbus or the campaigns of Carlos V; his first series dealt with the war of 1808–1814. Fact and fiction agreed that contemporary Spain was born of that tragedy. At around the time that Galdós published the first of the *Episodios*, the republican Fernando Garrido wrote that the uprising of the Spanish people against the French had been 'the most important political event in the history of our *patria*'.[43]

This version of events was still in circulation at the turn of the nineteenth century. The *Enciclopedia Espasa*, the great editorial work whose purpose was to present universal knowledge from a *Spanish* perspective, devoted five closely-written pages to describing what it called 'the admirable epic of the Spanish fighting the troops of the greatest commander ever seen'.[44] In 1908, all of Spain celebrated the centenary of the War of Independence with great pomp, largely in compensation for the humiliating defeats of 1898. Monuments were erected, congresses were held, *zarzuelas* were written, and there was even an opera composed called *Zaragoza*, whose librettist was none other than Pérez Galdós. Every city and social class made an effort to evoke, and pay tribute to, its particular contribution to the great national feat.

The myth was to surface for the last time in 1936 on the outbreak of war between two armed camps with diametrically opposed political views. Nationalists and Republicans both resorted to the exculpatory rhetoric of 'foreign aggression'. They coincided in the view that it was not a civil war but another attack on the nation, another fight for survival, in order to be faithful to themselves. Spain was now defending itself – according to preference – from Hitler and Mussolini on the one hand, or from the Judaeo-Masonic conspiracy orchestrated by Moscow on the other. For once, communists and anarchists found themselves in agreement. The anarchist daily *Solidaridad Obrera* declared that history was repeating itself in 'the epic struggle for national independence' from 'imperialist fascism', just as when 'the French troops began to believe themselves masters of the Peninsula' but were defeated thanks to 'the supreme faith that inspired the Iberian people in defence of their freedom'. This version was confirmed by the Communist *Mundo Obrero*: 'the heroic genius of Daoiz and Velarde, of Lieutenant Ruiz, of Malasaña, is embodied by the soldiers in the trenches of Madrid. Castaños, el Empecinado, the defenders of Zaragoza and Gerona are the historical predecessors of our military leaders of today. The cause is the same, upheld by the same people'. Franco was not slow to pay his tribute to this version of the past, and in a speech of 1941 he recalled that 'it is not the first time in our history that our young men have exchanged books for arms, for in a similar moment . . . when our other War of Independence . . .'[45]

With such a potent affirmation of identity, it appeared that nation-building had made a good start in the Spain of the nineteenth century. Whatever the true motives behind the conflict, the fact that it was remembered as a war of liberation against an attempt at foreign domination seemed to affirm the existence of the *nation*. Moreover, the exploit had been attributed to the *people*, bearer of the national identity, who had defended it tooth and nail after it had been given up for lost by élites corrupted by cosmopolitanism. Above all, this people had demonstrated the ability to defeat the previously invincible Napoleon, at the head of the greatest army in the world: what better demonstration of the existence of a deep-seated and unanimous sense of *españolidad* among Spaniards? What better proof of the invincibility demonstrated at Numancia and Sagunto surviving over the following millennia?

Nevertheless, the very success of the mythification of the war created its own problems, principally because the story of the anti-Napoleonic struggle took on a life of its own. This became associated with the idea of the *unity* or *independence* of the *patria*, but failed to become identified with a constitutionalist or modernising project. If history proclaimed that the defining feature of 'Spaniards' was their obstinate desire to overcome their disunity and to reject all foreign dependence, then there was nothing left to be done once these ends had been achieved. At most, safeguards had to be adopted in order to ward off potential aggressors, though who would possibly attempt to conquer the 'Spanish' when the latter had, on numerous occasions, overcome the greatest armies in the world? As the century advanced, the liberal revolution found itself in increasing difficulty and eventually it ground to a halt. At this point, all eyes turned instinctively to that other supreme national objective: independence. Consequently the upshot of the war was a self-serving myth centred on past achievements and adorned with routine references to the past glories of Numancia, Covadonga and other military exploits that confirmed the national fixation with independence.[46] As a result, the national myth was divorced from modernisation, except in the case of a small and isolated liberal élite.

A second problem caused by the success of mythification was that after the victory in the war of 1808–1814 the existence of a Spanish identity seemed so self-evident that no serious attempt was made to educate the masses in nationhood. It is one of the many contradictions of nationalism that its proponents consider nations to be *realities* or *natural* entities, while fully aware that a genuine effort has to be made in order to consolidate or to *shape* them. Like the heroes of myths and fairytales, they claim to be *awakening* them, giving us to understand that nations exist but they also slumber. Sometimes, however, revealing phrases slip out. Much later on, Francoism introduced a series of compulsory courses at various stages of the educational system entitled '*Formation* of the national spirit'. If nations were basic realities upon which human history and societies are founded – as nationalists like to claim – then patriotic sentiment would naturally emerge and individuals would not require it to be instilled. The chauvinistic Antonio de Capmany declared with pride that the Spanish were a nation, unlike the Italians and Germans, who had failed to stand up to Napoleon because 'they are not nations, although they speak the same language' and so 'the general cry of 'Germans' or 'Italians' does not inflame the individual spirit because not one belongs to a whole'. At the same time, oblivious to the contradiction, he urged poets to sing the praises of Spanish heroes so that the people would be educated in the patriotic spirit that he took for granted.[47] In fact, Capmany was not far off the mark: one of the causes of the weakness of Spanish national feeling in the nineteenth century may have been that not enough effort was put into cultivating a sense of nationhood, possibly because the ruling classes took its existence for granted. Though an apparent contradiction, too great a confidence in the reality of a nation is prejudicial to the national cause.

No one, however, could have foreseen these obstacles at the time. Nation-building was proceeding smoothly. The Spanish identity that had been in the making for centuries seemed to have metamorphosed into modern nationalism, having overcome the exclusivity of the élite and finally spread to the lower ranks of society. Always keen to monopolise language, the politicians gathered in Cádiz freely deployed nationalist rhetoric. They reinforced the idea of the nation as the subject of political sovereignty, another crucial advance towards modern nationalism. This legal device coincided with the appearance of the 'people' on the stage of history with a leading role inspired by a single sentiment: the defence of the national identity. Thus the British contribution to the war was overlooked – just as the British forgot about Spanish collaboration in their histories of the *Peninsular War* – and the bond between the nationalism of the élite and the motivation of the men fighting in the provinces was taken as given. Today, however, we tend to regard the anti-Napoleonic combatants as being much more concerned with their grass-roots communities and the local abuses of the invading French troops. Still, forty years after the war the complexity of the conflict had been forgotten and there was a general agreement that 'Spain', or the Spanish people, had undertaken a 'War of Independence', or national liberation, against Napoleon, and won.

Notes

1 This is the main argument used by the anonymous leaflet *Quiénes sean los verdaderos patriotas de España*, c. 1812. On this war, see M. Artola, *La España de Fernando VII*, Vol. XXXII de la *Historia de España Menéndez Pidal*, Madrid, 1992, and G. Lovett, *Napoleon and the Birth of Modern Spain*, New York: New York University Press, 1965, Vol. I.

2 See Jovellanos' letter to Mazarredo, quoted by F. Etienvre, 'Preface' to A. Capmany, *Centinela contra Franceses* (London, 1988), p. 53; cf. A. Nieto, *Los primeros pasos del Estado constitucional*, Barcelona, 1996, p. 23 ('a civil war within an International one').

3 The 'Frenchified', or Joseph I's followers, always insisted on this idea; see *Quiénes sean . . .*, p. 1.

4 J. Canga Argüelles, *Observaciones al tomo II de la Historia de la Guerra de España*, London, 1830, p. 35. On the 'gallophobic' feelings in the war of 1793–1795, see J.-R. Aymes, *La Guerra de España contra la Revolución Francesa, 1793–1795*, Alicante, 1991, pp. 437–447.

5 Etienvre, 'Preface' to Capmany's *Centinela*, pp. 118–119 and 125. Battle cries in Conde de Toreno, *Historia del levantamiento, guerra y revolución de España*, ed. *Biblioteca de Autores Españoles* (B.A.E.), 1953, R. Solís, *El Cádiz de las Cortes*, Madrid, 1969, or Fr. S. López, *Despertador Cristiano-Político*, Mexico, 1809, p. 18.

6 See the aggressive 'Descripción del francés' in S. Álvarez Gamero, 'Libelos del tiempo de Napoleón', *Revue Hispanique*, XLV(107) (1919): 314–322.

7 See the seminal article by Richard Herr, 'Good, Evil, and Spain's Rising against Napoleon', in R. Herr and H. T. Parker (eds), *Ideas in History*, Durham, NC: Duke University Press, 1965, pp. 157–181.

8 López, *Despertador*, pp. 2, 9, 29. Cf. J. Herrero, *Los orígenes del pensamiento reaccionario español*, Madrid, 1971, pp. 226–241 and 245–256, and J. Tone, *The Fatal Knot: The Guerrilla War in Navarre and the Defeat of Napoleon in Spain*, Chapel Hill, NC: University of North Carolina Press, 1994, pp. 54–55.

9 Manel Risques, in M. Risques, A. Duarte, B. de Riquer y J. M. Roig, *Història de la Catalunya . . .*, p. 37. Cf. M. Pérez Ledesma, 'Las *Cortes* de Cádiz y la sociedad española', *Ayer*, 1 (1991):170–171.

10 Tone, *Fatal Knot*, pp. 55–56.

11 See López, *Despertador*, or *La Bestia de siete cabezas y diez cuernos o Napoleón emperador de los Franceses*, by an 'Andalusian Priest', reprinted in Majorca, 1809.Other quotes offered by F.-X. Guerra, *Modernidad e Independencias*, Madrid, 1992, pp. 167–168, who says that the argument had been used in the war of 1793–1795.

12 See J. Álvarez Junco, 'La invención de la Guerra de la Independencia', *Studia Historica. Historia Contemporánea*, 12 (1994): 75–99.

13 See, among many other testimonies, Mgr. de Pradt, *Examen del plan presentado a las Cortes para el reconocimiento de la independencia de la América española*, Burdeos, P. Beaume, 1822.

14 For the period 1821–1822, *Diario de Sesiones de Cortes (D.S.C.)*, 11–III-1822 (p. 302) or 19–III-1822 (p. 418); or *Minerva Española*, 1–V-1821, p. 206.

15 A. Alcalá Galiano, *Obras Escogidas*, Madrid, Biblioteca de Autores Españoles, 1955, Vol. LXXXIV, pp. 447, 454 and 457.

16 Kosca Vayo, Díaz de Baeza or Ramírez Arcas use neither the word nor the idea of 'independence'. Eusebio de Tapia more than once refers to 'the heroic movement of a people who rises to defend its independence', but never calls the war one 'of independence' (*Apuntes sobre los hechos principales de la Revolución de Sevilla en 1808*, 1810, pp. 202–205). But both Florencio Galli, *Memorias sobre la Guerra de Cataluña 1822–1823*, Barcelona, 1835, and E. Marliani, *Historia política de la España moderna*, Barcelona, 1840, refer quite naturally to the 'War of Independence'.

17 Alcalá Galiano's *Memorias* were written in the 1860s, although published later; but in his 1840s translation of Samuel Dunham's *History of Spain* as *Historia de España*, he entitles Chapter 3 of Vol. VI 'Principio de la Guerra de la Independencia'. Eduardo Chaos, in his 1851 appendix to Juan de Mariana's *Historia general de España*, entitles this period 'Fernando VII's reign' and 'The National Government', but in the thematic index appears as the 'War of Independence': this seems to prove that both names coexisted in those years.

18 Such a change is perceptible even outside Spain. See *A Catechism of the History of Spain and Portugal*, written by 'a Lady', London, 1849, p. 77

('that noble struggle for independence known as the Peninsular War') and L. A. Fée, *Souvenirs de la Guerre. . . dite de l'Indépendance*, 1842.

19 E. S. Morgan, *Inventing the People. The Rise of Poular Sovereignty in England and America*, New York, 1988.

20 Quoted by Guerra, *Modernidad e Independencias*, p. 323.

21 *Semanario Patriótico*, 22–IX-1808.

22 *Catecismo católico-político*, Madrid, 1808 (in *Catecismos políticos españoles*, p. 33). Cf. M. C. Seoane, *El primer lenguaje constitucional español*, Madrid, 1968, p. 55.

23 Guerra, *Modernidad e Independencias*, pp. 164 (*Proclama a los españoles*), 237 (Martínez de la Rosa) and 248 (Quintana); Argüelles, quoted by A. Gil Novales, in J. Antón and M. Caminal, *Pensamiento político en España*, Barcelona, 1992, p. 86.

24 'Peace with a tyrant? Eternal war / to usurpation! Let's all die / without freedom we kneel / deprived of fatherland. / Thus was the crowd's cry: war!' 'There is no fatherland where there are only oppressors and oppressed.' 'Without a fatherland we cannot sing its anthems.'

25 Maurizio Virolli, *Por amor a la Patria*, Madrid: Acento, 1977.

26 *Semanario Patriótico*, 15–IX-1808, p. 47, quoted by A. Dérozier, *Quintana y el nacimiento del liberalismo en España*, Madrid, 1978, p. 259. Much later, B. Pérez Galdós understood the importance of this point and he inserted, in the first chapter of his 'National Episode' *La batalla de los Arapiles*, a text published by *El Imparcial* saying 'those who are born in a slave country have no fatherland; they are like those flocks destined to feed us'.

27 A similar connection was made by B. J. Gallardo, *Alocución patriótica en la solemne función con que los ciudadanos del comercio de Londres celebraron el restablecimiento de la Constitución y la libertad de la patria*, London: A. Taylor, 1820, p. 6, or the priest Manuel Martínez, who preached at Valladolid when the 1812 Constitution was received, according to R. Serrano García, *La revolución liberal en Valladolid (1808–1874)*, Valladolid, 1993, p. 48. *La Abeja Española*, 2–V-1813, pp. 14–17.

28 On these conflicts, see J. H. Elliott, *La revuelta de los catalanes*, Madrid, Siglo XXI, 1972; H. Kamen, *La Guerra de Sucesión en España, 1700–1715*, Barcelona: Grijalbo, 1974; M. T. Pérez Picazo, *La publicística española en la Guerra de Sucesión*, Madrid: CSIC, 1966; on the Castilian *Comunidades*, standard works by J. A. Maravall, J. Pérez and Gutiérrez Nieto.

29 Weber, cited in J. J. Linz, 'Intellectual Roles in Sixteenth and Seventeenth-Century Spain', *Daedalus*, 101(3), 1972: 88.

30 A. Capmany, 'Discurso preliminar' to his *Teatro histórico-crítico de la elocuencia española*, Madrid, 1786–1794; *Centinela contra franceses*, pp. 45, 87, 91, 104 and 133; other quotes in Herrero, *Orígenes del pensamiento reaccionario*, pp. 223–225.

31 Both Jovellanos and Capmany quoted by M. Artola, *Los orígenes de la España contemporánea*, 2 vols. Madrid, 1959, Vol. I, p. 330. On Capmany see Portillo Valdés, 'Nación política y territorio económico', pp. 256–258.

32 See J. F. Fuentes, 'Concepto de pueblo en el primer liberalismo español', *Trienio. Ilustración y Liberalismo*, 12 (1988), p. 203: from being a cursed word in Joseph I's Spain, *pueblo* came to be the usual way to label the insurgent Spain. Reinoso, quoted by J.-R. Aymes, *La guerra de la Independencia en España (1808–1814)*, Madrid, Siglo XXI, 1975, p. 19; Blanco White, by P. Trinidad, in J. Antón y M. Caminal (eds), *Pensamiento político en la España contemporánea (1800–1850)*, Barcelona, 1992, p. 64.

33 *Semanario Patriótico*, 15–IX–1808, quoted by Guerra, *Modernidad e Independencias*, p. 241. *El Robespierre español. Amigo de las Leyes*, VI and XXVII, Cádiz, 1811, quoted by Fuentes, 'Concepto de pueblo', p. 199. B. J. Gallardo, *Diccionario Crítico-Burlesco: Diccionario razonado manual para inteligencia de ciertos escritores que por equivocación han nacido en España*, Madrid, 1820, pp. 138–140.

34 P. Salmón, *Resumen histórico de la Revolución de España*, Cádiz, 1812, Vol. I, pp. 277–278.

35 J. F. Fuentes, 'La invención del pueblo: El mito del pueblo en el siglo XIX español', *Claves de Razón Práctica*, 103 (1999): 60–64, and 'Pueblo y élites en la España contemporánea, 1808–1839 (reflexiones sobre un desencuentro)', *Historia Contemporánea*, 8 (1992): 24. A. Flórez Estrada, *Introducción para la historia de la revolución de España*, London, 1810 (B.A.E., Madrid, 1958), CXIII, p. 240.

36 *El Robespierre Español*, 23–V–1811. Fuentes, 'Invención del pueblo', p. 60; and J. Muñoz Pérez, 'Los catecismos políticos de la Ilustración al primer liberalismo español, 1808–1822'. *Gades*, 16 (1987): 194, 196 and 208–209.

37 López, *Despertador*, pp. 10 and 17.

38 Tone, *Fatal Knot, passim*; García de Cortázar and González Vesga, *Breve Historia de España*, Madrid, 1994, pp. 42 and 431; Pérez Ledesma, 'Las *Cortes* de Cádiz', pp. 171–172; J. Álvarez Junco, 'El nacionalismo español como mito movilizador: Cuatro guerras', in R. Cruz and M. Pérez Ledesma, *Cultura y Movilización en la España contemporánea*, Madrid: Alianza, 1997, pp. 42–43.

39 Espronceda, 'Al Dos de Mayo', in *Obras Poéticas*, I, Madrid, Espasa-Calpe, p. 145. ('It is the People! As waves, / it roars from the rough sea. / It hails the shining Spanish glories, / its ancient honour, its independence'.)

40 F. Garrido, *La España contemporánea: Sus progresos materiales y morales en el siglo XIX*, 2 vols. Barcelona: S. Manero, 1865–1867, Vol. I, p. 109; Fuentes, 'Pueblo y élites', pp. 25–26.

41 J. L. López Aranguren, *Moral y Sociedad*, Madrid: Edicusa, 1966, pp. 50–51.

42 Resolution to commemorate this date, approved by the *Cortes* on 1 May 1811 *D.S.C.*, 1810–1813, pp. 977 and 994–995). New debates and resolutions in 1812 (ibid., p. 3110), 1813 (p. 5152) and 1814 (*D.S.C.*, 1814, p. 163, 174, 241–243, 282, 297 and 317). New decisions, particularly in Liberal periods, throughout the nineteenth century: *Abeja Española*, 2–V–1820, *La Iberia*, 2–V–1870 and 2–V–1871. First bill on the raising

of a monument on 16–IV-1812 (see later debate in *Cortes*, 1814, *D.S.C.*, p. 146); again, in a new Liberal period, members of the *Cortes* admit the monument is still waiting and on 14–III-1822 take a new decision to build it; this same year, Canga Argüelles makes the proposal to build a National Pantheon (ibid., pp. 1246–1247).

43 See G. Triviños, *Benito Pérez Galdós en la jaula de la epopeya: Héroes y mon-struos en la primera serie de los Episodios Nacionales*, Barcelona,1987. Garrido, *La España contemporánea*, Vol. I, pp. 109 and 113.

44 'España' in *Enciclopedia Espasa*, Madrid, 1942, Vol. XXI, pp. 1018–1023.

45 See J. Álvarez Junco, 'Mitos de la nación en guerra', in S. Juliá (ed.), *República y Guerra Civil*, Vol. XL of *Historia de España Menéndez Pidal*, Madrid, Espasa-Calpe, 2004, pp. 635–682.

46 See J. M. Jover, 'Introducción', in J. M. Jover (ed.), *La era isabelina y el Sexenio Democrático (1834–1874)*, Vol. XXXIV of *Historia de España Menéndez Pidal*, Madrid, Espasa-Calpe, 1981. pp. XIII–CLXII.

47 Etienvre, 'Preface' to Capmany's *Centinela*, pp. 44, 46.

Part II

The nationalisation of culture

4

National history and collective memory

The nationalisation of culture

In 1815, following the second, definitive defeat of Napoleon, the most urgent requirement was the rebuilding of the political fabric of Europe, which had been torn asunder by the revolutionary and Bonapartist whirlwinds that had swept through it. In the fond belief that the turmoil of the previous twenty-five years had been no more than a passing madness, Tsar Alexander I and the Austrian Chancellor Metternich presided over a coalition of absolute monarchs that aimed to restore the *ancien régime* and, in the process, to disentangle complicated dynastic claims and hereditary rights. At the same time, the liberals continued to entertain the idea of creating a new order based on the 'nation'. This long-standing term, used in the Middle Ages to refer to linguistic communities, had acquired collective psychological traits during the Renaissance. It had developed a *volksgeist*, or way of interpreting and giving cultural expression to the world, with Romanticism, and had then taken on the meaning of a *moi commun* or *volonté générale* under the French revolution thanks to Rousseau's genius. It was on this general will that the liberals now based political legitimacy. The European 'nations' they had in mind were all vast territorial units: France, England, Russia, Austria, Turkey, Sweden ... and Spain. There could be no doubt in anyone's mind about the latter's status as a 'nation' given that the Spanish monarchy, which had been recognised for more than three hundred years, had recently gained a 'people', as made manifest in their resistance to Napoleon. Thus the identity whose emergence has been analysed in Part I suddenly appeared in the guise of a modern nation in 1808, at around the same time as most other entities of the same kind.[1]

In reality, neither Spain nor any of the other countries or societies mentioned above formed a community with the linguistic and cultural homogeneity of which nationalists dreamed. In essence, they were relatively stable monarchies or political bodies that embraced communities distinguished by multiple internal differences. However, the way individuals view the world around them forms part of this social reality; and the Europeans of that time began to believe that they were indeed divided up into *nations*. There were some areas, such as Germany and Italy, with cultures at least as homogeneous as those mentioned above, and which were customarily included on the list of European 'nations' – particularly when drawn up by liberals – but which were not, however, united or autonomous political entities. This was the weakness exploited by the constitutionalists, who continued to undermine the established order by means of the national idea. By denouncing the existence of nations that lacked political sovereignty, they thereby declared the powers that ruled them to be illegitimate. Today we are well aware that a perfect match between a culture and a polity is no more than a textbook fantasy, but the liberals, determined to limit monarchical power, were in no mood to quibble with details. In response to the conservative discourse based on hereditary legitimacy and a natural order sanctioned by God, they proclaimed the rights of *peoples* and *nations*.

This heralded the start of a period characterised by the frenzied affirmation of cultural identities; in other words, the construction or invention of myths, symbols and discourses referring to the collectivities called nations which, in order to lay claim to political sovereignty, had to demonstrate that they were the protagonists of history. In order for public opinion to accept this new vision of the world, it became essential to reorganise all knowledge, references and cultural symbols to fit in with the concept of the nation. This is a phase which the specialists call *cultural nationalism*. There is general agreement in attributing a leading role at this stage to intellectual élites, who have the ability to create and transmit cultural discourses and symbols of identification. According to a sequence proposed by Miroslav Hroch, once the cultural creation has been completed, the new-found identity will provide the basis for a programme of political demands; following that, these demands will gather momentum beyond élitist circles to become those of the population as a whole. It is then, explains Hroch, that what we call *nationalist movements* fully develop.[2]

These successive stages do in fact apply only to non-State nationalisms, which are also known as *peripheral* or *secessionist* nationalisms (or to be more exact, '*state-seeking*', as Charles Tilly defines them). In contrast, State (for Tilly, *state-led*) nationalisms, or those that develop under the protection of already existing political powers, as in the case of Spain, begin their development at the political stage without the need for the preliminary cultural phase. Every nationalism, and even every collective movement, has to define the constituent parts of the group and to draw the lines that separate it from foreign or alien elements. State nationalisms begin by having the State impose physical *borders* that generally lead to an awareness of cultural differentiation.[3] In the Spanish case, it was the monarchy that delineated the first limits of the group by establishing borders with France and Portugal, whose subjects it went on to define as 'foreigners' or 'enemies'. Non-state nationalisms require a more subtle approach, which is usually the product of their intellectual élites, who create, construct or invent – although they would say *discover* – a series of cultural landmarks that act as borders. For a long time, these landmarks were principally linguistic or religious, although they were always complemented by historical references, or, in other words, the evocation of a 'collective memory'. Such a memory will exaggerate not only the heroic deeds but, above all, the *affronts* – military defeats, humiliations, economic exploitation, massacres and atrocities – that the group has suffered at the hands of those foreigners or neighbours whom the mobilising élites are anxious to present as rivals or oppressors. From the 1850s to the early 1900s, the definition of such a group in linguistic, religious and historical terms tended to be filled out with pseudo-scientific formulations which based the collective personality on biological features that conferred a – necessarily superior – *racial* distinction on the group in question. As references to race were discredited by the horrors uncovered in 1945, and as European societies have become highly secularised, it is historical and linguistic justifications that now tend to hold sway in Western Europe.

However, drawing up borders of exclusion and identifying enemies is never enough. A group also needs *symbols of identification*, or borders of *inclusion*, such as language, distinctive clothing, emblems, flags, hymns, and monuments or places that represent the national tradition: a complete set of cultural elements that distinguishes those who belong to the collective 'We' and which prepares them to answer the call of the 'nation'. History is also relevant to this aspect because such symbols usually make some reference to a mythified ideal past, a Golden Age in which the community or brotherly ideal was realised, and to which the political project of *identity* aims to return. This is why nationalist leaders do not talk about reaching, achieving or imposing their objectives, but of *recovering* something they once had: an ideal situation (of unity, independence, hegemony) that was once *theirs* and was forcibly taken away.

The traditions having been invented and the national symbols constructed, these elements become *sacrosanct* in preparation for the political utilisation of the cultural artefact. There is no doubt that, in general terms, there has been a diminution of the sacred to the advantage of the civil and secular, but if one stops to consider nationalist movements, it is clear that the process of secularisation has been somewhat superficial or fictitious because the nation has assumed many of the functions, loyalties and even trappings of religion. The duties owed to the nation far outweigh the civic or political ones owed under the *ancien régime*. It is true that it is not easy to generalise about nationalisms because, although some have adopted openly fundamental, ethno-sacral formulas referring to would-be racial superiority or divine predilection, others have taken a more secularised approach to citizenship on the basis of territoriality and integration into a specific legal system. The former are termed *ethnic* nationalisms while the latter are *civic*. The most common type, however, combines elements from both. Thus civic references to political achievements often develop into a sense of superiority, or even a belief in a redemptive mission for mankind, which translates into a right to dominate others. This transforms civic nationalism into an ethnic one and the belief in privileged destiny.[4]

There are contradictions inherent in collective identities that illustrate the complexities concealed behind the apparent simplicity of a nationalist construct: defining the national *We*, destined to be the subject of such important political rights and responsibilities, is not a transparent or mechanical task. On the contrary, it is far from easy, since human societies constitute an immense melting pot of races, languages, classes, religions and territorial units of differing sizes, not to mention gender, age and all the other criteria that can be used in the formation of collective subjects. Each person combines different combinations of all these features and a mixture is obviously far more common than any adherence to a perfectly defined racial or cultural type. There is also a constant process of construction and reconstruction, allowing the defenders of identities to refer to past or present situations which, conveniently idealised, can lead to an infinite number of combinations, many of them diametrically opposed to one another. Those who manage to create a personality from the cultural elements available that is attractive to a sufficient number of followers will not only have won the first battle but also will have a decisive effect on all subsequent political struggles.[5]

The artistic and intellectual élites of the nineteenth century devoted a large part of their literary, pictorial, musical, historical and even pseudo-scientific efforts to national subjects. The most accomplished and spectacular movement was undoubtedly the Italian one. Lacking an existing state structure on which to construct the nation, the liberal élites strove hard to create a cultural identity. This was christened the *Risorgimento* – 'revival' or 'resurgence' – a term that referred to the *reappearance* of a personality that it was assumed had always existed and which had merely lain dormant. Once the unification of Italy had taken place in 1870, one of its leaders explained that although 'Italy' had been Italy, they now had to 'make Italians'. In effect, the Sicilians and the Venetians had to be persuaded to speak proper Italian – which is, in fact, Tuscan – and to understand that the speech of their parents and their grandparents was, apparently, only a *dialect*. It should be noted that the nationalist myth had to be deployed not only in order to found new countries where borders were altered, as in the Italian case, but also in those, such as Spain, where revolutionary change had taken place. Even the most firmly established monarchies had to disguise or reinvent themselves as 'nations' in order to survive as modern States. The British historian Eric Hobsbawm appropriately labelled this phenomenon as the *invention of tradition*.[6] Throughout Europe in the second half of the nineteenth century, books were written about national history, museums were built to enshrine national culture, civic monuments and altars were consecrated to the nation, and rituals and ceremonies were invented in celebration of the nation.

In Spain, the attempt to build a new political identity was based on a culture already sponsored by the State. Nevertheless, it was not the State itself which undertook this task but the political élites who supported modernisation, with the Constitutionalists of Cádiz (who succeeded the Enlightenment reformers) leading the way. The reasoning behind the new theory of *national* sovereignty was generally clear and convincing, but one essential point remained obscure: what exactly was the specific content of 'Spain', the collective identity that disputed the king's sovereignty and for which citizens were expected to sacrifice their personal interests? The reality of its existence was taken for granted and yet, as François-Xavier Guerra has observed, very little was known about Spain, the *nation*, or what it meant. Was it already a political entity or would it still have to become one? Was it 'a product of history or the result of a voluntary association'? Was it made up of autonomous individuals equal among themselves or by 'ancient political communities, with their estates and privileged bodies'? It was the Constitution of Cádiz which defined who 'Spaniards' were, something less obvious than one might think. Were the inhabitants of overseas territories Spaniards, for example? The deputies decided that they were, but not all of them because the Indians and people of African ancestry were excluded. That debate is not relevant here and would soon become redundant as a result of the independence of the colonies in the 1810s and 1820s, but it is indicative of the difficulties inherent in defining those eligible for political sovereignity.[7]

National identity was not, however, only a question of doctrine or principles. It was also necessary to arouse emotion. Identifying individuals with the nation, and securing their loyalty to it, required a leap of the imagination that would make tangible the collective personality to which so much power was attributed. If the intellectuals' version of the war against Napoleon had been true, the existence of an already deep-rooted identity would have made it unnecessary to consolidate sentiments favourable to 'Spain', but even they could not be sure that an appeal to national sentiment would have been sufficient. Rightly or wrongly, as the years went by it was felt that there was a growing need to reinforce patriotic sentiments and ideas: to clarify what it meant to be Spanish, to describe Spain from a geographical point of view, to list its monuments, to learn about its history, and, if possible, to *see* it and *touch* it in illustrations and public statues. Emotional commitment to the national myth and, as a result, its capacity to mobilise the citizenship would depend upon the success of this nation-building process. Twenty years after the Cortes of Cádiz, one disillusioned member of the first generation of liberals, Alcalá Galiano, believed that it had been an error for them to take the reality of the Spanish nation for granted; and, long before d'Azeglio, he declared that the task facing the liberals was to 'make of the Spanish nation, a nation, which it is not, nor has it been, up to now'.[8]

Lastly, there was the problem of political orientation. The 'Spanish nation' invoked in resistance to the French was, as we know, the rallying cry of the liberals in their demands for constitutional and social change. We also know that the identity inherited from the earlier period possessed a number of features that did not easily conform to their objectives. First, the inherited identity revolved around the monarchy, creator of the political entity with which both natives and foreigners identified 'Spain'. Consequently there was to be no easy, far less automatic, conversion to the collective entity of the 'nation'. Indeed, this was a major obstacle encountered by the liberals as they tried to strengthen their position against Fernando VII and, later, against Don Carlos. Second, the inherited identity was based on Castilian culture, dominant in the geographical centre where the court resided and throughout a large part of the kingdom, but by no means in all of it. To talk about the Spanish nation as a single, solid entity was partly a fiction, official culture deliberately overlooking the monarchy's fragmented historical inheritance. Third, Spain's cultural inheritance was based on the Catholicism of the Counter-Reformation, which clashed with religious tolerance and other *modern evils*. Thus the liberals found themselves with a serious problem in defining the 'Spain' that was crucial to their political project. On the one hand, they had to ensure that it was not identified solely, nor even primarily, with inherited religion, loyalty to the king or adherence to traditional values, but that it should form the basis for the construction of a modern State and a participative political structure. On the other, it was essential not to question the unity and strength of the political body they aimed to establish.

The cultural élites thereby set about remaking the political imagery and beliefs of the past in order to adapt them to the new 'national' requirements. Everything had to revolve around the nation, the only political subject and mobilising myth which had the power and credibility to rival the absolute monarchs, the bearers of the sovereignty and the charisma that was now being claimed by the new collective entity. Throughout the nineteenth century, the intellectual and artistic élites devoted themselves to a wide variety of activities, including poetry, novels, history, painting, music and scientific investigation. The peculiarity of this age is that almost everything, including the so-called positive sciences, exhibited national traits. In the cultural reworking inevitably undertaken by each new generation or era, the (probably unconscious) aim was to *nationalise*. How this process developed is the subject of this and the following chapter.

National history

History was to take priority when it came to adapting earlier visions of Spanish society to the national perspective. A common history, or what was later to be called a 'collective memory', was an essential part of the culture that, according to the nationalist conception, should be shared by all the citizens of the same State.

The term 'collective memory' was made fashionable in the twentieth century by the historian Maurice Halbwachs, one of the founders of the French school of the *Annales*. This requires a little explanation, as national history should be distinguished from memory in the strict sense. In everyday speech, 'memory' is understood as the ability to reproduce episodes or sensations in the mind which have been experienced in the past. Defined in this way, it is a faculty belonging only to individuals who are alive at the time they exercise it, and it can only relate to acts which have affected their own past. Strictly speaking, such a faculty cannot be 'collective' unless we believe, as some of the founding fathers of Sociology did, that societies are comparable to living organisms, and even that they possess a collective mind able to reproduce, consciously or not, past experiences lived by the forebears of that community. It is a very different matter to attribute a social or supra-individual aspect to individual memory to the extent that, in evoking the past, just as in establishing any other relationship with reality, one cannot disregard socially created cultural prisms. What this memory can never contemplate are experiences that occurred several hundreds or thousands of years ago, such as the Punic Wars or the siege of Numantia, because none of the individuals alive today were alive then. Although people can *imagine* past events, they cannot *reactivate* them in their minds because they did not experience them. *Secondary* memories are possible in relation to events experienced by generations in a recent past and whose reminiscences have been transmitted to their immediate descendants. A prime example is the Spanish Civil War of 1936–1939, related by its protagonists to children born during the post-war period. However, it is well known that a high degree of distortion occurs even among those involved in the event, and that this increases exponentially as a particular version is transmitted from one listener to another. When referring to the remote past, the distortion that occurs in orally transmitted versions is such that one can no longer talk about *memory*. On the contrary, this is *tradition*, which may consist of orally transmitted stereotypes or, more frequently, a combination of texts and memorials which, at a later date, are used to present a particular version of the past.

It is also useful to distinguish the national histories of the nineteenth century from 'history' as an academic discipline. The latter is a rational analysis of past events based on testimonies reputed to be true and guided by a scientific interest – that is, a desire to understand and explain the past. This kind of history leads inevitably to a narrative in which the subjects vary according to the field and the period under study. In stark contrast to this, nineteenth-century national histories dealt with the origins and vicissitudes of *a permanent community*, the nation, whose unity and permanence they sought to demonstrate. To this end, a collective saga was written, beginning with the founding fathers and distinguished thereafter by heroes and martyrs, defenders of the original community, who became the central part of the shared culture that integrated individuals into the new nation-State. Such constructs, just like the traditions and memorials that are regarded as constituting 'collective memory', are undoubtedly respectable and it could even be claimed that they have positive effects on the self-esteem and integration of the whole community. Nevertheless, just as the latter have little to do with the memory that, as living beings, we have of our past experiences, the former are far from being history in the sense of a knowledge of the past that aspires to be scientific. Ernest Renan, in his penetrating lecture on 'What is a Nation?', was quite clear about this: 'Forgetting about the past, and even historical errors, form an essential part of the making of a nation and, as a result, progress in historical studies is often dangerous for the national consciousness'.[9]

The whole matter becomes more complicated because this work, which began with the great historiographical renovation of the eighteenth century, was a by-product of the rationalist shift of the seventeenth century. It is indisputable that Hume, Muratori, Gibbon and Voltaire sought, primarily, to rectify the old histories in order to establish dates and events factually and to weed out the myths from unreliable chronicles passed down acritically by Baroque scholars. Another of their laudable aims was to move on from the history of Great Men to write about 'civil' history, according to the terminology of the age, which meant concentrating less on monarchical dynasties and battles and more on 'agriculture, manufactories, commerce, the fine arts', together with 'the origin, advances and alterations to our constitution, our political and civil hierarchy, our legislation, our customs'. These two quotations from Juan Francisco Masdeu and Gaspar Melchor Jovellanos reveal that, even if the Spanish Monarchy kept its subjects isolated from the seventeenth century's intellectual movements, by the eighteenth century, times were changing and the voices of these new historians were making themselves heard. Although Jovellanos complained at the end of the eighteenth century that 'the nation lacks a history', there had in fact been several decades of intense historical investigation. Maravall observes that in eighteenth-century Spain 'history is written without pause', 'excavations are carried out, archives and libraries are founded and reorganised' and 'in teaching syllabuses . . . history and related readings play a large part'.[10] And the history that was produced was of an amazingly high standard when compared with that of the earlier period – so credulous and full of unsubstantiated facts – as well as the later one – so distorted by nationalist passion.

However, this historiographic renovation was not inspired by scientific interest alone. The efforts at cultural standardisation of the *Real Academia de la Historia* on behalf of the monarchy have already been mentioned. Similarly, there was a nationalising objective to the interest in history of the politico-intellectual élites who collaborated with the reforming enterprises of Enlightenment scholars. The *Sociedades Económicas* founded Chairs in History to study not just any kind of history but the History 'of Spain'. Likewise, even *regional* associations and academies that devoted their time to historical studies oriented their work towards the *national* past.[11] The most popular classics to be republished were *Crónica General de España* by Alfonso X, *Los claros varones de España* by Hernando del Pulgar, the *Crónica* by Florián de Ocampo and a total of eight editions of Mariana between 1733 and 1804.[12]

The books being written were mainly histories of Spain. Following in the pioneering footsteps of Nicolás Antonio and the Marqués de Mondéjar came several other historians. Published between 1747 and 1779, the twenty-nine tomes of *España Sagrada* by the Augustinian Enrique Flórez were particularly successful, and they were not even the history of a nation but of an ecclesiastical institution. However, given the overlapping nature of the national and Catholic identities, this was to become the cornerstone for the future Catholic-conservative version of the national past.[13] The greatest historiographical effort of all was to come in the form of the *Historia crítica de España y de la cultura española* by Juan Francisco Masdeu, which the author himself described as a 'universal history of Spain' and which constituted the most serious attempt at writing a national history in the 250 years between Juan de Mariana and Modesto Lafuente.

Not only was the historiography of the eighteenth century less fantastic than that produced in the century of empire, it was also less messianic and less contemptuous of the rest of the world. Driven by critical zeal, Enlightenment scholars ridiculed traditional history and attacked the myths and anecdotes about Great Men to the point that Masdeu expressed serious doubts about the existence of El Cid. However, as Maravall points out, what they put forward as an alternative was 'knowledge about *nations*': the nation was the 'general framework of the historiographical vision'. This was not just another attempt at rivalling foreigners or of combating their 'prejudices' by brandishing the greatest possible number of patriotic deeds before them (the standard tactic since the end of the Middle Ages and typical of ethnic patriotism). At a time of nation-building, it was now a question of demonstrating a continuity of character or behaviour over the millennia. Enlightened historians attempted, in good faith, to strip away one kind of mythological knowledge only to lay the foundations for the next.[14]

It was on these foundations that the liberals built their nationalist mythology during the years in Cádiz. When their work was brought to a sudden halt by the return of Fernando VII in 1814, they tasted the bitterness of exile, which was as much of a shock for them as it had been for the Jesuits in the eighteenth century. Because France was going through the throes of a Bourbon restoration, the majority of the liberals went to England, where they learnt about literary romanticism and political moderation.[15] It would not be too much to say that, in the years they lived outside Spain, the liberals also grasped the importance of the national construct. While in exile they realised that it was necessary to define the Spanish 'personality', which they had taken for granted in 1808–1814, and that, above all, it was vital to ensure that their fellow citizens came to share the same outlook. One of the results of this understanding was the perceived need for a history of Spain.

The adoption of nationalistic sentiments reflected the romanticism that was sweeping through European cultural circles. Chapter 5 will consider the political significance of this new cultural current, one of whose effects was to define problems in terms of national identities. Art, for the romantics, was one of the manifestations of the 'spirit of the people', whether it was expressed anonymously through popular folklore and romances or whether it was revealed in the works of great artists. Consequently, bookshops and libraries in the romantic era were crammed with *national* publications, including books on national history. There were books that dealt not only with one's own nation but also, in cultural circles as cosmopolitan as those of France, England or Germany, with those of other countries such as Russia, Poland, Italy and, of course, Spain. Between 1831 and 1845, about ten *Histories of Spain* were published in France, England and Germany alone.[16]

One of the corollaries of Romanticism was the identification of national characters, which led Spain to be categorised as the representation of European *exoticism* or, to be more precise, *orientalism*. This image may be credited to Lord Byron and it was corroborated initially by Washington Irving and Victor Hugo, and later by Gautier and Mérimée. In positive terms, orientalism translated into beauty, melancholy, ruins, knightly honour, hedonism and intense passion but, as the beneficiaries of such eulogies knew only too well, in political terms it represented decadence or even barbarism. Turkey, supreme example of the oriental world, was also an empire in decay and soon to become known as the 'sick man of Europe'. Those Spaniards who had been forced into exile for political reasons were stunned to encounter this image of their country, so completely at odds with the one they had been taught. Much concerned, they recognised that there was a generalised 'incomprehension' of their homeland and a lack of appreciation of their national achievements. They also realised that the cultural construction of their nation lagged well behind and that it was urgent to catch up. Foreign historians introduced their work by declaring their astonishment at the non-existence of histories of Spain. 'Spain has no national history', exclaimed Charles Romey, 'the historical genius has not awakened in this great and unhappy people'. It was indeed astonishing: since that very early expression of ethnic patriotism which was Mariana's *Historia General de España*, published at the end of the sixteenth century, there had been an extraordinary gap right up to the beginning of the nineteenth. In 250 years, no one had been capable of producing a work to rival it; and with innumerable additions and appendices, it continued to be the text studied by schoolchildren. Not only were the emigrant liberals distinctly unhappy about the situation, but they were also unwilling to accept what foreigners wrote, given that, by definition, they were unable to understand the reality of Spain, even in the rare instances in which they took a sincere interest in the country. Inspired by such defensive sentiments, the most headstrong, like Sempere y Guarinos and Lista, began to write while still in exile. Others, like Alcalá Galiano and Escosura, returned to Spain with the intention of either setting to work or urging historians at home to do so.

This eventually led to the publication of the *Historia General de España* by Modesto Lafuente, whose thirty volumes, printed between 1850 and 1867, were to become the general reference work right up until the time of the Second Republic. This was not because it was the only one; after its publication came innumerable histories of this kind. As well as the many school textbooks (outstanding among which were those by Fernando de Castro), published between 1857 and 1875, histories of Spain were published by Fernando Patxot, Antonio Cavanilles, Aldama, Víctor Gebhardt, Cayetano Rossell, or Zamora y Caballero, each of them in several volumes, making a total of forty-three in all. In the 1890s came those of Morayta and, lastly, the *Historia General de España*, written by members of the Real Academia de la Historia and edited by the leading figure of Restoration politics up until his death in 1897, Antonio Cánovas del Castillo, comprising another twenty-one volumes. This does not include republication of the classics, such as those of Mariana himself, or the collection entitled *Glorias Nacionales* which reprinted the *Crónica General de España*, the *Anales de la Corona de Aragón*, the works of Zurita, Moncada, Mendoza, Melo, Conde, Solís, extracts from Garibay and Ferreras and a 'historical dictionary' of Spain that listed 100,000 persons and events. To write a national history of Spain was not an original idea of Lafuente but a collective obsession. Even his work became part of a subsequent collective effort when, after the edition of 1887, it was published with an additional section written by Juan Valera, Andrés Borrego and Antonio Pirala.[17] Hence the authors of the 'History of Spain' were an intellectual élite spread over several generations and dominating the mid- and late nineteenth century. They were responsible for the received version of the past in national terms that will be examined below.

The mythical framework of the narrative

The narrative of the new general histories of Spain was located within a framework that actually had very few innovative features when compared with that deployed in the mythological and chivalrous histories available until that time. The first page of any nineteenth-century national history described the land inhabited by the chosen people in terms that differed little from the earlier ones, which had tried to demonstrate the preference of the Almighty for a chosen kingdom or lineage. In the Spanish case, that history was the *Laudes Hispaniae*, which dated back to Isidoro of Seville, pioneer of a tradition that would be continued by historians and chroniclers throughout the Middle Ages right up to the Modern Age.

Spain – meaning the Iberian Peninsula – was, according to the traditional cliché, a 'privileged land' endowed with unrivalled natural advantages. 'This country enjoys clear skies, the climate is warm, the soil is fertile, the rivers abound in fish, and the hills in game and minerals', reads one textbook which appeared shortly before Lafuente's history. Another, some years later, referred to the mild climate of Spain, its 'mighty rivers' and fertile meadows where 'all kinds of grain, delicious fruits and exquisite wines' are cultivated. 'Delicious fruits' and 'exquisite wines' were expressions used by a third writer of the same period, who added 'excellent wood for building, all kinds of cereals and good grazing to feed every species of livestock'. Like everyone else, he emphasised the wealth of minerals in – on this occasion – the *privileged subsoil* ('gold, silver, copper, mercury, lead, zinc, iron abound') and ended, in hyperbolic fashion, referring to the 'infinite waterways' that 'continually fertilise the pleasant lands they flow through . . . in all directions'. It was, as Lafuente himself put it, a land in which 'all climates and all temperatures are to be found' to the point that 'if any state or empire could subsist on its own natural resources, suitably exploited, that state or empire would be Spain'.[18]

There is not a single work in which similar quotations could not be found. The most extreme example of them all was the work of Fernando Patxot. 'Not without good reason' he begins, did Greek writers locate the Elysian Fields in 'our *patria*', 'the most beautiful of lands'. The location of the Garden of Eden was not certain, but 'reason, tradition and well-founded conjecture' suggested that it had been in Spain, 'most favoured land, almost surrounded by the seas; balcony onto the world, with views to America, to the Pole, to Africa; at the head of Europe and the centre of all worlds'. This book, entitled *Anales de España*, opens with 'the act of creating the world'; 'thus, the first Spanish man was Adam' and 'the first Spanish woman was called Eve'. Throwing caution to the wind, the author concludes the introduction with a description of the first Spanish woman, and first of her species, in terms very different to that of the sinful Eve, the origin of all human misfortune: 'endowed with every charm, paragon of sweetness, delicacy, tender love, candour and innocence . . .'[19]

Without relinquishing the accepted tradition that the Spanish were God's chosen people, the works of the national era which can be regarded as equivalent to the *Laudes Hispaniae* were pursuing a different objective: namely, to bind the human group whose history was being told to its geographical setting in such a way that its ethnic traits would be so permanently and clearly differentiated from those of others that nobody could doubt its condition as a nation. 'Nature marks the borders of this wonderful land', wrote Victor Gebhardt in 1861, which explained the existence of a 'Spanish nationality so real and compact'. Modesto Lafuente began his masterwork with these lines: 'If any region or portion of the globe seems made or designed by the great creator of nature to be inhabited by a people united in body as a nation, this region, this country is Spain'. He also expressed his unshakeable faith in the existence of permanent national characteristics created by the Almighty (each people has a 'providential destiny', 'societies do not die'). It was a faith expressed many times throughout his text to the 'multiple' yet always 'united' Spanish people. The battle of Saguntum, for example, was an expression of 'that indomitable ferocity that has so often distinguished the Spanish people', while Viriathus was yet another of 'that kind of independent warrior that the Spanish lands have always bred.'[20]

In line with the traditional connection between geography and collective psychology that derived from Jean Bodin and was repeated by Montesquieu, these new histories anchored the social and cultural personality of the national collectivity in a territory of outstanding quality. This was complemented by a far from modest description of the physical and psychological characteristics of the people. Masdeu, in the eighteenth century, explained that the delightful Peninsular soil and climate were the cause of the good 'natural complexion' of its inhabitants, 'men who loved to be industrious, men with an enormous talent for the sciences and the fine arts, men of excellent character for society'. Nineteenth-century authors faithfully repeated that a man born under the 'beneficial influence' of a 'beautiful Peninsula whose soil produces all that can make one's life pleasant' will 'combine within himself eastern ardour and the power of reason of the inhabitant of the north'. 'Those native to Spain', another author continued, 'are of good bearing, sturdy, long-suffering, jealous of their freedom and independence, and quick-witted, as is proven by the large number of renowned Spaniards who have excelled down the ages due to the heroism of their military exploits, the daring of their discoveries and conquests, the depth of their knowledge and their investigations in the sciences, and their ability in the fine arts'. In short, Spain, as well as being 'renowned for its glories, great because of its conquests, beautiful because of its skies, rich because of its many products', has always been recognised 'in every age and in every country for the courage, good faith, suffering, sobriety and religion of its native people'. The conclusion to be drawn by children who read these phrases was 'that there are few peoples in the world who can glory in more heroic and memorable enterprises than [those of] *our* Spain'.[21]

These modern *Laudes Hispaniae* fulfilled yet another function which was indispensable for a mythology based upon such initially beneficent conditions: an explanation of *the origin of evil*, the causes of the misfortunes that befell the *patria*. It was not easy to find reasons for the many adversities that occurred, having begun with a soil so fertile, individuals so well-endowed and, above all, divine grace. The answer lay in the very richness of the territory, which had attracted successive waves of foreign invaders to the Peninsula, against whom 'the Spanish' had put up a resistance 'as strange as it was terrible'. 'The fertility and quality' of the soil of Spain, and especially its mineral wealth, had been the 'cause of constant war with Carthaginians, Romans . . .'. From time immemorial, the wealth of the Spanish lands had excited the greed of its neighbours and led to invasions and wars of liberation. Before the onset of these tragedies, however, there had been an age when the inhabitants of the country had enjoyed their *national* identity and the riches of their *own* lands without foreign interference. That first moment when the Spanish lived happily in their natural surroundings and were left to their own devices was explicitly associated by nationalist history with the bliss of paradise. Before the invasions, 'Spaniards were happy, free and independent; their customs simple; their needs few; and the means to satisfy them, abundant'. This idyll was wrecked by the arrival of the perverse foreigner, attracted by the 'proverbial wealth of our lands', who was allowed to enter in all innocence because of 'the natural simplicity of isolated peoples', and which prevented the latter from suspecting the wickedness that lurked in those sly foreigners. Abundance, happiness, simplicity and naivety, on the one hand; greed, cunning and malevolence, on the other. A dual belief that was clearly expressed by Vicente de la Fuente when he wrote that 'all the ancients portray the customs of those early peoples as pure and simple until they were corrupted by commerce and foreign domination'.[22] More memorable and easier to remember was the synthesis, written in rhyming couplets, by Father Francisco José de Isla in the eighteenth century:

> The free, happy and independent Spain
> opened itself unwarily to the Carthagians.

In the first line, we have the original Arcadia, a 'happy' place (precisely because it was 'free' and 'independent') and fully legitimate (for the same reason), whose recovery became the supreme national objective. In the second, the evil foreigner, cause of the departure from paradise and all subsequent evils.

This national personality, which was presented as rooted in the very geography of the land, also had to acquire the lustre of antiquity. It is the mission of nationalist history to trace remote ancestors and their deeds: so remote that, with luck, they will date right back to the beginning of time. In the Spanish case, this flank had been well protected for centuries by references to the founding of the nation by the mythical Tubal, grandson of Noah. There could be no greater antiquity because that was the second, definitive launching of the human species after the Biblical Flood, and the first division into peoples and races. This legend derived from the Roman historian Josephus and, as shown in the previous chapter, became firmly entrenched in the history of Spain of Juan de Mariana, who needed this kind of legendary 'fact' so that he could favourably compare the antiquity of the Spanish people with that of the Italians. The belief in Tubal came under regular attack during the Enlightenment as attempts were made to verify historical sources, but it continued to prevail for some time into the nineteenth century, though frequently with a warning that it was only a 'tradition'. Nineteenth-century Europe, dominated by competition between nations, considered it not merely allowable, like Mariana, but almost obligatory for a historian to glorify his own nation, even if he had to pay a very high intellectual price to do so. As Alcalá Galiano reminds us in referring to the theories that brought the Celts from Africa and not from Europe, some historical narratives were adopted in order to 'avoid an odious dependence on France'.[23]

These descriptions also give us an idea of the ideal portrait of the *natural* Spaniard prior to foreign contamination. In 1867, Monreal y Ascaso represented the early Spaniards as 'similar to the Spartans', 'as frugal in their eating habits as they were simple in their dress'; 'thus the Spanish must have lived for some centuries, more or less content, but independent'; and precisely because they 'loved their independence . . . they were ready to kill themselves rather than fall into enemy hands'. The same year, Orodea couples the 'sobriety' and 'agility' of the Iberians to the simplicity, vivacity, independence, 'asperity and candour' of the Celts, which combined 'courage with loyalty, religious faith with a love of their national liberty'. Shortly before that, Modesto Lafuente had established the accepted version of the 'virtues of the Spanish' since the dawn of time: first of all came 'valour', together with a 'tendency to isolation, a conservative instinct and an attachment to the past, trust in their God and love of their religion, constancy in time of disaster and suffering in time of misfortune, bravery, indiscipline, the child of pride and high self-esteem'.[24] All the basic elements are found in these quotations: sobriety, religiosity, independence and suicidal courage alongside individualism and anarchic tendencies. The political objectives of the myth are obvious: to extol a particular *character type* and underline its perpetuation up to the present day, except for those aspects – such as the tendency towards disunity – that are better avoided.

As can be seen, the one essential collective character trait of Spaniards in history which no author fails to underline is their *bellicosity* or *martial spirit*. 'We Spaniards have taken greater pains in the handling of our swords than our pens', says Ortiz de la Vega, paraphrasing Mariana. The early Spaniards were characterised by their 'fierce habits and indomitable spirit'; the 'dominant spirit' in the original Spain was 'martial' as is proven by 'the bloody and continuous wars that Spaniards endured', and they prized 'immortality for their valour and their deeds' above any other honour.[25] Following the method of citing a classical authority, these historians quoted the observation of Titus Livius that Hispania had been the first land outside Italy to be occupied by Roman soldiers and the last to be brought under their complete domination, which led him to conclude that 'the nature of both the land and its inhabitants is better suited to war even than Italy, as well as everywhere else in the world'. This quotation was usually preceded by many pages on Saguntum and Numantia, which were considered to be irrefutable evidence of a courage beyond measure. To these were added Viriathus – a *Lusitanian* leader, incorporated into the history of Spain when the term included the entire Peninsula and who was never removed from the list of *Spanish* leaders – and even Sertorius, a Roman who sought refuge in Hispania during one of the last civil wars of the Republic and whose history it was necessary to reinvent from beginning to end so as to present him as a champion of 'Spanish' resistance to foreign invasion. Once these detailed narratives of the avatars of the conquest came to an end, the accepted nationalist canon, especially in its school texts, tended to compress the next five centuries into a few lines describing how the Peninsula lived peacefully integrated into the Roman world.

Anyone with any sense of history finds this heroic version of the Roman conquest of Hispania difficult to accept. First, one must question whether this conquest makes sense in relation to the much more relevant fact of the Romanisation of the following five centuries. This was the longest era of peace and prosperity in Peninsula history, during which the territory was integrated into the Roman empire by means of a network of communications, administrative centres and a language, Latin, from which the future national language would derive. Secondly, one could dispute the events and even the duration of this conquest, since the first Roman legions to disembark in the Peninsula did not do so with the aim of occupying it but in order to fight the Carthaginians. Their limited expansion during the following period may be attributed partially to the internal dissension and the civil wars that engulfed the Roman republic; when that phase ended and the conquest began in earnest, Hispania was subjugated by Julius Caesar and Octavius Augustus. Thirdly, even if the Iberians proved more difficult to conquer than was customary, there is no reason to suppose it was due to a strong sense of identity and an iron determination to expel the foreign invaders. On the contrary, it may well have been because of the very fragmentation of the cultures and political entities that existed within the territory, since the subjugation of a mountainous and divided land is more arduous than that of a centralised, unified kingdom whose army or neuralgic centre can be neutralised in a single battle. All these considerations were passed over by nationalist history. Even evangelisation lost its relative importance in the eyes of nineteenth-century historians, compared with those of earlier ones, in spite of a general identification of the national character with Catholicism. Between 1830 and 1880, it was crucial to establish that 'Spaniards', with an awareness of their identity, had existed in Spain since the beginning of time and that they had always been resolved to put up a fierce resistance to any attempt at foreign domination and would not hesitate to give their lives in defence of the independence of the nation. National sentiments, projected blindly on the past, dulled the historical sensitivity of these writers who failed to understand the difficulties of individuals in such a remote age regarding themselves in broad comparative terms and aspiring to national sovereignty.

It becomes inevitable at this point to examine the truth behind Saguntum and Numantia, memorable tragedies that are ritually invoked to prove the existence of the Spanish character. Saguntum was a city colonised by the Greeks and allied with the Romans, whose siege and subsequent conquest by Hannibal led to the Second Punic War in the third century BC. Due to the fierce defence of the Saguntians – whom Titus Livius differentiates clearly from the *Hispanics* – the Carthaginian leader ordered that they would all to be put to the sword, which may well have hardened their will to resist. When the situation became desperate, they threw all their most valuable goods onto a pyre to avoid them becoming booty for the victors, and many threw themselves onto it as well. A similar episode occurred seventy years later in Numantia, only this time it was a people of Celtic origin fighting against Rome. According to Strabo's description, 'the Numantians, besieged upon all sides, endured with heroic perseverance, except for some few who, unable to do more, abandoned the walls to the victor'. To claim that these two episodes provide proof of the existence of a *Spanish character* that has persisted down the ages, marked by indomitable courage and an invincibility deriving from their predisposition to die in combat rather than surrender, once again makes it necessary to ignore crucial details, such as the Greek origins of the Saguntian population and the behaviour of the besieged in Numantia who, when the situation became desperate, took the not unreasonable decision to surrender.[26]

On this point, Juan de Mariana reveals the respect of the humanist for classical sources when writing about Saguntum, many of whose defenders, he writes, did kill themselves, while others were slaughtered and there were some 'taken prisoner'. Such was not the case when writing about Numantia, where the erudite Jesuit allowed himself to be carried away by his desire to rival the glory of Italy. Numantia was the 'terror of the Roman people' and the 'glory and honour of Spain'. 'The citizens took their very own lives', he continues, 'they killed themselves and all of their own'; and if any Latin author claimed that, on entering the smouldering ruins, the Roman legions found any of the defenders alive, 'they are contradicted by all the other authors': in other words, *all* of them resisted to the death, a case of unequalled collective heroism. The obsession for comparing Spain with Italy also overcame Masdeu, the great historian of the eighteenth century, for whom Numantia was the 'imperial terror' and ultimate proof of 'Spanish courage compared to Roman'. The myths of Numantia and Saguntum took on new life in the nineteenth century, first for their usefulness during the Napoleonic wars and later in stirring up romantic nationalism. For Modesto Lafuente, Saguntum was 'the most heroic city in the world', and from its charred remains 'sounded a voice that announced to future generations what Spanish heroism was capable of'. He knew that the Saguntians were 'of Greek origin' but justified himself by saying that 'we can already con-sider [them] to be Spaniards . . . after the four centuries or more that they had been living on our soil'. The inconsistency implied by the fact that the exceptional courage of the national character could be acquired by residence was irrelevant because there were plenty of other exam-ples to prove that this kind of 'indomitable' ferocity or courage had *always* characterised the Spanish people. Saguntum had been merely one example 'that we shall witness more than once', 'that demonstrates the unquenchable fire of the sons of this soil'; 'it was the first example of intrepidity overcoming all dangers, of the indomitable courage that has always characterised the Spanish people'. Furthermore, the resistance of the Saguntians and the Numantians was not just the expression of an instinctive and excessive bellicosity, but it was already dedicated to the service of a political cause that was no less than national independence, the freedom of the *patria*. Numantia, said Victor Gebhardt, was the 'only Spanish city that upheld national independence to the end'. Orodea claimed that Saguntum, 'that glorious and immortal city' proved 'how sweet is independence and how much free peoples can achieve', while Numantia was the 'model for peoples who die for their liberty, for their autonomy'.[27]

Such emphasis on martial prowess was not to everyone's liking. It was particularly embarrassing to those who had lived in Italy and become conscious of the general view that the Spanish victories in the centre of the old empire resembled a new invasion of *barbarians*, a people of undoubted military superiority but culturally inferior. And while Mariana had recognised the fact that for Spain to find itself with 'more exploits than writers' was to its 'no doubt considerable discredit', Feijóo in the eighteenth century had devoted two essays from his *Teatro Crítico* to the 'Glories of Spain', in which he appealed for a national culture that was not exclusively military but also successful in fields such as navigation, humanism and the arts. In the mid-nineteenth century, the historian José R. Angulo set out to list those Spaniards who had been famous in the arts and sciences down the centuries. He went back as far as the heroic myth of Tubal, which had been revamped for nationalist purposes, claiming that artistic inclination among the Spanish was very ancient for 'in the year 2904 of the world, Tubal invented music by observing the harmonious sounds emanating from the hammers in his brother's smithy'.[28] It was not much in the way of Spanish cultural achievement and there was not much more to offer, unless one includes religiosity within the sphere of culture, because that is certainly one area of exceptional Hispanic achievement, which will be examined extensively in the next chapter.

Connected with religiosity, as a sign of cultural development, was nobility, another of the values praised as being typically Spanish. The dominant spirit of old Spain was, according to another mid-century author, 'as religious as it was chivalrous'; the 'Spaniards' of early times might have been 'wanderers, hunters, independent', but they were 'always supporters of justice, always noble and generous' and they had preserved 'their nobility, their generosity, their love of justice and independence' up to the present day. In itself, this noble pride was considered worthy of admiration, but the negative feature of the 'national character' most commonly recognised by writers – namely, internal division and disunity – also derived from it. Nobility of character, comprising a set of elevated moral attributes was one thing; the knightly *ethos* – an insubordinate, partial attitude that challenged all authority – was quite another. Viriathus himself, that 'invincible' leader (being Spanish), but nonetheless defeated by the Romans, provides us with an excellent, early example of the harmful effects of that lack of unity. The situation was described in detail by a historian of 1867, who again established the link between geography and character: owing to the rugged land of the Peninsula that breaks it up into natural regions, in early Spain there were 'tribes or states independent of each other', who looked upon 'the others as if they were foreigners'. Consequently, their ability to resist truly foreign conquerors was diminished and 'Spaniards themselves, allied with the invaders, contributed to crushing the voice of the *Patria*'; the Roman armies, in particular, would have been rendered helpless 'if even half of Spain had come to the aid of Viriathus'. This opinion is to be found elsewhere: 'if the peoples of the Peninsula . . . had put aside their petty rivalries, uniting under his [Viriathus'] standard, Heaven alone knows what would have been the fate of Rome'. Viriathus, 'heroic martyr to beloved freedom . . . sustained a remarkable idea, his notion of unity'; his voice 'made the Republic tremble because it taught peoples the maxim that strength is to be found in unity, because it opened their souls to the greater good, which is independence and made them aware of their rights'. But 'a spirit of localism still predominated among such Spaniards, for whom unity appeared to be the most difficult of tasks'; 'those Spaniards who showed the world what the miracle of independence was capable of . . . were themselves unable to learn the simplest of maxims, that unity gives strength'.[29] Once again, the most succinct appraisal of the idea is to be found in the verse of Padre Isla from the previous century:

> el Español rendido / contra su libertad toma partido;
> pues su mano juntando a las ajenas, / él mismo se fabrica las cadenas.

All of the above were aspects of the narrative schema initiated by the *Laudes Hispaniae*, and were continued in order to show the existence of a people endowed with a permanent nobility of character, whose deeds could be traced back to the earliest days of recorded history. Its usefulness was such that the histories of Spain clung faithfully to it in spite of its implausibility, at least until the fateful year of 1898, when the break was finally made with that tradition. However, it was then replaced by a pessimistic version of both Spain's geography and the collective psychology of the Spaniards, often radically opposed to the earlier one, marked by the vision of a *black* Spain with parched lands and a people with *Cainite* tendencies. The reference to Cainism indicates that some of the earlier myths, such as the *lack of unity*, still held sway in national history, acting as a malign agency as powerful and omnipresent as *moral degeneration* had been in Christian histories. The negative factor took on a variety of guises depending on the overriding political problem of the moment. It was 'Cainism', or fratricidal tendencies, when it surfaced in times of civil war; it became 'feudal anarchy', or 'a turbulent nobility', in times of the breakdown of national unity, and was explained away as Hispanic individualism; it was also 'anarchy' of a very different type when, at the end of the nineteenth century, revolutionaries' bombs began to explode, which were also attributed to the idiosyncratic individualism that everyone took for granted; and it once again became the innate fratricidal tendency in the 'separatisms' embodied in Basque and Catalan nationalism not long afterwards. In short, nineteenth-century historians allowed themselves to be guided more by their political preoccupations than by a desire to comprehend the past. And as the great task of that time was the building of a State, the conclusion or moral of the national historical legend was, necessarily, that 'unity constitutes the strength and power of a State . . . A people divided by races, interests, or in any other way, is devoured by a cancer within that sooner or later must destroy it'.[30]

Of paradise, falls and redemptions

This completes the description of the blueprint within which national history was to prosper. It did so with few modifications in relation to previous mythologies because it remained faithful to the three classical states of paradise, fall and redemption. All Spanish national history, when transformed into legend or political parable, is merely a repetition of the first *fall*, or expulsion from the original *paradise* of that isolated, happy, independent Spain. Successive millennia have seen a long series of 'losses of Spain', always coinciding with the *invasions* of *foreign* or *alien* colonisers motivated by greed and aided in their incursions by the lack of internal unity; and each 'loss' supplements the number of *martyrs* who sacrifice themselves in useless attempts to preserve what is about to disappear.

It might be thought that the loss – or, in other words, defeat – of Spain so many times should have raised doubts about her ability to resist, and that so many waves of foreign invaders should have led to speculation over the survival of the national identity. Not so. The national personality was lost again and again but the desire to perpetuate it lived on, and its very survival in the face of such adversity demonstrated its providential power. For that reason, as one author concludes, Spain could be defined as 'the genius of resistance, always conquered and always rising up against the conquest'; seven (a magic number) successive invasions and 'how strange! No other people in the world have held onto their national character more tenaciously down the centuries'.[31] This was because each of the *falls* had been followed by a heroic *restoration*. Heroic, of course, because if falls had *martyrs*, restorations had *heroes*: there was always an extraordinary individual imbued with a tremendous sense of nationality (a sense of virtue which everyone should embody and which would duly be instilled in the future members of the collectivity for whom the historical fable was intended).

Far be it from anyone to attribute a single one of those defeats to the inferiority of the native people compared to the foreign invader. On the battlefield, above all, there was no question of being outclassed given that Spaniards' willingness to die rather than surrender made them invincible. All the defeats had resulted from a combination of foreign wickedness or 'betrayal' and the perpetual divisions among the native peoples. Yet again, Viriathus – held up as a *martyr* not a *hero* – was a good illustration. Added to the inability of the natives to unite under the flag of so great a leader was the treachery of the Romans who, incapable of defeating him in a fair fight, paid three assassins ('unworthy to be called Spaniards') to finish off the rebel, described as a living example of the 'military genius of the Spanish fighter, just as we have seen him appear in modern times': one of those 'unschooled fighters . . . who, from shepherds to outlaws, become generals'. According to another historian, this ignominious end was compounded by the depths of moral degradation to which the 'Spanish army' sank when, on the death of Viriathus, it capitulated 'after a shameful treaty was accepted by their new chief, as stupid as he was cowardly'.[32]

This reference to moral decadence is connected to the defeat of the Visigoths at the hands of the Muslims at Guadalete in 711, the 'loss of Spain' par excellence. As always, there was the inevitable *disunity* in the form of factional infighting under the ill-fated king Rodrigo, and there was *betrayal* in the guise of the Conde Don Julián who summoned the infidel invader and contrived his crossing of the Straits. But there was more. The Christian historical sources closest to those events were fully convinced of the providentialist paradigm that attributed the decline and fall of empires to the *moral decadence* exemplified by biblical Babylonia. Christian writers resorted to this archetype to explain the unexpected disappearance of the Roman Empire, and it was churned out again and again until the second half of the nineteenth century. Even then, Spanish historians continued to claim that the fall of Rome had been due to the 'lapse in moral customs, the corruption of military discipline and the despotism of cruel and effeminate Roman Emperors'.[33]

Consequently, it was accepted that the disaster of Guadalete, witness to the demise of another empire, was the product of the *moral decadence* of the Visigothic leaders. The reigns of two kings, Witiza and Rodrigo, came under merciless attack for their 'vices' from the earliest Asturian chronicles of the ninth century to the general histories of Spain. Almost twelve centuries after their deaths, it was still being written that Witiza 'indulged in all forms of excess' and that Don Rodrigo 'followed in his footsteps' or ' was no more prudent'. As a result, the Muslim conquest of Spain 'was neither long nor difficult' because 'the Visigoths, degenerate and enervated since the reign of Witiza, had become the most cowardly and effeminate of men'.[34] Some historians attributed the moral and physical degeneration of the formerly vigorous Goths to a period preceding the last two reigns. One of the historians was Juan Cortada, a liberal Catalan who distanced himself from the ecclesiastical versions but still echoed their refrain: the 'luxury and vices' of the Visigoths 'drained their courage and the energy that led them to conquer Spain' and 'the Gothic monarchy collapsed under the weight of its own vices, like the Roman empire'. Another was Joaquín Rodríguez, for whom the mere introduction of 'the Roman language and culture' had infected the Goths with a 'love of corruption, luxury and the uncontrolled frenzy of passion, that, enfeebling those strong arms, debased them'. Amador de los Ríos describes the 'effeminacy and corruption' of the grandsons of Recaredo and Wamba in more detail, expanding on the old idea of *dissipation*: 'it was all the feasting, tasty food and wine, that depleted their strength'; it was impossible, he concluded, that 'a people who had sunk into such a demoralised state would not be threatened by a great catastrophe'. Modesto Lafuente had the final word on the Visigoths as 'enervated by soft living', a situation that caused a 'providential intervention', that 'is never lacking ... when a society requires to be dissolved or regenerated'.[35] He did no more than give voice to a general belief. A century earlier, with his usual gift for synthesis, Padre Isla had versified the legendary exploit of the rape by King Rodrigo of *Cava*, the daughter of Count Don Julián, 'wanton pleasures' that were the culmination of the vices initiated by Witiza and which brought the ire of God down upon the Gothic throne:

Entregado Rodrigo a su apetito
triste víctima fue de su delito.

In another two lines he named the villain and spelled out the monstrous betrayal of his *patria*:

cuando Julián, vengando su deshonra,
sacrificó a su rey, su patria y honra.

In these descriptions, it is interesting to note the repeated correlation of the moral *degeneration* or *enervation* of the Goths with *effeminacy*, a term which in political language used to mean, and continued to do so until well into the twentieth century, the loss of physical strength as well as moral judgement or control. It is no coincidence that *virility*, as opposed to effeminacy, was dominant in the original paradise: 'the Celtiberian . . . never waited for the enemy to attack but went in search of him, to provoke him to a fair fight in manly fashion'. This subject will be discussed more broadly elsewhere, but it should be pointed out that decadence and effeminacy were to reappear in 1898, at a time when so many of the underlying tendencies in the political culture of that century were to come to a head.[36]

If the Muslim invasion was the most important of the 'falls' or exiles from paradise, then the most outstanding of the 'redemptions' or renewals of the national saga came, logically, shortly afterwards. Don Pelayo and a group of 'Spaniards' (an identification with the nation that was always denied to Muslims), who had taken refuge in the Asturian mountains, embarked upon the restoration of 'what would afterwards be called the Monarchy of the Spains and Indies'. The role of Pelayo is similar to that of any one of the other great heroes linked to the beginnings of Golden Ages: Tubal and Hercules in the original paradise; Ataúlfo, on establishing the Visigothic monarchy; Recaredo for establishing religious unity; Fernando III who pushed on with the Reconquest and was rewarded with sainthood; as well as the Catholic Kings, who accomplished the political and religious unity of the nation. To embellish his legitimacy, many versions claimed that Pelayo was a relative of King Rodrigo and therefore legal heir to the Gothic throne. However, for the purposes of national history, as opposed to the ancient dynastic chronicles, this was not a crucial asset. As Orodea explains, Pelayo might be 'Goth according to some, and Roman according to others'; what is clear is that he was 'courageous, Christian and Spanish', and that in the mountains of Asturias he raised 'the first cry of freedom, making it the most solemn moment of our history and the beginning of a new civilisation, a new *patria* and a new personality'.[37]

Thus began the *Reconquest*, a name – extraordinarily effective in its synthesis, though of much later invention – that designated the longest and most fertile of golden ages and the one in which the national

identity became definitively forged. The writers responsible for the
national historical canon were unanimous in declaring that the greatest
moment was when *Spain*, united, had fought for her 'independence'
or liberation, closely associated with the recovery of her religion. The
Reconquest, more than any other collective enterprise – including the
discovery and colonisation of America – expressed the essential fighting
and religious spirit of the Spanish people, the obstinate affirmation of
their collective personality against an invader who was not only foreign
but, worse still, an enemy of the true faith. It was an affirmation against
both the external enemy and the internal powers that tended to frag-
ment their unity or hinder its achievement. The *anarchic* tendencies of
the nobility of that time were incorporated into the national character
as the defect that made the country so difficult to rule. Unity became
the supreme criterion by which to judge monarchs: favourably if they
achieved it, and unfavourably if they did not, by the untimely division
of their kingdoms among their sons, for example.

Although this liberal version of the national legend dated back to
the eighteenth century, it came into its own at the time of the *Cortes* de
Cádiz (1810–1814). In 1811, the deputy García Herreros explained
that in Spain there had been a long period during which everyone,
including the king himself, respected the 'elemental laws'. These laid
down the 'limits of authority conferred upon [the monarchs] . . . the
conditions under which they were obliged to obey them', but the
coming of a *foreign* dynasty brought to Spain the 'usages and customs
of other States and governments': 'despotism sat upon the throne and
the law was replaced by arbitrary actions'. Two years later, against the
backdrop of the war against the French invader, Martínez Marina published his *Teoría de las Cortes*, a full-blown idealisation of the mediaeval
world. According to him, Spain had no reason to envy either France or
England in respect of parliamentary antecedents. In mediaeval times,
there had been representative assemblies similar to theirs that the king
was obliged by law to consult on important affairs of state. As Alberto
Gil Novales observes, Martínez Marina was attempting to identify
'the representative government known to the Middle Ages with the
one being set up in Cádiz'. This was emphasised by Flórez Estrada:
'the Cortes de Cádiz have done no more than re-establish some part
of our venerable Constitution which, in better days, championed our
freedom and the greater part of which was destroyed by . . . dishonesty
and violence during the reigns of Fernando V, Carlos I and Felipe II';
and Agustín Argüelles was to repeat the thesis when he presented the
Constitution of 1812 as the culmination of Spanish mediaeval history.[38]

It was therefore mediaeval 'Spain' that, in its struggle against the infidel invader, was held to personify the national character and to found the defence of its freedom and independence on the Christian faith. This did not constitute a problem for the first generations of liberals, and as late as 1850, Fernando de Castro, a liberal cleric, maintained a balance between liberalism and Catholicism when he concluded his *philosophical* study of the history of Spain by saying that the unity of the nation had been achieved under the triple 'influence of religious and monarchical sentiments combined with that of freedom'. In Chapters 6 and 7, we shall see how the bitterness of the fight against first absolutism and then Carlism made this fusion between freedom and religion more difficult to sustain from mid-century onwards. However, what really interested the liberals about the idealised Middle Ages was its institutions rather than its ideas or beliefs and, more particularly, the limits imposed upon royal power and the representative aspects of mediaeval councils and town councils. By praising the municipal *fueros* and the powers of the *Cortes* in the various kingdoms, and by citing the celebrated oath of kings before the *Cortes* of Aragón ('you, who are no more than each one of us, while we together are more than you'), they depicted the *Spanish* monarchy as not absolute, thereby trimming the mediaeval historical myth to reflect favourably on their constitutional revolution. 'Everything was national in those times', wrote one in 1840; 'everything displayed its own, particular, Spanish physiognomy. Our municipal system was different to that of other States in Europe; our people were not ruled by the feudal Code of other nations'. In the Statute of 1834, Francisco Martínez de la Rosa was to put this into practice by calling the members of the two representative chambers thus created *próceres* and *procuradores* instead of 'lords', 'peers' or 'deputies', which were less traditional terms: 'the name of procurator of the kingdom is more Spanish, more traditional; it reminds us that we have not gone begging to foreign nations for these institutions'.[39]

In another display of historicism, the Franco dictatorship also came to prefer the term 'procurators' to 'deputies'. Nevertheless, the institution made up of these procurators was no more than a front for the dictatorship, just as the idealisation of mediaeval institutions on the part of Conservative Catholicism was no more than a cover for its opposition to any representative system. In any event, any similarities between the mythical version of national history offered by the liberals and what was later produced by Francoist Conservative Catholicism ended at this point. The two versions diverged radically over the moment and causes of the fall that inevitably followed the Golden Age represented by the mediaeval Reconquest. They coincided in that their idealised mediaeval Spain reached its height under the Catholic Kings, the architects of national unity in both politics and religion. Conservative Catholicism, however, extended the Golden Age to the (first) Hapsburg kings, to a time when the providential path taken by the nation had been rewarded with imperial glory. The liberals, on the other hand, considered that, at the death of Fernando and Isabel the destiny of the *patria* had already been derailed by the ascent to the throne of those very same Hapsburgs, *foreign* kings who, ignorant of Spanish tradition and acting to further their dynastic rather than national interests, implanted absolutism.

The latter theory, known as *Austracism*, arose, like so many other things, at the end of the eighteenth century. It was an attempt to release the national entity from responsibility for the decline of the previous century. Masdeu had already expounded a theory that the imperial era of the Hapsburgs had brought Spain to a 'desperate pass' in which her manufactures and commerce had been ruined. Jovellanos thought that Spain had reached the height of its greatness in the Middle Ages, culminating with the reign of the Catholic Kings, and that its subsequent decline was due to the Hapsburgs destroying the hereditary 'constitution'. In the third of his *Marruecas*, José de Cadalso, after eulogising the Catholic Kings as 'princes who will be immortal among all who know the meaning of government', blamed the political course taken by Carlos I and Felipe II for having left the people 'exhausted by wars, made effeminate by the gold and silver of America, diminished by populating a new world, disillusioned by so much misfortune and desirous of rest'. The decline in the seventeenth century became inevitable with the additional problems of succession within the royal family itself. According to Cadalso, by the death of the last and weakest of the Habsburg monarchs, Carlos II, in 1700, Spain had become 'the skeleton of a giant': 'long wars, far-flung conquests, the demands of the first Austrian kings, the apathy of the last ones, the division of Spain at the start of the century, the continued drain of men for the Americas and other causes have halted . . . the advance of the flourishing state left by King Don Fernando and the Queen Doña Isabel'; Felipe V inherited a country 'with no army, navy, commerce, income or agriculture'.[40] Thus did Enlightenment thinkers lay the foundations for one of the pillars of nationalist mythology: the attribution of responsibility for the collective misfortunes to a 'foreign' element, in this case the Hapsburg dynasty. They did not take the next step of acclaiming the *Comuneros* of the 1520s as pioneers in the defence of national sovereignty in the face of monarchical despotism, which was left to revolutionary liberal nationalism.

The theory of Austracism was reformulated in far more explicit and aggressive terms during the liberal revolution of the early nineteenth century. At that time, history had become a political weapon, and the attacks on Carlos V and Felipe II were aimed at Carlos IV and Godoy or Joseph Bonaparte and his followers. The Austracist version was faithfully repeated by liberal historians over several decades, for as long as its anti-absolutist function continued to be useful. Even the moderate, Alberto Lista, in his continuation of the work of Mariana, blamed the 'Austrian dynasty' for having 'consumed all the resources that the nation possessed . . . in useless enterprises and wars', for having 'sacrifice[d] the treasures of the new world, national industry and agriculture and torrents of Spanish blood' for the 'dangerous illusion' of becoming masters of Europe. Shortly afterwards, Eugenio de Tapia wrote that, under the Catholic Kings, Spain had reached the height of mediaeval excellence, overcoming the endemic Spanish problem of the 'anarchy' of aristocratic privileges and the fragmentation of kingdoms and constituting 'a vigorous and healthy body' that was willing 'to submit to a central power, without forgoing the rights of a peaceful and well-defined freedom'. But the Austrians did not maintain this balance, and although some procurators from the cities still dared to speak out like their forefathers, 'what could the weak voice of patriotism achieve against a terrible power, buttressed by military force and the theocratic authority of the Inquisition? Spanish society had been completely transformed . . . Their despotic successors stifled that freedom and the people, poor, oppressed and hopeless, gradually became inured to the yoke of an ignominious servitude'.[41]

The *expulsion from Paradise,* considered by the liberals to be the immediate origin of all present evils, dated from 1521: the year that the *Comunero* rebellion was crushed in Villalar and its leaders executed by Carlos V. The *Comuneros* not only symbolised the fight against tyranny but also rebellion against domination by a foreign power; they were therefore liberals *and* patriots. Their initial mythification was, yet again, at the hand of Manuel José de Quintana, author of an 'Oda a Juan de Padilla' which was banned by the Inquisition in 1805 and published among his *Poesías Patrióticas* at the start of the anti-Napoleonic uprising. During the war, another great figure of early liberalism, Martínez de la Rosa, first staged *La viuda de Padilla* in the besieged city of Cádiz, a play that was still being performed to acclaim several decades later. The short-lived glory of the *Comuneros* as the ultimate martyrs for Spanish freedom and the *patria* undoubtedly reached its peak during the liberal *trienio* (1820–1823), with the staging of the one-act play *La sombra de Padilla,* the five-act tragedy *Juan de Padilla o los Comuneros* and others, including *El sepulcro de Padilla.* As luck would have it, the *trienio* coincided with the third centenary of the battle of Villalar and there were ceremonies and speeches from politicians, who fancied themselves as historians, to celebrate the rehabilitation of the *Comuneros* defeated three hundred years earlier. *Comuneros* or *Hijos de Padilla*, was also the name adopted by a society of Freemasons representing the radical liberalism of the period which had split off from the increasingly more moderate *Gran Oriente*. And that glory lingered on well after the brief *trienio*. Liberal historians and writers were to continue repeating the versions of Quintana and Martínez de la Rosa for a long time. Even at mid-century, it was still commonplace to read in liberal histories that 'Castilian freedom' drowned in Padilla's blood and 'no power could then constrain the despot'.[42] In 1850, Ferrer del Río published *Decadencia de España. Primera parte. Historia del levantamiento de las Comunidades de Castilla*, a work that, both in its title and from the very first page, makes a clear connection between the crushing of the Castilian rebels with the beginnings of patriotic decline: 'with their freedom, everything perish[ed], however much the laurels of war conceal[ed] their intense misfortunes for some time'. Ten years later, in the National Exhibition of Fine Arts of 1860, a painting called *Padilla, Bravo and Maldonado on the scaffold* by Antonio Gisbert caused a sensation and became the essential illustration in any history of the *Comunero* rebellion. Liberal opinion was scandalised when the painting failed to win the Exhibition's Medal of Honour; the Congress of Deputies decided to buy and exhibit it in their rooms, and a subscription was set up to present the painter with a crown of gold in substitution for the medal he was denied. Gisbert went on to become the favourite painter of the Progressive Party in particular and liberal opinion in general.

Because the nationalism of nineteenth-century liberals was not Castilian but Spanish, the *Comuneros* had to be complemented by other martyrs, defenders of other freedoms crushed by the Hapsburgs. It was Quintana, once again, who dedicated part of his poetic work to Juan de Lanuza and Pau Clarís who, together with Padilla, made up the symbolic trio of the end of freedom in Aragón, Catalonia and Castile respectively.[43] In 1805, Quintana had written his *Panteón del Escorial*, a pre-romantic poem in which the ghosts of the first two Hapsburgs admit to their responsibility for national decline. Among moans and groans from beyond the grave, flickering torches, creaking doors and cracking marble, the Emperor confesses to his son:

> Yo los desastres / de España comencé y el triste llanto
> cuando, expirando en Villalar Padilla / morir vio en él su libertad
> Castilla.
> Tú los seguiste, y con su fiel Lanuza / cayó Aragón gimiendo. Así
> arrollados

los nobles fueros, las sagradas leyes / que eran del pueblo fuerza y
   energía,
¿quién insensato imaginar podría / que, en sí abrigando corazón de
   esclavo,
señor gran tiempo el español sería?'

Having established the causes of the decline, the liberal version
of this national historical myth was less concerned with verifying its
development than with completing the cycle by describing collective
redemption, or the promise of it. For the liberal revolutionaries of the
early nineteenth century, there could be no doubt about this: they had
to pursue the 'reconquest of our freedoms', to immerse themselves in
'those principles that shaped the Castilian soul and were later destroyed
by Austrian despotism'.[44] This renewal of the *patria* had already begun
with the explosion of anti-Napoleonic popular feeling which, according
to them, was inspired by the desire to re-establish freedom in Spain by
means of a constitutionalist revolution. As for the events of 1808, they
could be explained within the most orthodox limits of the mythology:
just as the luxuries, sins and effeminacy of the last Visigothic kings were
responsible for the subjugation of Spain by the Muslims, the moral
degradation in the times of Carlos IV and Godoy had brought 'foreign
invasion' down upon her; but the 'magnanimous nation' which, in spite
of the depravations of the court, 'had lost none of its dignity, put up
a resistance to the usurper that recalls the times of the Muslim invasion'.[45] The greatest coincidence of all was that Asturias, where Don
Pelayo first raised his standard after the disaster at Guadalete, also had
the privilege of witnessing the first efforts to recover the *patria* at the end
of May 1808.

Thus it was that the 'War of Independence' came to be so deeply
lodged in nationalist mythology: as the jewel in the crown of the glorious series of reconquests of the patriotic paradise. The bellicosity
and obstinate defence of the national identity in the face of all foreign
aggression were also reaffirmed as permanent traits of the collective
character. The one novelty was that it was no longer the great individual
hero – a leader – but the people – a nation – who had led the process,
while the corrupt élites had surrendered to the French. New times
brought new modes of thought and new protagonists to the story. This
version satisfied the liberals because they expected a new redemptive
intervention from this same people when the *patria* groaned once again
under the yoke of another tyranny; it did not displease the conservatives, who saw in the people their fidelity to inherited beliefs and traditions. Thus the national myth fulfilled its integrating function. History

was no longer a school of morality in the abstract, as classical thinkers maintained; it had become a school of *patriotic virtues*.[46] There were moral lessons to be learnt but they were based on a set of incontrovertible truths that the discipline set out to prove: namely, the existence of the national entity from the beginning of time; the progressive advance of this entity towards political unity which was the maximum collective achievement, as opposed to wretched regionalist selfishness; and the passionate defence of that unity and its independence when threatened by foreign invasion. This led on to a supreme objective that was implicitly proposed as the guiding light for the conduct of all the members of that collective: the affirmation of national unity and independence; in other words, the strengthening of the State as it was at that time.

Notes

1 Around 1780, according to E. Hobsbawm, *Nations and Nationalism since 1780*, Cambridge: Cambridge University Press, 1990.

2 B. Anderson, *Imagined Communities*, New York, 1983, p. 71; M. Hroch, *Social preconditions of National Revival in Europe*, Cambridge: Cambridge University Press, 1985.

3 P. Sahlins, *Boundaries: The Making of France and Spain in the Pyrenees*, Berkeley, CA: University of California Press, 1989.

4 See H. Isaacs, *The Idols of the Tribe: Group Identity and Political Change*, New York: Harper and Row, 1975.

5 On mobilisation and collective identity, see A. Melucci, 'The Symbolic Challenge of Contemporary Movements', *Social Research*, 52(4) (1985): 789–815.

6 E. Hobsbawm and T. Ranger (eds), *The Invention of Tradition*, Cambridge: Cambridge University Press, 1983; The word *invention* may be a bit excessive if by it we understand a wholly free creation. D'Azeglio's famous sentence, p. 267.

7 F.-X. Guerra, *Modernidad e Independencias*, Madrid, 1992, p. 44; J. M. Fradera, *Gobernar colonias*, Barcelona, 1999, Chapter 2.

8 Antonio Alcalá Galiano, *Indole de la revolución de España en 1808*, 1839, in *Obras Escogidas, Biblioteca de Autores Españoles* (B.A.E.), 1955, Vol. II, pp. 309–325.

9 Quoted by Hobsbawm, *Nations and Nationalism*, p. 12; on the need to forget the true history, Anderson, *Imagined Communities*, pp. 199–201. For the Spanish case, P. Cirujano, T. Elorriaga and J. S. Pérez Garzón, *Historia y nacionalismo español, 1834–1868*, Madrid, 1985, pp. 85–91.

10 J. A. Maravall, 'Mentalidad burguesa e idea de la Historia en el siglo XVIII', *Revista de Occidente*, 107 (1972): 250–286; Masdeu's quote, p. 123. Jovellanos, B.A.E., Vol. XLVI, p. 341.

11 For instance, the Academia Sevillana de Buenas Letras, established as

'ultimate goal' 'to vindicate our *patria*'s glory' (F. Aguilar Piñal, *La Real Academia Sevillana de Buenas Letras*, Madrid, 1966, p. 189). For the Barcelona academy's statutes, approved by the king in 1752, the goal was, instead, 'to write a history of Catalonia'.

12 In 1733, first edition in Spain of its thirty volumes in Latin. Appearing the same year, José Manuel Miñana's appendix that would be added to Mariana's work in most future editions. Both Mariana's history and Miñana's appendix were published in Spanish in Antwerp, 1739. Two years later, a new appendix was added, written by Manuel J. Medrano. Other reprints in Valencia 1783, Madrid 1780, 1794–1795, 1804.

13 Main histories were J. de Ferreras, *Synopsis historica chronologica de España*, 16 vols, 1700–1727; Fr. F. de Berganza, *Antigüedades del España*, 1719; Pablo Yáñez de Avilés, *De la era y fechas de España: Chronología*, 1732; Manuel J. de la Parra, *Compendio de la Historia General de España, que comprende desde la fundación hasta el año de 1704*, Madrid, 1734; J. J. Salazar y Hontiveros, *Glorias de España, plausibles en todos los siglos*, Madrid, 1736; G. Mayáns y Císcar, *Orígenes de la lengua española*, 1737; N. de Jesús Belando, *Historia civil de España*, 3 vols, 1740–1741; J.-B. Philipoteau Duchesne, *Compendio de Historia de España*, translated by F. J. de Isla in 1756; L. J. Velázquez, *Anales de la Nación Española, desde los tiempos remotos hasta los romanos*, Málaga, 1759; J. Velázquez de Velasco, *Noticia del viaje de España . . . y de una nueva historia general de la nación*, and *Colección de documentos contemporáneos de la Historia de España*, both in Madrid, 1765; P. and R. Rodríguez Mohedano, *Historia literaria de España, desde su primera población hasta nuestros días*, Madrid, 1766–1791; F. Marín y Mendoza, *Historia de la monarquía española hasta 1777*, Madrid, 1777; E. Flórez, *España sagrada*, 1747–1779.

14 Maravall, *Estudios de historia del pensamiento español (siglo XVIII)*, pp. 116 and 129. Cf. A. Mestre, 'Ensayo, erudición y crítica en el cambio de siglo', and J. Alvarez Barrientos, 'Orígenes de la Historia de la Literatura Española', both in G. Carnero (ed.), *Historia de la literatura española: Siglo XVIII*, 2 vols. Madrid, 1995, Vol. I, pp. 51–60 and 108–123. On the 'national character', Salazar y Hontiveros, *Glorias de España*, pp. 24–32, 'Valor de la Nación Española'.

15 See V. Lloréns *Liberales y románticos*, Madrid, 1968.

16 S. A. Dunham, *The History of Spain and Portugal*, 3 vols. London, 1832–1833; M. M. Busk, *History of Spain and Portugal*, London, 1833; A. Paquin, *Histoire de l'Espagne et du Portugal*, 2 vols. Paris: Parent-Desbarres, 1836; B. Guttenstein, *Geschichte des Spanische Volkes*, 2 vols. Mannheim, 1836–1838; Ch. Romey, *Histoire d'Espagne depuis les premiers temps jusqu'à nos jours*, 9 vols. Paris, 1839–1850; E. Rosseeuw Saint-Hilaire, *Histoire d'Espagne depuis les premiers temps historiques jusqu'à la mort de Ferdinand VII*, 5 vols. Paris, 1836–1841; E. Marliani, *Histoire politique de l'Espagne moderne*, 2 vols. Brussels, 1840; V. du Hamel, *Histoire constitutionelle de la monarchie espagnole, depuis l'invasion des hommes du Nord jusqu'à la mort*

de Ferdinand VII, Paris, 1845. There are references to a *Geschichte von Spanien*, by F. Lembke, 1831, that I have been unable to find.

17 On these histories, see J. M. Jover, 'Caracteres del nacionalismo español, 1854–1874', *Zona Abierta*, 31 (1984): 1–22; P. Cirujano Marín et al., *Historia y nacionalismo español*; M. Moreno Alonso, *Historiografía romántica española*, Seville, 1979; and C. Boyd, *Historia Patria: Politics, History, and National Identity in Spain, 1875–1975*, Princeton, NJ: Princeton University Press, 1997.

18 J. R. Angulo, *Nociones generales de la historia de España*, Madrid, 1844, p. 5; S. Gómez, *Compendio de Historia General de España*, 1855, p. 13; M. Cervilla Soler, *Compendio de Historia de España*, Toledo, 1853, pp. 2–3; and M. Lafuente, *Historia General de España, desde los tiempos más remotos hasta nuestros días*, 30 vols, Madrid, 1850–1866, I, Chapter 1.

19 See Fernando Patxot, under the pseudonym M. Ortiz de la Vega, *Anales de España, desde sus orígenes hasta el tiempo presente*, Barcelona, 1857–1859, Vol. 1, pp. 3, 14, 16 and 19. Cf. J. C. Tárrega, *Compendio de Historia de España*, Toledo, 1859, for whom it was very likely that the Iberian Peninsula was 'the Earthly Paradise mentioned in the Holy Bible' (p. 15).

20 V. Gebhardt, *Historia general de España y de sus Indias*, Barcelona, 1860–1873, Vol. I, Chapter 1; Lafuente, *Historia General de España*, Vol. I, Chapters 3 and 6. On the persistence of the national 'way of being', Cervilla Soler, *Compendio de Historia de España*, p. 2.

21 J. Rodríguez, *Lecciones de cronología e Historia General de España*, Madrid, 1850, p. 6; Angulo, *Nociones generales*, p. 5; S. Gómez, *Compendio de Historia*, p. 13.

22 J. Ortiz y Sanz, *Compendio cronológico de la historia de España*, 6 vols. 1795–1803, Vol. I, p. 1; Angulo, *Nociones generales*, p. 17; B. Monreal y Ascaso, *Curso de Historia de España*, Madrid, 1867, p. 33; V. de la Fuente, *Historia eclesiástica de España*, 4 vols. Madrid, 1855–1859, Vol. I, p. 28; F. J. Isla's *Resumen de la Historia de España*, quoted next, is so brief and there were so many editions that giving specific page numbers is difficult.

23 In the eighteenth century, Mayáns, L. J. Velázquez, Mohedano, Masdeu and Ortiz y Sanz reject the myth of Tubal. And yet, in the nineteenth, J. R. Angulo (1844), A. M. Terradillos (1848), A. Alix (1848–1852), J. Rodríguez (1850), M. Cervilla (1853), J. C. Tárrega (1859), F. S. Belmar (1861), F. Sánchez y Casado (1867) and M. Merry (1876) accept it, although often preceded by a cautious 'according to tradition . . .' Alcalá Galiano, preface to his *Historia de España, desde los tiempos primitivos hasta la mayoría de edad de Isabel II*, 7 vols, 1844–1846.

24 B. Monreal y Ascaso, *Curso de Historia de España*, p. 20; E. Orodea e Ibarra, *Curso de Lecciones de Historia de España*, Valladolid, 1867, p. 9; Lafuente, *Historia General de España*, 'Introduction'.

25 Ortiz y Sanz, preface to *Compendio cronológico*; Alcalá Galiano, *Historia de España*, p. 31; Angulo, *Nociones generales*, pp. 30–31. Titus Livius' quote, next, *Ab Urbe Condita*, XXVIII, 12.

26 Titus Livius, quoted by A. Blanco Freijeiro, 'Los pueblos ibéricos', in *Historia de España: La España antigua*, Madrid, 1980, p. 95. Strabo, *Geografía*, bk. III, for instance in J. García Mercadal, *Viajes de extranjeros por España y Portugal*, Madrid, 1962, Vol. I, p. 127; other references to the bellicosity of the Iberian peoples, pp. 119, 122 and 130–131. Polibius, a less heroic version, *Historias*, III, 17, 10. Saguntum's siege, in Titus Livius, *Ab Urbe Condita* XXI, 14. No primary source mentions the massive suicide of all inhabitants of this town.

27 J. de Mariana, *Historia General de España*, Bk II, Ch. IX (Numantia, III, X); J. F. Masdeu, *Historia crítica de España y de la cultura española*, Madrid, 1783–1805, pp. 104–105; cf. Salazar y Hontiveros, *Glorias de España*, pp. 24–26 and 32. On the persistence of this myth during the nineteenth century, see Lafuente, *Historia General de España*, Vol. 1, Chapters 4, 5 and 7; Cervilla Soler, *Compendio de Historia de España*, p. 12; Gebhardt, *Historia general de España*, Vol. I, pp. 67 and 131; Orodea e Ibarra, *Curso de Lecciones de Historia*, pp. 30–31 and 43. Cf. Alcalá Galiano, *Historia de España*, pp. 31 and 39 (Numantia, 'sublime feat', 'unique in the world's annals').

28 Mariana, prologue to *Historia General de España*; B. J. Feijóo, *Teatro Crítico*, Biblioteca de Autores Españoles, Vol. LVI, pp. 194 and 210; Angulo, *Nociones generales*, pp. 31 and 174.

29 Angulo, *Nociones generales*, p. 145; M. I. Alfaro, *Compendio de la historia de España*, Madrid, 1853, p. 10; Monreal y Ascaso, *Curso de Historia de España*, p. 33; Tárrega, *Compendio de Historia de España*, pp. 25 and 28; Orodea e Ibarra, *Curso de Lecciones de Historia*, pp. 40–41; and Lafuente, *Historia General de España*, Vol. I, Chapter 5 (Numantia was also left alone by the Spaniards, 'divided, as usual'; Vol. II, Chapter 3).

30 Rodríguez, *Lecciones de cronología e Historia*, p. XIV.

31 F. Sánchez y Casado, *Prontuario de Historia de España y de la Civilización Española*, Madrid, 1867, p. 2.

32 A. Cavanilles, *Compendio de Historia de España*, Madrid, 1860, Vol. I, pp. 83–90; E. Paluzie Cantalozella, *Resumen de Historia de España*, 1866, p. 15; Angulo, *Nociones generales*, p. 26.

33 Angulo, *Nociones generales*, p. 36.

34 A. M. Terradillos, *Prontuario de Historia de España*, Madrid, 1848, p. 32; A. Alix, *Compendio de Historia General*, Madrid, 1848–1852, Vol. II, p. 25; and A. A. Camus, *Compendio elemental de Historia Universal*, Madrid, 1842, pp. 144–147.

35 J. Cortada, *Historia de España, dedicada a la juventud*, Barcelona, 1845, p. 125; Rodríguez, *Lecciones de cronología e Historia*, p. 71; J. Amador de los Ríos, *Historia social, política y religiosa de los judios en España y Portugal*, 2 vols, Madrid, 1875–1876, Vol. I, p. 18.

36 J. Álvarez Junco, 'La nación en duda', in J. Pan Montojo (ed.), *Más se perdió en Cuba*, Madrid, 1998, pp. 455–462; on this, see Boyd, *Historia Patria*, p. 95. Previous quote, Orodea e Ibarra, *Curso de Lecciones de Historia*, p. 13.

37 A. Costes, *Compendio de Historia de España*, Barcelona, 1842, p. 28; Orodea e Ibarra, *Curso de Lecciones de Historia*, p. 147.
38 A. Gil Novales, 'Francisco Martínez Marina', in J. Antón and M. Caminal, *Pensamiento Político en la España Contemporánea, 1800–1950*, Barcelona, 1992, p. 3. García Herreros, quoted by M. Pérez Ledesma, 'Las Cortes de Cádiz y la sociedad española', *Ayer*, 1 (1991): 173–174. Flórez Estrada, quoted by J. A. Maravall, 'El mito de la "tradición" en el constitucionalismo español', *Cuadernos Hispanoamericanos*, 329–330 (1977): 561. On Martínez Marina, see also J. A. Maravall, 'El pensamiento político en España a comienzos del siglo XIX: Martínez Marina', *Revista de Estudios Políticos*, 81 (1955).
39 See J. Tomás Villarroya, 'El proceso constitucional, 1834–1843', in J. M. Jover (ed.), *La era isabelina y el Sexenio Democrático (1834–1874)*, Vol. XXXIV of *Historia de España Menéndez Pidal*, Madrid, 1981, pp. 9–10 and 18–19. Castro, quoted by F. Díaz de Cerio, *Fernando de Castro, filósofo de la Historia*, León, 1970, p. 499; E. de Tapia, *Historia de la civilización española, desde la invasión de los árabes hasta los tiempos presentes*, Madrid, 1840, Vol. IV, pp. 383–384.
40 J. de Cadalso, *Cartas marruecas*, III, XXXIV and XLIV. On Jovellanos's thought in this matter, R. Herr, *The Eighteenth-Century Revolution in Spain*, Princeton, NJ: Princeton University Press, 1969, pp. 342–343.
41 Lista, quoted by H. Juretschke, *Vida, obra y pensamiento de Alberto Lista*, Madrid, 1951, p. 368. Tapia, *Historia de la civilización española*, Vol. III, pp. 129–131. This myth keeps full vigour during the 1868–1874 revolution, as can be seen in S. Ezquerra, *¡Los españoles no tenemos patria!*, Madrid, 1869, pp. 45–46.
42 Rodríguez, *Lecciones de cronología e Historia*, p. 281. Political plays during the revolutionary triennium (1820–1823), in G. Carnero, (ed.), *Historia de la literatura española: Siglo XIX*, Madrid, 1997, Vol. I, p. 295.
43 On Lanuza, see also *La capilla de Lanuza*, play by Marcos Zapata, 1872, mentioned in G. Carnero, *Historia de la literatura ... Siglo XIX*, Vol. I, p. 399.
44 J. Herrero, *Los orígenes del pensamiento reaccionario español*, Madrid, 1971, p. 238.
45 J. Díaz de Baeza, *Historia de la Guerra de España contra el Emperador Napoleón*, Madrid, 1843, p. II. On this, see A. Dérozier, *Quintana y el nacimiento del liberalismo en España*, Madrid, 1978, p. 122.
46 Boyd, *Historia Patria*, pp. 70–74, 80–81.

5

The arts and sciences enlisted in support of the nation

Literary creativity brings patriotic heroes to life

Only a hundred years ago, the newly created Nobel Prize for Literature was awarded to the great German historian Theodor Mommsen. At the time it was considered natural to include history among the narrative arts, although within only a few decades many historians would have felt affronted, preferring to classify themselves as social scientists. In support of this shift, some would have cited their sophisticated research techniques and the rationality of their interpretative formulations, while many more would have referred to the 'objective' nature of the facts and the documentary evidence upon which their historical studies were based (and which fictional narrative can, by definition, forgo). However, we need only think back to Chapter 4 on 'national histories' to realise how far historical accounts which have been accepted as true for generations can stray into a world of fantasy. It is not, in reality, difficult to pass from history to literature. 'Nation-building entails the invention of collective narratives', states Gregory Jusdanis in his suggestive book on Greek nationalism; 'members of the community tell each other tales that they have learned about themselves, their nation and their history'. Benedict Anderson maintains that what we call 'fictional creations' are only a little more fictitious than narratives of the 'collective memory' and are almost equally as efficient in constructing national identities. By reading the same stories in the same language, all partakers of these cultural products go on to share a mental universe, to imagine themselves in the same way, to identify with the same heroes and to revile the same villains. There is the added benefit that, as the fiction is created, the language is enriched and reinforced as the privileged instrument of cohesion of the imaginary community. According to Jusdanis, European nationalisms associate 'language, literature and nation'. 'Literature was the imaginary mirror in which the nation saw itself reflected, where individuals lived as members of that community', he observes. 'The literary canon works like the Bible', he continues, and 'it came to the fore in Western societies when the Bible lost its authority as the supreme text'.[1] I shall now examine how this national literary canon was formed in Spain.

The reinterpretation of literature in national terms began in the eighteenth century, as did that of the collective past, although it gathered pace in the nineteenth. Writers had of course produced fiction before the Enlightenment era, but they conceived of it in a different light. Having never known anything else, it is now virtually impossible for us to appreciate that writers have not always been classified by national criteria. Poets used to belong to the Parnassus or to the Republic of the Arts, where Calderón rubbed shoulders with Shakespeare and Racine, Erasmus with Luis Vives and Thomas More, and Garcilaso de la Vega with Camoens and Ronsard. Their *nation* – the place of birth which determined which language they wrote in – was secondary. Only midway through the eighteenth century did histories of literature begin to designate these works as *French, English* or *Italian*. Over the next two hundred years, such books went on to become the model for literary histories and artistic creation in general. In this new era, Vives would inevitably be classified alongside Nebrija and the Valdés brothers, while Calderón was destined to form a trio with Tirso de Molina and Lope de Vega, while Garcilaso was pigeonholed with Boscán.[2]

The eighteenth century was the century of Neoclassicism throughout Europe. It is generally recognised that in Spain it was a period of little literary value, with academic rigidity predominating over creative genius, and yet it was during this period that 'national' literature began to make its mark. As an aesthetic trend, Neoclassicism was defined as contrary to the baroque excesses typical of the previous period, which had, however, been the period of greatest literary and artistic creativity of the Hispanic monarchy, to the extent that it would later come to be known as the *Siglo de Oro* (Golden Age) of *Spanish* literature. It is therefore perfectly natural that this enlightened return to classicism was received with hostility by the more traditional artistic and intellectual circles which, in the words of François Lopez, branded it as a 'servile foreign phenomenon'. Herein lies the paradox: it was the '*extranjerizantes* (lovers of things foreign)' who not only began to write *national* literature but also to elaborate the very concept. The consequent dilemma reflected that of the political project: just as the only solution found to combat the loss of international influence under the last Hapsburgs had been the reform of many traditional institutions, practices and beliefs, in literature it was thought necessary to advocate classical models and disregard Góngora and Calderón.[3]

The first histories of Spanish literature appeared in the eighteenth century, only slightly later than in the other great European monarchies. Prior to these, there had been *Elogios* (Eulogies) of the Castilian, or Spanish, language of earlier centuries, from Nebrija to Covarrubias, with echoes still apparent in the work of the Valencian Mayans in the early eighteenth century, and in that of the Catalan Capmany towards the end. However, the *Ilustrados* or Enlightenment scholars were to initiate the transition from this model towards that of the 'History of Spanish Literature'. The difference lay in the fact that the *Elogios* emphasised the importance and splendour of Spanish literature, as compared to French or Italian, on the basis of not unreasonable universal criteria, which judged the language by its antiquity or sound, whereas the new national histories were more interested in *defining the nature* of the *Spanish* literary creation – as well as what, in general terms, was inherently 'Spanish' – in order to highlight original features which were beyond compare with those of other cultures.[4]

A *Historia literaria de España* was published in 1766 by the Rodríguez Mohedano brothers, who were also Franciscan friars. Twenty years later, Antonio de Capmany brought out the first of five volumes of his *Teatro histórico-crítico de la elocuencia española*, which included everything from *El poema del Cid* and the *Siete Partidas* to the writings of Padre Nieremberg. The intervening period saw the publication of the works of the exiled Jesuits Francisco J. Lampilla, Juan Andrés and Juan F. Masdeu, the second of which was chosen as a textbook by the Chair of Literary History created in 1785.[5] These Jesuits, who have already been mentioned as historians, reappear in this discussion about literature because their works were called histories of Spanish *literature*. This is because, before 1800, the term literature possessed a much broader meaning than today: not only did it refer to fiction but also to 'all knowledge that has written expression', including mathematics, music, botany, the sciences, the arts, customs, in short, 'the totality of human knowledge'.[6] Consequently these works were histories of culture in general while contributing to the concept of 'Spanish literature'.

It became indispensable to this concept to determine an index or bibliographical list of 'Spanish' authors and classics. This was compiled by digging out literary texts that went on to become classics of national culture. Maravall recorded the efforts to publish bygone authors: 'Azara [published the works of] Garcilaso; Mayáns, [those of] Vives, el Brocense, Nicolás Antonio; Llaguno, the mediaeval chronicles'. But in order to reinforce the idea of *national* literature, collections of works proved more efficacious than individual authors, however great they were. Principal among these were the nine volumes of the *Parnaso*

Español, edited by Juan José López Sedano, and the *Colección de poesías castellanas anteriores al siglo XV,* edited by Tomás Antonio Sánchez, which included the poem of *El Mío Cid,* Berceo, the Arcipreste de Hita and the *Libro del Buen Amor,* many of which had been impossible to find until then. It is worth noting how Tomás Antonio Sánchez justified his endeavour: he believed it necessary to put together a 'chosen series of the best authors of our nation' and Lope de Vega, 'when he chooses to polish his style', 'is not inferior' to the classical authors. In other words, these works were not published because of their outstanding literary quality but because they were *our* antiquities.[7]

Perhaps due to this very breadth of the concept of 'literature', this was linked to History in the eighteenth century in a way never to be repeated in subsequent periods. The best Enlightenment writers, such as Meléndez Valdés, Moratín and Jovellanos, wrote a number of works eulogising great 'Spanish' historical events and the preferred medium for this purpose was undoubtedly drama, which had the biggest impact on public opinion. No fewer than a hundred plays on themes of Spanish history were staged, many written by some of the most renowned authors of the day. In the words of Guillermo Carnero, tragedy 'was orientated towards themes of national history . . . from *Numancia destruída* by Ignacio López de Ayala to *Doña María Pacheco* by Ignacio García Malo, as well as *Ataúlfo* by Montiano, *Florinda* by Rosa María Gálvez and other mediaeval subjects such as *Guzmán el Bueno* by Nicolás Moratín, *Don Sancho García* by Cadalso and *Los Pelayos* by Jovellanos y Quintana'.[8] Almost all of these works were performed towards the end of the century, after 1770 and some even after 1800, coinciding with the second part of the reign of Carlos III and the reign of Carlos IV: years when it would seem that national sentiment was expressed through historical theatre. It is towards the end of this period that Moratín, who frequently invoked the expression 'national literature', was so successful.

The *littérateurs* were conscious that it was their politico-educational duty to encourage patriotic feeling among the people. In one of his *Cartas Marruecas,* Cadalso announced his wish to write a *Historia heroica de España* – the story of patriotic heroes – so that their memory would serve to educate the coming generations; and in *Los eruditos a la violeta* he recommended that young scholars, instead of wasting their time on sentimental readings, should concentrate on the great Spanish historians, from Mariana to Ferreras. The future *afrancesado,* Meléndez Valdés, once planned to stop writing pastorals on the beauties of nature and devote his literary energies to praising the 'illustrious deeds' of 'Spanish heroes' from the battle of Saguntum to the wars of Felipe V.

Jovellanos had the same idea when he advised a young poet from the Salamanca school to 'throw aside pastoral pipes' and raise the patriotic horn to his lips:

'para entonar ilustres hechos españoles, . . .
las hazañas, las lides, las victorias / que al imperio de lados casi inmenso
y al Evangelio Santo un nuevo mundo / más pingüe y opulento
    sujetaron'.

In even more radical terms, Antonio de Capmany, in his *Centinela contra Franceses*, exhorted poets to 'exercise their talent in popular rhymes and romances that awaken ideas of honour and patriotism, recounting the exploits of courageous captains and soldiers in both worlds, against Indians, against infidels, against the enemies of Spain in Africa, Italy and Flanders, because history offers so many. And with these ballads repeated in dances, in village squares, fiestas and theatres, they will nourish the people and waken them from their present indolence'.[9]

The century of Enlightenment saw something of everything: histories of Spanish literature, editions of Spanish classics, writing on national historical themes, exhortations to young poets to foment patriotic feeling . . . and all this was merely preparatory to the great nationalist explosion at the start of the nineteenth century. The name of Manuel José Quintana was first heard in about 1800 and he was soon to become the most famous poet and symbol of the new patriotic sentiment: a sentiment illustrated by poems such as '*A España, después de la revolución de marzo*', '*A Padilla*' and '*A la batalla de Trafalgar*', as well as his prose work called *Vidas de Españoles Célebres* which included, among others, Guzmán el Bueno, El Cid, Roger de Lauria, Pizarro, Las Casas and El Gran Capitán. Quintana may have been the outstanding 'national' author, the only one to achieve the honour of being included in the *Biblioteca de Autores Españoles* in his own lifetime (and who, in old age, would be named by Espartero to act as tutor to Isabel II so that the young queen – with little enthusiasm for her studies – would have a 'national' education), but he was by no means the only one. Juan Nicasio Gallego wrote *Al dos de Mayo* and the Duke of Rivas wrote on the battle of Bailén and General Castaños. The Supreme Central Junta itself understood the new function of literature as a weapon for mobilising the 'nation', in this case against foreign invasion, and it announced a poetry competition to commemorate the first anniversary of the siege of Zaragoza.[10]

Within the next twenty years, except for a very brief liberal period, those early progressive writers would be silenced or exiled from Spain and their attempts to create a national identity checked, just at the time when the Romantic whirlwind was sweeping through European cultural centres. Absolutism mistrusted innovation – which was, by definition, foreign and suspicious – even if it was literary and idolised a mediaeval, chivalrous and religious past rather than the mythological, pagan world of Neoclassicism. However, reverence for the past against the evils of modernity also set this early Romanticism at odds with the liberals, heirs to the Enlightenment ideals of modernisation and progress. Consequently, for a long time, Spain, the 'natural' home of Romanticism in the European imagination, failed to embrace the new literature except for the odd isolated theoretical discussion, and only later began to imitate it.[11]

However, the fashion for Romanticism was to last in Europe for a long time and, around 1830, its political leanings altered and it became aligned with the liberal faction. It was this liberal Romanticism that Blanco White, Espronceda, Martínez de la Rosa, the Duke of Rivas and Larra himself discovered and came to identify with, at the end of what is known as the *Ominous* decade (1823–1833). On the death of Fernando VII, the last absolutist king, in 1833, these exiles returned to Spain and, in addition to becoming leading political figures, introduced the new literary fashion. Within a couple of years, the plays *Macías* by Larra, *El moro expósito* by the Duke of Rivas and, most successful of all, *Don Alvaro o la fuerza del sino* by Ángel de Saavedra,[12] had all been performed.

At this point, the political significance of Romanticism rather than its literary or artistic merits becomes relevant because, as well as being an aesthetic trend, it represented a philosophical attitude with far-reaching political repercussions. Rooted in aesthetic feeling and intuition, this attitude allegedly produced a more profound and veritable sense of reality than that obtained through logical reasoning. Whereas the result of Enlightenment confidence in reason as the supreme guide to human actions, and its faith in the inevitable advance of culture as the key to social *contentment,* had been a serene personal equilibrium and, in the last instance, optimism as regards the future of humanity, the Romantics were to become renowned for their extremism and anxiety, the result of the contrast between, on the one hand, their immense aspirations, and, on the other, their own fragility combined with the *mediocre* reality around them.

From such a perspective, it is not difficult to find many literary works written by Spanish liberals in the first three decades of the nineteenth century that can be classified as Romantic. These works are full of pessimism, melancholy and desperation for their suffering *patria* and the failure of its struggle for freedom. '*¡Ay, Rodrigo infeliz! ¡Ay, triste España!*', wrote Espronceda in his *Pelayo*, grieving but resigned to what he believed was the unjust but inevitable decline of his race; concluding '*si es fuerza perecer como valientes, / perezcamos al pie del patrio muro*'. This evocation of the 'unfortunate *patria*', 'unhappy Spain', or 'wretched Spain' appears repeatedly in the writing of Martínez de la Rosa. For example, '*Cuánto, mísera España, de destrozos y ruina, / cuánto de luto y amargura y llanto / tu suelo amarga y tu beldad divina*' he writes in his *Sitio de Zaragoza*. And in the long *Oda a España* by the Catalan Baralt, there are plaintive references to the glorious past of Spain and its subsequent decline and even death:

> ¿Y piensas que, volviendo a lo pasado / los tristes ojos, hallarás consuelo?
> . . .
> De una nación en la marchita frente / el antiguo verdor nunca renace:
> la que vencida fue, vencida yace . . .
> ¡Señora del imperio / que uno y otro hemisferio unió del mundo! . . .
> ¿Dónde está de tu gloria el monumento? / ¡Oh, mísera cautiva!
> ¿No ves de tu poder el polvo al viento? / Llora sin tregua, España, tu
> amargura . . .[13]

As for Larra, in spite of being accused of *afrancesamiento*, it would be difficult to find any greater passion and distress than that which he felt about *españolismo* or 'Spanishness'. It is enough to read his defence of Spain's image abroad or his gloomy 'Here lies half of Spain; it was killed by the other half'. Over the years, Larra's pessimism about Spain's political future only increased and, combined with his personal unhappiness, contributed to his suicide at a moment when an *ennui vital* and Romantic desperation seemed to have taken hold of the country.

Never before had the misfortunes of the *patria* combined so effortlessly with the nostalgia and unhappiness of poets as when the latter were political exiles. Espronceda gave voice to this feeling in his elegy *A la Patria*, well-known lines written during his exile in London:

> ¡Cuán solitaria la nación que un día / poblara inmensa gente!,
> ¡la nación cuyo imperio se extendía / del Ocaso al Oriente!
> Lágrimas viertes, infeliz, ahora, / soberana del mundo,
> y nadie de tu faz encantadora / borra el dolor profundo . . .
> Un tiempo España fue . . .
> Mas ora, como piedra en el desierto, / yaces desamparada,
> y el justo desgraciado vaga incierto / allá en tierra apartada . . .
> Desterrados, ¡oh, Dios! de nuestros lares, / lloremos duelo tanto:
> ¿Quién calmará ¡oh España! tus pesares? / ¿Quién secará tu llanto?[14]

Nevertheless, it could be claimed that such patriotic laments are not Romantic in the strict sense of the term. The 'loss of Spain' had been mourned from the times of Jiménez de Rada in the thirteenth century. Lamentations for the misfortunes of the *patria* had become a literary genre in their own right in the times of the political critics of Felipe II. Distress about Hispanic Cainism are be found from Quevedo to the Generation of 1898; and as for the lament of the exile, it has such a long literary tradition that it goes back as far as Ovid in the time of classical Rome.

In fact, the writers of the school of Spanish Romanticism in the early 1800s had received a classical education. However passionate, the exalted patriotic poetry of the 'War of Independence' was 'a renaissance of contemporary epic poetry' rather than Romanticism.[15] It is interesting to note that there were countless verses written about the glory of Bailén but not about the anti-Napoleonic guerrillas, even though the latter corresponded far better to the Romantic prototype of the social outcast who makes war without conforming to conventional rules and hierarchies. Moreover, the political work of Mártinez de la Rosa and the Duke of Rivas, who produced the Royal Statute of 1834, was a monument to common sense, pragmatism and a limited freedom, totally divorced from any Romantic extremism. As for Larra, although it is true that he radiated intense personal anguish for the ills of the *patria*, he never let that overcome his enlightened political attitudes and preoccupations: he never doubted that the remedy for solving Spanish problems was greater education for both the middle and lower classes. In short, he was a rationalist who believed that Spain should progress towards a way of life and thought typical of the countries that had advanced further down the road to 'progress'.[16] It is from this faith in progress – the inevitable consequence of the spread of education – that all liberal literature derives its invincible optimism without which, incidentally, its support for a political cause would be inconceivable. Larra himself exhibited the solid optimism of the progressive when he wrote that 'in the end, sooner or later, the light of truth finally dissipates the fog with which the supporters of ignorance wish to conceal it, and the strength of opinion . . . is in time more powerful and irresistible'. This has little to do with Romantic desperation; and neither do the lines with which Espronceda concludes his tragic sonnet to the death of Torrijos and his companions: they are actually an incitement to action and a barely veiled promise of final triumph and future vengeance:

> Españoles, llorad; mas vuestro llanto / lágrimas de dolor y sangre sean,
> sangre que ahogue a siervos y opresores. / Y los viles tiranos con espanto
> siempre delante amenazando vean / alzarse sus espectros vengadores.[17]

If we understand Romanticism to be the predominance of 'passion' over reason, there is little of it to be found in the aforementioned texts, and not much throughout the rest of the century. Even before what was known as the 'realist' novel, there were no substantially different features to be found in the writers usually considered as Spanish Romantics.[18] Only Bécquer, Rosalía de Castro, Verdaguer and Maragall, in the second half of the century, wrote in a seriously Romantic vein in their *intimismo*, nostalgia and subjectivism; but they were not openly political writers. To find true distance from positivist rationalism and faith in progress, together with doubts about patriotic virtues, personal sorrow for the tragic destiny of the country, and an escape into intuition, aesthetics and intimate feelings in order to avoid the collapse of so many truths, one must await the Generation of 1898. Only then, in the works of Valle Inclán and Baroja, do we find writers who, from a political point of view, considered the Carlist guerrilla to be interesting as an anti-modern, marginalised and ultimately defeated human being.

There is, however, one element that, though dating from the eighteenth century, can be considered Romantic and is closely connected to our thesis: this is the belief in the new collective subject called the nation, which remained a constant throughout the nineteenth century and continued alive and well among the Generation of 1898. Labelling it Romantic does require an explanation. As well as offering fundamental balance and historical optimism, Enlightened rationalism provided the solid foundations for a *universalist* objectivism whereby conclusions could be reached on the basis of general agreement because reason was the faculty common to all human beings. Romanticism, in contrast, fragmented the foundations of universal knowledge by upholding feeling and intuition as the means for knowledge of reality. Passion, intuition and feelings were, by definition, subjective and different in every individual. Thus truths and values, like beauty, lost their axiomatic and objective character. Politically, this individualistic subjectivism was, in principle, subversive: not only did it lead to demands for artistic freedom from rules and conventional moulds, it also meant that any external imposition on the individual will could be rejected. Romanticism was a potentially libertarian philosophy, a breeding ground for rebels, and it is therefore obvious why it was mistrusted by absolutist regimes even though it hymned an idealised mediaeval world.

Subjectivism can be understood in collective as well as individual terms. The Romantic not only sought truth and beauty in the intimacy of his being, attempting to discover within himself an internal reality impossible to capture through reason, he also sought that reality in that which was primitive, popular and *natural*, not deformed by the artifices of civilisation. Traditional songs and legends were much to the liking of the Romantics because they were spontaneous manifestations of the popular spirit removed from academic constraints. The *Volksgeist* or 'spirit of the people' which inspired them was the intellectual foundation of the political 'I', the *moi commun* or *volonté générale* in which Rousseau believed. However, this collective body differed from that of Rousseau insofar as it was not based on the democratic will of citizens but on a transcendent organic reality far superior to their individual lives. The German Johann Gottlieb Herder expressed it better than anyone: 'nations' were living organisms, creations of the deity, which inevitably mediated between the individual and humanity. Their essential features were to be found in language, a divine gift and the most precious inheritance of each people, and in the historic past, the embodiment of the innate tendencies and aptitudes of each collectivity. The Romantic was not interested in the abstract, aprioristic, essential *Man*, the subject of revolutionary liberal rights, but in the individual being immersed in a given social reality and prevented from realising his destiny outside it. Even when the artist imagined himself to be making an individual work, he was expressing the *Volksgeist*, and only achieved true creativity if he was faithful to the collective genius: the rest was mere imitation lacking in power. The same applied to the citizen, who could only achieve his or her full political potential within the bounds of national reality and by being true to the national way of life as defined by history. Thus one arrived at fatalistic conclusions that were in open contradiction to the subversion implicit in Romantic subjectivism of the individualistic kind. Romanticism provided a philosophical ratification of nationalism, the new demand for loyalty to the State; and this was not a civic or democratic nationalism, but one based upon a collective 'destiny' that denied individuals any free choice or rational life project. It is no coincidence that it was during the Romantic period when the Count de Gobineau wrote *An Essay on the Inequality of the Human Races* which became the basis for modern racism, nor that the fascists later drank so deeply of Romantic sources.

From this perspective, there was undoubtedly political Romanticism in Spain. This should not be interpreted as meaning that Spanish nationalism was the first step along a road leading inevitably to fascism, but that nation-building was based upon concepts that were neither rational, voluntary, democratic nor civic. Every history of art or literature states without hesitation that the Romantics 'sought themes inspired by national history'. It would be more exact to say that

Romantic writers and historians *imagined* reality in national terms, or that they invented or reconstructed history to conform to a national bias. They did not break away from the work of Enlightenment scholars but merely continued and justified it doctrinally, given that the Romantics shared with them their very un-Romantic faith in progress, among many other things.

Creating the national identity in the literary sphere required, first, rounding off the standard version of the history of Spanish literature. This was done by selecting and re-editing the works that would make up the core of national classicism, including for example the various editions of *romanceros* printed from 1815 onwards and, especially, the *Biblioteca de Autores Españoles*. This was a collection of classics launched in 1846 by the Catalans Aribau and Rivadeneyra which became, in the words of Guillermo Carnero, 'an affair of State' as there had been serious parliamentary debate on the need to subsidise it.[19] Once a definitive list of authors had been established, it was divided up into a linear sequence of chapters and these were printed as books of national literary history. So urgent had the need for these become that the relatively limited creative ability of the cultural élites in the country was unable to rise to the occasion and, just like the political histories, the first Spanish literary histories were published outside Spain by the German Friedrich Bouterweck, the Swiss Simone de Sismondi and the American George Ticknor.[20] Finally, and partially as a defensive reaction against the (mis)interpretations of national culture written by Protestants, unable by their very nature to understand it, two histories of Spanish literature were brought out by national authors: one by Antonio Gil y Zárate and the other by José Amador de los Ríos, in 1844 and 1861 respectively. More were to follow by Milá y Fontanals, Menéndez Pelayo and, in the twentieth century, Menéndez Pidal.[21] Although it was not considered the best, it may be that the most influential was the first of these, as Gil y Zárate produced the only university textbook in existence just at the time when the history of Spanish literature became a compulsory subject – partly at his own insistence – in the new curriculum established by the Claudio Moyano Law of 1857; and above all because it laid down the criteria by which to define 'Spanish' literature. These criteria made it possible to assess works, authors and trends as either classics worthy of being taught or merely foreign imports to be consigned to oblivion. This was a logical consequence of Romantic nationalism: art only had creative power when the creator did not imitate but was true to the 'spirit of the people' to which he belonged. Gil y Zárate was not perhaps an acute nor generous critic, but Larra was both and yet he was no less obsessed with the idea that art, in Spain, should be 'Spanish' and he despised translations and imitations because 'only national pride allows nations to set out and succeed in great undertakings'.[22]

As well as writing the standard national literary histories, the Romantics directed their own literary endeavours towards 'national' subjects. While Agustín Durán was editing mediaeval *romances*, which he justified because the *romancero* represented 'the uninterrupted history of the past and the nationality that made it', the Duke of Rivas, Espronceda and Zorrilla were busy composing their own nineteenth-century *romances* because, according to Martínez de la Rosa (taking his cue from the German Romantics), that particular metric form was 'the national poetry of Spain'.[23] Moreover, these *romances* dealt with 'Spanish' themes from the mediaeval and imperial eras. Again, this was not an attempt to write history in order to *understand* the past but rather to *imagine* that past: to *invent* it aesthetically in order to consolidate readers' patriotic feelings. Anachronisms were therefore irrelevant. Although the Duke of Rivas placed his *Don Alvaro* in the sixteenth century, he had soldiers shouting '*Viva España!*' and his captain saying 'Come, let us fight our way through like brave men or die like Spaniards!', both of which are inappropriate for that period. More serious is the distortion in his *romance* entitled *Un castellano leal*, in which he describes the repugnance felt by the Count of Benavente when given an imperial order to provide lodging for the Duke of Bourbon, who had engineered the victory at Pavia by defecting from the 'French' army to the 'Spanish' one. The Count obeys the Emperor – or King, given the emphasis placed on the Spanish symbols that surround him – but goes on to restore his honour by setting fire to his own palace. Rivas was not only upholding chivalrous ideals, for which he had a great weakness; he was also elevating national sentiment because the Duke of Bourbon, over and above his betrayal of personal or family commitments – the ultimate felony for a noble of the sixteenth century – had betrayed 'France', the supremely dishonourable act for a European citizen of the nineteenth century.

The direct transmission of patriotic values was not, however, the main aim of these writers and neither did they, like the historians, make the nation the central figure of their work. The heroes of their tragedies and novels were exceptional individuals, valiant knights or unhappy lovers whose lives did, however, unfold within a 'Spanish' historical setting. This was the main contribution of literature to the creation of the national identity: imagining the background to *our* past, describing the scenarios and putting words into the mouths of *our* ancestors. Novels and plays were more successful than poetry in this endeavour.

The historical novel first saw the light in 1830, the year in which the government relaxed its controls and allowed into Spain the first translations of Madame de Staël and Walter Scott. Ramón López Soler then published *Los bandos de Castilla*, a work that unleashed a veritable flood of others including, to name just a few, *La conquista de Valencia por el Cid* by Kosca Vayo; *El doncel de D. Enrique el Doliente* by Larra; *Sancho Saldaña* by Espronceda; *Ni rey ni roque* by Escosura; *Doña Isabel de Solís, reina de Granada* by Martínez de la Rosa; *Cristianos y moriscos* by Estébanez Calderón; *El señor de Bembibre* by Gil y Carrasco in 1844 and, later, *El Pastelero de Madrigal* by Manuel Fernández y González. It was in the second half of the century, and on into the twentieth, that the great novelistic historical creation of the *Episodios Nacionales* by Benito Pérez Galdós would be published, but these stand in a category of their own and will be discussed later.[24]

The theatrical season of 1834–1835 saw the triumph of the first plays by the Duke of Rivas and Larra. In subsequent years, the major playwrights were García Gutiérrez (*El Trovador, Juan Lorenzo, Venganza catalana*), Hartzenbusch (*Los amantes de Teruel, La jura de Santa Gadea, La madre de Pelayo*), the playwright as well as literary historian Gil y Zárate (*Carlos II el Hechizado, Guzmán el Bueno, Don Alvaro de Luna, El Gran Capitán*) and, after 1850, Tamayo y Baus (*Locura de amor*) and the prolific Fernández y González, both dramatist and novelist. By 1870, Romanticism had completed its task of inventing the historical past as 'Spanish' in exactly the terms required by the national identity. At this point, mention should be made of Romanticism's greatest proponent, José Zorrilla. He was a poet and dramatist with an 'astonishing ability to versify', somewhat superficial and colourful but undeniably gifted. He was also, and was clearly aware of being, the 'only, the true national poet', the man who embodied Spain in the same way that Victor Hugo embodied France. He made the greatest contribution to spreading an image of the past in 'Spanish' national terms and can realistically be called the creator of national historical drama. Almost all of his tragedies, 'Legends' and historical poems deal with themes or historical settings that are 'Spanish'. The tragedies include *El rey loco*, about the Visigoth Wamba; *El puñal del godo*, on the defeat of the Goths by the Moors; *El zapatero y el rey*, about Don Pedro the Cruel; *El alcalde Ronquillo*, on the *comuneros; Traidor, inconfeso y mártir*, on Portuguese political Sebastianism; *Sancho García*, on Castile in the eleventh century; and *Don Juan Tenorio*, set against a military background in the times of Carlos V. Zorrilla once admitted to 'Speak in Castilian, die a Spaniard' and, in the introduction to his *Cantos del trovador*, he made this patriotic statement:

Mi voz, mi razón, mi fantasía / la gloria cantan de la patria mía . . .
Venid, yo no hollaré con mis cantares / Del pueblo en que he nacido la
    creencia;
Respetaré su ley y sus altares. / En su desgracia a par que en su
    opulencia
Celebraré su fuerza o sus azares, / Y fiel ministro de la gaya ciencia,
Levantaré mi voz consoladora, / Sobre las ruinas en que España llora.[25]

Many years later, even those who pointed out Zorrilla's defects such
as 'pomp, harmony, liking for . . . glitter rather than profundity' recognised that these were nonetheless 'the very defects of the Spanish
race'.[26]

And defects Zorrilla did indeed have. As a poet, the critics recognise
his 'frequent lapses into verbosity and decorative cliché'. They also
agreed about his conformism and moral superficiality, evident in the
happy ending that he tacks onto the drama of the diabolical Don Juan
Tenorio. Parallel with his tendency to accept conventional and acritical versions of great literary themes is his lack of scruples in adapting
the historical past to national coordinates. The best example of this
is perhaps *El puñal del godo*, a one-act tragedy based on the much
lamented 'loss of Spain' after the Moorish invasion. The action takes
place in a hermit's cave on an isolated Portuguese mountain where a
mysterious, tormented individual, who turns out to be none other than
the last Visigothic king, Don Rodrigo, has sought refuge. Theudia, a
Visigothic noble who has fled Muslim dominions appears on the very
anniversary of the defeat at Guadalete (*día de hiel, / de luto y baldón y
saña, / para la infeliz España*'). 'A bitter day' comments Theudia, ' it is
for me too' replies the king in disguise, ' and for every Spaniard / it will
be for as long as the sun / shines'. Judging by these lines, Zorrilla has
no hesitation in crediting the Visigoths with a sense of 'Spanishness'
and, furthermore, he believes it is eternal. After commiserating on the
harshness of destiny, the noble asks his companion if he is Portuguese,
giving us to understand that, in that case, he has nothing to do with the
drama unfolding between Visigoths and Moors. There is no question
that they are in a foreign land and, like a good king in exile, Rodrigo
asks for information about the Spanish situation: 'Does the Hispanic
people still preserve / any memory of past glory?' Theudia tells him that
Spain is 'prey to a savage people / to whom it pays homage, / and who
devastate and destroy it'. The 'savagery' is, of course, a nineteenth-
century concept, and it is pure invention – also typical of the nineteenth
century – to raise the Visigoths to a level of 'civilisation' superior to
that of the Muslims. Zorrilla certainly never missed an opportunity to
express his conservatism and rescues the honour of the aristocracy in

a couple of lines: the nobles 'all perished / at the hands of the Moors one by one'. The ex-king, his identity revealed to Theudia, asks him: 'Is there nothing left?' 'A corner of Asturias, where those who escaped / from that terrible defeat are come together' and where 'your brave cousin, Don Pelayo' has raised his standard. Thus the dramatist adopts the mediaeval tradition that conferred Visigothic legitimacy on the Asturian dynasty. Don Rodrigo then decides to abandon 'his sackcloth and ashes' and to go and 'fight for our Spain / and triumph or fall with Don Pelayo'. The tragedy ends with the arrival at the cave of the infamous Count Don Julián, whom Theudia had been pursuing (to take revenge, he tells us, 'on behalf of my *patria*'). Don Rodrigo recognises him and reproaches his betrayal, and the Count in turn accuses the king of 'lewdness', alluding to the legendary rape of *la Cava*. 'Dishonoured by you, I lost everything', admits Don Julián. He now wanted revenge by 'wiping out your race from among the nations'. They begin to fight but Theudia intervenes in time, snatches the dagger from Don Julián, and kills him. 'By avenging you, I avenged Spain'. Don Rodrigo leaves with Theudia to 'die as good men of our *patria*'. They mention that 'Portugal will give us free passage, as she gave us shelter', confirming how far removed Portugal is from the Moorish invasion of the Visigothic kingdom.

With Zorrilla, this Romantic reconstruction of the past in 'Spanish' terms reaches its height. The quintessential idea is that since the dawn of time Spain has existed in essence all on its own without, for example, Portugal. Yet it was not even Spain's physical borders that were most important to these authors but its moral traits, described in very conventional terms to make them acceptable to the vast majority of recipients of the nationalistic message. Writers offered little that was new in their descriptions of the patriotic character. Above all, they emphasised the warlike spirit of the *race*, or rather its reckless courage based on an absolute contempt for death, allied to a noble attitude towards life expressed through a sense of honour and pride in lineage. That weight of nobility fused with an unblemished monarchism was born, it would appear, of those kings who had led their troops into battle during the Reconquest.[27] In short, the Spanish character comprised a martial spirit, noble sentiments and support for the monarchy combined with deep religiosity. This religiosity was the result, like so many other things, of centuries of war against Islam, and which Zorrilla, like Gil y Zárate and the conservative nationalism identified with Catholicism which will be analysed in coming chapters, did not hesitate to interpret as ideological.

Regardless of their political sympathies, almost all the Romantic poets and playwrights idealised the Middle Ages. Zorrilla synthesises the shared clichés when he writes in his *Leyenda* entitled 'The wild white lily', that they were 'simple times' of 'pleasant memory', an age governed by 'glory and love', an age of prodigies and of great deeds, which we, 'beings without ideals', call fables. Thus the Middle Ages are represented as the supreme era of chivalry, of unanimous Christian, and fundamentally Castilian, religiosity. This latter trait is not always explicit or even generalised, but neither is it exclusive to the most conservative authors. Romantic interest in the regional did not usually extend beyond a sentimental attraction to the retrospective and picturesque, without questioning the benefits of centralisation. It was yet another consequence of the progress in which these curious Romantics had such confidence.

Another obligatory distortion was the disappearance of anything Moorish from *españolista* mythology. However much the Middle Ages were the preferred period of the Romantics in which to locate their works, they firmly believed that only what was Catholic was 'Spanish' within that era. It was only with considerable effort that they were able to incorporate the Eastern stereotype that international Romanticism projected onto Spain. But they were forced to adapt. Martínez de la Rosa, in spite of having devoted himself to literature since he was a young man, remained unknown in exile until he achieved international recognition with the première in Paris of *Aben Humeya*, a tragedy with a Moorish theme. It was also during his years in exile that the Duke of Rivas wrote *Moro expósito*. This was clearly what the international market expected of Spanish writers. After the death of Fernando VII, and the return from exile and subsequent success of the Spanish Romantics in the mid-1830s, they would always introduce an Eastern touch into their recreations of the mediaeval period; but these would only be on a superficial level, such as references to Córdoba and Granada, and in particular references to the noble bearing of the characters and the ceremonious language that was supposed to derive from the Arab world.

A final aspect missing from this idealised mediaeval world was any element of femininity. However much Zorrilla might profess a true 'worship of women' – which he claimed was an essentially Christian trait – honour was an essentially masculine virtue and women only felt its effects through 'gallantry'. The Spanish Romantics paid true homage to men. From the political angle, which interests us here, it is astonishing how insistently the national essence was described as *virile*, brute, strong or healthy as compared to the European *effeminacy* of the time, reflected in the taste for refinement, luxury and sophisticated entertainment. A prime example is Espronceda's 'Canto del cosaco' in which he describes 'degenerate' Europe with its

gente opulenta, afeminada ya. / Son sus soldados menos que mujeres.
Sus reyes viles mercaderes son. / Vedlos huir para esconder su oro.

It is a *virility* whose political significance should not be overlooked: it meant the resolution of conflict by violence; a violence linked by Romanticism to racial enthusiasm, which inclined the Spanish to draw their swords rather than to negotiate.[28]

In this way, the Spanish identity defined by the Romantics ties in with the aggressive racial nationalism of imperialist Europe in the second half of the nineteenth century. By that time, 'race' was a term that had entered the political vocabulary: to Quintana, Spaniards were a 'race of heroes', and to Zorrilla, a 'race of brave men'. The old obsession of Counter-Reformation Spain with untainted bloodlines was to be revived in the heat of the new racist theories of the mid-nineteenth century. And both the old racism and the new racism could easily be confused with simple, old-fashioned xenophobia. The Duke of Rivas, for example, increased the tone of aggressive nationalism in his historical romances as the years went by: his poems to the 'Spanish' military victories of the sixteenth century were inspired, according to him, by the purest of ideals – defence of the faith and the disinterested pursuit of martial glory – while Spain's European rivals were heretics, forerunners of the 'merchants' of the degenerate modern world. Both Rivas and Zorrilla particularly detested France, as had the anti-Enlightenment circles of the eighteenth century. It was as if France were the 'other', that threatening, aggressive neighbour which had been used so successfully by the nationalists everywhere to unite the community behind them. It is true that there was good reason to fear France when her armies had laid waste to Europe on Napoleon's orders, and they had crossed into Spain three times between 1794 and 1823, but Zorrilla was not referring to this when, to the very end of his days, he compared the loyalty of the 'Spanish lions' with the innate disloyalty of the Gauls; neither did Angel de Saavedra have any reason to continually allude to French treachery when he had spent a large part of his life on the other side of the border.[29] Bellicose nationalism constitutes part of the political conservatism of both writers; and xenophobia and, ultimately, racism were the logical conclusion to the Romantic vision of the political world, divided into ethnic units that were differentiated not only by physical features but by psychological and moral ones as well.

Thus the last generation of Romantics engineered a fundamental change in the national image: namely, to purge it of the excessively liberal orientation that this imaginary community had had at the outset by placing it above political rivalries, while incorporating a sufficient number of conservative features into this imagined community in order to make it acceptable to the majority of citizens. Its lack of acceptability had been its main problem in the first half of the century: the past that was idealised by politicians, historians and writers had been presented in almost exclusively liberal terms in accordance with the vision of progress and modernity advocated by the constitutionalists and feared by large sectors of public opinion. In *La viuda de Padilla*, for example, the young Martínez de la Rosa claimed that he wanted to write 'a history of my nation' but he had his main character say: 'Fortunate, for they died for the *patria*. Free, they lived, free, they died'. In the same way, Quintana wanted to portray a national hero in his *Don Pelayo*, but once again his intention, which alienated so many of his readers, is obvious when his main character says that he wants to fight to 'found another Spain and another *Patria* / greater and happier than the first'.[30] It was necessary to curb those paeans to freedom, political participation and religious co-existence if the Romantics wished to become national writers. That was essentially what happened in the mid-nineteenth century, in the years when political power was in the hands of the '*moderados*', the Duke of Rivas was President of the Royal Academy, and Zorrilla was acclaimed on the stage.

Towards the end of his life, José Zorrilla was proclaimed 'national poet'. Only Quintana before him had merited such an exalted high honour. The political differences between the two are a clear indication of the evolution in academic literature. Quintana became the national poet because he identified the nation with liberal constitutionalism. Fifty years on, Zorrilla was similarly honoured for the opposite reason: he had reclaimed chivalrous, Catholic, monarchic Spain.

Historical painting portrays the patriotic heroes in the flesh

The nineteenth century was the golden age of what is known as 'historical painting'. This was no coincidence because painting was another of the privileged cultural spheres that contributed to national image-building. However, this was not 'historical' painting in general terms, like the genre of earlier times that had produced so much to illustrate episodes in Greco-Roman or religious history. The 'historical painting' of the nineteenth century concentrated on *national* historical scenes, and such was its degree of success that the very expression has since come to be associated with this restricted meaning.

Like the literature and the history, historico-national painting originated in the eighteenth century, with which it is often assumed, erroneously, that the nineteenth had made a radical break. The rupture had actually occurred with the earlier period of 1500–1700, when political painting had been devoted to glorifying the dynastic houses on vast canvases or in frescoes, to be admired by all those who had access to the palaces. Even at that early stage, a certain connection was being made between the reigning family and the kings whom mythology located in Hispania or the Roman emperors born in Baetica. However, these were no more than pale forerunners of what the eighteenth century would bring. The Royal Academy of Fine Arts of San Fernando, founded in 1752, was created for the purpose of encouraging artistic and intellectual activities that were also deployed in the patriotic cause, as were the Royal Spanish Academy and the Royal Academy of History. To this end, painting and sculpture competitions were announced in which 'Spanish' historical themes began to upstage the traditional mythological or allegorical, and eventually religious, ones. Nevertheless, it was never going to be easy to eliminate such a deep-rooted tradition as that of representing great human acts of a 'moral and exemplary nature' in abstract terms.[31]

Within a century of the founding of the Academy, the step from abstract-allegorical to historico-national painting was complete. That period had seen painting reach new heights, with the two extraordinary pictures painted by Goya of the uprising against the French invader in Madrid on the Second of May 1808 and the executions by the French firing squad the next day, often considered to be the forerunners of a new kind of historical painting. Pictures of history were, according to the renowned art critic Pérez Sánchez, 'absolutely new' but he adds that Goya 'could not be understood' in his own time. They were in fact so new and so difficult to comprehend that it is debatable whether they can be included in this genre of national history in the same way as other works that became established in the following decades. Goya, although he enshrined the rebellious populace in the central figure shot in the *Dos de Mayo*, still reflected the brutality of all those involved in the struggle, and was horrified by these acts of war, just as he was when he went on to do his series 'The Disasters of War'. There were other paintings from these years, however, that did glorify patriotic heroism in such a manner as to account for the proliferation of this genre after 1850: Viriathus, Wamba, Pelayo, San Fernando and the Catholic Kings became increasingly popular at the expense not only of Scipio, Lucretia and Cincinnatus but also of the infinite number of saints and virgins who had inspired Hispanic painters in earlier centuries.[32]

For once, a precise date can be given as to when a genre began its rapid rise to popularity: 1856, the year of the first National Exhibition held by the Royal Academy of San Fernando. First prize was awarded to Luis Madrazo for his *Don Pelayo en Covadonga*, and the competition was such a success that it continued to held every two years. Instead of allowing a free choice of subject matter, the Exhibition took its 'National' epithet very seriously and openly encouraged the presentation of entries that exalted patriotic history. During the rest of the century, more than half the prize-winning paintings were historical, whether based on themes put forward by the Academy, taken from the mediaeval *romancero*, the 'History of Spain' by Padre Mariana or the recently published work by Modesto Lafuente. The prize money told its own story: the first prize in History received 90,000 *reales* compared with 37,000 *reales* for the first in genre, the 35,000 for the best religious painting and 17,000 for that in landscapes.[33] Given such incentives and in view of the *historicist* climate predominant in European painting as well – it should not be forgotten that historicism meant nationalistic exaltation – it is not surprising that over the next four decades the market was flooded with historico-patriotic pictures.

Experts tend to classify this kind of painting as academically inspired, eclectic in style and average in quality. None of this is to its detriment, from the point of view of nationalistic painting, as it is not unreasonable to suppose that, had it been more creative in the manner of the impressionists and the avant-garde artists of later generations, it would have been less comprehensible and therefore less efficient in the fulfilment of its mission. The objective is to assess these pictorial productions in terms of their political significance which is, in fact, what lent them importance in their own day as well. Both critics and the general public coincided in judging the pictures for their patriotic content rather than for their artistic skill. In 1881, the art critic Jacinto Octavio Picón claimed that the importance of a historical painting lay in what it represented, which needed to be always 'a deed of capital importance for a country or a race'.[34]

In conclusion, the function of these pictures was both political and educational. As another critic wrote in 1862, just when interest in this field was beginning to grow, 'a picture represents a famous deed and popularises and conveys it with greater ease than any other genre . . . What a high and noble enterprise it would be to perpetuate the history of the *patria* in great paintings. It would inspire artists to new heights and, once accomplished, would be a fitting medium for our people to receive encouragement in virtue and glory and punishment lessons'. These moral lessons were so important that they could not be restricted to the few who viewed the pictures *in situ*, or those who read about them in the press; they should be conveyed by means of engravings which, around this time, began to be included in history books and illustrated magazines like the *Semanario Pintoresco Español*, *El Museo Universal* and *La Ilustración Española y Americana*. In 1871, a revolutionary moment, the daily *La Discusión* campaigned for the magazine illustrations of the National Exhibition of that year to be sent free to 'as many libraries, athenaeums, clubs, circles, *tertulias* and cafés as desire them . . . that there be no village, however small . . . where the productions of our young painters and sculptors should go unrecognised'.[35] The possessive *our* is undoubtedly the most important word in the sentence: *our* artists imagining *our* past, which, when reproduced by the illustrated press, should be transmitted to citizens to make them truly *ours*.

One major difference between historico-national literature and history on the one hand and painting on the other is that the latter was overwhelmingly official in origin: as well as the competitions held by the Royal Academy, both houses of parliament – Congress and the Senate – the Crown itself, and even local institutions such as the provincial *diputaciones*, commissioned works and exhibited paintings on the walls of their palaces. The educated middle classes were not buying and hanging pictures in their libraries in the same manner in which they bought history books or romantic sagas, or went to the theatre to view historical tragedies. This was an officially inspired phenomenon, with *public* money being spent on painting. To some extent, the public funding restricts the significance of the paintings but adds to their value precisely because they express the vision that the State had of the nation; it reflects on official efforts to nationalise culture.[36]

Another difference between literary and pictorial Romanticism is that the former stressed private histories and heroes against the background of a national past whereas in painting, as in history, the leading figure was, directly, the nation itself. And it was no longer represented in an allegorical way as was the case with classicism, but personified by kings, heroes and martyrs. On occasion, the collectivity itself appears in a more direct manner, as in the *Don Pelayo en Covadonga* which won Luis Madrazo First Prize in the first National Exhibition: the hero is accompanied by a high-ranking ecclesiastical figure on a rock holding up a cross, and in the lower part of the painting appears a group of soldiers and villagers in various attitudes of patriotic praise, among which an austere and decidedly feminine figure on the left stands out, easily interpreted as Spain herself.[37] Even though this was still the Romantic era, it was the exception for a historical painting to tell a private story, although one that did was *Los Amantes de Teruel* painted by Muñoz Degrain in 1884. Even the nobility had no substantial role, although one imagines that the noble houses commissioned paintings that extolled the great deeds of their ancestors. This is an area requiring further investigation: there may be more works than we are presently aware of. If not, this highlights both the secondary role of the aristocracy and the need for political imagery to revolve around a single entity: the nation.

These two differences aside, there are no aspects of this pictorial production that differ from the themes and focus of history and literature. Historical paintings tell us nothing new about the characteristics of the Spanish personality: individuals were warlike, Catholic and chivalrous; the collectivity featured unity, liberty and independence; and the monarchy played an overwhelming role. The chosen subjects for transmitting this message were equally predictable: Saguntum, Numantia, Viriathus, Hermenegildo, Recaredo, Don Pelayo, El Cid, the battle of Las Navas de Tolosa, Fernando el Santo, Jaime the Conqueror, Roger de Flor, Guzmán el Bueno, the surrender of Granada, the Catholic Kings – especially Isabel – Boabdil, Columbus, el Gran Capitán, Cisneros, Juana la Loca, Carlos V and Felipe II.[38] There had never been any representations of many of these figures until the second half of the nineteenth century when historical painting became fashionable, and some of them were wholly mythical figures such as the Apostle St James, whose features the artist had no problem in inventing when portraying his intervention at the battle of Clavijo. From that moment on, not only St James but all of these figures were personified, thanks to the daring of the painters. While literature had put words into the mouths of *our* ancestors, painting gave them shape and colour and imagined them in visible form. It facilitated the fantasies of *our* past, but in a far from impartial way. In so doing, it transformed them into the predecessors of the contemporary nation-State, as well as *ennobling* the characteristics of the individual in what was, incidentally, an impersonal and predictable way (there can be no comparison with the classical and mythological heroes painted by Velázquez or Ribera, who had the audacity to imagine them as popular figures); finally, and perhaps most importantly, it dressed up this ideal entity on which the legitimacy of the State was based in what appeared to be a generally accepted system of values but which were actually *religious, monarchic* and *martial*. It is noteworthy, for example, that these artists made no attempt to represent the cultural or intellectual achievements of the nation. Admittedly, this could be for aesthetic reasons: Cervantes, Quevedo and Huarte de San Juan are less thrilling subjects than el Gran Capitán or Don Juan de Austria. Nevertheless, it is surprising that a professional artist would feel no inclination to depict Velázquez in action or Murillo in his studio.[39]

Perhaps because it belonged to a later period, painting continued to maintain its ideological polarisation for longer than literature. The controversial depiction of the *Comuneros* in the paintings by Antonio Gisbert in 1860 has already been mentioned, this being a key element in the liberal version of the destruction of Spanish liberties by absolutism. Antonio Pérez and Juan de la Lanuza, other martyrs of royal despotism, also came in for artistic attention. Episodes that reflected badly on the image of the absolute monarchs were only tackled by artists with liberal leanings. These included the expulsions of the Jews and the Moors, the sack of Rome by the troops of Carlos V, Felipe II and the story of his son Prince Don Carlos, who was to become a great European liberal hero at the hands of Schiller and Verdi.[40] The same Gisbert who personified the *Comunero* leaders was one of those willing to take on the subject of Don Carlos and, much later, in 1888, would also paint the execution of Torrijos and his fellow liberal insurgents by the absolutist monarchy. Faced with this *progresista* expression of the national past, the conservatives retaliated: the *Partido Moderado* declared its preference for Casado del Alisal, the very artist who had snatched first prize from Gisbert in the Exhibition of 1860 with *The final moments of Don Fernando IV the Summoned*, a work illustrating a case of divine punishment for the sins of kings. Shortly afterwards, with *The Surrender of Bailén*, the same artist was to portray contemporary national glories in the barely disguised style of Velázquez.

However, even liberal historical myths could not eliminate the greatest of the Hapsburgs from any representation of the national past, for theirs had been the most splendid period of history for several centuries. It would have been possible to avoid underlining the more human aspects of Carlos V, such as his retirement to Yuste; but it was this which proved most useful in highlighting his '*españolismo*'. Other subject matter of a more critical but undeniably spectacular and/or romantic nature could have been chosen, such as the autos-da-fé of the Inquisition, racial persecution or scenes from the conquest of America, and it is true that the American Empire is to be found more frequently in painting, due no doubt to the colour and spectacle, than in the history books or creative writing, but scenes portray the discovery rather than the conquest.[41] Even liberal historical painting avoided a critical vision of the past that could be interpreted as favourable to what later became known as the *Leyenda Negra*, considered to be anti-Spanish. The struggle between liberals and conservatives continued, but the former were lacking in the aggressive confidence that had inspired them during the first half of the century and, above all, they were not willing to damage the national image in the context of a highly competitive Europe.

Spanish painting and foreign painting on Spain within the same period were vastly different. While native painters were inventing scenes of the Visigoths (long-forgotten by everyone else) or of insignificant anecdotes from mediaeval Christian kingdoms, foreigners were painting scenes of Moorish figures and bullfighting, bandits and executions by the *garrote vil*, friars and *señoritas*. Both were a distortion of reality but orientated in opposite directions. Those who were building up a *Spanish* image from within focused on Catholicism and the fight to overcome Saracen invaders, while European Romanticism was intent upon emphasising the *oriental* features of the Spanish stereotype.

The great age of historical painting begun in 1856 was over by 1892. The *Y aún dicen que el pescado es caro* ('And they still say that fish is expensive') by Sorolla, and *Una desgracia* (A Misfortune') by Jiménez Aranda, which appeared in 1890 and 1892 respectively, were symptomatic of the new pictorial sensibility based on social issues. Like the influence of Zola in literature, the artistic influence of Courbet inspired *realism* in art. At the turn of the century, the avant-garde suddenly lost interest in national historical painting.

However, the reappraisal of what was 'Spanish' painting and art went on apace as the first histories of art came to be written, which were similar to the earlier histories of literature and politics. In the 1880s, Bartolomé J. Cossío, a pioneer in this field, explained that 'only works that carry the national stamp, that show distinctive features of the genius of this country', could be considered 'Spanish painting'. Members of the Generation of 1898 like Ángel Ganivet also believed that 'a masterpiece of art ... regardless of its author's purpose ... contains a meaning that could be called historic, concordant with national history'. Ramiro de Maeztu, believed that painting was the pre-eminent talent of the 'Spanish race'. Well into the twentieth century, Rafael Doménech wrote in his *El nacionalismo en el arte* that, though recognising that nations were difficult to define, he did not doubt 'the existence, over time, of a creative force within a specific community of men' and that there was a profound connection between 'style' and 'nationalism'. 'To study a nation' – he went on – 'one must begin with the period in which its life is fully defined, differentiating it not only from other human unions, but from all other nationalities'. Some years later Manuel Gómez Moreno and shortly afterwards Emilio Lafuente Ferrari were to go back no less than ten centuries to identify 'the first works that could in all justice be said to initiate the history of Spanish painting of a fully national character', which they claimed were miniatures by Mozarabic *beatos*. Moreno wrote that 'Spain became a nation in the period between 850 and 1030', while Ferrari explained that this occurred immediately after the 'historic catastrophe' of the 'Muslim invasion' and shortly after the legal and religious fusion achieved by the Visigoths, 'which would undoubtedly have been factors in the development of national feeling earlier than in other countries of Europe'. The illuminated codices should be considered 'as a Spanish, national artistic product'; they were the 'first chapter in Spanish art, in the full sense of the word'. For these art historians, who introduced political judgements with such alarming ease, the culmination of national painting had been reached in the seventeenth century with the Castilian and Andalusian schools (and particularly Ribalta, the prototype of Spanish realism, who was characterised, according to Elías Tormo, by 'that particular harshness, that honesty, that virile something, a little dishevelled, but vital . . .', and by a curious coincidence with the 'rude virility' that Camón Aznar discovered in the textures of Zurbarán, 'a racial painter because he paints the race'). The painter whom all agreed to have been supremely Spanish – with complete disregard for his origins – was El Greco, and opinion was also unanimous in labelling as anti-Spanish the art of the eighteenth century when 'the Bourbons, with no contact with nor love for Spanish tradition, brought foreign artists to their court . . . The few Spaniards who remained in contact with official art became the satellites of the stars, very often not as brilliant as the kings and their contemporaries believed'. Thus did art critics and historians add their grain of sand to this 'retrospective nationalisation' of painting.[42]

The paintings produced between 1856 and 1892 went on to enjoy a long career as illustrations for school textbooks. In later times of intense nationalisation, such as during the dictatorship of Primo de Rivera (1923–1930), they would be reproduced in other popular media such as postcards and postage stamps, commercial calendars and wrappings for the festive sweet of *turrón*. In the early years of Francoism, the modern media, particularly film, continued to faithfully reproduce these images, and eventually they became an indelible part of the imagery of the *Spanish past*.

In search of national music: 'Deliberate "alhambrismo"'

Some European countries that were undergoing the process of nation-building during the nineteenth century, such as Germany and Italy, enjoyed hugely successful cultural support from the world of music. By comparison, music with a national significance appeared remarkably late in Spain, bearing in mind the Romantic association between Spanish culture and innate musical sense. Musical creativity had been in manifest decline for a long time, since the great Renaissance period associated with Tomás Luis de Victoria, Félix Antonio de Cabezón and Francisco Salinas. Throughout the eighteenth century, the music of the court had been imported: the composers agreeable to the Bourbons had been Scarlatti and Boccherini, just as their artists had been Mengs and Tiepolo, but this had ruffled no feathers at the time, any more than did the fact that the royal bodyguards were Walloons and the royal family spoke French or Italian. With the advent of nationalism, however, the lack of home-grown music was felt to be a humiliation, although in response there was no overnight renewal of musical creativity among native composers. Of the 131 operas that had their début in the Royal Theatre during the nineteenth century, only 16 were Spanish, and of these, many of the librettos were in Italian (such as *L'ultimo Abenzerraggio* by Felipe Pedrell). The outcry began in the 1830s, just as Romantic nationalism was beginning to prevail in the theatre and the novel. In 1835, the musical publication *El Artista* complained that 'we have no musical genre of our own . . . is it not shameful that the Italians, the Germans, the French, the English and even the Russians have a national opera, and that we do not?'[43] It is indicative that this complaint is not about a lack of quality but the absence of indigenous music, and that the institution with which the comparison is made is so openly nationalistic and hierarchical: *even the Russians*, considered to be the least European, had something that *we* lacked. Of course, music composed in other European cultural centres – particularly Italy – continued to be enjoyed, but it was experienced as 'dependence' or even as a foreign cultural 'invasion'. The second half of the nineteenth century was dominated by an awareness that it was essential to escape from such a painful situation of inferiority and to 'restore' Spanish music or, to be precise, to create a 'national opera'.

The attempts at 'restoration' began around 1850 thanks to the efforts of composers such as Hilarión Eslava, Soriano, Gaztambide and Barbieri. They all tried to compose works that would overcome cultural dependence through the discovery of a 'Spanish essence', or genuinely national characteristic that would give meaning to their music. As a music critic explained in 1873, this differentiating characteristic had to be found in the 'elements that constitute our way of life and our own nationality'; in other words, in 'the history of the *patria*, its language, its early theatre, its traditions and customs, popular songs and dances, national anthems and marches'. Common to all these composers was their dedication to opera (considered to be 'the great unresolved subject of debate of the nineteenth century' by Casares y Alonso), usually based on themes from national history.[44]

But the years went by with no outstanding successes and the sense of deprivation became intolerable. In 1875, the journal *La Opera Española* was founded, and in its first edition declared: 'The hour has come for Spanish opera to cease to be a myth or a pretext for meetings and discussions by charlatans and blusterers', who, instead of working 'for the good of such a patriotic and uplifting enterprise', made of it 'a medium that should not survive by relying on public charity'. The publication declared its aim of working on behalf of a true Spanish opera, 'relying on the moral cooperation of all those who love the glories of our *patria*', and, as the same journal made clear, it was to be opera 'written by Spanish maestros and sung in the Castilian language'. In 1876, Baltasar Saldoni proposed that a bill be presented in the Cortes for the founding of a 'national opera' in Spain. Five years later, the music and bullfighting critic Peña y Goñi was still asking: 'Does Spanish opera exist? No, Spanish opera does not exist, it has never existed'. It is true that there were, in these decades, several serious attempts staged by the Teatro Real. One of these, *El príncipe de Viana* by Capdepón, first performed in 1885, caused a debate over the essence of the national lyrical genre, in which Bretón and Peña y Goñi himself took part. In the same year, in a long article entitled 'Más en favor de la ópera nacional', Bretón tried to convince other writers to use the Castilian language, 'as beautiful, simple and rich for singing as any other' (as 'its wonderful literature' proved). In spite of all these declarations and good intentions, a high-flying national opera still failed to emerge.

Song was yet another sphere in which a creative identity was sought. The main theorist and advocate was the Catalan Felipe Pedrell, who published a *Cancionero musical popular español* (Popular Spanish Musical Songbook) and the album *Noches de España*, the very titles of which expressed his concern with identifying a *Spanish* musical identity. In 1891, Pedrell went on to publish a manifesto called 'For our music: Some observations on the vital question of a national school for lyric-writing', in which he again blamed the lack of truly Spanish song on the blind imitation of the Italians, leading to a superficial picturesqueness (*pintoresquismo*). He felt that, like the German lied, great Hispanic song should be based upon popular songs, internalising the 'natural music' of the nation. Towards the end of the century, there was composed a type of song of Germano-Andalusian inspiration which has been dubbed 'salon populism' (the equivalent in music to the literature of Fernán Caballero), an example of which is the collection *Orientales*, based on texts by Victor Hugo and published in 1876. There were other songwriters who tried to imitate the more refined, intimate and melancholy French *mélodie*, similar in style to the literature of Bécquer. However, no great Spanish Romantic music was ever composed. What did prove successful in mid-century were popular *regionalist* melodies. Pedrell wrote many lieder in Catalan as well as composing music for the work *Los Pirineos* by Balaguer. Most important in Catalonia was the work of Josep Anselm Clavé, composer and conductor of the popular choirs of the Orfeó Catalá. These choirs led to a raising of what was then only *regionalist* awareness in Barcelona, as well as in Bilbao, San Sebastián, Pamplona and even Galicia; that this local awareness was integrated without difficulty into *españolismo* is demonstrated by the fact that one of the best-known productions by Clavé was *Gloria a España*. Nevertheless, these cultural networks would also merge easily with the peripheral nationalisms when these came into being after 1898: one example from the First World War years was *Diez melodías vascas* by Jesús Guridi.

There was, nevertheless, one style of music of definably Spanish origin and originality. Known as the *género chico*, it is a genre that includes not only music but any short theatrical performance such as a revue, cabaret, farce and, in a class of its own, the *zarzuela*. The latter dated back to the theatrical spectacles with musical parts performed at the royal hunting lodge called *La Zarzuela* since the seventeenth century. This traditional music had almost disappeared when, in the last quarter of the nineteenth century, works by Barbieri (*Pan y toros*, *El barberillo de Lavapiés*), Chueca (*La canción de Lola*, *Agua, azucarillos y aguardiente*, *La Gran Vía*), Bretón (*La verbena de la Paloma*) and Chapí (*La revoltosa*, *El rey que rabió*, *El tambor de granaderos*) took the world by storm. Although some of these writers also composed operas, they never achieved the same level of success compared to that of their *zarzuelas*,[45] and it is significant that the most popular of all, Federico Chueca, was probably the one with the least technical sophistication. The popularity of the *zarzuela* continued well into the twentieth century, with *Las bodas de Luis Alonso* by Jiménez and *Doña Francisquita* by Vives. During the Second Republic, *Luisa Fernanda* by Moreno Torroba and *Katiuska* by Sorozábal, the latter against the background of the Russian Revolution, were also highly successful.

The *género chico* was essentially a product of Madrid (no less than 'one of the unconscious forces of centralisation', according to Antonio Valencia). Not only was Madrid the centre of production, but the whole atmosphere of these works, and even the subject matter of many, was redolent of the capital. In contrast to literary or pictorial creations, and even opera or the earlier *zarzuela grande*, the action unfolding in the *zarzuela* was contemporary and its characters were recognisably local, everyday types. Although it was merely entertainment with basically non-political satire, inevitably there were some political references, yet these expressed what were thought to be essentially conservative opinions of consensus. Among these, the supreme consensual opinion, over and above any political discrepancies, was affirmation of the national identity. Not even the regional figures that so often appeared in the *zarzuelas* were interpreted as conflicting with the national Spanish identity. Naive expressions of satisfaction for great historical deeds were also typical, especially recent ones relating to the Napoleonic wars.[46] Some pieces from *zarzuelas*, such as the 'Marcha' from *Cádiz*, and 'De España vengo' from *El niño judío*, went on to become patriotic songs in wartime, including the war of 1895–1898 in Cuba, when the *zarzuela* articulated openly anti-American stereotypes, and the Moroccan conflict in the early twentieth century, when much of the received wisdom handed down about the Moors was resurrected.

Although the success of the *zarzuela* did not spread beyond Spanish borders, other compositions from almost the same era became renowned worldwide as 'Spanish music'. Its composers were unrivalled: Albéniz, Falla, Granados and Turina. They followed in the footsteps of the earlier generation – Bretón, Monasterio, Chapí – but went on to achieve the international recognition which these composers never found. Apart from their similar geographical origins – they were either Catalans or Andalusians – the new generation of composers had two characteristics in common: they had studied outside Spain and they based their musical oeuvre on Andalusian-Moorish themes, which were just what the international market identified as Spanish. The best known works of Albéniz, a native of Gerona, were *Cantos de España*, *Danzas españolas*, *Caprichos andaluces*, *Suite española*, *Suite La Alhambra* and *Suite Iberia* (which was divided into sections with titles like *Triana*, *Rondeña*, *El Albaicín*). Those of Granados, another Catalan, were *Iberia*, *Goyescas*, the *Capricho español* and *Danzas españolas* (the latter including the *Andaluza* and *Oriental* parts). Falla also ensured the national identity was present in the titles of works such as *Noche en los jardines de España*, and made good use of the Andalusian element, as did Turin in *Sevilla*, *La procesión del Rocío* and *Danzas gitanas*. One critic has spoken of the 'deliberate *alhambrismo*' of this kind of music, but Falla justified the 'deliberate nationalism' so typical of his generation and declared the *zarzuela grande* to be a mere imitation of Italian opera.[47]

Other fields relating to music used for nation-building were the written histories of Spanish music and the founding of semi-official musical institutions, both of which occurred comparatively late,[48] as did the music described above. Apart from a fleeting attempt by the Republicans during the Civil War, for example, no national orchestra was established until the time of Franco. The difficult process of the gestation of 'Spanish' music, in spite of the obsession of composers and critics with this idea, is merely symptomatic of the complexities of creating collective identities. None of this detracts from the music itself in any way: it was of a far higher quality than the historical painting of the nineteenth century and better even than the greater part of the literature dating from the Romantic period. All subsequent generations of music-lovers everywhere have enjoyed the music of Falla, Albéniz and their generation. Without questioning its intrinsic value, first should be pointed out how late it was written; second, the deliberate search for inspiration in popular folklore, with which it was only remotely connected in spite of Romantic-populist declarations to the contrary; third, the coincidence in style with the eastern vision of Spain cherished by international Romanticism; fourth, the displacement it caused of a radically different style of music like the *zarzuela*, of lesser quality certainly, but far more popular in the Spanish market; and lastly, the deliberate link made by means of title and themes with the great endeavour of the age (and object of this book): the creation of the national identity.

The contribution from supposedly impartial sciences: archaeology and ethnography

Some fields are considered to be strictly scientific or, in other words, to be removed from the distortions produced by political ideologies or moral values. It is to be expected of archaeology, a science born around the turn of the century which had become an academic discipline by the mid-nineteenth century. Nevertheless, excellent work carried out recently by the cultural historian Margarita Díaz Andreu has shown that, far from scientific impartiality, there is a close connection between the earliest excavations at prehistoric sites and nationalist concerns. The less a bias is noticed, the stronger it actually is, and this is exactly what happens when the nation is accepted as a fact and it is thereby taken as a natural preliminary coordinate on which to base a series of data to which the scientist then applies critical judgement.

Given that Romantic nationalism had elevated the mediaeval era to represent the Golden Age of Spanish identity, it seems logical that the search for ancient objects would have centred on that era. To some extent, this was the case during the years of disentailment, when so many ecclesiastical libraries and buildings full of artworks were sold off or destroyed, although part of the conservation task was undertaken by the first foreign hispanicists. In the field of archaeological investigation, it was in the following decades – the mid-nineteenth century – when official institutions such as archaeological schools and museums were first set up, generally in imitation of the French ones from a little earlier.[49] It is at this point, however, that one begins to observe the political dimensions of archaeology, as it took a major interest in the pre-Roman age idealised by nationalist historiography as 'free, happy and independent', in the words of Padre Isla. Special attention was paid to the remains of Saguntum and Numantia, of such exceptional symbolic significance for having heroically resisted 'foreign' assault, and therefore proof of the martial ferocity and love of national independence that were believed to be essential components of the national identity. Thus the nascent field of archaeology, an area of science requiring official permits and subsidies, concentrated its activities on just those places, although they were probably not the ones of greatest interest as regards the quantity of existing remains or even of greatest importance for uncovering the secrets of the remote past.

Excavations began in Numantia in 1803 and again in 1853, although on both occasions they were soon abandoned. In 1842, a commission was set up to build a monument on the site, another project that came to nothing. Eventually, the Royal Academy of History began to take a serious interest in the search for archaeological remains, and sponsored excavations between 1861 and 1867. It was no accident, observes Díaz Andreu, that these coincided with the period when Napoleon III ordered the excavation of Celtic remains in order to throw light on the French national past. The site was declared a national monument in 1882 and a commemorative effigy was unveiled in 1905 by no less than Alfonso XIII in person. Only some days earlier, the German archaeologist Adolf Schulten had had his licence to excavate there withdrawn because it was considered scandalous that a foreigner should be given access. It was granted instead to a national team led by José Ramón Mélida, the first Professor of Prehistory in Madrid and a recognised figure, but who specialised in Egyptology. Mélida understood what was expected of him and, in his first report on the excavation, he declared that 'the discovery of the ruins of the heroic city of Numantia was a national duty'; he admitted to excavating not only for scientific reasons but to explain 'through these relics, the historic event of which our *patria* is proud'. In 1919, the Museo Numantino was opened to display the articles discovered and its inauguration was attended, once again, by the King.[50] A similar situation occurred at Saguntum. The reconstruction of its fortifications was justified by M. González Simancas because 'although they no longer serve any defensive purpose, they have an incalculable value due to their glorious history, the last dazzling chapter of which was written in the year 1811'.[51] Consequently the resistance offered by the population of Saguntum to the Carthaginians was linked to that offered by the Spanish to Napoleonic troops two thousand years later, thereby reinforcing the belief in a national character that had persisted over the millennia.

However, the usefulness of these activities to the national cause was compromised by their tardiness. By the end of the nineteenth century, what was called 'cultural nationalism' was already on the rise among regional and local élites, and men such as Manuel Murguía in Galicia, Telesforo de Aranzadi in the País Vasco and Bosch Gimpera in Catalonia were all attempting to do the same as the archaeologists of Spanish nationalism but from the opposite perspective: they were seeking an ethnic identity from earliest antiquity that would justify *their* political pretensions. Bosch Gimpera, founder of the excellent school of archaeologists of Barcelona, managed to find remains of the 'democratic sense of life' of the Catalans in the excavations of Greek Emporion, the modern city of Ampurias.[52] In order to justify their contemporary political pretensions – which were perfectly legitimate in themselves – it was necessary to demonstrate the antiquity of the nation, which meant distorting the results of what was, in principle, a scientific activity.

In the Basque case, Telesforo de Aranzadi, with his *El pueblo euskalduna* of 1899, was an example of the transition from archaeology to anthropology, another – supposed – science that was in its infancy at the end of the nineteenth century. Aranzadi maintained that Basque skulls were 'of the pure race, distinct from all the other peoples of Europe because of their geometric configuration' and, moreover, that they had remained 'pure, isolated, independent' until that moment. This was not an extravagance of the author or of Basque nationalism but typical of the prevailing climate. The reformist Joaquín Costa linked archaeology and physical anthropology in relation to the 'Spanish race', and was interested in the figure of Viriathus. Some social scientists, who considered themselves very advanced, were also measuring skulls and facial angles and doing other tests of a similar nature in the final decades of the century. As Joshua Goode has explained, all this began in Spain in the 1860s with Pedro González de Velasco, a disciple of the Frenchman Paul Broca. In 1884, his follower Federico Olóriz y Aguilera began to collect as many skulls and skeletons as he could from hospitals, barracks and even families. Eight years later he had amassed some 8,700 items and, based on his observations, came to the conclusion that the Spanish type, in spite of originating from a racial admixture, was one of the best defined in Europe, that it had remained essentially unchanged since the period of Roman domination, and that it was homogeneous throughout the Iberian Peninsula. Its mixed and predominantly dolichocephalic features made it one of the 'superior' classes of Europe. These studies by Olóriz won him the *Prix Godard*, awarded by the Museum of National History in Paris. In spite of the fact that this kind of research was generally at odds with Christian creationism – which led to its popularity among the left – the influence of Olóriz was such that Menéndez Pelayo included a long section on Spanish anthropology in his second edition of the *Historia de los Heterodoxos* of 1911. The other major figure of Spanish anthropology at that time was Manuel Antón Ferrándiz, who had also trained in Paris. He focused his studies on the way in which the racial cross-breeding that had given rise to the contemporary Spaniard affected different kinds of behaviour. In his work, Antón not only used craneometric studies but also the influence of geography and particularly climate. From all of this, he deduced a physical anthropology that, in his opinion, should be the common scientific basis for sociology, psychology and criminology. To summarise Antón's main conclusion, the Spanish race was the most perfect representation of the Mediterranean type, the result of Libyo-Iberian influence from North Africa blending with a Syro-Arabian influence from the Middle East.[53]

To round off this reformulation of the cultural world in national terms, one last *technical* activity – with both scientific and artistic dimensions – that should be mentioned is architecture, which is comparable to painting and sculpture. From the mid-nineteenth century onward, it was felt necessary to study the *national* past in this field as well, and to *imitate* it. This *nationalist* awareness led to a period of 'historicist fever', and to quote the art critic Francisco Calvo Serraller, there was a 'pastiche of resurrections . . . among which an Arabic style – so romantically – was to play a very special part'. Those who got carried away by the Romantic paradigm went for a Neo-Mudéjar style, while those who preferred to assimilate Spain into Europe tended towards the Italianate, imitating the Plateresque. This led to a flurry of Neo-Roman, Neo-Gothic, Neo-Plateresque and Neo-Mudéjar buildings, all causing controversy about which ones were authentically Spanish. Francoism would later opt for the style of Juan de Herrera or for the so-called 'Imperial style'.[54] It is hardly necessary, at this stage, to examine the reasons for these efforts to imitate what was national rather than *good* architecture. It was all based on the premise that only by being true to one's own 'way of life' could high-quality, authentic creations be made. Everyone seemed to agree with the initial idea but the arguments started, as always, over what comprised that identity or way of life, aggravated by the fact that it was assumed that there was only *one*. In short, none of this architecture is memorable.

Though there are more cultural spheres to which the new national criteria were applied, it is enough to say that throughout the era, the

Arts and Humanities were dominated by the national obsession, and even the sciences were not immune.

Artists and intellectuals: mission accomplished

The situation of Spain at the end of the nineteenth century can be summarised in one sentence: the intellectuals had done their homework. As in all the old European monarchies which tried to survive modernity by becoming nations, the élites had (almost) managed to complete the construction of a cultural edifice that revolved around a Spanish past, Spanish art and Spanish science. As far as possible, they had made the most of inherited beliefs and traditions. Both early liberal concerns and Romantic extremes had been overcome and superficially incorporated. Spanish artists and intellectuals had imitated Europe to a considerable extent, in spite of their readiness to condemn it for its *lack of idealism* and *effeminacy* or *decadence*. None of this caused serious problems. It is probable that moderation, imitation and the appearance of autonomy were the features that made the new constructs acceptable. Within the modest creative potential of that society, Spanish literature, painting and, of course, music compared favourably with the parallel constructs of the French, British, Italian, Russian or German identities. National myth had been born.

One question that remains to be answered is the sociological definition or categorisation of the groups to which leadership of this phase of cultural nationalism should be attributed. Students of nationalist phenomena normally conclude that it tended to be the work of urban élites with political ambitions and the resources for creating and transmitting cultural symbols. There can be no doubt that Spain corresponds to this general model. Among the Constitutionalists of Cadiz, there were 90 members of the clergy (about 30%), 56 lawyers (18%), 49 public officials (16%), 39 army officers (13%), 15 university professors (5%, rising to 12% if one adds another 20 ill-defined professional intellectuals), 20 merchants (6.5%) and 14 nobles (less than 5%). Morales Moya sums up the composition of this group as 'jurists, public servants, professors, a smattering of nobility and an abundance of clergy, many of them of gentlemanly origins'.[55] This profile is not dramatically different to that for those who built the ethno-patriotic identity under the Hapsburgs. It has merely adapted itself to the general changes in society. There is also continuity between this group and the *ilustrados* of the 1700s, whom Fernández Sebastián calls 'champions of emerging nationalism' and who were, according to him, 'men of letters and men of the law, clerics, scholars, army officers, liberal professionals and writers'. The same groups, having become ideological radicals under the impact of the French Revolution and Bonapartism, then went on to lead and direct constitutionalism, based on the idea of national sovereignty. The same author describes them as 'liberal professionals, enlightened clerics, public servants, artisans, army officers, jurists and merchants.[56]

The composition of the modernising élites remained basically unchanged during the Liberal *Trienio* (1820–1823). Of the deputies in the Cortes from these years, approximately 33% were clergy, 25% intellectuals and professionals (of whom two-thirds were lawyers), 15% were army officers along with a similar number of public officials and professional politicians; the nobility remained at about 4%, and merchants and manufacturers or, in other words, the 'bourgeoisie' to whom so much is attributed, accounted for another 4%. If one looks at membership of the Patriotic Societies, or revolutionary clubs, according to the calculations of Gil Novales, a very high percentage belonged to the armed forces (anything up to 50%); public servants, deputies and politicians made up over 15%, and the clergy less than that; 10% of members could be classified as intellectuals and professionals, while merchants, manufacturers and proprietors (mainly of cafés) accounted for only 5%, and neither artisans and labourers nor the nobility ever made up more than 3%. The author concludes that the liberal régime was based on the support of 'the military, public servants and the clergy', although there were significant numbers of middle-class professionals.[57]

We also have accurate figures for the number of exiles during the Ominous Decade of 1823–1833. Alcalá Galiano recalled that they were army officers, lawyers, civil servants and writers; in other words, the same mix of urban middle classes 'that makes up the nucleus of the so-called liberal party in all countries'. Juan Francisco Fuentes, who has identified more than five thousand émigrés in Paris, says that there were 'professional army men, many still of aristocratic origins, members of the clergy – with a prevalence of military chaplains – intellectuals, professional politicians, proprietors, merchants and workers from every trade'.[58] Except for the last group, the profile of a public, professional, intellectual élite remains the same. It is not very different to the composition of the deputies of the *Cortes del Estatuto* of 1834, in which 23.4% were lawyers and 28.7% army officers, compared to 9% for manufacturers and merchants, according to data from J. Tomás Villaroya. Studies by Francisco Villacorta suggest similar numbers for active members of the Athenaeum of Madrid between 1836 and 1868, although, logically, there is a higher percentage of teachers and members of the academic world (around 30%, with an additional 13% being journalists), as well as 35% being employed in top government or administrative posts (rising to 48% if one includes professional politicians). An examination of their intellectual formation reveals that 41% of Athenaeum members were jurists and 26% humanists or with a degree in Philosophy and the Arts.[59] Last but not least, the meticulous research of Gregorio de la Fuente on the revolutionary élites of 1868 concludes that 'the political élites . . . were not renewed in any drastic way during the revolutionary takeover of power', except for the disappearance of the clergy and members of the court. He emphasises the weight of 'the liberal and teaching professions' among the revolutionaries and defines them en masse as 'an urban élite made up of lawyers, teachers and journalists, people who lived by the pen or the gift of oratory' and who put themselves forward 'as the middle classes, the people, or sometimes, above all when they were army members, as spokesmen or representatives of the *patria*'.[60]

It is stretching the bounds of reality too far to call these groups 'bourgeois' if the term is used in the strict sense of ownership of the financial resources and means of production of a commercial and industrial society. What these groups controlled were certain means of communication of growing importance as instruments of political mobilisation at a time when the mass cultural and educational market was beginning to grow: the daily press, university posts, the reputable legal practices, parliamentary seats and, at first, the pulpit. However, the clergy, in rural areas or further removed from the centres of power than the members of the *Cortes*, were from the outset more absolutist than liberal and, after the purges and selective promotions of Fernando VII, they opted for resisting liberalism en masse. In short, this first nationalist liberal élite could be described as an *intelligentsia* which, though it commenced with a large number of the clergy, became essentially *secular*. It is in this area alone in which there is a substantial change between 1812 and 1868.

As well as their urban nature and intellectualism, another feature of these élites is their statism or links with the centre of political power. Spanish nationalism is statist in nature and encouraged by élites who tend to be located in the political capital rather than other urban cultural centres, have connections with the bureaucracy, and place their expectations in government action. In contrast to their weak ties to the principal productive activities of an industrial society, there is no lack of data establishing connections with the administration. The élites either worked directly for the State or they were liberal professionals whose qualifications and consequent right to monopolise a certain branch of activity was granted by State authority. Even the clergy can be included within this category in the early stages because ecclesiastical posts in regalist Spain 'were often an administrative choice'.[61]

It is clear that they all expected the State to be the principal tool for the social and economic modernisation of the country. Consequently, one of their political aims was to reinforce the public authority which was the cornerstone of their strategy. This *statism* is a curious peculiarity of Spanish liberals, who trusted more in government than in either civil society or their own influence over the cultural market. In the same way as the enlightened reformists of the previous century, they always acted, or tried to act, from the political centre, divorced from the cultural diversity within the country and from local centres of power. They depended upon and trusted in the State as both nationalising and modernising agent, believing that it was the State which should solve social, economic and cultural problems and also undertake to transmit culture and foment national feeling. This feature places Spanish national-liberalism within what Liah Greenfeld has called the 'collectivist-authoritarian' model in comparison with the 'individualist-libertarian' model typical of Anglo-Saxon societies, where the pursuit of private wealth and the defence of individual freedom are considered legitimate, and possibly the most efficient, means of serving the community.[62]

There is one final issue. It is known that since the eighteenth century the reformist élites had adopted a modernising project that clashed with the earlier identity built up during the Counter-Reformation. As has been described in Chapter 4 and this chapter, they went on to redesign culture in national terms. If this task had been, literally, an 'invention' (the term made fashionable by Eric Hobsbawm and Terence Ranger), it could have been successful. During the Enlightenment, the reformists had within their grasp the fundamental means for imposing their projects on society as a whole, which was royal support. Subsequently, when the liberals took over and radicalised the Enlightenment plan, they had recourse to all the resources of the State, although only for brief periods, and considerable influence all of the time over national means of communication like the press.

However, 'nations' cannot be *invented* that easily. Invention is a term that suggests complete freedom for the author: creation *ex nihilo*, starting from nothing. Of course, the formula has proved useful to denounce the nationalist belief in nations as 'natural' realities, pre-existing and opposed to the 'artificial' political bodies which are States. In fact, rather than existing prior to political action, nations, just like States, have been constructed by human actors – whom we call nationalists – loaded with political intentions: consequently, it is they who are most concerned with making *their* creation appear natural and permanent.

But these actors do not work in total freedom; they cannot 'invent' identities within contexts where there are no cultural elements that favour their actions. In his 'Thesis on Feuerbach', the young Marx vehemently rejected determinism and declared that human beings *make* history, though not freely but *under given conditions*. What he said could similarly be applied to nations: a national identity is an 'imagined community' created by those who advocate a political project based upon it, but its creators do not work in a vacuum. There are given materials – which do pre-exist – that limit and condition the task. Thus, the appropriate term is *construction* rather than *invention*. To build a national identity, one must necessarily base it on symbols comprehensible to its followers, on established local power and communications networks, on older identities that may be regional or local, racial and religious. Each cultural reference, each element employed in the construction of the collective identity, has its own characteristics and potentialities; it can be used for many purposes or functions but not for all of them. In order to be successful, nations, and political identities in general, must be built with the appropriate cultural materials: in other words, with traditions and beliefs acceptable to all, or a significant part of, public opinion. The builders have to know how to 'press the right buttons', otherwise the project will be rejected as incomprehensible or nonsensical by its recipients.

This was precisely the problem of the Spanish reformists and revolutionaries: that they based their appeals for mobilisation on an identity invented by them in an overly arbitrary way, within a vacuum, resorting to a combination of cultural elements that were barely credible or downright incomprehensible to a majority of the population. When they tried to make it work, the degree of incompatibility between the cultural construct proposed by the liberals and the popular, particularly peasant, mentality was made patent. This placed the élites in an apparently desperate situation because they had lost the royal support enjoyed by their enlightened predecessors yet subsequently failed to carry the populace with them. However, a new and unexpected element intervened: they began to receive support from certain sectors of the armed forces, remodelled by the military reforms of the last Bourbons and shaken to their foundations by the Napoleonic Wars. As can be seen from the figures quoted above, apart from the intellectual circles and their limited spheres of urban influence through revolutionary newspapers and *Patriotic* clubs, military circles were the only ones in which the liberals – by means of secret societies – were truly in the ascendant. It was therefore natural that recourse to the army became their customary means of accession to government. To some extent, this was similar to the situation experienced by the reformist *Ilustrados* of the eighteenth century, who depended on the monarch's blessing, even though this was far removed, in principle, from their projects for rationalising power. It was far more similar to the situation of other autocratic reformists (however much they claimed to act in the name of the people) such as the supporters of Kemal Ataturk in post-First World War Turkey or many of the nationalist élites taking over post-colonial régimes in nineteeenth-century Latin America or twentieth-century Africa. In each case, they were secular, urban, *patriotic* élites – in that they were fervent creators of patriotic myths inspired by a genuine desire for progress in the country – who attempted to uproot traditional beliefs and institutions that they considered to be obstacles in the path of their modernising project. Conservative forces rallied to resist them, basing that resistance on the mobilising and rhetorical ability of clerical networks. The reformists, in turn, compensated for their weak social support by turning to the army, another modernising élite, though of a paternalistic and authoritarian bent at odds with society, that claimed to be acting in the name of public opinion; and its brutality and lack of tact contributed to the reaction – and popularity – of the counter-revolutionaries. This all led to the convulsions, especially the military *pronunciamientos* (or *coups d'état*), the Carlist Wars and the anticlericalism that raged throughout nineteenth-century Spain; convulsions that are better understood in terms of struggles between élites – the clergy, secular intellectuals, the army – than in the traditional terms of confrontation between classes or great ideological social forces such as, in this case, the liberals, self-declared defenders of the popular interest, and the absolutists, acting in the name of the privileged powers of the *ancien régime*.

In these circumstances, the State found itself under constant siege, subject to brusque changes in political direction, and lacking in legitimacy and resources. All of this affected the process of building a national identity: early on, it was presented in a consistently partial way, which made it generally unacceptable; later, when poets like Zorrilla and historians like Lafuente had come up with myths acceptable to the majority, the cultural construct had to be complemented by the State. This comprised, for example, editing textbooks in which to popularise the myths of patriotic history, building schools in which to socialise children growing up with the new identity, reproducing historical paintings and taking 'Spanish' music to rural areas, as well as setting up an efficient military service that would imbue young men with patriotic values. The State had to complete the task begun by intellectuals and, initially, it seemed clear that it would do so. From the moment the nation becomes the fundamental legitimising identity of the modern world, the State is the first to strengthen that identity, upon which it bases its demand for loyalty. In many countries, the State has, in fact, been the major entrepreneur of nationalism: it has devoted its cultural resources and bureaucratic instruments of classification, control and communication – so superior to those of non-State groups – to the creation or reinforcement of a homogeneous cultural space, common symbols, and an emotional link with the national identity of which it considers itself to be the supreme representative. In Spain, as we shall see, the State's attempt was irresolute and full of ambiguities, leading to many of the problems of the twentieth century. Still, at least the intellectual élites cannot be accused of not having created the fundamental myths of cultural nationalism.

Notes

1 Gregory Jusdanis, *Belated Modernity and Aesthetic Culture: Inventing National Literature*, University of Minnesota Press, 1990, pp. 28, 33, 46 and 61; B. Anderson, *Imagined Communities*, New York, 1983, chap. 2.

2 On this topic, see E. Baker, 'On the Formation of the Spanish National Literary Canon', unpublished paper presented at Tufts University, symposium on Spanish Nationalism, October 1996; A. Ubeda de los Cobos, '¿Zeuxis o Velázquez? La reivindicación nacionalista en la definición del primer neoclasicismo español', *Hispania*, LVI(1), 192 (1996): 51–62; J. Alvarez Barrientos, in G. Carnero (ed.), *Historia de la literatura española: Siglo XVIII*, Vol. I, pp. 105–111.

3 François Lopez, in Carnero (ed.), *Historia . . . Siglo XVIII*, Vol. II, p. 598; histories of Spanish literature, see Álvarez Barrientos, in ibid., Vol. I, p. 108 ff.

4 See J. C. Mainer, 'La invención de la literatura española', in J. M. Enguita and J. C. Mainer (eds), *Literaturas regionales en España*, Zaragoza, 1994, pp. 23–45. Among the *Eulogies* mentioned, Bernardo Aldrete, *Del origen y principio de la lengua castellana* (1606); Sebastián de Covarrubias, *Tesoro de la lengua castellana* (1611); Gregorio Mayáns y Síscar, *Orígenes de la lengua española* (1737).

5 P. and R. Rodríguez Mohedano, *Historia literaria de España, desde su primera población hasta nuestros días*, Madrid, 1766; F. J. Lampillas, *Saggio storico-apologetico della Letteratura Spagnola*, 6 vols, Genoa, 1778–81; J. Andrés, *Dell'origine, progressi e stato attuale d'ogni letteratura*, 7 vols, Bodoni, 1782–1799; and J. F. Masdeu, *Historia crítica de España y de la cultura española*, 20 vols, Madrid, 1783–1805.

6 Álvarez Barrientos in Carnero, *Historia de la literatura española. Siglo XVIII*, Vol. I, p. 109; and E. Baker, *La Biblioteca de Don Quijote*, Madrid, Marcial Pons, 1997, pp. 12–13. D'Alembert, in his preface to the *Enciclopédie*,

1751, says that history is divided in 'civil' (facts, undertaken by nations) and 'literary' (culture, knowledge, whose prime movers are men of letters).

7 J. A. Maravall, *Estudios de historia del pensamiento español (siglo XVIII)*, Madrid, 1991, p. 114. The *Colección de poesías castellanas* was printed in Madrid by Antonio de Sancha between 1779 and 1789.

8 G. Carnero, preface to his *Historia . . . Siglo XVIII*, Vol. I, p. XLVII. Cf. J. L. Cano, *El tema de España en la poesía contemporánea*, Madrid, 1964, pp. 14–16; or R. Herr, *The Eighteenth-Century Revolution Revolution in Spain*, Princeton, NJ, 1969, p. 342.

9 Cadalso, *Cartas marruecas*, XVI ('to praise illustrious Spanish feats, the victories that subjected an immense and opulent empire to the Holy Gospel'); Jovellanos, in E. Allison Peers, *Historia del movimiento romántico español*, 2 vols, Madrid, 1973, Vol. I, p. 77. Capmany, *Centinela contra Franceses*, ed. and pref. F. Étienvre, London, 1988, pp. 44 and 117.

10 According to G. Carnero in *Historia de la literatura española: Siglo XIX*, Madrid, 1997, Vol. I, p. 511, there was 'a revival of heroic poetry' at this time. It was the moment when Ramón de Valvidares wrote *La Iberíada*, following the *La Araucana* or *Os Lusíadas* model.

11 F. Buendía, in her *Antología de la novela histórica española, 1830–1844*, Madrid: Aguilar, 1963, confirms this late arrival of Romanticism in a country usually considered Romantic par excellence. On those debates, according to Ramón D. Perés, *Historia de la literatura española e hispanoamericana*, Barcelona: Sopena, 1954, p. 498, the earliest took place in 1823 and was published in *El Europeo*, Barcelona.

12 First literary journal totally committed to the Romantic fashion also appeared in Spain in the 1830s: *Cartas españolas* (1831–1832), *Revista Española* (1832–1836), *El Artista* (1837), *El Piloto* (1839–1840). On this topic, see V. Lloréns, *El romanticismo español*, Madrid, 1979; Carnero, *Historia . . . Siglo XIX*, Vol. I; Peers, *Historia del movimiento romántico*; Iris Zavala, 'La literatura: romanticismo y costumbrismo', in *La época del romanticismo (1808–1874)*, Vol. XXXV, 2, of the *Historia de España Menéndez Pidal*, Madrid, Espasa-Calpe, 1989, pp. 5–183; and D. Flitter, *Teoría y crítica del romanticismo español*, Cambridge: Cambridge University Press, 1995.

13 'You should not think that you will be consoled by looking back at the past . . . Past youth of a nation is never reborn: if you are defeated, you will lie defeated. You used to be the master of both worlds, where is your glory now? Weep, Spain, your bitterness'. All these authors are published in the *Biblioteca de Autores Españoles* (B.A.E.), Vols LXXII (Espronceda); CXLV, CXLIX, CLI and CLV (Martínez de la Rosa); C, CI and CII (Rivas); and CCIV (Baralt).

14 Espronceda, B.A.E., Vol. LXXII, pp. 31–32 ('How lonely is now the nation yesterday populated by crowds! The nation whose empire embraced from East to West! You are crying now, you, sovereign of the world, and nobody can erase the sign of pain from your face. Spain used to exist, a long time

ago, but now lies, abandoned, just like a stone in a desert, and the right-
eous one wanders in a far away land. We are exiled from our home. Let's
cry. Who can soften Spain's sorrows? Who can wipe your tears?"). Larra,
Biblioteca de autores españoles (B.A.E.), Vols CXXVII, CXXVIII and
CXXX.

15 See L. F. Díaz Larios, in Carnero, *Historia ... Siglo XIX*, Vol. I, p.
511. Donald Shaw, in ibid., I, pp. 317–18, underlines the Neo-classicist
education of Martínez de la Rosa, Larra and Rivas.

16 C. Blanco Aguinaga, I. Zavala and J. Rodríguez Puértolas, *Historia social de
la literatura española*, Madrid, 1978, Vol. II, pp. 91, 95, 97.

17 'Spaniards, cry, but with tears of pain and blood; blood that suffocates
serfs and oppressors. Despicable tyrants must feel threatened forever by
avenging ghosts.'

18 According to Alison Peers, from 1837 there was no Romanticism, but
eclectic literature, in Spain (*Historia del movimiento romántico*, Vol. II,
Chapter 1); cf. Flitter, *Teoría y crítica del romanticismo*, p. 122.

19 Carnero, preface to Vol. II of *Historia ... Siglo XIX*, Vol. II, p. XXXIV.
The MP who defended the subsidy for the B. A. E. was Cándido Nocedal.
The fashion of publishing *romanceros* was closely related to the German
influence, where mediaeval Spain was idealised as a Romantic World par
excellence. Jakob Grimm collected and published a *Flor nueva de romances
viejos*, in Vienna, as early as 1815. In Spain, Agustín Durán, in 1828–1832,
Romancero General, o Colección de romances castellanos anteriores al siglo XVIII
(later reprinted as Vol. X of B. A. E., 1849). In Berlin, 1856, F. J. Wolff and
Conrad Hoffmann published a *Primavera y flor de romances castellanos.*

20 Friedrich Bouterweck, *Geschichte des Spanischen Poesie und Beredsamkeit*,
Göttingen: Rowers, 1804; Simone de Sismondi, *Histoire de la littérature
espagnole*, Paris: Crapelet, 1813; and George Ticknor, *History of Spanish
Literature*, 3 vols, London: Murray, 1849.

21 Antonio Gil y Zárate, *Manual de Literatura*, 2 vols, Madrid: Boix, 1844;
and José Amador de los Ríos, *Historia crítica de la literatura española*, 7 vols,
Madrid: J. Rodríguez, 1861–1865. This process would continue throughout the rest of the nineteenth century. In general, see Mainer, 'Invención de
la literatura española'.

22 See Larra, 'Horas de invierno' ('nations, like individuals, live their own
life', etc.), in B. A. E., Vol. CXXVIII, 1960, pp. 290–291). Agustín Durán,
director of the National Library in Madrid, wrote in 1828 that theatre, in
order to be 'authentic', 'should concentrate on the country's history' and
express 'the feelings and moral judgements of their inhabitants' (quoted by
Zavala, 'La literatura: romanticismo y costumbrismo', p. 26).

23 Durán, preface to *Romancero General*, 1828–1833; Martínez de la Rosa,
Anotaciones a la Poética, Paris: Didot, 1827.

24 E. de Kosca Vayo *La conquista de Valencia por el Cid* (1831); M. J. de Larra,
El doncel de D Enrique el Doliente (1834); J. Espronceda, *Sancho Saldaña*
(1834); P. de la Escosura, *Ni rey ni roque* (1835); J. Cortada, *La heredera*

de Sangumi (1835); F. Martínez de la Rosa, *Doña Isabel de Solís, reina de Granada* (1837); S. Estébanez Calderón, *Cristianos y moriscos* (1838); E. Gil y Carrasco, *El señor de Bembibre* (1844); before 1830, R. Húmera, *Ramiro, conde de Lucena* (1823). On this topic, see Buendía, *Antología de la novela histórica española*; Carnero, *Historia . . . Siglo XIX*, Vol. I, pp. 384–398, 620–621; or Lloréns, *El romanticismo español*, pp. 295–325. Some of these authors (Cortada, Kosca Bayo) were also historians. For Pérez Galdós see Chapter 10, this volume.

25 'My voice, my heart, my fantasy, they all sing my fatherland's glory . . . Come, my songs will not offend the beliefs of that nation in which I was born; I will respect your laws and your altars. In your unhappiness, as well as in your opulence, I will celebrate your fortunes. I will raise my comforting voice on these ruins on which Spain weeps'.

26 Perés, *Historia de la literatura española*, p. 503; J. I. Ferreras, *El teatro en el siglo XIX*, Madrid, 1989, p. 55; Blanco Aguinaga et al., *Historia social de la literatura española*, Vol. II, p. 93.

27 Saavedra, duke of Rivas, was particularly prone to references to the nobiliary values embodied by the Spaniards: *Don Alvaro*, for instance, boasts of being a 'Spanish grandee', and one of the characters in *Amor, honor y valor* of having 'noble and Christian blood, revered by the whole world', which oblige him to comply with his duties.

28 See Álvarez Junco, *El Emperador del Paralelo*, Madrid, 1990, pp. 249–252, 264–265. Espronceda's quote comes from his 'Canto del cosaco' ('these opulent people, effeminate, their soldiers are less than women, their kings are abject merchants; see how they run to hide their gold').

29 See Rivas's early 'Declaración de España contra los franceses'; later, 'Maldonado' or 'La victoria de Pavía'. Zorrilla underlines French lack of loyalty towards the Spaniards in *El zapatero y el Rey*. On this, Lloréns, *El romanticismo español*, pp. 165–166.

30 Quintana's *Pelayo* had many imitators, among others Marchena, Martínez de la Rosa and Espronceda. See A. Dérozier, *Quintana y el nacimiento del liberalismo en España*, Madrid, 1978, p. 114.

31 José Luis Díez, 'Evolución de la pintura española de historia en el siglo XIX', in *La pintura de historia del siglo XIX en España*, Madrid, 1992, p. 71. On decoration of royal palaces and on San Fernando Royal Academy see Chapter 2 of this volume.

32 A. Pérez Sánchez, in *La pintura de historia*, p. 34, or Díez, ibid., pp. 70–73 and 76–77. The beginning of this genre is usually located in José de Madrazo's *La muerte de Viriato, jefe de los lusitanos*, painted in Rome *c.*1820.

33 T. Pérez Vejo, *Pintura de historia e identidad nacional en España*, Madrid, 2001, 309–311; according to this author, national history themes were as many as 87% of the total, and the Middle Ages occupied 37%, classical antiquity 35% and the Visigoths 10% (same percentage as for the Habsburg period).

34 J. O. Picón, quoted by Pérez Vejo, *Pintura de historia*, p. 527.

35 *La Discusión*, 4–X-1871; previous quote, *La Época*, 5–XI-1862, both in Pérez Vejo, *Pintura de historia*, pp. 412, 493.

36 See C. Reyero, *La pintura de Historia en España: Esplendor de un género en el siglo XIX*, Madrid, 1989, pp. 19–37 and 47–50.

37 C. Reyero, 'Los temas históricos en la pintura española del siglo XIX', in *La pintura de Historia*, p. 43.

38 Among the most renowned authors of these paintings, R. Martí Alsina, J. Madrazo, A. Muñoz Degrain, I. Pinazo, M. Santamaría, J. Moreno Carbonero, F. Pradilla, E. Rosales, S. Martínez Cubells, J. Espalter or J. Casado del Alisal, all of them active between 1855 and 1892. On this topic, see C. Reyero, *Imagen histórica de España (1850–1890)*, Madrid, 1987.

39 Exceptionally, Carlos V can be seen at Tizian's workshop (Parra Piquer, León y Escosura). Cervantes was also portrayed in Felipe II's army by E. Zamacois (1863) and in his Alger confinement by Muñoz Degrain (1918, an unusually late date for this kind of painting).

40 Antonio Pérez, painted by M. Ferrán (1864) and V. Borrás (1884); Lanuza, by C. Larraz (1859), M. de Unceta (1862), E. López del Plano (1864), M. Barbasán (1891) and V. Balasanz (1886); the sack of Rome, by F. J. Amérigo (1887); mediaeval pogroms of Jews, by V. Cutanda (1887); expulsion of Jews, E. Sala y Francés (1889); expulsion of Moorish, M. Gómez Moreno (1882) and G. Puig y Roda (1894); the last moments of Prince Don Carlos, A. Gisbert (1858).

41 See Carlos Reyero, *La época de Carlos V y Felipe II en la pintura de Historia del siglo XIX*, Valladolid, 1999, pp. 48–51.

42 Cossío, Ganivet and Maeztu quoted by J. L. Bernal, 'Pintura y nacionalismo: el caso español', in A. de Blas (ed.), *Enciclopedia del nacionalismo*, Madrid, 1997, p. 416. Rafael Doménech, *El nacionalismo en el arte*, Madrid, s. d., pp. 16–17, 60. E. Lafuente Ferrari, *Breve historia de la pintura española* (1934), 2 vols, reprinted in Madrid, 1987, quotes in Vol. I, pp. 37–40.

43 Quoted by E. Casares and C. Alonso, *La música española en el siglo XIX*, Oviedo, 1995, p. 22. On this topic, my sources will be T. Marco (ed.), *Historia de la música española*, Vol. 6, *El siglo XX*, Madrid: Alianza, 1982; F. Sopeña, *Historia de la música española contemporánea*, Madrid: Rialp, 1976; Teixidor y Barceló, *Historia de la música española*, 1996; and P. García Picazo, 'Música y nacionalismo', in A. de Blas (ed.), *Enciclopedia del nacionalismo*, Madrid, 1997, pp. 328–335.

44 The best known operas by Spanish composers were *Marina* (E. Arrieta), *Ledia* and *Don Fernando el Emplazado* (Zubiaurre), *Las naves de Cortés*, *La hija de Jefté* and *Roger de Flor* (Chapí), performed in Madrid, most of them in the 1860s and 1870s. In Barcelona, in the same period, *Edita de Belcourt* (Obiols), *Quasimodo* and *Cleopatra* (Pedrell), *Constanza* (Nicolau), *Inés y Blanca* (Adalid). Previous quotes and data from E. Casares and C. Alonso, 'La música del siglo XIX español: Conceptos fundamentales', in Marco, *Historia de la música española*, Vol. 6, pp. 92, 95, 108 and 111.

45 Such as *Los amantes de Teruel* or *La Dolores* (by T. Bretón).

46 See C. Serrano, 'Cantando patria. Zarzuela y tópicos nacionales', in L. García Lorenzo (ed.), *Ramos Carrión y la zarzuela*, Zamora, 1992; A. Valencia, in *El género chico: Antología de textos completos*, Madrid, 1962, quoted by Casares and Alonso, *La música española*, p. 92; J. Arnau and C. M. Gómez, *Historia de la zarzuela*, Madrid, 1979.

47 In *Nuestra música*, published in 1917. Bullfighting and Andalusian elements also in M. Penella, who staged *El gato montés* in 1916, whose *pasodoble* came to be the typical music interpreted in bullrings. On this topic, see T. Marco, *Historia de la música española* . . ., Vol. 6, pp. 6, 46 and 153.

48 Only in 1904–1915 were the Orquesta Sinfónica de Madrid, the Barcelona Sinfónica and the Madrid Filarmónica founded. As to histories of Spanish music, by the mid-nineteenth century M. Soriano had published one and B. Saldoni a biographical dictionary of Spanish musicians; in the 1890s, A. Peña y Goñi wrote *La ópera española y la música dramática en España en el siglo XIX*.

49 A Commission of Monuments was created in 1844, following the French model. Provincial museums come from that period also, and the National Archaeological Museum from 1867. In 1856 was founded the Escuela Superior de Diplomática (École de Chantres). All this, in M. Díaz Andreu, 'Archaeology and nationalism in Spain', in P. Kohl and C. Fawcett, *Nationalism, politics, and the practice of archaeology*, Cambridge: Cambridge University Press, 1991, pp. 39–56.

50 M. Díaz Andreu, 'Archaeology and nationalism', pp. 44–45. Mélida, quoted by Díaz-Andreu, 'Archaeology and Nationalism', p. 44. See the Bibliography for other publications by Díaz Andreu, from which I have taken most of this information.

51 M. González Simancas, *Memoria presentada a la Junta Superior*, Madrid, 1923, p. 4. It was at that time that the Valencian town known for several centuries as Murviedro recovered its ancient name of Saguntum.

52 The Institut d'Estudis Catalans created a 'Servei d'Investigacions Arqueologiques' in 1915. The Ikuska Basque Seminar of Ancient History was started in 1921.

53 F. Olóriz y Aguilera, *Distribución geográfica del índice cefálico del español*, Madrid, 1894; M. Antón Ferrándiz, *Doctorado de Medicina: Conferencias de Antropología*, Madrid, 1892, and *Programa Razonado de Antropología*, Madrid, 1897. All this, taken from Joshua Goode, 'From Racial Fusion to Cultural Alloy: Transitions in the Spanish Anthropological Conception of Race, 1890–1923', paper presented at the Iberian Study Group, Harvard University, on 20 November 1998.

54 F. Calvo Serraller, *La imagen romántica de España: Arte y arquitectura del siglo XIX*, Madrid, 1995, p. 175.

55 A. Morales Moya, 'El Estado de la Ilustración', in *Las bases políticas, económicas y sociales de un régimen en transformación (1759–1834)*, Vol. XXX of *Historia de España Menéndez Pidal*, Madrid, 1998, p. 126. Figures, in F. Villacorta Baños, *Burguesía y cultura: Los intelectuales españoles en la sociedad*

liberal, 1808–1931, Madrid, Siglo XXI, 1980, p. 12; and R. Solís, *El Cádiz de las Cortes*, Madrid, 1969, pp. 220–27.

56 J. Fernández Sebastián, 'España, monarquía y nación. Cuatro concepciones de la comunidad política española entre el Antiguo Régimen y la revolución liberal', *Studia Historica. Historia Contemporánea*, 12 (1994): 53–61.

57 A complete list of members of the Cádiz *Cortes* in M. García Venero, *Historia del parlamentarismo español (1810–1813)*, Madrid, 1946, pp. 533–536. For the period 1820–1823, A. Gil Novales, *Las Sociedades Patrióticas (1820–1823)*, Madrid, 1975, p. 973.

58 J. F. Fuentes, 'Censo de liberales españoles en el exilio, 1823–1833', *Cuadernos Republicanos*, 32 (1997): 34; cf. R. Sánchez Mantero, *Liberales en el exilio. La emigración política en Francia en la crisis del Antiguo Régimen*, Madrid: Rialp, 1975. According to V. Lloréns *Liberales y románticos*, Madrid, 1968, p. 24, most of those exiles were military. Alcalá Galiano, *Recuerdos de un anciano*, Madrid, 1878, p. 462, quoted by Fuentes, 'Censo de liberales', p. 31.

59 J. Tomás Villarroya, 'El proceso constitucional, 1834–1843', in J. M. Jover (ed.), *La era isabelina y el Sexenio Democrático (1834–1874)*, Vol. XXXIV of *Historia de España Menéndez Pidal*, Madrid, 1981, p. 21; Villacorta Baños, *Burguesía y cultura*, pp. 38–42 and 248–259.

60 G. de la Fuente Monge, *Los revolucionarios de 1868*, Madrid, 2000, pp. 233 and 244–245.

61 J. A. Maravall, 'Mentalidad burguesa e idea de la Historia en el XVIII', 1972 (included in his *Estudios de historia del pensamiento. . . siglo XVIII*, 1991), p. 117.

62 L. Greenfeld, *Nationalism: Five Roads to Modernity*, Cambridge, MA: Harvard University Press, 1992, pp. 10–12.

Part III

Conservative opinion: between religion and the nation

6

Catholicism and *españolismo*: from the *ancien régime* to Fernando VII

The shouts and cheers of those that rose up against the French during the summer of 1808 did not acclaim the Spanish nation but the king, Fernando VII, and, above all, Catholicism. Fray Simón López recalls that 'the cry of the nation . . . resounded everywhere', but adds that it was a cry of 'long live Religion, long live the Church, long live the Virgin, long live God, long live Fernando VII, death to Napoleon, death to the French'. This rousing exclamation would be heard later with only slight variations: 'Long live Fernando VII, long live Religion, long live the Catholic Church and death to the impious Napoleon with all his satellites and his anti-Christian, tolerant, schismatic France'. The nation ceded pride of place to the king and, in particular, to collective religious beliefs and the ecclesiastical institutions that embodied them. As Fray Manuel Amado noted, 'We did not do it for our *patria*; we acted as we did because our religion demanded that we act in that way.'[1]

All observers, including the French generals and even the Emperor himself (who classed the whole episode as a 'revolt of friars'), agreed that the Catholic clergy played a leading role in the anti-Napoleonic mobilisation. And there can be no doubt that for the majority of the insurgents their sense of civic duty in fighting the invader was rooted in Catholic doctrine. Among the heroes and symbols invoked during the war, St James the Apostle and local patron saints such as the Virgin of Covadonga in Asturias, the Virgin of Fuencisla in Segovia, or the Virgin of the Pilar in Zaragoza figured far more often than legendary warriors such as Don Pelayo, El Cid or Hernán Cortés. Even references to the *patria* were usually qualified by the addition of 'its ancient customs' or 'its holy traditions', among which the Catholic religion always came first. In the minds of the majority, Spain and Catholicism were one and the same thing.[2]

The identification between Spain and Catholicism was destined to continue for a long time, certainly well into the 1850s. The most striking aspect is that it survived, if not in opposition to, then at least relatively *detached from*, the national myth which, during the early decades of the Modern Age, was created and controlled by the liberals. This was because the idea of nationhood embodied a secular, autonomous vision of the State that was a far from welcome thought to the men of the Church, who included in their ranks almost all of the ideologues of Hispanic conservatism. Only as the century advanced did doctrinal shifts within conservatism allow it to shape national myths. The aim of this chapter is to describe the manner by which conservative circles, defined far more by their religiosity than by their identification with the State, gradually evolved towards a nationalist outlook. The first section looks at how closely Catholicism was identified with the Hispanic monarchy at the time of the Counter-Reformation. The second section examines the purges of the non-Catholic minorities in Iberian society in the fifteenth and sixteenth centuries, something which left a lasting imprint upon the way in which the dominant religiosity was understood. The third section analyses the significance of the celebrated 'alliance between the Altar and the Throne' in the final years of the *ancien régime*, an alliance that was never free of rivalry. Only then can one fully appreciate the complexity of the ties that bound Spanish identity to Catholicism at the beginning of the Modern Age and the subsequent role of religion in the great political upheavals of the nineteenth century.

Spain and the light of Trent

Menéndez Pelayo famously declared that Spain was 'the light of Trent'. Not only was the Hispanic monarchy of the Hapsburgs at the forefront of the fight against Lutheranism, it was also the theologians and canon lawyers of Salamanca and Alcalá de Henares who did most to elaborate a Catholic refutation of Luther's doctrines. After the first hundred years of the Early Modern Age, it was universally agreed that both the Hapsburg monarchy and its subjects were identified with the Holy Roman Catholic and Apostolic version of Christianity. Catholicism was not embodied in any particular king or dynastic house but in 'Spain'. Consequently the Counter-Reformation played a crucial role in determining collective identity within the Spanish monarchy, while in other countries this fell to the Protestant Reformation.

Benedict Anderson argues that in order for an identity to have been created in Spain that was similar to that of the Protestant countries it would have been necessary for the Church to encourage Bible-reading, thereby increasing both publications and literacy. As it was, the clergy did everything within its power to keep the people apart from theological discussions of any sort (including the more literate urban middle classes), and it never embarked upon nor tolerated the intense pamphleteering and propaganda that characterized Protestantism.[3] Counter-Reformist Catholicism had its own methods for transmitting its ideas without the need for reading. It used a variety of instruments for shaping beliefs, attitudes and behaviour that included the weekly sermon, sporadic missionary campaigns and the purging of heretics. These constituted the Catholic Church's fundamental means of communication with an illiterate population. The Church also encouraged certain cultural activities such as theatrical performances, which could be highly creative and through which ideological messages, such as those contained in the great mystery plays or the works of Calderón de la Barca and Lope de Vega, could reach the general public. Last, but not least, the Church had its own methods of dissuasion, primarily the Tribunal of the Holy Office – otherwise known as the Inquisition – which exercised a rigid control over the faithful, persecuted ethnic minorities and punished unorthodox behaviour. The Inquisition also had its own means of discrimination, in the form of the *estatutos de limpieza de sangre* or Statutes of Pure Blood.

The kind of identity fostered by the Counter-Reformation Church was therefore different to that of the northern Protestant Churches as a result of the differing channels of religious transmission. Instead of the silence and restraint of Lutheran pietism, the result of an inner vision of religiosity based upon direct communication with the divine and the personal responsibility of the believer, Catholicism encouraged the worship of sacred objects and places and the celebration of public acts and ceremonies through which God was revealed and his message explained. The sacraments were especially important: these outward, material acts had great spiritual significance because they altered the state of grace of the participants, and Spanish Catholicism took to such public acts and the worship of material objects like none other. The objects were naturally holy images for which Christians felt a special devotion; a *collective* devotion, it should be added, as the Saints, the Christs and the Virgins were peculiar to each region or city, neighbourhood or craft. Even when these images were small enough to be carried about the body or on clothes as an amulet or as a means of protection, in the form of medals, rosaries or scapularies, they were often worn in order to be visible, to be seen *publicly*. Even more important than the veneration of objects was the participation of individuals in ceremonies that were clearly both public and collective: as well as Sunday Mass, there were the fundamental rites of passage which the Church had converted into sacraments, including a Catholic baptism, marriage and burial. Also of particular importance were the processions, acts consistent with the occupation of specifically public spaces through which the faithful would parade and display the religious symbols of their community. Generally, these took place only on fixed dates during the year, such as Holy Week, but could also be improvised in moments of exceptional need, such as droughts or epidemics. Wearing a medal, attending Mass, taking the sacraments and, above all, forming part of a brotherhood and carrying on one's own shoulders a sumptuous baroque *paso* through the streets, all identified the participant as a member of a community.

This was not so much a *religion* as a *culture*. A culture which was typical of all Catholic Europe, and which, in contrast to Protestant culture, did not consist of a set of profound personal convictions nor of an intellectual comprehension of certain dogmas or beliefs. These differences, however, did not prevent the formation of equally powerful collective identities. In order to be a Catholic, it was not necessary – or even advisable, as one could easily be treading on dangerous ground – to be able to read or to uphold an orthodox, dogmatic interpretation of the Faith. Indeed, the Tridentine catechism recommended that, when faced with the slightest theological doubt, one should respond, 'Holy Mother Church has doctors who will know how to answer you'. Crucial to an understanding of Spanish Catholicism in the Early Modern Age was participation in the same acts as one's neighbours, thus demonstrating a public and unequivocal submission to the authority and dictates of the Roman Catholic Church as the exclusive exponent of the sacred message. Such complete acceptance of the Catholic Church as the unique interpreter of the revealed truth also implied acceptance of its social privileges. These were so great because, as the Church's earthly representatives explained, nothing was ever enough to 'honour God'.[4]

Given that visible and public activities were encouraged in order to make explicit the submission of believers to the Church, the kind of religious behaviour that resulted was noisy and festive – even in the celebration of dramatic events – and deeply rooted in paganism. All in all, it was radically different from the silent communication of the Lutheran with God. Although there was no connection with the Bible or with the printed word which, according to Anderson, were the cornerstones of collective identity in the Protestant world, the Catholic identity was nonetheless as intense and socially influential as the Protestant one.

Ethnic cleansing: the vain attempt to impose uniformity

At first glance, the identification of Spain with Catholicism would appear to be as immutable and incontrovertible as any natural, geographical feature. In reality, this is far from the truth. Contemporary Spanish society has shown this by its spectacular social and cultural transformation over the last fifty years, although one does not need to turn to the present. Just a hundred years before the time of Felipe II, in the second half of the fifteenth century, the Iberian Peninsula was a mosaic of cultures, which Christian Europe contemplated with incomprehension and distrust precisely because of its variegated identity.

Throughout the whole of the Middle Ages, Muslims and Christians had shared an existence in Hispania that comprised many more years of peace than of war, while the Jews occupied the gaps between Christendom and Islam in order to enjoy a degree of tolerance that they were unable to find elsewhere. Nevertheless, coexistence and tolerance should not be equated with an absence of tension. Persecution of the Jews had been known since the time of the Visigoths. It had also taken place in Muslim territory at the height of Almoravid and Almohad fanaticism, a period during which many Jews had taken refuge in Christian lands, but towards the end of the fourteenth century a renewed spirit of persecution flourished there, too. The massacres began in 1391 following a virulently anti-Semitic campaign by an Archdeacon of Ecija. They erupted again in 1412 in the wake of the zealous mission of Fray Vicente Ferrer, and reached a peak in the mid-fifteenth century in Toledo and other cities of Castile and Andalucía. In addition to these *pogroms*, discriminatory measures were adopted by the *Cortes*, such as the obligation of wearing special badges and the ban on carrying arms, dressing in fine fabrics or holding certain public offices. The Jewish population responded with mass baptisms, which generated a new problem in the form of the *conversos*, or converted. There were 200,000 to 250,000 '*conversos*' or '*marranos*' at the start of the reign of the Catholic Kings, comprising some 4–5% of the total population, but their conversion did not make them any more acceptable to 'old Christians'. It is true that, in many cases, the sincerity of their faith was more than suspect, but some embraced their new beliefs with unquestionable authenticity and yet were no better received.[5]

The conversions did not prevent the Peninsula from continuing to be a land that exhibited a degree of multiculturalism that shocked visitors from beyond the Pyrenees, where Muslims were unknown and the Jews had been expelled centuries before. The tales told by travellers, ambassadors and pilgrims show how they judged the civilisation and religiosity of the Peninsular kingdoms according to the common criteria of the age, that is, by the fertility of the soil, the courtesy of the inhabitants, and the relics and buildings devoted to worship within each region. Among Hispanic 'abnormalities', no informant failed to record with indignation the presence of numerous Moorish and Jewish subjects in kingdoms that claimed to be Christian. Gabriel Tetzel, an aristocrat from Nüremberg travelling in Castile and Aragón as part of the retinue of the Bohemian nobleman León de Rosmithal between 1465 and 1467, described the country as full of Jews and Muslims and, according to him, there were traces of the orient even in the customs and features of Christian subjects. As he journeyed through the lands of the Count of Haro, he was scared to be among so many 'murderous and wicked' people and observed with astonishment that the Count 'allows them all [Muslims and Jews] to live in peace'. 'They say that the Count is Christian', he concluded, but 'no one knows the religion that he professes.' Twenty years later, the Germano-Polish nobleman Niklas Poplau, or Nicholas de Popielovo, noted that 'throughout Aragón live Saracens, whom we Germans call rats' and he complained openly of royal tolerance, calling Queen Isabel herself a 'protector of Jews'.[6]

Foreign repugnance at the 'impurity' of the Peninsula's subjects could not but have influenced the Catholic Kings when they began to play a central role in European politics. Under heavy pressure from strongly anti-Semitic opinion at home, they considered that the time had come to dispense with religious and racial diversity. In so doing, they were seeking to achieve a dual objective: the most obvious one, which is always stressed by observers, was to reinforce the unity of the social body and avoid any kind of religious dissidence, which was presumed to be dangerous for the stability of the kingdoms. The other objective, which was doubtless of lesser importance but should not be underrated, was to make the breakthrough into Europe, to make Spaniards acceptable to the rest of Christendom. In 1478, Fernando and Isabel obtained papal permission to set up the Inquisition, whose initial purpose was to ensure the purity of faith among the *conversos*. The first actions of the tribunal were harsh in the extreme: although the numbers of the 'released' – a euphemism for those condemned to die at the stake – and of those otherwise found guilty continue to be the subject of debate, it is at least clear that under the first three inquisitors, Torquemada, Deza and Cisneros, the Inquisition claimed more victims than in the subsequent three centuries of existence. These Inquisitors chose to take exemplary action, whose purpose was not only to punish those guilty of crypto-Judaism, but also to terrify those tempted to turn back to their old religion. There is no other way of interpreting the burning in effigy of fugitives, which was the response to the exodus of *conversos*.[7]

As the jurisdiction of the Inquisition did not extend to practising Jews and Muslims, the Catholic Kings eventually decided to take action against them as well. On 31 March 1492, flushed with the success of their recent occupation of Granada, the Kings decreed the expulsion of all Jews from their dominions. Experts have long debated the numbers of people affected by this measure, but the most reasonable estimate is that some 150,000 left the country while about half that number opted for conversion. This created a vacuum in fields such as medicine, finance, royal administration and certain crafts which the Christian population was unable to fill, although it is true that the activities of the *conversos* partially compensated for the flight of expertise and also contributed to the great cultural flowering that took place in the following decades. From *converso* families came literary figures such as Fernando de Rojas, humanists such as Juan Luis Vives and, above all, mystics and religious reformers including Luis de León, Ignacio de Loyola, Teresa de Jesús and Juan de Avila, among many others. Great administrators such as Santángel de la Caballería and Antonio Pérez, and doctors such as Andrés Laguna, were also *conversos*. They were all sincere Christians, although there were others whose conversions were undertaken merely for appearance's sake. What is important is that all of them fell within the jurisdiction of the Holy Office because they had been baptised.[8]

As for the Muslims, a protracted error has crept into Spanish histories, which persists in referring to the *taking* or *conquest* of Granada. Properly speaking, this never happened. Granada was not conquered, but agreed on its *conditional surrender* following a lengthy siege. The *capitulaciones*, or terms of surrender, guaranteed its inhabitants the free practice of their language and religion, as well as the continuity of their traditional judges. These clauses were respected for the first ten years, the period in which Hernando de Talavera, who had been appointed Archbishop of the new diocese, attempted the conversion of Muslims by peaceful means and even made the effort to learn their language. Once he had passed away, and in view of the slowness of the conversion process, the king and queen appointed Cisneros in his place. The latter introduced compulsory baptisms, which caused the first, harshly repressed revolts in the Albaicín neighbourhood of Granada. Reneging on the promises signed only ten years earlier, a royal decree of 1502 obliged all Muslims to choose between baptism or exile. Although this brought the Muslim problem to an abrupt end, just as it had the Jewish question before, it created the *morisco* minority in the same way as the same measure had earlier created the *converso* minority.[9]

Coming from northern Europe, where prejudice against the non-Christian subjects of the Peninsular kingdoms was so strong, Carlos V was even less tolerant than the Catholic Kings. It is curious to note that Carlos's sentiments coincided with those of the peoples of Castile and Valencia, who were otherwise in rebellion against him. In 1520, members of the *Germanía* or brotherhood in Valencia forced the Muslims to be baptised under pain of death. It must have been the only issue on which the Emperor agreed with the Valencian rebels because five years later he ratified the measure, placing Valencian Muslims in the same dilemma as those of Granada in 1502 in having to choose between conversion or exile. A guarantee was given to those who opted for baptism: they would remain free from inquisitorial investigation for forty years, which seemed to be a promise of leniency with regard to false conversions. However, Pope Clement VII undertook to absolve the king from fulfilment of the oath and by the end of Carlos's reign the Inquisition was taking action against the *moriscos* as freely as it did against the Jewish *conversos*. In 1526, the year in which Carlos V moved with his Erasmian court to Granada and began to build his magnificent Italianate circular palace in the heart of the Alhambra, he decided for the first time upon radical acculturation. He brought the Inquisition to the city and forbade the use of the Arabic language or Arabic dress. These measures led to so much conflict that the authorities were forced to suspend them. Forty years later, his son Felipe II had them reinstated, which led to a great uprising in the Alpujarra mountains. On this occasion, it was decided to use force. Two armies, one of them under the command of Juan de Austria, were ordered to either kill the *moriscos* in the mountains of Granada or else scatter them throughout Spain.[10]

Pockets of resistance continued to exist, particularly in the kingdom of Valencia where the majority of the *morisco* population lived, until the end of the century, a period overshadowed by the Turkish threat along the Mediterranean coast. Given that the *moriscos* were regarded as a potential bridgehead for an Ottoman landing, it is not surprising that it was then that the idea of expelling them from the dominions of the Catholic monarchy began to take shape. In Valencia, where the *moriscos* made up 20% of the population and it was feared that their expulsion would have a dramatic effect on the economy, the Archbishop nonetheless declared that the *moriscos*, far from being useful, were 'sponging off the wealth of Spain'; others, in Castile, warned that the industry and fertility of the *morisco* families that had been driven from the Alpujarras would convert them into the dominant race of the kingdom. Finally, between 1609 and 1614, Felipe III signed a series of decrees for the expulsion of the *moriscos*. Between 250,000 and 300,000 people left the various Peninsular kingdoms for Tangiers, Tetuan, Oran or Tunis.[11] Some, who had become true Christians, resisted the forced deportations and voluntarily suffered the death penalty. 'We cry for Spain', says the *morisco* Ricote in Don Quixote, 'when all is said and done, we were born there and it is our natural home.' But other, less compassionate authors than Cervantes, rejoiced in the expulsion of the *moriscos*, 'enemies within of unconquered Catholic Spain', as 'the most honourable, excellent and heroic enterprise that any prince in the world has attempted'; 'once again Spain belonged entirely to those who were her children and these infidels returned to the lands of Africa from whence they had come'.[12] The old Hispania had finally been cleansed of the alleged ethnic impurities which had besmirched it during the Middle Ages.

With the expulsion of the *moriscos*, the non-Catholic minorities had all but disappeared from the Peninsula. There remained the *conversos* – or New Christians of Jewish descent – who, following a century and a quarter of Inquisitorial action, had been carefully vetted, as well as those *moriscos* scattered across the different kingdoms who had managed to pass undetected. Isolated from one another and anxious to cover their tracks, in a few generations these peoples had lost all memory of the religions of their forebears. By that time, however, religion had ceased to be the issue: expulsion had simply turned into racial cleansing, whereby all descendants of the old minorities were denied any position of respectability within Christian society. A new legal instrument called the *Estatutos de limpieza de sangre* was employed for this purpose, having been invented in the fifteenth century in order to deny *conversos* access to certain professions, religious orders, university colleges and even entire provinces, such as Guipúzcoa. At the time, the *Estatutos* had provoked a bitter debate, even leading to a conciliatory papal intervention to the effect that the *conversos* were no longer Jews and that all Christians, new or old, were worthy of the same respect. Unfortunately, a later Pope was prepared to sanction such measures, in this case Paul III. The popularity of the *Estatutos* spread during the reign of Carlos V, when they were adopted by the *cabildos*, or city councils, of Seville, Córdoba and Toledo, as well as by the universities of Salamanca and Valladolid and the Franciscan Order. They did not punish new Christians outright; the mechanism was actually more perverse in that it reversed the burden of proof and obliged the applicant for a post or pension to demonstrate his or her condition as an 'old Christian', this requiring evidence of four or five generations of baptism, the maximum that the archives of the time could provide. It seemed impossible to eradicate one's non-Christian past. As one fifteenth-century poet put it, with bitter humour:

Ollas de tocino asado / torreznos a medio asar,
oir misas y rezar,/ santiguar y persignar
y nunca pude borrar / este rastro de confeso.[13]

In 1547, a serious row erupted between the Archbishop of Toledo and the new and vigorous Society of Jesus, who refused to introduce an *Estatuto*, the reason being that some of its founders, including Loyola and Laínez, had been born into *converso* families. Academic debate continued for decades, as did the indecision of the Spanish government, which led Felipe II to forbid the application of the *Estatutos* for a brief period. By the end of Felipe's reign, however, the *Estatutos* had become widespread, and even the Society of Jesus was obliged to demand that its novices possess 'pure blood', while it rewrote the biographies of its founders to eliminate any reference to their *impure* racial origins.[14]

By the end of the sixteenth century, the integration of the descendants of *conversos* and *moriscos* into Spanish society was almost complete. The majority had lost any memory of their past. A few new-Christian families managed, after manipulating or faking documents, buying up land and adopting an aristocratic lifestyle, to acquire titles including that of Grandee of Spain, and to occupy high-ranking ecclesiastical posts. As Américo Castro above all has stressed, many of the writers of the *Siglo de Oro*, even those who constantly referred to those of Jewish or Moorish blood with contempt, were descended from *conversos*. Who knows how many Spaniards today, even among the ardent defenders of racial pride and National-Catholicism, do not also descend from such families?[15]

The identification of Spain with fanatical Catholicism led to its becoming an indelible part of the so-called *Leyenda Negra*. There was certainly some justification for this, but it does not cease to be a legend or at least a distortion of reality; by no means could all the inhabitants of the Iberian Peninsula be considered supporters of either absolutism or Catholic intransigence. Neither was such an attitude unanimous nor did it bear any relation to an innate collective psychological trait. On the contrary, in the Peninsular kingdoms of around 1500 there existed at one and the same time a rich and diverse cultural world, and a sensual, secular Renaissance, with groups of the followers of Erasmus as numerous as in the most cultured societies of Christendom. The same period saw the development of mystic tendencies, whose advocates practised an inner Christian spirituality akin to Lutheranism and supported reform of the regular clergy; a reform which was carried out, to a large extent, at the end of the fifteenth century and which partially explains the later failure of Protestantism to take hold in Spain. Even so, there were communities of Protestants in Valladolid and Seville, as indeed there were groups of illuminati. Economic and political structures were modern and dynamic, and criticism of monarchist policy led to rebellious movements such as the *Comunidades* of Castile, which were very advanced in comparison with practice in Europe. The triumph of the absolute monarchy, the Inquisition and the *Estatutos* was the result of an internal struggle that ended in victory for the most conservative sectors of the Catholic hierarchy. By imposing their version of the *imagined community* on Spain, it became necessary to 'purify' society of Jews, *moriscos* and Protestants. It is true that these sectors had previously caused certain problems but these only became insurmountable once the time came to build a national stereotype based on a homogeneous culture. Only then did anyone begin to think that other races, although they lived in 'Spain', did not form part of 'Spain'; at which point, their elimination became inevitable.

With regard to Spain's foreign relations, it is important to note how the attempt to impose Christian cultural uniformity was also an effort to overcome Spain's perceived eccentricity with respect to Europe. The purification process had originally been incited and encouraged by the rest of Christendom, and the expulsion decreed by the Catholic Kings brought them felicitations from the Pope and other Christian rulers. Hieronymus Münzer, a German noble who journeyed through the Peninsula in the late fifteenth century, recorded with evident satisfaction the demolition of the Jewish quarter in Granada and praised the king and queen for condemning false converts and renegade Christians to death. He encouraged them to do the same with the Saracens, even while admitting that they were excellent subjects. Shortly afterwards, in 1513, the Florentine ambassador and great political thinker Francesco Guicciardini noted that when the Catholic Kings had come to the throne 'the whole kingdom was full of Jews and heretics and the majority of people were tainted with this *infection*'.[16] Nevertheless, foreign mistrust did not end with the expulsion. The troops of Carlos V who sacked Rome were greeted with cries of '*marranos*', as Sverker Arnoldsson pointed out some years ago. Erasmus of Rotterdam refused the invitation of Cardinal Cisneros to visit Spain; *non placet Hispania*, he wrote privately on one occasion, and, although his motives are not known, Marcel Bataillon speculates that it was due to the secret anti-Semitism of this prince of humanists. Years before, in a letter in which he had advised a student to abandon his study of the Talmud and other 'foolishness', Erasmus wrote, 'in Spain there are scarcely any Christians'. In the mid-sixteenth century, Pope Paul IV voiced his low opinion of the Spanish, on account of their *tainted* blood, and even at the beginning of the seventeenth century Cardinal Richelieu was to opine that the Spanish were '*des marranes, des faux catholiques, des basanés*'. The Russians of the sixteenth century must have believed something similar as, without ever having visited the Peninsula, they called their inhabitants *Iverianin*, Iberians, a word which they confused with *Evreianin*, Hebrews. Alain Milhou observes that, 'as if it were a mirror image, Europe saw her new masters, the Spanish, as new Christians, while in the Peninsula [new Christians] were objects of suspicion in the eyes of the majority of old Christians'.[17]

The situation became greatly aggravated because the purging of the Jews and Moriscos coincided with the accession of the Catholic monarchy to European political hegemony. The testimonies that crossed the Pyrenees about the brutalities of the purification process, crystallised in the umbrella term 'Spanish Inquisition', became the argument for creating an image of Hispanic society based on intolerance and cruelty. Later on, the country's backwardness and its inability to adapt to modernity would also be blamed on its fanatical spirit. It is ironic that in the origins of that intolerance lay the attempt to become more modern (but in the worst possible sense) by creating a homogeneous, white, Christian society that would be acceptable to the rest of Europe. In order to demonstrate to Christendom that Spain formed a part of it, Spain had resorted to a 'modern' solution that would thrive in the nationalistic twentieth century: the cultural homogenisation of a country by the forcible elimination of its minorities. It was one of the first examples of 'ethnic cleansing' in modern Europe. As in all cases, it caused untold suffering and, to some extent, produced the opposite effect to that desired because it marked the Spanish stereotype with overtones of a very un-European brutality and primitivism.

The problem of Protestantism in Spain was slightly different to that of the non-Christian minorities because this was not a pre-existing ethnic group but a cultural phenomenon related to the new cultural 'climate' of the Renaissance. However, the criteria upon which a solution to the Protestant problem was based remained the same: a fear of internal division. The conviction that *unity of belief* is necessary for the stability of the social body became an obsession that, in spite of the radical changes in circumstances, was to survive as a political myth up to at least the end of the nineteenth century. In the *Siglo de Oro*, the immense majority of intellectuals, even those who were highly critical of the censorship exercised by the Inquisition over artistic creativity and scientific progress, regarded the religious unity enjoyed under the Spanish monarchy from the start of the sixteenth century as profoundly positive. To some extent, this is understandable as religious differences had plunged many countries north of the Pyrenees – including their powerful neighbour and rival, France – into a serious and lengthy crisis, which would prove to be an essential factor in maintaining the hegemony of the Spanish Hapsburgs.

In conclusion, a series of events led to the creation of a cultural identity among the subjects of the Spanish monarchy based upon the Catholicism of the Counter-Reformation. A largely common system of values had been internalised by the majority of that society's members and, as a result, they also shared a xenophobic distrust, if not a visceral hatred, of the heretics of northern Europe. This was added to their traditional enmity towards Muslims and the deep-rooted anti-Semitism that has survived to the present day in terms such as '*judiada*' (dirty trick) and '*marrano*' (filthy pig). To their many and varied geographical, professional, class and family identities (though not their political ones, which remain speculative for this era), all of these people would have added that of 'Christian', or, possibly 'Catholic', or, to be more exact, 'Holy Roman Catholic and Apostolic', and, given half a chance, 'old Christian' or 'of pure blood'. Words that would probably be spoken either with far greater pride or a far greater degree of anxiety (given the need for acceptance) than any other identifying reference.

The Altar and the Throne: a not altogether happy marriage of convenience

During the early modern age and a large part of the modern one, the 'Spanish Church' was an organisation *sui generis*, with its loyalties divided between universal Catholicism on the one hand and the Hispanic Monarchy on the other. In more graphic terms, it was obliged to serve two masters: it submitted to papal precepts on all dogmatic and liturgical issues without the least hesitation, but it was subject to the Spanish monarch in all aspects of daily life and it was he, in particular, who possessed the right of '*patronato*' or presentation of the men who would hold the bishoprics and all other ecclesiastical positions of any importance. This privilege had been granted by the Pope to the Catholic Kings after the conquest of Granada, although it had only pertained to posts in the old Muslim kingdom. The Kings skilfully manoeuvred to extend this right to include the whole of the New World when its conquest and evangelisation began. Their successors, Carlos V (after elevating his former tutor, Adrian of Utrecht, to the Papal See) and Felipe II (when he introduced the reforms decreed by the Council of Trent), then succeeded in further extending royal patronage to ecclesiastical positions throughout all the kingdoms of the monarchy. However, the *Rey Prudente*, not content with exercising control over these appointments, decided to arrogate to himself the right to grant the *pase regio*, or permission, for papal bulls and other pontifical documents to be published within his domains, as well as *recursos de fuerza*, procedural appeals that allowed civil tribunals to review ecclesiastical decisions.

The Church was also subject to constant pressure to increase its financial contribution to the formidable expenses of the Crown. It is true to say that the bishoprics and abbeys were by far the wealthiest members of society, and that they were exempt from State taxes. However, by requiring them to divert a considerable portion of their revenues to the State, they became indirect tax collectors for the civil administration. In more than one sense, therefore, the Church became another branch of monarchical bureaucracy. It was a case of regalism *avant la lettre*, which led to extremely serious conflicts between *Catholic* monarchs and successive Vicars of Christ whom, in theory, they defended more keenly than anyone else. These conflicts led to open war with the Papacy, to the execution by royal order of papal envoys, and to other tensions so violent that they almost led to the excommunication of such very Catholic monarchs as Felipe II and Felipe IV.[18]

By no means did the relationship between Church and State lead to such intimate union that one could talk of a *theocracy* in imperial Spain, although it is true that in the theatrical works of the *Siglo de Oro* the monarch was practically deified, possibly to make the supremacy of royal authority more comprehensible to the general public. Lope de Vega was particularly emphatic: '*Son divinidad los reyes / el rey sólo es señor, después del cielo*'. Vélez de Guevara wrote that 'the King is God on earth', and Moreto referred to the 'sovereign deity' of the king.[19] Nevertheless, the principal political theorists, who were, of course, members of the clergy, avoided a purely religious legitimation of power, perhaps in order that the Papacy need not consider the king his delegate and could claim any superiority over him in return for anointing him as holy. The same jurists from Salamanca who predominated at the Council of Trent always refused to merge the spheres of politics and religion and insisted on the autonomous origins of civil authority. Francisco Suárez, the greatest political theorist of Spanish scholasticism, was categorical: acknowledging that authority had a divine origin, as established by St Paul, he argued that all of creation had a divine origin and, furthermore, it was logical that only a superior being could establish moral obligations of such weight. However, the earthly subject of political authority was the people who, for Suárez, were a fully constituted legal and moral entity. Consequently, it was the people, and none other, who had to determine the form and powers of government, by means of some kind of original contract that empowered them even to resist those powers if the government overstepped its limits, violated moral law or failed to serve the community which had established it.

In his *Defensio Fidei*, Suárez took issue explicitly with the theory of the Divine Right of Kings as upheld by King James I of England, who based his pretension to be the Head of the Church upon the theory. Francisco de Vitoria, the other great political philosopher from Salamanca, held to similar doctrines. For him, the ultimate source of power was unquestionably divine but its immediate foundation was natural law; all power, including ecclesiastical power, was an institution of natural law and thus neither civil nor ecclesiastical power, orientated as they are towards different ends, could be subordinate to the other. In particular, Vitoria denied that worldly princes could consider themselves vicars or delegates of the Pope, because no one had granted him temporal dominion over the universe. In short, the Hispanic monarchy of the imperial era was based upon a political theory that justified absolutism, and one could even talk of an alliance between the Altar and the Throne. In other words, there was no *political theologism*, the opposite of what was to occur in the nineteenth century.[20]

The profound struggle between Catholicism and the monarchy, or between Church and State, came to a head in the eighteenth century as States expanded and *regalist* tendencies became more generalised. In Spain, where the last Hapsburgs had given much ground to ecclesiastical privilege, the new Bourbon dynasty of 1700 imported the regalist outlook of Louis XIV while deprecating the waning of royal power. It should be remembered that the entire state administration – including the standing army – consisted of no more than 30,000 people. This was nothing compared with the immense ecclesiastical bureaucracy which maintained, directly or indirectly, 150,000 to 200,000 people. Felipe V and his successors decided to take the offensive, and they did so on three fronts. Two of these were no more than the classic tactics that continued or escalated the policy of intervention in ecclesiastical matters pursued by the first Hapsburgs. The first was aimed at reinforcing patronage, the *pase regio* and other regalist rights, chiselling away at the ties that continued to bind the Spanish Church to Rome and completing its submission to domestic civil power, culminating in triumph with the Concordat of 1753. The second, designed to increase the pressure on their own Spanish hierarchy as well as on Rome, was to increase the amount from ecclesiastical revenues that was already flowing into royal coffers. Some success was also achieved in this area. The third line of attack was new: an attempt to reduce the power of the clergy over cultural issues such as the control of publications, which was in the hands of the Inquisition, and its monopoly over education, which led to such drastic measures as the expulsion of the Jesuits.[21] In spite of repeated accusations to the contrary, what no enlightened reformer seriously attempted to do was to diminish religious feeling or belief among the subjects of the Hispanic monarchy, far less to introduce other religions. Except in isolated cases, such as that of the Count of Aranda, the sincerity of the Catholicism of reformist ministers and intellectuals in the Bourbon era is not open to question. What angered them, and what they were determined to combat, was the kind of religiosity then dominant, which they believed to be an obstacle to the cultural progress of society. This belief was what inspired such measures as the prohibition in the time of Fernando VI of plays about saints, and in the time of Carlos III mystery plays. The magnitude and complexity of the Church at that time, as well as its involvement with the State, explains why a significant number of the clergy themselves – generally the upper echelons, which tended to be the most enlightened sectors – collaborated in this policy, which could well be classified as anticlerical. The acquiescence and even favourable response by leading members of the clergy to the news of the Jesuits' expulsion is a revealing example of that internal complexity.

In spite of a degree of collaboration, there were sectors – probably the majority and especially among the lower orders – which never forgave the reformists. Absolutism did not permit direct criticism of royal orders, although resentment of the Bourbons would later be expressed by the Catholic historians of the second half of the nineteenth century. In the eighteenth century there were harsh allegations against 'philosophers' and 'Jansenists': in other words, the intellectuals and ministers who defended the consolidation of royal power to the detriment of the ecclesiastical authorities. *La falsa filosofía* by Fray Fernando de Ceballos, *El Filoteo* by Padre Antonio José Rodríguez, *Desengaños filosóficos* by Fernández de Valcarce, and the works of Antonio X. Pérez y López, Antonio Vila y Camps and Clemente Peñalosa y Zúñiga, among many others, all express their opposition to enlightened and regalist reforms from the standpoint of the monolithic Catholicism that was supposed to characterise Spain.[22]

It was in these mainly ecclesiastical centres of opposition to Bourbon reforms that the Spanish conservatism of the modern age first saw the light of day. The immediate and instinctive line of defence against such reforms was to brand them as heretical. This was partially successful, as even some ministers and other high-ranking officials of the monarchy, such as Macanaz and Olavide, saw their careers brought to an abrupt end by an inquisitorial trial. The heresy of which they were accused was Gallicanism which, in Spain, went by the name of Jansenism, which was equally irrelevant to theological dispute.[23] Such exceptions aside, the Inquisition of the eighteenth century had ceased to be the fearful weapon that it had been in earlier times. Moreover, it had little autonomy of action in relation to royal policy given that its highest office-holders were appointed directly by the king. Those who opposed the Bourbon reforms therefore had to search for a second line of defence, which was to accuse their supporters of being '*afrancesados*', '*extranjerizantes*' or, in short, French or foreign sympathisers. It was then that the anti-regalist, anti-Enlightenment sector of the Church first began to claim identification with 'Spanish tradition' and it is here – and not in the Hapsburg era – that one must seek the origins of the future National-Catholicism.

The Hieronymite friar Fernando de Ceballos is perhaps the figure who best represents the ecclesiastical sectors opposed to enlightenment policies. His most famous work attacked enlightened rationalism – that 'false philosophy' – which was, for him, yet another expression of eternal human rebellion against the divine order, beginning with Cain and more recently personified by Luther. According to Ceballos, every society is founded on the repression of human instincts, perverted after the fall of Adam and Eve, and it was the aim of reformers to eliminate this controlling aspect that made them the enemies of all social order. Nevertheless, while Ceballos detested rebellion, this did not lead him to advocate unlimited monarchical power; on the contrary, he declared himself to be anti-absolutist, because every absolute monarch tended towards regalism, and what had to be defended above all else were the privileges of the Catholic Church. As a result, this formidable reactionary defended the right to resist civil authority when the latter exceeded its jurisdictions. This linked Ceballos to a line of ecclesiastical political thought dating back to the sixteenth century which had led the Jesuit Juan de Mariana to defend nothing less than tyrannicide (further proof that the relationship between Church and State had been less than fraternal).[24]

Another offensive was launched by Lorenzo Hervás y Panduro, an erudite Jesuit who had emigrated to Italy in the time of Carlos III. His work dates from 1794, when France had already suffered five years of revolutionary turmoil. The immediate danger was no longer regalism but revolution, which had deprived the Church of goods and privileges to a degree undreamt of by any king. Revolution for Hervás, like modern philosophy for Ceballos, was to be explained in terms of moral rebellion and was inspired by pride and, of course, its origins also dated back to Cain and Luther, although its more immediate perpetrators were Jansenists, regalists, philosophers and Protestants. In opposition to the revolutionary world and its satanic postulates of liberty, equality and national sovereignty, Hervás upheld a conception of society as a natural organism, of the same order as the family, with political power comparable in all aspects to paternal authority. It was the old idea of '*jus generationis*' expounded by Robert Filmer and the most conservative political theologists from the time of the first Stuarts, which took on a new lease of life in the reign of Louis XIV thanks to Bossuet, but which had been explicitly opposed by Suárez and Spanish scholasticism during the *Siglo de Oro*. From it, Padre Hervás deduced first the impossibility of accepting the idea of *patria* as a moral entity from which political rights and duties could flow, and secondly the illegitimacy of unitary national political representation, which could never substitute the fragmented representation of corporate interests. In contrast to the Hieronymite Ceballos, for the Jesuit Hervás the repository of sovereignty or social *reason* was exclusively the monarch. 'In civil society', he wrote categorically, 'its members defend the *Patria* by defending the Sovereign that gives it body'.[25]

Ultimately, the concerns of Ceballos and Hervás were much the same: namely, the defence of the rights of 'God' or, in other words, of the Church. But the former, writing before the Revolution when the idea of the nation was still in its infancy, only conceived of regalism, in alliance with modern philosophy, as the enemy of those rights. The latter, however, had seen the rise of a new enemy, the nation – the offspring of both modern philosophy and regalism – and found no better guarantor of the rights of the Church than the monarch, as did the absolutists in the *Cortes* of Cádiz a few years later. This was probably the reason why the ultra-reactionary work by Hervás was banned by none other than the Inquisition. Although it was a semi-State institution, in the struggle over the rights of Church and State the Inquisition tended to pronounce in favour of the Church, but on this occasion it favoured the construction of a new kind of national legitimacy. The unfavourable verdict on the book by Hervás was written by Joaquín Lorenzo de Villanueva, enlightened canon and future liberal *diputado* of Cádiz, and its publication prohibited by the Bishop Félix Amat, another *Ilustrado*. Those who banned the work were obviously not defending the revolution but the State; in the same way that, by denouncing the revolution, Hervás was not defending the State but the Church of God. Thus a conflict between the Spanish monarchy and the Church of Rome turned the Spanish clergy against one another, revealing how divided they were between their loyalty to the universal Church on the one hand and to the Spanish State, of which the Church was also a branch, on the other.[26]

The definitive link between anti-regalist, anti-*Ilustrado* rhetoric and the defence of Spanish tradition was to be forged in the years 1793–

1795, at the time of the War of the Convention, the joint crusade – which ended in fiasco – launched by European monarchs against the French Revolution. It is the first time that one can talk of a war 'of opinion', and it was therefore radically different from previous dynastic conflicts. And who better to inflame 'opinion' in Spain than the clergy, the only sector able to preach moral exhortations and make political proclamations that would reach large numbers of the populace? As the French Consul in Barcelona noted in 1794, 'the monks and priests animated the people', confirming the mobilising role that they were to repeat in 1808. These lower-ranking members of the clergy were not acting spontaneously but following orders from their superiors: in Barcelona itself, for example, the Bishop ordered his parish priests to say 'the litanies with prayers against heretics as in times of war' in their churches; and the Bishop of Valencia laid down the doctrine that it was a 'war of religion, a very just and holy war', which should rightfully be called 'war of God, because it is against atheists who deny his Divine Majesty'. Was it a little strange to find priests attributing the paternity of revolutions to the spirit of rebellion embodied in the recent past by rationalist philosophers? It was certainly during the war against the atheist and revolutionary French that the political cry of 'God, *Patria*, King', that would be heard so often forty years later under the banner of Carlism, first sounded.[27]

Although the conventional Spanish army was defeated and the war lost, the 1793–1795 campaign proved quite successful insofar as the population, effectively mobilised by the friars, put up a furious resistance to the French invaders, especially in Catalonia. The rhetoric based on identification of the *patria* with religion, a key device of future National-Catholicism, had made a relatively good start. The Church, as it had always done in the face of collective suffering, attributed the evils of war to divine wrath at collective sinning, but these sins now amounted to the use of 'Frenchified' garments and adornments. Under the pretext of praising what was 'Spanish', the preachers who had whipped up the resistance to the French now turned their oratorical skills to condemning sinful 'foreign' luxuries, fashions and behaviour. The authorities took this so seriously that they came to publish edicts prohibiting the use of the French style of dress in favour of short breeches and other traditional dress. In this manner, moral reprimand came to be mixed up with the defence of tradition and a culture of xenophobia. In 1793–1795, just as in 1808, there were numerous cases of the ill-treatment of the French who lived in Spanish cities, and it was so indiscriminate that even émigrés who had crossed the Pyrenees to flee the Revolution fell victim.[28]

The booklet most widely circulated during the war was *El soldado católico en guerra de religión*, written by a popular preacher called Fray Diego José de Cádiz. At first glance, it appears to be a patriotic tract, as Padre Cádiz decried the 'Frenchifying of customs' in the accustomed way. However, on closer examination, one begins to appreciate that the friar was not defending 'Spain' and far less the monarchy, but religion. The title itself emphasises the religious bias of the conflict: the *Catholic* soldier in a *religious* war. With similar rhetorical extravagance, there are repeated references to religion, the Church, Catholicism and the true faith at least once or twice a page on every one of the hundred or more pages, in contrast with Spain and *patria*, which are mentioned on only a couple of occasions in the entire text. If Padre Cádiz is to believed, it was not a war of Spain against France but of Catholic believers against the revolution; the revolution brought upon them by materialistic philosophers which had its precedent in the Lutheran rebellion, since both, as Ceballos had explained, expressed the eternal, sinful desire to liberate human animality from the yoke of divine law. The war against the French, concluded Fray Diego de Cádiz, was a war in support of religion, a holy war, a crusade in which Christ, in the form of the Church, opposed Lucifer, incarnate in modern philosophers.[29]

In short, the anti-modern bias of the political rhetoric that would be used so often by extreme Spanish conservatism in the decades to come was as follows: the current war was not specifically national but universal; in other words, it was not a question of defending Spain against anti-Spain or the enemies of the nation in whatever guise they appeared, but of defending the Catholic Church, Christianity or the true religion against the snares of Satan contained within rationalism and other modern constructs. This anti-revolutionary, but not specifically national, orientation is what was to characterise the initial identification of Spanishness with the most orthodox Catholicism at the outset of the liberal revolutions.

The Fernandian nightmare

By 1808, the ideological spadework for the propaganda campaign against the French had already been accomplished, especially during the War of the Convention. The latter campaign had been under the supreme command of Manuel Godoy, then recently promoted to the highest political offices. Fifteen years later, his career came to an abrupt end. In the interval, he set the country on a course that was very different to the one approved by the anti-enlightenment sectors which had supported him in the war of 1793–1795. In fact, he adopted the enlightenment programme of the previous reign. Although his enmity towards certain people, including liberals such as Jovellanos, is well known, this can be seen as typical of people in a position of unrestrained personal power, whereas his relationship with Moratín and Meléndez Valdés, for example, demonstrate that he was on good terms with the modernising élites. The negative image of Godoy is a reflection of ecclesiastical rather than intellectual opinion, as he stood up to the clergy in the best traditions of Bourbon regalism. The Church considered Godoy's programme of disentailment particularly intolerable, as this forced the sale of 10–15% of ecclesiastical property, which amounted to approximately one seventh of all the agricultural lands belonging to the Church.

Hence the propaganda of 1808–1814 was again based on the identification of *Spanish* with 'Catholic' and *French* with 'atheist' and 'sacrilegious'. As Javier Herrero observed some years ago, it turned the conflict into yet another holy war, another 'religious crusade'. The 'Letter of a prelate to parish priests', published in the *Diario de Santiago* in June 1808, was categorical in this respect: 'In such a conflict it is needful that you should accompany the unceasing fervour of your prayers with your most efficacious preaching and persuasion from the pulpit and in the confessional, in the churches and in the squares, in homes and in all public and private places, to stir your parishioners to take up arms in this holy religious war'.[30]

If the anti-enlightenment or (after Cádiz) anti-liberal sectors had followed this line of thought, they would have been able to make common cause with the nationalist sentiment taking hold across Europe so vigorously by that time. All they would have had to do was to cultivate the idea that they were the 'true Spaniards', since *España* was already identified with traditional *Catholicism*. By forging a collective identity on such terms, they would have been in a position to expel from the *imagined community* those liberals who, in their opinion, represented the rationalist threat to Catholicism. However, they failed to take advantage of the occasion and, by insisting so much on the defence of *religion*, they left the *nation* in the hands of the liberals.

One indication of the climate in which the anti-Napoleonic campaign unfolded was the pamphlet *Despertador Cristiano-Político* by Fray Simón López and published in Valencia in 1809, a work whose influence could be compared to that of the *Soldado católico* by Padre Cádiz in the anti-French conflict fifteen years earlier. Its subtitle speaks volumes: *It is demonstrated that the authors of the universal upheaval of the Church and of the Monarchy are the Freemason philosophers: the diabolical arts that they employ are revealed and the means of obstructing their progress are described.*

For the author, who was a *diputado servil* – one faithful to the king – in Cádiz and later rewarded by Fernando VII with the See of Valencia, the behaviour of the French was 'sacrilegious, perfidious, bloody, inhuman, irreligious' and Napoleon was the modern Anti-Christ personified, 'the Leopard of the Apocalypse', 'one of the seven heads of the Beast'. His followers were 'the philosophers of our time', the 'coalition of the irreligious, unbelievers, deists, atheists, heretics, apostates of France and of the whole of Europe' at whose head were the Freemasons and other demonic sects which had managed to bring down the Throne and the Altar and install deism in France and then tried to extend it to the whole of Europe where 'they find insuperable obstacles in the Clergy, Monarchs and Nobility'.[31] Observe that the good priest does not specifically mention Spanish forces opposing the impious revolution, but universal, or at least European, ones. Peculiar to the Spanish case is the fact that although such perfidious creatures had easy access into the country because it was ruled by their own (Godoy, the favourite who was the 'ambitious, lecherous, irreligious ... satellite of Napoleon'), until that moment it had managed to avoid the fate of other States in Europe 'thanks to the loving providence of our God, thanks to the unity of the holy Catholic Religion, which we profess to the exclusion of all false sects, to which our King and our kingdom undoubtedly owe their conservation and their independence'. In short, the fight is between the just or the believers against the conspiracy of materialistic philosophers and therefore of no national significance. It is true that 'all nations have turned their eyes to Spain' which stands out for her fierce resistance to the rising tide of malignancy, but her tenacity is due only to her Catholic *unity*, to the 'exclusion of all false sects'.[32]

This approach to the war with the French on the basis of the Catholic identity of Spain was apparently common to all the troops fighting Napoleon, including their leaders. And however much their enemies later questioned their Catholicism, the liberals in Cádiz were also generally believers and they had not the slightest intention of undermining the Catholic unity of Spanish society. It is enough to recall Article 12 of the Constitution, which declared the confessionality of the country with a commitment startling for any reader who associates liberalism with the religious neutrality of public power: 'The Religion of the Spanish Nation is *and shall be in perpetuity the only true Roman Catholic and Apostolic [one]. The Nation protects it with wise and just laws and forbids the exercise of any other*'.

Typical also of constitutionalist sentiment in Cádiz were the catechisms that today one would not hesitate to call *political* but which, in their day, were known, significantly, as *Catholico-political, religious-civil* or *religious, moral and political.* One of them stated, in a manner repeated almost literally by the rest, that the word *español* was the equivalent of 'good man'. This, it went on to clarify, meant a person whose ethical and political conduct was governed by the 'maxims of Jesus Christ and the Gospels'. His obligations, it continued, were three: 'to be a Roman Catholic and Apostolic Christian; to defend his religion, his *patria* and his law; and to die before suffering defeat'.[33]

However, this should not mislead us. It was one thing for the *diputados* to be Catholic and to continue defending the Catholic unity of the nation, but quite another for them to found the national identity on traditional religiosity or be prepared to perpetuate the privileged situation of the Church. The religious measures drawn up by the constitutional *Cortes* were aimed unambiguously at the reform of the Church and a reduction of its social power: the number of regular clergy was reduced, the State appropriated more ecclesiastical revenues and, above all, the Inquisition was abolished and freedom of the press was established. Of all the debates, the one that caused the greatest passion concerned the suppression of the Inquisition, an issue that had a special symbolic value for both absolutists (also known by the derogatory term *serviles*) and liberals. For the former, it ensured the religious unity that was regarded as an indispensable guarantee and exclusive privilege of the *Spanish* against fratricidal discord. For the latter, it represented the suppression of intellectual freedom, the main cause of *Spanish* decline under the Hapsburgs. Herein lay the dividing line between the two different kinds of Catholics and the two future visions of the Nation: the same line that had separated pro- and anti-Enlightenment supporters.

In Cádiz, the invocation of Catholicism in defence of the nation varied greatly. The anti-revolutionary and even anti-Enlightenment invective of the popular preachers did little for those who considered themselves the heirs of the Enlightenment and who pursued an openly revolutionary liberal legislative agenda. For the liberals, the struggle was designed to end first foreign tyranny and then domestic tyranny, for which it was necessary to establish a political system based on the principle of national sovereignty. Quintana's *Semanario Patriótico*, the principal organ of the constitutionalists, constantly urged the Spanish people to fulfil their patriotic duty but, as François-Xavier Guerra has pointed out, 'The subject of religion is conspicuous by its absence in every issue, with one single but significant exception: when, in November of 1808, Madrid was on the point of succumbing to Napoleon's troops, the people were called upon 'to defend Religion and the *Patria*', which is indicative of the mobilising force of the call to arms.[34]

In a similar but contrasting vein, the absolutists had an aversion to 'Spain'. Certainly they felt that the *patria* was of value, and even believed that they were its most genuine representatives. Still, they avoided mentioning it by name if at all possible, choosing instead to talk about the monarchy or religion. Their discomfort became even greater if, instead of Spain or '*patria*', the term 'nation' was used, as this hinted at 'national sovereignty', the true *bête noire* of the absolutists. The repugnance caused by references to the nation is illustrated by a short poem by the absolutist María Manuela López in 1813:

> Españoles, viles imbuídos / en el orgullo y voces seductivas
> de igualdad, libertad y, ¡qué delirio! / nación, independencia, ciudades,
> derechos naturales e imprescritos

Not only the term 'nation' but even 'independence' is condemned in this verse. Indeed, Fernando's absolutist supporters generally endeavoured to avoid glorifying the war. The decree that re-established the Inquisition even lamented the deterioration in the 'purity of religion in Spain' during the conflict as a result of the 'presence of foreign troops of diverse sects, all equally infected by their hatred of the Holy Roman Church'.[35]

The return of Fernando VII and his assumption of absolute power did not mean a restoration of the *ancien régime* in the strictest sense. Fernando responded to the destruction wrought by the war on the institutions and ideas of the absolutist era by placing his trust entirely in the hands of the Catholic Church, a radical rupture with the policy of his predecessors. Reluctant to found the political system on a principle as dangerous as the *nation*, Fernando had no alternative but to entrust the defence of his absolute monarchy to the same clergy that had preached during the wars of 1793–1808 that the political and social structures were untouchable because they had been established by God. Fernando returned to the Church the convents, properties and rights of which it had been deprived by Joseph Bonaparte and the constitutionalists, as well as re-establishing the Inquisition and even re-admitting the Society of Jesus to his kingdom (which was to return to the days of Carlos III rather than restoring the *ancien régime*). Other measures did not smack so strongly of restoration: the old councils, for example, became 'shadows of their former selves', as Artola states. At certain times, the king placed power in the hands of his confessor, an unprecedented move, and at others in a Council of State that comprised the most intransigent of absolutists, including his brother, the Infante Don Carlos, and those who were to become his most notorious followers, the Bishop of León and Fray Cirilo de la Alameda. Altogether, he augmented the power of the Church to a level approaching theocracy, an unheard-of situation. In exchange, the Church hailed him time after time as 'the anointed holder of the Throne', 'sweet Fernando', 'beloved Fernando', 'defender of the holy religion', and for having been 'triumphant over the horrendous monster of impiety.'[36] The king was unable to see that, in the new political world, he would have defended the crown more effectively by proclaiming himself 'first among Spaniards', the most heroic and long-suffering representative of 'Spain'.

When the Constitution of Cádiz was restored as a result of Riego's *pronunciamiento* in 1820, the supporters of Fernando raised levies against the revolutionary government which were not called 'patriotic' or 'national' but 'apostolic' or the 'army of the Faith'. The most extreme of the king's supporters also organised themselves into a body called '*royal* volunteers' in answer to the liberal national militia, but this was created 'in close collaboration with the Catholic Church', according to Artola. It is significant that the proclamation published in 1823 by the guerrilla friar known as *El Trapense* did not begin with a call to arms to 'Spaniards!' but with one to 'My brothers in Jesus Christ'. It also finished with 'Long live Jesus! Long live Holy Mary! Long live the Holy Roman Catholic and Apostolic Religion! Long live the King our lord!' The proclamations of the Royal Junta that was set up in Navarre during the *trienio* of 1820–1823 were also almost exclusively religious in nature: 'Brave and generous Navarrese: . . . Beneath the dense and deceitful veil of the Constitution, in place of the promised felicity, were concealed the altars of impiety in order to sacrifice upon them at one and the same time Religion, the King and the *Patria* . . . Know you well that its purpose (the pen shudders at these words) is to separate you totally from obedience to, and spiritual communion with, the Vicar of Jesus Christ. Know you that these barbarous monsters of iniquity who try to deprive you of your Religion are also the declared enemies of the Throne'.[37] The most extreme of liberals responded by calling themselves '*comuneros*'. Perhaps it was never so clear as during the *Trienio* that the nation was a specifically liberal myth which the absolutists attempted to counter by invoking religion.

For the liberals, it was bad enough that the revolutionary experiment of 1820–1823 failed and that Fernando was returned to power for a second time. What made it even worse was that this was the result of foreign intervention, thereby underlining the non-national nature of Fernando's absolutism. France sent to restore Fernando an army which was not, on this occasion, dedicated to the revolutionary Goddess of Reason, but to Saint Louis. Those who, only six years earlier, had denigrated France for being a hotbed of enlightened philosophy, corruption and atheism now applauded it enthusiastically. One of them, José

Antonio Llanos, in his *Memorias Poéticas*, reserves his highest praise for the 'valiant and generous Gaul', while condemning 'the libertine race', or Spanish liberals. A national framing of the conflict – of Spaniard against Frenchmen – is eschewed in favour of the universal, ideological war of Catholic against revolutionary. The poem mentions both the *Madre Patria* and Iberia, but not Spain, while the only person found worthy of the adjective 'holy' is Fernando.[38]

Back in absolute power in 1823, Fernando once again earned the epithet of 'holy' by throwing himself back onto the Church – a Church now reduced to its anti-enlightenment sectors as a result of the appointments and promotions that were pursued during the first period of his reign. Under pressure from the French, he nonetheless created the *Juntas de Fe* in order to continue the work of the Holy Office. Just like the Inquisition, the *Juntas* could condemn people to death but, hypocritically, their execution was left to the ordinary system of justice. The Valencian schoolmaster Antonio Ripoll was the last person to be burnt at the stake, three hundred and fifty years after the Holy Office had been founded. The *Junta* that condemned the unfortunate Ripoll was acting under instructions from the Archbishop of Valencia, the same Fray Simón López who had written the *Despertador* in 1809.[39]

During its final decade of 1823–1833, absolutism had the support of a number of what Pedro C. González Cuevas has termed 'legitimating theologians', including Atilano Dehaxo Solórzano, José Clemente Carnicero and Francisco Puigserver. According to this author, the most important cultural and ideological undertaking of the period was the *Biblioteca de la Religión*, edited by the Cardinal of Toledo, Pedro de Inguanzo, who had been a leading absolutist *diputado* in Cádiz. This comprised French and Italian counter-revolutionary writers who dealt with the Pope and the Catholic faith while highlighting the evils of impiety and the punishment of unbelievers.[40] Opinion in Spain may have been deeply divided over Fernando, but the most conservative sectors in Europe were delighted with him. In 1824, no less than Joseph de Maistre, the great champion of the Catholic Counter-Revolution in the Latin world, dedicated his *Six Lettres sur l'Inquisition espagnole* to defending the institution that had safeguarded Spain's spiritual unity. Spain was the model for the alliance between Altar and Throne; an alliance that was perhaps circumstantial but nevertheless far closer than in the time of Felipe II. It was, in fact, an anti-national alliance between two supra-national powers: on the one hand the Altar, embodied in the Pope and the various territorial branches of the Church, and on the other the Throne, represented by the coalition of absolute monarchs.

Apología del Trono y el Altar was the very title of a work published in

1818 by the Capuchin monk Rafael de Vélez, which Javier Herrero considers to be 'the most systematic construction of reactionary ideology of the age'. Rewarded after the first restoration, like Fray Simón López, with a bishopric, his career continued to prosper after the second in 1823, when he was appointed Archbishop of Santiago. His general political theories are not relevant here, but it is enough to say that Archbishop Vélez found all rational or scientific approaches to political theory to be suspect, including Aristotle and the most distinguished names of Catholic scholasticism. He considered the 'science' of public law and political economy to be particularly dangerous as, according to him, it was destructive of the social order. It was from this 'science' that the Constitutionalists had derived their 'false' if not openly 'heretical principles', such as that nations preceded kings. 'Were there ever children without parents?', asked Vélez rhetorically. No less heretical, in his eyes, was the assertion that kings were born in order to serve nations and not nations for kings. Instead of continuing scholastic thought, Vélez was representative of the absolutist mindset, reiterating the ideas of Filmer and Bossuet that had been taken up by Hervás: society is ordered like the family and it is constitutively hierarchical. Power is always transmitted from superior to inferior and never the other way around. The king receives his power directly from God, whom he represents while he reigns – and before whom he is solely responsible – and magistrates receive power from the king, whom they in turn represent and to whom they answer. Only the sovereign, the bearer of divine authority and the guarantor of order, possesses political legitimacy. The nation does not exist in this sense. According to Vélez, the sovereignty of the people is not only absurd, it is sinful. Those who advocate it, or demand popular participation in legislation, are claiming powers that do not correspond to them and which offend not only the sovereign, but also the divine order.[41]

In conclusion, Spanish political literature in the reign of Fernando, like the propaganda of the 1793–1795 war and most of that of the 1808–1814 conflict, was fuelled by anti-enlightenment, anti-revolutionary *Catholic* polemicists, whose thinking diverged from the *Spanish* scholastic tradition. Although the most prominent of these thinkers were later acclaimed by Menéndez Pelayo and even by some relatively recent Francoist historians, they lacked both originality and quality in comparison not only with the outstanding figures of earlier eras of Spanish intellectual history, but even with the other European counter-revolutionary thinkers of their time. It is precisely the absence of originality that is most striking in their work as well as its *afrancesamiento*, however strange this might seem in such stubborn defenders of the

Spanish tradition or 'way of life'. The whole period was one of little creativity within Catholic thought in general, while in Spain it was limited
to the imitation, even plagiarism, of French and Italian polemicists.

By choosing not to present himself as the personification of an
'eternal Spain', of the glorious nation that had just defeated the
invincible Napoleon, Fernando VII showed that he failed to understand
that the most conservative sectors of the Church disliked the nation
precisely because such a myth could strengthen the power of the State.
It did not occur to him that his chosen followers were not going to
welcome his own attempts – as *Head of State*, for he was not a religious
authority – at building a strong State, even though his purpose was very
different to that of the liberal nationalists.

Carlism, another lost opportunity

The last ten years of the tragic reign of Fernando, from the intervention of the Hundred Thousand Sons of Saint Louis to the death of
the king in 1833, is still known today as the 'Ominous Decade'. The
history books tend to dismiss these years in a few lines, as a black
period of terror and obscurantism, but it was also the time when the
rapprochement between Altar and Throne finally came to an end.

It could be claimed that the alliance first began to break down as
early as 1824, the year in which it was recognised that restoring the situation to its previous state was impossible: the dire financial straits of the
Treasury prevented it from returning certain property to the Church,
while the allies had refused to countenance the reintroduction of the
Inquisition. It could also be argued that the first cracks appeared in
1826–1827, when the death of João VI of Portugal led to a liberal revolution and civil war in which the Spanish court was heavily involved. Or
the cracks might be said to date from 1830, when the Bourbons were
supplanted in France by Louis Philippe d'Orléans, who established a
liberal monarchy, and when Fernando, who had married for the fourth
time, finally found himself with an heir, although she was female and
in delicate health. Hard-pressed by the wretched state of affairs at the
Treasury and the impossibility of obtaining new loans, the absolute
monarch found himself obliged to resort to a group of what González
Cuevas calls 'bureaucratic conservatives' (of the sort known under
Francoism as 'technocrats'), who undertook a series of modernising
changes. The Minister of Finance, López Ballesteros, belonged to this
group and, at a later date, so did Cea Bermúdez and Javier de Burgos.
One of the measures taken by López Ballesteros was the creation of a
Ministry of Development. Today, its functions would be considered

more technical than political, but the clergy interpreted them as an attack upon the structure of the *ancien régime* and the social functions that had traditionally corresponded to themselves. Protests soon followed. The police corps, another Bonapartist invention, was created in 1824 and soon came up against 'strong opposition from those who preferred the re-establishment of the Inquisition, considered to be more efficient and more reliable in combatting the liberals'. The 'royal volunteers' in particular demanded that the king suppress the police force.[42] They reasoned that there was no need for the police – an invention of the Freemasons – if there already existed within the Spanish tradition an institution of such proven efficacy in maintaining religious unity and social peace as the Inquisition.

Mixed in with cries of 'death to the police' and 'long live the Inquisition' came, for the first time, shouts of protest from hard-line absolutists against their illustrious idol, Fernando. In November 1826, the 'Federation of Pure Royalists' published a manifesto that repudiated Fernando VII in the harshest terms ('the debility, stupidity, ingratitude and bad faith of that unworthy prince, of that parricide'). There are doubts about the authorship of the document, but the following year there was a royalist rebellion against Fernando known as the *guerra dels Malcontents* which was to be the prelude to the Carlist wars of the 1830s. The rallying cries were along the same lines as the manifesto but without the insults to the king: 'long live religion, long live the absolute king, long live the Inquisition, death to Freemasonry and all occult sects'. When he rebelled in Reus, Rafi Vidal claimed that his aim was to 'sustain and defend with our lives the sweet and sacred names of religion, king and Inquisition'. The names of the ultra right-wing secret societies that conspired against Fernando in his last years clearly coincided with this religious, not national, orientation: *La Purísima*, the Exterminating Angel, the Apostolic Juntas, the Army of the Faith, etc.

In spite of the reverence in which the absolute monarch was held, this was a rebellion against his policies. In reality, the king was timidly endeavouring to modernise the State. Those in revolt defended the Inquisition and the convents, asylums and hospitals that the State was trying to replace with a police force and a Ministry of Development. The ultra-absolutists had forced the government into an impossible situation because 'it could not deal with any of the fundamental social issues'. In other words, the government was unable to adapt the State to meet the needs of the moment. Nor could it modernise the economy 'without its attempts being considered as a capitulation to liberal or enlightened thought'.[43]

At this point, the absolutist extremists who rejected the king's

policies began to broach the idea of the Infante Don Carlos as an alternative to Fernando. What were the merits of Don Carlos and what was
his programme? According to Artola, his ideology 'is so barren as to
defy analysis. It is devoid of any idea beyond a total surrender to the
will of God'. This opinion does not seem to be an exaggeration: among
the most significant of his papers are the oft-quoted recommendations
given by Don Carlos to his brother at the height of the crisis in the
summer of 1826: 'Let there be holy fear of God and there will be good
customs, virtues, peace, tranquillity, joy and all'. The manifesto of the
'Federation of Pure Royalists', in which the name of the pious Infante
was first mooted, read: 'Let us make the air resound with hymns of
praise to entreat the help of the Almighty . . . Let us place in his divine
hands the future destinies of our beloved *patria* . . . Let us proclaim as
its leader his August Majesty Señor Don Carlos V, because the virtues
of this prince, his adherence to the clergy and to the Church are even
greater guarantees'. However much Don Carlos claimed to be following in the Spanish tradition, there are clearly no precedents of such an
openly theocratic programme.[44]

Upon the death of the disastrous Fernando in 1833, the supporters
of his brother rebelled. Although the ostensible reason for the rebellion was the issue of the succession, this was merely 'the pretext that
serv[ed] to unleash the conflict that existed between two political tendencies and, more especially, between two social groups that refused
to coexist. The first Carlist war is fundamentally a belated combat in
defence of the socio-economic structures of the *ancien régime*'. Indeed
it was, but this analysis overlooks that fact that its purpose was also to
defend a political theocracy of a type unknown under the *ancien régime*.
It comes as no surprise that the Church was so heavily involved in the
Carlist uprising because the Church network was, without a shadow
of a doubt, the means of mobilising the Carlists, just as it had mobilised other forces in the wars of 1793–1795, 1808, 1822 and 1827,
and just as it had refrained from doing as a result of the invasion of the
Hundred Thousand Sons of Saint Louis in 1823. As soon as the rebellion began, a 'secret Regency' was set up, two of whose three members
were the General of the Jesuits and the Bishop of León. Fray Cirilo de
la Alameda, the Franciscan Archbishop of Cuba and ultra-absolutist
ex-member of the Council of State under Fernando, would become
a member of the equivalent Carlist institution and preside over the
Council in the absence of the pretender.[45]

It is no exaggeration to say that Carlism was the most important
politico-social movement in nineteenth-century Spain. However, there
is no general agreement among historians over the reasons for its

success. Given that Carlism was a populist movement rooted in an emotional rather than an intellectual appeal, scrutiny of its symbols and slogans may be more instructive than its ideology. Among the symbols is the flag with the cross of Burgundy, sometimes known as the cross of Saint Andrew, a symbol of apparently religious significance but also used as a dynastic emblem by the Spanish Hapsburgs as Dukes of Burgundy. For a Bourbon to raise a Hapsburg standard could only signal their intention of re-establishing a counter-reformist, imperial monarchy. That aside, it is not in any sense a national symbol. As for the anthem, it praised the excellences of the Holy Tradition, which indicates adherence to the beliefs and institutions of their predecessors. The best known phrase was 'God, *Patria*, King', which was repeatedly invoked and merits close attention. The first word of the triad is 'God' and the fact that it comes first is significant in itself. There can be no doubt about the religious orientation of the Carlist army, which was sometimes called the 'Army of the Faith'. A proclamation by the Carlist colonel Basilio García in 1834 invoked 'the most holy of the throne and the altar' and ended with an appeal to join 'the ranks of the friends of our good God' with a 'long live religion and long live Carlos V!'. Don Carlos was once moved to name the *Virgen de los Dolores* as supreme commander of his armies. It was common for the Carlist troops to attend mass and even to say the rosary on a daily basis. There can be no question about the unequivocal Catholicism of the Carlists. There is no great mystery to this religiosity: it is a case of traditional Counter-Reformation Spanish Catholicism, which was under threat from the increasing number of functions appropriated by the State. Opposition to State expansion goes some way to explaining the support for Carlism from certain sectors of the nobility and other privileged groups on the periphery, which clung to the idea of the 'traditional monarchy' and the mediaeval '*fueros*' as a means of impeding the advance of the State.

Less clear is the meaning of the second word in this triad, '*Patria*'. It had been included for a long time and was cited by absolutist orators during the wars of 1793–1795 and 1808, as well as during the uprising of the *Malcontents*. Under Carlism, it became a commonplace, as in 'We have duties to the king, the *patria* and the religion' or 'we deserve the blessing of God, the love of the sovereign and the gratitude of the *patria*'. Not one of the references to the *patria* can be taken as an expression of nationalism. The content of '*patria*' is not just different but almost the opposite of 'nation'. The latter concept took for granted the existence of a collective subject that was, or could become, the bearer of sovereignty. In order for such a possibility to be realised, it was necessary to construct a series of myths, related to the past, in which the great virtues of the chosen people were highlighted in their collective exploits or in those of their individual heroes. Carlism makes no such references to Spanish heroes such as Viriathus, Don Pelayo or El Cid, nor to collective deeds such as the conquest of America. It does eulogise the *patria*, but the term refers to no more than a collection of 'traditions': fundamental beliefs, privileges, laws and institutions that were by no means exclusive to Spain but typical of every *ancien régime* in Europe. The '*patria*' was embodied in the King and Religion, and that was as true for a Spanish legitimist as it was for any of the Austrian, Russian and particularly French absolutist volunteers who fought for Don Carlos. '*Patria*', in short, was empty of meaning.[46]

The third word is 'King', which at first sight appears to be as clear as the word 'God'. 'Who can save Spain, apart from God and its legitimate king?' asked the Bishop of Urgel. To be a 'Royalist', or faithful to the King, meant essentially to submit oneself blindly to the monarch, to accept royal absolutism, and to recognise the unlimited authority of the legitimate heir to the crown. But Fernando VII was legitimate and yet absolutists had *not* submitted to his orders in 1826–1827; neither did they accept his annulment of the Salic Law. Decades later, they also refused to submit to other Carlist pretenders as soon as they detected any sign of divergence from the orthodox line of thought: Juan III was delegitimised by the Princess of Beira, and the Duke of Madrid, Carlos VII himself, by Ramón Nocedal, who argued that the pretender had 'legitimacy of origin' but not 'of exercise'. In other words, loyalty to an absolute king was *not* blind. However much the movement defined itself as *Carlist*, the basis of its identity was not founded on any kind of personal fidelity to Don Carlos or his legitimate successors. On occasion, this was admitted by the theorists: Joaquín Muzquiz went so far as to say that the aim of the movement was to 'found a new nationality on the Catholic idea, before which the old peoples and their old legitimacies disappear'.[47] This is an extraordinary text: it discusses the foundation of a new identity which, although it is called a 'nationality', is not national but Catholic. Confronted by the latter, the 'old legitimacies', including both the national and the dynastic, disappear. The only basis for legitimacy is Catholicism. Thus, the only authority to which Ramón Nocedal would submit after he had dared to challenge the pretender and found the *Partido Integrista* was that of the Pope, who finally ordered him to disband his party. 'King', the third concept, proves to be almost as flimsy as '*Patria*'. Only one is unequivocal: God, to which might be added, Religion and Catholicism.

Pérez Galdós, in his *Episodios Nacionales*, repeatedly viewed the Carlist wars as the confrontation of 'religion' and 'freedom'. The incompatibility between traditional religious identity and the new national legitimacy reached such a pitch that, on more than one occasion, the figure of the Carlist friar was described as entering *pueblos* with the cry of 'Long live religion, long live the king, down with the nation!' on his lips. Pío Baroja recalled a friar by the name of Orri and nicknamed *Padre Puñal* who was famous for his 'Death to the nation!' Galdos also describes absolutist crowds shouting the same thing.[48] The right detested the word 'nation'. The Isabelline or liberal troops referred to themselves as 'nationalists', which is ironic given that, just one hundred years later, during the civil war of 1936–1939, it would be the insurgent right that adopted the same terminology. In both cases, these were civil wars with international implications: during the Carlist war the liberals received considerable help from the British, though this was played down for domestic reasons. By contrast, the Carlists had no such reservations about resorting to international appeals for men, money and arms, though with little success. They were, however, joined by some French and Central European volunteers; these were legitimists who fought in Spain for the cause they would have liked to have defended in their own countries and who regarded it as a common cause. One of the French legitimists, the Comte de Villemur, was named Minister for War by Don Carlos in 1834. A fictional Carlist in the *Episodio nacional* complains about not receiving more international assistance, claiming that 'here we are fighting for the cause of all the powers, for legitimate thrones, against revolution and Jacobinism'. Indeed, the Carlist *Boletín* of 1838 maintained it was in the interests of 'all the governments of Europe', of 'all civilised peoples', to help Don Carlos 'stifle the revolution'. Most significant of all was the moral support which the Carlists received from the Pope, who refused to recognise Isabel II for a long time. In return, they became heavily involved in the Italian struggles, taking up the cause of the Pope as their own.[49] All of this points to the tenuous patriotic or national nature of the movement. In the twentieth-century civil war, however, when the Nationalists had become the right, they benefited from the crucial support of Nazi Germany and Fascist Italy, but, true to their national role, it was now they who made a huge effort to conceal the fact. On this occasion, it was their rivals who boasted of the international support and of the weapons received from Stalin. At the beginning of the twentieth century, a strong identification with national sentiment had become a feature of the right, while the left had diluted it with references to numerous other modern political myths, such as equality, democracy, progress and social revolution. At the beginning of the nineteenth, the situation had been the opposite: the left portrayed itself as national while the loyalties of the right were divided between nation, dynasty and, above all, religion.

The counter-revolutionary world vision: the Church against the evil of modernity

The culmination of the counter-revolutionary vision in Spain is repre-sented by the later work of Juan Donoso Cortés, the great mid-century reactionary, whose thought underlines just how far removed that vision was from nationalism. Juan Donoso Cortés, Marqués de Valdegamas and the Spanish ambassador to Paris during the revolutionary events of 1848, was one of the few political thinkers from the Peninsula whose political thought had any impact in Europe. This may be precisely because his work was not centred on Spanish problems. He portrayed a conflict that was not between Spain and anti-Spain, but between Catholicism and the demons of modernity: materialism, immorality, and the revolution that was destroying civilisation. And he was unpar-alleled in the apocalyptic manner in which he expressed that struggle. Believing himself to be a new Augustine of Hippo witnessing the col-lapse of the Roman Empire, he conceived of his *Ensayo sobre el catoli-cismo, el liberalismo y el socialismo* as a new *City of God*, setting out the final great battle between Catholic civilisation and rationalist error.[50] For him, as for Hervás y Panduro, Ceballos, Barruel, De Maistre and Alvarado, the origin of the problem was to be sought in rationalism. 'Reason follows error wherever it goes', was one of the aphorisms at which he excelled. One of his formulations, as categorical as it was arbitrary, described the successive incarnations of 'rationalist error': in the seventeenth century it was Protestantism, in the eighteenth century it was enlightenment philosophy, in the nineteenth century it was liberalism, which by 1848 had revealed its true face: socialism. This was an anarchic socialism, as personified in Pierre Joseph Proudhon, in whom Donoso had identified the new anti-Christ, the leader of the revolutionary hordes who were coming to destroy all excellence and all civilisation; a tide of destruction that would lead to an egalitarian tyranny of unimaginable dimensions. All Donoso Cortés could think of to counteract this revolutionary wave was for a 'religious reaction', for a 'Catholic dictatorship'. He clamoured for it not only for Spain but also for Europe, as he believed the problem extended far beyond national borders.[51]

Except for the force of his arguments – and the quality of his prose – there is nothing in the work of Donoso Cortés in 1848 that had not been written by Alvarado or Barruel thirty and fifty years before.

'Behind every political issue there is always a religious issue', went another of the axioms that made him famous. This sums up what all of them had to say: that modern rationalism was a satanic theology, that it had inevitably evolved from Protestantism to Enlightenment philosophy, revolutionary liberalism and, finally, socialist egalitarianism and anarchic barbarism. Just like the other counter-revolutionary thinkers considered in this chapter, Donoso believed in the absolute incompatibility between Catholic civilisation – based on submission to natural hierarchies and the repression of base instincts – and any socio-political organisation that was founded on natural reason and the satisfaction of earthly desires. As Begoña Urigüen concludes, 'the most radical principle of Donoso's anti-*moderantismo* [is] the irreconcilability between truth and error, between Religion and Philosophy, between the Church and Revolution'.[52]

Of most interest here is the fact that there is still no room for the nation in the ideas of this outstanding representative of Spanish conservatism in the mid-nineteenth century. The nation continued to be as suspect to him as it had been to the theorists of absolutism in the time of Fernando, a suspicion which was no doubt fanned by the nationalist fervour which he witnessed at first hand during the revolutions of 1848. Those who, he wrote, 'worship popular sovereignty worship an absurdity . . . In the normal state of societies, the people do not exist, only interests, . . . opinions, . . . parties' exist.[53] It is understandable that he should have been at odds with González Bravo, a politician with a liberal background who was moving towards extreme conservatism, but who based his position on a radical affirmation of the rights of the Spanish nation. Donoso, in contrast, took a European point of view. His inspiration came from Augustin Barruel, from Joseph de Maistre and from all the Franco-Italian anti-Enlightenment thought (Bergier, Nonotte, Valsechi, Mozzi) that had also influenced Vélez and Alvarado. Far more cosmopolitan than they were, Donoso felt openly European; he wrote for a European public and published his *Ensayo sobre el catolicismo* in French as well as Spanish. In the final years of his life, he also wrote a *Llamamiento a los conservadores* (the European ones) and did what he could to achieve an anti-revolutionary alliance of the continental Christian monarchies to counteract the liberal policy of the British – which included appeals to Louis Napoleon and the retired Metternich. It was an alliance that was to have been sponsored and protected by the Church, the only entity truly capable of saving societies from the 'danger of death' by which they were threatened.[54] Donoso's wisdom was passed on through Louis Veuillot and had a clear influence on Pope Pius IX and his *Syllabus*.

Two last aspects of conservative thought will also illustrate its explicitly anti-national bias. The word *nacionalismo* was first used by Abbot Barruel in his *Memorias para servir a la historia del jacobinismo* of 1798, in which he makes it clear that he regards the phenomenon as yet another perversion of modernity. Eugene Kamenka explains that, for Abbot Barruel, nationalism meant 'the bringing down of legitimate governments whose right to exercise authority is based on divine will or hereditary rights', which was linked to the 'terrible spirit of freemasonry and the Enlightenment, rooted in selfishness'. In the words of the abbot, when *'nationalism,* or national love, replaces a general love towards humanity . . . it becomes a virtue to expand at the expense of those who do not belong to your State . . . to despise foreigners, deceive them, insult them. This virtue receives the name of *patriotism,* in other words, *egotism'*. This counter-revolutionary abbot certainly had a point when he claimed that nationalism was an expression of collective egotism. Nevertheless, he was not the appropriate ideologue to promote Spanish nationalism as interpreted in Catholic-conservative terms.

Further, the conservative world felt only distrust of nationalism. For Metternich, the Austro-Hungarian Chancellor, nationalism was one of the first examples of the dangers of modern politics. In the 1840s, the Vatican flirted with the idea of making the Papacy the focal point of Italian unity, but the revolutionary whirlwind of 1848 eliminated that possibility for good. Thereafter, the previously liberal Pius IX opposed the idea of the nation just as he opposed that of liberalism. Not even the Catholic nationalism of Poland was supported by the Pope. In 1864, after seeing his Papal territories seized by Italian nationalists, he published his famous *Syllabus,* in which, holding faithfully to the theories of Barrruel, Joseph de Maistre, Alvarado and Donoso, he condemned all and sundry: rationalism, deism, tolerance, liberalism, socialism and nationalism. In sum, reconciliation of the See of Peter with 'progress, liberalism *and modern civilisation*' was impossible. Over time, and with no little hesitation and difficulty, his successors have modified this position. This is just as well, for if the Catholic Church had indeed made no concessions to modernity it would have eventually become an increasingly marginal and eccentric faith with a steady reduction in the number of its followers.

It is significant that, in Spain, the only ones to greet the appearance of the *Syllabus* with any enthusiasm were the *integristas* of Ramón Nocedal, who were so conservative that they eventually became unacceptable even to the Carlists. Ramón Nocedal considered himself to be the intellectual heir of Donoso Cortés and in that respect, at least, he was right. Pidal y Mon, the leader of moderate Catholicism, who brought a large number of old Traditionalists into the fold of *canovista* conservatism around 1880, was also right when he branded the influence of Donoso Cortés on Spanish Catholicism as a 'calamity'.[55]

In conclusion, Spanish conservatism in the second half of the nineteenth century had begun to rectify its thinking of earlier decades. It would continue to identify with Catholicism and to defend the *'patria'* and sacrosanct 'Spanish traditions', but it would also begin to combine the former with the latter in an amalgam that, much later, would come to be known as *National-Catholicism*. By accepting and developing the idea of *nation*, it became integrated into the modern world. This is not a value judgement: modernity is not necessarily either positive or negative, but survival is impossible without being a part of it. For better or worse, Spanish Catholic conservatism made the minimal adjustment required in order to survive in the modern world.

Notes

1 S. López, *Despertador Cristiano-Político*, Valencia, 1809, pp. 17 and 18; M. Amado, *Dios y España: o sea, Ensayo sobre una demostración histórica de lo que debe España a la Religión Católica*, Madrid, 1831, Vol. III, p. 261.

2 Napoleon, according to R. Nürnberger, quoted by P. C. González Cuevas, *Historia de las derechas españolas*, Madrid, 2000, p. 67. Invocations, in F.-X. Guerra, *Modernidad e Independencias*, Madrid, 1992, p. 158.

3 In spite of the high number of university students in sixteenth-century Spain (a number that would drop sharply in the seventeenth), according to R. Kagan, *Students and Society in Early Modern Spain*, Baltimore, MD: Johns Hopkins University Press, 1974.

4 G. Hermet, *Les catholiques dans l'Espagne franquiste*, Paris, 1980–81, Vol. I, p. 63.

5 Etymology of *marranos*, see J. Caro Baroja, *Los judíos en la España moderna y contemporánea*, Madrid, 1978, Vol. I, p. 129; for prosecutions, see Y. Baer, *Historia de los judíos en la España cristiana*, Madrid, 1981, Vol. II, or B. Netanyahu, *The Origins of the Inquisition in Fifteenth-Century Spain*, New York, 1995; figures of *conversos*, discrepancies between A. Domínguez Ortiz, *Los judeoconversos en la España moderna*, Madrid: Mapfre, 1991 p. 41, and B. Netanyahu, *Los marranos españoles*, Valladolid, 1994, pp. 203–211.

6 J. García Mercadal, *Viajes de estranjeros*, I, pp. 295–296, 309–326 and 328–417; J. Liske, *Viajes de extranjeros por España y Portugal en los siglos XV, XVI y XVII*, Madrid, 1878, pp. 46 and 55–57.

7 See, among others, J. Meseguer Fernández, *Historia de la Inquisición en España y América*, Madrid, 1984, Vol. I, pp. 395–397. According to P. Dedieu, by 1540 Judaism was already 'a residual phenomenon'(quoted by A. Domínguez Ortiz, *Los judeoconversos*, p. 36); according to A. Milhou, around 1525–1530 Cryptojudaism had been essentially dismantled in

Spain. See his 'La cultura cristiana frente al judaísmo y al islam: identidad hispánica y rechazo del otro (1449–1727)', *Monarquía católica y sociedad hispánica*, Fundación Duques de Soria, 1994, pp. 1 and 18–19.

8 Different figures in Caro Baroja, *Los judíos*, I, pp. 198–205; Baer, *Historia de los judíos*, II, pp. 649–650; Netanyahu, *Los marranos españoles*, pp. 203–211; and Milhou, 'La cultura cristiana', p. 15.

9 R. Villa-Real, *Historia de Granada*, Granada, 1991, pp. 151–152.

10 Ibid., p. 166.

11 See H. Lapeyre, *Géographie de l'Espagne morisque*, Paris, 1959; J.-P. Le Flem, in M. Tuñón de Lara (ed.), *Historia de España*, Barcelona, 1982, Vol. V, pp. 95–96; Milhou, 'La cultura cristiana', p. 16; J. Reglá, *Estudios sobre los moriscos*, Valencia, 1964; or J. Linz, 'Five Centuries of Spanish History: Quantification and Comparison'in V. R. Lorwin and J. Price (eds), *The Dimensions of the Past*, Yale University Press, 1972, pp. 190–192.

12 Fray Marcos de Guadalajara and Pedro Aznar, quoted by R. García Cárcel, 'El concepte d'Espanya als segles XVI i XVII', *L'Avenç*, 100, 1987, p. 44.

13 Antón del Montoro, quoted by A. Domínguez Ortiz, *Los judeoconversos*, pp. 255–256.

14 On the *Estatutos*, see A. Sicroff, *Les controverses des statuts de pureté de sang en Espagne du XVe au XVIIe siècle*, Paris, 1960. Cf. Domínguez Ortiz, *Los judeoconversos*, pp. 137–172.

15 On the *cristianos nuevos*, see A. Castro, *La realidad histórica de España*, 3rd edn, Mexico, 1966 and several other studies. According to J. J. Linz, 'Intellectual Roles in Sixteenth and Seventeenth-Century Spain', *Daedalus*, 101(3), 1972: 69, no more than 10% of sixteenth-century intellectuals and 6% in the seventeenth came from a *converso* family.

16 Münzer, in García Mercadal, *Viajes de extranjeros*, I, pp. 53–54, 85, 111–115, 149 and 171–172. Guicciardini, 'Relación del viaje (1512)', in ibid., I, 609–623.

17 S. Arnoldsson, *Leyenda Negra: estudios sus origines*, Goteborg, 1960, p. 31. Bataillon and Richelieu in Milhou, 'La cultura cristiana', pp. 12 and 14. Russians, in J. H. Billington, *The Icon and the Axe: An Interpretive History of Russian Culture*, New York, 1966, p. 70.

18 See, for instance, A. Domínguez Ortiz, *El Antiguo Régimen: los Reyes Católicos y los Austrias*, Madrid, 1973, pp. 220–239.

19 Quoted by J. A. Maravall, *Teatro y literatura*, pp. 126–127 and 132–133.

20 On Suárez, see C. Valverde, 'La filosofía', in *El Siglo del Quijote*, Vol. XXVI of the *Historia de España Menéndez Pidal*, Madrid, 1986, pp. 103–110. On Vitoria, V. Beltrán, *Francisco de Vitoria*, Barcelona, 1939, pp. 157ff. On both, A. Dempf *La filosofía cristiana del Estado en España*, Madrid, 1961, pp. 106–159.

21 See A. Morales Moya (ed.), *Las bases políticas, económicas y sociales de un régimen en transformación (1759–1834)*, Vol. XXX of the *Historia de España Menéndez Pidal*, Madrid, 1988, pp. 90 and 138.

22 J. Herrero, *Los orígenes del pensamiento reaccionario español*, Madrid, 1971, pp. 91–133.

23 On Macanaz, see C. Martín Gaite, *El proceso de Macanaz: Historia de un empapelamiento*, Madrid, 1970. On Jansenism, R. Herr, *The Eighteenth-Century Revolution in Spain*, Princeton, NJ: Princeton University Press, 1969, pp. 398–434; Herrero, *Orígenes del pensamiento reaccionario*, pp. 71–89; F. Lafage, *L'Espagne de la contre-révolution*, Paris, L'Harmattan, 1993, pp. 49–76.

24 On Ceballos, see Herrero, *Orígenes del pensamiento*, pp. 91–104; and J. L. Abellán, *Historia crítica del pensamiento español*, Madrid, 1984, Vol. IV, pp. 151–155.

25 Hervás y Panduro (1735–1809), *Historia de la vida del hombre*, with a volumen devoted to the Frenche Revolution, and *Las causas de la Revolución de Francia*, 2 vols (1794). On him, J. Herrero, *Orígenes del pensamiento*, pp. 151–181.

26 The Amat-Villanueva-Hervás episode, in Menéndez Pelayo, *Historia de los heterodoxos españoles*, Madrid, 1986, bk VI, chap. III; cf. Abellán, *Historia crítica del pensamiento*, IV, p. 152.

27 J.-R. Aymes, *La Guerra de España contra la Revolución Francesa (1793–1795)*, Alicante, 1991, pp. 413–419, 439–446. 'Por Dios, el Rey y la Patria'in 1793, according to R. Gambra Ciudad, *La primera guerra civil de España (1821–1823)*, Madrid, 1950, p. 100.

28 Aymes, *La Guerra de España*, pp. 422 and 440.

29 On Fr. Diego de Cádiz, see Herrero, *Orígenes del pensamiento*, pp. 142–147; or Abellán, *Historia crítica del pensamiento*, IV, pp. 162–165.

30 Herrero, *Orígenes del pensamiento*, pp. 222–223; quote of *Diario*, pp. 227–228; 1808 war as a crusade, also in Abellán, *Historia crítica del pensamiento*, IV, pp. 165ff.

31 S. López, *Despertador Cristiano-Político*, Valencia, 1809, pp. 1–4, 6 and 12.

32 Ibid., pp. 17 and 30. On this pamphlet, Herrero, *Orígenes del pensamiento*, pp. 251–256.

33 *Catecismos políticos españoles*, Madrid, 1989, pp. 17 and 19.

34 Guerra, *Modernidad e Independencias*, p. 249.

35 The marquise of Rumblar character, in Pérez Galdós'*National Episodes*, mistrusted the British for being 'blind to the trae and only Church'(*Cádiz*, XXVIII). M. M. López'poem, in *Los afectuosos gemidos de la nación española*, Cádiz, N. Gómez, 1813 (*Vile Spaniards, infatuated with pride and seductive words of equality, freedom and – how lunatic! – nation, independence, cities, natural and imprescriptible rights.*)

36 M. Artola, *La burguesía revolucionaria (1808–1874)*, Madrid, p. 51; and *La España de Fernando VII*, Madrid, 1992, p. 869; A. M. Moral Roncal, *Carlos V de Borbón (1788–1855)*, Madrid, 1999, pp. 113, 119, 173.

37 Artola, *España de Fernando VII*, p. 864. *El Trapense*, in P. de Montoya, *La intervención del clero vasco en las contiendas civiles (1820–23)*, San Sebastián,

1971, p. 352. Royal Junta in Navarre, in Lafage, *Espagne de la contre-révolution*, p. 105.

38 J. A. Llanos, *Memorias poéticas, o Llantos de la Madre Patria por los efectos de la Ominosa Constitución*, Madrid, 1824, pp. 15, 19–20 and 26–27.

39 Artola, *España de Fernando VII*, p. 862.

40 González Cuevas, *Historia de las derechas*, p. 77.

41 R. Vélez (1777–1850), Capuchin friar, published in Cádiz, during the war, *El Sol de Cádiz* (1812–13) and *Preservativo contra la Irreligión* (1812). On him, Herrero, *Orígenes del pensamiento*, pp. 264–267 and 294–300; or Abellán, *Historia crítica del pensamiento*, IV, pp. 168–171.

42 Artola, *España de Fernando VII*, p. 865; previous quote, in p. 857; protests against the Ministry, pp. 922–923; objections to the police, in 1826, in F. Lafage, *Espagne de la contre-révolution*, p. 111.

43 Artola, *España de Fernando VII*, p. 873.

44 Ibid., p. 884.

45 Ibid., pp. 925–926, 943 and 945. Cf. W. Callahan, *Church, Politics and Society in Spain, 1770–1874*, Cambridge, MA: Harvard University Press, pp. 147 and 151. Alameda, 'Instituciones del Estado carlista', in R. M. Lázaro Torres, *El poder de los carlistas: Evolución y declive de un Estado, 1833–1839*, Bilbao, 1993, pp. 73 and 102.

46 The reference to an ethnic *patria* also guaranteed the Catholic and monarchical character of Spain, according to Lafage, *Espagne de la contre-révolution*, pp. 105–106.

47 V. Garmendia, *La ideología carlista (1868–1876)*, San Sebastián, 1984; bishop of Urgel, p. 234; Muzquiz, p. 236.

48 'Freedom' vs 'religión', in Pérez Galdós, *La campaña del Maestrazgo*, chap. VII; '¡Muera la Nación!'and '¡Vivan las caenas!'cries, in *Los Cien Mil Hijos de San Luis*, chap. XXX; '¡Viva el Rey absoluto! ¡Muera la Nación!', chap. XXXVI. *Padre Puñal*, in Baroja, quoted by Montoya, *Intervención del clero vasco*, p. 36.

49 See J. Canal, *El carlismo*, Madrid, 2000, p. 153. Pérez Galdós, *De Oñate*, chap. V. *Boletín de Navarra y Provincias Vascongadas*, 16-II-1838, quoted by Lázaro Torres, *El poder de los carlistas*, pp. 11–12.

50 J. Donoso Cortés, *Obras Completas*, Madrid, 1946, Vol. II, pp. 368, 409 and 437. Cf. J. Álvarez Junco, 'Estudio preliminar'in Juan Donoso Cortés, *Lecciones de Derecho político* [1835], Madrid, 1984.

51 Even a Francoist author such as F. Gutiérrez Lasanta in *Donoso Cortés, el Profeta de la Hispanidad*, Logroño, 1953, and despite the title, interprets Donoso, above all, as a 'European'. On Donoso's irrationalism, rather than Romanticism, see V. Lloréns, *El romanticismo español*, Madrid, 1979, pp. 557–559.

52 Donoso Cortés, *Obras Completas*, 1970 edn, Vol. II, p. 312; satanic theology in socialism, Vol. II, pp. 597–600. B. Urigüen, *Orígenes y evolución de la derecha española*, Madrid, 1986, p. 60.

53 Donoso Cortés, *Obras Completas*, ed. 1946, Vol. I, pp. 197–198.

54 Donoso Cortés, *Obras Completas*, ed. 1970, Vol. II, pp. 653, 894–895 y 910; J. T. Graham, *Donoso Cortés, Utopian Romanticist and Political Realist*, Columbia, MO: University of Missouri Press, 1974, Chapter 9. On the French-Italian counter-revolutionary thinkers behind him, see Abellán, *Historia crítica del pensamiento*, IV, p. 179.
55 Urigüen, *Orígenes y evolución de la derecha*, p. 55.

7

The 'Two Spains'

Romanticism: the Catholic essence of Spain

The restoration of the *ancien régime* throughout Europe in 1815 following the defeat of Napoleon also saw the emergence of a new literary and philosophical movement: Romanticism. In Spain, the Romantic movement provided the opportunity for national identity to be remade in a Catholic image. Although the chronology of Spanish Romanticism has been the subject of much debate among literary historians, there is general agreement that a key role was played in its introduction into Spain by Johann Nikolaus Böhl von Faber, a native of Germany naturalised Spaniard as Juan Nicolás Böhl de Faber who, in 1814, published an adaptation of some lectures on history of theatre given in Vienna by August Wilhelm Schlegel. In the adaptation, the cause of Spanish Baroque theatre, which had been disregarded for a century and a half because it did not conform to neoclassical rules, was championed, especially the work of Pedro Calderón de la Barca, who was regarded not only as displaying great poetic imagination but also a profound Catholic spirituality. Böhl de Faber's passionate defence of the Baroque literary style was closely bound up with his own visceral anti-liberalism. Moreover, his wife, Francisca Ruiz de Larrea, published a pamphlet in the same year in which she claimed that the 'ancient character of the nation' and the 'race of the Pelayos' were both indissolubly linked to Catholicism and the absolute monarchy.[1]

Together with their Romanticism and conservatism, the Böhls manifested an appreciation of the *Spanish* identity as one of the most *Romantic* in Europe. Böhl de Faber, like Schlegel, was a follower of Johann Gottfried Herder, for whom both language and literature were 'national' insofar as they expressed a certain mentality and outlook. Herder regarded Spain as one of the most clearly defined nations in Europe in terms of its own 'way of life', but the Spanish national spirit, as expressed in the work of Calderón de la Barca, was the one most consistent with the new Romantic style. This was because Spanish

literature was replete with the chivalrous, heroic, religious and monarchic values typical of the mediaeval world that modern Europe was in
danger of relinquishing. From the perspective of German Romanticism,
Spain had already revealed its defined personality and literary dimension during the Middle Ages in such works as *El Cantar del Mío Cid*,
reaching a peak of perfection with the poetry and drama of the *Siglo
de Oro* or Golden Age. This creativity was thought to have declined
in the eighteenth century when the *afrancesamiento* (or increasingly
French outlook) of the Spanish court had caused poets and dramatists
alike to neglect the work of Calderón for the neoclassical style. The
eighteenth century was therefore regarded as essentially anti-Spanish,
suggesting that enlightened rationalism, the philosophy of progress, and
the cultural and political values of the modern European world were
incompatible with the Spanish mindset or outlook.[2]

Had the ideologues surrounding Fernando VII possessed any fore-
sight, they would have applauded the effort made by Schlegel and
Böhl de Faber to rehabilitate Calderón and Spanish Baroque literature. Nothing could have identified the *ancien régime* as the defender
of national, Spanish values –as opposed to foreign ones– more appropriately than the Romantic and literary vision of Schlegel and Böhl de
Faber. If Calderón's drama, as Guillermo Carnero writes, had come to
be regarded as 'consubstantial with the national character', then respect
for his values would have become a 'question of patriotism'.[3] As it was,
for the Spanish political right at that time the concept of the *nation* produced only fear, and fear was stronger than the desire for propaganda.
The absolute king was either incapable or unwilling to take advantage
of the conservative nationalism that was inseparable from the burgeon-
ing Romantic movement. Never having incorporated into his own
discourse the patriotic language now common among his most enlightened subjects, Fernando was even less likely to look favourably upon
Romanticism, a literary style for which conservatism felt no sympathy
whatsoever. It was of little import that the new fashion in literature
had, from the outset, been associated with a defence of the past against
modernity. Fernando's supporters viewed it solely as a disturbing and
unruly phenomenon, *lacking in rules* and typical of modern rebellious-
ness and disorder. In the same way that, in politics, they kept their distance from 'the nation' and clung to religion and dynastic legitimacy, in
intellectual and aesthetic matters they remained wedded to the classics.
Neither Romanticism nor any other creative or innovative movement
managed to make any headway in Fernando's world. Romanticism
only grew in popularity after the death of the king, by which time it was
already linked to liberalism.

The most famous Spanish Romantic authors, Martínez de la Rosa, Espronceda, Larra, and the Duque de Rivas were all liberals – radical in their youth, but increasingly less so as the years went by. By about 1850, some twenty years after Fernando VII had been laid to rest in the Pantheon of the Monasterio del Escorial and 'moderate' (in fact, highly conservative) liberalism had been consolidated, the majority of these Romantics were either dead or had joined forces with conservatism.

From around 1840, Romanticism began to become acceptable within conservative circles. In 1841, Javier de Burgos revived the ideas of Schlegel and Böhl de Faber, and Gil de Zarate, one of the architects of the modern Spanish historiographical approach to literature, followed suit a year later.[4] In this late Romantic period, the most popular and influential literary figure was no longer the elderly and now highly conservative Duque de Rivas, nor the late lamented Larra or Espronceda, but José Zorrilla, who has often been dubbed the 'national poet'. As J. I. Ferreras points out, Zorrilla achieved such prominence because of his condition as 'Christian and Catholic' and because he knew how to depict 'Castilian values . . . patriotism and Spanish independence', while disregarding 'any problem of current importance'. In effect, a large part of the poet's success was due to his ability to adapt the national stereotype to the Catholic and monarchical principles of conservatism. Zorrilla had a preference for the Middle Ages, in which many of his plays and poems were located. His 'Spanish' Middle Ages contained '*moros*', who were not Spanish but 'invaders' and who were rightly expelled from a territory that did not belong to them. The *community imagined* by Zorrilla was, by definition, Catholic. As a good Romantic, Zorrilla went beyond the mere identification of Spain with Catholicism and identified himself with both. In writing poetry, he recalled 'the *patria* in which I was born and the religion in which I live. A Spaniard, I seek inspiration in our soil. A Christian, I believe that my religion is more poetical than paganism'. As he declared in one of his poems, '*cuando hoy mi voz levanto, / cristiano y español, con fe y sin miedo, / canto mi religión, mi patria canto*'.[5]

The last exponent of this line of conservative thought, whose description as Romantic was looking increasingly dubious, was *Fernán Caballero*, who was none other than Cecilia Böhl de Faber, the daughter of Nicolás Böhl and Francisca Larrea. Cecilia was a highly educated woman, as familiar with classical Spanish literature as with German and French Romanticism. Her work is of exceptional interest for the purposes of this book. On the one hand, she believed in the existence of nations as permanent entities: 'No, nationalities are not erased at the stroke of a pen nor with a false aphorism, nor with some universal style of dress'. *Fernán Caballero* not only believed in nations but also that Spain stood out among them: 'Oh, Spain! . . . mother of countless saints and warriors and scholars . . . What models you have given to the world in every field . . . it would be difficult to find a nationality more genuinely fine and elegant than the Spanish one'. For *Fernán Caballero*, as for her father, Spanish identity was embodied in the social order and the mental world of the *ancien régime*. It was in this idealised world before the revolution of 1789 that she placed her most successful novels. *La Gaviota*, *La familia de Alvareda* and *Clemencia* all had a strongly conservative political bias and they were all published following the great upheavals of 1848. In each one, she idealises a rural world that represents religiosity and the hereditary hierarchies in contrast to the cities that she describes as dens of 'cynical sensualism' and licentiousness. Even capitalism is reprehensible to this diehard conservative. In mediaeval times, when 'faith and enthusiasm reigned', gold was used for noble and worthy causes, while the modern world deployed it for 'iniquitous gain'.[6]

The most interesting political aspect of *Fernán Caballero*'s work is that her conservatism fuses with her romantic belief in nations and that her vision of Spain is not the negative image projected by the *Leyenda Negra* in the sixteenth and seventeenth centuries and by the *Ilustrados* of the eighteenth. She accepted that Spain was a nation in decline, but decadence was beautiful to a Romantic. And the fact that Spain was unable to adapt to modernity demonstrated her spiritual superiority over the rest of Europe. It was also true that Spanish society was intolerant, bordering on the fanatical, but this expressed its deep and genuine religiosity compared to the superficiality of other societies, which cynically accepted the heretic and the atheist. Cecilia Böhl de Faber thereby modified the perception of Spain abroad that had first been shaped by Lord Byron and Washington Irving, and later by the French Romantic travellers Victor Hugo, Gautier, Dumas and Mérimée.

Böhl de Faber's impact within Spain was probably greater than that without. Together with Zorrilla and the last Duque de Rivas, *Fernán Caballero* helped make the idea of the 'nation' respectable in conservative circles. At last, nationalism and Catholicism had begun to find common ground, but the process could only be completed when the national myths had been refashioned in the Catholic image. Above all, it was necessary to recover for the Catholic cause the greatest national myth of the nineteenth century – namely, the war against Napoleon – which had been allowed to sink into oblivion under absolutist rule. Meanwhile, the liberals had transformed their version of the conflict into a national-liberal epic under the name of the 'War of Independence' in which the Spanish people had fought for their 'liberty'. The new denomination had been so successful that the Catholics could not hope to change it. However, they aimed to reinterpret the significance of the struggle, explaining that the Spanish people had been motivated by religion to fight.

As early as 1814, Francisca Ruiz de Larrea, mother of *Fernán Caballero*, had written that the troops opposing Napoleon 'breathed their last for their God and their King'. In 1831, Fray Manuel Amado claimed that 'it is to our Religion, and to it alone, that we owe that tenacious struggle'. 'Religion, *Patria*, King: those were the noble words spoken by the heroes of the Second of May as they breathed their last', wrote *El Católico* on the anniversary of the Second of May in 1840, and there are thousands of similar quotations. *El Siglo Futuro*, many years later, put the final touch to this interpretation. Declaring that the Second of May was the '*fiesta* of traditionalism' and a 'silent protest against all modern civilisation and the modern State', *El Siglo Futuro* also insisted that '"God, *Patria*, King" was the cry of the people on the Second of May' and that they 'died fighting against liberalism'.[7] Thus conservative Catholicism tried to rework the Second of May as a fiesta of traditionalism against the modern State. This attempt to reinterpret the anti-Napoleonic insurrection, perhaps because of the conservative rejection of the modern State or because the effort was made too late, was never entirely successful. The Second of May celebration would always remain a manifestation of moderately secular, liberal values. Even the last conservative governments of Isabel II banned its celebration. Nonetheless, beginning at mid-century and thanks to conservative Romanticism, 'Spanishness' was to be identified with the Catholic religion, royal absolutism and an aristocratic outlook. This had its advantages as regards Spain's image in international circles, but above all it provided the basis for a viable conservative political programme at home.

The liberal assault on the Catholic past

As the century advanced, and especially from 1860 onwards, even the least observant could see that radical changes were taking place in both Spain and Europe. In Europe, the revolutions of 1848 had caused the overthrow of the 'bourgeois monarchy' of Louis Philippe in France and certain other royal houses of lesser importance but, above all, they had brought down Metternich and anything that resembled a holy alliance. In Spain, Carlism appeared to have failed, from both a military and a political standpoint, although there was, in fact, still one more long and bloody war to come. Its first defeat of 1839–1840 had been followed by a second one in 1849, and then a fiasco in 1860 when the two sons of the first Don Carlos were captured on the Catalan coast. They avoided execution by renouncing their rights, upon which the Carlist claim fell to a third brother, Don Juan, '*Juan III*', who was a mild-mannered man with liberal inclinations, divorced from a very devout wife. He even attempted a reconciliation with Isabel II, which caused one Carlist faction, led by none other than the Princess of Beira, widow of the first Carlist pretender, to repudiate him. In a manifesto entitled 'To Spaniards' (for nationalism had even begun to penetrate among the Carlists), the Princess declared her stepson Don Juan a traitor to legitimist principles and proclaimed the new leader of the movement to be his eldest son, yet another Don Carlos, the self-styled '*Carlos VII*'. But theocratic absolutism was weak and divided, and everyone recognised that its time was running out. That same year, 1868, many Carlist politicians, under the leadership of Cándido Nocedal, who still held to certain liberal values, began their return to parliamentary government.

Not even the Church was any longer what it had been. It had seen the loss of almost all its lands and a drastic reduction in the number of its monks and nuns following the process of disentailment that stretched from 1835 to 1860.[8] Its support of Fernando VII and the Carlists had eroded its prestige, and as the liberal movement ceased to be the whirlwind that threatened to topple thrones and altars, the time seemed to be right to begin some form of reconciliation. The theoretically liberal Queen Isabel II was moving closer to a position of Catholic conservatism, known by then as neo-Catholicism, owing to the influence of a very devout royal clique, whose leading lights were Sister Patrocinio, *la Monja de las Llagas*, and Father Claret, royal confessor since 1857. It also included the royal consort himself, Don Francisco de Asís, who had even been involved in the foolhardy Carlist venture on the Catalan coast. The differences between the two branches of the Bourbon family were diminishing fast and there was constant discussion about matrimonial unions.[9] Clearly the clergy had motives for abandoning Carlist insurrectionism: demands for the return of the absolute monarchy and the Inquisition were becoming increasingly anachronistic, while pragmatism dictated that the Church should be well-placed within the oligarchical, parliamentary system in order to ensure, at the very least, control of the educational system and a comfortable allowance for the clergy. The Concordat of 1851 had granted both these things on condition that the Church recognise the legitimacy of Isabel II and accept disentailment as a *fait accompli*.

With the overwhelming of the Papacy by Italy's occupation of its territories in 1860, the Catholic Church did not find itself in a position to take a strong line. In the fateful year of 1860, the symbolic threshold of a new era, the Pope had lost all the territories over which he had ruled as monarch since the early Middle Ages, except for the city of Rome, which he only managed to hang on to for another ten years. It was during the Christmas of 1864 that Pius XI declared war on the modern world with the publication of the *Syllabus* and the *Quanta Cura*. It was a sign of desperation and no one rejoiced at their appearance except the Carlists and their counterparts in other countries. In 1869, with Garibaldi's troops at the gates of Rome, '*Carlos VII*' wrote in a letter to the Pope that 'the bravest crusades went out from Gothic Spain against the Crescent, and the most enthusiastic armies will go out from Carlist Spain against the sect that originated in the seventeenth century and which, since then, has unfortunately brought down thrones and increasingly enfeebled the Catholic faith'.[10] If the sect to which he was referring were Freemasonry, he would have said the eighteenth century; if it were Protestantism, he would have said the sixteenth; but having read Hervás and Vélez, the date was correct, and the 'sect' was rationalism, the root of all modern evils.

As the liberal revolution abated and the monarchy became more conservative, nationalism started to gain in respectability. It was no longer associated with radicals, arsonists and barricades in Spain and France (although the Italian and Polish liberals were very different), but with a placid bourgeoisie that read in the daily paper of the latest exploits of the *national* army in some skirmish usually in some far-off corner of Africa or Asia. Around 1860, the feelings of every well-bred Spaniard would be stirred by talk of the 'War of Independence', which was the most memorable demonstration in recent history of the invincibility of the 'race' – a word newly propelled into the political vocabulary. Between 1857 and 1863, in one of the few periods of relative tranquillity at home, premier General O'Donnell embarked upon his 'prestige policy': a series of imperial adventures of minor significance compared with those undertaken by neighbouring States, but none the less sufficient to stretch the impecunious public purse to its limits. The great European powers were taking part in a furious race for world domination and, if only in imitation, the Spanish élites had to show some sign of colonial ambition. O'Donnell was intent on pursuing this objective, and especially the dream of ruling northern Morocco, which concentrated all the aggression of mid-nineteenth century *españolismo*.[11]

The novelty of the conflict in Morocco was that it led liberal nationalism to converge with Catholic nationalism. This can be seen, for example, by the unanimous support for the declaration of war by the diverse political forces represented in the *Cortes*. Expressive of their conversion are two documents of very different origin. The first is the pastoral addressed to the troops leaving for the front by the Archbishop of Madrid, the second is a ringing article with the same purpose by the Republican Emilio Castelar. 'You are', said the Archbishop, 'the heirs of the victors of Covadonga, Las Navas and El Salado . . . You are going to the front to fight . . . with the enemies, not only of your Queen and of your *patria*, but also of your God and your religion . . . March away, conquer, overcome the enemies of the *patria*, who are those of your God.' The harangue by Castelar went as follows: 'Soldiers: you carry in your weapons the holy fire of the *Patria*. The cause of civilisation is your cause. Heaven has chosen you to fulfil the grand objective of modern history. You are going to open a new path to the glorious idea of progress . . . Victory awaits you, heaven blesses you.'[12] The discourse is different: one emphasises the defence of religion and the other underlines the civilising mission, but there are points common to both that would have been unthinkable twenty years earlier.

In order to be able to embrace nationalism without reservation, the conservative ideologues had to find an honourable place for Catholicism in the national mythology. The priority had been to appropriate for themselves the anti-Napoleonic struggle, showing it to be an explosion of national-religious sentiment, and this they had duly accomplished. The next step had been to introduce the Catholic message into O'Donnell's colonial adventures by means of the fusion of modern imperialism with the age-old idea of a crusade against Islam. The third step, still pending, was of a more intellectual nature and consisted of playing up the positive role – the *founding* role – of the Church in the new biography being written about the nation. Until then, it had been the liberals who had rewritten the history books in national terms and had presented the highly idealised Middle Ages of Castile and Aragón as the pinnacle of splendour and the paradigmatic expression of the 'Spanish way of life'. The features highlighted by the liberals from this golden age were the municipal *fueros* and a *Cortes* that limited the power of the monarch, although they were unable to deny that these formed part of a Catholic Spain in conflict with Islam. As for the loss of their paradise, the liberals laid the blame on a foreign royal house that had imported an absolutism alien to the Spanish character. In this way, Catholicism remained relatively free from responsibility for the nation's misfortunes.

Since the time of the constitutionalists, however, the Church had been an accomplice in the repression orchestrated by Fernando VII and the Carlists. Accordingly, the liberals abandoned their initial ingenuous optimism and now adopted a much more critical attitude towards both the monarchy and its ally, the Church. What first began to be questioned in the 1840s and 1850s was no less than the role of Catholicism in the history of Spain. Attacks upon specific bodies of the Church, such as the Inquisition, were nothing new. The Holy Office had been the target of criticism by modernising élites since the eighteenth century, and there had been bitter debates about it in the *Cortes* of Cádiz before the decision was taken to abolish it. The most far-reaching and best-documented critique was to appear in 1817–1818 in France. The *Histoire critique de l'Inquisition espagnole*, by the canon Juan Antonio Llorente, was an impassioned denunciation of the methods of the Holy Office and an (exaggerated) estimate of its victims. For the first time, a work was based on abundant documents from the tribunal itself, these having been taken by the abbot when he had gone into exile in 1814.[13]

Sempere y Guarinos, who was also in exile in France, launched a more broadly based attack by attempting to undermine the mythic stature of the Catholic Kings in his *Considérations sur les causes de la grandeur et de la décadence de la monarchie espagnole*. For the first generation of liberals, Fernando and Isabel had been the culmination of a happy mediaeval age and the last truly 'Spanish' monarchs. But Sempere y Guarinos observed that it was they, and no one else, who had created the Inquisition and expelled the Jews. He defended them to a degree on the grounds that they had acted under popular pressure. He also believed that the effects of these measures had not been entirely negative, in part because the Inquisition had saved Spain from the wars of religion which had been so disastrous for other countries (a widespread belief at the time), and in part, and more originally, because the expulsion of the Jews must have benefited the country as the precious metals that they were prohibited from taking with them made it possible to finance the American enterprise, thereby creating the foundations for the greatness that distinguished Spain during the following century.[14]

Although he was writing in 1826 and from exile, Sempere y Guarinos still retained some of the balance and restraint typical of the enlightenment era. Writing in an equally erudite tone at about the same time was José Antonio Conde, the first great Spanish Arabist, dedicated to recovering the legacy of the other non-Christian peninsular culture. In his *Historia de la dominación de los árabes en España*,[15] he brought to light previously unknown documents, either because they had been stored in inquisitorial archives or simply because a knowledge of the languages in which they were written did not exist. It is curious that, in spite of its enormous influence on peninsular culture, the Moorish legacy did not pose a serious dilemma because, according to Roberto López Vela, there was general agreement in considering them 'foreign invaders' and 'the enemies of Spain'. Sempere y Guarinos, for example, did not explore the expulsion of the Muslims in 1502 by the Catholic Kings.

A far closer and more contentious bond was that between the national 'essence' and Jewish culture, particularly that of the Jewish *conversos*. With their being the intimates of kings, having a huge influence over Spanish intellectual creativity during the Renaissance and the *Siglo de Oro*, it was difficult not to consider *conversos* as 'belonging'. At the same time, they were seen to be *traitors to the nation* in more than one sense. Despite this, the retrieval of the cultural legacy of the Jews had begun during the Enlightenment, when José Rodríguez de Castro published a monumental *Biblioteca Española* which contained a list of the works by Peninsular rabbis, whether written in Hebrew, Latin or a romance language, with a short summary of their contents. This was during the reign of Carlos III, a period of peace compared to the turbulent times ahead, and a time when a government could propose to abolish the decree of Jewish expulsion in order to promote the repopulation of the country, but the project was eventually ruled out by his son, Carlos IV. His grandson, Fernando VII, reiterated the ban on Jews returning to his dominions. Anti-semitism was still very much alive in anti-enlightenment circles, proof of which are the vicious smears of Vélez, Alvarado and others regarding the supposed hatred of the Jews towards Spain and their conspiracies against the *patria*.[16] Thirty or forty years later, this animosity had increased exponentially, but it was not a one-way street. In other words, not only did the Catholic right hate Jews and 'dissidents', but liberals and other 'dissidents' hated the Catholic Church. Anticlerical feeling reached a peak during the *Trienio* (or Triennium) of 1820–1823. The Inquisition, abolished in Cádiz and re-established in 1814, was again abolished. When the bands of '*Apostólicos*' rebelled, the most radical liberals responded with the first massacres of monks, including the lynching of a priest called Vinuesa. Ten years later, after yet another period of absolutism, most clergy actively supported the Carlists. The situation had only got worse. In 1834 and 1835, the slaughter of priests was extensive. Then Álvarez Mendizábal became prime minister and the State expropriated and sold Church lands. Moreover, between 1835 and 1843 the unimaginable happened: in Spain, the land of the Virgin Mary, the most Catholic of countries, there were *Protestant* missions. The political confusion at the time had resulted in an unregulated and partial religious tolerance that allowed at least two evangelical missionaries to enter through Gibraltar; one of them, George Borrow, known as *don Jorgito el de las Biblias*, was to become rightly famous for his vivid account of his journey through the lands of Andalucía and Castile, as well as for his empathy with gypsy culture.[17]

In spite of the success of Borrow's tale, the reception of the Protestants was generally cool. It is true that, between 1840 and 1870, the rift between intellectuals and Catholicism was clearly widening but, as Vicente Lloréns relates, the majority of intellectuals 'lived in unbelief, remote from religious concerns' or they adhered to a personal Christianity removed from any strict orthodox interpretation.[18] A small group of Protestants was formed, but its members were mainly the political exiles who had spent much of their time in England. The best-known were José María Blanco White, José Muñoz de Sotomayor, Lorenzo Lucena, Doctor Matamoros and Luis Usoz y Río. Though few in number they were very active and, with the help of biblical societies in London and Scotland, they began to bring out publications in Spanish. One of them, the Quaker Usoz y Río, devoted his time to collecting and publishing Spanish Protestant literature of the sixteenth century which, between 1847 and 1865, ran to twenty-four volumes.[19]

In reality, neither Protestants, Muslims nor Jews constituted a serious practical problem. From a theoretical point of view, however, they had the potential to cause enormous conflict: the thread that connected these three ostensibly different cases was that they all raised doubts as to whether Catholicism was, in fact, a permanent feature of Spanish identity. Although the debate took the form of an academic argument over historical issues, it obviously had profound political significance, which explains why it created such controversy. At issue was the *essence of Spain* and, with it, the direction which the country should take at such an important time. The books in defence of the religious minorities no longer accepted the simplistic idealisation of the Middle Ages and the Catholic Kings. Neither did they attribute Spain's subsequent decline to the Hapsburgs. It had been the Catholic Kings, those most Spanish of monarchs, who, in founding the Inquisition and decreeing the expulsion of the Jews and Muslims, had greatly damaged the economy and excised sections of society and culture that could no longer be regarded as 'foreign'. Royal decision-making, in conjunction with ecclesiastical intolerance, were therefore responsible for the subsequent impoverishment and decline of the country. To nationalists, such a burden of guilt might outweigh the beneficial effects traditionally attributed to unity of belief as an antidote to internal discord.

The most determined of the authors who took upon themselves the task of restoring the non-Catholic minorities to the history of Spain was Adolfo de Castro y Rossi, a native of Cádiz. His assault on the standard version began with a history of Spanish Jewry in 1847, followed by two other works: a history of Spanish Protestants 'and their persecution by Felipe II' in 1851, and a 'philosophical examination' of the causes of Spanish decline in 1852. Basically, Adolfo de Castro blamed the Church in collusion with the Monarchy for the decline. According to Castro, the Jews had arrived in Spain as early as the first century AD and lived peacefully in Spain until the conversion of Recaredo caused them to suffer 'extremely cruel' discriminatory measures. Tolerated by the Muslims, they had contributed more than anyone else to the cultural flowering of Córdoba, but the Christian north had been too ignorant to benefit from their knowledge as it continued to persecute, to slander, and to discriminate against Jews with 'fables invented by ignorant old women'. The Catholic Kings culminated the cycle of persecution by introducing the Inquisition, which proceeded to depopulate and sow fear first in Andalucía and then throughout the whole of Spain. Contrary to the usual presumption of 'idealism' on the part of the Catholic Kings, allegedly willing to sacrifice the interests of the economy for the sake of their religious beliefs, Castro argued that Fernando and Isabel planned the expulsion in order to avoid paying the huge debt that they had incurred with the Jews as a result of the war with Granada. Worse still, the Kings had taken advantage of the situation to force the Jews to leave behind their precious metals. 'In this manner', concluded Castro, 'Fernando V concealed his ambition and greed beneath a cloak of Christian piety.' Much the same motives were behind other measures, such as the expulsion of the Muslims and the persecution of heretics, whose property was shared out among accusers, inquisitors and the royal exchequer.[20]

In Castro's second book, which dealt with the Spanish Protestants in the time of Felipe II, he laid bare the historical responsibilities of the clergy, whose 'scandalous disorderliness' had been common knowledge since the Middle Ages: 'there was no sort of vice or wrongdoing which the clergy, to their misfortune, did not embrace'. Nevertheless, the main target of this criticism was not so much the Church as Felipe II himself, whom he judged harshly as a 'Spanish Nero' and a 'natural tyrant'. As a result, 'the sciences, virtue, courage and a greatness of spirit, along with prosperity, noble sentiments and the true honour of an illustrious and generous Spain, fell at the feet of Felipe II', only to be replaced by 'the triumph of ignorance, vice, cowardice, poverty, base feelings and the dishonour of a nation'.[21]

In 1852, Adolfo de Castro published his masterwork, a 'philosophical essay' on 'the principle causes of the decline of Spain'. Predictably, the clergy and the monarchy were the main culprits of Spain's decline. It was the clergy who pressured Isabel to establish the Inquisition, make war against the Moorish kingdom of Granada and expel the Jews. Thus 'the Spanish nation did not found this execrable tribunal. Its originators were kings and churchmen, against the wishes of many persons who resisted it with armed force'.[22] Carlos V, a foreign king, continued in the same manner as his grandparents, by 'governing against the laws' of Spain. Science was wrecked, while Jews and Protestants sought refuge in Venice. Flanders and Portugal rebelled and the territories were reduced to utter prostration under Carlos II, a 'puppet [king] at the whim [of] monks and priests'. This sad finale was the result of Fernando and Isabel. By sowing the seeds of imperial greatness, they had also sown 'the seed of their perdition and ruin'.[23]

The works of Adolfo de Castro and others, such as the lengthy *Historia de las persecuciones políticas y religiosas en Europa* by Fernando Garrido, must have had a considerable impact. The image of Felipe II or the *Rey Prudente* (Prudent King), for example, was considerably tarnished. The popular historical novels of the second half of the century took for granted the gloomy and sinister personality of Felipe II, master of the Monastery in El Escorial. Castelar's celebrated image of the Spanish empire was of a 'shroud spread over the planet.'[24] The *Leyenda Negra*, now embraced by the liberals, began to shape popular perception of the national past. Conservative Spain could not tolerate such a vision of the country's history.

The counteroffensive: The 'neo-Catholics'

In the time of Fernando VII, the close identification of Spain with Catholicism was not even a matter for debate. By the 1830s, however, it had become necessary to offer a justification. In 1831, Fray Manuel Amado wrote a three-volume work entitled *Dios y España, o sea, ensayo sobre una demostración histórica de lo que debe España a la Religión Católica*. In 1837, in *El Amigo de la Religión*, Francisco de Paula Garnier defended the cultural splendour of the Spain of the Hapsburgs and explicitly denied that religious intolerance could have produced any kind of decline. Later in the 1840s, the Catalan priest from Vic, Jaime Balmes, launched his public campaign to unite the two concepts of Spain and Catholicism and went on to become the most coherent exponent of this idea.

Standard histories tend to bracket Balmes with Donoso Cortés as the two leading lights of Spanish Catholic conservative thought in the first half of the nineteenth century, inferring that their political approaches were parallel. This is not the case, and the substantial differences between them are clearly apparent in relation to the issue of national identity. In general terms, Balmes is neither as apocalyptic nor as extreme as Donoso. He avoids the grandiose historico-theological approach typical of the latter and he does not adopt a siege mentality towards the modern world, but prefers instead to formulate concrete problems and to seek reasonable solutions to them. It is also doubtful that his thinking was Carlist in nature.[25] It is true that he worked hard to reconcile the liberal and Carlist branches of the dynasty, but his ideo-logical suppositions were very different from those of the theocratism of Vélez or Alvarado.

For Balmes, the power emanating from God resided within the community, which transferred this power to its rulers. The crucial point is that the community about which he was thinking was Spain, which he understood as a *nation* with *Catholicism* as an essential part of its being. Its history, particularly of the mediaeval period, had been founded on the two pillars, or 'social powers', of religion and monar-chy: in other words, Catholicism and the militarism of the king and his nobles. The 'unhappy nation' of the nineteenth century could only be 'regenerated' or achieve stability by a return to the two principles that had underpinned it in the Middle Ages. These are what Josep M. Fradera calls Spain's 'pre-constitutional' principles: the monarchy and Catholicism.[26]

Balmes once wrote that 'it is not politics that has to save religion, but rather religion that has to save politics'. These words sound like Donoso's – religion has to save the nineteenth century from the dangers of revolution – but they are not. They are not offered as a general panacea for Christian civilisation but as a solution to the specific case of the Spanish nation. In other words, Balmes is not claiming that religion is the foundation of *all* authority, but that it *is* the foundation of the specific *national* community that is Spain. It is perhaps an exag-geration to say, like Joaquín Varela, that there is an 'intense national-ism' in Balmes, as there does not appear to be any, either Spanish or Catalan. In his most ambitious historico-philosophical works, he explains the great political struggle of modern times as a confrontation between Catholicism and Protestantism, the ultimate representative of rationalism. Still, it is true that Balmes, unlike Donoso, was heavily influenced by the Romantic belief, derived from Schlegel and Böhl de Faber, that nations were the protagonists of history. For Balmes, Spain was a nation. Its fundamental, historical 'way of life' was 'of a specific character that distinguishes it from the other nations of Europe.'[27]

When discussing Balmes, one inevitably uses the word 'nation' ad infinitum because he does so himself. It is worth noting the difference between the title of his weekly periodical, *El Pensamiento de la Nación*, and those of the Catholic-conservative press of the previous generation: in the 1820s, absolutist organs were called *El Amigo de la Religión, El Realista* or *El Restaurador*. In the 1830s, Carlist organs were *El Amigo de la Religión Cristiano-Católica y de la Sociedad, La Voz de la Religión,* or *El Genio del Cristianismo*. In the early 1840s, the conservative press was still going by names such as *El Católico, La Voz del Católico* or *La Cruz*. The appearance of Balmes's periodical marked a turning-point in the type of name used, which symbolised the evolution of this current in relation to the idea of the nation. Indeed, from the time of *El Pensamiento de la Nación,* titles began to appear such as *La España, El Pensamiento Español, El Diario Español, El Español, El Correo Español* and *La Nación*.[28]

Balmes was the mouthpiece of a neo-Catholic group[29] which was active at a difficult time for the Spanish Church, which had suffered not only the recent dissolution of the monasteries and the disentailment of its lands but also its defeat in the Carlist War of 1833–1840 and the threat of General Espartero, the national leader who had considered creating some kind of specifically national Church, apart from Rome. The neo-Catholics worked in defence of traditional ecclesiastical interests and, thanks to their influence at court and the fall of Espartero in 1843, they managed to bind the Church to the State by means of the Concordat of 1851 and the seats reserved in the Senate for prelates. For almost a quarter of a century, the religious question ceased to be quite so controversial, until it erupted once again over the issue of the freedom of worship and the so-called 'university question'.

Before examining the political debate, we should take a look at the academic response to those who were trying to rehabilitate Spain's non-Catholic past. The first serious refutation came from José Amador de los Ríos, a moderate liberal who published his *Estudios históricos, políticos y literarios sobre los judíos en España* in direct response to the work of Adolfo de Castro, in 1848. Faced with the chronic unrest caused by feuding noblemen and an irrational populace, kings could, according to Amador de los Ríos, find themselves *forced* to intervene with sometimes drastic measures that were politically necessary, although financially and economically prejudicial. One of these measures had been the expulsion of the Jews, a grave intellectual loss for the country but necessary in order to progress with the nation-building project planned by the Catholic Kings. 'The masses applauded it', claims Amador de los Ríos, though the decision did demonstrate a certain 'ingratitude' on the part of Fernando, given that the Jews had financed the war against Granada. Amador recognised minor defects in the Catholic Kings, but did not accept that Fernando and Isabel displayed 'fanaticism'.

On the contrary, it was important for them to solve the problem of the widespread animosity towards the Jews and, above all, to construct the political unity of Spain, 'which could not be done without first ensuring religious unity.'[30]

Amador de los Ríos maintained a similar ambiguity in judging the Inquisition. He explicitly refuted Llorente, Puigblanch, Sempere and Adolfo de Castro, denying the rapacity of which they accused King Fernando: the Crown had neither established the Inquisition nor expelled the Jews in order to appropriate their wealth but in order to 'constitute and strengthen the dual unity of the Spanish monarchy'. As proof of his objectivity, Amador referred to Prescott, for whom the object of the Inquisition had been to achieve 'uniformity of beliefs . . . an indispensable and reliable guarantee' at a time when 'the political unity of the nascent Spanish monarchy' was being constructed. Consequently the Holy Office was not the result of a spirit of persecution but of the dangers of heresy: the political unity of Spain simply could not permit dissension and internal strife. A harsh solution, it put an end to the endemic disturbances against Jews and *conversos*, and it 'saved Spain from the dreadful wars of religion that were to rage in Germany, France, England and the Netherlands'. Amador admitted that the tribunal was later 'discredited' by fanatical and ambitious men, and that the Inquisition became a 'terrible impediment to the philosophical progress of the human spirit'. The situation became even worse after the loss of the 'prodigious talent' of Felipe II. His son expelled the *moriscos*, which, in Amador's judgement, was not justified by 'any of those great necessities that justify desperate solutions'. The decline intensified and, under Carlos II, with the nation in the hands of the 'theocratic element' and 'prey to every calamity', the Inquisition even stood 'above the head of the sovereign'. As a result, the Tribunal not only hampered the country's intellectual development, but also became an obstacle for the State itself.[31]

The interpretation of Amador de los Ríos was an immediate success and assured his admission into the Royal Academy of History. Moderate liberalism accepted it as gospel, and Modesto Lafuente, the historian with the greatest readership, followed it word by word. This was a sensible thing to do: Amador had restored the self-esteem so necessary for the nation-building process by means of an eclectic interpretation of history that praised the deeds of Spaniards without renouncing modern liberties. Nevertheless, however much he shielded himself behind the work of Prescott and Washington Irving, Amador's impartiality was *sui generis*. His anti-semitic bias, for example, was evident. From the very first page, he denied the Jews the status of 'nation'. They were a 'race' that would always be condemned by 'divine will' to have no *patria*, no home or temple. 'They will live at the mercy of other nations', he exclaimed. In an effort at restraint, however, Amador recommended that they should not be hated, but that their work should be valued and their mistakes treated with leniency. The best punishment for the Jews was to integrate them and for their racial peculiarities to disappear. This had been the policy followed by wise mediaeval monarchs like Alfonso X, who understood the importance of the Hebrew minority for the economic and intellectual development of his kingdom. It had not been successful in the longer term, among other reasons because Christian people had kept alive their hatred of the Jews, unable to forget their collaboration with the Muslim invader. If the Jews had felt a 'love of the *patria*', insisted Amador, reiterating his anti-semitic prejudices, they would have defended 'Spain', but their racial indifference to the land in which they lived, their 'greed' and the memory of 'old hatreds and . . . past offences' led them to connive in 'the loss of the Goths'. The Jews contemplated the downfall of their former hosts with indifference, if not with complacency, and even helped the Saracens to enter cities which it would have caused much bloodshed to take by force.[32]

It was in this context that the *bienio progresista* (1854–1856) arose, a brief period of liberal government which nonetheless witnessed, for the very first time in the history of Spain, the discussion of a constitutional article which would have permitted non-Catholic religious worship. Balmes was dead and the *neo-católico* group was marginalised as the majority of its members had failed to gain seats in the *Cortes*, but Cándido Nocedal had unexpectedly become its fervent supporter. Hitherto, Nocedal had been little more than a journalist and promising politician who ascribed to a middle-of-the-road *moderantismo*. Indeed, he had been seen as a potential contender for leadership of the embryonic *Unión Liberal*, a party that brought together *moderados* and *progresistas*. This was not to be: leadership of the party that would shift conservative liberalism towards the centre went to O'Donnell and Ríos Rosas. An increasingly conservative Nocedal signed up to neo-Catholicism, the hard right of the Moderate Party, and then, following the revolution of 1868, he joined the Carlists. The turning point in his ideological evolution may have been the debate of 1855, when he gave a forceful and brilliant defence of the Catholic essence of Spain.

The *progresista* constitutional bill included an article that, after declaring the Catholic character of the Spanish state and guaranteeing the payment for Catholic priests with public money, stated that 'no Spaniard or foreigner will be persecuted for their opinions, as long as they do not manifest them in public acts contrary to religion'. The impassioned speeches that were made for and against that article fill three hundred pages of the *Diario de Sesiones* of the *Cortes*, and what was discussed in depth was the historical and fundamental Catholicism of Spain. According to Victor Kiernan, this was 'the first complete examination of the Church and the State in the history of Spain'. For Nido y Segalerva, the *Cortes* discussed the problem of religious freedom in Spain for the first time since 'the days of Recaredo'.

The speaker for the liberals was Fernando Corradi, who reiterated the standard ideas about the harm wrought to the country by religious intolerance. Nocedal answered in national terms: Spain existed as a nation and had attained its political and cultural zenith thanks to Catholicism. His thesis is summed up in his statement that 'the Spanish nation, which is only known in Europe for its religious unity and respected for it, would cease to be so if Spaniards did not all have the same religion, the Catholic one, which is, without a shadow of a doubt . . . the most pronounced feature of the Spanish physiognomy, as it has always been'. In other words, Nocedal approached the religious unity of Spain in the same way as Balmes, as an 'eminently Spanish' matter not open to debate and certainly not 'one of those that men of different political schools can cross swords over'. For that reason, he believed that he himself represented 'all Spaniards, the true national opinion' in that debate, since the Spanish people 'do not belong to any party' but were simply 'religious and Catholic'. The mistake of the Carlists, he added, voicing another of Balmes's opinions, had been to appropriate Catholicism for their faction when it was a national characteristic.[33]

In 1866, as Isabel II's hold on power was weakening and rival factions were squaring up to one another over their respective versions of national history, the first episode of what was called the 'polemic over Spanish science' took place in the academic world. The origin of the controversy was the inaugural speech made by José Echegaray on becoming a member of the Academy of Sciences in March of that year. Right at the beginning, the mathematician announced that he was not going to acquiesce in 'the custom that demands national glorification in acts such as these'. It was true that, in the Córdoba of the Ummayads, Spain had been 'the centre of learning in Europe' and that Alfonso X, 'king of immortal memory', had surrounded himself with 'Arabs and Hebrews'. Still, this was not 'Christian Spain', for 'those glories are the glories of the Spanish Arabs'; and 'if we cast out their past glories from our history, as we cast out their unfortunate descendants from our land, that was also theirs, not one will remain that belongs to us alone'. Since the Renaissance, and particularly during the seventeenth century, mathematics had developed in Europe at astonishing speed, 'but what about our Spain? What analytical discovery, what geometric truth, what new theory carries a Spanish name?' The histories of science written abroad did not mention a single Spaniard. The eighteenth century, he continued, was 'yet another glorious century for Europe, yet another of silence and shame for our Spain'. In short, if one discarded 'those centuries in which Arab civilisation made Spain the country that led the world in science', it was not possible to write a history of Spanish mathematics because, since the fifteenth century, our people 'have not had any science'. 'Mathematical science', he insisted, 'owes nothing to us; it is not ours; there is no name associated with it that Castilian lips can pronounce without an effort.' Echegaray argued that this vacuum had nothing to do with an 'unfitness of race' or a 'radical and congenital inability' because the Spanish had more than demonstrated 'boldness of thought, flights of imagination, strength of desire' in other fields, and no other faculties were necessary to make science. Neither should political upheavals be blamed, because other peoples – among them, the Dutch, 'groaning under the weight of our fierce domination' – created science 'amidst war'. 'There has been a cause, and an external cause at that', concluded the mathematician. He did not mention it, but it was clear: the Catholic religion in general and the Inquisition in particular had destroyed the scientific development of the country.

Echegaray's speech soon brought a response, though not from the neo-Catholics but from Felipe Picatoste, a liberal, even radical, teacher of mathematics, who later became a Republican and was the author of a wide variety of works, including a history of Spain. The speech of Echegaray had wounded his national pride. 'The great misfortune of this country', he claimed, 'is that its sons, far from defending it, incriminate it, and far from glorifying it, they blame it and help to deny a past in which there was surely much good of which we are ignorant because we do not want to know about it'. It was a poor rejoinder, however: Picatoste was unable to contest Echegaray's thesis with concrete evidence.[34]

In the final years of Isabel II's reign, conspiracies, imprisonments and executions formed a tense backdrop to the ideological battle that was raging. The neo-Catholics, the true ideologues of her régime, had begun to exert their doctrinal influence some ten or fifteen years earlier and, by the mid-1860s, they were at the height of their political influence, especially over the throne. Nevertheless, they were beginning to lose their creativity and prestige as their members grew older and the régime with which they identified began to collapse. Their major concern at the time was education. The Moyano Law had been passed in 1857, but the provisions for its application took several more years. Whenever they were debated in parliament, the reactionaries fought to introduce amendments and additions that would guarantee the Church's doctrinal control. The neo-Catholics took a prominent part in these debates and even Pedro José Pidal, old and sick as he was, tried to contribute, but when he spoke of Spain and Catholicism he was so overcome with emotion that he began to weep and was unable to continue. His death in 1865 was another blow to the neo-Catholic group. The Syllabus had been published some months earlier. The Pope's anti-liberalism and the conflict over the 'Roman question' drew the neo-Catholics closer to the Carlists, the majority of them uniting with the latter following the revolution of 1868.

Spain became a nation under Recaredo

History had to be rewritten in order for the national entity called 'Spain' to be identified with Catholicism. This was a task undertaken by a number of authors in the last years of Isabel's reign, a delay of many years in comparison with the national histories produced with a liberal bias.[35] In some cases, their works were really histories of the Spanish Church, recycled and disguised as national histories; in others, as in that of Vicente de la Fuente, a history that could well be classified as national was presented as ecclesiastical. Without exception, they formulated the first version of the National-Catholic myth, which would culminate in the work of Menéndez Pelayo.

The original subject of these narratives is not the nation. They do not begin with the claim that 'Spain' existed since time immemorial or that the population was made up of 'Spaniards'. Like the absolutists in the time of Fernando VII, these writers created a biblical setting and made their subject the figures who preceded the People of God. Some of the authors, such as Merry, declared their belief in the biblical version of creation, openly rejecting the 'absurd doctrine of the Englishman Darwin'.[36] Difficult as it was, they managed to find a place for 'Spain' in the biblical tale. Though faintly ridiculous, they maintained the references to Tubal as first inhabitant of the Peninsula. Thanks to Tubal, 'this country, then uninhabited, blossomed into life with peoples, having religion, monarchic government and laws', important original features that would be part of the nation throughout its history. Other authors, such as Francisco Belmar, established an even closer connection by describing how, 'when the waters of the Flood abated, between the Pyrenees and the Straits of Gibraltar, appeared, by order of God, ... the beautiful country known by the agreeable name of Spain'. He also has the Church rise up triumphant from the catacombs, linking the two events by claiming that 'the people and the kingdom that refused to serve her [the Church] would perish ravaged by solitude'. Moreover, 'the greatness and prosperity that was reserved for the Spain of the future was to follow the same vicissitudes as the Catholic Church.[37] According to every mythical archetype, the triumphs and failures of the collective identity are explained in terms of its loyalty to, or betrayal of, its origins. For these authors, it was fundamental to establish Spain's origin as a religious one.

Another means of linking the collective identity to religion from the start was to emphasise the innate religiosity of the first inhabitants of the Peninsula, called 'Spaniards'. They were not only religious but, long before the spread of Christianity, they were instinctively monotheistic and contrary to idolatry. In spite of the fact that these authors had absolutely no evidence with which to support their claims, just as we have none today, they could claim that 'these peoples scarcely fell into idolatry, or not at all'; that 'the natural religion of Tubal' consisted of 'a single God, creator of the Universe'; that the customs of these early peoples were 'pure and simple, until they became depraved by trade and foreign domination' and that once 'conquered by the Romans, the Spanish soon received, along with their civilisation, all the shortcomings of their polytheism.'[38] In contrast to the nationalist version, *monotheistic religiosity* takes pride of place over *martial prowess* as the essential feature of the primitive Spaniards.

The climax of this religiosity came with the preaching of Christianity, which all authors insisted was a spectacular success. In the eighteenth century, Padre Flórez had claimed that Spain was the first country to be converted to Christianity, although at that time this had to do with a competition for primacy between the various branches of the universal Church. By contrast, in the era of nationalism the very identity of the nation was at stake. For Sánchez y Casado, the spread of Christianity 'was very fast and took place very shortly after the death of the Saviour'. 'Spain received it with enthusiasm', added Orodea, 'because Christianity was the religion of free peoples'. Merry confirms that Spain was 'one of the first nations of the world to hear and to follow the holy doctrine of Our Lord Jesus Christ'. Belmar explains the significance of this: the 'primitive Spaniards' had already revealed 'the noble heart of Spain' in their struggles against the Carthaginians, Romans and other invaders, but that was not sufficient to 'recast the different races of her inhabitants into one single one'. 'It was reserved only for Christ crucified', he continues, 'to make different peoples one single people.' With the coming of Saint James the Apostle, 'one of the most glorious nationalities of Europe' was founded.[39] The idea was simple enough: the Catholic religion created the Spanish nation.

Saint James the Apostle, rather than Tubal, was therefore the founder of the nation. And although the National-Catholic historians provided no new evidence, they would admit to no doubts as to the arrival of the Apostle in the Peninsula. Castellanos de Losada insists that the Spanish people were 'one of the first peoples to have had the joy of seeing the clear light of the Gospel, and [it happened] while Holy Mary was still alive, who deigned to visit our *patria* and indicated to James the Apostle ... the site on which he must erect her church'. As De la Fuente stresses, this has been a 'general, constant and unanimous' belief, while Merry calls any who doubts these 'wonders' as 'unwise', claiming elsewhere, without a shred of evidence, that James 'dwelt for nine years in the Peninsula'.[40]

The arrival of the Visigoths is particularly revealing, especially the first two centuries of their rule when, as Aryan Christians, they imposed their heretical doctrine on a supremely Catholic country. This exposes the inherent limits to the adaptations of ecclesiastical history to the national version. The 'Spain' of the early Visigoths was hardly the paragon of myth. The conversion of the Franks to Catholicism had taken place in the time of Clovis, a century before Recaredo, and the Catholic Franks and the Aryan Goths had fought several wars during the following century. Which side should the historian who was both a Spanish nationalist and a devout Catholic support? This was no small dilemma. In the end, Catholic conservative historians opted for the religious element, rather than the national one, as Manuel Ortiz y Sanz had done at the end of the eighteenth century. According to this version, the Catholic Franks triumphed over the Visigoths because God was on their side. Thus the 'Spaniards' were defeated when they sided with heretics. This account was still sanctioned by Menéndez Pelayo almost one hundred years later.[41]

A similar dilemma arose with Saint Hermenegildo, the prince who rebelled against his father, King Leovigildo. Early Catholic chroniclers had had a difficult time justifying the action of Hermenegildo, and a nationalist of the nineteenth century, concerned with legitimising the State, should have shown even greater severity towards the rebel, but fidelity to the Church proved greater than that to the State. Some authors, such as Cavanilles, denied that there was a rebellion, while others, such as Monreal, conceded that there was a rebellion, but argued that it was not led by the prince. More militant authors, such as Merry, admitted that Hermenegildo rebelled against his father, but considered that such a war was 'just'. The point is that Hermenegildo, unlike his father, was a Catholic convert. Despite his rebellion – a crime of State and an offence against paternal authority – Hermenegildo was considered a hero because of his Catholicism.[42]

The appearance of Recaredo on the scene was a cause for celebration as he heralded the true founding of the nation. All authors mention this fact and praise him mightily. One of the most eminent, Belmar, calls Recaredo 'the apostle of his people and the founder of the Catholic monarchy in Spain' who 'liberated' the country from the Aryan heresy. Vicente de la Fuente explains that Aryanism was 'the religion of the conquerors, of the barbarians', 'the Protestantism of the early centuries', while Catholicism was 'the religion of Spaniards, of civilisation and the ancient Roman culture'. It symbolised 'freedom for the oppressed Spaniards, enlightenment, civilisation, the fusion of races and national unity'. Merry concluded that, under Recaredo, 'the Spanish nation' became the most advanced in seventh-century Europe 'owing exclusively to the clergy, to the Spanish episcopate'.[43]

As with the liberal histories, the problem that these mythical interpretations encountered was how to explain the demise of the harmonious, paradisiacal situation that they described. The Visigothic monarchy collapsed after just one battle. The poverty of their arguments do not differ much from those of the liberals: the fall was caused by the personal 'vices' of two kings, proof of the 'degeneration' of an entire people. According to Belmar, Witiza was possessed of the wildest passions and the basest of vices, while Don Rodrigo's life was distinguished by its 'licentiousness' and the 'oppression of his subjects'. Likewise, Manuel Merry describes how the Visigoths were 'plunged into the most awful chaos of corruption and immorality', initiated by the 'profligacy of the emperors'. Only the clergy, insisted Merry, maintained 'their energy and religious feeling' and rebuked the monarch.[44]

Nevertheless, there had to be a positive side to Recaredo's labours. Indeed, almost as soon as the Visigothic reign came to an end, Spain was able to rise up and 'recover her nationality', writes Belmar. 'When the Spanish people', he continues, 'found themselves in the fog of the most ignominious servitude for having turned away from God, they understood that only by retracing their steps could they recover their lost independence.' Thus Don Pelayo put his trust in the Virgin and the result was the first miraculous victory over the Moors. Orodea claims that 'in the mountains of Asturias [Pelayo gave] the shout of freedom, which was the most solemn moment of our history and the start of our civilisation'. Merry insists that 'the Christian religion, *patria* and loyalty' were the foundations of 'our nationality' in the Middle Ages and of 'the great, extremely fertile principles that prepared the giant civilisation and enlargement of our beloved *patria* . . . in the powerful reigns of Carlos V and Felipe II'.[45]

After Don Pelayo came the glorious mediaeval epoch, the golden age not only for liberal historians but also for Catholic-conservative ones, although with some variations. For the latter, all glory derived from the struggle against the Muslims, not from the existence of political freedoms and the peaceful coexistence of different cultures. Padre Flórez had already portrayed El Cid and Fernán González as 'renowned conquerors of Moors, full of zeal for the Faith and endowers of churches'. Merry referred to the appearance of James the Apostle in Clavijo as 'one of the days of greatest glory for the Spanish nation'. The pinnacle of the Middle Ages was the accession of the Catholic Kings, 'the most brilliant period of patriotic history', when Spain 'recovered the unity that it had in the times of the Goths' and 'the nation was reborn full of life'. Yet another author claimed that 'the era in which the Catholic Kings flourished' was 'brilliant', when 'the most eminent men in politics, in administration, in the moral sciences, in the noble and mechanical arts, in commerce, in navigation and in the military excelled'.

The question of religious unity is a polemical one because it includes, for example, the expulsion of the Jews. The majority of authors are less than sympathetic, enumerating the catalogue of evils perpetuated by the Hebrew people: their usurious practices, the terrible plot hatched to deliver Spain to the Arabs, 'their pride, their duplicity, their black arts'.[46] Others explain that it became necessary to take measures to *protect* the Jews. As a result, the King and Queen had stipulated that they should live 'alone in their *juderías*', but their expulsion became 'inevitable'. Monreal believes that the kingdom suffered a blow 'from a material and economic point of view' as a consequence of the expulsion, but that 'the Spain of those times was acting in obedience to noble and lofty intentions'. The most hard-line, as usual, is Merry, for whom Fernando and Isabel created the Inquisition against the Jews because they had 'hard and repeated evidence that they worked untiringly to persuade Christians to abjure their faith' and hatched 'insidious plans with the Hebrews of other kingdoms'.[47]

Closely connected to the Jewish question, the Inquisition was always, at the very least, regarded in a positive light. Unlike Vélez and Alvarado, who had demanded that the Holy Office be retained, none of these authors did so. Still, they believed that 'religious unity, the basis for national [unity]', in the words of Sánchez y Casado, was due to the Holy Office. And they regarded the religious minorities of the mediaeval era as a political danger. Cavanilles maintained that 'many of the conversions were not sincere' and that 'they tried to stir up the country', and even that they had 'called in the forces of the Turk'. In any case, he concluded, 'let us remember that past centuries should not be judged by the ideas of the present'. Protestants were executed by Felipe II, according to Sánchez y Casado, because the king had 'good reason and the applause of the people'. Although their numbers were few, the danger was greater than would appear, explained Vicente de la Fuente, since 'Protestantism had passed the Pyrenees and already was almost acclimatised to Spain'.[48]

In contrast to liberal historians, National-Catholic ones viewed the early Hapsburgs in an exceptionally positive light. Felipe II, in particular, was 'one of the most firm defenders of the Catholic Church . . .a counterweight to Protestant politics', 'a great historical figure'. Don Felipe was a hard-working and diligent king, a model of prudence, talent and discretion, and all the crimes and evils imputed to him were pure invention. His entire dynasty followed a similar line of conduct. Sánchez y Casado admitted that Felipe III did not have the 'military and political qualities that make a great king', but he was 'very well-endowed with domestic virtues'. However, no one could beat Manuel and Antonio Merry in their devotion to the House of Austria: 'those kings who subordinated all their acts to religion, to which they subject social life and present themselves to the world as the true standard-bearers of Catholicism'. After the expulsion of the Moors decreed by Felipe III, 'the damages that liberals assumed were suffered by industry, commerce and agriculture [were] illusory'. Felipe IV and Olivares were also 'two very honourable figures', and only Carlos II suffered from 'a weak constitution and a pusillanimous character'.[49]

The Bourbons, however, were the antithesis of the Hapsburgs. The differences with the liberals became insurmountable. For the Merrys, writing at the time of the ruling dynasty, 'the *race* of the Bourbons' signalled that 'genuinely Christian Spanish policy had come to an end'. According to the Merrys, they 'only looked after material interests' and wished to subject the Church to their authority as well as 'humiliate the upper classes' and 'take away the people's freedoms'. Carlos III, acclaimed by liberalism and Freemasonry, was himself a pious king, but forgot 'the moral interests . . . that give solidity and stability' to a people. 'His indiscretion', they continued, 'opened the gates of the kingdom to revolution.' Moreover, the expulsion of the Jesuits was far crueller than that of the Jews or the Moors. In sum, the Merry brothers were much more interested in defending ecclesiastical privileges than in strengthening the Spanish State. On this issue, they even criticised the Catholic Kings for going 'too far' in their defence of the royal prerogative.[50]

Menéndez Pelayo, who later synthesised this vision of the past better than anyone else, expressed his rejection of the Bourbons even in the title of a section of a book: 'Accession of the French dynasty'. The great theorist of National-Catholicism treated the Bourbons in the same way that the liberals had treated the Hapsburgs: by denouncing them as foreigners. 'Never did greater affronts befall *our race!*', he began. *Foreign* generals commanded *our* armies and the palace was inundated by a 'plague of *foreign* arrivistes'. Moreover, 'the immunities [of the Church] were violated by the servants of the Duke of Anjou.'[51] The issue of regalism is reminiscent of the Aryan Visigoths: when the idealised Spain of the narrative clashes with the Church, the loyalties of the National-Catholic historian are divided, and when forced to choose between them, he places the Church above Spain.

With the odious eighteenth century out of the way, the national odyssey culminates in the uprising against Napoleon. At this point, the National-Catholic narrative coincides entirely with the historiography of the liberals, except for its stress on the role of the Church in the uprising and the religious motive behind the rebellion. As Sánchez y Casado writes, 'the uprising was not the work of Kings, [who were] prisoners in France, nor of councils, submissive and complaisant to the invader, nor of the enlightened classes from which the *afrancesados* came, but from the true Spanish people, led and inspired by the clergy'. Nocedal also insisted that 'the nation rose up for its God, for its King and for its *Patria*'.[52]

The aim of all these histories was to demonstrate that the Spanish national identity had been formed by the Catholic religion. An innate religiosity had existed prior to the preaching of Christianity and it had lasted right through to the heroics against Napoleon. Thus the destiny of Spain lay in the 'defence of Catholicism'. Even in the nineteenth century, Spain continued to be the defender of both Catholicism and civilisation in the face of the dislocating doctrines of modernity. In this way, Catholic-inspired nationalism fused with the Catholic mentality of resistance to the assault of modernity so typical of the nineteenth century. Spain remained true to itself in withstanding the onslaughts of foreign incomprehension, just as the Popes had to endure the waves of rationalist materialism. The real goal of some of these authors was to unite the two causes: Belmar, more clearly than anyone, explains how Spain has always defended the temporal sovereignty of the Pope and how that simply corresponds to the natural order of the universe, since 'the Almighty has placed in the firmament of heaven ... two supreme dignities: pontifical authority and royal power'.[53] It was a way of representing Spain which obliged it to continue deploying its army as guarantor of what remained of the Papal territories against the Italian nationalists.

The incompatibility between this vision of history and that of the liberals is clear. They coincide insofar as the backbone of the narrative follows the classical mythical sequence of Paradise-Fall-Redemption and, in both cases, Paradise has clearly been 'Spanish', and the exodus from it has been due to ill-fated foreign influences. However, from that point on, the periods to which these mythical phases refer, and the ethical and political values associated with them, vary hugely. For the liberals, their golden age was in the Middle Ages, symbolised by the freedoms of the *fueros* and the royal oath to the Aragonese *Cortes*, which all disappeared under the yoke of the Hapsburgs. Redemption, or a return to that contented era, therefore entailed an affirmation of national sovereignty and individual rights. For Catholic conservatives, their Hispanic paradise had existed under Carlos V and Felipe II, while the fall had been the result of 'weak' kings and the imitation of enlightenment models.

The Revolution of 1868 and the Canovist Restoration

In Spain, the final third of the nineteenth century began with the revolution of September 1868, which led to the exile of Isabel II, the child queen who had awoken such high hopes for a liberal monarchy three decades before. 'This woman is impossible', was the conclusion of even General O'Donnell, who was the most competent of all her premiers. Before her fortieth birthday, the plump Doña Isabel was forced to cut short her summer holiday in San Sebastián and cross the border into France. The men who had brought about her downfall then called elections to a constituent *Cortes*; and it was in the ensuing parliament, when the issue of the relationship between the State and Catholicism was debated, that freedom of worship was enshrined in a constitution for the very first time. The famous discussion over the two opposing conceptions of the nation, between the Republican Emilio Castelar and the Carlist Vicente Manterola, took place during the course of that debate. They represented, respectively, the secular-liberal conception and the Catholic-conservative one. The liberals won in a moment of revolutionary exhilaration and because Castelar was their spokesman. As both a Catholic and a Republican, he was a *rara avis* among the Hispanic élite of that century, though what swayed the public in his favour was his gift for oratory.

Vicente Manterola, a canon from Vitoria, was no match for Castelar. Scholarly, but lacking in imagination, he confined himself to restating the central idea of Balmes, Nocedal and Pidal: that Spain was inconceivable without Catholicism. 'Relinquish the religious idea, the Catholic idea, and you will have completely relinquished the history of the ancient and noble Spanish people', he declared. If Spain became 'ensnared in the loathsome toils of free-worship', that day 'its name would have disappeared from the map of civilised peoples'. Castelar attacked the canon's claim that one could not be a Spaniard 'without having burnt into one's flesh the mark of a religion compulsorily imposed'. This replicated the old pagan system whereby 'the king was also the Pope', but modern politics was based on the notion that the State – by which in fact he meant the nation – did not have a religion because 'the State does not confess, the State does not receive Holy Communion, the State does not die'. Castelar went on to observe that the State had not always been intolerant in religious matters. Neither Manterola nor anyone else could name a king more beloved of Catholicism than the saintly Fernando III, and yet 'he had allowed [the conquered Moors of Seville and Córdoba] to have their mosques, he left them their own judges'. In a single sentence, Castelar summed up the mythical view of national history propounded by the liberals: 'in Spain, the ancient is freedom; the early modern, despotism'. The Republican *diputado* went on to affirm that with early modern despotism and intolerance came decline. The Jews were expelled, and in response to Manterola's contempt for the subsequent cultural loss ('apart from some trinkets and that cottage industry in slippers, I don't know what the Jews produced'), Castelar reminded him of the names of some of the descendants of those expelled in 1492, from Spinoza to Disraeli, who could have become the 'glory [of] the Spanish nation'. Faithful to the anti-Semitic prejudices of conservative Catholicism, Manterola, with some audacity, even declared that the Hebrews were a race condemned by God to wander bereft of a *patria*, which was why they could never be 'a people with their sceptre, with their flag or with their president'. 'If such a thing should ever come to pass', he claimed, 'the Word of God' would have been killed.

Castelar could not foresee that, only eighty years later, the State of Israel would exist, with its flag and its president, but he still gave a forceful rejoinder: he did not believe in an inexorable destiny weighing upon peoples because he was 'more Christian than that' and he had faith in divine mercy. As he compared the religion of implacable justice with the religion of love and forgiveness, he was inspired to make this famous peroration: 'Great is the religion of power, but greater still is the religion of love. Great is the religion of implacable justice, but greater still is the religion of merciful forgiveness. And I, in the name of this religion, in the name of the Gospel, I come here to ask you to put religious freedom at the head of your fundamental code of law.' 'The Chamber was in an uproar', recalled the writer Benito Pérez Galdós, 'everyone was shouting.'[54]

The religious tolerance established by the Constitution of 1869 proved to be long-lasting, the result of its acceptance by more flexible conservatives such as Antonio Cánovas del Castillo, who became the architect of the Restoration Monarchy once the *pronunciamiento* of 1874 brought the revolutionary period to its end. Just as a series of political régimes came and went during the six years of the *Gloriosa* (1868–1874), the right went through a number of different phases in its identification with the nation. This was shaped by events in France. The defeat of Louis Napoleon's army by Bismarck in 1871 led to Paris being convulsed by 'the Commune'. The version of events that reached the rest of the world was a tale of horror: the destruction of monuments, the profanation of churches, the theft of property, and the introduction of free love. This was allegedly inspired by a mysterious society, 'The International', whose ultimate aim was worldwide revolution. The Prussians and the French were united in their condemnation of Parisian subversion. What shocked them most was the toppling of the Vendôme column, erected in honour of Napoleon, a symbol of the military glory of the nation. This seemed to the French and Prussian authorities a negation of the most fundamental social values, an inhuman act.

Inhuman was in fact what Ríos Rosas, leader of the *Unión Liberal*, called the few hundred *communards* who had sought refuge in Spain following the crushing of the revolution. Ríos Rosas declaimed before the *Cortes* that these exiles be returned to France, where they would probably be shot. His argument was that the *communards* had abandoned 'all patriotic feeling'. 'Men who abandon their family', he continued, 'their village and their Nation are destitute of all moral feeling, they are not rational beings, they cannot be the citizens of any *patria*'. Thus the *patria* had come to form part of the feelings and beliefs not just of every civilised person, but of every human being. By not being human, by not recognising either family or religion or *patria*, the *communards* had to be returned to France. And they were.[55]

Fear of the International did not cease with its repression. Shortly afterwards, in 1872, a journal called *La Defensa de la Sociedad* was first published in Madrid. Its collaborators included names from across the political spectrum, whether *progresistas, unionistas, moderados* and *carlistas*. What brought people of such widely differing political outlooks together was the spectre of 'internationalism' casting its shadow over Europe. The first issue of the journal explained, in apocalyptic terms, how 'a vast, growing, cunning association has appeared in the midst of nations': note 'in the midst of nations', not 'in Europe', and far less 'in Christendom', for, by this time, even the right now viewed reality through the prism of nationalism. Among the International's 'tyranni-cal designs' was the destruction of property, the family, religion and, last but by no means least, the *patria*. The aim of the International was to eradicate from the hearts of workers the idea of the *patria*. 'Love of one's *patria* is not incompatible with a love of humanity', explained the journal, but rather it is a love 'that God has placed providentially in the hearts of men' so that humanity 'can progress towards its growing perfection'.

The conservatives had come a long way in their attitude towards the nation since the times of Barruel, Alvarado and even Donoso. For the counter-revolutionaries of the first half-century, the national identity had been an invention of the rationalist anti-Christ whose preten-sion was to utilise it in order to seize sovereignty from the absolute monarchs, the visible representatives on earth of God. By 1871–1872, however, the anti-Christ had become the International which, accord-ing to Bravo Murillo, was comparable to Nero because if Nero 'was a monster [who] killed his mother', 'the International wants to kill the Catholic Church, dearly beloved mother of the young and the poor'.[56] The Church still waged war against the Satan of modernity, but Satan now appeared in the guise of internationalism, while Catholics, the defenders of authority and the social order, were distinguished by their love of the nation, in this case Spain. All that was needed was to convince public opinion of the complete identification of Spain with Catholicism and the conservative social order in order for political battle between 'Spain' and the 'anti-Spain' to be joined, the latter now manifest in a subversion that had always been international in its origins.

In 1875, the Bourbon dynasty regained the Spanish throne, now in the person of Alfonso XII, son of the deposed Isabel. The premier was Cánovas del Castillo and the Constitution that was approved in 1876 was his work. Cánovas was not prepared to accept major amend-ments to the institutional part of his bill, and the text drawn up by the commission of notables that he headed was sanctioned by Congress after only brief debate. Nonetheless, Cánovas was confronted by his own allies, the old *moderados* and neo-Catholics, over the issue of the Catholic unity of Spain, and a fierce debate took place. The bishops and their spokesmen insisted not only that the greatness of Spain was indis-solubly linked to Catholicism but also that tolerance was synonymous with social dissolution. Despite this opposition, Cánovas succeeded in having Article 11 passed, which established the Catholic confessionality of the State while authorising the private practice of other faiths.[57] In exchange, Cánovas rewarded the neo-Catholics with the Ministry for Development. As this included Education, the neo-Catholics contin-ued to exercise authority in an area which they still considered their fiefdom. In the mid-1860s, they had used the Ministry to ensure that teaching contained 'nothing contrary to Catholic dogma or sound morals'. In 1865, they had stripped Emilio Castelar of his professorial Chair and dismissed the rector of the *Universidad Central*, Juan Manuel Montalbán, when he defended academic freedom of speech, which had led to serious student protests. A year and a half later, Manuel de Orovio, the Minister for Development, clamped down even further by expelling Julián Sanz del Río, Fernando de Castro and Nicolás Salmerón from the same university, which also prompted the resigna-tion of Francisco Giner de los Ríos. All of them were readmitted to their posts after the revolution in 1868, when Fernando de Castro took up the post of rector. Following the Restoration in 1875, Orovio returned as Minister and reinstated the disciplinary measures of ten years earlier. The Krausists, expelled from their university posts for the second time, decided to have nothing more to do with the State and they founded the *Institución Libre de Enseñanza*, or Free Institute of Education. This was tolerated because, as Cánovas explained, the constitutional monarchy allowed for freedom of education as long as this was private. What it could not countenance, in fulfilment of the Concordat, was any public institution that did not comply with Catholic dogma. Yet it was in the *Institución Libre de Enseñanza* that the individuals that were to head the country's political and intellectual renovation during the first third of the twentieth century were to be educated.[58]

At almost the same time as the constitutional debate and the purge of the Krausists in 1876–1877, the two visions of 'Spain' clashed in the second round of the unresolved controversy over Spanish science. This was rekindled by the inaugural speech of a new member to the *Academia Real Española*, the poet Gaspar Núñez de Arce. His chosen theme was the decline of the nation under the Hapsburgs and, in line with standard liberal thinking, he devoted his dissertation to dem-onstrating 'the influence that religious intolerance and the constant, terrible intellectual repression resulting from it has exercised over our literature'. In response, Juan Valera gave a far more nuanced interpreta-tion: while accepting that religious fanaticism had withered 'the fresh-ness and flowering of our own great traditional culture' before its time, he believed that 'the age of greatest Catholic devotion, of greatest reli-gious intolerance' had also been the 'most fecund of our national life'. It was not that he, like the neo-Catholics, was eager to exaggerate the 'literary and scientific' achievement of that epoch, for he admitted that 'in the sciences we have counted for very little'. Where he diverged from Núñez de Arce was in attributing literary and scientific failure to inquisitorial intolerance and monarchical despotism, claiming that both had existed in other countries. 'People were tortured, burnt alive, subjected to terrible torments' in France and England as well, and there had also been 'an alliance between theocracy and royal power to oppress the people'. Yet these countries advanced despite such despotisms, while Spain 'fell behind'. In short, scientific discovery was dependent upon other factors – perhaps 'the spontaneity and enthusiasm of the nation' – not upon savage inquisitors or tyrannical kings.[59]

The philosopher Manuel de la Revilla joined into the debate by publishing an article that largely supported Núñez de Arce. He rejected Valera's parallels between religious persecution in Spain and that in France or England. The latter two were the 'offspring of fury and violence, rather than cold and systematic cruelty', while in Spain there had been a 'slow but uninterrupted bloodletting' under the control of an 'implacable, systematic and tenacious theocratic power'. Revilla's hard-line interpretation was contested by a young man of twenty who united neo-Catholic fervour with formidable erudition. His name was Marcelino Menéndez Pelayo. He maintained that it was wrong to talk of Spanish scientific backwardness in the seventeenth century and above all that blame should not be attached to the Inquisition as this had never interfered 'in sciences that do not touch on dogma'.[60]

Revilla was supported by Gumersindo de Azcárate, who declared that national scientific activity had been stifled for three centuries by a State obsessed with preserving the purity of the faith. Menéndez Pelayo's riposte to Azcárate was backed up by Gumersindo Laverde and Alejandro Pidal y Mon, the new leader of the neo-Catholics.[61] The philosopher José del Perojo responded that in the field of philosophical inquiry there had been no outstanding contribution from Spain nor any school that could be called Spanish. Neither was he in any doubt that 'the scientific progress of our people' had been paralysed by the Inquisition. 'The list of men of scientific merit who perished in the fires of the Inquisition is long', he affirmed, and 'in the end, all fell silent, and the silence of the grave reigned over our scientific and intellectual activity'. In short, there had been no great scientists in imperial Spain, and not because 'our ancestors' were 'incompetent'. On the contrary, he concluded that the defenders of the Inquisition had protected the faith but 'in exchange you made us crude and uneducated.'[62]

The controversy then ground to a halt. The most intelligent thinkers on both sides, including Menéndez Pelayo, came to the tacit recognition that there was a certain amount of truth to both arguments. Thereafter, the subject of national decline became depoliticised in academic circles. What eventually gained general acceptance was Valera's idea that blame for the decline did not necessarily lie with the Church or the monarchy but in a kind of 'internal disaster'. The century thereby drew to a close in a atmosphere of brooding, pessimistic nationalism, with little faith in the potential of the Spanish race, which the military defeat of 1898 at the hands of the USA would only serve to accentuate.

The National-Catholic offensive: anniversaries and congresses

Against this backdrop of political and cultural pessimism, Cánovas established a political system that was governed essentially by pragmatism and, as far as possible, he avoided the great metaphysical questions of religion and the national essence. In 1881, he handed over power to Sagasta knowing that, among other things, the professors expelled five years earlier would be readmitted.[63] This occurred without much fuss because the National-Catholics were embroiled in another, mainly internal, controversy. In 1878, three years before Sagasta came to power, Pope Pius IX had died after the longest pontificate in history. His successor, Leo XIII, a much broader-minded man who felt hampered by the doctrinaire positions adopted by Rome over the previous decades, initiated a timid rapprochement with the modern world. The new guiding principle of the Vatican was *ralliement*, which meant coordinated action within the new parliamentary systems, the progressive abandonment of monarchical absolutism, and support for the political parties closest to the Church for the purpose of defending its interests according to the principle of 'the least bad government possible'. This was what the German *Zentrum*, or moderate Catholic party, had done and similar attempts were being made in Belgium and France. In Spain, it was Alejandro Pidal y Mon, the son and ideological heir of Pedro José Pidal, who decided to take this route. He had evolved in exactly the opposite direction to the son of Nocedal. Instead of taking refuge in a fundamentalist *integrismo*, as Nocedal had done, he founded the *Unión Católica*, which provided pro-Carlist Catholicism with the opportunity to participate in parliamentary politics under the umbrella of the liberal conservatism of Cánovas, although without becoming formally integrated into the latter's party. The political programme of the *Unión Católica* comprised the defence of the *patria*, religion and property 'against the revolutionary invasion'[64] in that order, with the *patria* placed before religion. It was an attempt to resolve the conflict between Catholicism and the nation once and for all, with the former being subordinated to the latter. Still, the ideal entity known as 'Spain' would be radically and fundamentally Catholic. This is what had been proposed by writers and politicians like Balmes and Pedro Pidal and historians like Amador de los Ríos. Now the second Pidal wanted to extend this idea, to transform it into a mass ideology and to attract the Carlists. In order to achieve this, it was necessary to organise public acts and mass meetings, so his movement began to commemorate past deeds and figures that would define the national identity in Catholic terms. This gave rise to the idea of celebrating *anniversaries*: between 1881 and 1892, celebrations were held in honour of Calderón, Murillo, Santa Teresa de Avila, Recaredo, the Discovery of America and other, lesser protagonists and events.

The celebration of anniversaries was a custom unfamiliar to Spain. There had recently been gatherings in Rheims, Freibourg and Florence which had aimed to defend *Catholicism* and to rally *Catholics* at an international level under the leadership of the Church or the Pope himself. The enemy was still modernity, and its henchmen of 'the secret societies' were to be opposed by steadfast, wholesome Catholic associations.[65] The thinking of Pidal and the *Unión Católica* in 1881 was slightly different. Although their intention was certainly to uphold Catholicism, they hid this behind the term 'Spain'; or, to put it another way, theirs was a form of nationalism wherein the nation was identified with the True Faith. The ideal pretext was the bicentenary of the death of the poet and dramatist, Pedro Calderón de la Barca. The idea that Calderón was *the* national poet and the embodiment of Spanish values was exactly what Böhl de Faber had argued in vain seventy years before. All the Catholic press, including the Carlist element, joined in the celebration. For *El Fénix*, the paper that suppported Pidal, Calderón was an 'eminently Catholic spirit' and the 'glory of Spanish theatre'. Even the Carlist *El Siglo Futuro* declared him to be the 'national poet': he was '*españolísimo*, ow[ing] nothing or very little to the Greeks, Latins or Italians'. 'For Him he wrote', it declared, 'like Him he thought and felt, and he spoke to Him in His own language.'[66]

The press of other political persuasions could not ignore these celebrations, but any identification with the Catholic-conservative vision was avoided. The Canovist paper, *La Época*, said that it was important to 'honour truly great men, the defenders of great ideas, those who, putting their personal interests aside, have sought only the elevation of their *patria*'. *La Correspondencia de España*, a non-partisan paper, exclaimed: 'what nation, what literature, at least in modern times, has drama as rich and as national as ours?' *La Iberia*, supporter of Sagasta, held itself aloof, claiming that Calderón's best work was that 'in which he gives free rein to his genius and does not respect Catholic ideals, but rises above them'.[67]

The success of the Calderón anniversary celebration led to a quest for more candidates. April of 1882 coincided with the bicentenary of the death of Murillo, so he was portrayed as the ultimate *Spanish Christian* painter. On this occasion, it was more of a local event in Seville, promoted by a Jesuit. Nevertheless, he received the support of the Catholic press while the *Real Academia de Bellas Artes* in Madrid organised an event to pay tribute to the artist which was attended by King Alfonso XII. As Murillo could not be made representative of ultramontanism, *El Siglo Futuro* simply exaggerated his national and religious significance: 'the glory of this Spanish Christian artist will be celebrated in true Spanish and Christian fashion, thanks to a truly Christian and truly Spanish spirit.[68]

More tumultuous than the bicentenary of Murillo was the three-hundredth anniversary of the death of Santa Teresa of Avila, which also took place in 1882. By this point, Spanish Catholics were consumed by the struggle between the *unionistas* of Pidal and the Carlists of Nocedal, who presented themselves as 'pure' Catholics in comparison with what they considered to be the hybrid Catholic liberal beliefs of Pidal's *mestizo* supporters. Nevertheless, it was the latter who enjoyed the support of both the Pope and the highest ranks of the ecclesiastical hierarchy, as well as having greater resources at their disposal. As a result, not only did they celebrate the anniversary of the blessed Saint, but they also crowned it with a pilgrimage to Rome during the course of which they were received by the new Pope.[69] As Nocedal's supporters were unable to match the organisational capacity of Pidal's, they issued instructions not to attend the anniversary events organised by the *mestizos* and, to compensate, they launched a campaign to 'inundate' the Vatican with telegrams in which they expressed their loyalty to the Pope, begged for his blessing, and informed him of the acts which they themselves had held in celebration of the Saint, who was an 'honour to the Church and to Spain' and a 'glory which all other nations lack'. In his speech to the *unionistas*, the Pope praised Spanish Catholicism in general terms while eschewing all criticism of the Carlists. The Pontiff had also invoked 'the nation that is celebrated everywhere for the strength and constancy of its faith and for its profound association with the Catholic religion', which *El Siglo Futuro* interpreted as disapproval of those who advocated 'alliances or truces with the modern Spanish State'. Such a degree of distrust of the State in what was essentially a political movement was extraordinary.[70]

In 1889, by which time Cándido Nocedal was dead, the great

unifying celebration that conservative Catholicism had been waiting for finally arrived. This was the thirteen-hundredth anniversary of the conversion of king Recaredo, which the organisers, among whom were Menéndez Pelayo, Alejandro Pidal, Ortí y Lara and the Marqués de Comillas, hailed as 'the Conversion of Spain to Catholicism' or 'the Catholic Unity of Spain'. The fusion between Catholicism and nationalism was complete: 'Catholic Unity', the organisers declared, 'is the foundation of all our national glories'. The anniversary was therefore to be 'an eminently religious and eminently patriotic festivity'. Recaredo was regarded as having brought about not only political and religious unity but also social and racial unity, as he had forged from 'hostile and enemy races a single, cohesive people'. As the 'true light' had come so 'early to our *patria*', thousands of Spaniards had 'offered themselves up as martyrs to regenerate their *patria*' in defiance of the Romans. Under Recaredo, the nation had been created 'in the material sense' as well as in a spiritual one through its recognition of 'the Holy Roman Catholic and Apostolic Religion as the formal principle of its essence and nationality'. Thus Catholic unity became 'the constituent law of the Spanish nation'. As the Bishop of Oviedo concluded, Spain 'was constituted and formed by bishops and monks'.[71] The 'Prayer' that the Catholic press printed daily during the anniversary celebrations is of particular interest: 'Almighty and Merciful God, who through our Catholic King Recaredo and the Fathers of the Toledan Council cast out from our *patria* the Arian wickedness; grant that . . . we should work fervently for the restoration of our Catholic Unity and the social empire of Your Only Begotten Son . . . Heart of Jesus, reign over our Spain!' The 'social empire' of the Heart of Jesus was one of the watchwords of militant Catholicism in the time of Leo XIII.[72]

The aim of 're-Catholicising' society and creating an anti-revolutionary movement could no longer be accomplished without the nationalist ingredient. All the anniversaries mentioned were actually *counter*-anniversaries: while the Spanish Catholics were commemorating Calderón in 1881 as a response to the centennial of Voltaire, celebrated three years earlier by the French Republicans. The year of Murillo, 1882, was also that of Luther. And in 1889, the remote anniversary of Recaredo coincided with the much more recent centenary of the French Revolution, which included a Universal Exhibition in Paris and the opening of the Eiffel Tower. What could be more representative of the evils of modernity than Luther, Voltaire and the French Revolution? The anniversaries of the Marquis de Pombal and Giordano Bruno were also celebrated at around the same time, these revealing an 'ill-concealed hatred of the Church of Jesus Christ', declared *El Siglo*

Futuro. 'If Satan had an anniversary', the Carlist daily affirmed grimly, 'the anniversary of Satan would be celebrated'. The difference between France celebrating its Revolution and Spain its Catholicism was 'thirteen centuries of Spanish Catholic glory and the ever-glorious Spanish influence throughout the world', compared to one hundred years 'of appalling moral and intellectual depravity'.

What distinguishes the aforementioned celebrations from the anti-revolutionary pronouncements of the absolutists, the Carlists or Donoso Cortés is that their promoters, instead of looking for international events with which to bolster opposition to the atheistic revolution, counterattacked with *Spanish* anniversaries. *El Siglo Futuro* claimed that 'we are in the time of anniversaries', whereas in reality it was *always* a time for anniversaries, and the ones to be celebrated were dictated by political interests, not by the calendar.[73] The anniversary of Saint Francis of Assisi, for example, also fell in 1882, on 29 October, but it passed unremarked except by the friars of his order. The reason? He was not Spanish.

There was still one more major anniversary to come: 1892, the four-hundredth anniversary of the 'discovery of America'. The period around the Twelfth of October was full of meetings, processions and publications, many of them government-sponsored. The rhetoric about the 'providential mission of the Catholic Church and the Spanish nation in the discovery of the New World' was repeated ad nauseam. Of course, the providential mission to further the spread of Christianity corresponded to the Church but, in the Americas, for no less providential reasons, it had also fallen upon Spain. Moreover, the decade of the 1890s was distinctive because it marked the height of European imperialism. It is therefore hardly surprising that during this celebration, together with the voyage of Columbus and the Spanish colonisation of the Americas, articles in favour of a new war in Morocco and *españolismo* on the island of Cuba appeared.[74]

After so many celebrations, no one could harbour any doubts about the legitimacy of Catholic participation in politics any longer. Power had ceased to radiate from a remote and heavenly God or from His representative, the Universal Church. It was now incarnate in human figures such as Recaredo and San Fernando, who constituted 'the Spanish tradition'. It was emphasised again and again that the 'Spanish tradition' coincided with the 'Christian tradition', but it is likely that, in the nationalist climate of the late nineteenth century, it was much easier to grasp and identify with the former. To a large extent, the Church *nationalised* its message during this process, ceasing to broadcast it as universal in order to adapt to the new world of nations.

Marcelino Menéndez Pelayo, the young academic who had plunged into the controversy with Perojo and Revilla in 1871 and who, only five years later, had become a professor and the brightest star in the firmament of Spanish Catholic thought, played a major role in the anniversary of Calderón in 1881. Spain had not produced a Catholic apologist of comparable knowledge and ability for perhaps centuries, not to mention the enthusiasm that he brought to the cause. He had considered the homage to Calderón as too pagan and festive, and too biased towards the State. In other words, it was all well and good to pay tribute to Calderón and other Spanish literary and political giants, but he perceived a reluctance by the organisers to identify them with Catholicism and the Hapsburg empire. At a banquet, he proposed a toast 'to the Catholic faith, which is the cornerstone, the essence and the greatest and most beautiful feature . . . of our literature and our art', 'to the House of Austria . . . standard-bearer of the Church, emissary of the Holy See', and 'to the Spanish nation, amazon of the Latin race, for which it was the unyielding shield and barrier against German barbarism'. These were words which, according to Javier Varela, 'established him as the champion of the extremists'.[75]

It was Menéndez Pelayo who created the definitive intellectual framework for the Catholic-conservative version of nationalism that had been developing over the preceding fifty years. For him, it was an incontrovertible truth that Spain possessed a well-defined cultural personality, one which was different to that of the rest of Europe and identified with the Catholic tradition, and whose moment of greatest splendour had been the Catholic Kings and the Hapsburgs. In his epilogue to the *Historia de los Heterodoxos españoles*, a work published in the early 1880s, he summarised his thesis in a few memorable lines. Thanks to Rome, Spain acquired 'unity of language, of art and of law'. But a deeper unity was lacking, he insisted: 'unity of belief'. Only through this did a people 'acquire a life of its own and consciousness of its unanimous strength . . . Christianity gave this unity to Spain. Because of it, we were a nation, and a great nation, instead of a throng of disparate peoples, born to be a prey to the obstinacy of a covetous neighbour. Spain, evangelist of half the world; Spain, hammer of heretics, light of Trent, sword of Rome, cradle of Saint Ignatius . . . that is our greatness and our unity. We have no other'.[76] In his opinion, this great Catholic tradition had remained unyielding until the end of the seventeenth century, even under the last of the Hapsburgs. The decline had set in with the Bourbons, owing to the imitation of foreign models and the attempt to introduce *artificial* fashions and beliefs. The deviation from the national way of being had continued with the onset of the liberal revolutions. At the end of the nineteenth century, Menéndez Pelayo believed that he was witnessing 'the slow suicide of a people . . . chasing after the empty *trompe l'oeil* of a false, artificial culture instead of cultivating its own spirit, which is the only thing that redeems and ennobles a race'. The Spanish were on their way to becoming a group of rootless individuals who 'flee from all contact with their thought, disown all there is in the History that made them great . . . and contemplate with stupid eyes the destruction of the only Spain that is known to the world, the only one whose memory has virtue enough to delay our agony.'[77]

Menéndez Pelayo's *Historia de los Heterodoxos españoles*, his outstanding early work, might lead one to think that he harboured a multicultural vision of the national past, but this was not the case. In his view, the heterodox were no doubt members of the Spanish 'race' in terms of birth and blood, but the idea of 'race' also included a certain way of life and thought that was exclusive to it, and in which religion played the central role. The heterodox, those children of Spanish blood who were not Catholics, were an aberrant, *antinatural* species.[78] In this way, Menéndez Pelayo not only put the finishing touch to the intellectual creation of National-Catholicism, but launched the idea of the *anti-Spain*. He was identifying the enemy *within*. At that point, conservative National-Catholicism became complete.

Notes

1 G. Carnero, *Historia de la literatura . . . Siglo XIX*, Madrid, 1996, Vol. I, pp. XL and 110–123. Cf. D. Flitter, *Teoría y crítica del romanticismo español*, Cambridge: Cambridge University Press, 1995, pp. 8–18; and see V. Lloréns, *El romanticismo español*, Madrid, 1979, pp. 11–28.
2 C. Blanco Aguinaga, I. Zavala and J. Rodríguez Puértolas, *Historia social de la literatura española (en lengua castellana)*, Madrid, 1978, Vol. II, pp. 89–90.
3 Carnero, *Historia . . . Siglo XIX*, Vol. I, p. 111.
4 On these literary debates, see Flitter, *Teoría y crítica del romanticismo*, pp. 39–64, 127–139, 165 and 177–178.
5 Carnero, *Historia . . . Siglo XIX*, I, pp. 363–371 and 498–505; Lloréns, *Romanticismo español*, pp. 425–428 (*When I raise my voice, I do it as a Christian and as a Spaniard; I sing of my religion, of my fatherland*).
6 Lloréns, *Romanticismo español*, pp. 594ff.; Carnero, *Historia . . . Siglo XIX*, I, pp. 112, 658, 664. Quotes from *Clemencia* and *La familia de Alvareda*. One of the conservative characters depicted in *Clemencia* declares at some point to be frightened when hearing the word *nation*: 'we, Spaniards, may be far away from being perfect, but, thank God, we are not a *nation*'.

7 M. Amado, *Dios y España*, 3 vols, Madrid, 1831, III, pp. 260–261. *El Católico*, 2–V-1840, 'Madrid, Dos de Mayo'. *El Siglo Futuro*, 2–V-1881, 'El Dos de Mayo', and 2–V-1882, 'Guerra de la Independencia'.
8 See figures in V. Cárcel Ortí, *Historia de la Iglesia en España*, Madrid, 1979, Vol. 5, pp. 139–142, 160–163, 184 and 219–225. On this topic, cf. J. Sáez Marín, *Datos sobre la Iglesia española contemporánea (1768–1868)*, Madrid, 1975, and M. Revuelta, *La exclaustración, 1833–1840*, Madrid, 1976.
9 J. Canal, *El carlismo*, Madrid, 2000, p. 154.
10 Quoted by B. Urigüen, *Orígenes y evolución de la derecha española*, Madrid, 1986, p. 517.
11 On this war see next chapter.
12 Quotes from J. Álvarez Junco, 'El nacionalismo español como mito movilizador. Cuatro guerras', in R. Cruz and M. Pérez Ledesma (eds), *Cultura y Movilización en la España contemporánea*, Madrid, 1997, p. 48.
13 P. Sáinz Rodríguez, *Evolución de las ideas sobre la decadencia de España*, Madrid, 1962, pp. 116–121; J. A. Llorente, *Historia Crítica de la Inquisición en España*, Paris, 1817–1818.
14 M. Sempere y Guarinos, *Considérations sur les causes de la grandeur et de la décadence de la monarchie espagnole*, Paris, 1826, Vol. I, pp. 54–55, 59, 80–83, 127–129, 164.
15 J. A. Conde, *Historia de la dominación de los árabes en España*, Barcelona, 1821–1823.
16 J. Rodríguez de Castro, *Biblioteca española*, 2 vols, Madrid, 1781–1786.
17 Menéndez Pelayo wrote repeatedly on these Protestant missions, emphasising the dangers for 'Spanishness'. A more reasonable version in Cárcel Ortí, *Historia de la Iglesia*, Vol. 5, pp. 196–197.
18 Lloréns, *El romanticismo español*, p. 561.
19 Among other sixteenth-century writings, he published Raimundo González de Montes, *Artes de la Inquisición española*; Juan de Valdés's two *Diálogos*, *Alfabeto cristiano* and *Ciento diez consideraciones*; Cipriano de Valera's Spanish translation of Calvin's *Institución religiosa*. On Usoz y Río, who had studied in Bologna and held a chair on Hebrew in Madrid, see Lloréns, *El romanticismo español*, pp. 559–561.
20 A. de Castro y Rossi, *Historia de los judíos en España*, Cádiz, 1847 (see pp. 36–37, 45, 119–122, 130, 136); accusations against Fernando the Catholic, in Castro y Rossi, *Historia de los protestantes españoles y de su persecución por Felipe II*, Cádiz, 1851, pp. 243–247.
21 *Historia de los protestantes*, pp. 14, 241, 392–393, 416, 420, 424–425. Harsh opinions on Felipe II repeated in his *Examen filosófico sobre las principales causas de la decadencia de España*, Cádiz, 1852, pp. 72, 89.
22 *Examen filosófico*, pp. 2, 15 and 26.
23 Ibid., pp. 37, 57, 129 and 158.
24 E. San Miguel, *Historia de Felipe II, Rey de España*, Barcelona, 1867; Castelar, quoted by Sáinz Rodríguez, *Evolución de las ideas*, p. 119; J. M. Nin, *Secretos de la Inquisición*, Barcelona, 1855; M. Fernández y González,

286 Conservative opinion: religion and the nation

Martín Gil: Memorias del tiempo de Felipe II, 2 vols, Madrid, 1854; R. Ortega y Frías, *La sombra de Felipe II*, Madrid, 1892.

25 See conflicting opinions by Melchor Ferrer and Federico Suárez, for instance, in J. Varela Suances, 'Preface' to J. Balmes, *Política y Constitución*, Madrid, 1988, p. LIII.

26 J. Balmes, 'Consideraciones políticas sobre la situación de España', quoted by J. M. Fradera, *Jaume Balmes: Els fonaments racionals d'una política católica*, Barcelona, 1996, p. 229.

27 Varela Suances, 'Preface', pp. LXIII and LXXI; previous quote, on politics and religion, ibid., p. XXIX. On his Catalan 'provincialista' identity, ibid., pp. XLIX–L ('Intense nationalism', p. XLVII), and Fradera, *Jaume Balmes*, pp. 180–182 and 197ff. On Balmes, cf. J. Tomás Villarroya, 'El proceso constitucional (1834–1843)' and 'El proceso constitucional (1843–1868), in J. M. Jover (ed.), *La era isabelina y el Sexenio Democrático (1834–1874)*, Vol. XXXIV of the *Historia de España Menéndez Pidal*, Madrid, 1981, pp. 5–70 and 199–260.

28 Other titles in I. Sánchez Sánchez, 'La Iglesia española y el desarrollo de la buena prensa', in *Les élites espagnoles à l'époque contemporaine*, Pau, 1982, pp. 42–43.

29 On this group, also called 'monárquico-nacionales' (Gabino Tejado, Pedro J. Pidal, Aparisi y Guijarro, Ortí y Lara, Navarro Villoslada, Cándido Nocedal), see F. Cánovas Sánchez, *El Partido Moderado*, Madrid, 1982, pp. 192ff.

30 J. Amador de los Ríos, *Estudios históricos, políticos y literarios sobre los judíos de España*, Madrid, 1848; see also his *Historia social, política y religiosa de los judíos en España y Portugal*, 2 vols, Madrid, 1875–1876. Amador adds that the Jews lend the money for a war that left them indifferent, since they did not feel any kind of patriotism (*Estudios*, pp. 156 and 194–198).

31 Typical of Amador is his judgement on Felipe II, 'with a fanatical façade but politically skilful'. See *Estudios*, pp. 172–175 and 514–518.

32 Ibid., pp. 19–21 and 648–651.

33 B. Urigüen, *Orígenes y evolución de la derecha*, pp. 115–120. V. G. Kiernan, *La Revolución de 1854 en España*, Madrid: Aguilar, 1970, p. 146.

34 E. and E. García Camarero, *La polémica de la ciencia española*, Madrid, 1970, pp. 162, 166–167, 175–186, 191–197.

35 A. Cavanilles, *Compendio de Historia de España*, 5 vols, Madrid, 1860; F. S. Belmar, *Reflexiones sobre la España, desde la fundación de la monarquía hasta el fin del reinado de San Fernando*, Madrid, 1861; J. Amador de los Ríos, *Historia crítica de la literatura española*, Madrid, 1861; J. Ferrer de Couto, *Crisol histórico español y restauración de las glorias nacionales*, Havana, 1862; B. Monreal y Ascaso, *Curso de Historia de España*, Madrid, 1867; F. Sánchez y Casado, *Prontuario de Historia de España y de la Civilización Española*, Madrid, 1867; E. Orodea e Ibarra, *Curso de Lecciones de Historia de España*, Valladolid, 1867; V. de la Fuente, *Historia eclesiástica de España*, 5 vols, Madrid, 1873–1875; M. Merry y Colón, *Historia de España*, Seville,

1876. The seminal study on this topic is Carolyn Boyd, *Historia Patria*, Princeton, 1997.

36 M. Merry y Colón, *Historia de España*, p. 23. Merry also wrote a *Compendio de Historia de España*, dedicated 'To the Spanish Episcopate'.

37 Belmar, *Reflexiones sobre la España*, pp. 9–11.

38 B. Monreal y Ascaso, *Curso de Historia de España*, p. 20; Merry y Colón, *Historia de España*, p. 59; and De la Fuente, *Historia eclesiástica de España*, Vol. I, pp. 28 and 35.

39 Sánchez y Casado, *Prontuario de Historia de España*, p. 32; Orodea e Ibarra, *Curso de Lecciones de Historia*, p. 54; Merry y Colón, *Historia de España*, p. 114, and *Elementos de historia crítica*, p. 83; Belmar, *Reflexiones sobre la España*, p. 13.

40 S. Castellanos de Losada, *Memorándum Historial*, Madrid, 1858, p. 191; V. De la Fuente, *Historia eclesiástica de España*, Vol. I, p. 46; Merry y Colón, *Historia de España*, p. 114; Merry and Merry, *Compendio de Historia de España*, p. 18.

41 J. Ortiz y Sanz, *Compendio cronológico de la Historia de España*, 6 vols, Madrid, 1795–1803, Vol. II, pp. 96–101. M. Menéndez Pelayo, *Historia de los heterodoxos españoles*, Madrid, 1986, I, III, VI.

42 Cavanilles, *Compendio de Historia de España*, Vol. I, pp. 210–211; Monreal y Ascaso, *Curso de Historia de España*, p. 61; Merry and Merry, *Compendio*, p. 31.

43 Belmar, *Reflexiones sobre la España*, pp. 17–23; V. De la Fuente, *Historia eclesiástica de España*, Vol. II, pp. 198 and 230; Merry and Merry, *Compendio*, p. 38.

44 Belmar, *Reflexiones sobre la España*, p. 29; Merry and Merry, *Compendio*, p. 24; and Merry y Colón, *Historia de España*, pp. 83–84.

45 Belmar, *Reflexiones sobre la España*, pp. 33–35; Orodea e Ibarra, *Curso de Lecciones de Historia*, p. 147; Merry y Colón, *Historia de España*, p. 133, and *Elementos de historia crítica de España*, Seville, 1892 p. 243.

46 Orodea e Ibarra, *Curso de Lecciones de Historia*, p. 118; usury and conspiracies, Monreal y Ascaso, *Curso de Historia de España*, p. 70, and Merry and Merry, *Compendio*, p. 34.

47 Cavanilles, *Compendio de Historia de España*, Vol. V, pp. 25–26; Monreal y Ascaso, *Curso de Historia de España*, pp. 272–273; Merry and Merry, *Compendio*, p. 133.

48 F. Sánchez y Casado, *Prontuario de Historia de España*, pp. 212 and 302–328; Cavanilles, *Compendio de Historia de España*, Vol. IV, pp. 316–319; Monreal y Ascaso, *Curso de Historia de España*, p. 268; De la Fuente, *Historia eclesiástica de España*, Vol. V, p. 224.

49 De la Fuente, *Historia eclesiástica de España*, Vol. V, pp. 230–231; Merry and Merry, *Compendio*, pp. 146, 163, 168–174, 181, 190–193; Sánchez y Casado, *Prontuario de Historia de España*, pp. 304–328, 347, 377–378. The Comunero revolt, so important for Liberal historians, is usually neglected here.

50 Merry and Merry, *Compendio*, pp. 181–182 and 190; Merry y Colón, *Elementos de historia crítica*, III, p. 41ff.; and Belmar, *Reflexiones sobre la España*, pp. 583–584.
51 Menéndez Pelayo, *Historia de los heterodoxos*, VI, I.
52 Sánchez y Casado, *Prontuario de Historia de España*, pp. 484–485; C. Nocedal, 'Preface' to G. M. de Jovellanos' *Obras*, Madrid, 1858, p. XXXIII.
53 Belmar, *Reflexiones sobre la España*, p. 31 (see also pp. 51 and 59: 'priesthood and monarchy, the two beacons of the world'; the kings, 'rulers of society as representatives of the Almighty').
54 S. Petschen, *Iglesia-Estado: Un cambio político. Las Constituyentes de 1869*, Madrid, 1975, pp. 55–57, 158–159 and 299–300; E. Oliver, *Castelar y el período revolucionario español (1868–1874)*, Madrid, 1971, pp. 81–87; Pérez Galdós, *España sin rey*, chap. X.
55 See J. Álvarez Junco, *La Comuna en España*, Madrid, Siglo XXI, 1971, p. 95.
56 *La Defensa de la Sociedad*, reprinted in *Revista de Trabajo*, 1973, pp. 205, 208, 228 and 299.
57 See J. Varela Ortega, *Los amigos políticos*, Madrid, 1975, p. 94–103 and 118–121.
58 On university purges, see P. Rupérez, *La cuestión universitaria y la noche de San Daniel*, Madrid: Edicusa, 1975; M. Peset and J. L. Peset, *La Universidad española (siglos XVIII y XIX)*, Madrid, 1974, pp. 753–763; and J. L. Abellán, *Historia crítica del pensamiento español*, Madrid, 1984, Vol. IV, pp. 422, 460, 642, and V (I), 146–150.
59 J. Valera, *Discursos académicos*, in *Obras completas*, Madrid, 1905, Vol. I, pp. 269, 275, 290, 292, 296, 302.
60 García Camarero, *La polémica de la ciencia*, pp. 210–211, 213, 216, 226, 231–238, 247 and 239–268.
61 Revilla, *Revista Contemporánea*, Vol. III, 1876, pp. 503ff., quoted by García Camarero, *La polémica de la ciencia*, 201–08 and 231–38. Azcárate, *Revista de España*, 7–IV–1876, later included in his *El self-government y la monarquía doctrinaria*, Madrid, Ed. San Martín, 1877. Menéndez Pelayo, *Revista Europea*, Vol. VII, 30–IV–1876, pp. 330ff., quoted by García Camarero, 209–30 and 239–68. On this debate, see E. J. Capestany, *Menéndez Pelayo y su obra*, Buenos Aires, 1981, pp. 3–38; and J. Varela, *La novela de España*, Madrid, 1999, pp. 35–38.
62 Perojo, 'La ciencia española bajo la Inquisición', *Revista Contemporánea*, 15–IV–1877, included in García Camarero, *La polémica de la ciencia*, pp. 269–307; quotes in 269, 270, 279, 297 and 299. Pidal y Mon, *La España*, 17 and 24–III–1877. On Laverde, see Abellán, *Historia crítica del pensamiento*, V (I), pp. 350–355, 360–363.
63 The Sagasta first Liberal government coincided with anti-semitic pogroms in Tsarist Russia, that provoked a massive Jewish exodus towards Turkey and the Austro-Hungarian Empire. Sagasta offered to accept in Spain

Sephardic Jews, and a 'Centro Español de Inmigración Israelita' was formed in Madrid, led by Isidoro López Lapuya and Angel Pulido Fernández. See I. González García, 'El antisemitismo europeo y español contemporáneos: Las raíces históricas de una diferencia', *Boletín de la Institución Libre de Enseñanza*, 17, 1993, pp. 81–86; and A. Pulido Fernández, *Españoles sin patria y la raza sefardí*, Madrid, 1905.

64 See F. Lafage, *L'Espagne de la contre-révolution*, Paris: L'Harmattan, 1993, pp. 161–165.

65 'Los congresos católicos', *El Siglo Futuro*, 8 and 29–X-1875.

66 *El Fénix*, 25–V-1881; *El Siglo Futuro*, 25–II-1881.

67 *La Época*, *La Correspondencia* and *La Iberia*, 25–V-1881. See Menéndez Pelayo's lectures in 1881, *Calderón y su teatro*, published in Buenos Aires, 1946; Calderón's *Poesías inéditas* were published by Biblioteca Universal, Madrid, 1881, Vol. LXXI; marqués de Molins's lecture at the Real Academia de Morales y Políticas, Madrid, Gutenberg, 1881; the Universidad Central also published a *Memoria* devoted to the event, Madrid, Estrada, 1881; see also P. de Alcántara García, *Calderón de la Barca: Su vida y su teatro*, Madrid: Gras, 1881; or F. Picatoste, *Memoria premiada por la R. Academia de Ciencias Exactas*, Madrid: Aguado, 1881.

68 'Centenario de Murillo', *El Siglo Futuro*, 3–IV-1882.

69 *El Siglo Futuro*, 3–IV-1882; *La Unión*, supplement to the daily issue 1–IV-1882.

70 *El Siglo Futuro*, 14, 16 and 21–X-1882, supplement to 15–X-1882. *La Unión*, 22–IX to 17–X-1882, 22–IX-1882, 27–IX-1882, 2–X-1882ff.

71 *El Siglo Futuro*, 1–V-1889; bishop of Orense, 5–V-1889. Cf. *La Fe*, 29 April to 22 May.

72 *El Siglo Futuro*, 1 and 8–V-1889.

73 *El Siglo Futuro*, 8 and 14–I-1889; cfr. 28–I-1889.

74 *El Siglo Futuro*, from October 11 to 24, 1892 on Morocco; 9–VI-1892 on Cuba; 27–VII-1892, León XIII's letter.

75 Varela, *La novela de España*, p. 47; toast, in A. Botti, *Cielo y dinero*, Madrid, 1992, p. 37.

76 Quoted by Sáinz Rodríguez, *Evolución de las ideas*, pp. 568–569.

77 Menéndez Pelayo, *Historia de los heterodoxos*, 'Epílogo'.

78 See for instance F. Gutiérrez Lasanta, *Menéndez Pelayo, apologista de la Iglesia y de España*, Santiago de Compostela, 1958, pp. 190–201: heresies, an 'exotic plant' in Spain, because they are opposed to our 'race', our 'traditional soul'.

Part IV

The successes and failure of Spanish nationalism in the nineteenth century

8

An identity in search of a purpose

Aspirations and reality: what is the nation for?

The nineteenth century was convulsed by revolutions and other political upheavals that were perceived by many contemporaries as catastrophic occurrences. Yet it was also the age of steam and of the railway, of industry and the Exhibitions in London and Paris. Scientific discoveries brought hitherto undreamt-of changes to everyday life and most of the people that lived through them felt as though a new era was dawning, something that they frequently regarded with an optimism and a belief in progress that verged on the utopian. For them, the progression of humanity towards ever greater levels of political freedom, material well-being and moral rectitude was inexorable thanks to the continual advance of the empirical sciences that promised to reveal in a quantifiable fashion the mysteries of every facet of life, including the most obscure feelings and impulses. But not all progress was peaceful. Technological advances also contributed to military superiority, and Europeans became the masters of the world. Not only was it the century of political revolution and scientific discovery, it also saw the culmination of European power, with the British, French, Dutch, German and Belgian empires expanding across Africa, Asia and Australasia. In 1900, the small European sub-continent, which covers barely one tenth of the total global landmass, ruled over three-quarters of the lands and inhabitants of the planet; its per capita income was five times higher than in other parts; its financial centres controlled commerce and investment all over the world; and its literature, arts and languages were studied and imitated everywhere. As Eric Hobsbawm has declared, 'Never in history has there been a more European century and never will there be another one in the future.'[1] Given such a context, the generalised contemporary belief in the superiority of the white race and its providential mission to rule and civilise the world is perhaps comprehensible.

The sensation of crisis and backwardness that reigned in Spanish political and intellectual circles throughout the whole of the nineteenth century was a product of this context. It was not Europe as a whole that dominated the world, but certain European powers, while the remainder felt excluded. Today we know that, in spite of the political instability and the civil wars, the period was not so calamitous for Spain. Between 1800 and 1900, the population rose from 10 million to 18 million, almost doubling in size, and yet the persistent famines of earlier times did not recur, which can only mean that agricultural production was growing faster than the population, while output may actually have almost tripled. Although only concentrated in certain areas, industry also developed, and the major cities doubled in size twice during the century. The modernising process was slow in comparison with that in Britain, France or Germany but in no sense was it a failure. However, a generalised sense of frustration prevailed among Spanish élites because, as they looked into the mirror of the great European powers, they saw only stagnation and inferiority.[2]

This was mainly because advocates of the old Hispanic monarchy attributed to it not only the quality of a *nation* but also that of a great European or world *power*. As a result, it only bore comparison with Britain, France and Austria or, once unified, with Germany and Italy. Turkey and Russia were both considered beyond the pale, given their barbarism and/or doubtful European credentials. And nobody would accept the demotion of Spain to the level of Belgium, Poland or Romania which were, nonetheless, those States with a similar degree of international power in the nineteenth century.

Spain's elevated sense of place within the European and world hierarchy was a consequence of the leading role played by the Hispanic monarchy for some three hundred years, from the end of the fifteenth century when the *tercios* of the Gran Capitán arrived in Italy, to the Napoleonic era at the start of the nineteenth century. Spain had been a hegemonic power in Europe and America for the first half of that period, and, though much diminished in the second, remained the ruler of an immense empire in the Americas as well as becoming the main ally of the powerful France from 1700 onwards. Spain's condition changed abruptly just as Fernando VII became king, and the Spanish monarchy was plunged into sudden and almost total obscurity. After three centuries when it had taken part in *all* the major armed conflicts of the Western world, during the nineteenth and twentieth centuries Spain took part in *none*. In 1815, the Congress of Vienna, which redrew Europe's borders after the defeat of Bonaparte, was a clear demonstration of the low esteem in which the great powers held the monarchy of Fernando VII, when they satisfied almost none of his demands.[3] Historians and political observers even failed to recognise Spain's only recent international intervention of any relevance, namely, the fierce popular resistance to the Napoleonic occupation which had been a far from negligible factor in the final collapse of the Emperor. The 'War of Independence', the pride of modern Spanish patriotic sentiment, was known abroad as *the Peninsular War* or *la Guerre d'Espagne* – just another of Bonaparte's campaigns – and the whole world attributed the victory over the Corsican to the Duke of Wellington. 'Who put up such a heroic resistance to Rome at Numantia and Saguntum but the Spanish? Who was it that tenaciously and vigorously resisted the aggressor against the liberties of the peoples of Europe during our time?' bemoaned Bartolomé J. Gallardo in 1820. Ten years later, Canga Argüelles complained that while the English had reaped huge benefits from their victory over Napoleon, the Spanish, whose 'indomitable ferocity' he had failed to overcome, had resisted with indescribable sacrifice but only managed to 'ensure their independence, even at the cost of the devastation of their land and the ruin of their industry'.[4]

It is probable that European contempt for the Spain of Fernando VII had little to do with the country's domestic political problems. Fernando was an absolute monarch, he obstinately opposed any constitutional reform and he lived within a vortex of intrigues – but the same could be said of the Tsar in Russia and Metternich in Austria. The exception was British parliamentarianism, not the absolutism of Fernando. It was not this that caused Fernando to lose international standing and credibility, but his incapacity to prevent the loss of the empire in the Americas. In the course of the conflict with Napoleon, the colonies, with the exception of Cuba and Puerto Rico, declared their independence, and the troops sent by the king a decade later failed to recover them. Just at the time when the other European powers began to extend their overseas empires, Spain became a third-rate power overnight, being thereby reduced to the peripheral situation which it had occupied centuries earlier before it had become a unified monarchy. After having played a leading role on the world stage for so long, this diminution of Spain's status was hard to take.

In domestic circles, however, it was not the loss of the colonies that caused the greatest impact. Within the Hispanic court there had been a long-standing, deep-rooted and disproportionate Eurocentrism and, as a consequence, battles that had led to the acquisition of huge swathes of the Americas had never figured as prominently in the patriotic annals as inconsequential victories over the French, Protestants or Turks. Far from celebrating the discovery and conquest of the New World, there was even a certain tendency to blame the imperial expansion for many of the misfortunes of the *patria*, a tendency that the historical mythology invented by the liberals only served to reinforce.[5] In any case, the modernisers of the early nineteenth century were too absorbed in the fight against absolutism. Their main goal was to achieve a free and *enlightened* political system in place of tyranny and fanaticism, leading them to disregard the role of the State on the international stage. This explains why Rafael de Riego, the colonel who in 1820 diverted the troops in Cádiz from their task of re-establishing Spanish rule in the Americas to carrying out an internal coup, was elevated to the status of patriotic hero by the liberals when, for *reasons of state*, he should have been convicted of high treason. However, it was one thing for the liberals not to judge the loss of the colonies as catastrophic and quite another for them to fail to perceive the dramatic loss of influence it caused in relation to the outside world. They wrongly attributed this to the absolutism and obscurantism of the *Fernandino* era, which merely increased their resentment of the Throne.

That the liberals' assumptions were wrong was demonstrated by the growing importance of colonial empires throughout the nineteenth century as both the foundation and the visible proof of the greatness of a *nation*. As the decades went by, the bonds that had linked nationalist sentiment to constitutionalism, popular sovereignty and individual rights, all of which originated together in the times of the American and French Revolutions, were severed. Colonialism, or the possession of an empire, became the supreme criterion by which not merely a State, but the *nation* which it represented, was judged. In the words of the architect of the Restoration system of 1875–1923, Antonio Cánovas del Castillo, the colonisation of savage peoples was the 'new crusade' or 'divine mission' that 'educated and progressive nations' had to undertake in order to 'extend their own culture and introduce progress everywhere, educating, elevating, perfecting mankind'.[6] Concealed behind the rhetoric of the crusade for civilisation were the crude realities of territorial expansion and economic influence, and these led to a fierce competition between the great European States that was to culminate in the Great War of 1914–1918. Moreover, the imperial creed took a particularly irrational turn by its embrace of the racist doctrines which became fashionable in the mid-nineteenth century with the publication of works such as those of the Marquis de Gobineau and the popularisation of social Darwinism. Empires demonstrated the superiority of *races*. This was yet another factor that aggravated the Spanish identity crisis because the loss of empire, in addition to the problems of adapting to modernisation, was eventually interpreted as a sign of racial inferiority or 'degeneration'. Spain became the most eloquent example of the decadence of the Latin races in comparison to the

Anglo-Germanic races of northern, Protestant Europe, in the same way that Russia and Turkey became representative of the Slavic and Arabic races respectively. The Spanish could not bear to be likened to either of the latter, particularly as this made their European credentials suspect. In a speech to the Athenaeum in Madrid in 1870, Cánovas del Castillo himself recognised that the master races of the future were Germany and England.[7] The shocked reaction among the educated classes to the losses of Cuba, Puerto Rico and the Philippines in 1898, inconsequential in comparison to the earlier loss of the empire in the Americas, is an indication of the degree to which, since the beginning of the century, national standing had become associated with empire.

Thus, at the end of the nineteenth century, colonial expansion was one of the principal problems of Spanish nationalism. The other was the paralysis of the liberal revolution. As we know, attempts to transform the complex, though imprecise, Spanish ethno-patriotic sentiment that had evolved during the *ancien régime* into a modern nationalist identity had been the self-appointed task of the liberals, who considered it necessary to legitimise the power that they exercised in opposition to monarchical absolutism. At stake was far more than the control of government: it was the modernisation of society by means of 'a secularising, civilising project for the future', to quote Borja de Riquer.[8] It was also a project that diverged sharply from the political and cultural traditions introduced at the height of the Counter-Reformation and which were still deeply ingrained throughout the country. These traditions included, primarily, the unlimited paternal power of the monarch and his duty to uphold and protect the religious beliefs of the majority of the population, which meant a zealous intransigence towards any form of dissent. It was not easy to create a collective identity that would provide the foundation for a progressive political project based on this kind of language, which was the only one that the populace could understand. In Spain, it was inevitable that the liberal discourse, at least in its early stages, would fall on stony ground. Until well into the nineteenth century, the masses were to respond to appeals from those sectors of the clergy and nobility that were opposed to the modern mindset.

Nevertheless, impressed by the people's resistance to the French, and under the influence of Rousseau and Romanticism, the liberals gave their discourse a more populist stamp. In denial of the evidence, they claimed to speak in the name of the *people*, and the most radical even stirred up mass demonstrations in the few urban areas where they exercised some influence. According to François-Xavier Guerra, they justified their claim to power on the basis of 'assuming representation of the *people* in a symbolic way. It was a dual symbolism of word and deed: the *people* express themselves by means of the *pronunciamiento* or rising: they *act* through the rebel leader and they *speak* through the intellectuals, who are the authors of the declarations that always accompany the action. This dual symbolism is indicative of the two essential elements of the political class of that era: the men of the sword and the men of the quill, that is to say, army officers and lawyers'.[9] The two were, effectively, the principal supporters of the modernising élites, although there were also many civil servants, independent professionals and some members of the *bourgeoisie* (such as financiers, industrialists and merchants), to the limited extent that the latter was involved in politics. This was a very small minority in a country so overwhelmingly rural and isolated from European cultural trends except in a few bastions of cosmopolitanism and tolerance, such as the commercial city of Cádiz.[10] Irene Castells has written that 'the strength of absolutism under Fernando VII is explained by the fact that the majority of Spaniards accepted it'. It is significant that, on his return from France, Fernando was able to annul the Constitution of 1812 and imprison its authors without the slightest protest or opposition from the general public. Conspiracies were only hatched in select circles. Alcalá Galiano, one of the most prominent activists of the period, once explained that the insurrectional model prevailing until the death of Fernando VII aimed to force the King to accept the Constitution while avoiding the radicalism of the French Revolution. The army was therefore the ideal instrument to implement change as well as to defend the new institutions against their enemies without the need to resort to popular intervention.[11] In short, the liberal revolutionaries were élitist, while those who actually enjoyed mass support, especially in rural areas, were the defenders of the *ancien régime*. The latter were not slow to mobilise armed opposition to the liberal régimes or to cheer *¡Vivan las ca[d] enas!* ('Long live slavery!' – as opposed to the liberal cry of 'Long live freedom!') when the liberals fell. However, because both Romanticism and Rousseauan idealisations were so alien to their tastes, they resisted the use of popular rhetoric for some decades.

The fact that the liberals could summon so little public support among the masses did not mean that they lacked political clout. In such a hierarchical society, the support of the educated élites and, more important, their military connections, gave them tremendous influence. Although they were unable to hold on to power for any length of time, they were fully capable of discomfiting the governments of the traditional élites and even to remove them briefly from power. This resulted in the constant political instability of the nineteenth century.

Eventually, after endless failure, persecution and exile, many liberals began to understand how isolated they were from the 'people' whom, in theory, they represented and served. Only then did their thinking begin to change on at least four major points: they gave up populism, they developed a healthy scepticism in relation to the virtues of the Spanish *race*, they abandoned their optimistic, ingenuous vision of national history and, in consequence, they moderated their political programme to such an extent that all radical reform was erased from it. As regards the first point, in a debate about who should be granted the suffrage, Alcalá Galiano himself, the distinguished liberal of the *Trienio*, stated that 'it is not the democratic element that we should be seeking but the true liberal element, which is one of progress in knowledge and enlightenment'. Shortly afterwards, the historian Estanislao Kosca Vayo explained that the time had come to acknowledge that the Spanish people were 'religious and warlike, proud of their own ignorance, . . . separated from other nations because they do not travel' and that this gave rise to the apparent paradox of seeing 'the same masses who, in rallying to the cry of independence, seemed to want to secure their civil liberty [but then] rise up in favour of tyranny'.[12] Thus the liberals recognised the distance that separated them from majority opinion. In the second place, this was to affect their perception of Spaniards as a collective. Until the mid-1830s, it was commonly stated that they were a united, solemn and judicious people, far removed from the squabbling and political strife typified by the *feminine inconstancy* of the French. After the first Carlist War and the upheavals of the period 1834–1843, the Spanish people were subsequently perceived as a cruel, unbalanced and passionate race of extremists. Thirdly, the liberals abandoned the naive interpretation of Spanish history advocated by the first generation and based on an idealisation of the Middle Ages in Castile and Aragón as a period of democracy and tolerance. Among both the mid-century Moderates and the end-of-century liberal-conservatives there prevailed a sense of pessimism that is best represented by the leader of the latter, Cánovas del Castillo, a historian who specialised in the study of the decline of the Spanish Hapsburgs. Unlike Adolfo de Castro some years earlier, he was not seeking to hold either the monarchy or the Church accountable. For Cánovas, the cause of the problem was rooted in some profound perversion of the country itself because, according to Pérez de Ayala, 'he did not believe in the Spanish people . . . he deemed them unfit and unworthy'. This opinion is confirmed by Antonio Ramos Oliveira: Cánovas 'had the fixed conviction that Spain was finished'. This explains the fourth and last major change, both synthesis and consequence of the others: the exceptional moderation of the political objectives of Spanish liberalism, which occurred before the time of Cánovas. The Moderate (theoretically, the *liberal*-moderate) Party of the 1840s, with the Constitutionalists of Cádiz still pre-eminent, no longer defended any of the fundamental points of the early liberal programme, such as local democracy, freedom of the press and parliamentary control over the executive. According to Borja de Riquer, by mid-century, their aims had been reduced to two: to maintain law and order and to make their peace with the Catholic Church.[13]

Eric Hobsbawm regards nineteenth-century European nationalism as defined by two political programmes: liberal revolution in the first half and imperial expansion by the State in the second. If we accept this simplistic but ultimately defensible interpretation, Spanish nationalism at the end of the century had failed on both counts. As regards internal political reform, the liberal revolution had stalled, while in external terms the remains of the colonial empire were about to be lost. We have seen how Spanish pride in the nineteenth century centred on independence, an objective that had been realised early on, and that this resulted, as explained by José María Jover, in a 'retrospective' and self-satisfied nationalism that lacked a 'creative imagination with regard to the future'.[14] Why, therefore, make an effort at nation-building? What purpose or political programme could be served by nationalist rhetoric? If Spanish nationalism aimed to survive, it had to invent a *raison d'être* for itself, and this is the issue which shall be tackled here.

The imperial dream: The 'politics of prestige' of O'Donnell

Faced with the stagnation of domestic political reform, the objective with which Spanish nationalism had originally been identified, the most obvious reorientation was towards the expansion of the State's territorial borders, in a similar manner to other European countries. This could have led to the *defence* of existing borders, the immediate goal of so many other nationalisms, but the peculiarity of Spain is that it was not in conflict with neighbouring European States and, in contrast to those in Central and Eastern Europe, the borders in the south-west had been stable for a considerable length of time – including the one with Portugal, though frontier posts were kept on the alert – and these were ratified after the Napoleonic turmoil. The only possible territorial dispute would have been over the minute territory of Gibraltar, which was considered *unredeemed* and of huge symbolic value to domestic opinion. For the purposes of Spanish nationalism, the *Peñón*, otherwise known as the Rock, could have played a similar role to that of the Alto Adigio or Trieste for the combative and always exemplary Italian nationalism. However, Spain could not possibly consider challenging

Great Britain, the foremost world power. It was even more unthinkable to challenge their rival, France, over the French Basque Country or Roussillon or Sardinia, not only because of French strength but also because of the internal tensions that might be unleashed. It is now agreed that, once Napoleon had disappeared, there was 'no real foreign threat to Spanish security', and 'Spanish nationalism . . . did not aspire to lands unrecovered beyond [its] borders, and was not reactivated by participation in either of the two World Wars'. Enric Ucelay da Cal and Borja de Riquer have concluded that the absence of foreign territorial conflict, which has continued up to the present day, was actually 'a disadvantage for the nation-building process because the sense of unity deriving from being under attack diminished without being replaced by any other collective sense or purpose, as occurred in other neutral countries such as Switzerland and Sweden'.[15]

Juan Linz, one of the authors quoted above, has written that the idea of colonial expansion in Africa gathered momentum in Italy after 'it failed in its diplomatic attempts to extend the borders of the Italian nation beyond the northern boundary'. As a result, the 'energy of national affirmation' driving Italian society forward found its outlet abroad, and 'internal class conflict' was transformed into 'conflict between nations, or renewed imperialism, which we will find as one of the main ingredients of Fascism'. This could be a description of Spain, barring the reference to irredentism, which exhibited little more than querulous and impotent resentment over Gibraltar. Another project having similarities with Italian nationalism in the nineteenth century was integrative nationalism, or Pan-Iberianism, which will be examined later in this chapter, but it was scrapped in its infancy. The closest parallel between Spain and Italy was the attempts at colonial expansion on the African continent. However, it was not because the 'energy of national affirmation', which Juan Linz identifies in Italian society, had suddenly emerged in Spain and required an outlet: José María Jover observes that Spain's ventures 'were not, in origin, the result of the vitality of a nationalist project present in Spanish society'. It was a mimetic enterprise spearheaded by certain government sectors, which saw in imperial expansion the means of diverting or relieving chronic domestic political tensions.[16]

This strategy can most readily be identified with the Liberal Union, the party led by General Leopoldo O'Donnell, and almost all the events relating to it took place between 1858 and 1863. This was the only period of true *moderation*, in the sense of political balance or centrism, throughout the entire reign of Isabel II, and it offered a breathing space which allowed for a concentrated effort to be made in the imperial sphere. It became known as O'Donnell's *Politics of Prestige* and included military expeditions to Cochin-China, Morocco, Mexico, the Dominican Republic and El Callao (the principal port of Peru).[17] All were of minor importance compared to those being undertaken by the major European powers at that time, but they did set the wheels of the new patriotic rhetoric turning. Ultimately, the rhetoric proved to be the most successful aspect of these ventures! The principal venture of the politics of prestige, the Moroccan War of 1859–1860, pompously named the 'War of Africa', gave rise to such huge patriotic enthusiasm that, even today, the traces remain in ritualised military discourse, wherein names like Prim, the Castillejos and Wad-Ras are spoken of in almost the same breath as those of Hernán Cortés, Lepanto or the *Tercios* in Flanders.

Even before the first shots had been fired in the campaign at the end of 1859, the press had unanimously presented the military offensive about to take place in the north of Morocco as the occasion to demonstrate to Europeans the durability of the Spanish monarchy as a great power, or, in the language fashionable at the time, as a *superior race*, with the right to its imperial slice of the world. Representatives of the most diverse political tendencies coincided in emphasising how important it was to demonstrate the *strength* of Spain to the outside world. Above all, it was necessary to demonstrate this to the Moroccans, as the rumour had spread 'even among those African barbarians' that the former Castilians were 'impotent to avenge the insults to their honour'. However, a re-reading of the texts suggests that the true target of the action was 'the world' – that is, Europe – which had to be made to understand that Spain continued to be one of its great powers. 'With the eyes of Europe upon us, we shall show that we are no longer the decaying, indolent nation of times past . . . We are going to prove that the vigorous blood of heroes still flows through our veins . . . heroes whose renown still echoes in the immortal pages of history'.[18]

Only by bearing these intentions in mind can one begin to understand the euphoria generated by the favourable though meagre result of the Moroccan war. Not only did it lead to a spate of works boasting of the glorious deeds of the *patria*, but these reached a greater number of readers than any political event had ever done before. The *Diario de un testigo de la guerra de Africa*, by Pedro Antonio de Alarcón, became the most widely read book of these events; it was said that the author earned more than half a million *reales* and received more than twenty thousand letters of congratulation from all over Spain.[19] The conquest of Tetuan proved that the *country*, the *nation* or the *race* was among the elect, the *superior*, the ones who had the right and the duty to dominate and civilise the world. It had been a 'titanic struggle' in which the 'ever-victorious' Spanish troops had matched 'their historical reputation', and in which 'the behaviour of our army in the current war empowers us to believe that nothing has diminished the traditional qualities of the Spanish'. The Arab race – it was explained to the public – 'appears to be blessed with an irresistible fury . . . when it is favoured by fortune; but it lacks the perseverance in misfortune that is only possessed by peoples who have reached a certain degree of civilisation'. The conduct of the Spanish army had demonstrated its high racial quality by doing 'what few armies in the world have done. Raw and inexperienced as it was, it has fought with the intrepidity of veteran troops . . . Even the French . . . have not achieved such a prolonged series of victories on African soil in such a short time'.[20]

According to this interpretation of the war of 1859–1860, with which all the political forces of the time appeared to be in complete agreement, the Spanish people had overcome their *prostration*. The republican politician Emilio Castelar, whose superb oratory had begun to captivate audiences, said in characteristic style: 'This great nation, prostrate and vanquished, which daily took another downward step towards the abyss' had risen up and continued 'the interrupted work of its civilisation'. 'This warlike people who stood firm between the Crescent and Christian civilisation . . . continues its great sacrifices, offering the lives of its sons in a homage to universal civilisation.' As Castelar's newspaper had explained on the outbreak of war, the blood spilt in honourable international conflict as opposed to lamentable civil discord would fulfil an important function: it would 'nourish the tree of our nationality'.[21] That was exactly its purpose.

The conclusion to be drawn was clear: Europeans had to admit that they had been mistaken in relation to Spain and to recognise her standing once more. 'We were looked upon in disdain by Europe, which easily forgets the high qualities of the Spanish race', but Europe now knows that 'Toledan blades and Spanish sinews conserve their old mettle' and from today 'we shall be appreciated for our true worth'. 'Spain . . . should soon be one of the leading military and mercantile powers in Europe.'[22] A highly gratifying interpretation, at least for domestic consumption, since the European powers took little notice of such a minor armed skirmish, but it set a dangerous precedent for future wars, such as that of 1898, whose results were not as auspicious for the Spanish troops.

The 'War of Africa' was important for another reason. While the Franco-Spanish expedition to Cochin-China had already been presented in some circles as a continuation of the conquest and evangelisation of the Indies, the taking of Tetuan was looked upon as an extension of the Reconquest, the oldest of the nation's founding myths. It was this aspect that attracted the Catholic-conservative political factions. As has been repeatedly stated, the Spanish nation-building process had been undertaken by liberals and progressives in the early nineteenth century, while conservative forces had remained loyal to the traditional justification of political power in terms of dynastic legitimacy and the defence of Catholicism, always harbouring serious reservations about the suspiciously secular and democratic theory of popular sovereignty. In 1859, however, the possibility of embarking on a new crusade against the Moor struck a conservative chord. The association between *españolismo* and Catholicism made nationalism a far more attractive prospect to many who had previously been dubious about it, and this included the Archbishop of Madrid and Patriarch of the Indies, D. Tomás Iglesias y Barcones. He addressed the troops leaving for the front in a *Pastoral Letter* in which he said 'you are the heirs to the victors of Covadonga, Las Navas and El Salado . . . through [your] veins runs the blood of those who, after seven hundred years of fighting and glory, were able to free Europe and banish to the scorching deserts that you are going to cross the forefathers of those whom you are now going to fight'; 'you are going into combat to fight against the heathen . . . enemies, not only of your queen and your *patria*, but also of your God and your religion'.[23] It was the beginning of a new approach to nationalism. In the decades to follow, conservative leaders and ideologues would insist on identifying patriotic history with Catholicism, and they mobilised public opinion by invoking national identity in the call to join the crusade.

This unlikely common ground between the Archbishop of Madrid and the republican Castelar was one of the most significant aspects of the mobilisation: both were issuing a call to fight for the *patria*, although the former allied it with religion and the millennial war against Islam and the latter with progress and civilisation – causes equally blessed by Providence. The popular Pedro Antonio de Alarcón exemplified this fusion of Spanish patriotism with Catholicism and the civilising mission when he expressed surprise that he himself, who had written incendiary anticlerical pamphlets a few years earlier, now felt such religious fervour on the taking of Tetuan: 'Does all this mean that the war has made me neo-Catholic?'[24] To some extent, this was so. Spanish nationalism was becoming *neo-*. To put it another way, the war of 1859–1860 was an important step along the road to the acceptance of nationalism on the part of the Spanish right, defined, until then, by their Catholicism. Patriotism now received the blessing and support of the clergy and the absolutist élites who, up to that moment, had adhered to the idea of legitimacy through religion and tradition. This was yet another illustration of the fact that religion and *patria* are not incompatible. The Moroccan war was the fulfilment of the last testament of Isabel I, the Catholic Queen, the continuation of the Reconquest, both a crusade and the defensive reaction of a proud and independent people against a foreign invader.

Castelar, however, added the civilising mission, a notion common to all European imperialists of the period. The fulfilment of a *civilising*, as opposed to an *evangelising*, providential destiny was what differentiated the republican nationalist outlook from the Catholic-conservative one. Nevertheless, the majority of the arguments were common to both: the invincibility of the Spanish people; their racial superiority over the Arabs; the idealism and disinterestedness that Spain displayed in this kind of enterprise, being driven only to defend national *honour* (in contrast to other colonising powers who pursued *material* gains); and, above all, the need to fight in order to restore Spain's national image in the eyes of Europe, to reverse the decline and to overcome the passivity, hidden beneath the guise of neutrality, that dogged a nation undeservedly absent from European expansion. Statements such as 'we are going to show Europe that we are no longer the weak, indolent nation of recent times' or 'Europe has to understand that we are still worthy descendants of the victors of Pavia, Bailén and Lepanto!' reveal the aim of impressing the great powers, of demonstrating to them that Spain also had the right to take part in the parcelling-out of the world. *Españolismo* – whether it was based on religion as the right desired, or a higher level of civilisation as Castelar claimed – was the motive for extending the sphere of influence of a State that, recently demoted from empire to nation, was demanding to be promoted to the imperial division.

No territorial gains were, in fact, made from this series of campaigns, unless one counts the slight increase in influence over northern Morocco after the war of 1860, when the Spanish army occupied Tetuan for several months. This relieved Berber pressure on the *presidios* or strongholds of Ceuta and Melilla, which allowed them to continue extending their fortifications in the following decades. Even then, domineering Britain, whom the bellicose press of the time constantly referred to as the 'Perfidious Albion', vetoed any serious expansion of Spanish influence over the Sultanate. The results of the glorified 'War of Africa' were ultimately disappointing. O'Donnell, however, must have considered them sufficient for the purposes of domestic propaganda as he planned further colonial adventures. Two of these took place in the year after the Moroccan campaign, undoubtedly in the heat of the enthusiasm generated by the latter.

The first episode was an armed expedition, in conjunction with France and Britain, which was sent to the Mexico of Benito Juárez under the pretext of demanding that the Mexican government pay its international debt. Its real intention was to intervene in Mexican domestic politics by imposing Maximilian of Austria as Emperor, a venture that ended in defeat and the execution by firing squad of the unfortunate Hapsburg. The commander-in-chief of the Spanish expeditionary force was Juan Prim who, moved by personal political ambition, took the prudent decision to withdraw his men and thus extricate Spain from the fiasco, which became a humiliation primarily for Napoleon *le petit*, who was behind the scheme. The following year, General Norzagaray, perhaps following Prim's example and with equally good judgement, decided to retreat from Indochina. Spain, consequently, managed to avoid becoming entrapped in what was to become one of the most terrible conflicts of the twentieth century. The second episode was the voluntary reincorporation of the Dominican Republic into the Spanish Crown, an offer made by President Pedro Santana, encouraged and supported by Francisco Serrano, Captain General of Cuba. On this occasion, the monarchy of Isabel II was made to look ridiculous because, in less than a year, the new administration had alienated Dominican public opinion to such an extent that protests broke out and it decided to use force against the enemies of the colonial restoration. The dispatch of troops only led to a bloodbath and failed to prevent the abandonment of the whole enterprise in 1865.

Under O'Donnell's next government, there was a futile war with Chile and Peru that began in 1866 with the declaration of a naval blockade of the two countries. As it was folly to attempt to patrol a six-thousand-kilometre coastline with a squadron of half a dozen ships in such poor condition that it encountered serious difficulties in navigating the Straits of Magellan, the Spanish vessels took refuge wherever they could and spent weeks wondering what to do. Finally, they decided to shell the cities of Valparaiso and El Callao for a few hours, where there was hardly any artillery that could respond. They then turned around and sailed back to Spain proclaiming victory. The greatest contribution of this expedition to nation-building was the romantic phrase of Admiral Méndez Núñez when warned of the dangers of taking his squadron halfway around the world: 'better honour without ships than ships without honour.'[25]

'From an objective and realistic perspective' – concludes José María Jover – 'the history of these military expeditions is a sad and sterile story.' Nonetheless, 'Africa, Prim, El Callao, the ships and the honour came together to create a certain mythology that was incorporated into the new image of Spain forged during the Isabelline era.' For domestic consumption, there can be no doubt that they achieved a certain impact, although the bitterness of the Cuban War of 1895–1898 was later to erase them from the collective memory. What they definitely did not do was to lay the foundations for re-establishing an empire. Although the national press alleged that Europeans were 'astonished' at the exploits of the Spanish troops, the outside world was not impressed and Spain continued to occupy a peripheral, virtually non-existent, position in the scramble for colonies. In spite of this, it was the most intense moment of nationalisation based upon dreams of empire in the whole of the nineteenth century, and it was also the only military mobilisation between the devastating though idealised war of 1808–1814 and the far less damaging but more difficult to assimilate war of 1898. At any rate, the imperial surge was short-lived: the expeditions begun in the late 1850s had come to an end by the mid-1860s, and once again Spain withdrew into a neutrality which the most realistic politicians and thinkers of the era, from Balmes to Cánovas, had always advocated. It was to become the Spain of the *recogimiento* or 'withdrawal', a euphemism for marginalisation or passivity.[26]

Although in practical terms Spanish imperialism was over, in terms of bravado it remained alive and well for the rest of the century. In the 1880s and 1890s, public opinion manifested itself in the form of noisy and sometimes violent demonstrations in support of various colonial claims, as in other European cities. The most memorable of these took place in 1885, when news came through of a provocative incursion by one of Bismarcks's frigates into the Caroline Islands, a forgotten archipelago but routinely included as part of the Spanish empire in Australasia. Acts of vandalism ensued outside the German legations in Madrid and Barcelona. Similar demonstrations took place in 1893, when enlargements to the fortifications of Melilla encroached upon the grounds of a mosque and led to armed attacks by the Berbers, causing many losses among the Spanish troops, including a general. The streets of the main cities filled with angry demonstrators demanding that the insult be avenged. Tensions rose and another Moroccan war began to appear inevitable, but the Sultan backed down, promising not only to pay a symbolic indemnity and to punish the aggressors himself but also – and this was the key to the agreement – to place Moroccan troops – the *moros del rey* – in the area to prevent more attacks. This meant, in effect, that the Sultan accepted the continued enlargement of the fortified area.[27]

Such outbursts of enthusiasm are usually described as *popular* and this is certainly how they were labelled by contemporaries. There was even some interest in presenting them as involving the working people: a demonstration held in Madrid in 1885 was described by *La Iberia* as composed of 'a mass of 2,000 men, largely workers', who 'shouted and clapped nonstop and cheered Spain, the integrity of the *patria* and the sons of labour'. However, in the written and illustrated testimonies of these events, there are more frock coats and bowler hats than long shirts and peaked caps.[28] We should not deceive ourselves: these were upper-middle-class phenomena, involving educated professionals and intellectuals, many with liberal and even republican tendencies. When describing another demonstration of 1885, *El Globo* observed that there were 'beautiful, elegant *señoritas*, as well as people from the well-to-do classes, who led a respectable life'. Furthermore, the protests in Madrid that year started in the cafés around the Puerta del Sol, such as the Casino, the Círculo de Moret and La Gran Peña, all venues which catered for intellectuals rather than the working man. They are also situated in the same areas where the liberal patriotic societies and clubs of earlier times had had their headquarters. The usual route chosen by the demonstrators took them past the Círculo Militar and several barracks, the most important culminating outside the Athenaeum, whose illustrious members crowded onto the balconies waving the Spanish flag and cheering wildly for the army and the navy. In Barcelona, the city council initiated the protest, offering corps of 'Catalan volunteers' like those that had been sent to the war of 1860. Local councils were also the organisers in Palencia and other cities. In Granada, the demonstration was organised by 'many respectable and representative persons'. In San Sebastián, it began with a meeting in the Casino de la Concha, convened by 'the press'. In Córdoba, it was the idea of the *Sociedad de Amigos del País*. In the province of La Coruña, 'patriotic indignation' burst forth during a visit from Castelar, who was received 'with music, national anthems, applause, bunting, flowers, etc.'. All of these marches traversed the main roads of each city, not the working-class suburbs, and the balconies of the wealthy neighbourhoods were hung with bunting and 'luxurious flags' as a sign of support. It goes without saying that the conduct of the forces of law and order in dealing with these indignant patriots was exemplary, even though the latter smashed windows, tore down coats of arms and destroyed the façades of the German legations.[29]

Consequently the national-imperialists of the second half of the nineteenth century were a replica of the national-liberals of the first half: they were the intellectual and professional middle classes who looked to the armed forces for support. Members of intellectual and military circles were responsible for the founding of the *Real Sociedad Geográfica* in 1876 and the *Sociedad Española de Africanistas y Colonistas* in 1883, institutions which were behind the setting-up of small colonies in Río de Oro – the future Spanish Sahara – and Río Muni – Spanish Guinea. It should be noted that these expeditions were not necessarily associated with political conservatism; in fact, the republicans – with rare exceptions such as Pi y Margall – were decidedly in favour of them, largely through conviction but also undoubtedly inspired by opportunism, because it enabled them to expose the government's passivity on the international stage.

Certainly, left-wing support for an assertive colonial policy did not preclude the approval of the right. On the contrary, the enthusiasm with which the latter had backed the 1859–1860 Moroccan war had only intensified by this time. During events in Melilla in 1893, the Cardinal Primate Monescillo said that he followed 'with sympathy . . . the patriotic movement that the nation begins' and acknowledged 'the heroes' who emerged 'to encourage and fortify them with our applause'. The Cardinal then took the liberty of comparing himself to the Catholic Kings: just as they had 'called upon our forefathers before the walls of Santa Fe . . . before the ferocious attacks of the Riff, after conferring my blessing on all those going to fight against the Moorish hordes, I say: 'Spaniards, to Melilla!' He went on to link patriotism to the exclusively Catholic religiosity of the nation by saying that he supported the Spanish army 'with all the energies of patriotic love', but also with 'all the vigour of religious feeling and all the power of Catholic unity'. The exiled Queen Isabel II seized the opportunity to relate the conflict of 1893 to that of 1860, when she still reigned, confessing to 'the pleasure that fills her soul to know of the enthusiasm of the army and all social classes to maintain the good name of Spain and its immaculate glory intact'; if war broke out, she announced, her heart would be 'with our soldiers, who, with the help of God and their unquenchable courage, will once again achieve victory and new laurels for our beloved nation'.[30]

Nevertheless, these demonstrations of nationalist fervour were but pale imitations of the ones taking place in Paris, London and Berlin. True imperialist ultra-nationalism, similar to that which led European crowds to demand and applaud the declaration of war in 1914, was not to surface until the final years of the century, in the heat of the Cuban conflict. What then appeared is described by Borja de Riquer and Enric Ucelay da Cal as 'an almost neurotic preoccupation with identity', a hyper-sensitive nationalism, reflected in names such as that of the Puerto Rican 'Unconditional Spanish Party'. This type of discourse, they observe, was 'unknown in Spain until the impact of the second cycle of colonial wars in the 1890s', and it was introduced 'above all by the military press'.[31] It is indisputable that this jingoism was widespread during the years of the Cuban War, but once again the question should be asked as to whether it was not just a phenomenon restricted to the educated urban classes, with little impact on the immense majority of the country, particularly in the rural areas.

The impression one gets from these testimonies is that, among the *popular* or lower levels of society – in other words, among the classes from which the soldiers were recruited and sent to die – these colonial adventures were received far more coolly, and even with apprehension. This can be deduced from their everyday behaviour, although there is no significant proof to indicate that they were either for or against the wars. It is enough to recall how scandalised journalists and intellectuals were at the indifference of the people of Madrid to the news of the sinking of the Spanish fleets in May and July of 1898, when the crowds continued to flock to the bullring and enjoy the spectacle as if nothing had happened. It is also worth noting the considerable increase in emigration to Spanish America by young men of military age while that war lasted, as well as the huge increase in the number of fugitives and deserters from the army, and the spread of anti-tax and anti-inflationary riots. All these are indications that what really concerned the lower classes was the rise in prices, the scarcity of basic foodstuffs and the fact that their sons were being taken away to die in the jungle.[32] It is also logical to assume that the weak and difficult socialisation of the Spanish population as regards their national identity throughout the nineteenth century meant that the lower classes could not have experienced these colonial adventures with the same emotional intensity as the educated – in other words, *nationalised* – middle classes.

However, the intense patriotic sentiments of the polite society of enthusiastic empire-builders did not extend as far as raising money or sending their sons to their death on the battlefield. The wealthy classes, in spite of being the habitual instigators and exponents of nationalist discourse, kept both their money and the lives of their offspring well removed from the war effort by evading taxes and paying a 'cash redemption' in order to avoid military service, or by sheltering behind the many legal exemptions. In practical terms, they thereby showed as little enthusiasm for the Nation-State as 'working people'.[33] With the exception of certain sectors, such as those with links to the armed forces, military service did not rank very highly on the scale of values of the Spanish upper and upper-middle classes, in contrast to the situation in Germany, for example. Even those responsible for the ship of State, who had established a system of conscription full of inconsistencies and privileges, made it clear that 'service to the *patria*' was not an honour but a duty, imposed especially on the lower classes; both the latter and the upper classes reacted appropriately by trying to eschew military service to the best of their ability.

In sum, Juan Linz describes Spain in the nineteenth century as 'the first country to suffer colonial losses . . . the only colonial power to lose its last overseas territories . . . and neither is it successful in its minor imperialist adventures in Africa'.[34] If to this we add Spain's many civil wars, the conclusion could not be more devastating for the building of a shared identity: the *Spanish*, unable to unite in action against anyone else, fought constantly among themselves. On the international front, the conflicts that took place between the Franco-Prussian War and the Second World War were undoubtedly one of the most powerful driving forces behind the growth of jingoism, especially at a popular level, among the great European powers. This was largely because their citizens, particularly the troops, were immersed in patriotism but also because their governments, in exchange for the massive involvement in the war effort that they demanded of their societies, conceded substantial gains in political participation and provided public systems of social welfare of previously unknown dimensions.[35] In the case of Spain, there were no foreign wars nor even threats to its borders, so that neither the process of strengthening patriotic feeling nor the involvement of society in the State began to develop. By not experiencing the nationalising war efforts of other major European countries, the political system failed to take the crucial step towards achieving legitimacy. Still, the other side to the argument is that, because Spain was not involved in more wars, its fragile State was not subject to the tensions that led to the dismemberment of the Austro-Hungarian and Turkish empires in 1918.

The other dream: The 'Iberian Union'

One objective which might have tied in well with active, expansive nationalism, and which had been an ideal of the Spanish liberal revolution during the greater part of the nineteenth century was the Iberian Union, an equivalent in the Iberian Peninsula to Italian or German unification. Nineteenth-century nationalisms tended towards unification – the creation of great States – in contrast to present-day nationalisms, where the prevailing trend is secession or the demand for independent governments and state privileges for increasingly small areas and cultures. As Jover notes: 'if new times [brought] the achievement of

German unification, of Italian unification, why not also Iberian unification?'[36] Incidentally, the elimination of borders was not simply a nationalist objective but formed part of the ideal of progress as it had come to be formulated since the eighteenth century. The federal manifesto of 1869 connected nationalism and progress in the following manner: 'the United States of Europe, which are the ideal of our century, can and should begin in Spain'. This was not, in the strict sense, *Spanish*, but *Iberian* nationalism, although there can be no doubt that it was one of the possible culminations of *españolismo*, which would have willingly dissolved into a pan-Peninsular entity.

The unity of the Peninsula was an aspiration with a long history, although until the nineteenth century it had nothing to do with nationalism but rather with territorial ambitions and plans for the annexation of kingdoms devised by a succession of – mainly Castilian and Portuguese – kings. All the agreements and manoeuvres, wars and marriages had led to only one period of union between Spain and Portugal, between 1580 and 1640, but the fact that it continued to be propounded was no coincidence: the idea of Iberian unity was based not only upon the proximity of the kingdoms and the obvious geographical unity of the peninsula but also on cultural affinity. During the Middle Ages, the élites communicated in the main languages of the Peninsula without difficulty. The Castilian poets spoke Galician-Portuguese in the fourteenth and fifteenth centuries, just as the Portuguese Camóens and Gil Vicente or the Catalan Boscán wrote in Castilian in the sixteenth and seventeenth centuries. The greatest disengagement occurred in the eighteenth century, when international alliances placed Portugal on the side of the British, and Castile and Aragón on the side of the French. A new rapprochement took place during the Napoleonic Wars, and so did the first attempt at union of the modern era, still according to the dynastic formula: it consisted of the claim to the vacant Spanish throne by the Infanta Carlota Joaquina, daughter of Carlos IV and wife of the Portuguese king João VI. It was a petition that the *Cortes* in Cádiz took very seriously and discussed twice but ultimately rejected, based on their fear of the absolutist ideas of the princess.

In the following decades, the vicissitudes of the liberal revolution, similar in both countries, brought about an approximation of like-minded political groups. The liberals, frequent companions in exile and connected through the Grand Masonic Lodge of Madrid, which spanned the Peninsula, repeatedly planned a Peninsular union under a single constitutional régime as a defence against the Europe of the Holy Alliance. The most promising opportunity arose after the Portuguese dynastic crisis of 1826, which led to the Miguelist civil war, similar to the Spanish Carlist War of the following decade. In Portugal, to quote Teodoro Martín, both absolutists and liberals 'sought the support of their Spanish coreligionists, accepting Iberian commitments'. The Spanish émigrés in London, particularly Flórez Estrada and Andrés Borrego, made contact with the constitutional candidate Pedro IV, offering him a joint throne. The proposal had the support of the most significant Portuguese liberals of the time. After the July Revolution in France, the talks intensified in Paris, led by Juan Álvarez Mendizábal for Spain and Mousinho da Silveira for Portugal. However, the death of Fernando VII and the shift towards moderate liberalism by the new Regent, María Cristina, left the project on the back burner. Another fifteen years went by before a new gathering of exiles brought the leftists together once more. The Iberian Club was set up in Paris at the height of the 1848 disturbances, and some four hundred Spanish and Portuguese democrats, among them the socialist republican Sousa Brandão, paraded through the French capital waving a flag of four stripes – white, blue, red and yellow – which was to be the flag of a 'united Iberia'.[37]

Until mid-century, Iberian union was generally a liberal plan and, although it failed to take off, it was regularly advanced as a theoretical proposal in the press and in books and pamphlets until the 1860s. Teodoro Martín mentions projects for Peninsular unity put forward by republican organs such as *El Huracán* of Madrid or *El Nacional* of Barcelona in 1840. The romantic political writer Almeida Garrett, who was so influential in the cultural reawakening of the Portuguese identity with his *Viajens na minha terra*, also believed that Portugal could not survive in isolation from Spain. *A Revolução de Septembro* and *O Progreso*, in Lisbon, along with *La Iberia* in Madrid and *La Corona de Aragón* in Barcelona published articles, news of meetings and proposals for the reduction or elimination of customs tariffs between the two countries. One of the most regular contributors of these articles was Sinibaldo de Mas who, in 1850, published *La Iberia*, a pamphlet subtitled 'Report in which the political, economic and social advantages of the union of the two Peninsular monarchies as a single nation are proven'. The idea had originated in the episcopal palace of Macao among a group of Spanish and Portuguese friars. As Sinibaldo de Mas himself emphasised in later editions, from that moment on the proposal began to gather momentum: in 1850, a weekly called *Revista del Mediodía* was first published in Lisbon in Castilian and Portuguese; *A Peninsula*, published in Porto two years later, also supported the unionist project, as did *La Iberia Militar*, in 1853. Also in Porto, in 1854, an anonymous book appeared giving thirty reasons for union. In Lisbon in 1855, Carlos José Caldera was editing the bilingual *La Revista Peninsular*, with collaborators from both countries; and six years later, the *Revista Ibérica de Ciencias, Política, Literatura, Arte e Instrucción Pública* appeared in Madrid. Lastly, in Lisbon in 1859, the republican Sixto Cámara published *A União Iberica*, with a prologue by Coelho, in which he proposed practical measures that would lead to a closer relationship between the two countries. These included the construction of the Madrid-Lisbon railway, telegraphic communications, the mutual concession of political rights, the standardisation of weights and measures, the abolition of tariffs, the founding of a Peninsular Athenaeum and other societies for promoting the idea of unity, and compulsory education in both languages. But, once more, none of these proposals ever came to anything.[38]

A far more feasible option under serious discussion in mid-century was that of revitalising the old plan of dynastic union. The issue was raised in 1846 during negotiations for the marriage of Isabel II. Of the list of candidates, the Progressives wanted her to marry Pedro V or, failing that, for her younger sister, the Infanta Luisa Fernanda, to marry the future Luis I. The plans were opposed by both Moderates and Carlists, but the possibility arose again when the Spanish revolution of September 1868 left the throne vacant. Prim, the strongman of the moment, sponsored a Portuguese candidate, either King Fernando or his son Luis, and in January 1869 he authorised Fernández de los Ríos to undertake negotiations with the Portuguese king. Yet again, the project foundered, partly due to the doubts and fears of the Portuguese of being absorbed by Spain, but also due to the opposition of France and Britain to the creation of a single State in the Peninsula.

The September revolution rekindled interest in the Iberian idea among republicans as well, so that the years 1868–1873 saw the greatest number of unifying projects of the century. The plan was to create an Iberian Federation inspired by the ideas of Proudhon and sponsored by Casal Riberio and Henriques Nogueira on the Portuguese side, and by Orense and Pi y Margall on the Spanish side. The latter included it as part of his plan in *Las Nacionalidades*. The proclamation of a federal republic in Spain in 1873 made it seem immediately attainable and there were many contacts that year which led, among other things, to the foundation of a Hispanic-Portuguese Association, whose President was Salmerón. Once more, however, the plan succumbed to traditional Portuguese fears of absorption as well as, on this occasion, to the pessimism induced by Spanish political instability.

This brought any realistic possibility of success to an end. Any further projects became increasingly utopian and less acceptable. In 1881, Fernando Garrido wrote *Los Estados Unidos de Iberia* and nine years later Rafael María de Labra spoke in support of the Iberian idea in the Spanish Congress, guaranteeing that union would not diminish Portuguese independence. Either because the idea still seemed attractive or because it provided an opportunity for the republican movement to demonstrate its strength, in 1893 large numbers of Portuguese, including deputies, newspaper editors, professionals and financiers, attended the Spanish Republican Congress held in Badajoz, which was chaired by a joint presidency of Salmerón and Magalhães Lima. In 1895, the latter, who was editor of *O Século* in Lisbon, published *La Federação Iberica* – the Iberian Federation – an organisation which he claimed would lead to a Latin and, ultimately, a world federation. In those years, there was also an Iberian League, for which Oliveira Martins was the correspondent. The 1890s saw the Portuguese crisis of the *Ultimatum*, which led to a brief renaissance of Iberianism in order to promote the defence of *Latin nations* in the face of Anglo-Saxon ascendancy, but Anglophobia fostered the Portuguese identity, not Iberianism, and also led to a surge in republicanism. After one failed attempt in 1891, the monarchy finally fell in 1910, and with the coming of the Republic, the nation was guaranteed. Between 1890 and 1926, Portugal lived what Rui Ramos calls its 'second foundation', a stage of intense nationalisation mainly in the hands of masonic-republican and civic associations. The present-day flag and shield of Portugal date from this period, as well as the national anthem and standardised spelling. In the meantime, Portuguese freemasonry had split from Spain in 1880, forming a *Gran Oriente Lusitano* which excluded the Spanish lodges. Everything began to point to Hispanophobia rather than Iberianism. It was a triumph for the civic association *Primero de Decembro* (created to celebrate Portuguese independence from Castile in 1640) when, in 1886, it financed the monument to the *Restauradores* in the centre of Lisbon, which has become one of the symbols of Portuguese identity. Portuguese, not Iberian, identity had taken hold. It is curious that it had surfaced in the course of debates on Iberianism and, to some extent, in reaction to the plan for unity. The 1880s and 1890s were years of commemoration in both Peninsular States, but while Spain was celebrating the Catholic identity of the nation, Portugal was toasting its independence from Spain. The moment for union had passed.[39]

The Iberian project was over and, in spite of the support from certain political (mainly liberal) and cultural élites in both countries, the fact is that it had never been popular. There had been no lack of political opportunities for its achievement, above all those provided by a vacant throne or a possible royal union, but the international climate, in the form of British and to a lesser extent French opposition, was not favourable. It would, however, be unfair to attribute its failure to external factors as these would have been unlikely to have prevented a strong drive for unification within the Peninsula itself. Such unifying schemes continued into the twentieth century, with Catalan nationalists showing particular interest, but they became increasingly unrealistic and lacking in support. By the time of the dictator General Miguel Primo de Rivera (1923–1930), the only organisations claiming to be *Iberian* were anarchist.

There was one last possibility for an expansion of Spanish nationalism abroad: Pan-Hispanism or the unity of all of the Spanish-speaking Americas, including the old colonial metropolis. This was another equally unrealistic concept, close to the hearts of certain minority political élites for a long time. Initially, when Bolívar conceived his grandiose plans for Hispanic union in the 1820s, the wars of independence were too recent for the *madre patria* or 'motherland' to be included in such a project. From 1847, the time of a congress held in Lima, proposals for a confederation of the Hispanic world tended to include Spain. Isidoro Sepúlveda observes that, in a similar way to Iberianism, there were two tendencies in Pan-Hispanism: the more conservative one, represented by Ferrer de Couto, which sought to restore 'the foundations that raised Spain to its age of greatest splendour', whereas the liberal one, represented by Castelar, 'broke away from imperial dreams and . . . saw in the projection towards America the means of regenerating Spain'.[40] Overall, the unifying initiatives came from the New World rather than from Spain because, although anti-colonial rhetoric still existed, Hispanophilia had overcome Hispanophobia. In contrast, Spain was largely indifferent and inactivity ruled in government circles. One of the few initiatives worth mentioning was the creation of the Ibero-American Union in Madrid in 1885, which edited a journal of the same name. There was, of course, a flurry of Pan-Hispanist projects and speeches in 1892, on the four-hundredth anniversary of the Discovery. As in the case of Portugal, pessimism as regards the degeneration of the Latin race combined with the shadow of a formidable Anglo-Saxon power brought forth proposals for a defensive political confederation. None of these came to fruition due to insurmountable internal rivalries as well as the opposition not only of the United States but also of Britain and France. From the Spanish point of view, the most important contribution of Pan-Hispanism was the declaration of the *Doce de Octubre*, the twelfth of October, as the fiesta of *La Raza* – the race – in 1912, on the initiative of the Ibero-American Union, and promoted to the status of national fiesta by the Maura government in 1918. Zacarías de Vizcarra and Ramiro de Maeztu were later to create the concept and the myth of '*hispanidad*' or Spanishness, one of the pillars of anti-liberal, Catholic conservative nationalism in the first decades of the twentieth century. This led to the founding of the *Consejo de la Hispanidad* and the *Instituto de Cultura Hispánica*, both official institutions of Francoism, which nonetheless produced more hollow rhetoric than tangible results.[41]

Notes

1 E. J. Hobsbawm, *The Age of Empire, 1875–1914*, London: Vintage, 1989, p. 18; figures, in P. Kennedy, *The Rise and Fall of the Great Powers*, New York, 1987, pp. 148–149.
2 See D. R. Ringrose, *Spain, Europe and the 'Spanish Miracle', 1700–1900*, Cambridge: Cambridge University Press, 1996, pp. 65–66, and L. Prados de la Escosura, *De imperio a nación: Crecimiento y atraso económico en España (1780–1930)*, Madrid, 1988, pp. 129–131. Less optimistic figures in G. Tortella, *El desarrollo de la España contemporánea: Historia económica de los siglos XIX y XX*, Madrid, 1994, pp. 43–63; or J. Palafox, in J. P. Fusi and J. Palafox (eds), *España, 1808–1996: El desafío de la modernidad*, Madrid, 1997, pp. 104–114 and 195–211.
3 See M. Artola, *La España de Fernando VII*, Madrid, 1992, pp. 565–578.
4 B. J. Gallardo, *Alocución patriótica en la solemne función con que los ciudadanos del comercio de Londres celebraron el restablecimiento de la Constitución y la libertad de la patria*, London, R. y A. Taylor, 1820, p. 10; J. Canga Argüelles, *Observaciones al tomo II de la Historia de la Guerra de España, que escribió en inglés el Teniente Coronel Napier*, 3 vols, London, 1830, Vol. I, pp. 36–37.
5 The poet J. Quintana, at the very moment when Spanish colonies were becoming independent, blamed the corruption of public spirit in recent centuries to the 'arbitrary power' established by the Habsburgs in Spain and the 'immense accumulation of wealth' caused by the empire in the Americas; see F.-X. Guerra, *Modernidad e Independencias*, Madrid, 1992, p. 245.
6 'Discurso en el Ateneo', 1882, quoted by C. Dardé, 'Cánovas y el nacionalismo liberal español', in G. Gortázar (ed.), *Nación y Estado en la España liberal*, Madrid, 1994, p. 219.
7 Quoted by J. M. Jover, 'Restauración y conciencia histórica', in *España: Reflexiones sobre el ser de España*, Madrid, 1997, pp. 334–340. Cf. E. Demolins, *A quoi tient la supériorité des Anglo-Saxons*, Paris, 1890.
8 B. de Riquer, 'Aproximación al nacionalismo español contemporáneo', *Studia Historica*, 12 (1994): p. 12.
9 Guerra, *Modernidad e Independencias*, p. 362. The military were an essential part of the cultivated élite, and very often the only ones with mathematical and technological education (see for instance M. Murphy, *Blanco White: Self-Banished Spaniard*, New Haven, CT: Yale University Press, 1989, p. 30).

10 R. Solís, *El Cádiz de las Cortes*, Madrid, 1969, esp. Chapters 2, 3 and 8; or J. L. López Aranguren, *Moral y sociedad*, Madrid, 1966, pp. 51–52.

11 I. Castells, 'Antonio Alcalá Galiano', in J. Antón and M. Caminal (eds), *Pensamiento político en la España Contemporánea (1800–1850)*, Barcelona, 1992, pp. 123, 125 and 131. Cf. Alcalá Galiano's *Memorias*, in *Obras Escogidas*, *Biblioteca de Autores Españoles* (B.A.E.), Vol. LXXXIII, 1955, p. 392.

12 A. Galiano, quoted by Castells, 'Alcalá Galiano', p. 128. E. de Kosca Vayo, *Historia de la vida y reinado de Fernando VII de España*, Madrid, 1842, Vol. I, p. 285.

13 Cánovas and Ramos Oliveira, quoted by C. Dardé, 'Cánovas y el nacionalismo', p. 232; B. de Riquer, 'Reflexions entorn de la dèbil nacionalització espanyola del segle XIX', *L'Avenç*, 170 (1993): 9; and 'La faiblesse du processus de construction nationale en Espagne au XIXe siècle', *Revue d'histoire moderne et contemporaine*, 41/42 (1994): 355.

14 J. M. Jover, 'Caracteres del nacionalismo español, 1854–1874', *Zona Abierta*, 31 (1984): 22.

15 B. de Riquer and E. Ucelay, 'An Analysis of Nationalisms in Spain: A Proposal for an Integrated Historical Model', in J. Beramendi et al. (eds), *Nationalism in Europe: Past and Present*, Santiago de Compostela, 1994, Vol. II, p. 280. Previous quotes, from S. Payne, 'Nationalism, Regionalism and Micronationalism in Spain', *Journal of Contemporary History*, 26 (1991): 479; X. M. Núñez Seixas, 'Historia e actualidade dos nacionalismos na España contemporánea: unha perspectiva de conxunto', *Grial*, 128 (1995): 506; and J. Linz, 'Los nacionalismos en España: una perspectiva comparada', *Historia y fuente oral*, 7 (1992): 130.

16 J. Linz, 'El Estado-nación frente a los Estados plurinacionales', in E. D'Auria and J. Casassas, *El Estado moderno en Italia y España*, Barcelona, 1992, p. 74. J. M. Jover, 'Preface' to *La era isabelina y el Sexenio Democrático (1834–1874)*, Vol. XXXIV of the *Historia de España Menéndez Pidal*, Madrid, 1981, p. XCII.

17 On these events, J. Tomás Villarroya, 'El proceso constitucional (1843–1868)', in J. M. Jover (ed.), *La era isabelina*, pp. I–CLXII and 315–340; J. Bécker, *Historia de las relaciones exteriores de España durante el siglo XIX*, Madrid, 1924–1926, Vol. II; and J. W. Cortada, *Spain in the Nineteenth-Century World: Essays on Spanish Diplomacy, 1789–1898*, London, 1994, Chapters 2, 5 and 6.

18 *Las Novedades*, 7–II-1860; *La Iberia*, 11–IX-1859, 26 and 27–X-1859; *La Epoca*, 4–XI-1859. Cf. J. Álvarez Junco, 'El nacionalismo español como mito movilizador. Cuatro guerras', in R. Cruz and M. Pérez Ledesma (eds), *Cultura y Movilización en la España contemporánea*, Madrid, 1997, pp. 35–67.

19 The Spanish Royal Academy also offered a prize for poems celebrating the Moroccan triumph, and some of them were published by the Imprenta Nacional in 1960. Many years later, this war would be the topic of Pérez

Galdos 'national episode' *Aita Tettauen*. On this war, see M. C. Lécuyer
and C. Serrano, *La Guerre d'Afrique et ses répercussions en Espagne*, Rouen,
1976; or Bécker, *Historia de las relaciones exteriores*, Vol. II, pp. 409–457. On
Alarcón's popularity and earnings, J. Altabella, *Corresponsales de guerra: Su
historia y su actuación*, Madrid, 1945, p. 88.
20 *La Epoca*, 6 and 16–I-1860.
21 E. Castelar, *La Discusión*, 18–X-1859 and 6–II-1860.
22 *La Epoca*, 2–II-1860; *Las Novedades*, 7 and 8–II-1860; *La Esperanza*,
7–II-1860.
23 *Carta pastoral* del Arzobispo de Madrid de 2–XI-1859. For the conservative view on these wars, see F. Gaínza, *Campaña de Conchinchina*, Manila,
1859, quoted by J. M. Jover, *La civilización española a mediados del siglo
XIX*, Madrid, 1991, p. 169; Bécker, *Historia de las relaciones exteriores*, Vol.
II, pp. 365–368 and 459–469; or Cortada, *Spain in the Nineteenth-Century*,
p. 29.
24 P. A. de Alarcón, *Diario de un testigo de la Guerra de África*, Madrid, 1931,
Vol. 2, p. 120.
25 See M. van Aken, *Pan-Hispanism: Its Origin and Development to 1866*, Los
Angeles, 1959, pp. 107–115.
26 Jover, 'Preface' to *La era isabelina*, pp. XCII, CXLVIII and CXLV.
27 See H. Driessen, *On the Spanish-Moroccan Frontier*, New York: Berg, 1992,
p. 37; A. Rodríguez González, 'El conflicto de Melilla en 1893', *Hispania*,
XLIX(171) (1989): 235–266; A. Llanos Alcaraz, *La campaña de Melilla de
1893–94*, Melilla, 1994; M. Fernández Rodríguez, *España y Marruecos en
los primeros años de la Restauración (1875–1894)*, Madrid, 1985.
28 See the engraving published by *La Ilustración Española y Americana*, in
G. Menéndez Pidal, *La España del siglo XIX vista por sus contemporáneos*, Madrid, 1989, p. 77. On these demonstrations, J. P. Fusi, *España:
Evolución de la identidad nacional*, Madrid, 2000, p. 190.
29 *El Globo*, 5 to 10–IX-85; editoriales sobre el conflicto en sí, 27 and 28–
VIII-1885 and 11 and 14–IX-1885. *La Iberia*, 28–VIII-1885 and 5 and
7–IX-1885; *El Siglo Futuro*, 5 and 7–IX-1885.
30 Quoted by Rodríguez González, 'El conflicto de Melilla', pp. 246–247.
Even the Carlist pretender to the throne supported the Spanish claim on
the Caroline Islands, and encouraged his followers to fight for 'Spain's flag
and honour' (*El Siglo Futuro*, 10–IX-1885).
31 De Riquer and Ucelay, 'An Analysis of Nationalisms', pp. 293–294.
32 See N. Sales, *Sobre esclavos, reclutas y mercaderes de quintos*, Barcelona, 1974;
and 'Servei militar i societat: la desigualtat enfront del servei obligatori,
segles XVII–XX', *L'Avenç*, 98 (1986): 721–728; C. Serrano, *Le tour du
peuple: Crise nationale, mouvements populaires et populisme en Espagne, 1890–
1910*, Madrid, 1987, pp. 12–53 and 285–299; and S. Balfour, *The End of
the Spanish Empire (1898–1923)*, Oxford: Clarendon, 1997, Chapter 4.
33 See figures in M. Pérez Ledesma, 'La sociedad española, la guerra y la
derrota', in J. Pan-Montojo (ed.), *Más se perdió en Cuba*, Madrid, 1998,

pp. 113–114: the 10 million pesetas received by the Spanish State were multiplied by four in 1898, which means about 25,000 young men exempted from military service, 10 per cent of the total called to the army; if we add the legally exempted and physically handicapped, in all only about 50 per cent of the enlisted actually went to the army.

34 Linz, 'Los nacionalismos en España', p. 130.

35 See R. Bendix, *Nation-Building and Citizenship*, New York, 1964; Ch. Tilly, 'Cambio social y revolución en Europa: 1492–1992', *Historia Social*, 15 (1993): 71–98.

36 J. M. Jover, 'Federalismo en España. Cara y cruz de una experiencia histórica', in G. Gortázar, *Nación y Estado en la España liberal*, p. 122; or Jover, *La civilización española*, p. 147.

37 T. Martín Martín, *El iberismo: una herencia de la izquierda decimonónica*, Madrid, 1975; by the same author, 'El movimiento iberista en el siglo XIX', *Homenaje a A. Domínguez Ortiz*, Madrid, 1981, pp. 649–662; and 'El movimiento iberista en el siglo XX', *Estudios de Historia de España: Homenaje a M. Tuñón de Lara*, Universidad Internacional Menéndez Pelayo, 1981, Vol. III, pp. 305–315.

38 S. de Mas, *La Iberia: Memoria sobre la conveniencia de la unión pacífica y legal de Portugal y España*, Madrid, 1854. On Almeida Garrett, see J. A. Rocamora, 'Causas do surgimento e do fracaso de nacionalismo ibérico', *Analise Social*, Lisboa, XXVII, 122 (1993): 631–652. All other data in T. Martín Martín, *El iberismo*.

39 Further reading on Iberianism, F. Catroga, 'Nacionalistas e iberistas', in J. Mattoso (ed.), *Historia de Portugal*, Lisboa, 1992, Vol. 6; L. Moreno, *La federalización de España: Poder político y territorio*, Madrid, 1997; J. A. Rocamora, *El nacionalismo ibérico, 1792–1936*, Valladolid, 1994; H. de la Torre, 'Portugal, un nacionalismo anti-español', *Revista de Occidente*, 17 (1982), and 'Iberismo', in A. de Blas (ed.), *Enciclopedia de nacionalismo*, Madrid, 1997. Later evolution of Iberianism, and connection to Catalanism, I. de Ribera y Robira, *Iberisme*, Barcelona, 1907, and *O Génio Peninsular*, Oporto, 1914; or J. Cases Carbó, *El problema peninsular*, de 1924. King Alfonso XIII's projects, around the First World War, in J. Nido y Segalerva, *La Unión Ibérica: Estudio crítico e histórico de este problema*, Madrid, 1914.

40 I. Sepúlveda Muñoz, 'Nacionalismo español y proyección americana: el pan-hispanismo', in J. Beramendi et al. (eds), *Nationalism in Europe: Past and Present*, Santiago de Compostela, 1994, Vol. II, pp. 317–336.

41 Sepúlveda Muñoz, 'Nacionalismo español'. Cf. Van Aken, *Pan-Hispanism*, and F. B. Pike, *Hispanismo, 1898–1936. Spanish Conservatives and Liberals and their Relations with Spanish America*, Notre Dame, IN, 1971.

9

The 'crisis of penetration' of the State

Historians differ: was it a weak State or an oppressive State?

In 1973 Juan Linz, the pioneering scholar of Spanish nationalism, identified the essential problem of the State in the nineteenth century as one of a 'crisis of penetration'. According to Linz, the Spanish State was unable to influence society either by means of its educational institutions or else by creating symbols that were acceptable to the majority of its citizens. In the early 1980s, José María Jover put forward a similar theory, which has been advocated even more forcibly thereafter by Borja de Riquer, for whom the growth of regional nationalisms in the twentieth century has been due less to the strength and intolerable centralising pressures of *españolismo* than to its very weaknesses – in other words, 'to the ineffectiveness of the state nationalising process' in the nineteenth century, the outcome of which was 'a weak Spanish identity'.[1]

The leading writers on this subject therefore seem to agree that Spanish nationalism confronted a problem at least as serious as the imprecision of its political objectives: namely, the weakness and lack of involvement of the State, the institution which, in theory, should have taken the greatest interest in implanting and developing national identity. Yet, as argued in Chapter 2, almost all of the efforts to construct a Spanish cultural identity in the century of liberalism were the result of private or semi-private initiatives, almost always undertaken by groups which I have called the *intellectual élites*. These tended to have some connection with the State, often because they were, or aimed to be, public officials, but also because they believed in the State as the main agent of social modernisation. In spite of this, they did not act in the name of a State institution. The rulers or *statesmen*, on the other hand, played only a secondary and unenthusiastic role in the nationalising process, even though 'the liberal state', in seeking to enhance its legitimacy, 'should have been the principal agent of national unification, the great protagonist of nationalisation and, with the political, juridical, fiscal, economic, cultural and educational resources at its disposal, should have eradicated the differences existing between citizens and between the ancient historic communities'.[2]

The passivity exhibited by these rulers may be partly explained by the fact that the century of nationalisation coincided with a chronic lack of public resources and, more importantly, with a state in permanent political crisis. There is no phenomenon more characteristic of nineteenth-century Spain than the instability exposed by the alarming succession of political *crises*. It began with the rising in Aranjuez and the insurrection in Madrid on the Second of May of 1808, and continued with revolutions, sudden shifts from parliamentarianism to autocracy and back again, dynastic and régime changes, as well as the loss of the American colonies, and, with them, the loss of the Spanish monarchy's remaining international relevance. It took the Spanish State some seventy-five years to evolve 'from empire to nation' and, after losing the colonies, it had to adapt to its new condition of nation-State without any general agreement as to its essential features. It would be difficult to exaggerate the extent to which this undermined the legitimacy of national political authority. Borja de Riquer remarks that the State was constructed 'in the course of a long and bloody civil war', in addition to which this took place 'during a period of international and domestic decline', to quote Ignacio Olábarri.[3] Civil war – or political strife of a similar intensity – together with international decline and (the perception of) domestic political weakness were what formed the backdrop to Spanish politics between 1808 and 1898.

It is nonetheless undeniable that the politico-administrative structure of the modern Spanish State was created at more or less the same time as those of its neighbours. Although there was no blueprint for the new State, there was at least agreement about the need to transform the complex imperial and absolutist structure of the *ancien régime* into one that was appropriate for the Peninsular territories. This new structure was expected to organise and control society much as its predecessor, the imperial monarchy, had done, but without going so far as to establish public services. From the time of the *Cortes* of Cádiz, or possibly earlier given that the Gallic model was adopted by the modernisers of the Enlightenment, the idea that everything should be planned, ordered and overseen from a central nucleus – the capital and seat of government – began to gain ground. This model, which gained in prestige following the initial success of Napoleon in France, won the approval of the State-planners, although, as we shall see, it is debatable whether it was ever put into practice. Even so, the mere fact that it was proposed with such conviction converted it into a crucial factor thereafter.[4]

The French politico-administrative model first appealed in relation to the question of territorial and judicial standardisation. This was an ambition cherished by the liberals in Cádiz, though they had no time to execute it. It was universally agreed that territorial standardisation was justified because it was a means of eliminating inequalities, but there was another, implicit (and possibly unconscious) objective, which was to create a *single image* of the social body. The nation had to be made visible, almost tangible, and one way of achieving this was to divide up the territory in such a standardised fashion that it came to appear as one 'common' unit. This intention was announced, but not implemented, by the Constitution of Cádiz ('a more convenient division of the Spanish territory will be made, when circumstances permit', Article 11). Of greater appeal to the majority of deputies was the French system of *préfectures* or departments, but it was vetoed, having been introduced by the government of their enemy, the despised Joseph Bonaparte or *Pepe Botella*. However, this was the system that was eventually adopted, at least formally, having been expeditiously decreed in 1833 on the death of Fernando VII by the old *afrancesado* and enlightened reformist Javier de Burgos.[5] In order to avoid any whiff of Gallicism, it was decided to use the old term 'province', with which the *ancien régime* had designated the diverse and relatively autonomous territories of the Hispanic Monarchy and which was far removed from the Napoleonic model. From that time on, the *provincia* became the basic unit of centralised organisation, partly because all were similar to one another in territorial terms and partly because each had a unipersonal authority at its head known as the *jefe político* (political head) or civil governor, an unelected post whose incumbent was chosen by, and represented, the Ministry of the Interior. Subordinate to the civil governor was an elected corporation, the *Diputación Provincial*, but this was not, as José María Portillo observes, the expression of a 'federative principle' but merely a 'curb on despotism'.[6]

Judicial standardisation was equally important. This consisted of the reorganisation and codification of the chaotic amalgam of laws dating back to the Middle Ages, a system 'partly common to, and partly peculiar to, each kingdom, or piece of one, in spite of the appearance of unity adopted after the work of the compilers', following M. Artola's description. Napoleon, with his extraordinary authority and organisational ability, had managed to carry out this task in France, it being one of his most astonishing achievements. In Spain, however, there was no comparable period of reformist zeal, so the task dragged on, stagnating in the backwaters of the liberal revolution. The process began in the reign of Fernando VII with the Mercantile Code, continued under

Isabel II with the Penal Code, and was further developed by the Laws of Civil and Criminal Procedure during the *Sexenio Revolucionario* (1868–1874). Towards the end of the century, under the Restoration, it culminated with the Civil Code of 1888. The long list of sponsors underlines the continuity of effort behind it and the diversity of support which it enjoyed, and the substantial nature of the results can be judged by the fact that they remained in force for an average of 150 years, till the end of the Franco dictatorship in 1975.

Other areas that underwent reform included the central State structure. This was divided into an executive branch, which comprised eight ministries, a legislative branch, which was made up of two chambers, and a completely new judicial system – all of which remained almost untouched, as regards its essential features, until the political crisis of the 1930s, and in some respects it was to last for a further fifty years. In the economic sphere, the Stock Exchange of Madrid was created in 1831 and a unified tax system was created by the Mon reform of 1845. From 1856, the bank which had been known successively as the Bank of San Fernando, of San Carlos and of Isabel II, finally became the Bank *of Spain*, with a monopoly on the issue of money from 1874. Six years earlier, the revolution of 1868 had decreed the existence of an official Spanish currency, which was given the Catalan name of *peseta*. In 2002, 134 years later, it ceased to exist after the introduction of the euro.

All of the above suggests that the nineteenth-century Spanish State exhibited a notable degree of organisation and stability. If one surveys the *Gaceta Oficial* (the Official Gazette), this attests to the existence of a single, centralised power that endured over time. In practice, however, the politico-administrative structure was far more fragmented and less integrated than the laws would suggest. 'The political élites confused uniformity and centralisation with nationalisation', observes Borja de Riquer. What is worse, they confused theoretical uniformity and centralisation with their practical realization.[7] The State they created was actually very limited. Tangible expressions of the new official reality were the centrally nominated civil governors that ruled each province, the standardised laws that covered the entire country and the new (or renamed) public buildings in each provincial capital. Still, it is doubtful that this new structure was representative of society, that it channelled the latter's demands or that had it had any meaningful influence over the population; so doubtful, in fact, that many considered it to be at least partly fictitious. One does not have to turn to the radical thinkers for such an opinion. The philosopher José Ortega y Gasset, with his unerring ability to produce ringing epithets, spoke of the 'real

Spain' and the 'official Spain', two worlds which scarcely touched one another. Scrutiny of the fictitious and *official* nineteenth-century State is therefore crucial to any analysis of Spain's nation-building process.

As regards the Spanish State's weakness, it has to be said that there is no general agreement on the matter among historians and that this is one of the few issues of recent Spanish historiography to have caused heated debate. Back in the 1970s, Bartolomé Clavero criticised the theories put forward by José Antonio Maravall regarding the existence of a 'modern State' in Spain from the time of the Renaissance. Maravall claimed that the Spanish monarchs, since the reign of the Catholic Kings and the first Hapsburgs, had been able to delimit a territory, unify the law, regulate economic activity and even create a certain unitary collective image. Clavero, on the other hand, argued that the concept of 'State' could not be applied to this structure because it was such a diverse amalgam of kingdoms and *señorios* (seigneurial fiefdoms) in which the Weberian requisite of a monopoly on legitimate violence did not exist, and that what prevailed was a 'lack of control of the Law by the State'. Francisco Tomás y Valiente entered the debate on the side of Maravall, although he preferred to denominate this State as 'absolutist' rather than *modern*.[8]

Focusing on the modern era, Andrés de Blas insists that there was a fully formed State in nineteenth-century Spain and that this was never questioned at the time. For this very reason, he believes that 'a recourse [to nationalism] was relatively unnecessary in Spanish life'. 'The stability [of] an established State', he claims, 'lacking a serious policy of expansion and without important domestic challenges . . . is a key factor in understanding the tardy nature of Spanish nationalism.' In the 1980s, Juan Pablo Fusi argued 'that the Spain of the nineteenth century was already a fully fledged, mature nation, which [was found] partially wanting and threatened by emerging peripheral nationalisms only after the crisis of 1898'. Borja de Riquer responded in the early 1990s by claiming the opposite: namely, the 'predominance of a *real localism*' owing to the 'relative failure of the liberal State in the nineteenth century to forge a nation by means of an effective nationalising policy'. Fusi has since recognised the failure of nationalisation, but continues to differ regarding the detail. He traces the problem to the poverty and instability of the State itself, while Borja de Riquer blames 'the nature of the Spanish political élite', which introduced centralising measures that were almost impossible to enforce. Núñez Seixas and Olábarri also highlight the weakness of the national political élites, which would put them in the same camp as Riquer, while de Blas has consistently reiterated that the Spanish State was the equal of other contemporary states.[9] Given the lack of consensus on this issue, I shall tackle it point by point.

The first obstacle facing the nineteenth-century State was its doubtful legitimacy. Whatever the outlook of those in power – absolutist, liberal-progressive, moderate, republican or monarchic – many citizens simply did not consider the government a legitimate one or recognise its authority. The more conservative governments suffered less from this inability to attract public support because they did not base their legitimacy on the popular will, and, by introducing fewer changes, they depended to a lesser extent on society's acceptance. This did not, however, prevent them from facing the hostility of a significant sector of the population. As for the liberals, they either had to moderate their reformist projects or saw them blocked early on and, with no channels of communication open to the rural majority, also failed to gain any substantial support for their political vision. Borja de Riquer has frequently observed that there was little 'democratic consensus' or 'popular prestige' surrounding the liberal régime because the parties were not representative and because the citizens did not receive any political rights in exchange for their acceptance of the system: in short, there was 'little socialisation of political life'. Along similar lines, Núñez Seixas maintains that 'the official parties proved to be incapable of organising themselves on solidly based regional structures' and that 'it was difficult for potential citizens to feel themselves to be an integral part of the political nation given that the State was imposed upon them'.[10]

A second problem was more practical: the nascent State, in aspiring to legitimacy, was incapable of creating public services, principally because it lacked the resources to do so. The chronic impoverishment of the Spanish monarchy throughout the nineteenth century was undoubtedly one of the main causes of the weakness of the liberal State and, consequently, of its negligible contribution to the nationalising process. The monarchy, heavily indebted under the last two kings of the *ancien régime*, was not only deprived of its American revenues at the start of the modern era, but also had to deal with a country that had been devastated by the Napoleonic War, which was followed twenty years later by the no less devastating Carlist War. The indebtedness of the Treasury was so great that, for much of the century, approximately one-third of the annual budget was earmarked for the payment of interest on the debt. Successive governments, whose funds derived almost exclusively from the sale of disentailed land and an increase in the national debt, were impotent to implement new measures or to provide public services for their citizens.

Any regime which was so manifestly lacking in stability, legitimacy and resources was inevitably going to experience serious problems in endeavouring to carry out an ambitious plan of Statist centralisation. Worse still, both the physical terrain and the extant administrative system of Spain were highly fragmented. Not a single European traveller had anything good to say about the system of communications of the mountainous Iberian Peninsula until at least 1875, when the first railway lines were completed. In 1910, more than 4,000 of the country's 9,200 *pueblos* still remained isolated, even by road. It is hardly surprising that local centres of power were so successful in resisting the statutory provisions that, time and time again, decreed their disappearance. The most obvious case is that of the *foral* regions, whose opposition to the standardisation of laws and taxes was so effective that they were able to extract legal exemptions from common laws, such as the *foral* appendices to the Civil Code and the special tax arrangements for the Basque-Navarrese provinces. Indeed, the tension between Statist centralisation and the defence of traditional privileges and exemptions was one of the principal reasons for the Carlist wars, and, ultimately, for the emergence of Catalan and Basque nationalism, though these extreme examples lie beyond our scope. The most habitual response to the pursuit of centralised standardisation was covert resistance, as a result of which the local powers reached a tacit pact with the liberal State. This came to be known as *caciquismo*, which was not simply a vestige of remote feudal privileges but a new phenomenon that resulted from the merger of the residual hierarchies of the *ancien régime* with new local élites created by disentailment. *Caciquismo* should not be regarded as an agreement between *real* local powers and *theoretical* centralisation, because the former could not afford to ignore the directives coming from Madrid and were, in fact, forced to compromise; in other words, the State exercised *real* power. The pre-eminence of the cities designated as the forty-nine provincial capitals, in comparison with the limited power wielded by other localities of a similar size, also demonstrates that the power of the central government was not to be ignored.[11]

Regional and local fragmentation thereby coexisted alongside a de facto central power. A further source of fracture within the State was the party and personal divisions which dominated political life and which were reflected by the tendency to regard the public administration as an inheritable property that was parcelled out to private individuals or bodies. The civil governor, the embodiment of the State in the provinces, 'acted far more like a leader of the party in government than as a representative of the State administration', remarks De Riquer. Indeed, 'centralisation was, in practice, much more of a political instrument subordinated to party interests than a coherent general principle of State organisation and nationalisation'.[12] Something similar could be said of the civil service that grew very slowly throughout the nineteenth century. The appearance of a State bureaucracy in Spain coincided with that in France and Germany, which suggests that the Spanish State was similar to that of the more advanced countries. In the Spanish case, however, it is doubtful that the bureaucracy devoted the bulk of its efforts to the creation and maintenance of public services. On the contrary, the upper-middle classes exploited the system for their own ends, above all as a source of income and influence for their own familial and social circles. This is certainly the impression that Benito Perez Galdós, who was fascinated by officialdom, gives in his novels. The State in Spain therefore existed, but it was not only badly managed but also treated as if it were a personal sinecure of the élites, while the vast majority of the population perceived it as an impenetrable maze, alien to their needs, but with the power to impose arbitrary rules and decisions that could threaten their very livelihoods.

All observers described the Spain of the nineteenth century, and even the early twentieth century, as a *provincial* country, so fragmented that the reach of government did not extend to many of its remoter corners. These descriptions may have been exaggerated, and there may also have been a more efficient though less visible side to centralisation, but they continue to prevail amongt modern historians. According to Ignacio Olábarri, 'Spain, in the nineteenth and twentieth centuries, continued to be a plural reality, with extreme territorial contrasts in every sphere (demographic, economic, social, cultural, religious, etc.)'. For De Riquer, the 'legal means of State action were, for decades, extremely weak and barely articulated'. Juan Pablo Fusi agrees: 'the Spain of the nineteenth century was a country of theoretical centralism but real localism and regionalism. For many years, it was simply a network of regions that were badly communicated and poorly integrated ... Localism dominated Spanish social and political life well into the twentieth century'. Ortega y Gasset famously declared that the reality of Spain was the province and that the influence of Madrid extended a mere six kilometres from the capital.[13] Yet other European States, even those generally considered to be the most successful, were also highly fragmented and riven by regional particularism.[14] The general, if mistaken, perception was that fragmentation and localism were greater in Spain than in other countries, with the exception of Austria and Turkey.

It is not difficult to imagine the frustration experienced by the architects of the Spanish Nation-State when, in an effort to replicate the European models they so admired, they tried to extend the jurisdiction of the State to areas such as education, public welfare, and the registration of births and deaths, all of which had been in the hands of the Catholic Church for centuries. After overcoming endless obstacles and resistance, the State-planners managed to pass the appropriate laws, but the application of the reforms was then thwarted by a lack of money and civil servants. One of the few unifying endeavours that was undertaken by the Spanish State was the construction of the railway network, but this was achieved by means of concessions to (foreign) private companies, not with public funds. The roads, on the other hand, depended on the State, and they did not reach an acceptable standard until the time of Primo de Rivera in the 1920s. As for the benefits of the welfare state, these were not made available until well into the twentieth century, and did not become widespread until the time of Franco.

Thus the ministries were hopelessly underfinanced and understaffed, with the result that the Spanish monarchy was unable to carry out in a satisfactory manner any of the tasks that have defined modern Nation-States. The monarchy was unable to create a State that provided a national infrastructure, supplied public services and redistributed the nation's wealth. Neither could it integrate the population in a political sense nor, as a result, could it forge a national culture or enhance its legitimacy as the representative of the *nation*. The government was obliged to delegate most of its day-to-day tasks to the *caciques*, who controlled the local power networks and who furnished the executive with the votes that it required at election time. In exchange, these local powerbrokers demanded a free hand to interpret the law as they saw fit. All citizens were aware that it was far more important to be on good terms with the *cacique* than to abide by the law. Accordingly, it was the State – which was unable to guarantee rights or supply public services – that was to be avoided, while the *cacique* provided protection.[15] Though this alienated people from the law, and fostered a cynical atttitude towards it, the State was nonetheless forced to rely on the exercise of local power by the *caciques*, who thereby maintained the status quo insofar as every region had *its own law* and there was little or no development of a truly national culture.

The nationalisation of the masses: education, military service, symbols and monuments

No mechanism is so crucial to the building of a nation as a free, obligatory State educational system. Spain's politico-intellectual élites were aware of this as early as the Enlightenment. The Constitution of 1812, in its 'Preliminary Discourse', affirmed that 'the State, no less than the soldiers who defend it, needs citizens who raise up the nation and promote its felicity with all manner of culture and knowledge. Therefore one of the first concerns that should occupy the representatives of a great and generous people is public education. This has to be general and uniform . . . So that it is national in character and so that public opinion can address the great objective of forming true Spaniards and honest men who love their *patria*, it is essential that the management of public education should not be put into mercenary hands'. On the basis of these principles, the Constitution laid down the obligations of the State to establish and maintain a school system that embraced all the *pueblos* in the kingdom. This led to the bill that was drawn up by the poet Quintana in 1813, which, for the very first time, envisaged the public education of all the citizens. The deputies of Cádiz displayed a commendable clarity of thought but, like everything else that they proposed, it came to nothing.

The liberals of the *Trienio* (1820–1823) tried to establish a General Regulation of Public Education, which was less ambitious than Quintana's plan because it assigned only a supervisory function to the State – not a monopoly – but they also failed. The next attempt was in 1834, with the establishment of the *Escuelas Normales Femeninas* and a plan for a State educational system with a minimum period of free, obligatory schooling. Yet again, political events thwarted the project. The same occurred under the Moderates in 1845, when Pedro José Pidal drew up a new plan for free education which was boycotted by his own party. Only in 1857 did the *Cortes* finally pass a General Law of Public Education, which was put forward by the conservative Catholic Minister for Public Works, Claudio Moyano. In outline, it did not differ much from the project originally presented by Quintana in Cádiz: public education would be unified under the joint control of Church and State and it would be imparted at three levels within a centralist model of crushing rigidity and simplicity. Primary education would be compulsory for all children between six and nine years of age and the schools would be established in all municipalities of over 500 inhabitants. Secondary education would be imparted in *institutos* in the provincial capitals, and higher education would be pursued at a number of universities in the regional capitals. Doctorates were reserved for the 'Central University' in Madrid.[16]

At last, there seemed to be a plan for the *nationalisation of the masses*, to use the term coined by Georges Mosse.[17] It had been an uphill struggle but, in 1857, a law had finally been passed that established a single, overarching *national* system of education, including a period of compulsory schooling for all children. This was the same decade in which the first modern *Historias de España* were published, so in a very short time there were also nationalising textbooks, exemplary among which were those of Fernando de Castro. Furthermore, Moyano's Law was destined to last: its basic concepts and levels remained in force until the 'massification' of the educational system in the final years of the Franco régime. Unfortunately, it was a largely theoretical triumph, as shown by its inadequate application for at least fifty years, thereby highlighting the narrowness of the parameters within which the Spanish State moved at that time. Unable to fund the educational system, the State simply decreed that municipal councils – which had just been deprived of their major source of income in 1855 as a result of disentailment – would be responsible for the building and upkeep of the primary schools, while the provincial *diputaciones* were made to run the *institutos* or second-ary schools. As Francisco Comín and Carmen García write, 'central government shirked its commitment to provide certain public services in the knowledge that they would be equally disregarded by local cor-porations lacking the necessary resources'. The long-term results were entirely predictable: by 1898, forty years after Moyano's Law had been passed, almost half the schools had still not been built and 60 per cent of children of primary school age were still not in school. More than 60 per cent of the entire population continued to be illiterate, compared to 50 per cent in Italy, 17 per cent in France, and some 5 per cent in Britain and Germany. The majority of those who could read and write had studied in private institutions, almost all of which were Catholic colleges. Where State schools did exist, the teachers were paid so little, and so late, that their penury became proverbial.[18]

This failure in education, as well as having a profoundly negative effect on the nationalising process, is indicative of two basic problems that explain the conduct of Spanish rulers in the nineteenth century: the *lack of resources* and, equally important, the *lack of political will*, insofar as the State chose to spend the money that *was* available to it on other things. An analysis of public spending reveals a highly militarised administration: in 1885, payments to the armed forces absorbed 49 per cent of the State budget for personnel, and between 1850 and 1890 the army, navy and Interior Ministry between them accounted for over 60 per cent of total State spending. Given that the country was rarely at war, it must be concluded that the main function of the armed forces was domestic, as Manuel Balbé explained some years ago. Included in this expenditure is the Civil Guard, or rural police force, which proved to be the only national entity created in the nineteenth century that achieved an undisputed degree of efficiency. In fact, the maintenance of law and order was the one service that the Spanish State could guarantee, though it employed methods that were so primitive as to be excessive within the European context of the time. Consequently the armed forces were the most visible branch of the national administration, a symbol of the State's presence in society. Apart from military spending, the other major item in the State budget was the allocation for the upkeep of the Catholic Church and clergy which, in the watershed year of 1898, equalled that for public works, and was five times that for education. Only after the crisis of 1898 did the situation begin to change, when the Ministry of Public Education was set up and the government assumed responsibility for primary education. Spending on public education subsequently rose from 1 per cent to 4 per cent of the national budget.[19]

Why was State education so neglected? Was it simply because during the Restoration 'the intensity of nationalism does not seem to have been very great', as argued by Carlos Dardé?[20] We should not be deceived by the sporadic outbreaks of patriotism during, say, the conflict over the Caroline Islands in 1885, or earlier, during the War of Africa in 1860. There had been no decisive nationalising plan during the two 25-year periods (1843–1868 and 1875–1900) under conservative rule. As under the reign of Fernando VII (1814–1833), the politicians believed that religion was the guarantee of their subjects' subordination. Education was consequently left in the hands of the Church. The conservatives were not only subject to irresistible pressure from the clergy but almost certainly shared the conviction that the formation of good Catholics was just as important as that of good citizens or patriots. Right from the period of right-wing domination under Fernando VII all education was placed under direct ecclesiastical control. What neither the absolutists under Fernando VII, nor the Moderates of General Narváez, nor the conservatives of Antonio Cánovas and later Antonio Maura ever seem to have understood was that the Catholic Church was not only anti-liberal but also anti-Statist. From this perspective, the Catholic Church was an obstacle to nationalisation.

In short, the Spanish State made no concerted effort to provide State schools in which, in the words of Pierre Vilar, 'to make Spaniards'. Religious schools thrived to such an extent that their share of all schools grew from 10 per cent in 1860 to some 30 per cent in 1920; and, naturally, they 'made' Catholics. According to the Law of 1857, the history of Spain was not taught at elementary level, but 'Christian Doctrine and Notions of the Holy Story' was.[21] Not only were the history of Spain and civic values omitted, to the benefit of the catechism and Christian morality, but, when it proved easier to do so, Christian doctrine was taught in Basque, Catalan or Galician instead of the official language of the State. This was where Spain differed so radically from France. The latter was a country that had inherited a linguistic diversity comparable to that of Spain, but which, in two or three generations, wiped out the many varieties of *patois* and instilled Parisian French as the national language on the pretext of eradicating illiteracy. According to the study by Eugen Weber, the compulsory State education system set up by the Third Republic from 1880 onwards was the main tool in this process. It caused a severe conflict with the Vatican, which led to the Pope's denunciation of the Napoleonic Concordat and to the rupture of diplomatic relations. During the conflict, tens of thousands of teachers in holy orders were forced into exile from the land of the old *fille aînée de l'Église*, many of whom found refuge in Spain and contributed to the growing number of private schools under the Restoration. A comparison of the two countries becomes inevitable: 'in contrast to what happened in the France of the Third Republic', writes Carlos Serrano, in Spain 'schools were not able to play a central role as an instrument of national integration . . . The administration was incapable of implementing a linguistic policy that would have made Castilian the common language of all Spaniards. The Catalans, Galicians and some Basques never attended national schools, they did not need to communicate with the rest of Spain, they spoke their own languages and they could get by without Castilian (which they only needed to speak if they emigrated to Spanish America)'.[22] It is evident that this was one of the keys to the shortcomings in the development of a national identity in Spain during the twentieth century. Spain remained linguistically richer and more diverse than France, and, as a result, suffered from greater problems of national integration.

Military service was an equally eloquent example of a lack of both political will and financial resources. As Eugen Weber has shown, in France military service was a crucial means of integrating the French rural population into the new national identity. It is no coincidence that French historians have been more aware than Spanish ones of the absence of this nationalising instrument in Spain. Pierre Vilar has compared Spain at the end of the nineteenth century to the France of the Second Empire, when military service was bedevilled by exemptions and when it was permissible for some recruits to be substituted for others. Given that sacrifice for the *patria* was justified on the grounds that the latter embodied an ideal of *justice*, or equality before the law, a military service that was avoided by the rich could not be considered *patriotic*: 'how to preach *sacrifice for the patria* if not everyone is a soldier?' In the *Communist Manifesto*, Marx had written that the proletariat had no homeland, and that the poor could feel no patriotism. Similarly, Thiers excluded the lower classes from the electoral system because they had no vested *interest* in the running of the nation. In Spain, there was less theorising but the same sentiment was to be found in both popular and highbrow literature. An example of the latter is the bitter tale by Clarín entitled *El Sustituto*, which tells the story of a young gentleman who sends one of his tenants to do military service in his stead. Resigned, the peasant goes off to war, consoled by the thought that his mother will receive a pension if he is killed in combat. As the recruits depart, the young man, his master, is commissioned by the local council to write an ode to those who are about to offer their lives for the *patria*. Popular literature has left us this even more corrosive comment:

> Hoy, en todo momento, / los pobres, la gentuza, la morralla,
> dan su sangre en los campos de batalla / y los ricos su oro,
> al seis por ciento . . .[23]

After the battle of Sedan in 1870, France blamed its defeat by Germany on the discriminatory system of recruitment that was then scrapped by the Third Republic and replaced by a truly universal military service. This is exactly what neither rulers nor legislators were to do in Spain at any time during the nineteenth century. It is true that the lack of resources was partly to blame – it is not cheap to maintain barracks, armaments and uniformed troops to a reasonable standard – but if the will to integrate all social strata into *service for the patria* had existed, riding roughshod over hereditary hierarchies, at least the attempt would have been made. Not that there is any reason to think that this would have altered popular feeling: only by coercion is it possible to tear sons away from their parents, send them far away and subject them to discomfort and sacrifice for long periods, often at serious risk to their lives. There would always have been popular opposition, just as there was in other countries. Nevertheless, military service would have achieved a nationalising effect in relation to many of those conscripted by bringing them out of their isolation and making them live alongside others, whom they would have begun to see as *compatriots* from other *regions*; by making them practise a language that they would have come to consider as *common* to all; and by subjecting them to a powerful rhetoric on the necessity of placing the *good of the patria* above and beyond individual or local interests. The desertion rate would still have been high, especially in time of war, because it was high in all armies at that time, but at least the armed forces would have been *national*. The appalling reputation of the Spanish army was summed up by the radical left, which described the military contribution of the lower classes as a 'blood tax' levied on the poor. It is therefore difficult to avoid the conclusion of Núñez-Seixas that the army 'never fulfilled the unifying role in Spain that it played in other European States, where military service was obligatory for all citizens'. According to Núñez-Seixas, not only the system of recruitment but all aspects of the army were 'crudely classist', from the policing functions of the armed forces, so closely identified with the defence of the existing system of land ownership, to the system of insurance to purchase an exemption from the call to arms.[24]

In comparison with maintaining an army, it is far cheaper to create and propagate a range of national symbols, which are essential for the spread of nationalist sentiment. Eric Hobsbawm coined the term 'the invention of tradition' to refer to the process of creation by nineteenth-century European States of their flags, anthems, commemorative ceremonies, festivities, monuments, memorial stones, street names and many other symbols and rituals that were intended to be the expression of a collective entity in existence since time immemorial. Although the process reached its height in the years prior to 1900, it had begun about a century earlier and, initially, Spain had advanced at the same pace as the other monarchies. Jovellanos and Meléndez Valdés expressed their wish to introduce popular fiestas with rituals and songs that would familiarise the people with the great historic deeds of the *patria*. It might even be claimed that Spain led the way, since 'national flag' was a term that figured in the decree by which Carlos III stipulated the use of an oblong ensign by the navy consisting of three horizontal stripes, red at the top and bottom with a double width of yellow in the middle. It was also during his reign that the '*Himno de Granaderos*' was first composed and played. This was to become the future royal march, although no one would have thought to call it a 'national anthem'. However, the decree referring to the flag, signed by the king, refers to 'my' navy, a possessive adjective indicative of the prevailing mentality, which was still far from any *national* significance of the ensign. On the other hand, although Spain set out early on the road to nationalisation, the process would be seriously hampered by the tempestuous political climate of the nineteenth century.

The flag is, of course, the first symbol required by any collective that aims to create a sense of nationhood. There never was a single flag common to the complex collection of kingdoms over which the Hapsburgs and the first Bourbons ruled, far less a national one, however much it was claimed in the nineteenth and twentieth centuries that *Spain* achieved *national unity* under the Catholic Kings. The troops of Carlos V and Felipe II used a variety of heraldic or regional emblems and, in order to identify one another, red cockades or the crosses of

Burgundy. Under the Bourbons, the cockade became white and the fleur-de-lis was added to the common symbols. In 1785, Carlos III then introduced the red and yellow flag for the navy, and his successor extended its use to fortified seaboard towns eight years later. During the Napoleonic War, there was a proliferation of standards and flags for the different regiments but the bicolour ensign of Carlos III began to take pride of place because Cádiz, as a maritime stronghold, had raised it as a symbol of resistance against the French. It then became the liberal emblem and was adopted by the National Militia, as a result of which Fernando VII restricted its widespread use, although he respected its maritime function. During the first Carlist War, it was flown by the troops of the Regent, María Cristina, and in 1843, shortly after the conflict ended, a law was promulgated to extend its use throughout the army. However, despite frequent claims to the contrary, this did not mean that there was now a national flag: it was purely for military use and would never have been flown over ministries or other public buildings. Minor legal changes affected its status during the reign of Isabel II, but when the Moroccan war began in 1860, the country enthusiastically embraced the colours and, finally, in 1868, the revolutionaries adopted the flag definitively as a national one. It was a little late in the day. The Carlists opposed it, of course, as they remained loyal to the white flag with the cross of Burgundy, but so did the Royal Academy of History, in whose name Cánovas wrote a report – of great historical good sense – refuting the antiquity and national character of this symbol. Over time, even the republicans changed tack, adding a purple stripe to the red and yellow ones that derived from the famous liberal mythification of the Castilian *comuneros* of the 1520s. In 1869, Fernández de los Ríos actually proposed to the *Cortes* that the bicolour flag be changed for a tricolour one. The measure was not officially adopted but it appears that both the tricolour and the bicolour were used during the fleeting Republic of 1873. From the time of the Restoration, the bicolour flag, which was considered both liberal and monarchical, was used exclusively but with so little enthusiasm that not until 1908 was it officially decreed that it should be flown on all public buildings, and only in 1927 did it become mandatory for it to be flown on all merchant shipping. The Second Republic of 1931 reintroduced the purple stripe, which was promptly removed by Franco in 1939. Only since 1977, when the recently legalised Communist Party embraced the red and yellow flag, has it finally been accepted as a common symbol by all those who consider themselves *Spaniards*.

Less well established than the flag, although almost equally polemical, has been the national anthem. The *Marcha de Granaderos* was composed in the eighteenth century and played on all state occasions throughout the nineteenth without being granted official standing. The *Himno de Riego* was played under liberal governments and during the Republics of 1873 and 1931–1939. Between the Republics and during the mobilization for the Cuban War of 1868–1878, the troops embarked to the strains of various tunes, of which the *Marcha* from the *zarzuela* (or operetta) *Cádiz* was among the most popular. The streets were also filled with patriotic crowds among whom left-wing supporters might well have been chanting the Marseillaise, the *French* revolutionary composition, to express their support for the *Spanish* cause. Finally, in 1908, the *Marcha de Granaderos*, now called *Marcha Real*, was chosen as the national anthem, but when, in early 1931, in the final months of the reign of Alfonso XIII, the chief musician of the Royal Corps of Halberdiers, Bartolomé Pérez Casas, adapted the score, he registered it as his own composition in the General Society of Authors and his heirs continued to receive royalties every time it was played, right up until the end of the twentieth century. It is impossible to imagine a greater degree of privatisation of a public symbol! Even worse was the fact that neither in 1908, nor after the Civil War of 1936–1939 when the victorious régime ratified the *Marcha Real* as the national anthem, were any words written in accompaniment, although several unofficial versions existed, one of which was written by José María Pemán that became quite popular under Franco ('Long live Spain, raise up your arms, sons of the Spanish people, which rises up anew'). With the introduction of democracy in the late 1970s, it was decided once again to leave the anthem without words in view of the difficulty of reaching a consensus. This has meant that, as in the case of the flag, not only did the indecision continue until the late twentieth century, but even then the opportunity was lost to introduce one of the most effective mechanisms for internalising a patriotic identity: a collective song that makes those singing it feel part of a transcendent entity, superior to their individual lives.[25]

A third essential symbol of nationhood that was also lacking in the nineteenth century was a *national* fiesta or holiday. An obvious date was the Second of May because it was politically acceptable from the absolutists (later the Carlists) to the Republicans (when they came to exist), while encompassing all the liberal tendencies. The idea of commemorating the date went back a long way: it was first announced by the *Cortes* of Cádiz in 1811, only three years after the event itself, with the Napoleonic wars still raging. Of course, anything to the liking of the Cádiz liberals was enough to alienate the régime of Fernando VII, and for two decades, the date, like the yellow and red flag, was ignored. When it was revived in the 1830s, the impetus had been lost and the day failed to become a great national festivity. It was not, on this occasion, a problem of resources: there were many fiestas throughout the country and one of them, on 25 July, even had a certain national air as it had been dedicated by the Catholic Church to St James, the Patron Saint of Spain. Only in a very few circles was there any sense of the need for a secular patriotic celebration. By mid-century, the Second of May had become a day of festivities in Madrid, with both a religious and a civic content, and the celebration was paid for by the town council, which considered the events commemorated to be of great local importance. As Isabel II's reign drew to a close, the *fiesta* became more contentious because of its liberal bias, and it was even banned by some of the last Isabelline governments. During the revolution of 1868–1874, it regained a certain popularity, but times had moved on and its vulgar, xenophobic tendencies – one of the biggest diversions was to beat up any passer-by who might be French – meant that more progressive groups, such as the internationalist workers, spoke out against it. The Restoration prohibited the celebration once more, and by the time of the Second of May's centenary, the army had turned it into a day of homage to Captains Daoiz and Velarde – a means of glorifying the armed forces. It is difficult to conceive of a more blatant example of historical distortion as, in the first moments of the insurrection, the two captains had been the exception among their comrades-in-arms in actually opposing the French.[26]

Not until after 1910 would the government finally decide to introduce a national holiday of commemoration and call it such. It was not the Second of May, with its civic-liberal connotations, neither was it St James Day, bound up with the idea of the 'Catholic unity' of Spain. It was the Twelfth of October, the date on which Christopher Columbus reached the island of Guanahaní and which Europeans call the 'Discovery of America'. This could be seen as the triumph of a secular, expansive nationalism of an imperial kind, but it was also the day on which the *fiesta del Pilar* had been held for centuries in celebration of the miraculous appearance of the Mother of God to the evangelist of Spain. The ambiguity remained: the power of the State and the nation were celebrated jointly with Christianity.

The indecisiveness apparent in the choosing of all these major national symbols is equally visible in the lack of monuments to honour national values and national heroes and their deeds. On the death of Fernando VII in 1833, there was still not a single patriotic monument in Madrid. Ornamental structures were not, in fact, a strong feature of Spanish cities, and there were remarkably few in Madrid. Kings had resided in the palaces of Aranjuez and La Granja in preference to

Madrid and paid scant attention to their capital city. A portrayal of the nation was also absent from the royal palaces, whose symbols, decorations, gardens and fountains limited themselves to the depiction of mythological or allegorical themes in the style of Versailles which, in their turn, had imitated those of Renaissance Italy, upon which Felipe II had already modelled the palaces of El Pardo, El Bosque and Aranjuez itself.[27] In short, in the early eighteenth century, the court resided in two royal palaces and there were only two monuments in their gardens of any political significance: the equestrian statues of Felipe III and Felipe IV, both gifts from the Medici in the previous century, and both celebrating *royal* power, not *national* glory. Carlos III beautified Madrid in many ways, including the vast church of *San Francisco el Grande* close to the palace, the great arch of the *Puerta de Alcalá* and the *Paseo del Prado*, flanked by a science museum and botanical gardens and crowned at each end by the mythological sculptures of Cybele and Neptune. Nevertheless, these monuments were not representative of the glory of the nation either. They were not designed to embellish Madrid as the *capital* of the State but as the royal *court* or residence. Fernando VII added the *Puerta de Toledo* and he changed the purpose of Villanueva's magnificent building from natural science museum to art gallery, where he exhibited the royal collection of paintings instead. In due course, the *Museo del Prado* was to become a truly *national* art gallery, although it has never been called this.[28]

It was left to the liberal revolution to establish a new symbolic order in the urban centres of the *nation* and, above all, in the *capital* of that nation. The public spaces had to be filled with models of the new patriotic morality, which honoured the *fathers of the patria* as a shining example for future generations. The monument of paramount importance to the early liberals was one dedicated to those killed by the French in May 1808, the symbolic date on which Spain had emerged as a modern nation. The *Cortes* made the decision as early as 1811 but the project was shelved until the death of their arch enemy, the last absolutist king, twenty years later. Even then, there were delays owing to further political changes, bureaucratic obstacles and empty coffers. Eventually, in 1840, a liberal government, no doubt spurred on by the imminent burial of Napoleon's remains in *Les Invalides* in Paris, completed and inaugurated the monument situated to one side of the *Museo del Prado*. At last there was a symbol of undeniably national significance in the busiest and most respectable avenue of the capital, and yet it received little attention except on the Second of May, during ceremonies which included a Requiem Mass.

In 1850, the new parliament building of the Spanish *Cortes* was inaugurated in the Carrera de San Jerónimo. Although in a central part of the city, the building was not located in a strategic position, without either the height or the perspective appropriate to such a symbolic building. Ten years later, an emotional scene took place inside when all the political groups, with rare unanimity, backed the declaration of war against Morocco proposed by O'Donnell. In the euphoria of victory, it was decided to add two bronze lions – one on either side of the steps leading up to the main entrance – cast from the metal of cannons captured from the enemy. This was a common custom at the time, which Georges Mosse has studied in the case of Germany. According to Mosse, a monument of this kind symbolically subjugates and humiliates the enemy in perpetuity by turning his weapons into a lasting reminder of defeat. In addition, the strength of the victors is measured by the prestige of the vanquished. In this case, the enemy, symbolically reduced to the brace of lions, was merely a motley collection of irregular troops involved in a conflict that was blown out of all proportion as the 'War of Africa'. Nineteenth-century Spain, incapable of measuring up to the great powers, expressed the limits to its own power and ambition in the very bronzes calculated to glorify its achievement.[29]

The building of monuments turned into an obsession in the last two decades of the century. In Madrid statues were not only raised to monarchs and military leaders, such as Isabel the Catholic Queen, the Marqués del Duero, Espartero and Don Alvaro de Bazán, but also to explorers and artists, such as Columbus, Calderón, Murillo, Goya and Velázquez. They were generally placed around the *Museo del Prado* at the time of the centenary celebrations in the 1880s. The most significant and most ambitious patriotic monument was the *Panteón de Hombres Ilustres*, an idea cherished since 1839, approved thirty years later by the *Cortes* of the glorious revolution. It was to be located in the Church of *San Francisco el Grande*, from which, in the grandiose project put forward by Fernández de los Rios in his book *El futuro Madrid*, a broad avenue would bisect the old city and lead up to the *Cortes*. It would be a monument, he said, 'to educate the Nation in the example of its eminent men, to show to the living the reward for a fruitful existence and to augur a succession of great citizens worthy of being buried in that precinct'. The nationalising bent of the liberal élites is unquestionable and, as usual, they were following the European example: here we can see the influence of the French *Panthéon National* installed by the Revolution in the church of *Sainte Geneviève*; the influence of the Italian tombs of the great men of Tuscan (by then, national) culture brought together in *Santa Croce* in Florence; and the influence of the British gallery of statesmen and other luminaries buried in Westminster

Abbey. The great avenue dreamed up by Fernández de los Ríos was never begun, though, during the revolution of 1868–1874 time was found to exhume the remains said to belong to the Gran Capitán, Garcilaso, Quevedo, Calderón, the Duque de Aranda and Gravina and to have them reburied in the church of *San Francisco el Grande* with all the pomp and ceremony that they deserved. With the coming of the Restoration, however, those unfortunate relics were secretly returned to their places of origin. It was then planned to build a true Pantheon which would be the annex to a great basilica to be built to the south of the *Museo del Prado*. The annex came to be built with 'a neo-Gothic, neo-Byzantine cloister with an Italian bell tower . . . an eclectic and exotic design' and, at the end of the nineteenth century, the bodies of a number of the century's politicians were laid to rest within it. The building of the basilica, however, was to drag on for far longer and it was only finished after the Civil War, in the 1940s, an era that was far from propitious for the execution of large-scale projects, particularly those in honour of liberal politicians. Once again, the original grandiose plan came to nothing. Today, this is one of the most forgotten corners of Madrid.[30]

The turn of the century saw plans for other national monuments, such as the one to commemorate the combatants of the war of 1898. It was a homage to the 'Disaster' that, as Carlos Serrano joked, became a real disaster when it collapsed and was never rebuilt. The statue to Alfonso XII next to the lake in the *Parque del Retiro* was much more a success, although it took far longer than planned. It was a small-scale imitation of the one dedicated to Victor Emmanuel in the Campidoglio in Rome, but it was in honour of the king rather than the nation. Overall, nineteenth-century national monuments in Spain were neither numerous nor impressive. Other cities which built monuments, mainly between 1880 and 1900, tended to celebrate locally born notables, with the ever-present ambiguity of intention between national and merely local pride.[31]

A comparison between the paucity of national monuments and the abundance of Catholic ones is inevitable, and it highlights yet again that the only collective personality to rival the national one was the Catholic Church. It is not a question of Catholic buildings with a religious func-tion and built with Church funds or donations from the faithful, but overtly *public* symbols such as the statues to the Sacred Heart of Jesus located in highly strategic places. This particular devotion dated back to the eighteenth century and, after becoming a favourite among the Jesuits, achieved popularity in Rome in the second half of the nine-teenth, to the point that Pius IX declared it 'the queen of devotions'.

Moreover, Leo XIII consecrated the world to the Heart of Jesus. From the moment that the *Sacré Coeur* in Montmartre was dedicated to it, on the same hill where the cannons had been placed to crush the Paris Commune, many of the great Catholic-conservative movements of the period were founded upon it. In Spain, the two principal cities each had a monument of this kind: Barcelona, on Mount Tibidabo, over-looking the urban sprawl from the heights, and Madrid, on the *Cerro de los Ángeles*, a small elevation but one of huge symbolic value as it was considered to be the geographical centre of Spain. The latter was inaugurated by Alfonso XIII in a solemn ceremony during which he consecrated the country to the Sacred Heart. Thus, the greatest monu-ment of his reign was a religious one, while the stone memorials to the troops that fought in Cuba and the Philippines, to the conquerors of the New World and to the insurgents that defied Napoleon, were never finished. Although there were plenty of national centenaries and other occasions, and no lack of ideas, nothing ever happened. As a result, the population was never *nationalised* by grandiose patriotic monuments.[32] Franco, who had the monument on the *Cerro de los Ángeles* rebuilt after the Civil War and *re-consecrated* the country to the Sacred Heart, was the only one to create a vast and impressive edifice imbued with, from his point of view, national significance. This was *el Valle de los Caídos* or the Valley of the Fallen, though this represented a forced and partial act of nationalisation with which much of the population did not identify.

It was much easier and cheaper to change the names of streets than to build monuments. The liberals understood this and, from the moment they first took power, they hastened to rename the main squares of towns and *pueblos* as 'Plaza de la Constitución'. It was a simple idea with a symbolic content similar to the French custom of planting 'trees of freedom'. The absolutists created fewer symbols, but they understood the importance of erasing those of the enemy and, within hours of their return to power, commemorative tablets were torn down and consti-tutional name plates defaced. During the long periods of Moderate power, the rulers chose not to change names in order to avoid treading on anyone's toes. The only cluster of street names of patriotic signifi-cance in Madrid (usually with a liberal bias) dates back to the 1830s, but this was very much a product of the times: the war with the Carlists, the disentailment of Church lands and the destruction of monasteries and convents. Otherwise few new street names were created, though new names occasionally had to be found as a result of urban redevel-opment or because the old names were considered ridiculous. One way or another, the names *Colón, Hernán Cortés, Pizarro, Cervantes, el Dos de Mayo, Bailén, la Independencia, Daoiz y Velarde* and *Espoz y*

Mina became part of Madrid's topography.[33] Once the city walls were demolished in 1868 and the city grew outwards with the new suburb of Salamanca, a large number of streets had to be named – but how times had changed! With rare exceptions such as *Padilla, Bravo* and *Maldonado*, the new street directory drew upon the names of contemporary politicians, such as *Serrano, Narváez, Espartero (Príncipe de Vergara), O'Donnell* and *El Doctor Esquerdo*. It is revealing to compare Madrid with Barcelona. The *Eixample* district of Barcelona, which was planned at around the same time, enumerated the territories and glorious deeds of the Catalan myth in all its mediaeval splendour: *Córcega, Rosellón, Provenza, Mallorca, Valencia, Aragón, Nápoles, Cerdeña, Sicilia,* and so on. Whether this affirmation of Catalonia expressed the glory of Spain or represented an embryonic, alternative nationalism is unclear: there is probably a bit of both. Clearly the planners of the *Eixample* were aware that a street directory could further the development of a collective identity among its citizens, a fact of which the rulers of Madrid appeared to be ignorant.

In conclusion, it is no easy matter to pronounce on the strength or weakness of the nationalising process. The facts appear to support those who believe in its weakness: the process was tenuous and most of the responsibility fell to the State, which played an unsatisfactory and insufficient role. Nevertheless, tenuous, insufficient and weak are all relative terms. There is overwhelming evidence for Spain's weakness as long as one compares it with France, but it is far less damning if we consider other countries on the European periphery, such as Portugal. And there is no doubt at all of Spain's nationalizing progress if the comparison is made with earlier periods in Spanish history when a *national awareness* was completely non-existent. In other words, efforts were undeniably made during the nineteenth century to create and extend a new *national* image of the political collectivity which, up to that point, had been known to the world as an empire or as a monarchy that ruled over diverse territories. There were numerous obstacles to the process, but not everything was lacking. The shortcomings of the flag, the national anthem and the national monuments notwithstanding, there were a number of *places of memory* (to use Pierre Nora's famous term), which are sacred *loci* in which the culture of the *patria* is venerated. Since the time of Fernando VII, there has been a truly national art gallery, although not under that name, and during the reign of his daughter an opera house was built that was called 'royal', just like the eighteenth-century academies, but whose purpose, like the latter's, was *national*. Isabel II was still on the throne when the foundations were laid for a 'National Library' and a 'Spanish' theatre, and a series of painting exhibitions were held that were unquestionably national in both name and nature. Shortly afterwards, a *national* historical archive and a *national* archaeological museum were opened. It was all done in imitation of other countries, particularly France, but towards 1900 the idea of the nation had taken root and there was even a sense that it had always existed. In other words, the tradition had been 'invented'. An *official image* of Spain had been created: a Spain as it was seen by the leading figures of State and as they wanted it to be seen by others. And that image was now clearly distinguishable from that of the reigning monarch although his or her portrait continued to hang in public buildings, and in many ways the monarch continued to represent the country.

So, how weak was that process? To make an accurate assessment, we would need to know more about the overall number of monuments in the country, who planned them, who paid for them and how many of them could be considered national rather than local.[34] As well as monuments, we would have to look at other symbolic indicators such as stamps and coins. It appears that the effigy of the monarch and the traditional coat of arms gradually gave way to a female figure who represented the nation – a process that quickened between 1868 and 1870, when the country had no monarchy. Allegorical and cultural themes were also introduced into banknotes between 1875 and 1900. We would also have to consider the image of the country that was presented by its governments in the international exhibitions held between 1859 and 1900. As far as we know, there was a predominantly Moorish influence until 1878, whereas from the Paris exhibition of 1889 onwards there was a distinct shift towards the plateresque, which was then considered to be the *Spanish* style. But who was it that decided the national style and why did they do so?[35] There is also much work to be done on the evolution of people's names, a field recently explored by Carlos Serrano in which clear national meanings often reveal themselves. We have hardly begun to scratch the surface in these areas, all of which are of great interest for politico-cultural history.

When all these sources have been analysed, one would have to make a comparison not only with France, which has been the *exceptionally* successful *ideal* model of the Nation-State, but also with those countries who were in a similar situation to that of Spain. Only then would we be in a position to discuss whether Spain was an anomaly or was in fact *average*, given its circumstances. I would advance the hypothesis that, although Spain nationalised less than France and although there was none of the enormous enthusiasm of the Italian *risorgimento* for reformulating culture in national terms, greater efforts were made in Spain than in either Austria or Turkey, to name two political entities that disintegrated after the First World War. In effect, there is little proof other than the final outcome of the process: if the State survived, then nationalisation had achieved some success, but if it was fragmented, then the 'nation'-building process was weak. Unfortunately, this reasoning is circular: to discover whether the nation is strong, one looks to the State, but the strength of the State is also determined by the force of national sentiment. Somehow this causative circle must be broken. In the Spanish case, it is worth noting that the State survived in spite of the stresses and strains it endured throughout the twentieth century. This suggests that the nationalising process of the nineteenth century certainly made progress, but without the drive to ensure an entirely satisfactory outcome.

Notes

1 J. Linz, 'Early State-Building and late Peripheral Nationalisms against the State: The Case of Spain', in S. N. Eisenstadt and S. Rokkan (eds), *Building States and Nations*, Sage, 1973, Vol. 2, pp. 32–112; J. M. Jover, 'Preface' to *La era isabelina y el Sexenio Democrático (1834–1874)*, Vol. XXXIV of the *Historia de España Menéndez Pidal*, Madrid, 1981; B. de Riquer, 'Reflexions entorn de la dèbil nacionalització espanyola del segle XIX', *L'Avenç*, 170 (1993): 8.

2 B. de Riquer, 'Aproximación al nacionalismo español contemporáneo', *Studia Historica*, 12 (1994): 11–29.

3 De Riquer, 'Reflexions entorn de la dèbil nacionalització' p. 9; I. Olábarri Gortázar, 'Un conflicto entre nacionalismos. La "cuestión regional" en España, 1808–1939', in F. Fernández Rodríguez (ed.), *La España de las autonomías*, Madrid, 1985, p. 105.

4 See A. Gallego Anabitarte, 'España 1812: Cádiz, Estado unitario, en perspectiva histórica', *Ayer*, 1 (1991): 143.

5 See A. M. Calero, 'Liberalismo y división provincial', *Revista de Historia Contemporánea*, 3 (1984): 5–31; and A. Nieto, *Los primeros pasos del Estado constitucional*, Barcelona, 1996, pp. 238–294. On the *préféctures* created by Joseph Bonaparte, see G. Dufour, 'Le centralisme des *Afrancesados*', in C. Dumas (ed.), *Nationalisme et littérature en Espagne et Amérique Latine au XIXe siecle*, Lille, 1982, pp. 11–23.

6 J. M. Portillo Valdés, 'Nación política y territorio económico: El primer modelo provincial español (1812)', *Historia Contemporánea*, 12 (1995): 272; Muñoz Torrero's quote, pp. 267–268.

7 De Riquer, 'Aproximación al nacionalismo español', p. 17.

8 For a synthesis of this debate, and bibliographical references, see G. Martínez Dorado, 'La formación del Estado y la acción colectiva en España, 1808–1845', *Historia Social*, 15 (1993): 102–103.

9 X. M. Núñez-Seixas, 'Los oasis en el desierto: Perspectivas historiográficas sobre el nacionalismo español', *Bulletin d'Histoire Contemporaine de
   l'Espagne*, 26 (1997): 501; B. de Riquer, 'Sobre el lugar de los nacionalis-
   mos-regionalismos en la historia contemporánea española', and J. P. Fusi,
   'Revisionismo crítico e historia nacionalista (A propósito de un artículo de
   Borja de Riquer)', both in *Historia Social*, 7 (1990): 105–126 and 127–134;
   A. de Blas Guerrero, *Sobre el nacionalismo español*, Madrid, 1989, p. 16.
10 De Riquer, 'Reflexions entorn de la dèbil nacionalització', pp. 11–12; X.
   M. Núñez Seixas, 'Questione nazionale e crisi statale: Spagna, 1898–1936'
   Ricerche Storica, XXIV(1) (1994): 99.
11 Isolated villages, in D. R. Ringrose, *Imperio y península: Ensayos sobre historia económica de España (siglos XVI–XIX)*, Madrid, Siglo XXI, 1987; or J.
   P. Fusi, *España. Evolución de la identidad*, Madrid, 2000, p. 169. Resistance
   to centralisation, Olábarri Gortázar, 'Un conflicto entre nacionalismos',
   pp. 90–96; cf. A. Robles Egea (ed.), *Política en penumbra: Patronazgo y clientelismo políticos en la España contemporánea*, Madrid, 1996.
12 De Riquer, 'Aproximación', p. 17.
13 Olábarri Gortázar, 'Un conflicto entre nacionalismos', p. 95; De Riquer,
   'Reflexions entorn de la dèbil nacionalització', p. 11; Fusi, *España:
   Evolución de la identidad*, pp. 165 and 169; J. Ortega y Gasset, in his *La
   redención de las provincias*.
14 In his classical study, *From Peasants into Frenchmen: The Modernization of
   Rural France, 1870–1914*, Stanford, CA: Stanford University Press, 1976,
   E. Weber suggests that France was not culturally homogeneous until 1914.
   The Austro-Hungarian empire had the maximum diversity, but regional
   particularism was strong in Italy and there were serious tensions with
   Prussia's leadership in Germany. In Great Britain, Wales and Scotland
   lived like separate bodies, far away from the Nation-State ideal. On this
   topic, see Núñez Seixas, 'Questione nazionale e crisi statale', pp. 93–97.
15 See R. Cruz, '"El más frío de los monstruos fríos": La formación del Estado
   en la España contemporánea', *Política y Sociedad*, 18 (1995): 81–92.
16 On this law, previous projects and subsequent legal reforms, see M. Puelles
   Benítez, *Educación e ideología en la España contemporánea*, Barcelona, 1980.
17 G. Mosse, *The Nationalization of the Masses: Political Symbolism and Mass
   Movements in Germany from the Napoleonic Wars through the Third Reich*,
   Ithaca, NY: Cornell University Press, 1991.
18 F. Comín and C. García García, 'Reforma liberal, centralismo y haciendas
   municipales en el siglo XIX', *Hacienda Pública Española*, 133 (1995): 91–92.
   Figures, in Puelles Benítez, *Educación e ideología*; C. Boyd, *Historia Patria:
   Politics, History, and National Identity in Spain, 1875–1975*, Princeton, NJ:
   Princeton University Press, 1997, pp. 8–12, 22–24 and 45–46; and M.
   Vilanova and X. Moreno, *Atlas de la evolución del analfabetismo en España de
   1887 a 1891*, Madrid, 1992.
19 P. Tedde, 'Estadistas y burócratas: El gasto público en funcionarios durante
   la Restauración', *Revista de Occidente*, 83 (1988); De Riquer, 'Reflexions

entorn de la dèbil nacionalització', pp. 10–11; and M. Ballbé, *Orden público y militarismo en la España constitucional*, Madrid, Alianza, 1983. Expenses for secondary education were taken up by the central State in 1887. Oddly, university level was the only field where Spain had a percentage of students comparable with that of the main European countries (as C. E. Núñez explains in *La fuente de la riqueza: Educación y desarrollo económico en la España Contemporánea*, Madrid, 1992, Chapter 8).

20 C. Dardé, 'Cánovas y el nacionalismo liberal español', in G. Gortázar (ed.), *Nación y Estado en la España liberal*, Madrid, 1994, p. 231.

21 P. Vilar, 'Estado, nación patria, en España y Francia, 1870–1914', *Estudios de Historia Social*, 28/29 (1984): 7–41, at 17. Ley Moyano, in J. L. Abellán, *Historia crítica del pensamiento español*, Vol. V-1, Madrid, 1987, pp. 400–404; or M. Puelles Benítez, *Educación e ideología*, pp. 142–157; for leaning of conservative governments towards religious education see Boyd, *Historia Patria*, p. 29.

22 De Riquer, 'Reflexions entorn de la dèbil nacionalització', p. 13; Núñez, *La fuente de la riqueza*; E. Weber, *Peasants into Frenchmen*, pp. 303–338; and J. Linz, 'Politics in a Multi-Lingual Society with a Dominant World Language: The Case of Spain', in J. G. Savard and R. Vergneault (eds), *Les États multilingues: problèmes et solutions*, Quebec, 1975, pp. 367–444.

23 Vilar, 'Estado, nación, patria', pp. 26–30 (*Today, and always, / the poor, the mob, the rabble, / give their blood in the battlefields, / and the rich give their gold, / at six per cent*).

24 X. M. Núñez-Seixas, 'Historia e actualidade dos nacionalismos na España contemporánea: unha perspectiva de conxunto', *Grial*, 128 (1995): 503–504; C. Serrano, 'Prófugos y desertores en la guerra de Cuba', *Estudios de Historia Social*, 22–23 (1984): 21–35; N. Sales, *Sobre esclavos, reclutas y mercaderes de quintos*, Barcelona, 1974; cf. A. Feijóo Gómez, *Quintas y protesta social en el siglo XIX*, Madrid, 1996.

25 C. Serrano, *El nacimiento de Carmen: Símbolos mitos y nación*, Madrid, 1999, Chapters 4 (anthem) and 5 (patriotic *zarzuela*). On the origin of the anthem, F. Redondo Díaz, 'Leyenda y realidad de la Marcha Real española', *Revista de Historia Militar*, 54 (1983): 63–89. Royalties on the anthem, in *El País*, 21–XI-1993, and M. A. Aguilar, 'Saludos al himno', ibid., 11–X-1997. Symbols and monuments in general, Núñez Seixas, 'Los oasis en el desierto', pp. 505–507, with an excellent bibliography.

26 On bullfighting as national *fiesta*, see Serrano, *El nacimiento de Carmen*, Chapter 13. On the prohibition of the celebration of the Second of May in 1863, F. J. Orellana, *Historia del general Prim*, Barcelona, 1872, Vol. II, p. 473–474. Internationalist workers against this festivity in 1870, A. Lorenzo, *El proletariado militante*, Madrid, 1974, pp. 155ff.

27 J. Brown and J. H. Elliott, *A Palace for a King*, New Haven, CT: Yale University Press, 1980, pp. 31, 38–41 and 48. Cfr. V. Juaristi, *Las fuentes de España*, Madrid, 1944, Chapter IV.

28 See S. Juliá, D. Ringrose and C. Segura, *Madrid: Historia de una capital*, Madrid, Alianza, 1994.
29 29 G. Mosse, *Fallen Soldiers: Reshaping the Memory of the World Wars*, Oxford: Oxford University Press, 1990; J. Álvarez Junco, 'La nación en duda', in J. Pan Montojo (ed.), *Más se perdió en Cuba*, Madrid, 1998, p. 448; Serrano, *El nacimiento de Carmen*, Chapters 7–11.
30 Project on National Pantheon, see Archivo del Congreso de los Diputados, Serie Gral., leg. 108, exp. n° 447 (1858). Its style, M. Alpuente, 'Sic transit gloria mundi', *El País*, 15–VII-2000.
31 Monument to the 'Disaster', C. Serrano, *El nacimiento de Carmen*, Chapter 10; on local monuments, see list in C. Reyero, *La escultura conmemorativa en España: La edad de oro del monumento público, 1820–1914*, Madrid, 1999.
32 For the monument at the *Cerro de los Ángeles*, and other civic monuments that failed, see Serrano, *El nacimiento de Carmen*.
33 R. de Mesonero Romanos, *Nuevo manual de Madrid*, Madrid, Biblioteca de Autores Españoles (B.A.E.), Vol. CCI.
34 See Serrano, *El nacimiento de Carmen*, Chapters 7, 8 and 10; and Reyero, *La escultura conmemorativa*.
35 See J. Gallego, 'Artistas españoles en medio siglo de Exposiciones Universales', *Revista de Ideas Estéticas*, 86 (1964): 297–312; R. Gómez López-Egea, 'La arquitectura a través de las exposiciones Universales', *Estudios e Investigación*, 20 (1980): 61–69.

10

Heading towards 'disaster'

'What a country!': The 'Peral affair'

In 1811, at the height of the war against the French, an Asturian priest sent a letter with a somewhat unusual proposal to the constitutional *Cortes* assembled in Cádiz. He offered to walk from *pueblo* to *pueblo* the length and breadth of the country while bearing an image of Spain. The image would be of a venerable matron in mourning, on her knees and raising her hands to heaven in supplication. At the base of this image would be the inscription: *'La Madre Patria pide a sus amantes hijos la ayuden lo que puedan en el presente conflicto'*. The alms thereby collected would be sent to replenish the coffers of the armies fighting Napoleon. Some fifty years later, Bernardo López García, a little-known poet from Jaén, was to achieve everlasting fame thanks to a single poem which, for the next hundred years, was to be found in all the poetry anthologies and would be memorised and recited by successive generations of schoolchildren. It was entitled 'To the Second of May' and its opening lines were:

> Oigo, Patria, tu aflicción / y escucho el triste concierto
> que forman, tocando a muerto, / la campana y el cañón[1]

These are just two examples of the way that Spain was commonly depicted by those who considered it to be *their* nation. In the era of nationalism, when nations first came to be represented in graphic and literary form in Europe, when Britain invented proud *Britannia* and France the brave and virtuous *Marianne*, Spain was frequently thought of as a sorrowful mother dressed in mourning. Although López García also refers in the same poem to his *patria* in grandiose terms:

> y tú, soberbia matrona / que libre de extraño yugo
> no tuviste más verdugo / que el peso de tu corona

it is doubtful that he imagined a 'matron' in the style of the *Serenissima* of Venice, as painted by Titian with her opulent curves adorned with

350   *Successes and failures of Spanish nationalism*

jewels while she reclined languidly among silks and velvets. The Spain of the past had always been a dignified, austere and, above all, fearsome figure, and yet it was now seen by the poet – and many of his fellow citizens, to judge by the response – as a mother in distress, wandering among smoking ruins and funeral drapings, despairing at the death of her children and scorned by those whom she had once ruled. This was nothing new in Mediterranean culture: it was, in fact, a transposition of the traditional *Mater Dolorosa* of Catholic imagery. For anyone brought up within Mediterranean Catholicism, it was the easiest image of all to evoke: Mary weeping at the foot of the cross.

As well as drawing on Catholicism, such an image also had a characteristically Hispanic flavour. I have already described how, towards the end of the sixteenth century, when Felipe II was still king, the Spanish élites were dominated not only by a feeling of domestic decline but also by one of foreign incomprehension. Under Felipe III, when Spain was still the hegemonic power of Europe and its armies were fighting on several fronts, Quevedo depicted Spain as a humble, patient figure subjected to constant attack from its proud and insolent enemies. This generated xenophobia but also self-pity, something which can be detected among contemporary political writers who were obsesssed with the idea of decline.

Artists at that time did not yet represent 'Spain' but the monarchy. The monarch had never doubted the need to surround him or herself with the greatest possible number of symbols of power: on his or her head a crown, the expression of majesty; on the crown a cross, denoting the religious filiation and divine grace visited upon the throne; to one side a lion, terrible but peaceful, the representation of the force of nature; occasionally a set of scales in the hands of the monarch, the promise of justice and equity; and finally, allusions to the dominions of the reigning house together with classical references to the virtues of its members. These representations of royalty were very similar and almost interchangeable throughout Europe. An artist's workshop had no difficulty in adapting a picture to celebrate one particular dynasty, even though, years before, it had originally been painted in honour of another. Very little of all the paraphernalia with which artists surrounded the idealised monarchs of the *ancien régime* made reference to any specific qualities of either the kingdom or the dynasty, and none was significant in national terms. There are certain allusions which are specific to Spain as a consequence of its Atlantic empire, such as the two globes on which the throne is often placed, in representation of its dominion over both hemispheres. Very rarely, however, do we see Aztec or Mayan peoples or abundant tropical fruits, which would have been symbols more indicative of the Americas. There are constant references to religion, which the monarchy would always defend, and there is also a focus on military victories, which is not exclusive to the Hapsburgs and Bourbons but typical of royalty everywhere else at the time. Not even among the monarchies which acted as patrons of the sciences, leading to the creation of the Royal Society in Britain and the royal academies in France, were there any references to the new rationalist vision of the world – such as, for example, by including telescopes or compasses, or the triangles and plumb lines which became two symbols of the Freemasons. This was still a representation of the monarchy, not the nation.

The national entity began to take on a visible form at the time of the liberal revolutions. Spain, like France and Britain, came to be differentiated from the royal house, and almost immediately it became an instrument of political propaganda. There has, on occasion, been a *Juan Español*, or 'John Spaniard', dressed up as an Aragonese peasant, but Spain is habitually a female figure, though not a sensual Venus. Rather, she is an upright, warlike and just Minerva. In accordance with monarchical tradition, this figure of Spain-as-a-woman wore a crown topped with battlements in reference to Castile as the core of the national entity and believed to have originated in the monarchy of Asturias-León in the early wars against Islam. However, as political instability mounted, the image of Spain in the nineteenth century changed. The female figure came to be depicted in an increasingly precarious state. By mid-century, she was usually thin and her clothes threadbare because she was exhausted by the politicians and made desperate by the infighting among her children, as well as being hounded by pretenders to the throne (following the overthrow of Isabel II), decrepid, moribund, and sometimes even crucified. She was still accompanied by the lion, but it had become an emaciated or domesticated animal, often chained and even yoked to the carriage of some political charlatan.[2] In the final decades of the century, the Spanish no longer imagined their nation as a 'proud matron' or a fierce lion. The pride and the ferocity had been subdued by petty tyrants and she suffered on account of the sad fate of her offspring.

This painfully negative image does substantiate what has been said about the problems and obstacles afflicting Spanish nationalism during the nineteenth century. De Riquer and Ucelay have noted that 'the difficulties of consolidating a liberal national programme for Spain in the nineteenth century meant that, towards the 1890s, although both upper and lower classes tended to accept a *Patria* identified with the State, they were so critical of it that ironical complaints about its incompetence became a part of everyday speech (*'What a country!'*)'.[3] This is borne out by the cartoons of the satirical press: a plaintive patriotism, full of lament, based on the idea of the Mother *Patria* lying prostrate with a serious, even mortal illness, while she craves the love of her children and implores their aid. In contrast to the imperial epic of proud Victorian England, best expressed by Kipling, in contrast to the sentimental, high-flown, populist patriotism of Victor Hugo, and in contrast to the cultural pride and passionate intensity of the heroes of Verdi and Manzoni, literary works taught Spanish children to take pity on Spain. This was because Spain, the mother, sought the affection of her children in a manner peculiar to her: either from her bed, where she lay ailing and forgotten by her ungrateful offspring (who had been seduced by foreign fashions), or from the pillory, where she tamely endured the ridicule of insolent underlings like the *Perfidious Albion*, the conceited and superficial *Frog* or the overpowerful *Teuton*.

Nevertheless, this patriotism was scornful as well as tragic. In order to survive, the *españolito* – the little Spaniard – learned to mock his misfortunes and smile with resignation at them. What a country! What a shame! Whatever happened, how predictable it all was! And yet, how curious! And also, how very 'us'! The 'us', naturally, meant that the nationalising process had not been a complete failure as the national entity had at least produced a sense of identification, even if this was bereft of pride.

It should not be overlooked that the villains who martyred Mother Spain were almost always *politicians*. Nineteenth-century satirical imagery depicts them either as leeches who suck the lifeblood from the nation or as the most mischievous and wretched of sons who drive their mother to distraction with their strife. Pérez Galdós was convinced of this and, in the introduction to the *Episodio Nacional* entitled *Gerona*, he wrote that the 'shameful behaviour of the parties' and 'the discord at the top had not spread to the common people of the country, who retained a certain savage innocence . . . for which reason the uniformity of feeling on which nationality was founded was still powerful.'[4] The belief that political parties divided the nation appears almost constantly as a feature of Spanish political culture in the nineteenth and twentieth centuries. Yet this amounts to a basic misunderstanding of the function exercised by the political sphere in a representative system, which consists of keeping public debates and conflicts of interest from spiralling out of control and making coexistence impossible. It suggests that, in Spain, parliamentary politics were ushered in prematurely, necessitated by the French invasion and the absence of the king and that, although the Constitution was initially welcomed as a substitute for the paternalist monarch and as a panacea for all the evils afflicting the *Patria*, it was deemed a failure as soon as the representatives of the people were divided up into parties and began to fight among themselves. Politicians soon came to be seen as the *cause* of the divisions and therefore responsible for the evils engulfing the country.

Withstanding this perverse world of politics and the wicked *Father-State*, were the wholesome, all-powerful *People*, the redeemer of moribund *Mother* Spain. It was Pérez Galdós who best expressed this belief in his great saga of the *Episodios Nacionales*, in which the leading role is played by the Spanish *People*. The central theme of this series of no fewer than forty-six novels is Spanish society in the nineteenth century. Several of the main characters are clearly representative of the *People (*or the national *race*, the term in vogue at the time). Santiago *Ibero* (from Iberia), for example, is a valiant army officer who is both a Christian and a liberal and, though quarrelsome, he is an honest adversary insofar as he detests conspiracies and secret societies. Jerónimo Ansúrez is a 'Celtiberian', gypsy-like vagabond, who has preserved 'the pristine vigour of his race' and who originates from that 'indomitable race that will not tolerate the yoke of tyrants'. Pérez Galdós firmly believed in the essence of a people, an overarching, ahistorical, constant identity, a 'form of being' compressed in time and space, without substantial differences between 'regions', although these did manifest nuances of character. Mythification is evident in his search for this race and a description of its avatars. Paloma Aguilar observes that the *Episodios Nacionales* are anti-epical, which is typical of the pessimistic nationalism of the time.[5] Galdós never ceased to declaim that what he wanted to write was the story of the everyday life of the people, not a story of military heroics or political intrigues. Wars form the backdrop to the *Episodios*, and it is clear that the novelist takes an interest in military strategy and techniques, but he is not writing a nationalist epic with a military bias. His hero is the nation. As the saga unfolds, the author also reveals that he is telling a tale of disaster, one that is *contrary to reason*. The History of Spain is a 'History of the Absurd', 'which, by God!, is already lasting longer than it should.' One of his characters, Santiuste, re-baptised as *Confusio*, ends up writing the history of Spain not as it happened but *as it should have happened*.

Gilberto Triviños remarks that Galdós always chose a narrative schema that ended in disappointment as each series begins with enthusiasm and finishes with a 'gilded mediocrity' that inevitably includes a loss of enthusiasm for public affairs. The first series starts with the thrilling discovery of patriotic feeling by Gabriel Araceli at Trafalgar, but, by the end of the ten novels, he has learnt to detest war, having also encountered the 'carnage' concomitant with military exploits. The same thing happens to Salvador Monsalud in the second series, to Fernando Calpena and Santiago Ibero in the third, and to Santiuste *Confusio* in the fourth. In the fifth, all the political unrest, all the passion and all the drama of the nineteenth century run aground on the 'foolish peace' of the Restoration, and *Tito* Liviano takes over as the roguish, sceptical chronicler of events, being more interested in his love life than in the destiny of the nation. Cánovas, both strongman and mastermind of the new political system, artfully expressed the general attitude towards Spain in a well-known phrase that Galdós reproduces in his final *Episodio*. In contemplating the conditions necessary for Spanish nationality, while the Constitution of 1876 was still under debate, the great statesman from Málaga mused that 'they are Spanish . . . all those who can be nothing else'.[6]

In short, the most extensive literary work ever about the national entity presents the Spanish people as noble, unselfish, heroic and unfortunate, but by no means 'glorious' in traditional terms. It is undoubtedly the Good People who are the epic hero, in contrast to the bad politicians and the Evil Father-State, a maleficent monster that has Mother Spain held fast between its talons. Due, however, to the politicans' lack of organisation and uncontrolled passion, they stagger from one disaster to the next. They wish for the redemption of the *Patria* – one could even say the *Matria* – but constantly fail.

This aspect of the myth is perhaps illustrated even more effffectively by a real, historical person by the name of Isaac Peral than by literary figures. None the less, Peral underwent such a transformation in the public eye that he could also be considered a created figure, though one with no known author, thereby increasing his significance. Peral is said to have invented the submarine. He was acclaimed by the contemporary press and by subsequent biographers as the supreme incarnation of the 'martyr' of historico-national mythology: the hero who suffers, sacrifices himself and dies for the *patria*. I shall first look at the story through the eyes of the general public.In 1885, at the peak of the 'patriotic fervour' that resulted from the 'perfidious German occupation' of the Caroline Islands, as one of Peral's biographers writes, came the news that a Spanish naval officer had solved the problem of sailing underwater. Ever since the creation of steel hulls it was known that it would become possible to build submarines, and naval engineers of all sorts had set to work to make them a reality. The advances were progressive but partial. Encyclopaedias do not attribute the finished product to any single inventor. In Spain, however, it was said that 'a Spaniard had invented the submarine'. The Naval Ministry approved the blueprints drawn up by Peral and allocated him the funds necessary to build a prototype. Legend takes over when a number of faults are detected during the first trials. Public opinion, and later biographers of our hero, put these down to 'sabotage'. It was claimed by one biographer that an anti-Peral faction was paid for by 'some foreign power'. It was all very vague but the 'sabotage' had two sources: foreign enmity and homegrown envy (the greatest 'defect' of the 'national character'). Supposedly, Peral refused the offers of 'foreign governments' because he was too much of a patriot.   In September 1888 the submarine was launched. Trials continued throughout 1889 and 1890, apparently with some success: on one occasion the machine remained submerged for seven minutes, on another occasion it reached a depth of six or even ten metres.

The inventor's popularity began to rise. The most popular writers of the time, including Echegaray, Pérez Galdós and Dicenta, began to write about him. The international press – according to legend – followed events closely. Cartagena and other cities agreed to change the name of their main streets to 'Isaac Peral'. However, further problems then ensued. The government's reports became less enthusiastic. One suspects that, though Peral's vessel was capable of short immersions, he had not produced a vessel capable of fighting on the high seas. However, public opinion was convinced that the project's shortcomings were the result of manipulation, rivalry and bureaucratic negligence. The months went by and work came to a halt. A report of December 1890 finally withdrew official support from the venture. Within two or three years, Isaac Peral had been forgotten, a clear demonstration of the 'people's ingratitude'. He was dogged by an ongoing illness. Eventually, he was operated upon in Berlin. The operation was a success but led to an infection, which developed into meningitis. He finally died on 22 May 1895. It is claimed that the entire diplomatic corps of Berlin filed past his embalmed body, this being proof of the universal recognition of his merit. By contrast, when the body arrived in Spain, few were there to receive him, a further display of the country's ingratitude. He was not even buried in the Pantheon of Illustrious Seamen. Finally, in 1927, a mausoleum was built by the dictator Primo de Rivera, and in 1965, the remains of his vessel, which years earlier a liberal Minister of the Navy had tried to sell off as 'scrap iron', were transported to Cartagena by Franco, yet another dictator.[7]

The Peral affair, which received huge press coverage at the time, is highly symbolic. Fusi calls it 'the catalyst of popular patriotism', and indeed it was. Still, the Peral affair also revealed how the Spanish people saw themselves. Over and above his inventive ability, Peral represented goodness, patriotism, chivalry and sacrifice. What more did the Spanish people need in order to triumph over their enemies? And if victory escaped them through no fault of their own – like the storms that dispersed the 'Invincible' Spanish Armada – what more did they need to have a high opinion of themselves? If things went wrong, it was somebody else's fault, usually a politician's. Politicians were the ones who haggled over Peral's invention, who denied him funds, and who tried to sell the submarine for scrap. There were also his detractors in the Navy, the general public who abandoned him, and the journalists who forgot about him. It appeared that there was something phagocytic about the national body that led it to devour its most illustrious sons. The abandonment of the Peral project affected the way in which the 'Disaster' of 1898 was perceived. If such a 'significant invention' had had the backing it deserved, the country might have had a flotilla of submarines that would have avoided the catastrophes of Cavite and Santiago.

One of Peral's biographers, Fernández Rúa, took advantage of the affair to vindicate a long list of great Spanish inventors who had never been recognised, not even by their compatriots. In the sixteenth century, for example, Blasco de Garay allegedly made 'the first attempts to sail under steam', in the eighteenth century Salvá y Campillo invented wireless telegraphy, and in the nineteenth century Francisco de Paula Martí produced the fountain pen thirty years before Parker but 'did not know how to industrialise its manufacture'. Moreover, the invention of experimental toxicology, the laryngoscope, the photographic plate, Torres Quevedo's dirigible and La Cierva's autogyro were all pressed into service to refute the opinion that Spaniards 'lack creative power in technical and scientific fields'. Finally, the biographer used the Peral affair to refute the accusation made by Masson de Morviliers, one hundred years after the event. The pattern is clear: failures were due to the indifference of leaders, the pettiness of political rivalries and a racial incapacity to benefit from, and commercialise, talent.

By taking pity on Peral and so much wasted genius, Spain was taking pity on itself. By blaming politicians and the State, Spaniards exonerated themselves from their inconsequential international role. They blamed the State for the straightforward reason that the nation was not yet fully identified with it. These simplistic takes on reality are revealing but they do not constitute great tragedy. This is not tragedy in the Polish or Russian style, and, although the satirical press did sometimes present Spain as Christ on the cross, nineteenth-century Spain was not overwhelmed in the same way as Quevedo, who seriously believed that his *patria* was a martyr among nations. The dominant perception in the nineteenth century was a sceptical, uncommitted humour reminiscent of picaresque realism. It is the age of Galdós: there are no splendid epics or exalted nationalism, rather the anti-epic, characterised by disillusionment, mockery and despair.[8] Literature and satirical engravings alike adapted themselves to Spain's international situation.

Myths are a construct that have to be good enough to satisfy an undemanding public. A nationalistic public is not demanding: it *wishes* to believe in its myths and distrusts anyone who subjects them to critical scrutiny. In the Spanish case, the public wanted to believe in a discourse that praised an ancient identity that was obstinately defended against successive waves of invaders and recently reinforced by the 'War of Independence'. Those who felt part of that identity felt that it compensated them for the hardships they suffered, even though these were greater than those endured by the peoples of the principal European powers. However, Spain was not trying to compete with them. This was the celebrated 'withdrawal' to which Cánovas referred, a euphemism for marginalisation or passivity, although resignation or *hibernation* might have been more apt. Following the revolutionary vicissitudes of the first seventy-five years of the nineteenth century, any ambition to make the State the driving force for the social and economic modernisation of the country had withered away. Moreover, Spain's rulers dared not attempt to extend its borders, either by means of an *Iberian Union* or a new overseas empire. Consequently citizens were fed memories of past glories, invariably based on the resistance to foreign invasion, the affirmation of their own identity and *independence*. This amounted to the self-satisfied 'retrospective nationalism' described by José María Jover, which was an easy option in political terms insofar as the nation's independence had already been won.

Those children fortunate enough to attend school were taught a set of conformist ideas about how proud they should feel to be Spanish. They learnt that they belonged to a people who had chosen and achieved freedom, having overcome innumerable obstacles; that these people had once been the supreme world power; that they had disinterestedly pursued the defence of the Catholic religion rather than succumbing to petty ambitions characteristic of earthly power; that the nation's decline had been caused by the wickedness of their enemies combined with a certain naivety of their own, not to mention a fatal propensity for disunity and the imitation of foreign models. Last, but not least, not even Napoleon's army, the most powerful in history, had been able to subjugate such an obstinate, rebellious people. All this empty posturing was taught daily in the schoolroom and routinely repeated on important occasions. In reality, however, it was understood that life had little to do with the heroic virtues of the national past and everything to do with cunning and, above all, choosing one's *political friends* carefully, although everyone, even the *caciques*, complained about the misfortunes of the *patria*, which were always attributed to some unspecified culprit. If there were no foreigners present to humiliate *us*, jokes would even be made at the expense of the nation. The grand rhetoric of nationalism was fundamentally empty. In the words of Machado, the years went by 'With that monotony / that measures empty time'.

1898: 'Disaster' and 'Regeneration'

Up until 1898, it could be said that nation-building in Spain had been achieved with some degree of success. Though feeling somewhat infe-rior to its more wealthy neighbours and with visible colonial scars, the nation had so far survived without amputations to its Peninsular body and had even held on to a part of its possessions in the Americas and Australasia, not to mention the promise of a future in Africa.

However, reality is never far away. A State cannot survive by resting on its laurels. National projects cannot merely look to the past, but have to look forward to future goals. Even the past must be adapted or rein-vented in order to meet the needs of the moment. Without a forward-looking programme – at that time, Spanish nationalism had none – the field is left open for rivals to demonstrate that the 'nation' sleeps.

In the Spanish case, this rude awakening came in 1898. The United States of America, though a young country *with no history* – as claimed by the Spanish press, scandalised that a brash newcomer should have the temerity to make its mark in the world – was already the world's leading industrial power and there was pressure from within industrial and political circles to expand its political influence in the Caribbean and the Pacific. In both areas, particularly the nearby Caribbean, the old Spanish monarchy offered a perfect target for such ambition. Spain's colonial territories were a long way from the metropolis, poorly defended and diplomatically isolated in a world full of alliances. Last, but not least, Spain still endured a bad press in the Anglo-Saxon world as the 'scourge of heretics'. This made it easy for the sensationalist press in America to persuade the general public of its calumnies in relation to the descendants of the Spanish Inquisition. President McKinley, under pressure from Congress, the lobbies and the press, agreed to support the Cuban rebels. The Spanish government under Sagasta had no alternative but to declare war, knowing full well that it would lose. In two naval battles lasting only a few hours, the Spanish fleets of the Caribbean and the Philippines were annihilated and the government had to surrender all that remained of the empire.[9]

The immediate political and economic consequences of the loss of empire were not catastrophic. Economically, imperial fortunes were reinvested at home and more than compensated for the loss of the colonial markets, while the national debt which had accumulated during the war was quickly paid off thanks to the tax reforms that Chancellor of the Exchequer Fernández Villaverde had been able to impose in the aftermath of the shock. Politically, the paralysis and infighting within the Carlist and Republican oppositions, together with the relative flexibility of the system under Cánovas, meant that there were no revolutionary scares. There was, however, a very serious crisis of conscience. Within the international arena, Spain's standing reached a historical low. A few days after the destruction of the first fleet, in May 1898, the British prime minister Lord Salisbury made a famous speech to parliament in which he said that there were 'great nations, whose enormous power grows year by year, which increase their wealth, extend their territories, perfect their organisation', but that there were also 'societies which we could call dying nations [where] bad government shows no signs of improving but worsens with each day that passes'. 'That cannot last', he concluded: the 'living nations' have to take over the territories of the 'dying nations'. He did not mention Spain by name but nobody doubted that, together with the Ottoman empire, it was the most obvious example of a *dying nation*.

More important than the international repercussions were the domestic ones. The educated middle classes with a nationalist awareness may not have known about the speech by the British premier but the perception was the same: the Cuban War had demonstrated the *disastrous* situation of the country. There had been a complete lack of international support; shortfalls in equipment and the appalling conditions endured by the national service recruits demonstrated the deficiencies of the State; the puffed-up rhetoric prior to the conflict was an indication of how manipulative the government was; and the fact that the mass of the populace had demonstrated complete indifference to the conflict could only be seen as symptomatic of an imminent death. Yet the intellectuals, journalists and other creators of national opinion, who had stoked the jingoistic fires in the months before the conflict to the extent that the government had been left with no option but to declare war, now exempted themselves from all blame. As for popular indifference, it showed that the masses had *not* been indoctrinated to the same extent as the middle classes. The people were lacking in schools, national fiestas, rites, symbols and monuments while suffering a surfeit of *caciques*, inequitable national service, and administrative inefficiency and arbitrariness on a daily basis. The upshot was a generalised patriotic scepticism.

Still, the nationalising élites, prey to the racial attitudes of their age, believed that the masses had been struck by a deep-seated affliction. The acidic humour, the self-pity and the lack of patriotic pride of the popular classes had begun to worry those who had taken the problem seriously for some time. As early as 1860, Fernando Garrido had written a book entitled *La regeneración de España*; and Lucas Mallada had published his famous *Los males de la Patria* ('The Ills of the *Patria*', an expression that became proverbial) in 1890, eight years before the 'Disaster'. The era that was known as 'the 98' had been a long time coming. When it arrived, it triggered *El problema nacional* by Macías Picavea, *Las desdichas de la Patria* by Vidal Fité, *Del desastre nacional y sus causas* by Damián Isern, and *Los desastres y la regeneración de España* by Rodríguez Martínez. And that was just the beginning. Over the next fifty years, a whole literary genre was to develop in relation to the *problem of Spain*. There is no doubt that the educated middle classes were very concerned by the situation but their way of expressing nationalist sentiment was typical: they succumbed to the belief that the Mother *Patria* was at death's door and her children must come to her aid.

Intellectuals of the *Generation of '98* and the 'regenerationists' were drawn from right across the political spectrum. Although the phrase 'regeneration of the *Patria*' was endorsed by everyone, it embraced a wide variety of programmes which coincided only in the need for radical reform. The new climate ushered in a period of more active and effective nationalism that found past glory and imperial aspirations (with the exception of Morocco) to be suspect, and which concentrated on modernisation at home. The upheaval made possible the tax reforms that eliminated not only the war debts but also the national debt that had encumbered the State for over a century. And, from that time on, diverse regimes with very diverse programmes undertook the building of schools, dams and roads.

Spain continued to remain aloof from international politics and this was all to the good. In their zeal to avoid exposing the State to international conflict, its leaders chose to stand aside from the Great War of 1914–1918. What would have happened if Spain had taken sides? If it had lost, an implosion would have taken place of the magnitude that destroyed the Austro-Hungarian and Ottoman empires. If it had won, a decisive reinforcement of the national identity would have occurred, as in France and Britain. Many intellectuals declared themselves in favour of siding with the Allies precisely because they considered popular patriotism to be a priority and hoped for a victory that would strengthen it. The government decided otherwise, and under the umbrella of neutrality the country enjoyed unprecedented prosperity. Before the war, during the relative stability of the Maurist era, progress had been made in the electrification of industry and the rebuilding of the fleet. After the war came the boom of the 1920s, when the dictator General Miguel Primo de Rivera injected large sums of public money into the economy. By then it was clear that change was in the air: the economy was growing, the cities doubled their population in thirty years, the rural population and illiteracy both fell by 20 per cent in the same period and, with the incorporation of women into the labour market and public life, customs were changing rapidly. In short, the political crisis of the 1930s was not produced by secular oppression and poverty but just the opposite: it was the result of growth and change, and the imbalance between a modern, urban, lay society and rural Spain where traditional Catholicism and the rule of the *caciques* still held sway. By 1935, the country was at a point in its development that would not be reached again until twenty years later. Without the political disruption of the Civil War of 1936–1939, it is not unreasonable to think that the great leap forward in modernisation would have started twenty years earlier.

An essential part of the post-1898 programme was a determination to achieve the long-deferred *nationalisation of the masses*. One of the features of the war that had most astonished commentators had been popular indifference to the news of the naval disasters. They agreed that the people felt very little patriotism and that the most obvious means of augmenting it was an intensive policy of education. As Vicente Gay wrote shortly afterwards, it was necessary to 'create the nation, to educate *Spaniards*'.[10] One of the most visible results of this regenerationist momentum was the Ministry of Public Education, set up in 1900, which in turn appointed a Junta for the Promotion of Studies, whose declared – and largely successful – aim was to train academics so that Spain could share in the advances of European science. Another of the Junta's achievements, the Centre for Historic Studies, appeared to have an equally scientific goal in the fields of humanities and the social sciences, but as its brief was to distil the historical essence of the nation, it was far more ideologically motivated. Ramón Menéndez Pidal was chosen to be its director: he was an impeccable representative of the 'ideal' Spain, a member of the prestigious Pidal family, whose conservative politicians and thinkers had managed to combine Catholicism with nationalism. He had acquired his erudition from his mentor, the great Menéndez Pelayo (though they were unrelated). To his connections with conservative Spain was added the liberal, secular tradition of the *Institución Libre de Enseñanza*, with which he had been in close contact since the turn of the century. Don Ramón, to all appearances a believer in scientific positivism, devoted himself to seeking the key to the Spanish 'racial character' in history and, naturally, he found it: in the Castilian language and 'spirit'.[11]

The State became active in promoting nationalisation in many other ways. In 1908, it sponsored the centenary celebration of what everyone now called the 'War of Independence'. It was no longer an event restricted to Madrid and neither was it merely official: local notables and institutions now competed to make the celebrations a memorable event. The same year, it was decreed that the national flag should be flown on all public buildings, while the following decade saw the introduction of the *Fiesta de la Raza*. It was then that Eduardo Marquina wrote the words for the national anthem that began: 'Ask, Spain! Your children will give to you.' While the State was responsible for much of the nationalising effort, the intellectuals were not to be left out, however critical they might have been. In 1905, all of them, old and young, radical and conservative, came together in homage to Cervantes, on the three-hundredth anniversary of the publication of *El Quijote*. Cervantes was the perfect political symbol because his work was open to multiple interpretations: from a National Catholic one by Alejandro Pidal to a Nietzschean one by Navarro Tómas, not forgetting a rationalist one by the scientist Ramón y Cajal, an anti-bourgeois one by the journalist *Azorín* and a merely 'entertaining' one by Valera.[12] In 1909, they made another show of their enthusiasm for *national* literary heroes with a homage to Larra and, in 1913, they could be seen in support of Ortega y Gasset in the *Liga para la Educación Política* (the League for Political Education) whose declared 'generational mission' was to educate the public in national values.

In short, it was an era of intense, even compulsive, nationalisation, which aimed to recover the ground lost during the nineteenth century. Nation-building was an essential part of the regenerationist programme, since the national ideal legitimised the fight against 'local egotisms' and particularly *caciquismo*, which was unanimously accused of being at the root of all the country's ills. It was recognised that there was '[a] need to end the divorce between the official world and social reality'[13] or, in other words, to transform the politico-administrative structure into a true vehicle for the expression of social demands. This was too contentious, as the Second Republic of the 1930s was to show, and, for the time being, the path chosen was that of least resistance: the encouragement of simple, optimistic jingoism, which ignored the criticisms and concerns of the '98 intellectuals. It was symbolised by the patriotic songs about the new war in Melilla at the start of the 1920s, such as 'Little Spanish soldier boy, brave little soldier boy' and 'Little

flag, you are red, little flag, you are yellow'. This patriotism, full of sentimental diminutives, became quite popular, but the bad news from the
front meant that the pitiful tone never entirely disappeared. While girls
played with their skipping ropes, they sang:

> I shan't wash or brush my hair / I shan't wear my *mantilla*
> till my fiancé comes back / from the war in Melilla.
> I shan't wash or brush my hair / I shan't wear my ribbon blue
> till my fiancé returns / from the mountain of Gurugú.

The mountain of Gurugú was, in fact, the very place from which they
would not return.

When General Primo de Rivera seized power in 1923, and two years
later brought the war in Morocco to its victorious conclusion, this
kind of acritical *casticismo* reached its peak. Under Primo de Rivera,
the *patria* – not the king – became the symbol of unity as opposed
to *politicians* (including the *caciques*). The dictator exploited the idea
of the *patria* as a unifying force in contrast to the divisiveness of
politics. It is no coincidence that his single party was called the *Unión
Patriótica*: 'Union', in contrast to the 'fragmentation' of liberal politics,
and 'Patriotic' because the concept of the *Patria* united Spaniards in
contrast to the private interests and political ideologies that divided
them. Under the command of the General, a man of uncomplicated
ideas, literacy was promoted, there was much talk of hygiene and racial
improvement, the cataloguing of national monuments was announced,
and banknotes and postal stamps were printed with illustrations of the
historical paintings of 1856–1892. Similar motifs proved popular on
calendars, sweet wrappers and packets of cigarette papers. These were
the years of the crossing of the Atlantic by the four-man crew of the
'Plus Ultra' plane, the Ibero-American Exhibition in Seville (for which
a model of Columbus's caravel the *Santa María* was built) the building
of the mausoleum for Peral and the repatriation of the body of Angel
Ganivet. *Plazas de España* were built in Madrid, Seville and Barcelona,
and the latter seized the opportunity provided by the International
Exhibition to recreate an archetypal *Spanish pueblo*. However much the
intellectuals loathed the dictator – and they did, particularly towards the
end of his mandate – they joined in the nation-building effort. Breaking
with a centuries-old tradition, they expressed their liking for flamenco
and bull-fighting: an *andalucista* like García Lorca was not the only one
to weep at the death of the bullfighter Sánchez Mejías, while a serious
philosopher like José Ortega y Gasset admitted to his friendship with
the bullfighter Domingo Ortega. This acceptance of the romantic, ori-
entalist stereotype of Spain by its élites ran parallel with a neo-Romantic

revival from abroad with the arrival of Ernest Hemingway, Waldo Frank, Havelock Ellis, Gerald Brenan and Robert Graves. The Americans had forgotten the insults of 1898 and decided that in Spain they had found, to quote Hemingway, 'the only good people left in Europe'. A 'virgin' country, claimed Waldo Frank, that was 'faithful to itself'[14] and which stood in contrast to the brutality of the Great War and a declining and corrupt civilisation.

'Faithful to itself', meaning that it had been unchanged for centuries, was just what Spain was not. It was changing at considerable speed and beginning to catch up with the more advanced parts of Europe, largely as a result of its reaction to its humiliating performance in 1898. Spanish nationalism had finally found a substitute for the liberal revolution proposed a hundred years earlier and eventually abandoned: the *regeneration*, the *Europeanisation* and, ultimately, the *modernisation* of the country. The only problem with this mission was that it had been discovered too late. The younger generations, with a more intense and radical political awareness, began to distance themselves from the project and to embark upon others which were incompatible with *españolismo*, such as the international labour movement and rival national identities.[15] It would be easy to assume that the most urgent and threatening of these two alternatives, and the one that would most galvanise public opinion over the following decades, would be the danger of a social revolution. It was certainly a problem and the Spanish labour movement held onto its internationalist beliefs far longer than other movements in Europe. With hindsight, however, it is clear that the most serious threat to *españolismo* came from the peripheral nationalisms, and primarily *catalanismo*, which had been created by the city that had always rivalled Madrid: Barcelona.

The emergence of identities to rival the Spanish one

The origins of the peripheral nationalisms date back to the Romantic era, which rediscovered the cultural differences that existed in the Peninsula just as it had done in so many other parts of Europe. According to Borja de Riquer, it was the educated minorities who conducted the 'search for elements of ethnicity and identity . . . in their region'.[16] This was yet another *invention of tradition*, similar to that of the State nationalisms, provided that the term 'invention' is not taken too literally (as if the non-Castilian languages and cultures had not existed previously in the Peninsula). Minority cultural groups with creative potential, but not officially recognised by the State, could find no means of survival other than by counterattacking the State *risorgimenti* with their own *renaixenças* or *rexurdimentos*, which became the foundation for later demands for an autonomous political space. Thus, while Modesto Lafuente and José Zorrilla dubbed as 'Spanish' the situations and characters from times past when no nation existed, intellectuals in Barcelona applied themselves to the creation of literary and historical myths that would convince the inhabitants of Lerida or Tortosa, for example, that they were *Catalans*, and that the correct way of speaking *their* language was the way ordained by Barcelona, an urban centre that championed a political project to challenge that of Madrid.

These cultural movements, which at the outset had no political ambitions, eventually made way for the nationalist movements. In spite of this, there was no direct causal relationship between Romanticism and political nationalism: the same literary phenomenon took place in the Languedoc and in Wales, for example, and it did not automatically generate demands for political autonomy. In the Spanish case, the example of Galicia is the most telling. If the origins of dissension had been a purely ethnocultural phenomenon set in motion by the literary minorities of each region, Galician nationalism would have been an equally or even more powerful force than Catalan or Basque nationalism. Galicia was a territory with clear boundaries, a language, and specific social problems (concerning the *foros*) which could have been presented as the product of colonial oppression. There was also a Galician literary *Rexurdimiento* comparable to the Catalan *Renaixença*, but *galleguismo* remained a minority phenomenon for a very long time. Other elements must be added to the combination of ethnocultural factors and literary Romanticism.[17]

Among these elements are a number of socio-economic factors, but these do *not* include the delay or 'failure' of industrialisation or of the 'bourgeois revolution', as has so often been claimed. Neither did Spain lack a 'process of social and economic modernisation' – another way of saying the same thing – that went hand in hand with the political process. If that had been the case, it would have been impossible to associate nationalisation or *españolismo* with modernisation. Neither do I think that De Riquer is right to blame a bad communications network – in comparison with the French, British or Germans ones – for preventing the development of a *national* market.[18] If these factors had been in any way decisive, powerful State nationalisms would have been the preserve of advanced countries. There was backwardness, bad communications – even worse than in Spain – and a failure of the industrialising process in Portugal and Greece, for example, without them generating a conflictive national identity or secessionist problems. Quite the opposite: an exaggerated nationalist rhetoric served to compensate for the frustrations deriving from a lesser degree of economic development.

The specifically Spanish problem was not so much that the country was backward but that its development was uneven, which naturally led to a similarly uneven process of cultural modernisation. Nicolás Sánchez Albornoz described the situation of Spain in the nineteenth century as 'a dual economy', in which areas at the forefront of industrial development, mainly in the province of Barcelona and the *ría* or tidal river of Bilbao, existed side by side with agricultural areas of extensive cultivation, mostly inland. The methods used to farm the land were outdated and produced very low yields, so that agriculture could only survive by means of highly protectionist tariffs. The early differences in economic development became increasingly marked, dramatically so in the last quarter of the century.

The two major industrial zones developed around the cities of Barcelona and Bilbao, the only ones that could begin to compete with the political capital, Madrid. Barcelona, especially, was not only as rich but also as well populated as Madrid and, by the end of the century, it was well connected with Paris, the cultural capital of Europe. The city of Bilbao was itself the result of developments in mining and metal-lurgy. The region was less well populated and less well communicated with than the area around Barcelona, but the concentration of wealth was no less spectacular and connections with London, the world finan-cial centre, were relatively easy, although its financial networks were also well integrated with those of Madrid. What made Basque national-ism less threatening than *catalanismo* for many decades was the rural and Carlist bias of its ideologies, which caused leading Basque intel-lectuals to distance themselves from nationalism and move to Castile. In the case of Galicia, not only did it lack the industrial development that would have given weight to regionalist demands but there was also no single pre-eminent city where leading intellectuals could meet and orchestrate a confrontation with Madrid. Moreover, dissatisfied élites had their own means of escape: emigration. It could be said that Galician nationalism first saw the light of day in Madrid and Buenos Aires.

Núñez-Seixas describes this situation in terms of 'territorial tensions' generated by the 'lack of correlation between the geographical sources of economic power and of political power.'[19] In other words, the crux of the matter was not low or limited industrial development per se but the fact that it was restricted to small enclaves, none of which coincided with the centre of political decision-making. Madrid was not a great industrial centre and neither did it have the European connections that could have transformed it into a focal point of cultural life. The same applies to the geographical areas from which its political leaders were recruited, mainly Andalusia and Castile.[20] Neither the State capital nor the politicians' home areas were the most economically or culturally advanced parts of the country.

As shown in the previous chapter, the nationalising efforts of the State were limited or insufficient. Sociologists such as Linz and historians such as Jover, De Riquer, Núñez-Seixas and Fusi have all pointed out the relative vacuum created by the lack of cultural vitality on the part of the Spanish State in the nineteenth century. A simple comparison between the implantation of a French identity in the Basque and Catalan areas to the north of the border and the weakness of *españolismo* in those to the south is sufficient evidence of this.[21] Nevertheless, we have seen that the State *did* make an effort and *did* manage to create and implant its symbols. A number of State institutions were established and housed in splendid buildings that were the reflection of a very visible political and administrative apparatus. These include the royal palace, the parliament buildings of the *Cortes* and the *Senado*, and the offices of the *Presidencia del Gobierno* and the various ministries. The problem remained that all of these edifices were in Madrid, as were most of the few existing national monuments. The writers and artists responsible for the 'invention of tradition' in the form of novels, history books, paintings, plays and zarzuelas during this period also resided there. The question, therefore, is not whether national cultural constructs existed during the nineteenth century but how far their influence extended. They were almost certainly overly restricted to the capital, which was sufficient to satisfy the central political élites and also to rule the least developed, most central areas of the country, which remained within the sphere of influence of Madrid. It was clearly insufficient to attract the more developed areas, especially the two major cities, which were not going to be so easily seduced by a capital of little significance in comparison with the European centres with which they associated.

It must be recognised that Madrid, the capital of a centralised bureaucracy on which, in theory, everything depended, *was* of little significance. Fusi reminds us that, at the beginning of the nineteenth century, 'for someone like Alcalá Galiano, who came from a flourishing and elegant city like Cádiz', Madrid was 'a poor, ugly and dirty city, far removed from being a true Court'.[22] Some thirty years later, Balmes, a Catalan of measured and conservative character, lived for a time in Madrid and felt compelled to write: 'With no sea, no river, in the heart of a desert, with no industry, no life of its own, Madrid is nothing by itself, but because it is the court, it is a colony of civil servants rather

than a city of importance.' At around 1850, Madrid had a population of 250,000 inhabitants, which was a quarter the size of Paris and
one-tenth that of London; and, continues Fusi, 'it lacked everything
that defined a great modern city of the time: boulevards, garden
squares, great avenues, luxury stores, elegant houses, street lighting,
monuments, theatres, opera, urban transport, stations, hotels, banking
houses'.[23] Nevertheless, Madrilenians were very pleased with their city.
'From Madrid to heaven', went the refrain from a zarzuela or operetta.
According to Ortega, the only 'creative culture' to emerge in Madrid
was '*madrileñismo*', a cult to the city itself. This may have contributed
to the idea that they were living in the centre of a functioning State,
and of a strong and visible nation. This appears to be at variance with
the impression of the peripheral élites, particularly in Barcelona, who
were living the *febre de l'or* (gold fever) and artistic modernism, and who
cheerfully travelled to Paris but lacked any enthusiasm for the journey
to Madrid, especially if they were obliged to beg for vital political
measures, which made them feel positively resentful.

Socio-economic differences and the resulting cultural imbalances
were an important part of the origins of the *fin de siècle* national problem
but they were not, on their own, sufficient. Italy, for example, suffered
from even greater differences than Spain. Núñez-Seixas observes that
'between Lombardy and Sicily, the contrasts were more extreme than
between Catalonia and Extremadura',[24] but at that point, the élites
and the political activity of the State came into their own: in northern
Italy, the intelligentsia became the driving force behind a nationalising State, which achieved unity and stood up to both Austria and
the Vatican in the process. It then embarked upon colonial wars, and
eventually engaged in European wars from which, to all appearances,
it emerged victorious. In Spain, the peripheral élites were neither the
inventors nor the champions of a modernising liberal State, which never
embarked upon any successful international adventures. Juan Linz has
explained that 'the crisis of Spanish national identity . . . would not have
happened if the Spanish State had had the international successes of
France, and if Spanish culture had been as creative and dynamic as that
of other European countries'.[25] In other words, State weakness and a
limited cultural creativity preceded the crisis of the nation.

That weakness reached critical proportions in 1898. Prior to that, as
Blas and Laborda comment, during the nineteenth century, 'none of
the principal political problems of the age offered a serious challenge to
the State'. The Carlists, who were the true subversive opposition, never
questioned the national identity or State reality and the 'Catalan question' did not become a threatening political question until after 1898.[26]

Perhaps it was due to the protracted existence of a political structure corresponding to the name of 'Spain' and to the powerful stimulus given to the national identity by the war against Napoleon, together with the mythification of history and culture undertaken by the liberals and the international success of the Andalusian stereotype created by the Romantics of a Spanish identity that was assumed to be eternal. It is true that the State, by avoiding international strife, had been able to stand its ground without apparent problems. It is also true that official-dom made no attempt to reinforce the national identity, but neither was there a redoubtable opposition movement trying to raise any alternative flag. Only in the last quarter of the nineteenth century, in the two industrial metropoli that eclipsed Madrid in economic terms, did there emerge élites who were prepared to make that challenge. It is curious that, in order to do so, they imitated many of the symbols and myths that were a part of the legacy of *españolista* mythology. Basque nationalism, for example, was based on the 'purity of blood' that excluded Muslims and Jews, and on the existence of a millenarian identity founded by Tubal, the grandson of Noah, to which it had obstinately clung despite successive waves of invasions.[27] *Vasquismo* as well as *catalanismo* adopted many of the forms of victimhood of the *Mater Dolorosa* previously reserved to *españolismo*. In any event, alternative identities came of age or, to put it another way, became truly popular movements after the terrible demonstration of incompetence on the international stage by the State in 1898.

That year was as crucial for the peripheral nationalisms as it was for Spanish nationalism on account of the fact that one version of regenerationism placed its hopes for 'purification' and political modernisation in the developed regions. Macías Picavea declared that 'the sad central mesetas where both Castiles lie exposed and unprotected' would be the death knell of Spain if the 'living members' of the national body – Catalonia, Valencia, Asturias, the Basque country – turned against the Madrilenian oligarchy.[28] However, this obliged the existing 'regionalisms' to make radical changes in their political orientation. National histories are always full of irony and it would be amusing if they were not so often tragic. In the Iberian case, it is astonishing how the two main non-State nationalisms were able to manoeuvre to their advantage in a highly contradictory situation. Both of them, but particularly the Basques, had always had links with Carlism, an anti-modernising movement that prided itself on being a bastion of resistance in the face of the progressive Jacobinism of the *españolista* élites. As if by magic, they had to transform themselves into champions of Europeanisation and modernisation. For a long time, this situation left the two movements with their hands tied, contradicted by their own élites, who had been seduced by the modernising vision of Jacobinism.

In the meantime, Spanish nationalism evolved in exactly the opposite direction, away from its secular-progressive origins towards national-Catholicism. As de Riquer and Ucelay have acutely observed, both State and non-State nationalisms reacted *against* their initial ideological tendencies: 'in the Spanish case, the original liberal bias that led to an *institutional nationalism* was rejected by the *new identity-based nationalism* born of the colonial conflict. In the case of the peripheral nationalisms of Catalonia, the Basque Country and Galicia, the tendency was to move away from the highly conservative founding movements that attempted to monopolise the new cause'.[29] This led to many of the internal problems that these movements were to suffer at a later date, such as the dramatic choice faced by Basque nationalists on the outbreak of civil war in 1936: whether to support Franco or the Republic. The decision was made almost with the toss of a coin: in fact, there was a split, and while the leaders of the Partido Nacionalista Vasco (Basque Nationalist Party) chose to support the Republican cause, the Carlists in Alava and Navarre sent more volunteers than any other part of Spain to swell the insurgent forces.

Reactive *españolismo*

We have taken a brief look at the peripheral nationalisms because they provided Spanish nationalism with yet another reason for its existence. As well as 'regeneration' or internal modernisation, which was accepted by all political forces after 1898, there was now also the issue of *anti-separatism*, or the defence of the State against breakaway nationalisms. In terms of social mobilisation theory, Spanish nationalism became a *reactive* movement – as opposed to a *proactive* one – because it was neither creative nor aggressive. It merely adopted an attitude of distress or endurance quite appropriate to the representations of Spain as *Mater Dolorosa*. Its aim was overwhelmingly conservative and, at least until Franco's death, the one that achieved the most lasting success of all those embraced by Spanish nationalism. Borja de Riquer also defines this nationalist variation as reactive rather than 'integrative', which was entirely appropriate for 'the most reactionary, most anti-democratic and most socially regressive ideological sectors'. While it is true that *españolismo* was dominated by the most conservative sectors, it should not be forgotten that elements remained of nineteenth-century Jacobinism and the post-'98 regenerationist movement.

This conservative nationalism can be described as 'unitary and authoritarian, very concerned about the danger of separatism and inclined to militarism'.[30] The armed forces, driven by revenge after the humiliation of 1898, felt especially drawn by this reactive patriotism, which led them to interfere in political life once again following the respite under the Restoration of 1875–1898. They began by assaulting the editorial offices of Catalan publications in 1905 which supposedly questioned the unity of the nation and ended up by securing a 'Law of Jurisdictions' in 1906 that would allow offences against the *patria* or the honour of the armed forces to be tried by court-martial. Núñez-Seixas suggests that the armed forces identified closely with a Spanish nationalism that, 'frustrated in its foreign expansion', vented its discontent on the 'enemy within': the *separatist* nationalisms and the revolutionary left, both of which were deemed to be 'anti-Spanish'. Thus the army intervened in the Spanish politics of the twentieth century much as it had done in the nineteenth. However, it no longer did it do so in defence of the constitutional order but in defence of the *nation*, and against its *disintegration*. Eventually, de Riquer continues, 'the increasingly conflictive and hysterical dialectic beween this integral ultra-Spanish nationalism and the peripheral nationalisms [became] a key element in the crisis of the parliamentary system'. In effect, Primo de Rivera took advantage of the alleged threat to the unity of the *patria* to overthrow the Constitution of 1876, as did pre-fascist thinkers to declare that parliamentarianism had run its course. In the first half of the nineteenth century, the armed forces conspired constantly to introduce a Constitution, but in the twentieth century, inspired by the fear of the disintegration of the State, rebelled against constitutional régimes. Still, there is a certain coherence insofar as both cases concern the State and in both cases the intervention of the army was carried out in the name of the *nation*: but one that had been transformed from its liberal, modernising beginnings to become an aggressive, authoritarian pillar of the traditional social order.

Conservatism, or defence of the existing social order, became the ultimate objective of Spanish nationalism in the early twentieth century following the stagnation of the liberal revolution and the thwarting of colonial expansion in the previous century. This version of Spanish identity was naturally the one preferred by Catholic-conservative groups which had assumed nationalism as a safeguard against revolution. National-Catholicism had occasionally been at the service of expansionist objectives, such as the Moroccan War of 1859–1860, but, with few exceptions, its political interests were ecclesiastical rather than national. One only has to recall the conclusions of the Catholic centennial congresses of the 1880s: to say the rosary, protest at the situation of the Pope, consecrate Spain to the Sacred Heart, organise apostolic missions and ensure that education followed Catholic dogma. These were thankless objectives for a nationalist. From a Catholic perspective, the only attitude possible before a modern world full of threats was a defensive one. Initially, such threats appeared limited to the Church and the absolute monarchy, the 'divine order' of the *ancien régime*, but the sedition continued to spread. The defence of individual freedoms and restrictions on royal power became demands for 'democracy', or participation in government, and then 'socialism', or workers' rights. The conservative world was convinced that *everything* was at threat: religion, property, the family, even the nation, which had originally been the creation of the liberal revolution against the absolute monarchy. By this means, 'Spain' came to be the incantation to ward off the diabolical genie that threatened the social order.

By this stage, the 'nation' had become opposed to social revolution. According to Andrés de Blas, Cánovas, the architect of the Restoration régime, 'continually exaggerated the strength of an egalitarian flood that, at the least sign of weakness, would sweep away the pillars of shared coexistence . . .; in this state of permanent threat, once the bulwark of Christian resignation has been breached, the State will be the only instrument capable . . . of saving society'.[31] The State was the instrument, the nation was now the justification or ideology, and the U-turn was complete: from being revolutionary in 1820, it had become counter-revolutionary one hundred years later. As Eric Storm writes, 'nationalism was primarily an answer to the fear of the fragmentation of the nation into social classes'. Nonetheless, he recognises that this was a slow process because 'the absence of any serious threat to social stability either from within the country or from outside prevented extreme nationalism from achieving a firm footing in Spain'.[32]

By the 1930s, however, the threats had become serious. The social and cultural changes of the previous thirty years led to the political upheavals of the Republic and the Civil War. Urbanisation, industrialisation, secularisation and labour unrest had all taken place at such speed that they had an unbearable destabilising effect on a society that was so traditional and hierarchical. Once the monarchy fell in 1931, the Second Republic that replaced it raised unduly high expectations. Its main inspiration was the secular-progressive nationalism of the previous century and the mission of its founders was to strengthen the State, promote education, and undertake a cautious redistribution of property. Sadly, improvements were too long in coming, the revolutionary left began to make maximalist demands and the political process developed into a free-for-all. This led to the spectacular success of the first mass Catholic party in Spanish history, the *Confederación Española de Derechas Autónomas* (The Spanish Confederation of Autonomous Rightists), a party that won more deputies than any other in the same year – 1933 – that it was founded. Its ideology is revealing: it preached traditional Catholic conservatism on the one hand while talking the language of radical nationalism on the other; in other words, it represented itself as a patriotic organisation that would defend Spain against its dissolution at the hands of the *anti-Spain*. But 'Spain' was not only Catholicism, it was also the system of inherited social power – order, property, family, tradition, authority, anti-liberalism and anti-Enlightenment – while 'anti-Spain' was not only revolution but also modern civilisation, the 'godless' materialistic, secular, urban world. By bringing to bear the long-established and powerful networks of communication and mobilisation of the Church to spread this ideology, it is not hard to understand the rapid success of the party of José María Gil Robles.

In response to the Republican threat, a broad coalition was formed of all the conservative sectors. This encompassed the Catholics, frightened by modern secularisation; the traditional spheres of economic power, horrified by the 'social revolution'; and the armed forces, who were called upon to safeguard the 'nation' against the 'separatism' they so detested. The army led the coup of July 1933 against the Republic in the old praetorian tradition, but on this occasion it could not claim victory and neither did it admit defeat. The result was a stalemate that degenerated into a long and bloody civil war, exacerbated by the international situation and the eagerness of the two extremes of the European political spectrum, fascism and communism, to supply arms. Like all wars, the Civil War of 1936 simplified the options, and the whole array of existing and potential nationalisms were reduced to two: the 'Republican' option, successor to the nineteenth-century secular-progressive movement and the regenerationism of 1898, or the 'National' Catholic-conservative option. The latter perpetuated the age-old division of the Spanish right between its loyalty to God and its loyalty to the *Patria*. Still, its confusion was limited compared to that of the Republican side, which, along with its genuine nationalist enthusiasm, added an eclectic mix of left-wing myths, promises and political values to its propaganda, including progress, freedom, democracy, education, civism, equality, social revolution, federalism, or its opposite, Statist Jacobinism. None of the great modern political myths were missing, and the essential message was diluted. In contrast, the Francoists concentrated their propaganda on what was *national*: it was no coincidence that the rebels called themselves, and were called by others, the 'Nationalists'. They were better versed than their opponents in using the myth of the nation. Yet again, that myth demonstrated its unparalleled strength.[33]

However, even among the victors, the message was not *exclusively* national. Crosses could be seen among the red-and-yellow flags and all the rallies and military parades were preceded by a mass. Ledesma Ramos and other purist Fascists were not happy with that combination when they merged with the Falange in 1933, and they opposed the confessional overtones that the leaders closest to traditional conservatism introduced into the Falangist programme. As nationalists, they were right: God and the *Patria* could travel together, but only if the myths were realized in such a way as to remain under the control of the State; if the Church could reserve some part of the State to itself, then Fascism lost its purity.

Although the nationalisation of political life had been thorough between 1931 and 1939, a period in which not even the most remote village remained unaffected by events, the *nationalisation of the masses* of the next ten years reached an almost hysterical intensity. After the trauma of war and the destruction of the traditional lifestyle in so many parts of the Peninsula came an exhaustive process of nationalist propaganda. It was as if Spanish nationalism had to be imposed, forcing itself on society to as great an extent as the two World Wars had on the major European countries. In short, it had to compensate for the all the inactivity, all the obstacles and all the ambivalence of the nineteenth century. Unfortunately, it was an obligatory and brutal nationalisation based on the negation and destruction of half the country. There is not a single author who does not agree that the nationalising policy of the victors was based not upon integration but upon 'repression and coercive indoctrination'. 'At no time', as Borja de Riquer comments, 'did Francoism attempt to transmit a really new idea of Spain that might have appealed to a large number of those defeated in the civil war.'[34]

The régime also lasted far too long. It outlived its Fascist contemporaries in 1945 partly because of its identification with Catholicism and partly because of the protection it received from the United States within the context of the Cold War. However, by the 1960s and 1970s, on the periphery of a prosperous and democratic Europe which was choosing to unify, Franco's Spain was an embarrassing anachronism associated with economic and cultural backwardness, political oppression, clericalism, and an overweening military and police presence on the streets. Because *catalanismo* and *vasquismo* had stood up to the régime, they were hailed as emblems of democracy and modernity, far removed from their Carlist origins and the brutal methods that continued to be employed by radical *vasquismo*. This led to the dual and ambiguous legitimation of the nation in Article Two of the Constitution of 1978, which is the result of the transaction – the *consensus* of the Transition – that left the issue of sovereignty undefined between the 'Spanish nation' as an 'indisoluble' unit and the 'nationalities'. Both nationalisms survived. Both, to a certain extent, had failed because, according to Juan Linz, 'the failures and limitations of the peripheral nationalisms against the State and even within the State' were the result of the 'limited success' of Spanish nationalism in the nineteenth century.[35] Both had failed, but each had sufficient strength to make life difficult for the other. In recent years, *españolismo* has tried to establish links with 'constitutional patriotism', a civic and pluricultural ideal, in order to distance itself from Francoism. Its survival will depend on the success of this association.

Notes

1 'I know about your sorrows, oh Fatherland [lit., Motherland], and I hear the sad funeral concert played by the bell and the gun'. Asturian priest ('the Fatherland begs [its] beloved children to help [it] as much as they can in the present conflict'), in G. Lovett, *Napoleon and the Birth of Modern Spain*, New York University Press, 1965, Vol I, p. 332.

2 These images in *El Papagayo*, 1842, or *Gil Blas*, 1864–1865, among others.

3 B. de Riquer and E. Ucelay, 'An Analysis of Nationalisms in Spain: A Proposal for an Integrated Historical Model', in J. Beramendi et al. (eds), *Nationalism in Europe: Past and Present*, Santiago de Compostela, 1994, p. 291.

4 See the 'National Episodes' *Gerona*, Introduction; *El Grande Oriente*, XVI; *Mendizábal*, XXXIII; *Narváez*, V–VI; *Bodas Reales*, V; *De Cartago a Sagunto*, XXI; *Amadeo I*, IX.

5 P. Aguilar, 'Pérez Galdós, Benito', in A. de Blas (ed.), *Enciclopedia del Nacionalismo*, Madrid, 1997, pp. 409–411.

6 History of the 'people' in *Mendizábal*, II, for instance. Aguilar, 'Pérez Galdós'; and G. Triviños, *Benito Pérez Galdós en la jaula de la epopeya*, Barcelona, 1987, p. 193. Cánovas's sentence, repeated by Pérez Galdós in *Cánovas*, Chapter XI.

7 J. Zarco Avellaneda, *Isaac Peral y Caballero*, Alcoy, 1986, pp. 16, 22, 28, 31, 44 and 50; cf. J. L. Fernández-Rúa, *Inventores españoles*, Madrid, 1954.

8 P. Aguilar, 'Pérez Galdós'; on Quevedo, see R. Lida, quoted by Triviños, *Benito Pérez Galdós*, pp. 197 and 200–203.

9 There is an immense bibliography on the 1898 Spanish defeat: see for instance J. Pan-Montojo (ed.), *Más se perdió en Cuba*, Madrid, 1998; or S. Balfour, *The End of the Spanish Empire*, Oxford: Clarendon, 1997.

10 *El regionalismo ante el nacionalismo y el imperialismo modernos en la formación de los Estados*, Valladolid, 1908, pp. 23–24, quoted by X. M. Núñez-Seixas,

'Historia e actualidade dos nacionalismos na España contemporánea: unha perspectiva de conxunto', *Grial*, 128 (1995): 513.

11 See his Preface to the second volume of the *Historia de España* edited by him, p. XLI: 'We take for granted the permanence of racial traits, a well-known phenomenon'.

12 See E. Storm, *La perspectiva del progreso: Pensamiento político en la España de fin de siglo*, Madrid, 2001, pp. 289–303.

13 B. de Riquer, 'Aproximación al nacionalismo español contemporáneo', *Studia Historica*, 12 (1994): 11–29 at p. 20.

14 Hemingway, quoted by E. F. Stanton, *Hemingway and Spain*, Seattle: University of Washington Press, 1989, p. XIV. Waldo Frank, *Virgin Spain*, London, Jonathan Cape, 1926.

15 See J. L. Guereña, 'Del anti-Dos de Mayo al Primero de Mayo. Aspectos del internacionalismo en el movimiento obrero español', *Estudios de Historia Social*, 38/39 (1986): 91–103.

16 De Riquer, 'Aproximación', p. 23.

17 A classical account on Catalan nationalism in J. Pabón's *Cambó*, Barcelona: Alpha, 1952, Vol. I, pp. 98–99, basically followed by I. Olábarri Gortázar, 'Un conflicto entre nacionalismos. La "cuestión regional" en España, 1808–1939', in F. Fernández Rodríguez (ed.), *La España de las autonomías*, Madrid, 1985, pp. 110–111. On Languedoc and Wales, see X. M. Núñez-Seixas, 'Questione nazionale e crisi statale: Spagna, 1898–1936' *Ricerche Storica*, XXIV(1) (1994): p. 98. As for the Galician case, see J. J. Linz, 'Early State-building and Late Peripheral Nationalism against the State: the Case of Spain', in S. N. Eisenstadt and S. Rokkan (eds), *Building States and Nations*, London, 1973, Vol. 2, pp. 90–92.

18 De Riquer, 'Aproximación', pp. 12 and 16.

19 Núñez-Seixas, 'Questione nazionale e crisi statale', pp. 99–100; structural differences, in Olábarri, 'Un conflicto entre nacionalismos', pp. 94–100.

20 Costa Pinto and Núñez-Seixas, 'Portugal and Spain', p. 174.

21 J. M. Fradera, 'La política liberal y el descubrimiento de una identidad distintiva en Cataluña', *Hispania* LX/2, 205 (2000): 273–302.

22 J. P. Fusi, 'Centralismo y localismo: la formación del Estado español', in G. Gortázar (ed.), *Nación y Estado en la España liberal*, Madrid, 1994, p. 87.

23 Balmes, *Escritos políticos*, Madrid, 1950, II, p. 380, quoted by M. Puelles Benítez, *Educación e ideología en la España contemporánea*, Barcelona, 1980, p. 126 ; J. P. Fusi, *España: Evolución de la identidad nacional*, Madrid, 2000, pp. 170–173.

24 Núñez-Seixas, 'Questione nazionale e crisi statale', p. 93.

25 J J. Linz, 'Los nacionalismos en España: una perspectiva comparada', *Historia y fuente oral*, 7 (1992): 133.

26 A. de Blas and J. J. Laborda, 'La construcción del Estado en España', in F. Hernández y F. Mercadé (eds), *Estructuras sociales y cuestión nacional en España*, Barcelona: Ariel, 1986, p. 475.

27 See J. M. Sánchez Prieto, *El imaginario vasco: Representaciones de una*

conciencia histórica, nacional y política en el escenario europeo 1833–1876, Barcelona, 1993.

28 M. Picavea, *El Problema Nacional,* 1899; reed. Madrid, 1993, p. 195.

29 De Riquer and Ucelay, 'An Analysis of Nationalisms', p. 295. On the Spanish origins of Catalan myths, de Riquer and Ucelay, 'An Analysis', p. 276; on Basque mythology, Sánchez Priento, *El imaginario vasco,* or J. Juaristi, *Vestigios de Babel: Para una arqueología de los nacionalismos españoles,* Madrid, 1992; on the support received by Catalan, Basque and, to a lesser degree, Galician nationalisms from local élites and the Catholic clergy opposed to the expansion of the state, see Núñez-Seixas, 'Historia e actualidade dos nacionalismos', p. 507. On the shift of Catalan nationalism towards a much more modern programme, around the 1905–1906 political crisis, see J. Álvarez Junco, *El Emperador del Paralelo,* Madrid, 1990, Chapter 8.

30 De Riquer and Ucelay, 'An Analysis of Nationalisms', pp. 295–296; X. M. Núñez-Seixas, 'Questione nazionale e crisi statale', p. 101, and 'Historia e actualidade dos nacionalismos', p. 515.

31 A. de Blas, 'Cánovas del Castillo y el lugar de la nación', in A. Cánovas del Castillo, *Discurso sobre la nación,* reed. Madrid, 1997, pp. 37–38.

32 Storm, *La perspectiva del progreso,* p. 370.

33 J. Álvarez Junco, 'El nacionalismo español como mito movilizador: Cuatro guerras', in R. Cruz and M. Pérez Ledesma, *Cultura y Movilización en la España contemporánea,* Madrid: Alianza, 1997, pp. 63–66.

34 De Riquer, 'Aproximación', p. 28. On the relative failure of the Francoist neo-nationalisation, X. M. Núñez-Seixas, 'Historia e actualidade dos nacionalismos', pp. 523ff.

35 Linz, 'Los nacionalismos en España', p. 135.

Select bibliography

Abellán, J. L., *Historia crítica del pensamiento español*. Madrid: Espasa-Calpe, 1984–1989.

Aguilar, P., 'Pérez Galdós, Benito', in A. de Blas (ed.), *Enciclopedia del Nacionalismo*. Madrid: Tecnos, 1997, pp. 409–411.

Alarcón, P. A. de, *Diario de un testigo de la Guerra de África*, 2 vols. Madrid: Rivadeneyra, 1931.

Alcalá Galiano, A., *Historia de España, desde los tiempos primitivos hasta la mayoría de edad de Isabel II, con arreglo a la que escribió en inglés el Dr. Dunham* , 7 vols. Madrid: Sociedad Tipogr., 1844–1846.

Alfaro, M. I., *Compendio de la historia de España*. Madrid: Vda. de Hernando, 1853.

Alix, A., *Compendio de Historia General*. Madrid: Cabrerizo, 1848–1852.

Almirall, V., *España tal como es*. Barcelona: Librería Española, 1886.

Alvarado, F., *Cartas críticas que escribió (. . .) El Filósofo Rancio*, 5 vols. Madrid: E. Aguado, 1824–1825.

Álvarez Junco, J., 'La invención de la Guerra de la Independencia'. *Studia Historica. Historia Contemporánea*, 12 (1994): 75–99.

Álvarez Junco, J., 'The Nation-Building Process in Nineteenth-Century Spain', in Clare Mar-Molinero and Angel Smith (eds), *Nationalism and the Nation in the Iberian Peninsula: Competing and Conflicting Identities*. Oxford: Berg, 1996, pp. 89–106.

Álvarez Junco, J., 'El nacionalismo español como mito movilizador: Cuatro guerras', in R. Cruz and M. Pérez Ledesma (eds), *Cultura y movilización en la España contemporánea*. Madrid: Alianza, 1997, pp. 35–67.

Álvarez Junco, J., 'La nación en duda', in J. Pan-Montojo (ed.), *Más se perdió en Cuba: España, 1898 y la crisis de fin de siglo*. Madrid: Alianza, 1998, pp. 405–475.

Amado, M., *Dios y España: o sea, Ensayo sobre una demostración histórica de lo que debe España a la Religión Católica*, 3 vols. Madrid: Eusebio Aguado, 1831.

Amador de los Ríos, J., *Estudios históricos, políticos y literarios sobre los judíos de España*. Madrid: D. M. Díaz, 1848.

Amador de los Ríos, J., *Historia crítica de la literatura española*, 7 vols. Madrid: J. Rodríguez, 1861–1865.

Amador de los Ríos, J., *Historia social, política y religiosa de los judíos en España y Portugal*, 2 vols. Madrid: Fortanet, 1875–1876.

Angulo, J. R., *Nociones generales de la historia de España*. Madrid: R. de la Sota, 1844.

Arco y Garay, R. del, *La idea de Imperio en la política y la literatura españolas*. Madrid: Espasa-Calpe, 1944.

Arnoldsson, S., *Leyenda Negra: Estudios sobre sus orígenes*. Goteborg: Statens Humanistiska Forskningsrad, 1960.

Aróstegui Sánchez, J., 'El carlismo y la Guerra Civil', in *Historia de España Menéndez Pidal*, Vol. XXXIV, pp. 71–140. Madrid: Espasa, 1978.

Artola, M., *Los orígenes de la España contemporánea*, 2 vols. Madrid: Instituto de Estudios Políticos, 1959.

Artola, M., *La burguesía revolucionaria (1808–1874)*. Madrid: Alianza/ Alfaguara, 1973.

Artola, M., *La España de Fernando VII*, Vol. XXXII of *Historia de España Menéndez Pidal*. Madrid: Espasa-Calpe, 1992.

Artola, M., *La Monarquía de España*. Madrid: Alianza, 1999.

Asensio, E., 'La lengua compañera del imperio'. *Revista de Filología Española*, 43(3–4), 1960: 398–413.

Ayala, F., 'El *problema* de España', in *España, a la fecha*. Buenos Aires: Sur, 1965, pp. 99–125.

Ayala, F., *La imagen de España*. Madrid: Alianza, 1986.

Aymes, J.-R., *La guerra de la Independencia en España (1808–1814)*. Madrid: Siglo XXI, 1975.

Aymes, J.-R., *La guerra de España contra la Revolución Francesa (1793–1795)*. Alicante: Instituto de Estudios 'J. Gil-Albert', 1991.

Balfour, S., 'The Lion and the Pig: Nationalism and National Identity in Fin de Siècle Spain', in Clare Mar-Molinero and Jo Labanyi, *An Introduction to Spanish Cultural Studies*. Cambridge: Cambridge University Press, 1996.

Balfour, S., *The End of the Spanish Empire (1898–1923)*. Oxford: Clarendon Press, 1997.

Battaner Arias, M. P., *Vocabulario político-social en España (1868–1873)*. Madrid: Real Academia Española, 1977.

Belmar, F. S., *Reflexiones sobre la España, desde la fundación de la monarquía hasta el fin del reinado de San Fernando*. Madrid: La Esperanza, 1861.

Bennassar, B., *Historia de los españoles*, 2 vols. Barcelona: Crítica, 1989.

Beramendi, J., 'Bibliografía sobre nacionalismo y cuestión nacional en la España contemporánea (1939–1983)'. *Estudios de Historia Social*, 28–29 (1984): 491–515.

Beramendi, J., 'La historiografía de los nacionalismos en España'. *Historia Contemporánea*, 7 (1992): 135–154.

Beramendi, J., Núñez Seixas, X. M., and Maíz, R. (eds), *Nationalism in Europe: Past and Present*, 3 vols. Universidade de Santiago de Compostela, 1994.

Blas Guerrero, A. de, *Sobre el nacionalismo español*. Madrid: Centro de Estudios Constitucionales, 1989.

Blas Guerrero, A. de, *Tradición republicana y nacionalismo español*. Madrid: Tecnos, 1991.

Blas Guerrero, A. de, and Laborda, J. J., 'La construcción del Estado en España', in F. Hernández and F. Mercadé (eds), *Estructuras sociales y cuestión nacional en España*. Barcelona: Ariel, 1986, pp. 461–487.

Blinkhorn, M., 'Spain: The *Spanish Problem* and the Imperial Myth'. *Journal of Contemporary History*, 15 (1980): 5–25.

Botrel, J. F., 'Nationalisme et consolation dans la littérature populaire espagnole des années 1898', in C. Dumas, (ed.), *Nationalisme et littérature en Espagne et Amérique Latine au XIXe siècle*. Lille: Presses Universitaires de Lille III, 1982, pp. 63–98.

Botti, A., *Cielo y dinero: El nacionalcatolicismo en España (1881–1975)*. Madrid: Alianza, 1992.

Boyd, C., *Historia Patria: Politics, History, and National Identity in Spain, 1875–1975*. Princeton, NJ: Princeton University Press, 1997.

Brown, J., and Elliott, J. H., *A Palace for a King*. New Haven, CT: Yale University Press, 1980.

Cabanes, F. X., *Historia de la Guerra de España contra Napoleón Bonaparte*. Madrid: D. M. de Burgos, 1818.

Cadalso, J. de, *Cartas Marruecas*. Madrid: Cátedra, 1984.

Callahan, W., *Church, Politics, and Society in Spain, 1770–1874*. Cambridge, MA: Harvard University Press, 1984.

Calvo Serraller, F., *La imagen romántica de España*. Madrid: Alianza, 1995.

Camus, A., *Compendio elemental de Historia Universal*. Madrid: Mellado, 1842.

Canal, J., *El carlismo: Dos siglos de contrarrevolución en España*. Madrid: Alianza, 2000.

Canga Argüelles, J., *Observaciones al tomo II de la Historia de la Guerra de España, que escribió en inglés el Teniente Coronel Napier*, 3 vols. London: D. M. Calero, 1830.

Cánovas del Castillo, A., *Historia de la decadencia de España, desde Felipe III hasta Carlos II*. Madrid: Biblioteca Universal, 1852–1854.

Cánovas del Castillo, A., *La nación, su origen y naturaleza* [1882]. Reprinted by Biblioteca Nueva, Madrid, 1997, preface by A. de Blas.

Cánovas del Castillo, A., *La escarapela roja y las banderas y divisas usadas en España*. Madrid: Fortanet, 1912.

Cánovas Sánchez, F., *El Partido Moderado*. Madrid: Centro de Estudios Constitucionales, 1982.

Capestany, E. J., *Menéndez Pelayo y su obra*. Buenos Aires: Depalma, 1981.

Capmany, A. de, *Centinela contra franceses*, ed. and pref. Françoise Etienvre. London: Tamesis Books, 1988.

Capmany, A. de, *Teatro histórico-crítico de la elocuencia española*, 5 vols. Madrid: A. Sancha, 1786–1794.

Carande, R., *Carlos V y sus banqueros*, Madrid: Sociedad de Estudios y Publicaciones, 1965.

Cárcel Ortí, V.(ed.), *La Iglesia en la España contemporánea (1808–1975)*; Vol. 5 of *Historia de la Iglesia en España*. Madrid: La Editorial Católica, 1979.

Carnero, G. (ed.), *Historia de la literatura española: Siglo XVIII*. Madrid: Espasa-Calpe, 1995.

Carnero, G. (ed.), *Historia de la literatura española: Siglo XIX*. Madrid: Espasa-Calpe, 1997.

Caro Baroja, J., *El mito del carácter nacional: Meditaciones a contrapelo*. Madrid: Seminarios y Ediciones, 1970.

Caro Baroja, J., *Los judíos en la España moderna y contemporánea*, 3 vols. Madrid: Istmo, 1978.

Caro Baroja, J., *Las falsificaciones de la historia (en relación con la de España)*. Barcelona: Seix Barral, 1992.

Casares, E., and Alonso, C., *La música española en el siglo XIX*. Oviedo: Universidad de Oviedo, 1995.

Castellanos de Losada, S., *Memorándum Historial: Nociones de la Historia Universal y participación de España*. Madrid: F. del Castillo, 1858.

Castro, A., *La realidad histórica de España*, 3rd edn. México: Porrúa, 1966 [1954].

Castro, A., *Origen, ser y existir de los españoles*. Madrid: Taurus, 1959.

Castro, A., *Sobre el nombre y el quién de los españoles*. Madrid: Taurus, 1973.

Castro, F. de, *Historia profana general y particular de España*. Madrid: F. Martínez García, 1853.

Castro, F. de, *Resumen de Historia general y de España*. Madrid: F. Martínez García, 1850–1863.

Castro y Rossi, A. de, *Historia de los judíos en España*. Cádiz: Imp. de la Revista Médica, 1847.

Castro y Rossi, A. de, *Historia de los protestantes españoles y de su persecución por Felipe II*, Cádiz: Imp. de la Revista Médica, 1851.

Castro y Rossi, A. de, *Examen filosófico sobre las principales causas de la decadencia de España*. Cádiz: Imp. F. Pantoja, 1852.

Castro y Rossi, A. de, *Costumbres públicas y privadas de los españoles del siglo XVII, fundado en el estudio de las comedias de Calderón*. Madrid: Gutenberg, 1881.

Catalán, D., 'España en su historiografía: de objeto a sujeto de la historia'. Preface to Menéndez Pidal, R., *Los españoles en la historia*. Madrid: Espasa-Calpe, 1962.

Catecismos políticos españoles, arreglados a las Constituciones del siglo XIX. Consejería de Cultura. Comunidad de Madrid, 1989.

Cavanilles, A., *Compendio de Historia de España*, 5 vols. Madrid: J. M. Alegría, 1860.

Cepeda Adán, J., 'La Historiografía', in *Historia de España Menéndez Pidal*, Vol. XXVI, *El Siglo del Quijote*, I, pp. 523–643. Madrid: Espasa-Calpe, 1986.

Cervilla Soler, M., *Compendio de Historia de España*. Toledo: S. López Fando, 1853.

Cirujano Marín, P., Elorriaga Planes, T., and Pérez Garzón, J. S., *Historia y nacionalismo español, 1834–1868.* Madrid: C.S.I.C., 1985.

Clavero, B., *El código y el fuero: De la cuestión regional en la España contemporánea.* Madrid: Siglo XXI, 1982.

Clemente, J. C., *Bases documentales del carlismo y de las guerras civiles de los siglos XIX y XX,* 2 vols. Madrid: Servicio Histórico Militar, 1985.

Conde, J. A., *Historia de la dominación de los árabes en España,* 3 vols. Madrid: 1820–1821.

Corcuera, J., 'Nacionalismo y clases en la España de la Restauración'. *Estudios de Historia Social,* 28–29 (1984): 249–282.

Cortada, J., *Historia de España, dedicada a la juventud,* 2 vols. Barcelona: J. Bastinos, 1845.

Cossío, M. B., *Aproximación a la pintura española* [1884]. Reprinted by Akal, Madrid, 1985.

Costes, Adèle, *Compendio de Historia de España.* Barcelona: Verdaguer, 1842.

Cueva, J. de la, 'Cultura y movilización en el movimiento católico de la Restauración (1899–1913)', in M. Suárez Cortina (ed.), *La cultura española de la Restauración,* Santander: Sociedad Menéndez Pelayo, 1999, pp. 169–192.

Del Río, A., and Bernadete, M. J., *El concepto contemporáneo de España: Antología de ensayos (1895–1931).* Buenos Aires: Losada, 1946.

Dérozier, A., *Quintana y el nacimiento del liberalismo en España.* Madrid: Turner, 1978.

Díaz-Andreu, M., 'Archaeology and Nationalism in Spain', in Ph. Kohl, and C. Fawcett (eds), *Nationalism, Politics and the Practice of Archaeology.* Cambridge: Cambridge University Press, 1991, pp. 39–56.

Díaz-Andreu, M., 'El pasado en el presente: la búsqueda de las raíces en los nacionalismos culturales. El caso español'. In J. Beramendi et al. (eds), *Nationalism in Europe: Past and Present,* I. Santiago de Compostela: 1994, pp. 199–218.

Díaz-Andreu, M., 'Ethnicity and Iberians: The Archaeological Crossroads between Perception and Material Culture'. *European Jounal of Archaeology,* 1(2), 1998: 199–218.

Díaz de Baeza, J., *Historia de la Guerra de España contra el Emperador Napoleón.* Madrid: Boix, 1843.

Díaz-Plaja, G., *España en su literatura.* Barcelona: Salvat, 1969.

Diccionario Bibliográfico de la Guerra de la Independencia Española (1808–1814), 3 vols. Madrid: Servicio Histórico Militar, 1944–1952.

Díez, J. L. (ed.), *La pintura de historia del siglo XIX en España.* Madrid: Ministerio de Cultura, 1992.

Díez del Corral, L., *La monarquía hispánica en el pensamiento político europeo: De Maquiavelo a Humboldt.* Madrid: Revista de Occidente, 1976.

Domínguez Ortiz, A., *La sociedad española en el siglo XVII,* 2 vols. Madrid: Consejo Superior de Investigaciones Científicas, 1963.

Domínguez Ortiz, A., *El Antiguo Régimen: los Reyes Católicos y los Austrias.* Madrid: Alianza, 1973.

Domínguez Ortiz, A., *Los judeoconversos en la España moderna*. Madrid: Mapfre, 1991.

Donoso Cortés, J., *Obras Completas*, 2 vols. Madrid: Biblioteca de Autores Cristianos, 1946.

Dumas, C. (ed.), *Nationalisme et littérature en Espagne et Amérique Latine au XIXe siècle*. Lille: Presses Universitaires, 1982.

Elliott, J. H., *Imperial Spain, 1469–1716*. London: Penguin, 1970.

Étienvre, F., 'Preface' to A.Capmany, *Centinela contra franceses*. London: Tamesis Books, 1988.

Ezquerra, S., *¡Los españoles no tenemos patria!*. Madrid: J. Peña, 1869.

Fernández y González, M., *Martín Gil: Memorias del tiempo de Felipe II*. Madrid: Gaspar y Roig, 1854.

Fernández Sebastián, J., *La génesis del fuerismo: Prensa e ideas políticas en la crisis del Antiguo Régimen (País Vasco, 1750–1840)*. Madrid: Siglo XXI, 1991.

Fernández Sebastián, J., 'España, monarquía y nación: Cuatro concepciones de la comunidad política española entre el Antiguo Régimen y la Revolución liberal'. *Studia Histórica. Historia Contemporánea*, 12 (1994): 45–74.

Ferrer de Couto, J., *Crisol histórico español y restauración de las glorias nacionales*, Havana: Vda. de Barcina, 1862.

Ferrer del Río, A., *Decadencia de España. Primera parte. Historia del levantamiento de las Comunidades de Castilla*. Madrid: 1850.

Ferreras, J. Ignacio, *El teatro en el siglo XIX*. Madrid: Taurus, 1989.

Flitter, D., *Teoría y crítica del romanticismo español*. Cambridge: Cambridge University Press, 1995.

Flórez, E., *España sagrada: Teatro geográfico-histórico de la Iglesia de España*, 51 vols. Madrid: A. Marín, 1747–1779.

Flórez Estrada, A., *Introducción para la historia de la revolución de España*. London, 1810.

Fox, E. I., *La crisis intelectual de 1898*. Madrid: Edicusa, 1976.

Fox, E. I., *Ideología y política en las letras de fin de siglo (1898)*. Madrid: Espasa-Calpe, 1988.

Fox, E. I., *La invención de España*. Madrid: Cátedra, 1997.

Fradera, J. M., *Jaume Balmes: Els fonaments racionals d'una política católica*. Barcelona: Eumo, 1996.

Franco, D., *España como preocupación*. Madrid: Alianza, 1988.

Fuente, V. de la, *Historia eclesiástica de España*, 4 vols. Madrid, 1855–1859.

Fuentes, J. F., 'Pueblo y élites en la España contemporánea, 1808–1839 (reflexiones sobre un desencuentro)'. *Historia Contemporánea*, 8 (1992): 15–34.

Fuentes, J. F., 'La invención del pueblo: El mito del pueblo en el siglo XIX español'. *Claves de Razón Práctica*, 103 (1999): 60–64.

Fusi, J. P., 'Revisionismo crítico e historia nacionalista (A propósito de un artículo de B. de Riquer)'. *Historia Social*, 7 (1990): 127–134.

Fusi, J. Pablo, 'Center and Periphery, 1900–1936: National integration and Regional Nationalisms Reconsidered', in F. Lannon and P. Preston,

Elites and Power in Twentieth-Century Spain. Oxford: Clarendon, 1990, pp. 33–40.

Fusi, J. P., *España: Evolución de la identidad nacional.* Madrid: Temas de Hoy, 2000.

Fusi, J. P., and Niño, A. (eds), *Vísperas del 98: Orígenes y antecedentes de la crisis del 98.* Madrid: Biblioteca Nueva, 1997.

Galli, F., *Memorias sobre la Guerra de Cataluña 1822–1823.* Barcelona: A. Bergnes, 1835.

Gambra Ciudad, R., *La primera guerra civil de España (1821–1823).* Madrid: Escelicer, 1950.

García Arenal, M., *Los moriscos.* Madrid: Editora Nacional, 1975.

García Camarero, E. and García Camarero, E., *La polémica de la ciencia española.* Madrid: Alianza, 1970.

García Cárcel, R., 'El concepte d'Espanya als segles XVI i XVII'. *L'Avenç,* 100 (1987): 38–50.

García Cárcel, R., *La Leyenda Negra: Historia y opinión.* Madrid: Alianza, 1992.

García Cárcel, R. (ed.), *La construcción de las historias en España.* Madrid: M. Pons, 2004.

García Melero, J. E., *Arte español de la Ilustración y del siglo XIX.* Madrid: Encuentro, 1998.

García Mercadal, J., *Viajes de extranjeros por España y Portugal.* Madrid: Aguilar, 1962, 3 vols.

Garmendia, V., *La ideología carlista (1868–1876): En los orígenes del nacionalismo vasco.* San Sebastián: Diputación Foral de Guipúzcoa, 1984.

Garrido, F., *La España contemporánea: Sus progresos materiales y morales en el siglo XIX,* 2 vols. Barcelona: S. Manero, 1865–1867.

Gebhardt, V., *Historia general de España y de sus Indias,* 7 vols. Barcelona: Luis Tasso, 1860–1873.

Gil Novales, A., 'Francisco Martínez Marina' and 'Agustín de Argüelles', in J. Antón and M. Caminal (eds), *Pensamiento político en la España contemporánea, 1800–1950.* Barcelona: Teide, 1992, pp. 1–18 and 79–118.

Gómez, S., *Compendio de Historia General de España.* Madrid: Rivadeneyra, 1855.

González Cuevas, P. C., *Historia de las derechas españolas.* Madrid: Biblioteca Nueva, 2000.

Gortázar, G. (ed.), *Nación y Estado en la España liberal.* Madrid: Noesis, 1994.

Graham, J. T., *Donoso Cortés, Utopian Romanticist and Political Realist.* Columbia, MO: University of Missouri Press, 1974.

Green, O. H., *Spain and the Western Tradition: The Castillian Mind in Literature, from El Cid to Calderón,* 4 vols. Madison: University of Wisconsin Press, 1963–1966.

Greenfeld, L., *Nationalism: Five Roads to Modernity.* Cambridge, MA: Harvard University Press, 1992.

Guerra, F.-X., *Modernidad e Independencias.* Madrid: Mapfre, 1992.

Gutiérrez Lasanta, F., *Menéndez Pelayo, apologista de la Iglesia y de España*. Santiago de Compostela: El Noticiero, 1958.

Herr, R., 'Good, Evil, and Spain's Rising against Napoleon', in R. Herr and H. T. Parker (eds), *Ideas in History*. Durham, NC: Duke University Press, 1965, pp. 157–181.

Herr, R., *The Eighteenth-Century Revolution in Spain*. Princeton, NJ: Princeton University Press, 1969.

Herrero, J., *Los orígenes del pensamiento reaccionario español*. Madrid: Edicusa, 1971.

Hervás y Panduro, L., *Las causas de la Revolución de Francia* [1794]. Reprinted in Madrid, Atlas, 1943.

Iglesias, C. (ed.), *Símbolos de España*. Madrid: Centro de Estudios Políticos y Constitucionales, 2000.

Isern, D., *Del Desastre nacional y sus causas*. Madrid: Minuesa, 1899.

Jover Zamora, J. M., 'Sobre los conceptos de monarquía y nación en el pensamiento político español del siglo XVII'. *Cuadernos de Historia de España*, Buenos Aires, XIII (1950): 101–150.

Jover Zamora, J. M., 'Preface' to *La era isabelina y el Sexenio Democrático (1834–1874)*, Vol. XXXIV of *Historia de España Menéndez Pidal*. Madrid: Espasa-Calpe, 1981.

Jover Zamora, J. M., 'Caracteres del nacionalismo español, 1854–1874'. *Zona Abierta*, 31 (1984): 1–22.

Jover Zamora, J. M., *La civilización española a mediados del siglo XIX*. Madrid: Espasa-Calpe, 1991.

Juaristi, J., *Vestigios de Babel: Para una arqueología de los nacionalismos españoles*. Madrid: Siglo XXI, 1992.

Juaristi, J., 'El Ruedo Ibérico: Mitos y símbolos de masa del nacionalismo español'. *Cuadernos de Alzate*, 16 (1997): 19–31.

Kagan, R., *Students and Society in Early Modern Spain*. Baltimore, MD: Johns Hopkins University Press, 1974.

Kirkpatrick, S., *Larra: El laberinto inextricable de un romántico liberal*. Madrid: Gredos, 1987.

Lafage, F., *L'Espagne de la contre-révolution*. Paris: L'Harmattan, 1993.

Lafuente, M., *Historia General de España, desde los tiempos más remotos hasta nuestros días*, 30 vols. Madrid: Mellado, 1850–1866.

Laitin, D. D., Solé, C., and Kalyvas, S. N., 'Language and the Construction of States: The Case of Catalonia in Spain'. *Politics and Society*, 22(1), 1994: 5–29.

Lampillas, F. J., *Saggio storico-apologetico della Letteratura Spagnuola*, 6 vols. Genoa, 1778–1781 (translated to Spanish from Italian, Zaragoza, 1782–1784).

Lapeyre, H., *Géographie de l'Espagne morisque*. Paris: SEVPEN, 1959.

Lázaro Torres, Rosa María, *El poder de los carlistas: Evolución y declive de un Estado, 1833–1839*. Bilbao: P. Alcalde, 1993.

Lécuyer, M.-C., and Serrano, C., *La Guerre d'Afrique et ses répercussions en*

Espagne: Idéologies et colonialisme en Espagne, 1859–1904. Rouen: Presses Universitaires de France, 1976.

Linz, J. J., 'Intellectual Roles in Sixteenth and Seventeenth-Century Spain'. *Daedalus*, 101(3), 1972: 59–108.

Linz, J. J., 'Five Centuries of Spanish History: Quantification and Comparison', in V. R. Lorwin and J. Price (eds), *The Dimensions of the Past*, Yale University Press, 1972, pp. 177–261.

Linz, J. J., 'Early State-building and late Peripheral Nationalism against the State: The Case of Spain', in S. N. Eisenstadt and S. Rokkan (eds), *Building States and Nations*, London: Sage, 1973, Vol. 2, pp. 32–112.

Linz, J. J. 'Politics in a Multi-Lingual Society with a Dominant Worl Language: The Case of Spain',. iIn J. G. Savard and R. Vergneault (eds), *Les États multilingues: problèmes et solutions*. Quebec: Université Laval, 1975, pp. 367–444.

Linz, J. J., 'Los nacionalismos en España: una perspectiva comparada'. *Historia y fuente oral*, 7 (1992): 127–135.

Linz, J. J., 'El Estado-nación frente a los Estados plurinacionales', in E. D'Auria and J. Casassas, *El Estado moderno en Italia y España*, Barcelona: Universitat de Barcelona/Consiglio Nazionale delle Ricerche, 1992, pp. 71–87.

Liske, J., *Viajes de extranjeros por España y Portugal en los siglos XV, XVI y XVII*. Madrid: Medina, 1878.

Lloréns, V., *Liberales y románticos*. Madrid: Castalia, 1968.

Lloréns, V., *El romanticismo español*. Madrid: J. March/Castalia, 1979.

Llorente, J. A., *Mémoire historique sur la révolution d'Espagne*. Paris: Plassan, 1814, 2 vols.

Llorente, J. A., *Historia Crítica de la Inquisición en España*, 4 vols. Paris, 1817–1818.

López, S., *Despertador cristiano-político*. Valencia: 1809.

López Alonso, C., 'El pensamiento conservador español en el s. XIX: De Cádiz a la Restauración', in F.Vallespín (ed.), *Historia de la Teoría Política*. Madrid: Alianza, 1993, Vol. V, pp. 273–314.

Lovett, G., *Napoleon and the Birth of Modern Spain*. New York: New York University Press, 1965, 2 vols.

Macías Picavea, R., *El problema nacional: Hechos, causas, remedios*. Madrid: V. Suárez, 1899.

Mainer, J. C., 'La doma de la quimera: Ensayos sobre nacionalismo y cultura en España'. Bellaterra: Universidad Autónoma de Barcelona, 1988.

Mainer, J. C., 'La invención de la literatura española', in J. M. Enguita and J. C. Mainer (eds), *Literaturas regionales en España*, Zaragoza: Instituto Fernando el Católico, 1994, pp. 23–45.

Mallada, L., *Los males de la Patria y la futura revolución española*. Madrid, 1890.

Mar-Molinero, C., and Smith, A., *Nationalism and the Nation in the Iberian Peninsula*. Oxford: Berg, 1996.

Maravall, J. A., *Teoría del Estado en España en el siglo XVII*. Madrid: Instituto de Estudios Políticos, 1944.

Maravall, J. A., *El concepto de España en la Edad Media*. Madrid: Instituto de Estudios Políticos, 1954.

Maravall, J. A., 'El pensamiento político de España a comienzos del siglo XIX: Martínez Marina'. *Revista de Estudios Políticos*, Madrid, 1955: 81.

Maravall, J. A., *Las Comunidades de Castilla: Una primera revolución moderna.* Madrid: Revista de Occidente, 1963.

Maravall, J. A., 'Sobre el sentimiento de nación en el siglo XVIII: la obra de Forner'. *La Torre*, Puerto Rico, XV(57) (1967): 25–56.

Maravall, J. A., *La oposición política bajo los Austrias*, Barcelona: Ariel, 1972.

Maravall, J. A., *Estudios de historia del pensamiento español: Siglo XVII.* Madrid: Cultura Hispánica, 1975.

Maravall, J. A., *Estudios de Historia del pensamiento español (siglo XVIII).* Madrid: Mondadori, 1991.

Mariana, J. de, *Historia general de España* [*Historia de Rebus Hispaniae*, 1592–1605]. Madrid: Biblioteca de Autores Españoles, 1950.

Marías, J., *La España posible en tiempos de Carlos III.* Madrid: Sociedad de Estudios y Publicaciones, 1963.

Marliani, E., *Historia política de la España moderna*, Barcelona: A. Bergnes, 1840.

Martín, M., *El colonialismo español en Marruecos.* Paris, Ruedo Ibérico, 1973.

Martín Gaite, C., *El proceso de Macanaz: Historia de un empapelamiento.* Madrid: Moneda y Crédito, 1970.

Martín Martín, T., *El iberismo: una herencia de la izquierda decimonónica.* Madrid: Edicusa, 1975.

Mas, S. de, *La Iberia: Memoria sobre la conveniencia de la unión pacífica y legal de Portugal y España.* Madrid: Rivadeneyra, 1854.

Masdeu, J. F., *Historia crítica de España y de la cultura española*, 20 vols. Madrid: A. de Sancha, 1783–1805.

Menéndez Pelayo, M., *Historia de los heterodoxos españoles.* Madrid, Ed. Católica, 1986.

Menéndez Pelayo, M., *Calderón y su teatro.* Buenos Aires: Emecé, 1946.

Menéndez Pidal, R., *Los españoles en la historia.* Madrid: Espasa-Calpe, 1947.

Merriman, R. B., *The Rise of the Spanish Empire, in the Old World and the New.* New York: Cooper Square, 1962.

Merry y Colón, M., *Historia de España.* Seville: A. Izquierdo y Sobrino, 1876.

Merry y Colón, M., *Elementos de historia crítica de España.* Seville: A. Pérez, 1892.

Merry y Colón, M. and Merry y Villalba, A., *Compendio de Historia de España.* Seville: J. Mª Ariza, 1889.

Monreal y Ascaso, B., *Curso de Historia de España.* Madrid: M. Tello, 1867.

Montero, F., *El movimiento católico en España.* Madrid: Eudema, 1993.

Montoya, P. de, *La intervención del clero vasco en las contiendas civiles (1820–23).* San Sebastián: Izarra, 1971.

Moral Roncal, A. M., *Carlos V de Borbón (1788–1855).* Madrid: Actas, 1999.

Morales Moya, A. (ed.), *Las bases políticas, económicas y sociales de un régimen en transformación (1759–1834)*, Vol. XXX of *Historia de España Menéndez Pidal*. Madrid: Espasa-Calpe, 1998.

Moreno Alonso, M., *Historiografía romántica española: Introducción al estudio de la historia en el siglo XIX*. Seville: Universidad de Sevilla, 1979.

Moreno Luzón, J., 'Mitos de la España inmortal'. In C. Forcadell, P. Salomón and I. Saz (eds), *Discursos de España en el siglo XX*. Zaragoza: Institución Fernando el Católico, 2009, pp. 123–146.

Münzer, J., *Viaje por España y Portugal (1494–1495)*. Madrid: Polifemo, 1991.

Nation et nationalités en Espagne. Paris, Fondation Singer-Polignac, 1985.

Netanyahu, B., *Los marranos españoles*. Valladolid: Junta de Castilla y León, 1994.

Nido y Segalerva, J., *La Unión Ibérica: Estudio crítico e histórico de este problema*. Madrid: P. de Velasco, 1914.

Nieto, A., *Los primeros pasos del Estado constitucional*. Barcelona: Ariel, 1996.

Nin, J. M., *Secretos de la Inquisición*. Barcelona: J. Bosch, 1855.

Nocedal, C., 'Discurso preliminar' to G. M. Jovellanos, *Obras*, Biblioteca de Autores Españoles. Madrid: Rivadeneyra, 1858.

Núñez Ruiz, D., *La mentalidad positiva en España: desarrollo y crisis*. Madrid: Túcar, 1975.

Núñez-Seixas, X. M., 'Questione nazionale e crisi statale: Spagna, 1898–1936'. *Ricerche Storica*, XXIV(1), 1994: 87–117.

Núñez-Seixas, X. M., 'Historia e actualidade dos nacionalismos na España contemporánea: unha perspectiva de conxunto'. *Grial*, 128 (1995): 495–540.

Núñez-Seixas, X. M., 'Region-building in Spain during the 19th and 20th centuries', in G. Brunn (ed.), *Region und Regionsbildung in Europa: Konzeptionen der Forschung und empirische Befunde*. Baden-Baden: Nomos Verlagsgesellschaft, 1996, pp. 175–210.

Núñez-Seixas, X. M., 'Los oasis en el desierto: Perspectivas historiográficas sobre el nacionalismo español'. *Bulletin d'Histoire Contemporaine de l'Espagne*, 26 (1997): 483–533.

Núñez-Seixas, X. M., *Los nacionalismos en la España contemporánea (siglos XIX y XX)*. Barcelona: Hipòtesi, 1999.

Núñez-Seixas, X. M., 'La construcción del Estado-nación español en el siglo XIX: ¿Éxito incompleto o fracaso relativo?', in *L'Estat-Nació i el conflicte regional: Joan Mañé i Flaquer, un cas paradigmàtic, 1823–1901*. Barcelona: Publicacions de l'Abadia de Montserrat, 2004, 7–31.

Núñez-Seixas, X. M., 'La questione nazionale in Spagna: Note sul recente dibattito storiografico'. *Mondo Contemporaneo*, Turin, 2 (2007): 105–127.

Núñez-Seixas, X. M., and Sevillano Calero, F. (eds), *Los enemigos de España: Imagen del otro, conflictos bélicos y disputas nacionales (siglos XVI–XX)*. Madrid, Centro de Estudios Políticos y Constitucionales, 2010.

Olábarri Gortázar, I., 'Un conflicto entre nacionalismos: La 'cuestión regional' en España, 1808–1939', in F. Fernández Rodríguez (ed.), *La España de las autonomías*. Madrid: IEAL, 1985, pp. 69–147.

Onaindía, M., *La construcción de la nación española: Republicanismo y nacionalismo en la Ilustración*. Barcelona: Sine Qua Non, 2002.

Orodea e Ibarra, E., *Curso de Lecciones de Historia de España*. Valladolid: Hijos de Rodríguez, 1867.

Ortega y Frías, R., *La sombra de Felipe II*. Madrid: San Martín, 1892.

Ortega y Gasset, J., *España invertebrada*. Madrid, 1921.

Ortiz y Sanz, J., *Compendio cronológico de la historia de España*, 6 vols. Madrid, 1795–1803.

Ortiz de la Vega, M. (Patxot y Ferrer, F.) *Anales de España, desde sus orígenes hasta el tiempo presente*, 6 vols. Barcelona: Cervantes, 1857–1859.

Paluzie Cantalozella, E., *Resumen de Historia de España*, Barcelona, 1866.

Pan-Montojo, J. (ed.), *Más se perdió en Cuba: España, 1898 y la crisis de fin de siglo*. Madrid: Alianza, 1998.

Pasamar, G., and Peiró, I., *Historiografía y práctica social en España*. Zaragoza: Prensas Universitarias, 1987.

Payne, S., *Politics and the Military in Modern Spain*. Stanford, CA: Stanford University Press, 1967.

Payne, S., 'Spanish Conservatism, 1834–1923'. *Journal of Contemporary History*, 13 (1978): 765–789.

Payne, S., 'Nationalism, Regionalism and Micronationalism in Spain'. *Journal of Contemporary History*, 26 (1991): 479–491.

Pedregal y Cañedo, M., *Estudios sobre el engrandecimiento y la decadencia de España*. Madrid: F. Góngora, 1878.

Peers, E. A., *Historia del movimiento romántico español*, 2 vols. Madrid: Gredos, 1973.

Peiró, I., *La Guerra de la Independencia y sus conmemoraciones*. Zaragoza: Institución Fernando el Católico, 2008.

Pellistrandi, B., *Un discours national? La Real Academia de la Historia entre science et politique (1847–1897)*. Madrid: Casa de Velázquez, 2004.

Pérez Galdós, B., *Episodios Nacionales*, 46 vols. 1872–1912.

Pérez Ledesma, M., 'Las Cortes de Cádiz y la sociedad española'. *Ayer*, 1 (1991): 167–206.

Pérez Ledesma, M., 'La sociedad española, la guerra y la derrota', in J. Pan-Montojo (ed.), *Más se perdió en Cuba: España, 1898 y la crisis de fin de siglo*. Madrid: Alianza, 1998, pp. 91–149.

Pérez Vejo, T., *Pintura de historia e identidad nacional en España*. Madrid: Universidad Complutense, 2001.

Peset, M. and Peset, J. L., *La Universidad española (siglos XVIII y XIX)*. Madrid: Taurus, 1974.

Petschen, S., *Iglesia-Estado: Un cambio político. Las Constituyentes de 1869*. Madrid: Taurus, 1975.

Picatoste, F., *Estudios sobre la grandeza y decadencia de España*, 2 vols. Madrid: Hernando y Cía., 1887.

Pidal, P. J., *La unidad católica de España*. Madrid: Revista de Legislación, 1880.

Pike, F. B., *Hispanismo, 1898–1936: Spanish Conservatives and Liberals and Their Relations with Spanish America*. Notre Dame, IN: University of Notre Dame Press, 1971.

Portillo Valdés, J. M., 'Nación política y territorio económico: El primer modelo provincial español (1812)'. *Historia Contemporánea*, 12 (1995): 248–277.

Powell, P., *Tree of Hate: Propaganda and Prejudices Affecting U.S. Relations with the Hispanic World*. New York: Basic Books, 1971.

Prado, A., *La literatura del casticismo*. Madrid: Moneda y Crédito, 1973.

Prados de la Escosura, L., *De imperio a nación: Crecimiento y atraso económico en España (1780–1930)*. Madrid: Alianza, 1988.

Puelles Benítez, M., *Educación e ideología en la España contemporánea*. Barcelona: Labor, 1980.

Pulido Fernández, A., *Españoles sin patria y la raza sefardí*. Madrid: Teodoro, 1905.

Quintana, M. J., *Obras Completas*. Madrid: Biblioteca de Autores Españoles, 1946.

Real Academia de la Historia, *España: Reflexiones sobre el ser de España*. Madrid: R. A. H., 1997.

Real Academia de la Historia, *España como nación*. Madrid: Planeta, 2000.

Redondo Díaz, F., 'Leyenda y realidad de la Marcha Real española'. *Revista de Historia Militar*, 54 (1983): 63–89.

Reglá, J., *Estudios sobre los moriscos*, Valencia, Anales de la Universidad, 1964.

Revuelta, M., *La exclaustración, 1833–1840*. Madrid: Edica, 1976.

Reyero, C., *Imagen histórica de España (1850–1890)*. Madrid: Espasa-Calpe, 1987.

Reyero, C., *La pintura de Historia en España: Esplendor de un género en el siglo XIX*. Madrid: Cátedra, 1989.

Reyero, C., *La escultura conmemorativa en España: La Edad de Oro del monumento público*. Madrid: Cátedra, 1999.

Ringrose, D. R., *Spain, Europe and the 'Spanish Miracle', 1700–1900*. Cambridge: Cambridge University Press, 1996.

Riquer, B. de, 'Sobre el lugar de los nacionalismos-regionalismos en la historia contemporánea española'. *Historia Social*, 7 (1990): 105–126.

Riquer, B. de, 'Reflexions entorn de la dèbil nacionalització espanyola del segle XIX'. *L'Avenç*, 170 (1993): 8–15.

Riquer, B. de, 'Aproximación al nacionalismo español contemporáneo'. *Studia Historica*, 12 (1994): 11–29.

Riquer, B. de, and Ucelay, E., 'An Analysis of Nationalisms in Spain: A Proposal for an Integrated Historical Model', in J. Beramendi et al. (eds), *Nationalism in Europe: Past and Present*. Santiago de Compostela, 1994, Vol. II, pp. 275–301.

Robles Egea, A. (ed.), *Política en penumbra: Patronazgo y clientelismo políticos en la España contemporánea*. Madrid: Siglo XXI, 1996.

Rocamora, J. A., *El nacionalismo ibérico, 1792–1936*. Valladolid: Universidad de Valladolid, 1994.

Rodríguez, J., *Lecciones de cronología e Historia General de España*. Madrid: Calleja, 1850.

Rodríguez de Castro, J., *Biblioteca española*, 2 vols. Madrid: Real Gaceta, 1781–1786.

Rodríguez González, A., 'El conflicto de Melilla en 1893'. *Hispania*, XLIX(171) (1989): 235–266.

Rodríguez Mohedano, P. and Rodríguez Mohedano, R., *Historia literaria de España, desde su primera población hasta nuestros días*. Madrid: Pérez de Soto, 1766.

Romero Tobar, L. (ed.), *Historia de la literatura española: Siglo XIX*. Madrid: Espasa-Calpe, 1998.

Rozenberg, Danielle, *L'Espagne contemporaine et la question juive*. Paris: Presses Universitaires de Mirail-Toulouse, 2006.

Sáez Marín, J., *Datos sobre la Iglesia española contemporánea (1768–1868)*. Madrid: Editora Nacional, 1975.

Sahlins, P., *Boundaries: The Making of France and Spain in the Pyrenees*. Berkeley, CA: University of California Press, 1989.

Sáinz Rodríguez, P., *Evolución de las ideas sobre la decadencia de España*. Madrid: Rialp, 1962.

Salazar y Hontiveros, J. J., *Glorias de España, plausibles en todos los siglos. . .* Madrid: Ariztia, 1736.

Salmón, P. M., *Resumen histórico de la Revolución de España*. Cádiz: Imp. Real, 1812.

San Miguel, E., *Historia de Felipe II, Rey de España*, 2 vols. Barcelona: Maneso, 1867–1868.

Sánchez Albornoz, C., *España, un enigma histórico*. Buenos Aires: Edhasa, 1960.

Sánchez y Casado, F., *Prontuario de Historia de España y de la Civilización Española*. Madrid: 1867.

Sánchez Mantero, R., *Liberales en el exilio: La emigración política en Francia en la crisis del Antiguo Régimen*. Madrid: Rialp, 1975.

Schmidt, B., *El problema español, de Quevedo a Manuel Azaña*. Madrid: Edicusa, 1976.

Seco Serrano, C., *Militarismo y civilismo en la España contemporánea*. Madrid: Centro de Estudios Económicos, 1984.

Sempere y Guarinos, J., *Considérations sur les causes de la grandeur et de la décadence de la monarchie espagnole*, 2 vols. Paris: J. Renouard, 1826.

Seoane, M. C., *El primer lenguaje constitucional español (las Cortes de Cádiz)*. Madrid: Moneda y Crédito, 1968.

Serrano, C., *Final del Imperio: España, 1895–1898*. Madrid: Siglo XXI, 1984.

Serrano, C., *Le tour du peuple: Crise nationale, mouvements populaires et populisme en Espagne, 1890–1910*. Madrid: Casa de Velázquez, 1987.

Serrano, C. (ed.), *Nations, nationalismes et question nationale*. Paris: Ibérica, 1994.

Serrano, C., *El nacimiento de Carmen: Símbolos, mitos y nación*. Madrid: Taurus, 1999.

Serrano, C. (ed.), *Nations en quête de passé: La Péninsule ibérique (XIXe–XXe siècles)*. Paris: Université de Paris-Sorbonne, 2000.

Shubert, A., *A Social History of Modern Spain*. London: Unwin Hyman, 1990.

Shaw, D., *A Literary History of Spain: The Nineteenth Century*. New York: Barnes and Noble, 1972.

Shubert, A., and Álvarez Junco, J. (eds), *Spanish History since 1808*: London: Arnold, 2000.

Sicroff, A., *Les controverses des statuts de 'pureté de sang' en Espagne du XVe au XVIIe siècle*. Paris: Didier, 1960.

Solís, R., *El Cádiz de las Cortes: La vida en la ciudad en los años 1810 a 1813*. Madrid: Alianza, 1969.

Storm, E., *La perspectiva del progreso: Pensamiento político en la España de fin de siglo*. Madrid: Turner, 2001.

Tapia, E. de, *Historia de la civilización española, desde la invasión de los árabes hasta los tiempos presentes*, 2 vols. Madrid: Yenes, 1840.

Tárrega, J. C., *Compendio de Historia de España*. Toledo: J. de Cea, 1859.

Tate, R. B., *Ensayos sobre la historiografía peninsular del siglo XV*. Madrid: Gredos, 1970.

Terradillos, A. M., *Prontuario de Historia de España*. Madrid: V. Hernando, 1848.

Tomás Villarroya, J., 'El proceso constitucional (1834–1843)' and 'El proceso constitucional (1843–1868)', in J. María Jover (ed.), *La era isabelina y el Sexenio Democrático (1834–1874)*, Vol. XXXIV of *Historia de España Menéndez Pidal*, Madrid: Espasa-Calpe, 1981, pp. 5–70 and 199–370.

Tone, J., *The Fatal Knot: The Guerrilla War in Navarre and the Defeat of Napoleon in Spain*. Chapel Hill, NC: University of North Carolina Press, 1994.

Toreno, conde de, *Historia del levantamiento, guerra y revolución de España*. Madrid: T. Jordán, 1835–1837, 5 vols.

Tuñón de Lara, M., *Medio siglo de cultura española*. Madrid: Tecnos, 1970.

Unamuno, M. de, *En torno al casticismo*. Madrid, 1895.

Urigüen, B., *Orígenes y evolución de la derecha española: el neo-catolicismo*. Madrid: Consejo Superior de Investigaciones Científicas, 1986.

Valera, J., *Obras completas*, Vol. I, *Discursos académicos*. Madrid: 1905.

Valls Montes, R., *La interpretación de la historia de España y sus orígenes ideológicos en el bachillerato franquista (1938–1953)*. Valencia, I. C. E., 1984.

Valverde, C., 'La filosofía', in *El Siglo del Quijote*, Vol. XXVI of the *Historia de España Menéndez Pidal*, Madrid: Espasa-Calpe, 1986, pp. 79–155.

Van Aken, M., *Pan-Hispanism: Its Origin and Development to 1866*. Los Angeles, CA: University of Southern California Press, 1959.

Varela, J., *La novela de España: Los intelectuales y el problema español*. Madrid: Taurus, 1999.

Varela Ortega, J., 'Aftermath of Splendid Disaster: Spanish Politics before and after the Spanish-American War of 1898'. *Journal of Contemporary History*, 15 (1980): 317–344.

Varela Suances, J., 'Introduction' to J. Balmes, *Política y Constitución*. Madrid: Centro de Estudios Constitucionales, 1988.

Vélez, R., *Preservativo contra la irreligión, o los planes de la Filosofía contra la religión y el Estado*. Cádiz, 1812.

Vilar, P., 'Estado, nación, patria, en España y en Francia, 1870–1914'. *Estudios de Historia Social*, 28–29 (1984): 7–41.

Villacorta Baños, F., *Burguesía y cultura: Los intelectuales españoles en la sociedad liberal, 1808–1931*. Madrid: Siglo XXI, 1980.

Viñao Frago, A., *Política y educación en los orígenes de la España contemporánea*. Madrid: Siglo XXI, 1982.

Wilhelmsen, A., *La formación del pensamiento político carlista (1810–1875)*. Madrid: Actas, 1995.

Periodicals cited

La Abeja Española
El Amigo de la Religión Cristiano-Católica y de la Sociedad
El Artista
Boletín de Navarra y Provincias Vascongadas
El Católico
El Censor
La Corona de Aragón
El Correo Español
La Correspondencia
La Correspondencia de España
La Cruz
La Defensa de la Sociedad
Diario de Santiago
Diario de Sesiones de Cortes
La Discusión
La Época
La España
El Español
La Esperanza
El Europeo
La Fe
El Fénix
Gaceta Oficial
El Globo
El Huracán

La Iberia
La Iberia Militar
La Ilustración Española y Americana
El Imparcial
Minerva Española
Mundo Obrero
El Museo Universal
La Nación
El Nacional
Las Novedades
La Ópera Española
El País
A Península
El Pensamiento de la Nación
El Pensamiento Español
El Piloto
El Procurador General de la Nación y del Rey
O Progreso
El Realista
El Redactor General
El Restaurador
Revista Contemporánea
Revista de España
Revista de Madrid
Revista del Mediodía
Revista Española

Revista Europea

Revista Ibérica de Ciencias, Política,
  Literatura, Arte e Instrucción Pública

La Revista Peninsular

A Revolução de Septembro

El Robespierre Español

O Século

Semanario Patriótico

Semanario Pintoresco Español

El Siglo Futuro

Solidaridad Obrera

A União Iberica

La Unión

La Voz de la Religión

La Voz del Católico

Index